Yates

GARDEN
GUIDE

HarperCollins*Publishers New Zealand*

Acknowledgments
We wish to thank the following for assisting with this book:
Allen Gilbert, Gordon Butler, Malcolm O'Reilly, Adrian Plowman, Don Huxley,
Judy Horton, Wendy Hucker, Deirdre O'Donnell, Sam and Michael Yates,
Bayer Australia Ltd and Kevin Handreck. Special thanks to Denise Cleverley,
Sue Linn, Nick Hayhoe, Graeme Leather and Margaret Sinclair.
Historical photographs and material are used by
kind permission of the Yates Company Archives and the Yates family.
Picture research by Jenny Mills.
Illustrations by Nicola Oram and Osmosis.

First published 1895

This edition published in New Zealand in 1998
by HarperCollins*Publishers (New Zealand) Limited*
P.O. Box 1, Auckland

Reprinted 1999, 2000

HarperCollins*Publishers*
31 View Road, Glenfield, Auckland 10, New Zealand
25 Ryde Road, Pymble, Sydney, NSW 2073, Australia
77-85 Fulham Palace Road, London W6 8JB, United Kingdom
Hazelton Lanes, 55 Avenue Road, Suite 2900, Toronto, Ontario M5R 3L2
and 1995 Markham Road, Scarborough, Ontario M1B 5M8, Canada
10 East 53rd Street, New York NY 10032, USA

ISBN 1 86950 286 8

Produced by Phoenix Offset on 113gsm Matt Art

FOREWORD

New Zealand, which has one of the highest rates of home ownership in the world, has always been a nation of gardeners. As successive generations have developed an interest in gardening — both for its intrinsic pleasure as an occupation and for its ability to enhance our homes — *Yates Garden Guide* has been New Zealand's most reliable source of gardening information.

Although it was first published more than one hundred years ago, and in spite of the plethora of gardening books that seem to continually flood the New Zealand market, *Yates Garden Guide* continues to hold its popularity. One of the main reasons for the book's enduring relevance has been its ability to change with the times while at the same time remaining true to its commitment to give practical, down-to-earth and workable advice.

Now, as *Yates Garden Guide* proudly moves into its second century of publication, and in keeping with Yates's forward thinking, we have given this seventy-fifth edition a completely new look. This is the most comprehensive update of the book in its history. It has changed to a larger format and is full of colour with completely new photographs and illustrations. The information has been revised and expanded, with an additional chapter aimed at junior gardeners and, as a result of our increased understanding of the fragility of our environment, guidelines for water-saving gardening. In addition, there are lists of top plants, and practical hints from a number of respected gardening authorities.

We are grateful to the many gardening experts who took the time to share their expertise, and appreciate their willing enthusiasm to be involved with this best-known of New Zealand's books. We would also like to thank the many other people who contributed their ideas, experience and support to this new edition.

For *Yates Garden Guide* is far more than just another gardening book: it has a special place in the hearts and minds of all New Zealanders and, indeed, is generally acknowledged to be the all-time best-selling New Zealand gardening book. This statistic reinforces the important place *Yates Garden Guide* has established and maintained in the New Zealand way of life. With the release of this new edition we are proud that it will now be able to delight, inform and inspire further generations of readers and gardeners.

Yates New Zealand Limited

CONTENTS

PART I: DESIGNING OR REDESIGNING YOUR GARDEN ... PAGE 1

PART II: PREPARING AND MAINTAINING YOUR GARDEN ... PAGE 31

PART III: PROPAGATING PLANTS ... PAGE 97

A POTTED HISTORY OF NEW ZEALAND GARDENING

A s we approach 2000, gardening in New Zealand is a national pastime, rated among our most popular leisure activities. Our garderns have probably reached an all-time high in their sophistication and diversity, but New Zealanders have always been great gardeners.

GARDENING FOR SURVIVAL

It started well before the arrival of the Europeans, at least 1000 years before, when the first voyagers from East Polynesia arrived in Aotearoa. The Maori brought with them a whole history of gardening, and were skilled adaptors and innovators when it came to surviving in a land vastly different from that from which they had come. They were challenged not only by different landforms, temperatures and weather patterns, but by new kinds of soils too.

Of the crops they brought with them from the tropics, five became staple to the Maori diet. For centuries, kumara, taro, yam, gourd and the pacific cabbage tree ('ti') remained the principal source of food, even though the plants that already existed in New Zealand were being incorporated into the diet too. They made good use of the cabbage tree species they found in New Zealand and the various trees and shrubs with edible roots, fruit and berries.

Archaeological findings paint a picture of Maori gardens that were productive, but also very handsome. Probably designed for ease of management as much as aesthetics, the vegetable plots of the early Maori were very orderly, arranged in neat patterns and rows. They were also graced with beautiful sculpture in the form of carved stone figures that had an important spiritual role.

These were statues of powerful gods. Crop failures were more likely to be attributed to their displeasure than the simple weather patterns. According to legend, Pani, the female goddess, gave birth to the first kumara tubers. The statue of Rongo, the male god of gardening and peace, would be placed at the head of the garden to watch over the growth of the plants.

When the first Europeans arrived, Maori gardening found a commercial opportunity as settlers came to terms with gardening in this strange new land. Maori became prosperous market gardeners, growing a range of vegetables, including some that they did not eat themselves. They were expert in the culture of potatoes, corn, turnips and cabbages, and also grew edible greens that were introduced by the Europeans. These included hua inanga (fat hen), paea (wild cabbage), and kohukohu (chickweed).

The land wars and the migration to cities brought dramatic change to the Maori way of life and by the mid 1900s much of their gardening culture was lost. These days, the revival of traditional Maori gardening is part of a movement towards relearning the old skills and knowledge.

EARLY COTTAGE GARDENS

Like the Maori, the first Pakeha to arrive in New Zealand gardened because they had to. It was a case of sheer survival. Barely comparable with today's notion of a cottage, their basic shacks were surrounded by bush, with no shops, and often miles from the nearest neighbour — a far cry from their homeland.

It is difficult to imagine how anybody found the time or resources to indulge in an ornamental garden. But the plants reminiscent of the 'Old World' brought considerable comfort in a strange, uncertain, new land. Flowers were grown in small plots at the front of the house, often intermingled with existing native plants.

In the mid 1800s, during the first big wave of immigration, creative gardening was fast becoming a pleasure that everyone could indulge in. Previously it had been the domain of the upper classes. Also at this time, it became fashionable for women to garden. Flower gardens became all the rage and this was the beginning of what we now identify as the cottage garden.

However, cottage gardens of the time were not necessarily recognised by their owners as such. The early 'cottagers' were working-class people whose cottage gardens were largely the result of the need to grow food and ornamentals in a limited space.

Fashion-conscious, middle-class gardeners of the time would most likely have been aspiring to the neatly manicured 'gardenesque' style which was in vogue in England. Any cheerful informality that they ended up with was probably not their ultimate goal.

Cottage gardens have changed over the decades and swung in and out of fashion, but to this day they are held in high regard. In the early part of this century design gurus such as Vita Sackville-West and Gertrude Jekyll in England and Edna Waling of Australia sang their praises and the 1980s marked a grand renaissance in the art of cottage gardening. Loved by so many gardeners, it seems their colourful simplicity will never lose its appeal.

A TAPESTRY OF STYLES

Contrary to popular belief, the cottage-style garden was not the only one adopted by the early colonists. New Zealand garden style was (and still is) influenced by English fashions of the time, as well as the affluence of the garden's owner.

In the early 1800s, formal gardens were fashionable in England, and New Zealand Mission gardens often boasted a round ornamental bed in front of the house. In these gardens were planted colourful plants such as petunias and poppies, dahlias and sweet William, stocks and geraniums.

Between 1840 and 1855 came the influence of a new style, the 'gardenesque'. Those who could afford it made gracious lawns with sweeping curves, and borders displaying neatly spaced flowering shrubs and perennials. The circular flower beds remained very popular but the overall layout became less symmetrical. Gardeners more concerned with survival than style continued in the cottage style, a few favourite ornamentals interspersed with vegetables.

When formality returned to fashion in Victorian times, toned-down versions of the bold parterres of formal English gardens sprang up around New Zealand. Even the humble cottage garden was planted in beds laid out in formal, geometric patterns.

The average Victorian garden was, in common with today's gardens, a private retreat from the world outside, but these were the days of the great plant hunters and well-off Victorians loved to show off their horticultural prowess. They collected everything from alpines to palm trees.

Lawns were very popular, as were plants with bold exotic looks. New Zealand plants became fashionable in England and palms from the tropics were planted here, along

A mixed perennial border in the colour-conscious cottage style of the 90s.

The influence of Victorian garden design can still be seen in New Zealand today, as in this formal garden in New Plymouth.

with the very popular flaxes and cabbage trees. Many Victorian gardens became a blend of different styles.

By the turn of the century, English garden designers of the informal persuasion were making their mark. The English country look was still quite formal in layout, but was planted with a lavish, informal abundance. The English designer, Gertrude Jekyll, is famous for her work at that time. Hers was a reaction against the stiff geometric layouts and brazen colour schemes of Victorian times. She was inspired by the simple cottage gardens of rural England and her influence on New Zealand garden style remains today.

In the early 1900s, prior to World War I, New Zealand gardens reflected a newfound stability and prosperity. Often divided into 'garden rooms', they featured rock and water gardens, tea houses, arbours, gazebos and ferneries, and a wealth of exciting new plants from all around the world. Garden structures were made from rustic materials, in keeping with the natural style of the times, but also using conveniently available local materials.

Breakthroughs in plant breeding included the first hybrid tea roses, and rambler roses which were frequently grown over arbours and verandahs. There was much interest in form and texture in the garden, with the use of grasses, bamboos and subtropical foliage.

Through the 1920s, '30s and '40s gardens became simpler under the influences of the war and economic depression. There was also the art deco movement and the advent of state housing. Smaller suburban sections spurred an interest in more compact plants and gardens became more clipped and formal than the cottage gardens of earlier decades.

Inevitably, under hard times, vegetable gardening prospered.

Not everybody struggled of course. Wealthy farmers of the 1920s and '30s employed the services of professional garden designers. Large park-like estates were established, with gracefully curving driveways, large terraced lawns, stone walls, summer houses and sunken gardens. Trees grew in clumps on the outer boundaries and formed grand entrance avenues.

As prosperity returned in the 1950s and '60s, garden designers started to concern themselves with 'lifestyle' and entertainment. The outdoor living area was, perhaps for the first time, regarded as an extension of the indoor living space, complete with barbecues, patios and pools. Courtyards became popular and 'Modern' was the style of the times.

The once essential vegetable garden started to diminish in favour of shrubs, roses, annuals and bulbs. If there was a vegetable garden it was likely to be Dad's domain. Women often took care of the front ornamental garden, or stayed indoors. The cover of the 1963 *Yates Garden Guide* clearly depicts this.

In the 1970s the natural garden was the way to go. Mass plantings of New Zealand natives prevailed under acres of bark mulch. This symbolised our new environmental awareness and carried on into the early '80s. The 'correctness' of the natural garden became so entrenched that, inevitably, there was a reaction against it.

Bursting with colour, nostalgia and Englishness, the late-twentieth-century cottage garden was born. Sales of colourful flowering plants skyrocketed, but the trend for informality remained. Until quite recently, most gardeners remained in favour of informal garden styles.

The 1990s have seen a resurgence of formal styles, even in vegetable gardening. We have less need to produce vegetables in our backyards than we did a hundred years ago, but the decorative potager has become highly fashionable.

In late-twentieth-century New Zealand there are cottage gardens, English country gardens, subtropical gardens, Mediterranean gardens, wild gardens and native gardens. Layer upon layer of influence and circumstance has resulted in an ever diversifying, always changing New Zealand garden style.

NEW ZEALAND PLANTS

Even in the early days, when acres of native bush were being cleared, native plants were appreciated as garden plants. They were often selected to be left in place when a house site was cleared, or planted among the exotics brought from home. Entirely native gardens were also known.

During Victorian times nursery catalogues listed vast collections of native plants. While exotic plants were being brought into the country, New Zealand natives were being taken out, and included among the interesting exotics displayed in fashionable English gardens.

It seems that native plants have always been promoted as both aesthetically pleasing and patriotic. For at least 60 years natives have dominated school gardens and (to a lesser extent) other public places.

The difference these days is a vastly larger palette of native plants to work with. Many of today's 'natives' were not in existence prior to the 1970s, when the native gardening boom stimulated a deluge of hybridisation and selection. Late-twentieth-century cultivars now supplement the true endemic flora with a wide assortment of different flower and foliage colour, and compact growth forms better suited to the smaller garden.

While the purist's all-native garden is not as prevalent as it was twenty years ago, natives remain very popular. They are incorporated into all styles of garden, as formal clipped hedges, rural shelter belts, bold tropical-style foliage, or flowering cottage garden plants. They are among the best for coastal gardens and indispensable where low maintenance is concerned.

HORTICULTURAL KNOW-HOW

The early New Zealanders, through necessity, were a knowledgeable lot when it came to gardening.

Driven by the need to survive and strong spiritual beliefs, the early Maori persevered against all odds, and developed sound horticultural skills such as mulching, soil improvement, forming raised beds and creating shelter.

The early settlers were people of an adventurous pioneering spirit who also had to learn fast to survive. Many brought with them a basic knowledge of gardening, and very early on were experimenting with all forms of gardening.

In the mid-1800s when horticulture was becoming very fashionable, colonial nurseries, seed merchants and garden writers sprang up as quickly as the expanding population.

By Victorian times the highly evolved art of fruit and vegetable gardening had been transported to New Zealand from England. It was indicative of the level of sophistication of Victorian gardeners that the productive, space-saving advantages of the espalier were well-known to them. They were also skilled at propagating, grafting and soil management and were very proficient in the use of animal manures. Gardening knowledge also came to New Zealand from the East, via the Chinese gold miners. Later, many turned their skills to market gardening.

In times of hardship, gardening knowledge was considered a great virtue. It was brought into school programmes and actively promoted for the good of all. Information was close at hand from the earliest years.

Horticultural societies had an educational role and also encouraged participation in gardening, and competitions for the biggest vegetables and most beautiful blooms became widespread. Books, magazines and articles on gardening, and nursery catalogues all fed the early New Zealanders' appetite for gardening information.

While there seems never to have been any shortage of published information on gardening, there's always room for another gardening book, as information keeps pace with the changing times. Even faster than the pace of fashion is the rate at which new plants become available. The first *Yates Garden Guide* was published in 1895, a booklet that was vastly different from this 1998 edition.

THE YATES STORY

The story of Arthur Yates begins in Manchester in 1826, when his grandfather, George Yates, the younger son of a cotton

192 Queen Street, 1906–1911.

manufacturer of Ashton-in-Makerfield, opened a grocery store and seed shop. Three years later he opened a branch store exclusively for seeds, and his eldest son, Samuel, aged fifteen years, was put in charge. The building of a great business in the production and distribution of seeds had begun.

Within a few years Samuel's trade had outstripped that of his father and he moved the store to larger premises. In 1855 he joined his father in partnership and in 1888 the business was transferred to him under the title Samuel Yates, Late George Yates and Son.

Over the years that followed, Samuel's five sons joined the firm: Harry, Arthur, William, Ernest and Percy. Our story concerns Arthur, the second son, who, because of his asthmatic condition and weak chest, was sent to New Zealand, where the family hoped the climate would improve his health.

For people of substance in England, New Zealand offered a life of more refinement than Australia. It was a smaller country, one more like England, and it lacked the stigma of a convict population. Arthur, aged eighteen, left his homeland on the sailing ship *Auckland*.

Arthur landed in New Zealand on 23 December 1879 after a troubled voyage. In an effort to restore his health, he worked for the first two years as a station-hand and shepherd on the back country runs of Otago and Hawke's Bay districts. From his experiences on the land, Arthur saw the opportunity for the supply of top-quality seeds.

In 1883 he opened a tiny seed shop, in a ramshackle wooden building on muddy Victoria Street West in Auckland. Takings on the first day were 1/6, expenses 2/6, but the business soon flourished and Arthur began travelling through the Waikato farmlands on horseback, seeking orders from the pioneer farmers.

In 1886 he visited Australia and travelled extensively on the eastern coast. On his return to New Zealand he sent a commercial traveller, Mr Hogg, to take orders for seeds in New South Wales and Victoria. A year later Mr Hogg leased premises in Sydney which acted as a branch for the Auckland operation.

Arthur was joined in New Zealand by his younger brother, Ernest, who arrived from Manchester in 1887. They formed a partnership, but before long Arthur decided

13 Albert Street, early 1940s.

he would move to Sydney as he felt the climate suited him better. He sailed across the Tasman leaving Ernest to manage New Zealand while he managed Australia.

Later, in 1906, the two brothers agreed to operate as two separate businesses in Auckland and Sydney, under the same name but managed separately. Each company retained close links with their father's business, Samuel Yates Ltd in Manchester. In the same year, the Auckland company transferred its business from 89 Queen Street to larger premises at 192 Queen Street.

In 1911 the company transferred again, to the newly erected shop and warehouse at 13 Albert Street, Auckland. Business was conducted from these premises until 1972, by which time the growth of the company made it necessary to move to a new complex at 270 Neilson Street, Onehunga.

In 1921 the first branch at Whangarei was opened. In the late 1920s the Auckland warehouse was further extended. The Christchurch branch was established in 1945, followed by Palmerston North in 1958, Wellington in 1960, and Hamilton in 1964.

In 1985 there was a takeover of the company by Equiticorp, and even though the Yates name remained, that was the end of the involvement of the Yates family.

Over the years all of the branches, with the exception of Christchurch, were closed. With improved delivery systems operating, all North Island customers were supplied from Auckland and South Island customers from Christchurch.

In September 1987, head office and the national warehouse moved to 4 Henderson Place, Onehunga. With the use of modern technology and improved efficiency it was possible to reduce the size of the warehouse to one-third the size of the Neilson Street complex. Another major transition for Yates New Zealand Ltd came in 1993, when the company was purchased by Arthur Yates and Company Pty Ltd, the Australian arm that was started by Arthur Yates over 100 years ago.

Between 1906, when Ernest Yates became principal of the New Zealand company, and 1985, when Equiticorp took over control, eight descendants of Ernest have served the company, namely: Eric, Ronald, Warwick, Norman, Jack, Richard, Scott and Phillip.

It is probably unique that the original firm of Samuel Yates Ltd of Manchester is today a subsidiary of the Australian company, and that descendants of George Yates managed the Manchester, Australian and New Zealand businesses right through until 1985.

The nursery on the rooftop of the Albert Street building, 1940.

PART I: DESIGNING OR REDESIGNING YOUR GARDEN

CHAPTER 1

ASPECTS OF PLANNING

A garden is for plants – and for people too. It's a place for enjoyment and relaxation, but it must also be functional and fit in with family needs and activities. Your degree of enthusiasm for gardening is an important factor to consider when planning your garden. Some people are never happier than when working in the garden, and others want a garden which is maintained without too much effort. Whatever your attitude, a garden should never become a burden or its upkeep a demanding chore.

These days, a variety of garden styles and designs can be selected, depending on your lifestyle or the type of house you have. Recently there has been a revival of interest in formal garden design, with straight-edged, square or rectangular beds and closely clipped hedges. Other gardens are closely planted with flowers and vegetables to give a crowded, cottage-like effect. Many new homes are built in bushland settings with the native plants and natural features retained wherever possible. Home design is changing too. A patio, terrace or deck for outdoor living and entertaining is often the focal point of modern, or modernised, houses, and there is a better blending of house and garden. New landscape materials – paving, pine bark and treated pine logs – have added new interest to planning a garden. Many of these are easy do-it-yourself materials, so you don't need to be an expert to use them.

No matter what sort of garden you choose, a plan is needed. Garden plans can be flexible, and alterations to an existing landscape may need only your labour and the cost of a few plants. A family's needs and interests do not remain static. For example, as children grow up, sandpits, swings and seesaws will no longer be of interest to them. Increasingly they will use the barbecue and swimming pool areas for recreation. Space to park additional cars may be required too. When planning your garden, long-term garden features should be located first, and places for short-term facilities fitted around these. This chapter outlines some of the principles involved in planning a pleasant and functional garden.

PATTERNS OF CLIMATE

Climate determines what plants you can grow. This applies to all plants – trees, shrubs, lawns, flowers and vegetables. Climate can be simply defined as a summation of the weather. In gardening, rainfall and temperature are the most important factors, with wind also to be considered in certain localities. The highest and lowest temperatures are more critical than the average temperature, because it is the extremes which cause problems with plant growth. This is important for the longer-lived species which may be damaged or destroyed by heat or cold. As a general rule, it is best to select plants for their particular temperature range. Rain, and when it falls, is important too. Although we cannot protect plants from excessive rain, we can supplement low rainfall in dry districts or in dry seasons by

> ## Hint
>
> *The large variety of plants on display in garden centres can be very tempting. However, in most cases it is better to grow large numbers of a small selection of plants successfully, than to plant a wide range of plants that do poorly. Choose carefully as small plants can grow into big trees.*
>
> DIANA SELBY
> LANDSCAPE ARCHITECT

TOP FIVE DECIDUOUS SHADE TREES

INDIAN BEAD TREE

Melia azedarach is a very handsome strong-growing tree with scented lilac flowers in spring and bright yellow fruits which persist into the winter months, long after the leaves have fallen.

SILK TREE

Albizzia julibrissin is an excellent choice for a small garden. Masses of fluffy pink flowers float atop layers of graceful foliage over summer.

GOLDEN ASH

Fraxinus excelsior 'Aurea' is one of the most majestic trees, with beautiful golden spring and summer foliage, stunning autumn colour and smooth golden branches providing a remarkable sight in winter.

ROBINIA 'FRISIA'

The brilliant butter-yellow summer foliage of this popular tree looks stunning against a dark background and provides excellent contrast to other plantings.

FLOWERING CHERRY

These spring flowering trees (*Prunus* cultivars) are greatly revered for their massed displays of delicate flowers. There are many different varieties to choose from, each with its own particular growth pattern.

INDIAN BEAD TREE

SILK TREE

watering. In many parts of New Zealand, gardens will need some supplementary watering.

New Zealand's climate is largely influenced by its latitudinal placement with a prevailing westerly wind-flow, its oceanic environment and its dominant mountain ranges. A succession of anticyclones and depressions constantly moving eastwards over the country determines the broad climatic pattern. However, their effects are rarely uniform over the entire country due to the above three factors together with a widely varying topography resulting in a complex weather pattern with many localised microclimates. The maps on page 4 and 5 show the range of soil temperature zones within New Zealand.

MICROCLIMATE

This description of climate zones in New Zealand is very general. Any district, city or town includes some locations where the climate is different from the general pattern. This difference may be due to one of many factors, including elevation, slope, aspect, proximity to the coast or lakes, or prevailing winds.

For example, northerly aspects are warmer than southerly aspects; hollows or flat sites at the bottom of slopes are cold and more liable

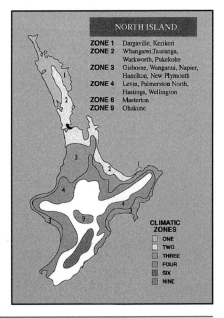

NORTH ISLAND	
ZONE 1	Dargaville, Kerikeri
ZONE 2	Whangarei,Tauranga, Warkworth, Pukekohe
ZONE 3	Gisborne, Wanganui, Napier, Hamilton, New Plymouth
ZONE 4	Levin, Palmerston North, Hastings, Wellington
ZONE 6	Masterton
ZONE 9	Ohakune

CLIMATIC ZONES
- ONE
- TWO
- THREE
- FOUR
- SIX
- NINE

to frost because cold air flows downhill. These small local climates are called microclimates. You can often create a microclimate in your own garden by providing extra warmth and shelter with a brick, stone or concrete building or wall. Plants themselves may provide microclimates. Shade-loving plants can be grown under the protection of trees. Also, frost-sensitive plants may succeed in the shelter provided by overhanging vegetation because radiation frosts are eliminated at that particular spot. You can build artificial microclimates too: bush or shadehouses, glasshouses and glass frames. These are discussed in Chapter 2.

ASPECT, SUN AND SHADE

Plants need light to carry out the process called photosynthesis. This allows them to make sugars (the starting point for more complex plant foods) from carbon dioxide in the air and water from the soil.

Many plants require full sunlight, but others tolerate shade in varying degrees. The preferred aspect for most New Zealand homes and gardens is north-east. This way, sun is received in the early morning and for most of the day. A north-east slope is even better, because it is warmer and protected from cold southerly and south-west winds. It

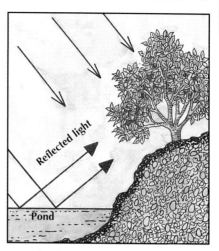

A pond reflects sunlight from the surface of the water and provides extra light for nearby plants.

is possible to build a house on almost any block of land so that the garden gets sufficient sunlight. In fact, many people prefer the front of the house to face south so that they can have the main garden and outdoor living areas at the back of the house for more privacy.

When planning a garden it is important to know the sunny spots and the areas shaded by buildings, trees and shrubs. A deciduous tree such as a liquidambar or a prunus planted on the north of the house will give summer shade but will let through winter sun. Alternatively, you could cover a north-facing terrace with a pergola and grow a deciduous climber like wisteria over it. The south and south-east sides of the house are suitable for shade-loving plants such as hydrangeas, azaleas and camellias. In many places, especially in warm temperate areas, the garden on the west side of the house receives full sun in the early afternoon, that is, the hottest part of the day. Winds from the west and south-west are another hazard. Tall shrubs on western and southern boundaries may be the best answer to problems raised by excessive wind. Individual trees, shrubs and smaller flowering perennials also compete with each other for light. How well various plants mix together is related to rates of growth and ultimate height and spread.

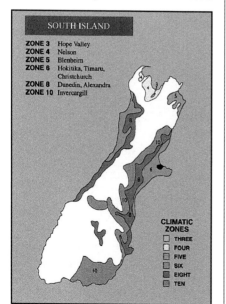

SOUTH ISLAND

ZONE 3	Hope Valley
ZONE 4	Nelson
ZONE 5	Blenheim
ZONE 6	Hokitika, Timaru, Christchurch
ZONE 8	Dunedin, Alexandra
ZONE 10	Invercargill

CLIMATIC ZONES
- THREE
- FOUR
- FIVE
- SIX
- EIGHT
- TEN

DESIGNING OR REDESIGNING YOUR GARDEN

DESIGNING OR REDESIGNING YOUR GARDEN

WIND PROTECTION

Plants grow better and people enjoy outdoor living more if they are sheltered from strong winds. Many parts of New Zealand are subject to extremes of wind and rain, the worst being the cold southerly winds of winter and spring and the hot westerly flows often predominant over Canterbury Plains in summer. North-east winds often cause problems in exposed areas on the east coast.

Windbreaks of trees, shrubs, hedges or fences on the south or west sides of a garden will give good protection for distances up to ten times the height of the barrier, and some protection at twenty times the height. Trees and shrubs planted on the south or west will not create a shade problem in your own garden, but their effect on neighbouring properties should be taken into consideration. If strategically placed, though, a belt of tall vegetation can provide an effective shelter zone when planted well back from garden or vegetable beds.

The best man-made wind barriers filter, rather than block, the wind. Slatted fences, lattice or perforated concrete blocks (with about 50 per cent opening) are more effective than solid paling fences or brick walls. Solid barriers create wind turbulence on both sides. Similarly, a tree or shrub with dense foliage will create turbulence, but lightly foliaged plants will filter wind and reduce its speed. Correct placement of suitable windbreaks prevents plant damage and creates a better microclimate for the garden. The effects of different windbreaks are shown below.

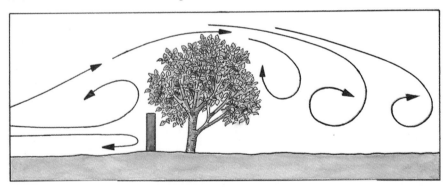

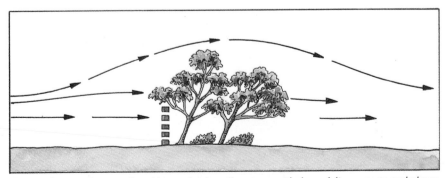

Solid barriers, such as a paling fence, a brick wall or trees with dense foliage, create turbulence on both sides of the wind barrier. Slatted fences and shrubs with light foliage, on the other hand, will filter the wind and reduce its speed.

A garden can fit in with existing bushland.

CONSIDER WHAT YOU HAVE

Bushland sites may include native trees or shrubs which it is desirable to retain. Disturb the ground as little as possible until you are ready to make improvements, otherwise weeds move in as soon as the natural cover goes. Rocky outcrops can also be worked into the garden design. Even a low-lying wet area may be useful. For example, an ornamental pool might be placed on the site and surrounded with bog plants.

Building subdivisions in older, settled areas often contain established trees and shrubs, which should be retained if at all possible. Subdivisions in areas which were previously farming land usually have little in the way of ornamental plants or existing features, so you have to start from scratch.

Another point to consider is the existing outlook from the house or from the garden. Pleasant outlooks can often be improved by using suitable plantings as a 'frame', while the reverse situation may apply to an unsightly outlook. This should be screened from view with trees, shrubs, a hedge or a garden wall. Privacy plantings will also give protection from prying neighbours, traffic noise and headlight glare.

SOIL TYPE AND DRAINAGE

This topic is described fully in Chapter 3 but a few points here may help in the planning stage.

Heavy clay soils are more fertile than light sandy soils, but invariably cause drainage problems. Sandy soils will often have a clay

Hint

Thorough planning is crucial if you want to establish a successful garden. Take careful note of the situation, climate and type of soil that you have, then choose appropriate plants. If you buy plants that are not suitable for your garden, you will just be wasting your money.

GORDON COLLIER
TITOKI POINT

subsoil, or a rock layer close to the surface which traps water, even on sloping ground. Usually a deep rubble drain on the high side of the block will divert run-off water or

DESIGNING OR REDESIGNING YOUR GARDEN

A slope filled with well-chosen plants can become a garden feature.

seepage from above. On very steep slopes, surface run-off water may be excessive. This problem is best overcome by terracing the slope with retaining walls.

Whatever type of soil you have – clay, sand or loam – remember that the topsoil is the most valuable. If a new house is being built it is a good idea to remove about 5 cm of topsoil from the site. Heap this good soil in an out-of-the-way corner for later use. Excess clay from excavations or trenches should be kept in the building area or heaped separately. It can be used for the base of rockeries or built-up beds, but in many cases it is best removed from the site entirely.

Hint

Don't rush into planting. Neighbourhood gardens are fabulous trial beds. Stroll around local streets and identify plants that are flourishing. They are the ones most likely to do well for you.

BOB EDWARDS
EDITOR, *COMMERCIAL HORTICULTURE*

Any part of the garden which has been excavated to clay subsoil will need to be covered with a generous layer of imported garden soil. It is best to purchase this from a reliable supplier.

After importing soil into the garden, encourage the appearance of any troublesome weeds by watering well and waiting for the weeds to appear. Low-toxic herbicides containing glyphosate (such as Zero), which will kill almost any plant without harming the soil, can be used to eliminate weeds before making garden plantings.

MAKING YOUR PLAN

After you have considered all the features of the section, both good and bad, the next step is to make a plan to scale. Use stiff white paper or graph paper for the base plan, with several sheets of tracing paper for transparent overlays.

House and site plans are drawn on a metric scale of 1:100 (a line 1 cm long on the plan will represent 1 m on the ground). Pads of graph paper are available from stationers, measuring 18 cm x 30 cm, a suitable size for an average block with a frontage of 15–18 m and a depth of 30 m. Use two sheets joined together for larger sections.

Make the base plan very clear so it can be seen through the tracing paper on which you will draw your garden designs. On the base plan show the boundaries of the land, the position of the house and existing features such as trees and shrubs. It is also a good idea to indicate the general contours or slope and note the position of steep areas, low-lying spots and shallow soil over rocky sections, because these may influence future planting schemes. Mark in the positions of all services, including electricity, gas, telephone, water (with tap positions), sewerage or septic systems.

Outside the boundary show compass points to give you an idea of sun and shade areas, and mark in the prevailing wind direction. Also indicate any unsightly aspects to be screened, or pleasant views to be retained. Use the first overlay of tracing paper to broadly define suitable areas for different purposes or activities. Further sheets can be used to plan the various areas in more detail.

There are two facets of home life to consider when planning a garden. The first

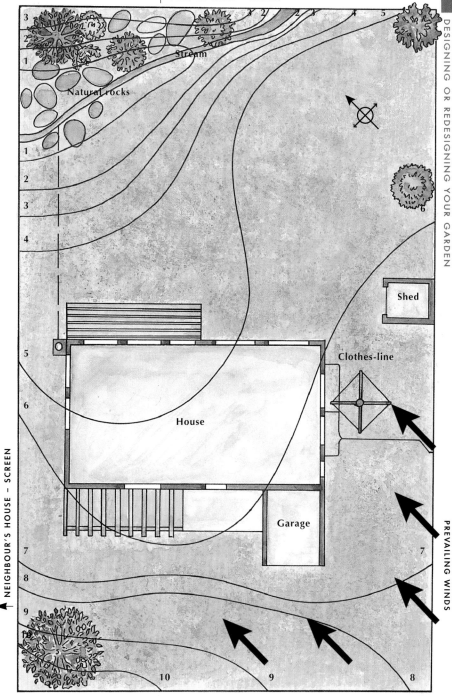

Base plan for a new garden.

DESIGNING OR REDESIGNING YOUR GARDEN

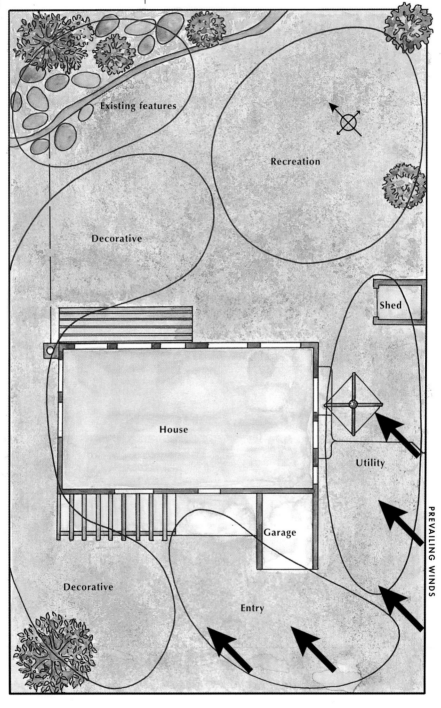

VIEW TO HILLS – RETAIN

Existing features

Recreation

Decorative

Shed

House

Utility

NEIGHBOUR'S HOUSE – SCREEN

PREVAILING WINDS

Decorative

Garage

Entry

First garden plan overlay showing main purpose and activity areas.

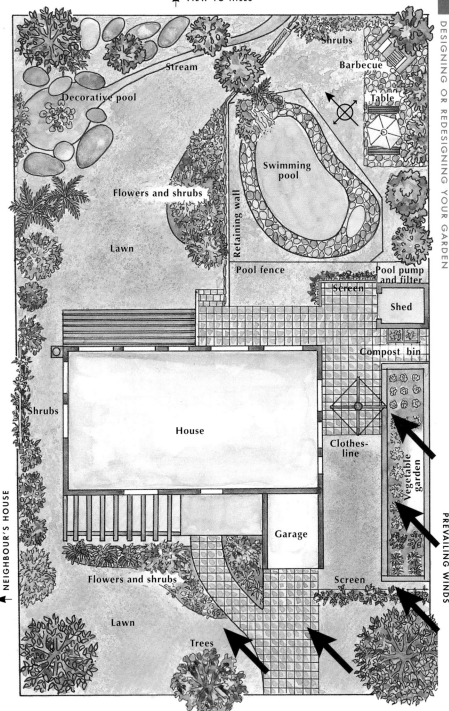

▲ VIEW TO HILLS

Stream

Shrubs

Barbecue

Decorative pool

Table

Swimming pool

Flowers and shrubs

Retaining wall

Lawn

Pool fence

Pool pump and filter

Screen

Shed

Compost bin

Shrubs

House

Clothes-line

Vegetable garden

PREVAILING WINDS

NEIGHBOUR'S HOUSE

Garage

Flowers and shrubs

Screen

Lawn

Trees

Second garden plan overlay showing final planting and garden layout.

DESIGNING OR REDESIGNING YOUR GARDEN

Hint

If a plant — whether a tree, shrub or perennial — doesn't look good where you have planted it, don't hesitate to move it. Relocate plants in winter to minimise transplantation shock.

MARY LOVELL-SMITH
CHRISTCHURCH *PRESS*

concerns routine activities which require utility areas, places for drying washing, for composting, for storing garbage bins, and for housing tools. A children's play area for a swing or sandpit could also be classed as a utility area. Your family may need more than one utility area. The outdoor recreational and entertainment aspects of family life call for areas of lawn, garden beds, shrubberies and trees, among which a barbecue or perhaps a swimming pool can be located. Plans for these areas must take into account nearby houses and views from windows in your own house

(views of the garden and views beyond the boundaries of the building block). Plans for the garden itself should be fairly simple at first. There will be plenty of opportunities to embellish later on. While you're planning, consider the long-term maintenance as well as the preparation of the site and the initial plantings. Too ambitious a plan may make the garden a millstone around your neck later on.

The siting of utility areas depends on the design of the house. Ready access to clothes lines, rubbish bins and children's play areas is necessary. Sunlight for the drying area and some sun and shade for a play area is required. A study of the diagrams showing the positions and lengths of shadows at different times of the year can help you decide where trees or tall shrubs can be placed. The utility area dealing with garden waste or compost is best located in a corner remote from the house. It can be quite effectively screened with medium-height shrubs.

The ornamental and recreational areas of a garden usually have lawns as their basic feature. Lawns provide open space and give an air of spaciousness to the garden.

A grape vine provides shade in summer and sun in winter for this outdoor eating area.

Garden trees should be chosen carefully. The size of a tree after ten or twenty years is an important consideration. Choose trees that will grow to a suitable size rather than trees that have to be regularly pruned to keep them within reasonable bounds. Some other considerations when selecting trees are: the vigour and extent of spread of root systems; deciduous or evergreen habit; the type of foliage; and flowering habit, time and colour. A poor choice might adversely affect the other plants in the garden through root competition and shading.

Shrubs can be used very effectively for boundary planting. Decide on the ultimate height desired and choose shrubs that will reach that height at maturity. Pruning and trimming to size can then be avoided and the plants will be free to follow their natural growth form.

A garden with shrubs as the only feature would be easy to maintain but visually rather monotonous. Low-growing perennials used along shrubbery frontages will give a changing pattern of colour. Evergreen perennials will produce the best effect but deciduous species (plants with bulbs, tubers or rhizomes that die back in winter) can be tucked in to give variation.

There is a tendency to overplant with shrubs in a new garden because there seems to be room for lots of them, but space for the shrubs to spread is essential. Shrubs in large pots or tubs should not be overlooked when garden plans are being made because, to some extent, these shrubs are mobile. The containers might be brought to where the plants can be seen to best effect when in flower, and relegated to a minor position at other times. Permanently placed container-grown shrubs are useful for softening paved areas.

Most gardens need some flowering annuals, not only for garden decoration but for providing blooms for cutting. Annuals grow in many shapes and sizes – tall, dwarf, compact, spreading – and the range of flower colours is enormous.

Do not overlook climbing plants. Because of their vertical habit they don't take up much room in the garden. Self-clingers (like ivy or Virginia creeper) can be grown on brick or masonry walls, and all types of climbers can be trained on fences, trellises or pergolas.

Shrubby native plants provide food and protection for small birds.

There are many ways of attracting birds to the garden. Some of the native shrubs and trees – such as rewarewa, kowhai, kaka beak and flax – will attract honeyeaters. Fruiting plants such as coprosma and wineberry will also provide sources of food. Plant a mixture of different-sized plants to attract birds and make sure that some of them have twiggy, shrubby growth that will provide shelter for the smaller birds. Provide a birdbath or some other safe source of water.

Hint

Never underestimate the role of the colours, shapes and textures of leaves in your garden. Be big and bold with foliage. Plenty of foliage is vital for creating a restful atmosphere and aesthetically it's a lot more forgiving than flowers.

MARY LOVELL-SMITH
CHRISTCHURCH *PRESS*

THE LOW-ALLERGEN GARDEN

The plants we grow in our gardens are not always beautiful and harmless. The months from August until March can cause sneezing, itchy eyes, a runny nose and extreme fatigue in people who are sensitive to pollen. Others may suffer seasonal asthma, or find that their asthma becomes worse during these months.

These symptoms can be significantly reduced with some careful planning of your garden. The plants which cause most trouble are very often in our own backyards. Many wind-borne pollens only travel short distances, so controlling pollen sources in your garden, especially near your windows, is important.

CREATING A LOW-ALLERGEN GARDEN

The most significant step you can take in planning a low-allergen garden is to choose bird- or insect-pollinated plants rather than wind-pollinated ones. Plants pollinated by birds and insects produce only small amounts of pollen. Most native trees and shrubs are pollinated by birds and insects.

Lawns can also produce a lot of wind-borne pollen. When mowing a lawn, protect your eyes, nose and mouth with a mask and goggles, or mow while the dew is still on the lawn.

Grow windbreaks or build high, climber-covered fences to reduce the amount of wind-borne pollen reaching your garden from neighbouring properties.

THANKS TO THE ASTHMA FOUNDATION FOR THIS INFORMATION

Weeds produce airborne pollen as well as taking valuable nutrients from the soil. Mulching helps to control weeds, but it is important that you use an inorganic mulch, since organic mulch like straw and hay may harbour moulds which are allergenic for some people. A suitable groundcover is a good substitute for mulch.

Lightly scented plants are preferable to strong scents, as these can act as an irritant and cause symptoms similar to those caused by breathing in pollen or mould spores.

OTHER THINGS YOU CAN DO

It is a good idea to stay indoors on hot, still days when pollen counts are high, or on very windy days. The best time to garden is in the early morning, before temperatures rise and the breezes increase, and also on cool, cloudy days.

Watch out for areas that may harbour moulds, such as shaded and southern sides of houses, and avoid digging in compost heaps, as these contain mould spores which could aggravate asthma or other irritations.

Be aware that washing dried outside may pick up pollen and cause allergic symptoms in the very pollen sensitive person.

CHOOSING SUITABLE PLANTS

Low-allergy plants include those that are pollinated by insects or birds only, or that are propagated by cuttings or grafting. Some plants you might like to try are:

GRASSES AND GROUNDCOVERS

- kikuyu • kidney weed (dichondra) • snow-in-summer • low-growing cotoneaster • Tasmanian violet

CLIMBERS

- clematis • Chilean jasmine • passionfruit • banksia rose • potato vine

SHRUBS

- azalea • rhododendron • camellia • gardenia • rosemary • heath banksia • kaka beak • tea tree

TREES

- magnolia • sweet bay • citrus • flowering almond, apricot and cherry • scribbly gum • silky oak • lilly pilly • cabbage tree palm

FLOWERS

- alyssum • aquilegia • foxglove • impatiens • lobelia • nasturtium • petunia • snapdragon

For a full list of suitable plants, contact your local nursery or Asthma Auckland. Enquiries: (09) 630 2293.

WHAT TO AVOID

THE FOLLOWING PLANTS SHOULD BE AVOIDED BY THOSE WHO SUFFER FROM ASTHMA:

- asteraceae family (daisies, chrysanthemums, calendulas, marigolds) • most introduced grasses • wattles • alder • ash • birch • she oak • cypress • elm • liquidambar • maple • white cedar • oak • olive • poplar • privet • walnut • willow

THE FOLLOWING PLANTS MAY CAUSE A PAINFUL RASH IF TOUCHED:

- primula • common or English ivy • poinsettia • rhus tree • *Grevillea* 'Robyn Gordon' and other cultivars • many bulbs

CHAPTER 2

FEATURES FOR YOUR GARDEN

A gardener with imagination and ingenuity can introduce many special features to make a garden more interesting and attractive. A garden provides plenty of opportunities for creative thinking. Many garden features can be created by the home gardener and there is a wealth of landscaping materials from which to choose. A do-it-yourself job may take a little longer, but it will give much more satisfaction than calling in a landscape consultant or contractor. This chapter aims to give you some first principles for the design and construction of garden features.

PATIOS AND TERRACES

Patio is a Spanish word meaning the inner court of a house. A terrace is defined as a promenade or place for leisurely walking. In the New Zealand garden scene, both words have come to mean an area which is an extension of the house with access to the living room, dining room or kitchen. Often these areas are uncovered, but in warm climates an overhead framework for creepers, shadecloth or clear sheeting can be a useful addition. The cover provides some shade, reduces glare, and allows the area to be used during hot or wet seasons. Enclosure on at least one side by a trellised vine can increase privacy.

It is best if a patio or terrace faces east, north-east or north in order to trap sun from early morning to mid-afternoon. Patios and terraces are ideal for outdoor meals. On flat sites it is usual to build them flush with garden beds or lawn, or with one or two shallow steps to the garden. A railing or low wall is needed on sloping sites, especially if young children are around.

The patio or terrace is ideal for outdoor pot and tub plants which need open sunlight and extra warmth. Container-grown vegetables and herbs are also popular.

The paving surface of the patio or terrace should be smooth (for walking and for the placing of outdoor tables and chairs) and easy to sweep and clean. Brick paving, which can be laid in many patterns, is popular, but may absorb stains. A less expensive alternative is pre-cast concrete paving blocks or slabs. Quarry tiles, which come in a wide variety of colours, shapes and textures, give a more formal appearance but must be laid on a concrete base. The tiles do not absorb stains and are easy to clean. Large split sandstone slabs need careful laying for an even surface, but dressed (sawn) slabs make one of the best paving materials. These have an attractive, non-slip, easy-to-clean surface which dries quickly after rain. Where the paving is set on a sand base, ants sometimes bring sand to the surface along joints. Weeds may germinate there too. Ants and weeds can be removed with one of the several suitable commercial products.

Hint

You can create continuity between living rooms and outdoor patios by using containers and plants with colours and styles that coordinate with your interior decor. The wide range of pots on the market makes it easy to find something to suit the colour scheme of your house.

DIANA SELBY
LANDSCAPE ARCHITECT

DESIGNING OR REDESIGNING YOUR GARDEN

COURTYARDS

Courtyards are usually open to the sky and are really an outside room. Some people prefer a covered courtyard – a vine covering a pergola, a roof of opaque fibreglass – as protection against direct sunlight. You can build a courtyard in a very small space, between house and garage or between the house and a boundary fence or wall. In warm climates, the zone between the house and the garage or carport can be roofed but left open at the ends. Termed breezeways, these areas protect car travellers arriving or leaving during rain, and provide an airy, shaded retreat in hot weather. Breezeways can be planted as is suggested for shady courtyards.

A courtyard usually contains more plants than a patio or terrace – in many cases it becomes a sort of transition between the garden and house. Choose courtyard plants carefully. Plants for shade or semi-shade are usually the most suitable but one side of the courtyard may be sunny at some times of the year. Low-growing shrubs are best in the sunniest parts. Groundcover plantings could include ferns, plants with small foliage and some flowering plants. Paved courtyards need the relief provided by plants in tubs or pots. Climbing or clinging plants can be effective in reducing the starkness of walls.

DECKS

A deck or timber platform offers another alternative for outdoor living. It is a natural choice for steep or rocky sites where flat land is scarce. It is less expensive to build a deck than to level the ground and erect a massive retaining wall.

You can use low-level decks on flat sites as an alternative to paving. This way you can extend the house at floor level, provide a non-slip surface adjacent to a swimming pool, or make a shady dining area around the trunk of a large tree. High-level decks need a safety rail. Decks of stained or treated timber are simple to maintain. Small gaps between decking boards allow quick drainage after rain and easy sweeping. Many do-it-yourself enthusiasts can build simple low-level decks, but a high-level deck is usually a job for an experienced

This attractive eating area serves as a sheltered outdoor room.

carpenter. The foundation area must be well drained to carry water away from the posts or piers supporting the deck. Container-grown plants soften and decorate open decks and the roofed verandahs which are features of many older homes. Choice of specimens for a container planting on a deck is influenced by the amount of sunlight reaching the flooring. Open decks are suitable for small, sun-hardy shrubs, while covered verandahs require plants for semi-shade. Low tables can accommodate ornamental plants in small pots.

BARBECUES AND SWIMMING POOLS

For many families the barbecue and swimming pool are the centres of outdoor entertaining and family recreation. These facilities can be used to best advantage if they are adjacent to one another or, better still, if they are integrated. In the latter case, a more spacious area may result because duplication of some plantings is then avoided. It is preferable to have the pool and barbecue sites in close proximity to the house. This makes the outdoor living areas an extension of the patio or terrace and the indoors. Also, from a practical point of view, the kitchen and bathroom are within easy reach.

The swimming pool itself should receive full sunlight for much of the day. This can be achieved to some extent by attention to another matter, namely, siting the pool where tall trees can't continually shed leaves into it. Shelter from wind can be provided by the house, shrubberies, hedges or vine-covered trellises. Pools need a surround of concrete tiles or other non-slip and waterproof material. Beyond the pool surrounds, a lawn is ideal, providing an area for outdoor furniture that will serve both pool and barbecue.

Trees take several years to reach a size where they will throw worthwhile shade, and many species have root systems that may cause problems for older pools. A creeper-covered pergola may be a much better means of providing shade near the pool. Trees need not be excluded, but they should be chosen from the list of trees of limited height, appropriate to the locality, and then planted as far from the pool as is practicable.

In New Zealand it is mandatory to have a safety fence around a swimming pool. Tall

Hint

When planning barbecue and swimming pool areas, don't forget to include lighting, especially to highlight changes in level that may be dangerous. Garden lights also increase the ambience of your outdoor living areas and can be used to highlight specimen plants.

MICHAEL GRAHAM
LANDSCAPE ARCHITECT

shrubs grown for windbreaks, screening for privacy, or visual effects outside a pool safety fence must be far enough away to prevent their use as aids to scaling the fence. Use lower shrubs, perennials and flowering annuals within the fenced section.

Essential pool equipment, such as the filter and pump, can be screened by low hedges. Abelia, box, corokia, and blue plumbago can be clipped to make a dense screen.

There is so much variation in climate zones in New Zealand that it must be left to individual home owners to work out the most appropriate plantings for their pool and barbecue areas. The use of tall species of palms, hibiscus, various bamboos and Australian frangipani, which warm-climate gardeners use to such good effect, would not be possible in cool–temperate regions. Checking your neighbourhood to see which plants grow well is probably the best starting point when planning what and where to plant.

Shrubs and a spreading tree will screen and shade a barbecue area. With that as a basis, more detailed plantings can be made according to individual preferences, micro-climates and garden design.

Views towards other parts of the garden from outdoor living spaces should always be retained. A decorative pool and its surrounding plants, or a big tree on a far boundary, should not be looked on as separate entities but rather as integral parts of the whole garden. The objective should be to have them all visible from various points both inside the house and in the garden.

DESIGNING OR REDESIGNING YOUR GARDEN

DECORATIVE POOLS

Decorative pools introduce movement and sparkling light to a garden and give a sense of coolness during the hotter part of the year. Informal pools can be located in shady places, although that makes it impossible to grow plants like waterlilies which require full sunlight. For part shade there are aquatic plants that are tolerant of partial sun. In the vicinity of a shaded pool the microclimate is such that shade-tolerant vegetation flourishes. Tree ferns, palms of limited size, variously sized foliage plants of many species, small ferns and cotula introduce a rainforest atmosphere, especially if there are overhanging trees and background shrubs.

Plantings around decorative pools should not be in a narrow band close to the edge of the pool. Make plantings up to several metres away from the poolside, using a variety of plants that are compatible with one another in size, foliage type and the form and colour of the leaves. A fairly open foreground, using mainly low-growing plants, puts the pool and its surrounding vegetation into a pleasant perspective. Pools need fish in them to control the aquatic larvae of pest insects, especially mosquitoes. The bright colours of goldfish enhance a pool's appearance, but remember that fish need projecting rocks or some other kind of shelter from predatory birds.

Hint

Combat mosquitoes in bowls or small ponds by adding a few drops of cooking oil to the water — it won't harm the plants but it will stop the larvae coming up for air.

MARY LOVELL-SMITH
CHRISTCHURCH *PRESS*

For informal pools, ready-made fibreglass liners are available in various shapes and sizes. Excavate a hole, slip in the fibreglass shell and you have an instant pool. More popular are the do-it-yourself pools which are constructed by lining an excavation of your own design with black polythene or flexible waterproof sheeting. Suitable grades of sheeting can be bought at nurseries and hardware stores. Also available are pool-making kits, with instructions and diagrams.

Having decided on the shape and size of your pool, you should allow enough flexible lining for the sloping sides, plus about 20 cm overlap all around so you can anchor it down. If you wish to keep and breed fish (which keep the pool clean and free of mosquito wrigglers) you will need to excavate part of the pool to a depth of about 45 cm. Ensure that this deep part is overhung with rocks or vegetation.

Some of the excavated soil can be used to form a rocky mound behind the pool or to build up the edges on the low sides. In the latter case, tread the soil down firmly. Lay the liner loosely, anchoring the edges with small stones, and fill with water. This gives firm contact between the sheet and the base, and allows you to check water levels accurately at all points. Build up low spots and shave off high spots as required.

Now lap the edges with stones to cover and anchor the liner in place. Use thinner stones at the front and wider slabs overhanging the water at the back. One or two large stones can project well over the water, but make sure they are counter-balanced in case someone stands on them. All stones and edges should be firm and well settled at this stage. When you are happy with the effect, siphon out the water and apply a 2.5 cm layer of cement (one part cement to three parts sand) as a permanent protection to the polythene. Keep the cement mix fairly dry. Starting at the lowest point, gradually spread the cement upwards and tuck under the stones. For easier working, place a hessian sack, an old mat or piece of carpet on the cemented bottom so you can stand on this without causing damage. When almost dry, smooth the cement by rubbing with a piece of hessian.

When completed, blend the pool into the surroundings with scattered rocks, boulders, pebbles or gravel. Ferns, Nile grass (*Cyperus papyrus*), New Zealand flax, irises and dwarf conifers are good subjects for pool surrounds. Do not plant large trees close by because the roots may damage the pool.

Formal pools, which may be circular, oval, square or rectangular, are often more appropriate in small gardens, especially in paved areas. The surround can be built in brickwork on a concrete slab, and can be topped with a coping slab. The brickwork should be cement-rendered with a mix of one part cement to three parts sand to which a waterproofing compound has been added. If the edge of the pool is built up 40–50 cm above ground level the coping slab can be used as a seat. A high surround presents a deterrent for small children but should never be regarded as childproof. Formal pools may be located in open places so that the structure and texture of the pool materials are displayed. Plantings around formal pools are usually restrained in order to give the pond plants themselves greater prominence.

In both informal and formal pools, pockets of brick or stone on the bottom can hold aquatic plants, or plants can be grown in sunken pots or wire baskets. Waterlilies (*Nymphaea* spp.) are the most popular, but there are many other attractive and useful oxygenating plants which will keep the water clean and fresh. Among them are sacred lotus (*Nelumbo nucifera*), arrowhead (*Sagittaria sagittifolia*), taro (*Colocasia esculenta*), pickerel weed (*Pontederia cordata*) and the native milfoil (*Myriophyllum propinquum*). If water plants become too rampant, as some species may do, thin them out before they take over the pool completely. A few floating plants, notably water hyacinth and oxygen weed, have been declared plant pests in New Zealand. They must not be used in garden pools.

DESIGNING OR REDESIGNING YOUR GARDEN

A decorative pond helps this garden to blend in with its natural surroundings.

The solid structure of this pergola is both aesthetically pleasing and functional.

PLAY AREAS

A playground is a great asset. It encourages youngsters to play out of doors and gives them a feeling of ownership of their own small part of the garden. For toddlers, a sandpit is a must. Locate it where spilled sand does not matter and construct it on a base of unmortared bricks or concrete pavers for good drainage after rain. A surround of concrete blocks or dressed timber (no splinters) can be used. Seesaws and swings suit older children but make sure they are soundly built and unlikely to cause mishaps. Swings should always have plastic seats. Smooth timber logs are quite attractive and kids will invent their own games climbing over or around them. For children who are old enough, a rope ladder on the limb of a large tree is a great attraction, especially if it leads to a cubby house. Play areas should be carpeted with rough lawn. Lawn is soft enough for jumping and falling on and good for rough-and-tumble games. If the area is too shady for grass, use pine bark, or even artificial grass, to soften falls.

PERGOLAS

A pergola was originally an arbour or covered walk at the bottom of the garden. Today, a pergola is commonly an extension of the house over a patio or terrace. In many respects it has taken over from the verandah of colonial days. A well-designed pergola is not only an attractive addition to your house but a structure to support vines or creepers and hanging baskets.

The structure must be strong if it is to carry a heavy creeper like wisteria or grape vine. Wooden posts 100 mm x 100 mm square, with load-bearing rails of 100 mm x 50 mm timber on edge and 75 mm x 50 mm cross-rails on edge, are standard in such constructions. You can use pine posts and rails for a more rustic look. Posts can also be brick piers or moulded concrete. Roofing is not necessary but some people use timber slats, shade cloth or translucent polycarbonate sheets.

SCREENS

Building sites are likely to become smaller, rather than larger, in future. The average new homesite is now 15–18 metres wide and 30–45 metres deep. This means that privacy from the street or from your neighbours is often at a premium. Trees, shrubs and hedges come to mind immediately, but in some situations there is not sufficient space for them to grow, and structured screens are a useful substitute.

There are many kinds of screen: brick, concrete blocks, stone, slatted timber, lattice, translucent polycarbonate sheets and toughened glass panels. Don't forget that screens must look good from both sides, your own and your neighbour's! Check with the neighbour first, then check local council regulations to see how high and how close to the boundary your screen can go. Many screens will support attractive, useful creepers and vines. (See Chapter 13.)

For full and permanent screening, choose species which are evergreen. Consider, too, the type of foliage, because some climbers are less than beautiful except when in flower. The weight of the vine when it has covered the screen is important. Some plants (such as

Hint

Thorny plants are best sited away from places where people pass in a hurry. Planting climbing roses on tennis courts and arches may seem a good idea, but unless they are thornless, running for that elusive ball or chasing the dog could turn into a painful experience.

DENNIS GREVILLE
GARDEN WRITER

wisteria) develop thick, woody stems and foliage in great abundance. They become too bulky and too heavy as time passes. Climbers with thin and flexible stems are easily trained over a screen and are still relatively lightweight when fully grown.

A lattice screen is softened by climbing roses.

TOP FIVE
FAST-GROWING TREES

VIRGILIA

'A short life but a gay one' is a truism for this rapid-growing South African tree. Virgilia is sometimes called 'tree-in-a-hurry' and has soft, finely divided leaves and mauve-pink spring pea blossoms. A great choice for a small garden.

EUCALYPTS

The most Australian of all trees, gum trees have more than 600 species, so there's one to suit every garden. The spectacular Western Australian flowering gum, which is most noticeable when it produces showy red blossoms, is now being grafted onto a hardy rootstock. This greatly extends the range of areas where it can be grown.

NEW ZEALAND NGAIO
(*MYOPORUM LAETUM*)

A very popular choice for coastal areas but equally as good elsewhere provided it is protected from heavy frost.

LEMONWOOD

Pittosporum eugenoides has handsome glossy green foliage, and a tolerance of poor soils that makes it a perfect choice for hedging or a fast-growing screen.

CASUARINA

There's a casuarina for every situation, from the seaside to the desert edge. On most species the fine, weeping branchlets droop gracefully.

Hint

One good specimen tree is worth its weight in gold. Select a tree that you really like, and that is suitable for your garden, and prepare the site well. It will pay dividends in the future. The choice of trees now is stunning.
GORDON COLLIER
TITOKI POINT

GARDEN TREES

A garden without any trees lacks the tall plants that give balance to the shrubs. There are trees whose natural growth pattern achieves a mature height of 6–8 metres, which is quite enough for most suburban gardens. Big trees are for large gardens. Several small trees planted near one another will, in time, enmesh their canopies.

The provision of shade in summer is one of the most important roles that trees play in a garden. In cool climates, deciduous trees may be preferable to evergreens so that summer shade will be replaced by sunlight in winter.

Whatever the type of tree, there will be a shaded area beneath for at least several months each year. This raises some difficulties with underplantings. The usual lawn grasses do not thrive, and weeds that favour shady places often flourish under trees. Laying paving under the tree and growing some plants in containers is one way of improving these difficult areas. An alternative solution is to plant lots of shade-tolerant plants under the tree. Some paving stones and a garden seat will work well in this shady spot. Plants with large leaves are often used because they impart an air of luxuriant tropical vegetation and because these types of leaves have evolved to make the most of the available light. Hostas, fatsia, Japanese anemone, clivia (an excellent plant for the deepest shade), daylily, bergenia, various euphorbias, acanthus and the native Renga lily, plus the colour of balsams, impatiens, cinerarias, primulas and polyanthus, and the fine foliage of ferns – these are only some of the plants that can suit difficult spots under trees. Where there is a group of shade trees, a mini

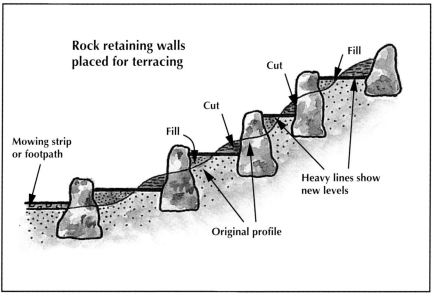

Rock retaining walls placed for terracing

Fill

Cut

Cut

Fill

Mowing strip or footpath

Heavy lines show new levels

Original profile

Rocks set on edge form rockery pockets on a sloping site.

rainforest effect can be achieved, especially if some light climbing plants are placed where it becomes possible for them to cling to the lower parts of tree trunks. Rainforest effects need not be confined to the northern climes. Densely planted areas with meandering paths can be developed using cool-climate plants too.

USE OF FLOWERING ANNUALS

Garden beds in full sun that are devoted entirely to annuals can create outstanding floral displays. With careful selection, other parts of the garden can be brightened by annuals. A small number of annuals will grow in less than full sunlight. The most shade tolerant are cinerarias, primulas, polyanthus, lobelia, bedding begonias, impatiens and dwarf marigolds. Alyssum, violas, portulaca, French marigolds, petunias and phlox are low-growing plants with a spreading habit that makes them suitable for foreground plantings, for sunny parts of rock gardens, or for use as edgings or ribbons of colour.

Most gardens can make use of flowering annuals outside the formal flowerbeds. Even a few brightly flowering annuals grouped in clumps can change a garden's appearance quite markedly.

TERRACING SLOPES

On level sites, a terrace garden can serve the same purpose as a retaining wall.

Terraces can be created with rocks, railway sleepers or treated pine logs. If building a rock garden, use ripped, rather than bush, rock. Collecting bush rock causes environmental damage and destroys the habitat of many tiny creatures.

On slopes, rocks are used to form pockets of terraced beds. Bury their large ends (to about one-third of their depth) in soil. Always use the largest rocks at the bottom of the mound or slope. Prostrate plants can cover rocks placed as water barriers. The plants will reduce the speed of flowing water while the underlying rocks, plus the plants' roots, will hold the soil.

Many terraces are overplanted in a desire to have an instant garden, but these will finish up as a shapeless mass of greenery. A happier approach is to plant alternate pockets with suitable perennials and keep the remaining pockets for colourful annuals to give a more interesting and varied effect throughout the year.

There are hundreds of suitable low-growing and prostrate plants. They are often specially listed in nursery catalogues.

DESIGNING OR REDESIGNING YOUR GARDEN

DRIVEWAYS, PATHS
AND STEPPING STONES

Driveways are a strictly utilitarian part of the garden but ideally should blend with the general design. There are many practical considerations to keep in mind. Keep the driveway as short as possible and, for convenience and safety, avoid sharp curves. The angle of approach to or from the street should not be too sharp, nor should the entrance be obscured by large trees or shrubs. If possible, provide a turning area in the garden so you don't have to back your car into the street. A turning area can also be used to wash the car, for a children's play area or just as parking space for a visitor's car. Sloping sites present special problems for driveways. The construction of driveway and garage may call for excavating, filling and wall-building. On very steep slopes falling away from the street, a suspended car ramp may be the answer.

Driveways need solid foundations to prevent cracking and sinking. Split sandstone slabs or bricks can be bedded on a 10 cm sand base. Gravel in various colours is quite a good surface, but is prone to weed invasion and to erosion on slopes. An asphalt driveway is best constructed by a contractor; you need an area of about 60 square metres to make it an economical proposition. Pavers are popular for driveway surfaces but must be laid on a well–prepared bed. They are relatively easy to lay, are easy to maintain and are available in quite a range of colours. A wide variety of designs can be achieved.

Concrete is cheap and needs minimal after-care. Its appearance can be improved by pressing coloured gravel into the surface before it sets. Concrete tracks are the least expensive solution. In warm to hot localities, turf growing between concrete car tracks is preferable to the pebbles or gravel that are sometimes used in cool climates.

A path need not be the shortest distance between two points except between house and utility areas, clothes-line, rubbish bin, garage or carport. A curved path is more interesting, provided the garden scene is attractive and interesting. Planning and building some paths can often be deferred until the garden is well established, when the best positions can be decided.

An informal path made of bricks set in a well-maintained bed of decorative gravel.

There are as many materials for paths as there are for driveways. The surface should be easy to walk on but foundations need not be as solid as for driveways and large paved areas. Gravel of many grades and shades is popular and may be contained by a brick or concrete border adjacent to lawn or flower beds. In localities where there is heavy rain from time to time, gravel tends to wash down slopes. Some paths can be informal to the extent that ground covers spill onto them from one or both sides.

Stepping stones may form a sufficient path across a lawn. The dotted-line effect is often more pleasing than a solid one, and does not divide the lawn into separate sections. Set flagstones or concrete paving slabs flush with the lawn on a sand base 4 cm deep. An occasional trim around the edges will keep them neat and tidy. Flat rocks or discs of sawn hardwood make good stepping stones for informal paths or rustic areas laid with pebbles, gravel or pine bark.

STEPS AND RETAINING WALLS

Both steps and retaining walls are almost inevitable on sloping land. Steps can be an attractive garden feature as well as giving access to a change in level. They should be wide and shallow for ease of walking up and down, especially for older people and very young children.

The riser (vertical part) should not exceed 15 cm in height, and the tread (horizontal part) should not be less than 30 cm deep. For brick steps, two courses for the riser and a tread as wide as one brick length plus one brick width is a comfortable combination.

Deep steps are often necessary on steep slopes. For long flights, incorporate a landing every ten to twelve steps. The landing can also be used as a place to change direction. A handrail is an asset where steps are steep. Steps are awkward to negotiate with lawnmowers and wheelbarrows, so a ramp may be a practical alternative. Ramps, however, take much more space to give an easy grade.

Split or dressed stone steps are popular. Bricks, concrete blocks, pavers or slabs are used in more formal situations. Horizontal logs, sawn timber decking, railway sleepers and large hardwood discs blend with informal or bush settings.

Treated logs have been used to build a solid retaining wall on a steep slope.

Retaining walls resist the downhill thrust of earth behind them. Again, brick, stone, concrete and timber may be used. Dry walls, any form of packed stone walling, whether cement is used or not, are more attractive and quite stable if they are less than 1.5 m high. The face can be sloped slightly backward for

Hint

When choosing trees for your garden, always check on the potential size of mature specimens, as sometimes the height given is that at five or ten years.

DIANA SELBY
LANDSCAPE ARCHITECT

greater stability. Drainage is important, too. If the wall is not to become a dam, provide weep holes every 2.5–3 m along the base of the wall.

Lay the largest rocks or stones at the bottom, bedding them in the soil. Between

DESIGNING OR REDESIGNING YOUR GARDEN

Hint
Although it might seem a
luxury, a glasshouse will pay
for itself in no time, as it
enables you to extend the
growing season of many
plants, ensuring greater
productivity. It's also a great
way to ensure the survival of
frost-tender plants.

NICK HAYHOE
YATES NEW ZEALAND

each row of stones distribute a 4 cm layer of soil and bring the filling soil up behind them. Then lay another row of stones and repeat the process. Each row of stones should be slightly behind the row below to make the batter or backward slope, about 5 cm for every 30 cm of height.

If trailing or rockery plants are to be grown in the 'wall garden', plant them as the wall is built, spreading their roots into the soil in the crevices. If the construction materials allow it, recesses which can be filled with soil to act as planting points should be provided. The best soil is a loam which can be easily spread and worked into crevices. Soil should be damp enough to hold together, but not wet. Sandy soils are difficult to use for this job and tend to flow out of the cracks when dry.

SHADEHOUSES

There are great many good reasons for constructing a shadehouse in the garden. A collection of orchids or container-grown ferns and foliage plants is one justification for having a shadehouse. A shadehouse is desirable when a number of potted indoor plants are in use. House plants benefit from having a spell outside in the shadehouse environment because they are then in better, brighter, circumambient light. Another use for a shadehouse is to make it an open-

This garden shadehouse has been built as an extension to the main house.

A small glasshouse is all that's required to give plants a good start in a cold climate.

fronted annexe to a patio or terrace. This is a particularly desirable arrangement in the warm temperate regions where relief from glare and, perhaps, additional shade from one side may make the environment more pleasant. Plants grown in tubs, troughs or pots on the patio become an extension of the shadehouse.

A shadehouse reduces direct sunlight, provides a cool, moist atmosphere and protects plants from hot, dry winds. When you build a shadehouse you create a microclimate for plants which may not survive in the open. Select a sunny aspect: a shadehouse should not be dark and dismal.

The size of the structure will depend on your enthusiasm for shadehouse plants and ferns. The frame must be solid – treated timber or steel tubing is best – and the uprights should be set solidly in concrete footings. The floor can be concrete too, but ashes, gravel, metal dust or pine bark are less expensive alternatives.

Lattice, wooden slats, or 10 cm wire netting threaded with tea-tree pieces can be used for shadehouse walls and roof, but shadecloth is an effective and long-lasting modern substitute. It comes in a number of colours and gives different percentages of shade ranging from 32 per cent to 92 per cent. Choose a grade which allows more, rather than less, sunlight – 32 per cent and 50 per cent are both good. A tap for watering

should be located near the door. Overhead mist sprinklers are more professional, but also more costly.

The most popular shadehouse plants are orchids (see Chapter 16) and ferns, but there are many other species that have brilliant flowers or coloured or variegated leaves which are suitable and attractive. Larger garden centres and those which specialise in shade plants usually have a wide range from which to choose.

GLASSHOUSES

In New Zealand, glasshouses are popular in cold-climate zones, especially in the South Island. If your hobby is growing delicate tropical and warmth-loving plants you will need some winter protection for them.

The construction of a glasshouse is not difficult and the use of standard glasshouse fittings simplifies the job considerably. The frame is made from 75 mm x 50 mm timber, or an all-steel structure can be made using galvanised pipe and pressed metal fittings. Width, length and height should be multiples of standard glass sheet plus an allowance for glazing bars. Building a small lean-to glasshouse on a blank wall of the house is an easier option. In this case, make sure the glasshouse is in a position to receive a reasonable amount of sun. In warm areas some shade cover for your glasshouse may be needed during the summer months.

PART II: PREPARING AND MAINTAINING YOUR GARDEN

CHAPTER 3

SOILS, COMPOST AND WORMS

To know your soil you should first understand how plants grow and manufacture food. Plants – from the smallest seedlings to the largest trees – are factories which take raw materials from the air, water and soil to build carbohydrates, proteins and fats. To do this they need a constant supply of raw materials and a source of energy – sunlight – to form roots, leaves, stems, flowers, fruits and seeds. Each part of the plant has a special job to do, but its performance depends on the cooperation of every other part.

Leaves and young stems are the real manufacturing sections. They contain a green pigment called chlorophyll which, in the presence of light, allows them to produce sugars from carbon dioxide from the air and water from the soil. This sugar production is called photosynthesis and is the starting point for more complex substances such as starches and cellulose. The plant proteins and amino acids which are so important for both human and animal nutrition are nitrogenous compounds synthesised in the plant tissues from nitrogen absorbed from the soil. Other plant nutrients are also absorbed from the soil.

HOW ROOTS DO THEIR WORK

Roots anchor a plant in the soil. Some plants have a long, strong taproot with smaller lateral roots. Others have a branched fibrous root system. Whatever form it takes, the root system absorbs water and dissolved nutrients from the soil through the root hairs (elongated cells just behind the root tip) and passes them to conducting tissue in the root, then on to the stem and other parts of the plant. Roots must respire (or breathe) to perform their task of absorbing and conducting efficiently, so a soil must be able to provide oxygen as well as water and nutrients.

SOIL TYPES

Some soils are better for growing plants than others. The terms rich and poor, good and bad, fertile and infertile are commonly used to describe these differences. The quality of the soil in your garden largely depends on the type of parent rock from which it is formed, on the influence of climate over hundreds of thousands of years and on what your house builder and previous owners have done to it. It is remarkable how much poor soils can be improved if you learn to manage them properly.

Soil is made up of mineral particles which vary in shape, size and chemical composition. Sand particles are quite large because they break down slowly. Other minerals break down more quickly into clay particles. These are extremely small – many thousands of times smaller than coarse sand – and they have an important effect on the physical and chemical properties of the soil. The size of the particles – coarse sand, fine sand, silt and clay – and the proportions in which they occur determine soil texture.

SANDY SOILS

Sandy soils have large particles with large spaces, called pore spaces, between them. They drain readily, have good aeration and are easy to cultivate. For this reason they are often called 'light' soils. However, very sandy soils are less effective at retaining water and nutrients than are other soils.

When slightly moist, good loam soil will stay together when shaped into a ball.

CLAY SOILS

Clay soils have small particles and little pore space. They store water well, often too well for good drainage and aeration, and retain plant nutrients. Clay particles act as soil colloids (substances in a glue-like state) and

LOAMS

All soils between the extremes of sand and clay are referred to as loams. They are mixtures of coarse and fine particles. They are divided into such categories as sandy loam (more sand than clay) and clay loam (more clay than sand). You can identify the soil in your garden by the feel in your hand when the soil is slightly moist.

- Sandy soil does not stick together and is coarse and gritty.
- Sandy loam sticks together, is friable (easily crumbled) and slightly gritty.
- Loam sticks together, is friable and not gritty.
- Clay loam sticks together, is slightly friable but easily moulded.
- Clay soil sticks together, is not friable, but rather it is easily moulded and sticky.

ORGANIC MATTER AND SOIL STRUCTURE

All soils contain some organic matter. It consists of the remains of plants and animals and the organisms (earthworms, slaters, beetles, bacteria, fungi, and so on) that are decomposing them.

Of the various components of plant remains, the proteins and carbohydrates are quickly broken down into simple chemicals that can be absorbed by both plants and bacteria, but the more resistant bits of organic matter remain as small fragments which form a dark brown material called humus. Particles of humus attract and hold nutrients on their surface in the same way as clay colloids. Humus particles bind mineral particles (especially fine sand, silt and clay) into aggregates or crumbs. These crumbs have relatively large pore spaces between them which help drainage and aeration. The addition of humus to heavy soils makes them easier to cultivate.

HOW TO IMPROVE SOILS

The water- and nutrient-holding ability of sandy soils can be improved by adding organic matter. Animal manure, leaf mould, spent mushroom compost, garden compost and green manure crops are all excellent additives when dug into the soil.

Animal manures are probably the best because they contain useful quantities of

---

Hint

The key to a healthy garden is to ensure a strong foundation by developing a good quality soil. It will take time and hard physical effort, and most likely some money, but it will repay you in the future with vigorous plant growth. Work plenty of compost into your soil and you will be rewarded with a clean, green environment.

DALE HARVEY
GARDEN WRITER

---

attract and hold nutrients on their surface. Clay soils can be difficult to cultivate and are often called 'heavy'.

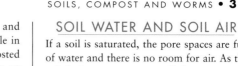

nutrients as well. Animal manures and mushroom compost are readily available in bags and sometimes in bulk. Composted 'green wastes' are also readily available, or you can make your own compost. Green manure crops are also a good source of organic matter but few home gardens have space to grow them nowadays. Peat moss is a good moisture-holding material but it contains negligible quantities of plant nutrients. Dry peat moss should be moistened before adding it to soil.

All organic materials will eventually decompose in soil and therefore must be renewed from time to time, especially in annual flower and vegetable beds which are continually cultivated.

Clay soils benefit from organic matter too, because it improves their structure by binding clay particles into crumbs. By adding coarse sand to heavy soils you make a permanent improvement in their texture. Spread the sand to a depth of 5–8 cm, then mix well into the topsoil to a depth of 15–20 cm. Gypsum can be incorporated into a clay soil and will help the soil to function more effectively. Add gypsum at a rate of about 0.5–1 kg per square metre of soil.

The crumb structure of clay and clay loam is destroyed if they are dug when too wet. Allow the soil to dry out for a day or two before digging. When cultivating any soil, only dig the topsoil. Do not dig so deeply as to bring subsoil (especially clay) to the surface.

SOIL WATER AND SOIL AIR

If a soil is saturated, the pore spaces are full of water and there is no room for air. As the soil drains, excess water, called 'gravitational water', moves downwards, leaving a film of water around each soil particle. The soil is now at 'field capacity', that is, it is holding as much water as it can against gravity. Sandy soils have a very low field capacity. Clay soils may have a field capacity ten times as great.

Some plants (especially vegetables with large leaves, like cabbage, cauliflower, lettuce and some vine crops) wilt readily in very hot weather. This is because they are losing water faster than the roots can take it up. Provided the soil is moist enough, the plants recover in the cool of the evening and the leaves are back to normal the following morning.

DRAINAGE

Too much water is also harmful to plants. In saturated soil, root respiration slows down due to a lack of oxygen. Soil bacteria and other soil organisms also need oxygen to function, so organic decay is restricted in wet soil. Another harmful aspect of wet soil is a decrease in soil temperature. Well-drained, friable soils are warmer than wet soils. A warm soil increases root respiration and plants grow faster. Bacterial activity also increases.

Fortunately, many garden soils have good natural drainage. Soils which have a high proportion of sand seldom present a problem unless there is a clay subsoil or rock layer close

STRUCTURE OF SOIL

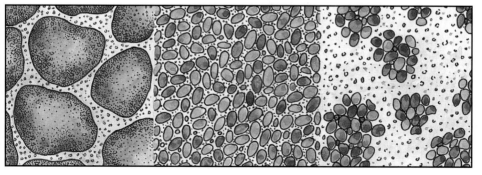

SANDY SOIL: large air spaces between particles allow free drainage but do not hold water or nutrients well.

CLAY SOIL: fine particles are tightly packed together, so drainage and aeration are poor.

IMPROVED CLAY SOIL: particles are aggregated into clumps, improving air space and drainage.

PREPARING AND MAINTAINING YOUR GARDEN

Hint

Soils of differing textures hold varying amounts of water, so an understanding of your soil type is essential. In general, sandy soils require regular light watering while clay soils should be watered heavily but much less frequently. Adjust irrigation system timers accordingly.

TERRY WALKER
ENVIROSCAPES

to the surface. On heavy soils, drainage improvement of some kind is usually needed. To check the need for drainage, dig a few test holes to a depth of 40–50 cm and inspect after heavy watering or rain. If water remains in the holes for 24 hours, some artificial drainage is required.

On sloping sites, a rubble drain running diagonally at the top of the slope to divert run-off water or seepage away from the garden

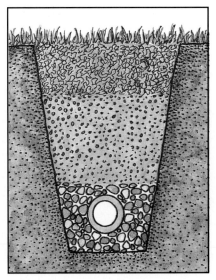

Drainage pipes – terracotta, cement or polythene – must be bedded in porous material such as gravel or coarse sand before the subsoil and topsoil are replaced.

may be sufficient. Dig the trench 40–50 cm deep and fill with rough stones to a depth of 15–20 cm. Cover with a layer of aggregate or gravel and replace the topsoil.

Another simple drainage method is to raise garden beds 15–20 cm above the surrounding surface. The sides of the beds should slope at 45–60 degrees. If gardens are surrounded by stone or brickwork, make provision for weep holes at the bottom of the surround.

If drainage is a major problem, a permanent herring-bone system made of terracotta, porous cement or slotted polythene pipes may be needed. In medium to light soils, set the drains 6–9 m apart and dig trenches about 60 cm deep with a fall of between 1 in 100 and 1 in 200 so that the pipes are self-cleaning. Pipes must be bedded in porous material such as aggregate, gravel or coarse sand. In very wet situations, it may be best to consult a drainage expert.

WATERING AND MULCHING

How much and how often you water plants depends on the soil type of your garden, the kind of plants you grow, your general climate and the time of the year. Microclimatic factors, such as slope, aspect or exposure to wind, will also affect loss of water from plants and soil. It is difficult to lay down rules for watering, but there are a few general principles worth knowing.

Sandy soils generally need more frequent watering than clay soils, but less water should be applied each time. Whatever the soil type, do not let it reach wilting point before you water again. Plants do not thrive on such 'on and off' treatment. Remember, a good soaking encourages deep rooting and soil stays moist for a long time. Light sprinkling, no matter how often you do it, encourages roots to stay at the surface. The subsoil gets drier and drier and becomes difficult to wet again without a lot of heavy soaking. Early morning or evening is considered the best time for watering, because evaporation rates are likely to be lower than in the middle of the day. In humid areas, however, evening watering over plants that are susceptible to fungal diseases will encourage such diseases to flourish, and therefore should be avoided. In the morning it is usually less windy, too, so the water spray goes where you want it.

In very dry weather, morning watering may help pollination and seed-setting in some vegetables, particularly sweet corn and beans.

Mulching is a good way of conserving soil moisture, especially in summer. A mulch is any soil covering which protects surface roots and reduces evaporation. It also helps maintain an even soil temperature and discourages many weeds from growing.

The best mulches are loose materials that allow most rain or irrigation water to run through to the soil. They must also allow free access of air to soil and roots. The depth of the mulch should vary with its coarseness, from shallow for the finest to thicker for the coarsest (2–8 cm). Garden compost, leaf mould, well-rotted animal manure, straw, pine bark, spent hops and sawdust are common mulching materials. Do not dig mulches into the soil (especially bark materials and sawdust). All will eventually decompose naturally and become integrated with the topsoil. Mineral substances, stones, pebbles, gravel and sand are used as permanent mulches in gardens planted with trees and shrubs. More recently, woven weed

Hint

Unexplained wilting of container plants may be an indication of too much water or a lack of drainage. Before you add more water, check that the drainage holes are not blocked. Yates Patio and Tub Mix will ensure even drainage.

THE TWO ANNS
A & A CONSULTANTS

mats have become available by the metre from garden suppliers. These effectively suppress weeds while still allowing oxygen and moisture to penetrate the soil. In ornamental situations they need to be anchored in place and disguised by a more attractive layer of something like pine bark.

TOP FIVE FLOWERS FOR ALKALINE SOIL

GLADIOLI

Gladioli usually flower about 100 days after planting the bulbs and can be grown in a wide range of climates.

HYACINTH

One of the best features of hyacinth flowers is their delightful perfume.

SWEET PEA

Sweet peas will grow most happily in soil with a pH between 7 and 8. This is why it is often recommended that soil be limed before planting.

LILAC

Lilac flourishes in harsh conditions, as long as the winters are cold.

GYPSOPHILA

Baby's breath is known as 'chalk plant' because it grows naturally on chalky limestone soils. It makes a splendid cut flower.

GYPSOPHILA

HYACINTH

LILAC

TOP FIVE VEGIES FOR ACID SOIL

POTATO

Grow potatoes to help break up the soil in a new garden. The crop will be a bonus.

PUMPKIN

Pumpkins are so tolerant that they'll grow just about anywhere – even out of your compost heap!

CUCUMBER

Like pumpkins, cucumbers have separate male and female flowers. Only the female flowers will develop fruit.

BEANS

Because they can make use of nitrogen from the atmosphere, bean plants will actually enrich the soil in your garden.

SWEET CORN

The only member of the grass family that is grown as a vegetable, sweet corn has spread from its original home in the Americas to become a staple food in many parts of the world.

PUMPKIN

BEANS

Overwatering is wasteful because it washes out plant nutrients. A common mistake is to overwater in winter when plant growth rate is reduced. (In the case of deciduous shrubs and trees, the plants are dormant.) If a plant is not growing actively, little or no water is needed.

Wet soil may also favour the spread of some fungal diseases, so it is best to keep mulch a few centimetres away from the stems of plants or the trunks of shrubs and trees. Such a moist area may encourage root rots to attack the plant at or near soil level.

Hint

When organic matter is dug into a clay soil, it is broken down by biological processes to form humus. This in turn increases the space between clay particles, so that air and water move freely through the soil crumb.

ALAN MCDONALD
YATES NEW ZEALAND

WATERING METHODS

There are dozens of kinds of sprays and sprinklers for watering gardens. Those which give a fine spray are generally preferred because large drops of water tend to pack the surface of heavy soils. Fine sprays also generally have a lower watering rate, which gives better penetration and less run-off on sloping sites. However, be aware that fine sprays allow greater evaporation.

A soaker hose, with small holes less than 30 cm apart, is useful for slow watering but must be handled carefully in a crowded garden of shrubs or annuals. The small holes may become blocked and this needs watching. The Aquapore hose is made from recycled rubber and allows water to seep through the tiny holes in the structure of the hose walls.

Ordinary garden hose has stood the test of time and is as popular as ever. Nozzles adjustable for spray width and droplet size can be hand-held or attached to a stand. A water-breaker nozzle such as the Plassay Delicate Water Spray Head is excellent for watering seed beds, small seedlings and plants in pots. It delivers a full volume of water in a soft and even spray.

Irrigation systems are reasonably priced and readily available. A system can be designed for individual needs and installed by a handyperson, or professional advice and installation may be preferred. Some systems incorporate automatic timing devices that switch sprinkler lines on or off according to a predetermined pattern and time span. Mini sprinklers that spray in various patterns are available to connect to these systems.

COMPOSTING

Mention the word composting to any keen gardener or hobby farmer and you can be assured of a lengthy discussion about materials, methods, special techniques with even secret recipes obtained from distant ancestors thrown in for good measure.

Anyone can make good compost, or can they? Some people will say that to produce good compost you only have to throw all your rubbish in a heap and let it rot. This is perhaps the oldest method of making compost and it will work eventually, provided that you have a good mixture of different materials in the composting heap. Actually, any material of plant or animal origin can be used to make compost.

This 'rubbish heap' method can be very slow, however, and although the usual range of microorganisms act in converting the rubbish to compost, conditions are often not ideal and the heap can take ten or eighteen months to mature.

Sometimes anaerobic (without oxygen) conditions develop, creating a wet and smelly heap; these heaps are eventually worked on by worms to complete the composting process. With this method you actually end up with a compost comprised of very rich worm casts (vermicast). If you have only one product in the compost heap, for example a high carbon source such as sawdust, it will not compost at all until a nitrogen source such as animal manure or grass clippings is thoroughly mixed into the heap.

The carbon–nitrogen ratio (C/N) is very important. Simply explained, it means that a

Well-rotted compost provides food for plants.

mix of both high carbon and high nitrogen materials must be placed in the compost pile. This is the food supply for all the micro-organisms that actually produce the compost, and a correct mix allows efficient and fast compost production.

Examples of high carbon materials are paper, wheat straw, sawdust and chipped wood products. Some high nitrogen sources are animal manures, including poultry and pigeon manure, human faeces, urine, grass clippings and green prunings from garden plants. Some materials have a reasonable C/N ratio and under ideal conditions will compost readily; examples of these are lucerne straw and grass clippings.

One composting mixture described by Kevin Handreck in *Gardening Down Under* (published by the CSIRO in Australia) is for leaves, sawdust and animal manure to be used in a volume to volume ratio of 1:1:3. Using a wheelbarrow as the measure, Handreck suggests you use one barrowload of leaves, one barrowload of sawdust and three barrowloads of manure. You may use any equivalent measuring implement at hand if no wheelbarrow is available or if that amount is too large for you to handle. The important thing to remember is that no matter what size heap you build, the ratio of materials should give you a good C/N ratio.

....

Hint

Succulents are great plants for difficult sites. When grown outdoors, they can take on vivid colours if stressed by a lack of food or water, by extremely low temperatures, or by high levels of ultraviolet light.

JODY LUSK AND RICHARD DAVEY
WAIRERE NURSERY

....

The C/N ratio is the single most important factor in composting, but there are other factors that aid the composting process. These are temperature, moisture, oxygen supply and the particle size of the material in the compost heap. The organisms that break down the organic material in the compost heap must also be available; these can be introduced by adding commercially available compost activators, animal manures, one spadeful of organically active soil, or a handful of compost from your previous compost pile.

A correct temperature range is necessary for composting. Positioning the compost pile or compost bin in a place where it will obtain plenty of sunlight can help, especially in areas with cold winters. But if your heap is large enough and is made correctly it should generate its own heat. Make sure that the heap does not become too dry during the initial activation period and in hot summer periods.

Once activated, a composting heap goes through various temperature changes. This is because different organisms are present in the various temperature regimes. These organisms have high rates of multiplication and can cause compost heaps to reach temperatures above 60°C, a temperature high enough to kill many weed seeds. However, since all parts of the heap may not reach these temperatures, it is just as well to keep weed seeds out of composting material.

Moisture is essential for the organisms in the compost pile. When building a compost heap it is important to moisten each layer as it is placed on the heap. If the compost gets too dry the microbial activity will cease; conversely, the compost must not get too wet and cold as the activity will also cease. Therefore, protect open heaps from rain during wet weather and check the compost heap regularly.

Adequate aeration is needed to provide the organisms in the compost heap with oxygen. There are many ingenious ways to add air to your compost heap.

● Place an open-layered design of bricks at the base of the heap so as to provide air channels.

● Tie stakes together or make tubes of plastic, reinforcement mesh or rolled-up chicken wire to form tubes. Place these vertically into the heap.

● Use plastic piping with holes drilled in a spiral design along the full length of the pipe. These can be inserted vertically into the heaps and are particularly useful in compost bins because the extra air speeds up the composting process.

● Turn over the compost heap at least once every day and you will greatly enhance the composting process and aerate the heap.

The smaller the size of the individual pieces of materials placed in your compost heap, the faster it will mature. Small pieces of material have a relatively larger surface area than big pieces, so organisms within the compost have a larger area to work on and will break down the material into compost at a much faster rate than would occur in compost heaps built with large pieces of material. To break down the materials you can use mulching machines, which are available in a large range of sizes (and prices). Mulching can be done with other cutting implements, such as rotary mowers with or without catchers.

The way the materials are placed in the compost heap will influence its successful operation. Materials with high moisture content, such as wet grass and fresh vegetable matter, should be mixed with another material that can absorb the excess moisture – for example, shredded paper, straw, or sawdust. If large pieces of materials are used they should be spread evenly through the heap, or placed at the base of the compost heap if you are using an open-air composting method.

Generally, compost heaps are built by having successive layers of materials (each 100–250 mm thick) interspersed with layers of organic fertiliser (manure) or a material with a high nitrogen content. Some methods suggest mixing all the materials together, then building the compost heap. Rotary bins are designed to mix the material every time the bin is turned around and are more efficient because of this feature.

Many compost designs incorporate the use of lime on each layer. This is unnecessary if you build the heap to provide good aeration; however, you may wish to sprinkle some lime into the compost to provide extra calcium. A number of compost recipes suggest the layering of soil on each layer of material that is placed into the compost heap. Soil will provide organisms, but commercial compost activators, animal manures, or one handful of compost from a previous heap will provide most of the organisms necessary.

Placing layers of soil within your compost heap is not recommended; too many home gardeners destroy their compost heaps this way and end up with a smelly, compressed, wet mix that will take a very long time to break down into compost. A layer of material such as sawdust should be used as an alternative to soil to seal the heap to prevent odours.

To have a nutrient-rich compost you should put nutrient-rich materials into the compost heap. To add nutrients to your heap, sprinkle on fertilisers. Moisturising the heap with a liquid seaweed, or applying Yates Compost Maker, will also provide micronutrients. Some forms of seaweed have been found to contain nearly all the free elements known to exist – including gold!

There are many different kinds of compost bins which can be effectively used. Here are some of them:

- Recycled plastic bins and 200-litre drums;
- Home-made wire mesh bins (place recycled paper, cardboard or plastic around the outside of these bins to enable them to compost quickly in cool weather);
- Bins made of polycarbonate or long-lasting plastic;
- Kit bins;
- Wooden bins;

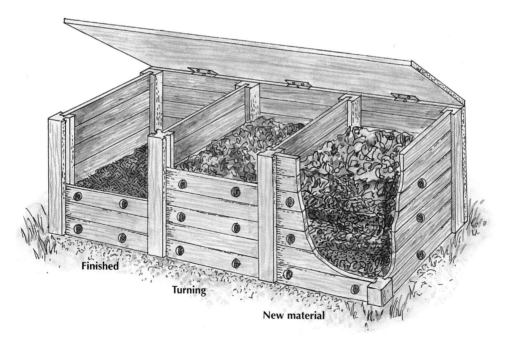

Finished

Turning

New material

If you have a number of bins, you can make use of completed compost while other heaps are at different stages of decomposition.

- Rotating bins;
- Ordinary plastic bags and thick, industrial-strength bags;
- Rubbish bins converted to compost bins by cutting out the base;
- Composting toilets, which are highly recommended as they do not contribute to groundwater and soil pollution like septic tank systems.

Do not use galvanised containers as they can supply toxic amounts of zinc to the compost.

All of the abovementioned bins have advantages and disadvantages. Compost bins which absorb heat, have good aeration, or are designed to be easily turned are more efficient, but providing you have the correct C/N ratio, moisture, warmth, and material that is of a small particle size, it is possible to compost in an ordinary plastic bag and obtain compost within a few weeks, even in winter.

There is no reason for anyone not to compost their kitchen and garden waste; 40 per cent of municipal waste can be turned into compost and up to 80 per cent of kitchen waste can be converted to compost.

....

Hint

Traditional compost-making can take quite a long time. To develop a richer, better compost in a shorter time, add Yates Compost Maker to your organic mixture.

CHARLIE GRAY
YATES NEW ZEALAND

....

You should encourage your local council to aid in the recycling and composting of community waste. Any person building a new toilet system, replacing the old, or installing a second unit, should think about installing a composting toilet. Compost from composting toilets is ideal and can be used directly on the garden. Health authorities now approve of these systems.

When compost is used in the garden it improves soil structure, provides nutrients and humus to the soil and plants, reduces water use by acting as an 'organic sponge' reservoir within the soil and provides you with the material for organically growing vegetables and fruit. Compost can be used to build a 'no-dig' garden which is easily maintained, is ideal for people of all ages, and is environmentally friendly (see pages 56–57).

WORMS

There are actually thousands of species of worms, ranging from the tiniest eelworms that can only be seen with the aid of a microscope with a magnification power of 300 000:1, to the gigantic Gippsland earthworms, found in Australia, that can grow to several metres in length.

The most common of all worms are the earthworms, those found living in the soil, under forest litter, or in rotting vegetation. Earthworms have been decribed as 'the living gut of this planet', an apt description since without earthworms it is very likely that there would be no life forms (as we know them) on this earth today. All plants and animals rely on worms, because worms mine the soil and recycle nutrients.

Worms burrow in the earth, aerating the soil structure and thus providing oxygen for billions of bacteria, fungi and other micro- and macro-organisms. These in turn provide the environment for plants to grow. Each day every worm digests about half its own weight of soil. This works out to be somewhere near 40–50 grams dry weight per year. If you have 200 worms per square metre, then that population can shift an incredible 80–100 tonnes of soil per hectare per year. Worms concentrate the minerals in the soil as it passes through their gut, so that the resulting worm casts can contain up to six times the available nitrogen, seven times the available phosphorus, twelve times the available potassium, and also increased availability of many of the minor elements such as calcium, magnesium and sulphur. In fact, worm casts can be said to be the complete plant food. You cannot put too much on your plants – worm casts won't burn plant roots or foliage.

Many worms mix organic matter into the soil, thus improving the structure of that soil. This can be seen as a dark area spreading down into the soil layer.

Taken a step further, by increasing the air supply to the soil, worms actually facilitate a massive build-up of soil organisms, which also allows roots of plants to grow deeper into the lower soil depths. Improved root growth gives better crop yields and reduces the demand for water due to surface evaporation around roots. Most organic gardeners and farmers rely heavily on the action of worms to implement their sustainable systems.

WORMS IN THE COMPOST CHAIN

Worms are the engines that convert your rubbish pile into compost; in fact, many composting techniques rely upon worms to convert waste into usable compost. In recent years worms have been used to convert sewage waste to compost, and landscape contractors are using worms to help rehabilitate areas spoilt by erosion, clearing, or mining operations. Many organic farmers and gardeners have begun 'seeding' their cropping areas with species of worms suitable for their farm areas or gardens.

GROWING YOUR OWN WORMS

Worm bins can be constructed from bath tubs, tin cans, boxes, old fish tank frames, bricks and wooden planking. Providing the container is about 25–30 cm deep, it will do. The bin should be placed in a position where it does not get too hot during the summer months. Home-garden worm farms made from recycled plastic are popular for disposing of household vegetable waste. Containers of worms are available for purchase but it is important to be aware that the species of worms that do the fastest job of breaking down organic material in bins and worm farms do not survive well in soils.

To breed worms successfully you must supply them with food which is high in nitrogen, such as kitchen waste, bread, straw, leaves, grass clippings, herbs and animal manure. Bran is often used too. In other words, worms thrive on anything you would customarily put in your compost heap.

The moisture content of a worm farm is important, since worms require water but dislike waterlogged soils. Each worm farm should have a removable cover to prevent

Worms can hasten the breakdown of organic matter into useful compost.

waterlogging of the worm bed during periods of rain. The bed should be kept moist but not saturated. Placing wet bags on the surface will reduce evaporation losses and create the darkness required by the worms. The

Hint

Earthworms are gardener's delight. They feed on organic compost, their burrows aerate the soil and their casts improve the friability of the soil, which is essential for healthy plant growth. Today, you can buy live worms to add to your garden.

ROD GIBBONS
LIVING EARTH

contents of your bin should consist of about 5 cm of loamy soil, then about 10 cm of the ingredients mentioned above, then another 5 cm of loamy soil. Check the worm bin weekly for moisture content and food supply.

CHAPTER 4

PLANT NUTRIENTS
AND FERTILISERS

About 250 years ago, farmers and gardeners started to ask the question 'What makes plants grow?' It was widely believed that soil humus was the source of carbon, which makes up the sugar and starch in plants, and that substances like saltpetre, lime and phosphates helped the humus to be more useful. It was not until 1840 that the German chemist Justus von Liebig proved that carbon came from carbon dioxide in the air and not from humus in the soil. He proved too that other nutrients were absorbed by plant roots as simple chemicals dissolved in soil water.

Great strides in the study of plant nutrition have been made in the last hundred years. We now know that, apart from carbon, hydrogen and oxygen, which plants get from air and water, about a dozen nutrients or elements are essential for plant growth. These nutrients are contained in the minerals and organic matter in the soil. The organic matter must be decomposed so that plant roots can absorb the nutrients as simple chemicals or parts of molecules called 'ions'.

We can supplement these sources of nutrients through applications of soluble fertilisers. It makes no difference whether plants obtain nutrients from decomposed matter or from fertilisers. Plants grow best when a combination of organic matter and fertilisers is available to them.

The nutrient elements that are essential to the growth of all plants can be divided into three groups. The major elements are needed in larger amounts than are the secondary elements, which in turn are required more than the trace (or minor) elements. In the following list, the names of the elements are followed by their symbols (as seen listed on fertiliser packages).

Major elements
nitrogen (N), phosphorus (P), potassium (K)
Secondary elements
calcium (Ca), magnesium (Mg), sulphur (S)
Minor elements
iron (Fe), manganese (Mn), copper (Cu),
zinc (Zn), boron (B), molybdenum (Mo)

A number of other elements, including chlorine, nickel, sodium and silicon, are also needed by at least some plants. None is likely to be deficient in home garden soils.

MAJOR ELEMENTS

Nitrogen, phosphorus and potassium, often called 'the big three', are the most important elements required by plants. Each is needed in large amounts and the presence or absence of any one of them has a dramatic effect on plant growth.

NITROGEN (N)

Nitrogen is an essential part of the proteins in plant (and animal) cells. It is also a necessary part of chlorophyll, the green pigment in plants, and is extremely important to leaf growth. Plants deficient in nitrogen are stunted, with pale green or yellow leaves, often with reddish tints.

Soil bacteria break down protein in organic matter into nitrogen-rich ammonium ions. Another group of bacteria lives in nodules or swellings on the roots of legumes (peas, beans, lupins, clovers, lucerne, acacias, cassia and many others). These bacteria are able to 'fix' nitrogen

PREPARING AND MAINTAINING YOUR GARDEN

in the air between the soil particles. The 'fixed' nitrogen is used by the host plant but, when the roots die, the nodules disintegrate and release nitrogen which can then be used by crops. (See 'Green manure crops' on page 51 of this chapter.) Most powdered and granular fertiliser mixtures contain sulphate of ammonia as the source of nitrogen.

Urea (46 per cent N) is a soluble, quick-acting form of nitrogen which is widely used in water-soluble fertiliser mixtures such as Thrive. When applied as a spray, some urea is absorbed through the leaves. Most, however, is washed into the soil and converted into nitrate nitrogen.

Potassium nitrate (13 per cent N) is a quick-acting source of nitrogen and potassium (36 per cent K). It is commonly used in water-soluble fertiliser mixtures.

Urea formaldehyde (38.4 per cent N) is also known as Ureaform, Nitroform or UF38. It releases some nitrogen within a few weeks but the remainder is broken down by soil bacteria over three or four months. The rate of release varies with soil temperature, and is slower in winter than in summer.

PHOSPHORUS (P)

Phosphorus forms part of the nucleo-proteins in plant cells, so it is important in growing tissue where the cells are actively dividing. It promotes the development of seedlings, root growth, flowering and the formation of fruits and seeds. A deficiency of phosphorus

leads to poor root development, stunted growth and often a purplish discolouration of the leaves. Most soils in New Zealand, although naturally deficient in phosphates, contain adequate levels for healthy plant growth in the average home garden. Phosphate fertilisers have been used extensively in agriculture for many years, as constant cropping continually removes this vital element from the soil. However, caution must be taken in applying these fertilisers around phosphate-sensitive plants such as the *Proteaceae* family, which includes proteas, leucadendrons, banksias and grevilleas. Many garden soils come to have very high phosphorus levels from additions of mixed fertilisers and poultry manures.

Superphosphate (9 per cent P) is the most common phosphorus fertiliser and is used in all powdered and granular mixtures. It is not completely soluble. It is a mixture of calcium phosphate and calcium sulphate, so it provides useful quantities of calcium (22 per cent Ca) and sulphur (11 per cent S) as well as phosphorus.

Mono-ammonium phosphate (22 per cent P) contains both phosphorus and nitrogen (12 per cent N). It is completely soluble, quick-acting and is a common ingredient in water-soluble mixtures such as Thrive.

POTASSIUM (K)

Potassium promotes chlorophyll production and plays an important part in the strength of cells and the movement of water in plants. It also helps plants resist disease and improves the quality of flowers, fruits and seeds.

Plants deficient in potassium have weak stems; their leaves, especially the older ones, may be floppy, with yellow or brown tips or scorched margins. Sandy soils in high rainfall areas are most likely to be deficient.

Potassium chloride (49.8 per cent K), also known as muriate of potash, is the most widely used of all potassium fertilisers. Its application should be avoided in areas where the water is salty.

Potassium sulphate (40 per cent K) also contains sulphur (16 per cent S) but is more expensive than potassium chloride. It is preferred for some crops, for example strawberries and potatoes. It is widely used in water-soluble fertiliser mixtures.

SECONDARY ELEMENTS

CALCIUM (CA)

Calcium is important in the construction and strength of cell walls in plants in a similar way as it is to the bones of animals. It also promotes proper functioning of growing tissue, especially in root tips.

Calcium neutralises acids in the cell sap and when applied to soil as lime plays an important part in reducing soil acidity. Calcium as a nutrient is rarely deficient unless the soil is extremely acid.

MAGNESIUM (MG)

Magnesium is a small part of the chlorophyll molecule so is important in photosynthesis. Lack of magnesium causes leaf yellowing, especially on the older leaves of plants, because magnesium, like potassium, is mobile in the plant and young leaves have first call on these two nutrients.

Most New Zealand soils provide adequate amounts of magnesium. The exceptions are those that have received excessive applications of poultry manures; the potassium in these can interfere with magnesium supply to plants. Some powdered fertilisers, and all water-soluble ones, contain adequate quantities of magnesium sulphate or Epsom salts (10 per cent Mg).

Dolomite (3–8 per cent Mg) is a poor source of magnesium. It must be applied in large quantities and is slowly released over two or three years.

SULPHUR (S)

Sulphur forms part of many plant proteins. It does not occur in chlorophyll but it is involved in its production. Sulphur deficiency shows up as yellowing of leaves and stunting of shoots, with symptoms similar to those of nitrogen deficiency.

In garden soils a deficiency is extremely unlikely because superphosphate (11 per cent S), sulphate of ammonia (24 per cent S) and all powdered and granular mixtures contain sulphur in adequate quantities. Organic matter also contains sulphur, but like nitrogen it is only available following bacterial breakdown to the sulphate form. In districts where sulphur deficiencies are known to occur, gypsum or calcium sulphate (15 per cent S) can be used.

TRACE ELEMENTS

The importance of minor or trace elements is not questioned but we must understand that they are needed only in minute quantities. Their excessive use may do more harm than good to the plants in your garden. In a normal garden situation, trace element deficiencies are not common.

All organic materials – animal manures, blood and bone, bone dust, compost and leaf mould – contain trace elements. Even superphosphate, which is made from rock phosphate, contains useful amounts. Trace elements are added to some proprietary fertiliser mixtures such as the Gro-Plus range, and also to water-soluble mixtures (such as Thrive) in small but adequate quantities. It is much easier and safer to use these products than to mix your own. Trace elements act as growth regulators or enzymes (starters) in building chemical compounds inside plant cells.

....

Hint

Read the label of bagged fertilisers and note the level of NPK in the product. If the fertiliser that you buy has a low concentration of NPK, you will have to apply more of it in order to feed the plants well. You only get what you pay for.

ELENKA NIKOLLOFF
YATES NEW ZEALAND

....

IRON (FE)

Iron is not a part of the chlorophyll molecule but small quantities must be present for its formation. Symptoms of iron deficiency include yellowing of younger leaves, because iron is relatively immobile in the plant. A deficiency is more likely in alkaline soils. All neutral and acidic soils naturally supply enough iron to most plants. If extra iron is needed, iron chelates release quickly but they last only a short time in alkaline soils.

MANGANESE (MN)

Manganese plays a similar role to iron but is needed to form proteins. Deficiency symptoms – again, more likely on alkaline soils – are yellowing of younger leaves, especially between the veins. Plants may also be stunted. An excess of manganese may produce toxic effects on very acid soils. These effects are overcome by liming to raise pH above pH 5.5 (see page 54).

COPPER (CU) AND ZINC (ZN)

Both copper and zink are enzyme activators. Lack of either element leads to leaf mottling, and yellowing in younger leaves.

In citrus trees zinc deficiency causes an abnormality called 'little leaf'. Copper and zinc deficiencies are more likely on very acid, sandy coastal soils but may also occur on peaty soils.

BORON (B)

Boron is important to growing tissue in young shoots, roots, flower buds and fruits. A deficiency leads to breakdown of internal tissue and corkiness, especially in apples, beetroot and turnips – often called 'brown heart'.

Tissue breakdown may also occur in the stems of celery and silver beet and in the flower buds of cauliflower and broccoli. Boron deficiency is more likely in alkaline soils or in those which have been limed heavily. There is a narrow span between not enough boron and too much. Even relatively small amounts of seaweeds and sea grasses can produce boron toxicity.

MOLYBDENUM (MO)

Molybdenum is needed for the conversion of nitrogen gas into plant protein. Deficiencies are most prevalent in high rainfall areas on acid soils. Very often an application of lime will release sufficient soil molybdenum to correct a deficiency. As little as 25 grams per hectare of molybdenum will correct deficiencies. Molybdenum deficiencies are common in cauliflowers, Brussels sprouts and other members of the cabbage family, causing the disease known as 'whiptail'. In home gardens, the use of one of the water-soluble fertilisers – all of which contain molybdenum in adequate quantities – will correct any deficiency.

INORGANIC FERTILISERS

The analysis of fertiliser materials is expressed as the percentage of nitrogen, phosphorus and potassium they contain, often called the N.P.K. ratio. Home gardeners will usually find it easier to use mixed 'complete' N.P.K. fertilisers than the separate compounds listed above, but the separate compounds are sometimes useful if only one or two nutrient elements are needed (for example, when there is already an ample supply of phosphorus in the soil).

N.P.K. mixtures come in powdered, granular and water-soluble form. There are dozens of brands and many formulations. Some powdered mixtures contain blood and bone as well as inorganic chemicals. Granular mixtures have the advantage of being free-running and of not setting hard in storage, so you can buy them in large quantities and have them on hand when you need them. Some of the more popular home garden packs, including the Gro-Plus range, contain a trace element mix.

POWDERED AND GRANULAR FERTILISERS

There are four basic groups or types of these fertilisers.

Group 1

Many of these, including Gro-Plus Complete Plant Food, have an approximate analysis N.P.K. 5:5:4. This analysis, which is relatively high in phosphorus, is recommended as a general garden fertiliser, especially for pre-planting or pre-sowing. Gro-Plus Lawn Starter has an approximate analysis of 4:6:3 and is designed as a pre-sowing mixture for lawn seed.

Group 2

These mixtures, including Gro-Plus Camellia & Azalea Food and Gro-Plus Rose Food, contain more nitrogen and potassium and less phosphorus. They have an approximate analysis of N.P.K. 10:4:6 or N.P.K. 10:4:10.

Group 3

These include lawn fertilisers which contain even higher quantities of nitrogen with an approximate analysis N.P.K. 13:2:4. These, including Gro-Plus Lawn Food, are designed

INORGANIC MIXED FERTILISERS

COMPLETE FERTILISERS	N%	P%	K%	REMARKS
Gro-Plus Camellia & Azalea Food	6.0	3.4	5.3	A balanced fertiliser for acid-loving trees and shrubs – azaleas, camellias, rhododentron, ericas, daphnes, gardenias, kalmias and hydrangeas. Nitrogen is present in both slow-acting organic form and in fast-acting ammonium form. The iron content in the fertiliser helps retain the correct soil acidity for acid-loving plants. Apply 100 g per square metre and repeat again each spring.
	Contains calcium and sulphur and a range of trace elements			
Gro-Plus Citrus Food	10.5	2.3	8.3	A balanced fertiliser to suit the demanding citrus tree, and other fruit trees. The nitrogen is present in both the slow-acting organic form and fast-acting ammonium form. Apply 200 g per square metre around the drip line (located under the outer foliage of the tree).
	Contains calcium and sulphur and a range of trace elements			
Gro-Plus Complete Plant Food	5.0	5.5	4.1	A balanced, all-purpose fertiliser for vegetables, flowers and shrubs. It contains trace elements. As a base dressing apply 100 g per square metre.
	Contains calcium and sulphur and a range of trace elements			
Gro-Plus Lawn Food	12.5	1.7	4.7	A balanced fertiliser for lawns with a high nitrogen content to promote dense leaf growth. The iron content produces a deeper leaf colour and promotes fine grass species, discouraging coarse grasses, weeds, worms and moss. Apply at a rate of 2.5 kg per 100 square metres in the spring and autumn on established lawns.
	Contains calcium and sulphur and a range of trace elements			
Gro-Plus Rose Food	8.0	3.7	7.1	Specially blended for roses, with a higher nitrogen and potassium content to encourage perfection in blooms. Apply at a rate of 100 g per square metre for established plants and at 300 g per square metre on older, larger bushes.
	Contains calcium and sulphur and a range of trace elements			
Gro-Plus Lawn Starter	3.6	6.3	3.3	An essential aid to establishing a new lawn. High phosphorus content helps root development. Apply at a rate of 100 g per square metre.
	Contains calcium and sulphur and a range of trace elements			

PREPARING AND MAINTAINING YOUR GARDEN

to replace the large amounts of nitrogen removed in grass clippings. They are also useful to apply as side dressings (fertiliser scattered around or along rows of plants) for leafy vegetables such as cabbage, cauliflower, lettuce and silver beet.

Group 4

The last group of mixtures are those designed for shrubs with shallow fibrous roots, such as azalea, camellia, daphne and rhododendron. These fertilisers contain large quantities of slow-acting organic material like blood and bone. They can be used safely without the risk of root damage, which can often occur when more concentrated mixtures are used. An example of these organic-based mixtures is Gro-Plus Camellia and Azalea Food, with an approximate analysis N.P.K. 6:3:5.

Hint

Healthy plants have a higher resistance to disease than unhealthy ones. If you feed your plants well and water them as required, they will resist most diseases. Be careful, though, as overfeeding and watering can make them more susceptible to disease.

DENNIS GREVILLE
GARDEN WRITER

WATER-SOLUBLE FERTILISERS

Thrive is a well-known water-soluble fertiliser. The main ingredients are urea, mono-ammonium phosphate and potassium sulphate or potassium nitrate. It also contains a balanced trace element mix.

The ingredients dissolve completely in water, so it is easy to apply in dilute solutions by watering-can or through a hose-spray attachment. It can be used safely as a nutrient booster for flowering annuals, vegetables, shrubs, indoor and outdoor pot plants – in fact, for every plant in the garden.

The N.P.K. analysis is higher, especially in nitrogen, than for powdered or granular fertilisers. The approximate analysis of Thrive is N.P.K. 27:5:9.

A special formulation, Thrive Flower and Fruit, with an N.P.K of 15:4:26, is specifically formulated to meet the needs of flowering and fruiting plants.

SLOW-RELEASE FERTILISERS

There is nothing really new about slow-release fertilisers. We have been using them for years: bone dust, blood and bone, animal manures and compost. All these organic materials must be decomposed before the nutrients are available. Pelletised manures like Gro-Plus Organic Sheep Pellets also act as slow-release fertilisers, because it takes some time before the nutrients dissolve out of them and become available to the plants.

CONTROLLED-RELEASE FERTILISERS

In slow- or controlled-release fertilisers the soluble fertiliser particle is protected with an exterior coating. Some coatings dissolve slowly, others expand to allow the fertiliser in solution to leach through the membrane. Paraffins, waxes, resins, polythene and sulphur have been used as coating materials. One of the best-known and most widely used is Multicote controlled-release fertiliser.

Multicote has a polymer resin coating which acts as a membrane. Water penetrates the membrane to dissolve the nutrients, which then diffuse out slowly through the plastic membrane and into the soil. When all the nutrients are released the plastic shell gradually breaks down.

The rate of nutrient release depends on soil temperature. This is appropriate because plants grow faster and take up more nutrients in warm soils. Release is not influenced by soil acidity or alkalinity or by bacterial activity in any way.

Multicote is available in New Zealand in bulk and in small home-garden packs. It is very widely used by the nursery and horticultural industries, and is available in a number of formulations, each with different release times (ranging from 40 to 700 days). It is a complete N.P.K. mixture, but doesn't contain trace elements. Trace elements can be added if necessary by spraying plants with water-soluble fertilisers such as Thrive.

The addition of Multicote is recommended for soil mixtures for seed beds, boxes and punnets, for a wide range of container-grown plants and for plants growing in restricted spaces such as rockeries.

ORGANIC FERTILISERS

These fertilisers include animal manures and animal or vegetable by-products. Animal manures contain small quantities of nitrogen, phosphorus and potassium, which vary with the kind of animal, its diet and the amount of straw or litter mixed with the manure. They are first-class materials for improving the structure of soils, but they must be added in large quantities to benefit the soil in this way. Spread them to a depth of 5–7 cm over the surface and dig them into the topsoil. Animal manure containing a lot of straw may cause a temporary nitrogen deficiency because bacteria decomposing the straw have first call and plants may suffer. So add extra nitrogen or, better still, a complete fertiliser

which contains at least 10 per cent nitrogen plus phosphorus and potassium.

LIQUID MANURE

Liquid animal manure watered onto leafy vegetables every week or two is an alternative fertiliser. The liquid is made by suspending a hessian bag filled with fresh manure in a large cask or drum of water. After a week the liquid is diluted with water (one part to three parts) for use. The drum is again filled and a week later the liquid is diluted with water (1:1). This is repeated a third time and the liquid used without dilution. This practice has been largely superseded by the use of water-soluble fertiliser mixtures. In areas where fresh manure is readily available, however, this is a viable method for organically fertilising your garden.

GREEN MANURE CROPS

Green manuring is another relatively inexpensive way of adding organic matter to the soil, but the system is usually confined to vegetable gardens when empty beds are lying idle in winter. In our climate, because there

ANALYSIS OF ORGANIC MANURES AND ORGANIC BY-PRODUCTS

MANURE OR FERTILISER	APPROXIMATE NUTRIENT CONTENT %		
	NITROGEN (N)	PHOSPHORUS (P)	POTASSIUM (K)
ANIMAL MANURE			
Cow	1.0	0.4	0.5
Fowl	2.1	1.6	1.0
Fowl (pelleted slow-release)	4.6	2.3	3.4
Horse	0.7	0.4	0.5
Pig	1.1	0.7	0.1
Sheep	1.8	0.4	0.5
ORGANIC BY-PRODUCTS			
Bone dust	3.0	10.9	—
Blood and bone	6.0	7.0	—
Yates Fish Emulsion	4.5	0.4	1.1
Yates Bio-Gold	10.0	4.0	6.0

are many vegetables which can be grown in winter, there is often little space left over for a green manure crop.

However, if you do have an empty bed there are several green manure crops you can use. Seeds of wheat, barley or oats can be broadcast at 30–60 g per square metre in autumn to provide a large bulk of material to dig into the soil in spring. Legume crops which add nitrogen through nodule bacteria in their roots are usually preferred. Suitable crops for autumn planting are lupins and mustard. The recommended seed rate is 15–30 g per square metre. Dig the crops in when they begin to flower in spring. A complete fertiliser must be broadcast at one-third of a cup per square metre when sowing all green manure crops.

Water the crops a day or two before digging them in. If the crop is very tall, flatten it and chop up with a sharp spade. After digging, keep the soil damp but not wet, then after three weeks dig the soil over again. It will take another three or four weeks for the organic matter to decompose. If there is any sign of yellowing in the following crop, give side dressings of a nitrogen fertiliser.

COMMERCIAL ORGANIC FERTILISERS

Easy-to-handle organic fertilisers are now readily available, with pelleted, slow-release poultry manure being the most popular. Products such as Gro-Plus Organic Sheep Pellets are widely used to fertilise plants in the ground and in containers, both in domestic and commercial situations.

Organic by-products of animal origin include bone dust, bone meal and blood and bone. Most of these fertilisers contain higher quantities of nitrogen and phosphorus than animal manure, but very little potassium. Nutrients are released slowly. Spread them at 125–250 g per square metre and dig into the topsoil. Blood and bone is often an ingredient of mixed fertilisers where a slow release of nutrients is desirable. For this reason it is included in Gro-Plus Camellia and Azalea Food.

An average analysis of animal manures and organic by-products discussed in this section is shown in the table on p. 51.

LIME AND pH

Even if all essential elements are present in a soil, it cannot be taken for granted that they are all available to plants. Availability depends very much on the acidity or alkalinity (amount of lime) in the soil. Just as we can measure temperature with a thermometer, so we can measure whether a soil is sour (acid) or sweet (alkaline). Acidity or alkalinity (sometimes called 'soil reaction') is measured on a scale of pH units. This scale ranges from pH units 0.0 (the most acid) to pH 14.0 (the most alkaline). The halfway mark, pH 7.0, is neither acid nor alkaline. Distilled water has a pH of 7.0. In soils, the pH ranges from pH 4.0 (strongly acid) to pH 10.0 (strongly alkaline), so soils can be rated accordingly.

If soil pH is too high or too low, some elements may not be available. This is shown in the diagram opposite in which the width of the horizontal bars gives the relative availability of each element at different pH levels. On strongly acid soils (pH 4.0–5.0) all of the major elements – nitrogen, phosphorus, potassium, calcium, magnesium and sulphur, and the trace element molybdenum – are poorly available to plants. As soil pH increases into the 7.5–8.0 range, phosphorus availability decreases, as do the availabilities of the other five trace elements.

In soils which are in the slight to medium alkaline range (pH 7.5–8.5), phosphorus again becomes unavailable, and so do the other five trace elements: iron, manganese, boron, copper and zinc. All plant nutrients are available between pH 6.0 and pH 7.0, with the best availability at pH 6.5 – a soil which is very slightly acid.

Hint

Hellebores (winter roses) cannot be overlooked as a choice of plant for winter colour. Top-dress them with sheep pellets, rather than blood and bone, to obtain the best results from your plants.

TERRY HATCH
JOY PLANTS

INFLUENCE OF pH
ON NUTRIENT AVAILABILITY

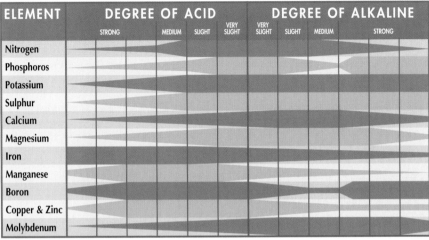

ELEMENT	DEGREE OF ACID				DEGREE OF ALKALINE			
	STRONG	MEDIUM	SLIGHT	VERY SLIGHT	VERY SLIGHT	SLIGHT	MEDIUM	STRONG
Nitrogen								
Phosphoros								
Potassium								
Sulphur								
Calcium								
Magnesium								
Iron								
Manganese								
Boron								
Copper & Zinc								
Molybdenum								

pH LEVEL   4.0   4.5   5.0   5.5   6.0   6.5   7.0   7.5   8.0   8.5   9.0   9.5   10.0

HOW PLANTS REACT TO pH

Most plants grow happily if the soil pH is between 6.0 and 7.0, but there are exceptions. Lime-intolerant plants – such as azaleas, camellias, ericas, gardenias and rhododendrons – prefer strongly acid soil (pH 5.0–5.5). Some others prefer a medium acid soil (pH 5.5–6.0). These include hippeastrum, cineraria, clematis, cyclamen, dianthus, ferns, fir trees, junipers, lupins, magnolias, orchids, veronicas and most bulbs.

Most vegetables and herbs thrive on soils with a pH between 6.0 and 7.0. Exceptions are potato, kumara and watermelon (pH 5.0–5.5). Many other garden plants will also tolerate a medium acid soil.

HOW TO CHECK pH

Most soils in New Zealand are of varying degrees of acidity. Strongly acidic soil is often referred to as 'sour soil' and, as mentioned previously, the availability of all the major nutrients decreases dramatically. Beneficial soil organisms also become less active. Constant addition of organic material and acidic fertilisers over time may cause extreme acidity. Observation of plant growth may show up indications of a possible pH imbalance. An imbalance may manifest itself

similarly to a nutrient deficiency or in generally poor growth. If applications of fertiliser fail to help the situation, it may be time to consider having your soil tested. You can do this through a garden centre, stock and station agent, or Agriculture New Zealand (who send soil samples away for analysis), or through a professional soil testing and plant analysis laboratory.

Commercial organic fertilisers are one way to ensure a healthy crop.

HOW TO RAISE pH

Lime contains calcium, one of the base or 'alkali' elements, and is used to raise the pH of acid soils.

Agricultural lime (calcium carbonate) is the best to use. It is finely ground, but takes some time to react with the acidity in the soil. All limestones contain some magnesium, but the dolomitic limestones and dolomite contain higher proportions. These are preferable for liming soils that have received heavy applications of poultry manures.

Hydrated lime or slaked lime (calcium hydroxide) can also be used. It is quick-acting in raising soil pH but should not be applied at the same time as fertilisers. A given weight of hydrated lime is equivalent to about 1.3 times that weight of agricultural lime.

Gypsum (calcium sulphate) is often used to improve soils containing high levels of sodium. It contains 23 per cent calcium and 15 per cent sulphur but it is not a liming material – in fact, it has a neutral or very slightly acid effect on soil. However, by displacing sodium, gypsum will improve the structure of soil.

Agricultural lime (or dolomite) can be applied at any time of the year and watered into the topsoil. The quantity required depends on soil type – sand, loam or clay – and the amount of organic matter in the soil. It is best to raise pH slowly rather than apply massive doses. The following quantities of agricultural lime are a guide to raising pH by one unit, say from pH 5.5 to pH 6.5.

SOIL TYPE	QUANTITY OF LIME (GRAMS PER SQUARE METRE)
Sandy soil	150–200
Loam	200–280
Clay soil	280–450

In gardens where the soil is known to be acid, lime is often applied at the above rates every year or two. This maintains a desirable pH, especially in annual flower beds and vegetable plots which are usually cropped continuously throughout the year.

There is no practical evidence that lime binds sand or clay particles into crumbs in a direct way. However, it does have an effect on soil chemistry, favouring bacterial activity and the decomposition of organic matter. The formation of humus particles, in turn, promotes a good crumb structure.

HOW TO LOWER SOIL pH

The best acidifying agent to lower pH on alkaline soils is sulphur. Be aware, however, that for all practical purposes it is not possible to lower the pH of soils with a pH above 8.3. Sulphates such as aluminium sulphate (alum) and iron sulphate are sometimes recommended. Sulphate of ammonia also has an acidifying effect if used over a long period. Peat moss will also lower pH, but the results are less predictable. The following quantities of sulphur are a guide for lowering the pH by one unit, say from pH 7.5 to pH 6.5.

SOIL TYPE	QUANTITY OF SULPHUR (GRAMS PER SQUARE METRE)
Sandy soil	30–60
Loam	60–90
Clay soil	90–120

When making soil tests, always record the area from which samples were taken, and the date of the test. If lime or sulphur is applied to correct pH levels, make a note of how much and when it was applied.

HYDROPONICS

Hydroponics is a system of growing plants without soil. If there is sufficient light, the right temperature, air to supply carbon dioxide to leaves and oxygen for the plant and its roots, we should be able to feed them water and nutrients for healthy growth.

Many experiments have been carried out in laboratories using water-culture methods. These gave precise information on the effect of each nutrient on plants. In true water culture, roots dip into a nutrient solution through which air is bubbled regularly so roots can breathe. More often, plants are grown in a combination of free-draining sand or gravel and an inert moisture-holding material and fed with a nutrient solution.

Carnations, lettuce and strawberries and a number of other crops have been successfully grown commercially in hydroponic beds.

There is new interest in this system of growing plants for vegetables, flowers and small shrubs. It has a special appeal to people living in flats or home units where there is a sunny balcony or patio but no outside garden.

Hydroponics is much the same as growing plants in tubs or pots – but without soil. Containers must have free drainage and plants must be watered and fed regularly. Several kits for hydroponic beds and planter boxes are available.

The advantages of hydroponics are that it involves no digging, few weeds grow, and very little maintenance is required, apart from regular watering and feeding. If you want to try your hand at hydroponics, fill a polystyrene trough with a mixture containing two parts coarse river sand, one part crushed charcoal and one part vermiculite, plus a tablespoon of Gro-Plus Complete Plant Food per bucket of mix. Sow three rows of baby carrots and water them regularly.

A comparatively easy and economical hydroponic nutrient solution can be made by mixing one part of Thrive with one part of nitrate of potash and a half part of Epsom salts. Dissolve at the rate of 5 grams (a level measuring spoon) to 5 litres of water and feed every few days as required. Before sowing or planting, work superphosphate into the growing medium at the rate of 1 kg per 10 square metres of surface (top) area. This will encourage stronger root growth and also supply calcium. Flush with clean water every week to prevent salt build-up. Repeat the application of superphosphate at monthly intervals.

Many nutrient mixtures for hydroponic gardening are made up to special formulas. Your local hydroponic supplier will be able to give you advice on these mixtures.

Pansies and Swan River daisies flourish in a vertical hydroponic set-up.

No–dig Gardening

A no-dig garden is just that – a garden bed made up of layers of organic materials that does not require back-breaking digging and tilling. Esther Deans, inventor of the 'no-dig' garden, recommends her method for all gardeners but says it is particularly useful for those physically unable to dig in the traditional fashion. Children, older gardeners, handicapped people or those confined to a wheelchair will find this method practical and toil-free.

WHERE TO PUT A NO-DIG GARDEN

A no-dig garden can go almost anywhere. It can be situated on a section of lawn or existing garden. It can be built over hard, rocky ground or even on top of a concrete slab. It is also possible to adapt the method to create an elevated garden. Use any type of frame or container, set at a convenient level, and line it with heavy-duty plastic punched with drainage holes and make the garden within the frame.

MAKING A NO-DIG GARDEN:

ON THE GROUND

1. Select a site, preferably in a sunny position.
2. Build a box frame with boards or bricks.
3. Place a 50 mm thick layer of newspaper (not cardboard or glossy magazine paper) in the bottom of the frame. Overlap the paper so there are no gaps.

CONSTRUCTING THE BED

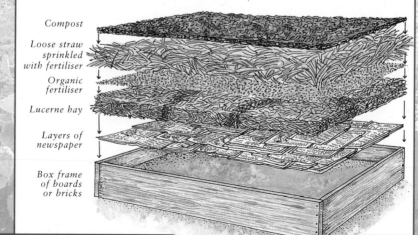

Compost

Loose straw sprinkled with fertiliser

Organic fertiliser

Lucerne hay

Layers of newspaper

Box frame of boards or bricks

4. Cover with pads of lucerne hay as they come off the bale.
5. Sprinkle on a dusting of organic fertiliser.
6. Cover with 20 cm of loose straw.
7. Scatter some fertiliser onto this layer.
8. Tip a circle of rich compost 10 cm deep and about 45 cm in diameter in places where seeds are to be planted.

ON ROCKY GROUND OR CONCRETE

1. Build a box frame with boards or bricks.
2. On the bottom spread a layer of decaying leaves, small sticks and pieces of seaweed to a depth of 10 cm.
3. Layer the organic materials as in the method above.

TENDING YOUR GARDEN

Do not dig a no-dig garden. It is both unnecessary and detrimental to the unique process. Simply replace new layers of compost, manure, lucerne and newspapers when necessary.

Rotate your crops. For example, when leafy summer crops have been harvested the layers of the garden will have composted down and merged into each other. Add another layer of compost and plant autumn seeds such as carrots, onions, cauliflower or cabbage.

Water during the early morning when evaporation is at its lowest.

Weeding will be minimal because the organic materials added to the garden should be weed free.

WHAT TO PLANT

Vegetable seeds and seedlings, flowering annuals, herbs, bulbs and strawberries all thrive in a no-dig garden. Use the following vegetable-growing schedule as a guide to obtaining a rich seasonal bounty from your no-dig garden.

VEGETABLE SOWING GUIDE

This is a guide for temperate regions. Consult an advisor at your local nursery if you live in a different climatic region.

SPRING

Sow seeds of French, climbing or scarlet runner beans, beetroot, carrot, corn, melon, pumpkin, radish and summer squash. Sow seeds or plant seedlings of cabbage, capsicum, celery, cucumber, eggplant, lettuce, marrow, silver beet, tomato and zucchini. Set in potato tubers.

SUMMER

Sow seeds of French beans, carrot, corn, beetroot and radish. Sow seeds or plant seedlings of Brussels sprouts, cabbage, cauliflower, capsicum, celery, tomato, leek, lettuce, silver beet, tomato and vine crops.

AUTUMN

Sow seeds of broad beans, bok choy, carrot, Chinese cabbage, peas, radish, spinach. Sow seeds or plant seedlings of broccoli, kohlrabi, leek, lettuce and onion.

WINTER

Sow seeds of pea, snow pea and spinach. Sow seeds or plant seedlings of lettuce and onion. Plant garlic cloves.

CHAPTER 5

THE WATER-SAVING GARDEN

Garden tradition, largely imported from England, has given many New Zealand gardeners ambitions to develop a lush, green garden that is full of plants with high water needs. Water is a seemingly unlimited natural resource. However, those who live in rural and small coastal settlements, where water supply is their own responsibility, have come to realise that water is the most precious resource, one that should never be taken for granted. In the cities, with expanding populations and environmental and cultural considerations involved in creating new water storage facilities, home gardeners must also learn to garden with less water. Some water authorities now charge by usage and this 'hip pocket' message will help emphasise the importance of not wasting water in the garden.

Water is fundamental to plant life and growth, acting as a communication network, transporting nutrients and other critical substances around the plant. Water is vital to all the important chemical reactions taking place in a plant and is also responsible for keeping a plant turgid by producing internal pressure. There are many plants which have adapted to using less water, or which have become very efficient at storing water, such as cacti and succulents. Moreover, there are many ways in which to cut down on water usage and still enjoy the lush green effect.

Gardening with less water requires some thought and planning, and changes to old habits. Here are a few simple hints that will help you cut down your use of water, while protecting the substantial investment you have put into that valuable asset: your garden.

MAKING THE MOST OF YOUR WATER

- Water in the morning or evening. This gives moisture time to penetrate so that it doesn't evaporate before it gets down into the soil.
- Train your plants in good water habits. Less frequent, deep soakings will train the roots to grow down into the soil. Light sprinklings (especially with a hand-held hose) are therapeutic for the gardener, but create problems for the plants. They encourage the roots to stay near the surface where they are more vulnerable to heating up and drying out.
- Train yourself – and your kids – in good water habits. Don't leave garden taps dripping, don't use hose water to clean paths and drives; a broom and some muscle is all you need!
- Water the roots of plants, not the leaves. Don't let precious H_2O blow away in the breeze. Use a soaker hose, a watering system, or direct the water into a plastic tube that carries the water straight down to the roots of the plants. (Hint: an empty soft drink bottle makes a great watering system for an individual plant. Fill with water, punch two small holes in the lid and upend the bottle beside a small plant. The water will gradually seep into the soil.)
- Mulch around your plants to conserve moisture in the soil. Make sure there is moisture in the soil before you mulch. Use manure, compost, newspaper, rocks, straw or whatever else you can get hold of. Don't allow mulch to touch the plant's trunk and don't use material that has been sprayed with a weedkiller. (See the section entitled 'Mulching' on page 62 of this chapter.)
- Use every drop of water. Rinse water from washing machines can be directed onto the roots of plants. 'Grey' water from baths can be mixed with soluble fertilisers such as Thrive – this will encourage the growth of healthy plants with vigorous root systems. A lightly fertilised lawn can use up to 30 per cent less water than an unfertilised one of the same grass type.

PREPARING AND MAINTAINING YOUR GARDEN

Strawflowers (also known as paper daisies) will add cheerful colour to a low water-use garden bed.

TIPS TO USING LESS WATER

- Group your plants according to their water needs. Put the plants that need the most water together in one part of the garden. If you have just one plant with high water requirements in a garden bed, it will mean that all the other plants in that bed will receive more water than they need.
- Give your plants the best chance of surviving dry periods: don't be tempted to grow plants that prefer shade in full sun. A vulnerable shrub in a hot, dry position will need much more watering to keep it in good condition.
- Fertilise your plants using liquid fertiliser. Dry fertilisers take water from the soil but soluble fertilisers like Thrive, which are applied in liquid form, will encourage plant growth without raising salt levels in the soil.
- Control weeds in the garden. Weeds are great competitors and they will fight with your garden plants for every precious drop. Use a glyphosate-based herbicide,

such as Zero, which won't affect the soil. Make sure that the herbicide doesn't contact your garden plants.
- Grow your garden on a smaller scale. Container gardening is fashionable and great fun. Use a good-sized pot, a quality potting mix that holds water (look for names such as 'patio and tub' mix) and group pots together so they stay cooler. Move the pots into the shade during very hot periods.
- Reduce lawn areas. Lawns can consume more water than almost any other part of the garden. Instead of lawn, a water-saving garden could use paving, pebbles, or drought-tolerant ground covers such as coprosmas, lamium, snow-in-summer (*Cerastium tomentosum*) or native hebes.
- Grow grasses that need less water such as kikuyu or buffalo grass. Kikuyu may be considered an objectionable plant and a weed in some instances, however it has its place especially on coastal sections where other forms of lawn are impossible to establish. It is totally drought tolerant but suited only to warmer areas as it is frost

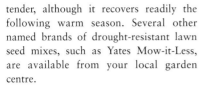

tender, although it recovers readily the following warm season. Several other named brands of drought-resistant lawn seed mixes, such as Yates Mow-it-Less, are available from your local garden centre.

● During very dry periods let the lawn die off completely – it is easier to replace lawn than trees and shrubs when the rain eventually falls again. When mowing, leave the grass longer than normal. Longer grass means a deeper root system, and the long blades shade the soil, which also helps keeps the soil temperature down.

● Train your lawn in good water habits, in the same way as you would train your other garden plants. Once the lawn is well established, give long soakings rather than short, light waterings. This will encourage a deeper, more hardy root system.

● Grow drought-tolerant plants. Many New Zealand natives have evolved to handle periods of water stress. Look for plants with small leaves, hard leaf surfaces or hairy leaf coverings. Exotics such as Australian, Californian, Mediterranean and South African plants can also cope well with water stress. In the flower garden grow Swan River daisy, coreopsis, Californian poppy, cosmos, portulaca and strawflower. Succulents and cacti have also evolved to handle low rainfall periods by combining water-storing stems and waxy leaf surfaces or, in the case of most cacti, no leaves at all (plants lose most water through their leaves).

Hint

In a drought, trim off the edges of the foliage of trees and shrubs that cannot be watered so less water is lost through transpiration.

MARY LOVELL-SMITH
CHRISTCHURCH *PRESS*

Once they are well established in the garden, many New Zealand natives, such as these Renga lilies, can handle periods of water stress.

WATER-SAVING PRODUCTS

There are many new products available to the home gardener that will help reduce water use in the garden. Water-storing polymer crystals are polymer 'sugars' that can hold hundreds of times their weight in water. Either mix the dry crystals into the soil before planting or, preferably, leave them to sit in water for a few hours before use. During this time they will swell up and change from their crystalline form into a soft gel. The gel provides a reserve of moisture for the plants' roots to draw on during dry periods.

Stressguard is another polymer product. Stressguard is a liquid that is diluted with water and sprayed over the plant surfaces. This thin film of polymer provides a flexible outer coating that allows the plant to function normally, but protects from sunburn and reduces water loss by as much as 50 per cent. Use Stressguard in situations where you are growing plants that might be slightly out of their climatic range, especially plants that would prefer a cooler climate.

When transplanting, spray a film of Stressguard over the plant before moving it from its original position. Even if the plant loses some roots during the move, the layer of Stressguard will help it to survive until the root system has had a chance to regrow.

A combination of good mulching and careful plant selection (here we see lamb's ear, Stachys lanata) *makes a successful water-saving garden.*

Soil wetters break the surface tension of the soil and allow the water to penetrate deeply. If soil or potting mix has dried out, or become compacted – as often happens with a frequently used lawn – it can actually repel water and shed it from the surface. Treatment with a soil wetter can often remedy this situation.

Above all, you should always keep in mind that mulching can reduce the amount of water you use on your garden by 50 per cent.

MULCHING

It is important to recognise the value of mulching materials as they can protect soils from the harsh sun, add organic matter to depleted soils, preserve moisture, reduce the need for irrigation, improve crop production, increase soil microbial activity, alleviate the effects of soil pollution, correct past bad farming practices, give plants humus, aid weed control, help in recycling waste material and build good soil structure. Mulch can be used to begin an easy, work-free garden area, control weeds in your garden, or help you build a no-dig vegetable garden (see pages 56–57).

Materials used for mulching include the following:

SAWDUST, WOOD SHAVINGS AND WOOD PULP

These are common components of potting mixes, and are best utilised by composting for two to eight weeks before use, preferably with animal manure. If fresh material is used without adding some nitrogen in the form of fertiliser or animal manure, you may see yellow leaves on plants, which is a sign of nitrogen deficiency. Fresh wood or bark chips or material from council mulchers will usually be mixed with some moist green plant material containing nitrogen. This mulch will need to be composted before use.

BARK CHIPS AND PINE BARK

Some eucalypt bark, for example redgum and blackbutt, and pine bark chips, contain resins which must be leached from the bark before use. Two weeks of leaching, composting or constant wetting with water will get rid of these plant-retardant resins. These make excellent, long-lasting mulches.

GRAVEL, STONES, QUARTZ AND SCORIA

These are often used for special landscape effects, for colour and form. It is not advisable for those gardeners who want to dig the soil in garden beds, as very often stones 'stray' from these areas and can ruin mower blades or mechanical equipment. Gravel is often used for driveways, small garden areas, or in pots.

PLASTIC SHEETING

Used extensively in landscaping during the 1950–70 period as the answer to all weed problems, it is no longer recommended since plastic builds up warmth, encouraging surface root growth, and thus plants are susceptible to being blown out of the ground by strong winds. Moisture builds up under the plastic, and little if any oxygen is allowed to permeate into the soil. If you use plastic sheeting it should be perforated to allow soil aeration, but it is much better to buy specially manufactured 'weedmats' that are made from woven synthetic material.

WEEDMAT

Specially formulated woven mesh is used for weed control and to allow water to penetrate

A thick layer of crop straw mulch will retain soil moisture and reduce weed competition for this citrus tree.

Hint

There is a huge range of mulches available. When using a mulch, ensure that the material is fully composted; this will guarantee that nitrogen compounds are available to your plants. For effective water retention and weed suppression, the mulch should be at least 5 cm deep.

ROD GIBBONS
LIVING EARTH

plant roots. The open mesh also allows oxygen to permeate into the soil. It is sold by the metre in varying widths.

PASTURE HAY

This is wonderful material, especially if obtained from an old disused haystack; however, new hay can be the source of grass seeds and weed seed, and should be composted before use, or covered with other mulching material to suppress weed seedling growth. It is readily obtained in small bales, in very large round bales (some biodynamically grown without using chemicals), or loose from disused or old haystacks.

CROP STRAW

This is ideal mulch. Usually with no weed seeds, it is high in carbon and only needs nitrogen added to it to help decomposition. Crop straw is often used to protect strawberries and vegetables from soil-borne diseases such as botrytis, thus preventing fruit rots developing. It is usually available either in small bales or loose.

LUCERNE HAY

Renowned as a fantastic mulch, it has its own carbon/nitrogen composition. It is very nutritious, composts well, and is used for no-dig gardens. A great activator for compost, it will compost quickly with the addition of milk or compost accelerator to encourage microbial activity. It is usually available in small bales and is relatively expensive.

PREPARING AND MAINTAINING YOUR GARDEN

Hellebores are a great plant to grow as they need minimal attention. In the summer they don't even need to be watered, as they should be dormant. They are also great for reducing water loss in the garden, as their prostrate form helps eliminate evaporation.

TERRY HATCH
JOY PLANTS

PEA STRAW

This soft material breaks down quickly, and is an ideal mulch, though it will contain some pea seeds that will self-germinate. These are easily weeded out, or plants can be left to grow to provide nitrogen to the soil. Adding activators such as milk will help decomposition. It is available in small bale form.

PROPRIETARY MULCHES

Named-brand mulches, such as Yates Rose and Shrub Mulch, are available in garden centres. Rose and Shrub Mulch is a blend of fine aged bark and Bio-Gold organic fertiliser, providing a balance of the major elements (N.P.K.) and trace elements, which slowly breaks down to supply additional nutrients and humus to the soil. Used as an integral part of your winter clean-up or in preparation of beds for spring, together with a summer application, your roses will be kept moist and well fed all year round.

EUCALYPTUS LEAVES

Eucalyptus leaves make a very good mulch which is slow to decompose. The leaves give a natural look to those areas planted with Australian native plants, but look equally attractive on any garden. They will decompose faster if shredded with a mulching machine before application. Because whole leaves 'fit' into each other, only thin layers are needed for good weed control.

Your own homemade compost makes one of the best mulches. Not only does it hold moisture, it also improves and enriches the soil.

PEAT MOSS

Peat moss from sphagnum peat bogs is expensive but can be an ideal mulch. Usually very acid, it can be used around acid-loving plants such as azaleas, camellias, boronias and potatoes. It is used also to correct the pH of highly alkaline soils. Large-scale use of peat is environmentally unsound because of the finite nature of peat resources.

GRASS CLIPPINGS

Fresh grass has a high nitrogen and moisture content and will compost well if high carbonaceous materials such as straw are mixed with it. If using for mulch allow it to dry out thoroughly in the sun before applying to soil or around plants.

COMPOST

Any well-prepared nutrient-rich compost is excellent to use in the garden. It provides humus and food for plants, will not burn plant roots and is an ideal material to help build up the microorganisms in the soil.

MUSHROOM COMPOST

A very good material, mushroom compost is excellent for plant growth, but check pH as some samples have high pH or high salt content, which will retard plant growth and make leaves curl. Always obtain mushroom compost from a reliable source.

RECYCLED WASTE

Many municipal councils are concerned about waste disposal and pollution of the environment by waste products and are now beginning to recycle some of this resource, partly by composting and mulching organic material and then selling this back to the general public or direct to farmers.

SEWAGE WASTE

Sewage is now also being recycled in many cities and towns to prevent pollution of waterways, ground water and the oceans. After composting, the sewage material is recycled as composts and fertiliser, incorporated into soil mixes or sold to farmers to help rejuvenate soils. One inherent problem with many forms of sewage waste is the heavy metal components, but this problem may be solved in future years.

Fallen leaves are nature's mulch. Don't waste them: spread them directly onto garden beds or add them to compost.

WORM CASTS

The best material available of all the mulching products, worm casts are obtainable from worm farmers. Many farms will probably be created in future years to recycle waste, so future supplies should be assured. Casts are high in plant food value, cannot burn plant roots, can be spread to any depth desired, and build up biological activity in your soil.

OLD HESSIAN BAGS

These are relatively cheap materials to spread upon the soil; plants are planted through the hessian, or it can be used as a base for sowing grass seed. It is an ideal material for this, as the fibres will rot away within a few months.

TAN BARK

A by-product of the tanning industry, the bark is from acacia (wattle tree) species. Expensive, but often sought for its landscape effect (it has a very dark colour), it is an acidic material with some residual resins that impede weed growth.

PREPARING AND MAINTAINING YOUR GARDEN

SEAWEED

Seaweed is an ideal mulch, but it will take a long time to decompose. Seaweed gathered from the shore line should be washed, especially if this mulch is used very frequently in the garden. Various forms are available, such as sea grass and kelp. Check with your local council or government department representative for permission to collect from the shore.

A 'gel' can be made by placing cut and dried pieces of kelp in a drum with water. Add some fertiliser, manure, or urine. This forms a gel that can be spread around plants or diluted with water and used as liquid fertiliser. Seaweed is nutritious and various species have been found to contain nearly all the elements known.

Seaweed provides nutrients and plant growth substances. Many organic growers use seaweed foliar or granular applications to provide micronutrients and a balanced food supply. Seaweed extracts are also thought to be beneficial in reducing the incidence of pests and diseases.

Hint

Laying newspaper in your garden can be really difficult if there's even a hint of a breeze. To stop it blowing everywhere, first soak it thoroughly in a wheelbarrow that has been quarter-filled with water.

NICK HAYHOE
YATES NEW ZEALAND

PAPER

Shredded paper or sheets of paper can be used as mulch. This material is ideal for preventing weed growth around newly planted trees, to use under other mulch material (usually 1–5 cm thick), or as the base for a no-dig garden. Note that newsprint does contain very small amounts of heavy metals. Paper has a high carbon content and will need a high nitrogenous material, such as

Overlapped sheets of newspaper are excellent for suppressing weeds. Once in place, cover them with an attractive mulch layer.

grass clippings or animal manure, to help break it down.

ANIMAL MANURES

All manures make great mulches and provide plants with food. Fresh manures must be used cautiously as you can burn plant roots. Used fresh, manures are spread to a thickness of 1–2 cm only, but if the manure is mixed with straw, wood shavings, sawdust, or other material it can be spread to twice this depth. If the manure has been composted for 1–2 months or more, or has been weathered for many months, then this material can be spread to a depth of 15 cm or more if needed. Some manures such as sheep manure may contain lots of weed seeds; composting sheep manure before use will kill these seeds.

CARPET UNDERLAY

A material recommended by permaculturists to prevent weed growth, carpet works well with blackberries. A readily available mulch source in urban areas, it can be laid and then holes or slits cut into the material so that plants can be planted through it.

NATURAL MULCH

Trees such as gums often have accumulated leaf mulch under them that can be utilised as a garden mulch. Deciduous trees also shed

Apply mulch in such a way as to avoid contact with the base of plants.

copious amounts of leaf litter that can be collected to make a natural-looking and effective mulch. Don't collect from reserves.

DRIED PINE NEEDLES

Though slightly acidic, pine needles can be used as a mulch. Used around strawberry plants to improve strawberry fruit flavour, the needles are long-lasting. They will, however, break down quickly if chopped up and composted with manure and a little lime.

KITCHEN WASTE

Many products found in the kitchen and home can be used as mulch, for example tea leaves, coffee grounds, hair clippings, rags (shredded), egg shells, shells from nuts, stone fruit seeds (crushed) and old telephone books (shredded).

INDUSTRY BY-PRODUCTS

Many products such as spent hops, feathermeal, or vegetable trash from greengrocers or market places can make useful mulch. Keep in mind that material that would normally go to the rubbish tip can be recycled, even if it may need composting before using as a mulch.

Hint

Succulents can withstand long periods without water, but for optimum growth regular watering, particularly during the summer, is necessary. If you are growing succulents in containers, water them when the potting mixture feels dry to the touch. Alternatively, break open a leaf — if it is moist and fleshy there is no need to water the plant.

JODY LUSK AND RICHARD DAVEY
WAIRERE NURSERY

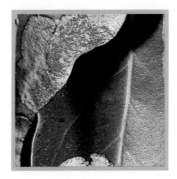

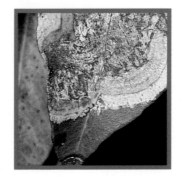

CHAPTER 6

PESTS, DISEASES AND WEEDS

You need not be an expert on pests, diseases and weeds to have a clean, healthy garden which will grow top-quality flowers, fruit and vegetables. Effective and relatively low-toxic sprays and dusts are available to control most pests and diseases and to eradicate the majority of weeds. The quick reference charts at the end of this chapter (see pages 86–92) tells you what pests and diseases attack your plants, how to identify them or their symptoms and what chemical to use.

It is important to know the normal, healthy appearance of plants so that problems caused by pests or diseases can be detected quickly. Early recognition of a problem gives you a good start in overcoming it. But it is not always a pest or disease which makes a plant unhealthy.

Inadequate watering may be the cause. If you allow soil to dry out to a depth of 5–10 cm below the surface, subsequent light watering, however frequent, will not let the water soak in to reach plant roots. The best way to overcome this is to water thoroughly for several hours until the soil is evenly moist throughout its depth. Overwatering and bad drainage can also be the cause of unhealthy plants, especially in the case of trees and shrubs. Overly wet conditions can impair root efficiency by preventing air (for respiration) from reaching them.

Low levels of nutrients or lack of fertiliser, and in some cases a deficiency of trace elements, may be the cause of poor growth. But soil analysis is complicated and does not always give a cut-and-dried answer to the problem of unhealthy plants. The simplest strategy is to use a mixed fertiliser which contains the major nutrients (nitrogen, phosphorus and potassium) plus animal manure, if available, or compost. (See Chapters 3 and 4.) However, never use fertilisers in excess of the quantities recommended.

CHEMICALS FOR THE HOME GARDEN

There is a wide range of chemicals available for ridding the garden of pests and diseases. Some of these are specific in their action while others are broad-spectrum chemicals and will control more than one pest or disease. Multi-purpose sprays are available, which contain one or more insecticides to control pests, combined with one or more fungicides to control diseases. These sprays are recommended, especially when there is some doubt as to the cause of the problem.

Whatever garden chemicals are used, it is important to stress that they should be used with care. Fortunately, chemical manufacturers have discarded many of the more toxic insecticides for garden use. Most garden chemicals can be used with perfect safety if directions are followed and simple precautions are taken:

- Read directions carefully before using and use only for the purpose stated on the label.
- Avoid contact of spray or dust with skin.
- Avoid breathing fumes from sprays or dusts.
- Avoid spraying or dusting on windy days. A calm, cloudy day is best for spraying.
- Avoid eating or smoking when spraying or dusting.
- Rinse spray equipment after use and wash face and hands with soap and water.
- Store sprays and dusts out of reach of children or in a locked cupboard.
- Do not harvest vegetable and fruit crops earlier than the withholding period (see tables pages 86–88 for insecticides and fungicides).

PREPARING AND MAINTAINING YOUR GARDEN

DUSTS OR SPRAYS?

Whether you use dusts or sprays, it is important to apply them so that all parts of the plant are covered. Dusts do not need mixing and are simple to apply. But dusts can be difficult to apply to larger plants and are easily washed off by rain or overhead watering. Generally, spraying gives a better and more even coverage of the plant surfaces, and therefore more effective control. Many gardeners find the pressure sprays, such as the Yates Maxi 2, 4 or 6 litre, to be the most convenient for the home gardener. Knapsack sprays, which can be carried over the shoulder, are also readily available and convenient. The Fynaspray is a less expensive bucket-type sprayer with a long spray rod and adjustable nozzle and a length of plastic tubing. For small balcony gardens, pot plants and glass or shadehouses a plastic mist atomiser will prove adequate.

For correct strength of sprays, always follow the manufacturer's directions exactly.

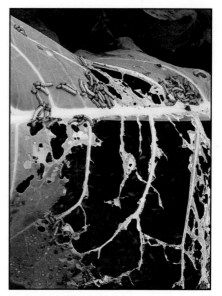

Many leaf-eating caterpillars can be controlled with Nature's Way Pyrethrum, a bio-insecticide.

Hint

Before mixing insecticides always read the directions to check compatability. When diluting concentrates, use one volume of water for all the different sprays. Don't dilute individual sprays then mix them together. Once you have mixed it, use it: sprays degrade in sunlight and become inactive.

DIANA SELBY
LANDSCAPE ARCHITECT

Do not be tempted to put in a little extra for good measure – it is unnecessary and can even be harmful. Most garden chemicals can be used in the same container, providing the hose and nozzle are washed out thoroughly immediately after use. Extra care must be taken to wash hormone herbicides from any containers or spray equipment used.

PESTS

Garden pests are generally members of the insect world – beetles, bugs, caterpillars, aphids or thrips – but also include tiny red spiders or mites. Snails and slugs are not insects but probably do as much damage as other pests.

Pests are controlled by insecticides, miticides and snail baits. Before we describe these pests in detail we will divide them into two broad groups: chewing insects and sap-sucking insects.

Chewing insects actually eat plant tissues – that is, leaves, stems, buds, flowers or fruits. Beetles, caterpillars, codling moth, cutworms and grasshoppers are included in this group. They are controlled by contact insecticides or stomach poisons. Snails and slugs are usually included in this group too because they are controlled by stomach poison baits in the same way as chewing insects.

Sap-sucking insects are those which suck sap from young shoots, flower buds, leaves and stems. They do not actually eat plant tissue so a contact or systemic insecticide (absorbed by plants into the sap stream) is needed to destroy them. The sap-suckers include aphids, thrips, mites and several kinds of bugs and scale insects.

Not all leaf-eating insects are caterpillars. In this case, the culprit is a beetle.

Most sap-suckers feed by inserting their sharp mouthparts (or beaks) into plant tissue and extracting the sap. This kind of feeding causes collapse of plant cells, destruction of tissues and wilting. Many virus diseases of plants are transmitted from one plant to another by sap-sucking insects.

CHEWING INSECTS
Caterpillars

There are many types of caterpillars which are usually the larval (caterpillar or grub) stage of moths such as potato tuber moth, cabbage white butterfly or tomato moth. The moths lay their eggs on the underside of leaves. The larvae of caterpillars hatch from the eggs and then feed on the leaves or fruit. Caterpillars can be controlled by Yates Carbaryl, Mavrik, Maldison, Target, Trigger Insect Spray or Bayer Baythroid.

Nature's Way Pyrethrum is a bio-insecticide with low human toxicity which controls leaf-eating caterpillars on cabbages and other crucifers.

Armyworms and cutworms

Another kind of caterpillar is the armyworm or cutworm, which is brown or green (or sometimes striped) and mostly feeds at night.

These caterpillars cut through the stems of seedlings or transplants. Drench around plants with spray-strength solutions of Yates Carbaryl.

Beetles, weevils, grasshoppers and crickets

Beetles and other insects which chew leaves and stems can easily be controlled by sprays of Maldison or Carbaryl. Black beetles are a serious pest in lawns, but also attack other plants. The adult beetles do some damage in spring but most damage is caused in mid-summer to early autumn. Carbaryl will give some control of adult beetles in spring, however the most effective control is Soil Insect Killer granules applied in January to kill the grubs.

Grass grubs in spring and summer, and porina caterpillars and crickets in late summer, may cause serious damage to turf

Hint

Hosta foliage is caviar for slugs and snails. When you see slug damage, cut the leaves right back to ground level, and lay a bait such as Blitzem or Mesurol around the plants. The snails will soon disappear and fresh, lush foliage will grow on your plants.

BARRY SLIGH
TAUNTON GARDEN AND NURSERY

grasses. The grass dies in patches for no apparent reason. Grass grubs live and feed on roots below the soil surface, whereas crickets and porina caterpillars live underground and emerge after dark to feed on grass foliage. Close inspection of the soil is advisable to confirm the presence of these pests. Soil Insect Killer applied in mid–late summer, depending on the pest and the climate, will control all three lawn pests.

PREPARING AND MAINTAINING YOUR GARDEN

Codling moth damage in an apple.

Pittosporum leafminer damage.

Bronze beetle is another irksome pest. The grubs live underground through autumn and winter, feeding on plant roots. In spring the adult beetles hatch out, often in great numbers, ready to devastate whichever plant they choose as their host. Orthene is a very effective systemic insecticide with which to eradicate bronze beetle in its adult stage. Mavrik is a better choice for flowering and fruiting plants.

Codling moth

Codling moth may cause serious damage in apples, pears and quinces. The moths lay their eggs on leaves and the developing fruit as flowering finishes. When the eggs hatch, the caterpillars burrow into the fruit. Apply insecticide spray (Carbaryl or Fruit Tree Spray) at petal fall and then at fourteen-day intervals until four or six sprays have been applied. All infected fruit should be removed and destroyed.

Bean fly

Bean fly may be a serious pest of French beans (both dwarf and climbing) in warm, subtropical areas. The small, adult fly lays eggs on the leaves and the larvae or maggots tunnel into the young stems which swell and

break. If detected, spray plants with Mavrik at intervals of seven to fourteen days to control the pest.

Leafminers

Leafminers are the larvae of a small fly. They tunnel through the leaves leaving scribble-like white markings, especially in cinerarias, nasturtiums, marguerites, spinach and silver beet. As the grubs are difficult to reach with contact sprays, systemic insecticides – Orthene or Shield – give best control.

Borers

Borers attack fruit trees and a number of ornamental trees and shrubs. The grubs tunnel into the trunk or branches, leaving a mass of sawdust or gum oozing from the hole. Probe the hole with a piece of wire and inject into it a contact insecticide such as Maldison or Carbaryl.

Snails and slugs

Blitzem or Mesurol are very effective against snails and slugs. Scatter the baits (as directed on the package) where seeds have been sown or seedlings transplanted. These pests are more active in cool, wet weather, so it is wise to spread baits in these conditions, especially under shrubs and hedges where snails and slugs shelter and breed.

Some plants, in particular flaxes and other sword-leaved plants, are favourite breeding spots. Most snail baits contain a pet deterrent for added safety to domestic pets. However, it is important to read the directions carefully.

Hint

If you are worried about children or pets eating slug bait in the garden, try using Blitzem granules instead of the more conventional pellets. These are very fine, and virtually invisible once spread on the soil. The granules are a little more expensive than the pellets, but they remain active much longer.

CHARLIE GRAY
YATES NEW ZEALAND

SAP-SUCKING INSECTS
Aphids

Aphids are small, soft-bodied insects which usually cluster on young shoots and flower buds or underneath leaves. There are many different species which vary in colour – yellow, bronze, green, brown, pink, grey and black. Aphids attack fruit trees (including citrus trees) roses, camellias, chrysanthemums and other ornamentals, a wide range of vegetables, flowering annuals, bulbs and even weeds. Woolly aphids are another type which give a white, fleecy appearance on the branches of apples, pears, hydrangeas and other shrubs. Aphids also transmit virus diseases such as broad bean wilt (on broad beans and sweet peas), potato mosaic and mosaic virus of stocks. Some weeds are alternative hosts for virus disease. Because aphids are small and often collect on the underside of foliage, they are frequently undetected. Small colonies multiply rapidly and can develop into a heavy infestation in a matter of days. Systemic sprays are most effective in controlling aphids. Shield or Confidor are excellent for shrubs, flowers and ornamentals because they persist in the sap for several weeks. For vegetables, Garden

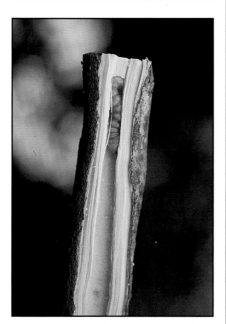

A cross-section of a branch shows how borer has attacked a citrus tree.

Although it looks like a slug, pear and cherry slug is actually a leaf-eating caterpillar.

Aphids are sap-sucking insects that can rapidly build up numbers when conditions are favourable.

Master, Maldison or Confidor are recommended because of their seven-day, three-day or one-day withholding periods.

Pyrethrum sprays, for example Nature's Way Pyrethrum, also provide some control but have short residual effect and plants can be reinfested in a few days.

Hint

When using chemical sprays, always follow the directions on the label. Always wear protective clothing, especially rubber gloves, a hat, mask and safety goggles or sunglasses. Don't spray on windy days as drift can affect other plants and people. Sprayfix helps reduce drift.

NICK HAYHOE
YATES NEW ZEALAND

Passion vine hoppers

Passion vine hoppers are tiny, quick-flying insects, often called leaf hoppers or lace wings. When disturbed they flick away quickly to another plant. Mature passion vine hoppers are easily recognised by their brown, lacy wings. The immature stage is characterised by a white fluffy tail and is equally as damaging. The best method of control is to use a systemic insecticide, such as Confidor, in November, to eradicate the juvenile insects. Excellent organic control can be achieved by trimming off and burning all plant material on which eggs have been laid. During winter pruning, look for thin twigs and tendrils with tiny, regularly spaced eggs laid neatly along them.

White flies

These small, white-winged, sap-sucking flies have become very prevalent in recent years. They usually attack annuals and vegetables, especially tomato, bean and vine crops. Target is one of the best controls for white fly. Mavrik is an excellent alternative for flowering or fruiting plants.

Although thrips are tiny insects, they can seriously disfigure flowers like roses. They are especially attracted to light-coloured blooms.

Thrips

Thrips are small insects about 1 mm long and just visible to the naked eye. They vary in colour from white through yellow and brown to black. Thrips attack the flowers, fruit and foliage of vegetable crops and ornamental plants. Roses, fruit trees, azaleas, gladioli, tomatoes, onions and beans are regular victims of thrip invasion. They also feed on a wide range of weeds. During hot weather, weeds dry up and the insects migrate to more attractive plants. Certain kinds of thrips transmit spotted wilt virus which may seriously affect tomato, lettuce and dahlias in summer. Thrips are often most difficult to control because the eggs are laid inside the plant tissue and the pupae and adults often feed on unopened flower buds. This prevents sprays and dusts from reaching the insects. Regular spraying with Super Shield or Mavrik will control them. A pyrethrum spray such as Trigger Insect Spray is recommended for small pot plants and indoor plants.

Bugs

These large insects are often called shield bugs because of their shape and tough exterior. They can be serious pests in summer.

The green vegetable bug is bright green in colour and about 1 cm long in adulthood, but more rounded and black and white or black and red in younger stages. It attacks beans, tomatoes, potatoes, sweet corn, vine crops, grapes, sunflowers, and other ornamentals.

Spittle bugs tend to be pests of cooler climate

As well as attacking plants, green vegetable bugs have an unpleasant smell.

PREPARING AND MAINTAINING YOUR GARDEN

gardens. Both the native spittle bug and the foreign meadow spittle bug cover themselves in a protective white spittle-like substance. They inhabit a large range of plants and may cause wilting, distortion and malformation of new growth. Douse spittle bugs with a gentle spray of water, to remove their protective coating, before spraying with an insecticide.

Bugs can be controlled by using any of several insecticides. Carbaryl and Baythroid are good contact sprays. Shield and Confidor are effective systemic sprays.

Mealybugs

Mealybugs are small insects covered with a white mealy coating; some have white hairs attached to their bodies. Heavy infestations can occur on citrus trees, daphne and other ornamental plants. Orchids and ferns, especially in shadehouses, can become infested too. They may also attack bulbs in storage and the roots of some plants such as polyanthus, liliums and ferns.

Confidor or Shield will control mealybugs, but use Confidor Aerosol on soft plants in a shadehouse. This also applies to indoor pot plants. Control root-infesting mealybugs by drenching soil at spray strength with the appropriate product.

Mites

The two-spotted mite (red spider) attacks a wide range of fruit trees (apples, pears, peaches), vegetables (tomato, beans, vine crops) and ornamentals (azalea, roses, marigolds).

Symptoms of two-spotted mite are bronzing or dull-grey mottling of the leaves. In heavy infestations leaves may drop. The tiny pinkish-red mites cluster on the underside of the leaves, often producing a mass of fine webbing. The two-spotted mite has become problematic because the use of insecticides has decreased the number of natural insect enemies, such as ladybirds.

Mites can be controlled by Mite Killer, a specific miticide, or by the insecticides Mavrik or Super Shield. Sulphur or lime sulphur, both of which are often used to control fungus diseases, will also give some protection against mites.

Scale insects

One of the most common scale insects in New Zealand is the white rose scale. Also present in large numbers is the brown scale, a common pest of both indoor and outdoor plants. Scale insects are easily recognised in their adult stage by the waxy, limpet-like

Mealybugs love to gather in protected parts of the plant, like the undersides of leaves.

Two-spotted mites discolour the foliage of affected plants.

Scale insects build themselves a protective covering.

structures which cover and protect the feeding insect. Spray plants with Conqueror Oil in December and again in January, before the young insects have secreted their waxy covering. Maldison or Confidor will increase its effectiveness. Several other scale insects are also present in New Zealand; these can be treated in the same way.

Hint

If you have mealy bug on your pot plants, it may pay to gently ease the plant out of its container to check if the roots are infected as well as the foliage. If they are, treat the plant by drenching the soil with Confidor. Immerse the entire root system of the plant in a bucket of Confidor solution until bubbles no longer rise. This will guarantee success.

THE TWO ANNS
A & A CONSULTANTS

DISEASES

Plant diseases are mainly caused by parasitic organisms called 'plant pathogens'. The pathogen may be a fungus, a bacterium, a virus or a nematode. In addition, there are non-parasitic diseases that will sometimes need to be controlled.

FUNGAL DISEASES

Most plant diseases are caused by fungi which may be carried in the seed, in the soil or on other plants or weeds. They spread quickly, especially in warm, humid weather, by means of microscopic spores which are distributed by wind or water. Rain or water-splash favours their spread. Fungal diseases fall into four main groups: mildews, rusts, leaf spots, and stem and root rots.

Mildew

Powdery mildew is a fungus which spreads a white or ash-grey film over the upper and lower surfaces of the leaves of plants – usually the older leaves. Powdery mildew is a common disease of roses, dahlias, zinnias, calendulas, sweet peas, and vine crops. The systemic fungicide Greenguard will control this disease. Also effective is an application of

PREPARING AND MAINTAINING YOUR GARDEN

Nature's Way Fungus Spray or Baycor Aerosol.

Downy mildew is often more widespread in younger plants and is recognised by downy, whitish tufts or spores and mycelia on the underside of the leaves. Downy mildew is common on grapes, vine crops, cabbages and other crucifers, onions, lettuce and stocks. Spray with Bravo. Regular application of the spray is necessary during rainy weather.

Rust

Rust fungus is easily identified by the many orange or red pustules on leaves or stems which break open and release masses of spores. Rust is a common disease of calendulas, snapdragons, geraniums, gerberas and beans. In recent years it has become a serious disease of poplar trees. The most effective spray to control rust is Baycor Aerosol. Good control is also obtained with sulphur, lime sulphur or Bravo.

Leaf spots

Leaf spots are easily seen and may be serious on roses (black spot and anthracnose). Leaf spots and blights are also common on tomato, potato, capsicum, carrot, parsnip, beet and silver beet, polyanthus, iris and many shrubs. Leaf spots are usually more serious in wet conditions. Sprays of Bravo, lime sulphur or Fungus Fighter will control most leaf spots.

On roses use Shield or Super Shield, as these products control a number of fungi and insect pests.

Yates Rose Spray and Yates Greenguard control both powdery and downy mildew as well as leaf spots and rust.

Stem rots and root rots

The causes of stem rots, root rots and collar rots are not easily determined but most are due to fungal pathogens which attack the conducting tissues of the plant, causing it to wilt and finally collapse.

Sclerotinia is a widespread fungus which attacks many soft-stemmed plants, including beans, lettuce, nemesias, linarias and other annuals. The stem rot and the fungus then form small, hard-fruiting bodies called sclerotia which fall to the ground. These develop a mycelium and, later, small toadstool-like structures which shed spores to restart the cycle.

Powdery mildew on a cucurbit leaf.

Azalea petal blight is a widespread fungal disease.

Petal blight of azaleas has a similar life cycle. Greenguard is a suitable spray to control azalea petal blight. Practise crop rotation with other crops.

Some fungal pathogens attack the stems or crowns of plants at ground level. These fungi are more active in damp conditions and poorly drained soils. Root rot or collar rot is common in delphiniums, carnations, gerberas, strawberries, cabbages and other crucifers. Fruit trees and shrubs may also be attacked. While dampness and poor drainage encourage these root and crown rots, some control can be achieved by drenching the soil around the plants with Bravo or Champion Copper.

'Damping off' disease of seeds and seedlings is discussed on page 101. The fungus causing this disease is soil-borne and most active under damp, cold conditions, so it is wise to dust seeds with a fungicide such as Captan before sowing them. This protects the seeds during germination. Damping off can also occur after seedlings have germinated. To prevent seedlings falling over at soil level, drench the area around them with Captan or Bravo as directed on the container. Using Black Magic Seed Raising Mix will also ensure a healthy result as it contains a fungicide to guard against damping off.

Hint
Fight fungal diseases in the garden by ensuring that air can circulate around plants. Space them further apart than recommended, and leave gaps in your shelter plantings.

MARY LOVELL-SMITH
CHRISTCHURCH *PRESS*

BACTERIAL DISEASES
Bacterial diseases are not common in the home garden, which is fortunate because there are virtually no chemicals available to control them efficiently. Black rot of cabbage and other crucifers is seen occasionally and there are also a few bacterial leaf spots of tomato and zinnia and a leaf and pod spot of beans (halo blight). Yates Fungus Fighter is an effective preventative treatment. None of these diseases is usually serious. Many bacterial diseases are seed-borne, but careful attention to hygiene in seed production and treatment by seed companies makes this source of infection unlikely.

PREPARING AND MAINTAINING YOUR GARDEN

Hint

Crop rotation will help control nematodes, as will companion planting: marigolds are particularly useful for this.

DEAN LAUGHLAN
ENVIROSCAPES

VIRAL DISEASES

Viral diseases are often found in the home garden. Spotted wilt of tomatoes, necrotic yellow of lettuce and broad bean wilt of broad beans and sweet peas can be quite devastating. Other viral diseases, like those causing striping in tulips and stocks and the greening of aster and gerbera flowers, do not usually affect the vigour of the plants.

Some other viral diseases gradually reduce the vigour and productiveness of the

Roses infected with virus have an unsightly appearance. Minimise the potential for infection by buying guaranteed virus-free plants.

plants they attack, especially perennials. Good examples are 'woody' fruit of passionfruit, crinkle leaf of strawberries, mosaic virus of potatoes, spotted wilt of tomatoes and mosaic virus of orchids. No chemicals will control the viral diseases of plants, so garden hygiene is most important in controlling infection. Plants suspected of viral infection should be removed and destroyed by burning. It is worthwhile to remove all weeds from the garden and surrounds because many weeds are alternative hosts for viral diseases. Lastly, some viral diseases are transmitted from one plant to another by sap-sucking insects such as aphids, passion vine hoppers and thrips. If you control these pests, the battle against viral disease is almost won.

DISEASES CAUSED BY NEMATODES

Nematodes or eelworms are minute, soil-inhabiting worms, some of which are useful in decomposing organic matter and others of which are parasites attacking the roots of plants and causing large swellings or galls. They are more prevalent in sandy soils than heavy soils. Tomatoes, beetroots, carrots, lettuces, cabbages, carnations and gardenias are susceptible to attack. Control by using Basamid granules, incorporating them into the top layer of soil and then watering. Do not grow susceptible plants in that part of the garden for one or two seasons.

Leaving the soil completely free of plants (including weeds) from spring to autumn is also a useful method of reducing nematode populations.

Another important nematode is the leaf nematode of chrysanthemums. Leaves show large, triangular dead patches and die off from the base upwards. The leaf nematode is often prevalent from late summer to early autumn when accompanied by extended rain periods. Control this problem by spraying with Rogor or Lebaycid when the lower leaves show damage.

NON-PARASITIC DISEASES

Poor growth of plants is not always caused by parasitic organisms. Environmental factors either in the atmosphere or in the soil may be the reason for unhealthy plants. These so-

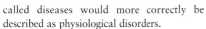

called diseases would more correctly be described as physiological disorders.

The influence of the atmosphere in which plants grow is important. Excessive cold often causes purple or red pigments to develop in the leaves of roses and many plants. Chlorosis (yellowing) of leaves occurs in others. In other cases, flower buds do not form properly or flowers are not pollinated. Low temperatures are the main cause of poor pollination in tomatoes and capsicum, especially in spring and early summer. This often leads to misshapen fruit called 'catface'. Vine crops often fail to set fruit at low temperatures or in cloudy weather, due to the absence of bees.

On the other hand, excessive heat, which is often combined with a dry atmosphere, causes wilting, scorching of leaves (tip burn) and other tender tissues (sunscald of tomato and capsicum), blossom drop in tomatoes and capsicums and faulty pollination in beans and sweetcorn (pollen blast).

Cold winds slow down growth and hot

winds increase moisture loss from plants and soil. Strong winds cause structural injury to leaves, stems, flowers and fruits.

Insufficient light results in soft, spindly growth, especially in seedlings, and may reduce flowering and fruiting in older plants.

In industrial areas of cities and towns, chemical pollutants such as sulphur dioxide and the exhaust fumes of motor vehicles produce hydrocarbons and oxides of nitrogen which can have toxic effects on plants. Fluorine, ozone and ethylene are other harmful gases which may cause yellowing of leaves or interfere with flowering and fruit formation.

Dust and smoke from factories can cause damage by blocking the stomata (breathing pores) of leaves and forming a film which prevents light from reaching the leaf surface. Some plants are more resistant to gases and dusts in the atmosphere, so gardeners who are unfortunate to live near these sources of pollution should restrict their plants to those which can best resist it. Your local nursery

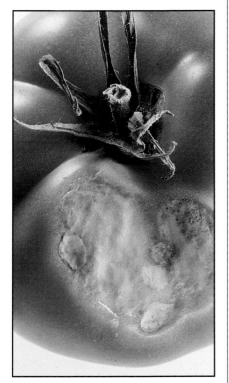

Sunscald on a tomato.

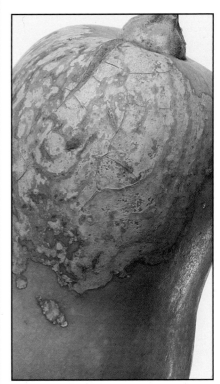

Cold damage on a butternut pumpkin.

PREPARING AND MAINTAINING YOUR GARDEN

Cold conditions have caused pigmentation in the leaves of these cabbages.

will be able to assist you with your selection. An application of lime will often correct the problem as it allows soil molybdenum to become more available to the plants.

The influence of soil factors on the growth of plants has been mentioned in the opening paragraphs of this chapter and also in Chapters 3 and 4.

The importance of adequate watering cannot be stressed too strongly. Insufficient water not only causes wilting; a disturbance in the even supply of moisture can be responsible for blossom fall in sweet peas and tomatoes and early fruit drop in citrus trees. Lack of water can also lead to the accumulation of salt (mostly as chlorides) in the soil, especially in container plantings and dry districts or those exposed to salt spray near the coast. Excess chlorides in the soil cause severe leaf scorch, especially on the leaf margins, and may eventually result in the death of a plant. Plants susceptible to this problem are beans, cabbages, cauliflowers, lettuces, onions, tomatoes, citrus trees, peaches, apricots and grape vines.

On very acid soils, all the important plant nutrients – nitrogen, phosphorus, potassium, calcium, magnesium and sulphur – are usually in short supply. (See Chapter 4.) A common disorder in tomatoes is blossom-end rot in which the fruit becomes sunken and blackened. This condition is caused by lack of calcium in the developing fruit. Blossom-end rot is aggravated by moisture stress in very hot weather, so regular watering and mulching of the surface will help control the problem. Overwatering should be avoided, however, because root absorption may be less efficient. An application of lime or gypsum (calcium sulphate) to the bed before planting will lessen the incidence of this disorder. Tip burn of cabbage and blackheart of celery are similar kinds of calcium deficiency.

A deficiency of magnesium shows symptoms of yellowing between the leaf veins, especially on the older leaves. It is not uncommon on acid soils. Susceptible plants are citrus trees, apples, grape vines, beetroots, tomatoes and members of the cabbage family.

The trace element molybdenum is also deficient in acid soil and causes a disorder called whiptail in broccoli, Brussels sprouts, cabbages and cauliflowers. The leaf blades become narrow and the margins of the leaves thickened and distorted. The application of water-soluble fertilisers – all of which contain molybdenum – will usually overcome this problem. Molybdenum deficiencies have also been recorded in lettuces, tomatoes and vine crops when these are grown on acid soil.

On alkaline soils, other elements are likely to be unavailable. This shortage applies particularly to iron and manganese, the lack of which causes chlorosis in young leaves of azaleas, rhododendrons, camellias and other acid-loving plants. Deficiencies of manganese can also occur in citrus trees, beetroots and tomatoes, especially in dry areas or on heavily limed soil.

Boron is another trace element which may be deficient on alkaline soil. Symptoms are usually associated with growing tissue such as shoots, buds, fruits and storage roots. Susceptible plants are apples (internal browning), broccoli and cauliflowers (hollow stems), beetroot (heart rot), silver beet and celery (stem cracking), swedes and turnips (brown heart).

Deficiencies of copper and zinc are not common but have been recorded on very acid, sandy, coastal soils and also on fertile, 'black earth' soils. Symptoms occur in the younger leaves, which are chlorotic and stunted. The disorder has been called little leaf or rosette in apples, peaches, apricots and citrus trees. Maize (which includes sweet corn) is also susceptible to zinc deficiency.

While trace elements are an interesting facet of plant nutrition, deficiencies of these are not common in a home garden where organic matter and mixed fertilisers are used. In addition, all the water-soluble fertilisers, such as Thrive, and some powder fertilisers, such as Gro-Plus products, contain trace elements in small but balanced quantities. Because trace elements are required in such small amounts by plants, their correct application is essential.

The use of specially formulated fertilisers is much safer and easier than applying trace elements separately or making up your own mixtures.

Careful plant selection can ensure that plants are healthy, even when growing in difficult situations like this exposed coastal garden.

PREPARING AND MAINTAINING YOUR GARDEN

PESTS AND DISEASES
OF FRUIT TREES

Apples, pears and quinces are attacked by codling moth. Aphids can also do damage — woolly aphids are a serious pest of apples, and green and black peach aphids are often a problem in peaches. (See previous sections under relevant headings for control of these pests.)

Black spot (apple scab) and powdery mildew of apples are controlled by sprays such as Yates Fungus Fighter. Apply when leaf buds show green tips, at pink bud stage and then after full bloom. Bitter pit of apples causes water-soaked spots on fruit and the pit turns brown, dry and spongy. It tends to occur more on young trees and is the result of calcium deficiency, usually due to very dry conditions. Apply rock sulphate or dolomite lime as part of your fertiliser program.

With stone fruits, a clean-up spray is neccessary while the trees are still dormant in June or early July. Spray with Champion Copper and Mavrik at early bud swell. Any dried-up fruit ('mummies') should be collected from around the base of the tree and incinerated.

Spray stone fruit with Bravo to control rust three weeks after flower fall and repeat at three-week intervals. Peach leaf-curl and shot hole of stone fruits is controlled by Champion Copper in the clean-up spray. A further spray in autumn at leaf fall is advisable. Brown rot is a destructive disease of stone fruits. The clean-up spray in winter helps to control brown rot, but this should be followed by spraying with Bravo at three to four weeks and one to two weeks before harvest. Collect and destroy any fruit affected with brown rot.

PESTS AND DISEASES
OF CITRUS TREES

The important pests of citrus trees are scale insects, aphids, red mite, mealybug and lemon tree borer. Mavrik sprayed at intervals of seven to fourteen days as required, will control most of these pests. It is especially useful over the flowering period as it will not interfere with honey bees once the spray has dried. Should scale insect or mealybug become difficult to control, a spray of Orthene and Conqueror Oil may be necessary. Lemon tree borer can be controlled

Black spot, a fungal disease, disfigures rose leaves and eventually leads to excessive leaf drop.

by injecting Maldison through the small holes created by the tunnelling larvae. Any pruning should be carried out in mid-winter when the adult insects are dormant.

A serious disease of citrus trees is lemon scab. Spray with Champion Copper when trees commence flowering in spring, followed by a second spray in summer at petal fall. Melanose is also a common citrus disease causing rotting of the fruit at the stem end and diebacks of branches and twigs. The sprays used to control lemon scab should also control melanose.

Sooty mould is caused by a black fungus which covers the leaves of citrus. It does very little damage, as the fungus survives on the sugary secretions from aphids or scale insects. If these pests are controlled, the sooty mould will disappear.

Collar rot attacks the trunks of citrus trees just above soil level. Yellowing leaves and cracking bark are the usual symptoms. Cut the bark back to healthy growth and paint the area with Bacseal Pruning Paint. Yellowing and dwarfing of leaves may also be due to lack of nitrogen and perhaps trace element deficiencies. See Chapter 4 for fertiliser recommendations.

LAWN PROBLEMS

Black beetles, grass grubs, porina caterpillars, army worms, ants and crickets are the main pests of lawns. For control, see previous section under the heading 'Beetles, weevils, grasshoppers and crickets' (page 71). The main diseases of lawns are brown patch and dollar spot. Both are caused by a fungus and usually occur in late spring, summer and autumn when the weather is warm and humid. Brown patch starts with small discoloured patches of grass which later spread to form irregular dead patches a metre or more in diameter. Dollar spot is very similar in appearance but the spots usually remain small and circular. A number of turf fungicides are available to control both diseases. Greenguard controls both brown patch and dollar spot and Captan is very effective against brown patch. Early spraying is essential, however.

Fairy ring forms a ring of green grass surrounded by an outer ring of dead grass with mushroom-like growths appearing

Sooty mould grows on the excretions from sap-sucking insects

occasionally in the affected area. The fungus responsible for fairy rings is very deep in the soil and the only complete cure is to remove the turf and soil to a depth of 20 cm from the affected area.

Algae (a green or black scum) and moss are usually problems in shaded, overwet or badly drained sections of the lawn. If these conditions are alleviated the grass will again cover the area. Slime moulds form small, steel-grey or black mounds on leaves and stems of grass in warm, moist weather. These are not parasites and do not injure the grass, although they may look unsightly. Slime moulds can be brushed off the lawn with a stiff broom. Moss may be controlled with Moss Killer or sulphate of iron, and algae with bluestone copper sulphate.

Hint

Lawn diseases are always easier to spot first thing in the morning when the dew is on the grass.

NICK HAYHOE
YATES NEW ZEALAND

PREPARING AND MAINTAINING YOUR GARDEN

RECOMMENDED HOME GARDEN

SOME COMMON NAMES OR REG. TRADE NAME	WITHHOLDING PERIOD (DAYS)	USED TO CONTROL
INSECTICIDES		
Ant Free	Not applicable	Ants
Ant & Spider Trigger Spray	Not applicable	Cockroaches, ants, spiders, fleas, silverfish, and other invading insects
Basamid	as directed	Root knot nematode and other nematodes
Baythroid Aerosol	1 or 7	Aphids, caterpillars, bugs, earwigs, thri
Carbaryl	3	Beetles, bugs, codling moth, grasshopp
Confidor	3–21	Aphids, thrips, mealybug
Conqueror Oil	3	Scales, aphids, caterpillars, mites
Derris Dust	1	Caterpillars, aphids, thrips
Maldison		Aphids, beetles, bugs, borers, caterpilla thrips
Mavrik	0–2 (56 – apples)	Caterpillars , aphids and mites
Nature's Way Pyrethrum	0	Caterpillars, aphids, thrips
Orthene	3–7	Bugs, thrips, codling moth, caterpillars
Soil Insect Killer	14	Grass grubs, various other lawn insect
Super Shield	7	Aphids, thrips, caterpillars, bugs, mites white fly
Target	7	Aphids, bugs, mites, white fly
Trigger Insect Spray	1	Aphids, thrips, caterpillars

INSECTICIDES AND FUNGICIDES

REMARKS

Controls common black ant.

Excellent surface spray. May be used indoors and outdoors. Kills and controls for up to three months.

Easy to use, systemic, gives up to 3 months' protection.

Low-toxic, broad-spectrum insecticide.

Low-hazard insecticide, component of many all-purpose sprays and tomato sprays.

A new insecticide with low toxicity. Poses minimal risk to most beneficial insects.

Two-way action control of chewing and sucking insects. Low hazard to bees.

Safer insecticide for leaf-eating insects but frequent dusting is necessary.

Low-hazard contact insecticide component of many all-purpose sprays.

Low-hazard, broad spectrum insecticide. Low hazard to bees. Thorough coverage of foliage is necessary. Low toxicity.

Low-hazard insecticide for the specific control of caterpillars.

Effective systemic insecticide for sap-suckers and chewing pests.

Effective control of grass grubs.

Broad-spectrum control and systemic spray.

Translaminar insecticide. Controls sap-sucking insects.

Good for a wide range of insects and plants. Low-hazard, relatively safe non-residual contact

PREPARING AND MAINTAINING YOUR GARDEN

SOME COMMON NAMES OR REG. TRADE NAME	WITHHOLDING PERIOD (DAYS)	USED TO CONTROL
FUNGICIDES		
Bravo	1	Leaf spots, brown rot, black spot, bitter rot, blight, downy mildew, anthracnose, septoria spot, leaf curl
Captan	7 or 14	Downy and powdery mildew, rust, blight brown patch and dollar spot of lawns, damping off (seedlings)
Champion Copper	1	Leaf spots, leaf blights, downy mildew, leaf curl (peaches), black spot (apples)
Fungus Fighter	1–7	Black spot, leaf curl, blight, bacterial diseases
Greenguard	14	Petal blight, powdery mildew on cucurbits, apples and grapevine; dollar spot (lawns)
Lime Sulphur	0	Leaf curl (peaches), black spot (apples), powdery mildew, rusts, also controls mit and some scale insects
COMBINATION SPRAYS		
Garden Master	7 or 14	Many insects and fungus diseases
Liquid Tomato Spray	3	Caterpillars, thrips, bugs, early blight, late blight, septoria spot
Rose and Ornamental Spray	Not applicable powdery mildew, rust	Aphids, thrips, caterpillars, black spot,
Shield	Not applicable	Black spot, powdery mildew, rust, aphid thrips, caterpillars
Super Shield	Not applicable	Black spot, powdery mildew, rust, aphid thrips, caterpillars, mites

REMARKS

All-purpose fungicide. Thorough spray coverage is essential.

Effective against a wide range of diseases. Ensure thorough coverage.

Widely used fungicide for many troublesome diseases. Component of many all-purpose sprays.

Suitable for use on most crops and ornamentals.

The most effective azalea petal blight spray available.

Useful fungicide for diseases of fruit trees. May cause leaf scorch of vine crops.

Convenient multi-purpose product.

Protects tomatoes from most insect pests and fungus diseases.

Controls insects and fungus on roses and other ornamental plants.

Systemic fungicide and contact insecticide suits all roses.

Systemic fungicide and contact insecticide suits all roses.

SPRAY PROGRAMMES

BERRY FRUIT		
TIME	MATERIAL	PEST/DISEASE
Winter	Champion Copper	Fungal and bacterial diseases
Bud burst	Champion Copper	Cane spot, cane wilt
Pre-blossom	Bravo, Carbaryl	Cane spot, cane wilt, brown beetle, leaf roller
Petal fall until 7 days before harvest	Bravo, Carbaryl	Downy mildew, botrytis, caterpillars
Immediately after harvest	Bravo, Maldison	Cane spot, bud moth, spur blight

CITRUS		
TIME	MATERIAL	PEST/DISEASE
October	Champion Copper, Orthene	Verrucosis, melanose, aphids
November (petal fall of main blossom)	Champion Copper, Orthene	Verrucosis, aphids
December (after flowering)	Champion Copper, Orthene, Conqueror Oil	Verrucosis, aphids, scale, red mite, mealybug
February	Champion Copper, Orthene, Conqueror Oil	Verrucosis, aphids, scale, red mite, mealybug
April	Champion Copper, Orthene	Verrucosis, aphids, mealybug
May	Champion Copper, Orthene	Verrucosis, aphids, mealybug
June	Champion Copper, Orthene	Verrucosis, scale

CURRANTS AND GOOSEBERRIES		
TIME	MATERIAL	PEST/DISEASE
Late July	Conqueror Oil	Scale, mites
Bud movement	Champion Copper	Leaf spot
Pre-blossom until harvest	Nature's Way Fungus Spray, Carbaryl	Fungus diseases, caterpillars
Post-harvest	Champion Copper	Clean up of fungal spores

FEIJOAS		
TIME	MATERIAL	PEST/DISEASE
May	Conqueror Oil	Hard wax scale
November/March	Maldison	Leaf roller caterpillar, scale

GRAPES

TIME	MATERIAL	PEST/DISEASE
August	Champion Copper, Conqueror Oil	Scale, mites, mildew, black spot
Bud swell	Champion Copper, Garden Master	Mites, caterpillars, mildew, black spot
Bud burst, pre-blossom, post fruit set and at 14 day intervals	Target, Nature's Way Fungus Spray	Downy mildew, powdery mildew, black spot, aphids, mealybug, leaf roller

PASSION FRUIT

TIME	MATERIAL	PEST/DISEASE
November to Feb at monthly intervals	Champion Copper, Maldison	Brown spot, mealybug, passion vine hopper
Winter at monthly intervals	Champion Copper	Grease spot

PIPFRUIT

TIME	MATERIAL	PEST/DISEASE
Dormant (winter)	Champion Copper, Conqueror Oil	Fungus diseases, insects and eggs
Bud swelling	Champion Copper	Fungus diseases
Pink (just prior to flowering)	Fungus Fighter	Black spot
Full bloom	Fungus Fighter	Black spot
Petal fall	Fungus Fighter, Maldison	Black spot, codling moth
3 weeks later	Fungus Fighter, Carbaryl	Black spot, powdery mildew, codling moth, leaf curling midge
3 week intervals to harvest	Manzeb, Carbaryl, Mite Killer	Add Mite Killer only if mites are a problem

ROSES

TIME	MATERIAL	PEST/DISEASE
Amateurs		
Winter	Champion Copper, Conqueror Oil	Scale mites, aphids, fungus diseases
From leaf bud movement at 2 weekly intervals	Super Shield or Shield	Black spot, powdery mildew, rust and insects. Also mites if using Super Shield
Connoisseurs		
Winter	Champion Copper, Conqueror Oil	Scale, mites, aphids, fungus diseases
From leaf bud movement at 2 weekly intervals	Bravo, Orthene Alternate with Super Shield or Shield. Mite Killer (if required)	Downy mildew, black spot, powdery mildew, insects Black spot, powdery mildew, rust, all insects and mites

PREPARING AND MAINTAINING YOUR GARDEN

STONE FRUIT

TIME	MATERIAL	PEST/DISEASE
Dormant	Champion Copper	Fungus diseases
Bud swell and bud burst	Champion Copper, Mavrik	Leaf curl, bladder plum, aphids, thrips, mites
Full bloom	Mavri, Greenguard	Brown rot, aphids, thrips, mites
Petal fall and 3 weeks later	Bravo, Mavrik Bravo, Mavrik	Brown rot, aphids, thrips, mites
3 week intervals to harvest	Bravo, Carbaryl	Brown rot, Oriental fruit moth, cherry/pear slug
During leaf fall	Champion Copper	Fungus diseases

STRAWBERRIES

TIME	MATERIAL	PEST/DISEASE
August/Sept	Champion, Conqueror Oil	Leaf spot, red mite
Pre-blossom and fortnightly	Champion Copper, Benlate, Garden Master	Botrytis, septoria and Alternaria leaf spot, caterpillars and mites

TAMARILLOS

TIME	MATERIAL	PEST/DISEASE
November/March at monthly intervals	Nature's Way Fungus Spray, Guardall	Powdery mildew, white fly, green vegetable bug, caterpillars

TOMATOES

TIME	MATERIAL	PEST/DISEASE
Sept–Oct	Champion Copper	Blight, bacterial speck
Nov–April	Target, Bravo or Tomato Spray	Early/late blight, insects

VEGETABLES

TIME	MATERIAL	PEST/DISEASE
Beans	Target, Champion Copper	Caterpillars, white fly, green vegetable bug, fungus diseases
Broad beans	Target, Bravo or Champion Copper	Aphids, rust, chocolate spot
Brassicas: cabbages, cauliflower etc.	Target	White butterfly caterpillars, aphids
Cucurbits	Target, Nature's Way Fungus Spray	White fly, caterpillars, powdery mildew
Carrots/parsnips	Soil Insect Killer	Carrot rust fly
Potatoes	Garden Master or Champion Copper	Tuber moth, blight

WEEDS

Weeds in the garden, especially annual weeds, can be eliminated to a great degree if they are prevented from flowering and forming seed. They can be controlled by hand weeding or hoeing, preferably when they are quite small, or by treating with a herbicide such as Roundup or Zero.

An extremely effective weed spray is glyphosate, commonly sold as Zero. This is a non-selective chemical which is ideal to control persistent weeds like paspalum, couch grass and sorrel. The chemical is translocated from the above-ground parts of the plant to the persistent underground parts. There is no residual herbicide action when glyphosate is sprayed onto the soil. The chemical is relatively safe to use but it is important to take care to prevent spray or drift spray from reaching useful plants. Glyphosate breaks down rapidly in soil or water.

Weeds near fences, trees and borders

Weeds, both grasses and others, are a nuisance if they trail over fences, around trunks of woody shrubs and trees or across borders and edges of gardens.

Weeds in paths and driveways

On areas such as paths, driveways, courtyards or tennis hardcourts, residual weedkillers can be used. There are many brands, such as Yates DAS. It is important to stress that this has a

> *Hint*
>
> *Don't procrastinate when it comes to weeding: the task is much easier when the plants are small and not covered in prickles, spines or seeds. Hoeing in the hot midday sun will fry weeds before they set seed. Just one hour of weeding can make such a difference to the look of your garden.*
>
> DALE HARVEY
> GARDEN WRITER

> *Hint*
>
> *One method of organic weed control for your garden is to pour boiling water over the offending plants. Within a day you will notice the effects as the weeds die off. This is particularly useful for weeds that are growing in the cracks of brick patios.*
>
> ROD GIBBONS
> LIVING EARTH

residual effect on the soil – usually for a period of at least six months – and that during heavy rain on slopes there may be some leaching of the chemicals into adjacent areas.

Perennial woody weeds

Large woody weeds like blackberry, lantana, briars, scrub and trees can be killed with specific herbicides such as Woody Weedkiller. Overall sprays control blackberries and other woody weeds. For trees and larger scrub growth, the chemical can be poured into holes bored in the trunk or into a frill ring cut

Lawn can be successfully grown under trees if shade-tolerant grasses are used.

PREPARING AND MAINTAINING YOUR GARDEN

WEEDKILLER FOR SPECIFIC APPLICATIONS

LOCATION/ PROBLEM	WEEDKILLER	COMMENTS
Driveway, paths, fence lines	DAS	Long-term bare ground control of a wide range of plants (8–12 months). Not for soils that are to be replanted within 12 months.
Garden beds	Zero, Roundup	Kills a wide range of plants, including grasses. Not effective on wandering jew. No residual effect on soil.
Quick knockdown, weeds around fences, posts, etc	Zero, Greenscape	Quick knockdown, short-term control. Good clean-up products.
Shrubberies	Zero	See above
Unwanted woody plants	Woody Weedkiller, Amitrole	Controls blackberry, lantana and saplings
Preparing for a lawn (see previous page)		
Lawn weeds	Turfix Lawn Weed Spray, Faneron, Prickle Weedkiller, Weed 'n' Feed Liquid	Selective control of broadleaf weeds in turf. Does not control grassy weeds. Read directions carefully before purchase. Slow acting.

around the trunk. The spray may drift in the wind and damage nearby plants, so take care to spray on a calm day.

Weeds in lawns

The best way to prevent weeds in lawns is to have healthy, vigorous turf which resists weed invasion. This is achieved by correct application of fertilisers, adequate watering and other maintenance practices. (See Chapter 9.)

However, weeds may still be a problem and a wide range of selective herbicides is available to control them. Lawn weeds can be divided into four groups.

Grassy weeds

Any grass which differs from the grass composing the lawn can be considered a weed. Some common grassy weeds are

paspalum, summer grass (or crabgrass), kikuyu and couch. In fact, couch grass in a bent lawn or carpet grass in a couch lawn could be regarded as weeds. Such weeds should be removed by hand or carefully treated with glyphosate, using a Zero Weeding Wand. Avoid touching desirable grasses in the lawn.

Clumping grasses such as paspalum or crab

Hint

A weed is simply a plant in the wrong place. A pear tree in an apple orchard is still considered a weed.

ELLABY MARTIN
NURSERYMAN

grass can be 'crowned' at the soil surface with a hoe or sharp knife. There is no need to remove the root system. Sedges can be discouraged by the installation of better drainage.

Broadleaf weeds

Marshmallow, dandelion, cat's-ear, plantain daisies, cudweed and chickweed are some of the common broadleaf weeds found in lawns. Products such as Yates Turfix Lawn Weed Spray and Weed 'n' Feed are effective in eradicating them.

Clover-like weeds

Clovers, hydrocotyle and creeping oxalis are the main weeds in this group. Yates Turfix Lawn Weed Spray will control clovers and other broadleaf weeds. Hydrocotyle Killer gives good control of hydrocotyle, creeping oxalis and other broadleaf weeds.

Fineleaf weeds

Cotula and Onehunga weed are the main fineleaf weeds found in lawns. Control can be achieved with either Yates Faneron or Prickle Weedkiller.

The weedkillers listed in the last three sections can be used on most lawn grasses. They should not be used on lawns composed of mixtures that include strawberry clover or white clover. Buffalo lawns are easily damaged by weed-killers, so exercise caution and read the label carefully before application.

The use of sulphate of ammonia, or lawn foods which contain it, will discourage weeds, especially broadleaf weeds and clovers. The herbicide effect is increased if the fertiliser is applied dry to a lawn which is damp with dew. Lawn sand – a mixture of equal parts of sulphate of ammonia, sulphate of iron and sand – is another method of lawn weed control. The mixture is applied dry at 4 kg per 100 square metres and the lawn should not be watered for a day or two. The grass may suffer a temporary burn but will recover rapidly. Yates Weed 'n' Feed Liquid is convenient for hose-on application both to fertilise lawn grasses and control broadleaf weeds.

Pesticides mentioned in this chapter are generally available throughout New Zealand. For advice on specific treatment of pests in your district, consult your local garden centre. Before buying or using any pesticide read the label carefully.

Five Garden Plants that can become Weeds

Watsonia

These do particularly well in sandy soil and in drier climates, and can become great invaders.

Tritonia (Montbretia)

This indestructible plant is also known as Crocosmia, but, whatever it's called, it can be bad news in bushland.

Agapanthus Orientalis

The most commonly planted form of agapanthus is excellent for covering large banks and other difficult sites, but the attractive blue and white flowers self-seed freely and may invade other parts of the garden. Many smaller-growing cultivars, more desirable for the home garden, are now available.

Bear's Breeches

Like agapanthus, *Acanthus mollis* is excellent for filling difficult to plant areas but also self-seeds freely. Flower stems can be pruned off before they set seed, to prevent the spread of undesirable seedlings.

Arum

Because they have a rhizomatous rather than a bulbous rootstock, arum lilies are not always classed as bulbs, but there's no doubt that they can become weeds, especially in damp spots.

ARUM

WATSONIA

PART III: PROPAGATING PLANTS

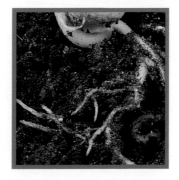

CHAPTER 7

SOWING SEEDS
AND RAISING SEEDLINGS

Seeds are formed in the flowers of plants by male pollen cells fertilising the female ovules or egg cells. Most plants have male and female parts in the one flower. Some, like sweet corn and vine crops, have male and female flowers on different parts of the same plant. Matai, willows and poplar trees have male flowers on one plant and female flowers on another.

Many annual plants are cross-pollinated, with the pollen being transferred by wind or insects (mostly bees) to other plants. The other plants may be of the same variety, of a different variety or sometimes of a different, but closely related, species. For this reason, plants grown from the seed of cross-pollinated plants may not be true to type unless special care is taken by seedsmen to prevent 'crossing'. Plant breeders use controlled cross-pollination to develop new varieties and, more recently, F1 (first filial generation) hybrids. Hybrid flowers and vegetables have special qualities of uniformity, vigour and tolerance to unfavourable conditions. Many hybrids also have greater disease resistance. Hybrids produce seed in the same manner as any other plant, but the seed of hybrid plants should not be saved because the next generation will not be uniform in its characteristics.

SEED STRUCTURE AND SEED LIFE

All seeds have two parts: an embryo, in which the shoot and root of the new plant are already formed; and storage tissue to feed the embryo when germination starts. The seeds you buy may look dry and lifeless but they do contain some moisture (8–10 per cent), and respiration (breathing) is going on at a slow rate, very much like a motor idling.

Like all living things, seeds will eventually die. They die faster when stored in warm, humid conditions, so it is difficult to keep them alive in tropical climates. Even in a mild climate, short-lived seeds (aster, carnation, gerbera, onion, parsley and parsnip) will begin to lose germination vigour in eighteen months or less. Seedsmen have overcome this storage problem by drying seeds to a low moisture content (4–7 per cent) and sealing them in moisture-proof packets. This way, respiration is slowed down further, and seeds maintain germination vigour for many years. Long-lived seeds (lupins, sweet peas, zinnias, capsicum, tomato and vine crops) maintain germination for several years under favourable conditions. However, to keep them in peak condition they too are sold in foil packets. If you are storing seeds at home, whether in foil or paper packets, always keep them in a cool, dry place.

HOW SEEDS GERMINATE
WATER AND AIR

Seeds must absorb 40–60 per cent of their weight in water to trigger germination. When germination starts they respire faster, so they need more air as well. When you sow seeds in soil, they take up moisture from the film of water surrounding the soil particles. The space between the particles (pore space) supplies the air. If the pore spaces are very small, as in silty or clay soils, there is too much water and not enough air. Sandy soils have large pore spaces and a good air supply but hold moisture badly. If you add moisture-holding materials (peat moss, compost or seed-raising mixture) to sandy soils, then you have the ideal combination for seeds to germinate: sufficient water and sufficient air.

PROPAGATING PLANTS

A seed carries its own food source for the growing seedling.

TEMPERATURE

Soil temperature is important, too. Most garden seeds will germinate if the soil temperature reaches 20°C. As the soil temperature decreases, germination becomes

....

Hint

Larkspur seeds need to experience a cold spell in order to germinate successfully. Simulate this by putting the seeds in your refrigerator for 14 days before you sow them.

MARY LOVELL-SMITH
CHRISTCHURCH *PRESS*

....

slower. There are some exceptions, however. A few spring-flowering annuals, such as alyssum, cornflower, gypsophila, larkspur, linaria, nemesia, polyanthus, poppy (Iceland)

and primula, germinate well at 15°C. Spinach (not silver beet) also germinates in cool soil.

Many summer-flowering annuals, such as amaranthus, celosia, coleus, gerbera, petunia, portulaca, salvia and zinnia, need a soil temperature of 25°C to germinate quickly. This also applies to warm-season vegetables such as beans, capsicum, sweet corn, tomato and vine crops. For example, bean seedlings may take between two and three weeks to emerge if seed is sown in early spring, but they will emerge in seven to ten days if the seeds are sown a few weeks later when the soil is warmer.

LIGHT

Many seeds will germinate successfully, regardless of the amount of light they receive but some seeds have evolved to have very special light requirements.

Some large seeds need darkness for germination, while others must be contacted by light. Those in this last category are usually quite small and should be thinly scattered onto the surface of the mix. They should then be pressed gently into the mix so that they are in contact with the moisture, but still exposed to the light. Do not cover with seed-raising mix or other material. Fine seeds should be watered carefully with a light misting or by immersing the seed tray in water. It is best to cover the seed tray with plastic wrap or glass. Alternatively, grow the seeds in a Yates Mini Greenhouse.

TIME FOR GERMINATION

Quite apart from temperature, some seeds germinate much faster than others, so it is important to know when to expect seedlings from the seeds you sow. Under good conditions, seedlings of aster, marigold, zinnia, beans, peas, lettuce, vine crops and the cabbage family emerge in six to ten days (often less).

Slow starters include begonia, cineraria, coleus, cyclamen, delphinium, larkspur, pansy, polyanthus, primula, verbena, parsley and parsnip. Seedlings of these may take three to four weeks to show, so keep the soil damp, but not wet, for this length of time.

The number of days for the seedlings of flowers and vegetables to emerge is given in the Sowing Guides in Chapters 10 and 18.

SEED TREATMENT

It is best to treat seeds with a fungicidal dust before sowing them. This protects the germinating seeds and young seedlings from a soil-borne fungus which causes the disease called 'damping off'.

You can use any fungicide dust, Captan or copper oxychloride. Add a small quantity of fungicidal dust to the seeds in the packet. Fold over the top of the packet and shake well for about five to ten seconds. This will give each seed a coating of fungicide. Plant seeds in Black Magic Seed Raising Mix, which contains a fungicide to prevent damping off.

SOWING SEEDS DIRECT INTO GARDEN BEDS

Many seeds can be sown direct into their garden situation. Direct sowing avoids double handling. Plants are usually more vigorous, because 'transplant shock' (damage to roots followed by temporary wilting) is avoided too. If you are running late with your plantings of flowers or vegetables, direct sowing can often make up for lost time.

Most plants recommended for direct sowing have relatively large seeds, but all have vigorous seedlings which can cope with conditions in the open garden. Popular flowers for direct sowing are alyssum, aster, balsam, calendula, celosia, larkspur, linaria, lupin, marigold, mignonette, nasturtium, nemesia, phlox, stock, sweet pea, sunflowers, verbena and zinnia.

Vegetables with large seeds (beans, broad beans, peas and sweet corn), and root crops such as beetroot, carrots, parsnip and turnip (all of which transplant badly), are direct sown. Many others, such as cabbage, Chinese cabbage, lettuce, onion, silver beet and spinach, take to this method too. You can sow late crops of tomato, capsicum and vine crops direct, too, but most gardeners prefer to raise early plants in punnets or pots.

PREPARING SOIL AND APPLYING FERTILISER

When sowing direct, prepare the garden bed a week or two beforehand. Always cultivate the soil when in a dark, damp condition to preserve a good crumb structure.

Preparing the garden bed a week or two before using it stimulates the germination of those weed seeds which are inevitably present in the soil. By removing these weeds the

The first leaves to open on a developing seedling are called the 'seed leaves'.

PROPAGATING PLANTS

Hint

Fresh seed usually germinates more successfully than older seed. Keep any unused seed in an airtight container in the refrigerator until it is next required.

JACK HOBBS
GARDEN WRITER AND BROADCASTER

gardener is then able to sow into a relatively weed-free seed bed. It is important that the germinating seed has as little competition from weeds as possible.

Before sowing, apply a complete fertiliser (such as Gro-Plus Complete Plant Food) with an approximate analysis N.P.K. 5:5:4. The high phosphorus content will ensure vigorous seedling growth immediately after seed germination. Fertiliser may be broadcast at one-third of a cup per square metre and raked into the topsoil before final levelling. When sowing seeds in rows or a definite pattern it is better (and more economical) to scatter fertiliser in a band 15–20 cm wide at one and a half tablespoons per metre where the seed is to be sown. Rake into the topsoil and level as before.

Large seeds (beans, broad beans, lupins, peas, sweet peas and sweet corn) are liable to burn if in direct contact with fertiliser, so it is best to apply fertiliser in a band to the side of the seed or just below it. There are two ways of doing this:

1. Open a furrow 15–20 cm deep, scatter fertiliser along the bottom at 30 g per metre and cover it with soil by raking the shoulders of the furrow. Then make a shallow furrow for seeds on top of the fertiliser band.
2. Open two furrows 10–15 cm deep on either side of a line where seed is to be sown. Scatter fertiliser at 15 g per metre along the bottom of each and cover in furrows as before. Then make a shallow furrow for seeds midway between the fertiliser bands.

Another method of direct sowing is to sow seeds in clumps or stations at the required distance apart. Scatter fertiliser in a band and rake in as before, or scatter the fertiliser at each position where seed is to be sown and mix it with the topsoil. Make saucer-shaped depressions at each station and sow a few seeds in each. Many bedding plants, including nemesia, phlox, stock and zinnia, can be sown in clumps about 20 cm apart. Usually, all seedlings can be retained without thinning to give a denser mass of colour. Seeds of lettuce, silver beet, spinach, and late sowings of tomato, capsicum and vine crops, can be sown in clumps (three to five seeds to each) in the same way. Thin each clump to the strongest seedling. With tomato and vine crops, retain two seedlings. Sweet corn is often sown in pairs and the weaker seedling removed after germination.

SOWING DEPTH

Sowing depth depends on seed size: the smaller the seeds, the shallower they are sown. As discussed, some actually need light to trigger germination. Others need to be kept in the dark.

When sowing direct, sow seeds of medium size in rows 12 mm deep. They can be covered with soil, but it is far better to cover with peat moss or seed-raising mixture. These light-textured materials hold moisture but have large spaces between particles to provide good aeration.

Large seeds (beans, peas, lupins, sweet peas, vine crops, etc) can be sown more deeply, at 25–50 mm. Always sow them into dark, damp soil at the bottom of the furrow. Then cover the furrow with soil and lightly

A wide range of flowers can easily be grown from seed.

tamp down with the back of the rake. Covering with compost or seed-raising mix is not necessary unless the soil is extremely heavy. Lightly rake the whole bed and spread a light mulch of compost. If the seeds are pressed into dark damp soil, further watering is usually not required until seedlings emerge. Too much moisture for these large seeds, especially in the first day or two, can be harmful to germination because water is trapped beneath the seed coat and excludes air for respiration. For this reason, do not soak beans, peas, lupins or sweet peas in water overnight before sowing.

SPACING SEEDS

The spacing of seeds, especially for those sown in rows or clumps, depends on the kind of seed to be sown. This is given in the cultivation notes on the reverse side of each packet. It is also shown in the Sowing Guide in Chapter 10 (see pages 144–153).

Sowing seed thinly can be difficult for home gardeners but, like most things, it is simple once you know how. First, make a V-shaped crease in the packet as a 'track' for the seeds. Then take the packet between thumb and fingers, but leave the index finger free to tap the packet. As you tap, seeds will shuffle along the crease and fall onto the soil. With a little practice you can tap out one or two seeds at a time. Alternatively, empty a quantity of seeds into the palm of the hand. Take a pinch of seeds between thumb and forefinger and sprinkle along the row or drop a few seeds at each station. Tiny seeds can also be mixed with a small amount of fine sand and sprinkled along the furrow.

MOISTURE CONTROL AND EARLY CARE

Apart from large seeds, which usually do not require extra water before seedlings emerge, most seeds must be kept damp, but not wet, until seedlings show through. This is most important for seeds which may take

Always water young seedlings with a fine, gentle spray.

PROPAGATING PLANTS

three to four weeks (or more in cool weather) to emerge. If you have used compost to cover the seeds, plus an additional mulch on the beds, you will have ideal conditions for retaining moisture, making water penetration easy and preventing surface soil from caking.

When seedlings have emerged, continue watering, but rather more thoroughly and less frequently, to encourage deep rooting. As a general guide, a seedling 2.5 cm high may have its roots at a depth of 5–7 cm, so there is not much benefit to be had from a light sprinkling which wets the surface soil only. For watering seeds and seedlings, always use a fine hose spray, a water-breaker nozzle or a watering-can with a fine rose.

Slugs and snails love young seedlings. Scatter Blitzem or Mesurol pellets over the bed a day or two after you sow the seed. Repeat the treatment when seedlings emerge, or sooner if the bait disintegrates in heavy rain.

RAISING SEEDLINGS

Seeds of many plants are best raised in seed beds, seed boxes, punnets and pots. The main reason is that the seeds are small and the seedlings lack the vigour and rapid growth of larger seeds. In raising seedlings, you have much better control over early growing conditions, light, temperature, soil mix, water and nutrients. Begonia, cineraria, coleus, cyclamen, poppy (Iceland), petunia,

polyanthus and primula are good examples of seeds that are best raised in this way. For example, petunia seedlings may take three or four weeks to reach a height of 2.5 cm, whereas marigold seedlings grow to that height in a week. Some flower seeds are expensive, so it is important to raise as many seedlings as possible.

There are, of course, many flower seeds which can be sown direct or raised as seedlings, just as you choose. This gives greater flexibility to your planting program. For example, you may have a bed of petunia or phlox still flowering well in late summer. Rather than sacrifice this colour display for an empty bed, raise seedlings of, say, nemesia, which will be ready for transplanting when the summer flowers are finished.

It is often more convenient to raise the seedlings of some vegetables, especially when you need only a few plants. This is particularly true of broccoli, cabbage, cauliflower, and of early plants of capsicum, eggplant, tomato and all the vine crops. Sow the seed in punnets and prick out seedlings into 10 cm plastic pots to grow on for another four weeks or more.

SOIL MIXTURES AND SEEDLINGS

Ordinary potting mixes are not ideal for raising seeds as they contain fertilisers which can burn delicate young roots, and their lumpy texture can obstruct the development of seedlings. Packaged seed-raising mix, such as Black Magic Seed Raising Mix, from a reputable manufacturer is suitable for growing most seedlings, but you can also make your own. You will need a mix which is open, friable and well drained. Sand, preferably coarse river sand, is the best material to meet this requirement. Do not use beach sand unless it has been thoroughly washed to remove salt. You will need a good moisture-holding material too. Choose from spent mushroom compost, garden compost or peat moss. When seedlings are transplanted, the young roots cling to the particles and so take moisture with them to the new spot in the garden.

For a start, try a soil mix containing one part garden soil, one part coarse sand and one part compost or peat moss (you will have to dampen the peat moss before adding to the mix). Add 30 g of a pre-sowing fertiliser, such as Gro-Plus Complete Plant Food, and 90 g of lime to each bucket of mix. The mix must be free-flowing and should not compress in the hand when damp. If your garden soil is very sandy, you will need less sand and more moisture-holding material. If your garden soil is heavy or contains a lot of organic matter, you will need more sand. Test the mix by filling a seedling tray or punnet and watering it with a fine spray. The mix should absorb moisture quickly, in a few seconds, and drain freely. If it does not, add a little more sand.

SEED BEDS

A permanent seed bed is a good idea in a large garden or if you wish to raise large numbers of seedlings. Select a sunny, sheltered spot in the garden, build it up 15–20 cm for drainage and contain it with boards or a brick surround. An area one metre square is a convenient size. To sandy soils add liberal quantities of compost or other moisture-holding material. On clay soils spread a 5 cm layer of coarse sand as well. Then add the mixed fertiliser at one-third of a cup per square metre and lime at one cup per square metre. Dig the bed over to mix the ingredients thoroughly to a depth of about 10 cm.

You will need some protection for young seedlings in an open seed bed. A frame of 50 mm x 25 mm timber, covered with flyscreen wire or 32 per cent shade cloth, is suitable. Make wooden legs at each corner or rest it on upright bricks. Use the frame to protect young seedlings from direct sunlight during the hottest part of the day. Don't keep seedlings covered all the time, otherwise they become soft and lanky. Give the seedlings more sun and less shade as they grow. The frame is useful for covering the seed bed in heavy rain, too.

SEED TRAYS, PUNNETS AND POTS

These are shallower than a seed bed and so do not hold as much moisture. They have the advantage, however, of being able to be moved about easily to give seedlings the required conditions of shade or sunlight. After sowing, the containers can be kept indoors to provide a rather higher and more even

Plastic wrap helps retain moisture around seeds during the germination period.

PROPAGATING PLANTS

Seedlings started in Jiffy peat moss pellets suffer no transplant shock.

temperature (especially in winter), and moved outside as soon as the seedlings emerge. Plastic trays, punnets and mini-punnets are already provided with good drainage, are easy to wash and clean, and can be used over and over again. You can fill these containers with soil mix, sow seeds and prick out seedlings while standing or sitting at a workbench – easier than squatting at the seed bed.

A recent innovation is the introduction of a variety of cell containers formed in the shape of an inverted cone. They are useful for raising seedlings from seed, as the seedling is easily removed from them with little or no

damage to the root system of the plant, thus minimising transplanting shock. The shape of the cone concentrates the development of the roots downward.

Fill the container of your choice with seed-raising mix to the top of the container. With a flat board, firm the mix to a level 6–12 mm below the rim of the container. (You can use the bottom of an empty tray or punnet for firming the soil, because the bottom is slightly smaller in area than the top.) Another method is to almost fill the container with dry soil mixture, dump it on the bench to level it and then water well with a fine spray until water seeps from the drainage holes. Alternatively, stand containers in shallow water until moisture seeps to the surface. With both these methods the soil mix is often too wet for immediate use, so leave for a day or two before sowing.

Another method of raising seeds favoured by many home gardeners and commercial growers is planting the seed in peat pellets. These are pellets of compressed peat moss which, when expanded by adding water, make a block of peat moss suitable for raising seeds or cuttings. When the plant is of suitable size for transplanting, the peat block, complete with plant, is put into the permanent position in the garden and no 'transplant shock' is encountered.

SOWING SEED

Before you sow, it can be helpful to dust the seed in the packet with a fungicide. The importance of this cannot be overemphasised.

When sowing in seed beds, mark out shallow rows or drills about 6 mm deep and 5–7 cm apart with the edge of a flat board or dowel stick. Scatter seed thinly along the rows by tapping seeds from the packet. Do not crowd seeds in the row. For every 2.5 cm of row, sow five to seven small seeds like primula or three to four medium-sized seeds such as aster, pansy or stock. Then sprinkle seed-raising mix to the required depth over the surface. Make sure the material you use is free-flowing and spreads evenly. This covering allows water to penetrate, forms a mulch to stop the surface drying out and protects seeds from washing away. Water well with a fine hose spray or a watering-can with a fine rose. For plastic seed trays, mark

Hint

Plant hellebore seed during February. Sow into seed-raising mix then cover with 2 cm of number 5 sand. Place outside under trees or shrubs; don't put it in a greenhouse because the temperature will rise too high and reduce germination rates. In most areas germination should occur during June or July.

TERRY HATCH
JOY PLANTS

out shallow rows or drills with a board or dowel stick as described for seed beds. Sow seed, cover with moisture-holding material and water gently as before.

An alternative method is to use a 'marking board'. This is a flat board, slightly smaller in area than the tray, with 100 evenly spaced flat-headed nails driven into it. The heads of the nails are approximately 12 mm in diameter and protrude from the board about 6 mm. Press the board firmly into the damp soil surface, leaving 100 shallow holes. If the soil is too dry, the holes will fill with loose soil. Tap out between two and four seeds in each hole. Then cover the whole tray with seed-raising mix or compost to a depth of 3 mm. Water well with a fine spray as previously.

Plastic punnets are ideal for very small seeds like petunia, begonias and primula. Your seed-raising mix should be damp and free from lumps or clods. After dusting seed with fungicide (this also helps you to see the fine seed more clearly), sprinkle seed over the surface. Firm down with a board or the bottom of an empty punnet. Water very gently. A thin layer of seed-raising mix over the seeds will keep them moist and allow light to reach them.

Punnets and mini-punnets are good for vegetable seedlings when you only need a few plants. Scatter about twenty seeds to a punnet or about ten seeds to a mini-punnet. This number will give you about a dozen or half a dozen seedlings respectively of broccoli, cabbage or tomato. Press into the damp mix with the bottom of an empty punnet, cover and water gently. For large seeds of pumpkin, cucumber, zucchini, marrow and other vine crops, use eight seeds to a punnet or four seeds to a mini-punnet. Press seeds into soil point down. Vine crop seeds need to be kept on the dry side, so do not overwater them.

GENERAL CARE OF SEEDLINGS

You must keep seeds moist but not wet until seedlings emerge. This may be seven to ten days for fast-germinating seeds but two to four weeks or more for slow starters. Check the Sowing Guides in Chapters 10 and 18 for approximate times.

Although the covering of moisture-holding

TOP FIVE FLOWERS TO GROW FROM SEED

SWEET PEAS

These blooms offer everything – fragrance, colour, ease of cultivation. To top it off, they make great cut flowers.

NASTURTIUM

Pots, hanging baskets, banks, borders: all can be brightened up with the cheerful colours of nasturtiums – and, as a bonus, they're edible!

MARIGOLD

These grow best in warmer weather, but in frost-free areas the smaller-flowered varieties will perform year round.

SUNFLOWER

Sunflowers seem to capture the colour and cheerfulness of the sun. The bright-yellow blooms add warmth to the summer garden.

DAHLIA

Dahlias are members of the daisy family that bloom during the hotter months. They develop a curious, potato-like tuber and can last for years.

DAHLIA

SWEET PEAS

PROPAGATING PLANTS

Hint

When pricking out seedlings always hold them by a leaf rather than the stem. Damaged leaves may recover, but a broken stem will not. Young seedlings are reasonably fragile, so hold them gently but firmly. Before you plant out your seedlings, harden them off in the garden for a week. This helps them adapt to their new environment.

JACK HOBBS
GARDEN WRITER AND BROADCASTER

material may appear dry on top, the soil underneath can be quite damp. Test this by scraping some of the covering away with your finger and feeling the dampness of the soil underneath. The same rule applies to seedlings once they are started. Keep them damp but not wet. As they grow stronger, thorough but less frequent watering is needed. Morning, rather than evening, watering is recommended. Seedlings require some shade when very young but, as they grow, they need more sunlight. This way, they become more accustomed to conditions in the open garden. Too much shade makes soft, lanky seedlings which transplant poorly.

For extra warmth, especially in winter, you can cover seed beds with glass or clear plastic until seedlings emerge. Remove the cover immediately seedlings break the surface. Don't use these coverings in direct sunlight – the temperature increases so much that the seedlings 'cook' as they break the surface. Trays and punnets may also be covered with glass or enclosed in clear plastic bags or cling film to increase temperature and prevent evaporation (both indoors and outdoors), but remove them when seedlings emerge. In very cold districts you may consider an electrically heated tray which fits under a miniature greenhouse and raises soil temperature by about 10 degrees.

Control slugs and snails by scattering Blitzem or Mesurol pellets on or around seed

Plastic wrap keeps seeds warm while they are germinating.

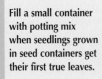

STEP 1 Fill a small container with potting mix when seedlings grown in seed containers get their first true leaves.

STEP 2 Lift the seedlings, holding them by their leaves. Gently tease out the roots of individual plants.

STEP 3 Make holes in which to transplant the seedlings using an old pen or pencil (often called a 'dibble').

STEP 4 Place seedlings in holes, firm the mix down and water. Keep out of direct sunlight for a week.

beds, trays or containers. If you don't do this you may wake up one morning to find no seedlings at all! Damping off can occur in seedlings after they have emerged, especially if the weather is humid and the seeds are sown thickly. If some of your seedlings start to topple over at soil level, immediately drench them with a weak solution of Champion Copper.

As soon as seedlings have their true leaves (after the first two seed leaves have emerged), begin fertilising with a soluble plant food, such as Thrive, at half strength.

PRICKING OUT

This is a way to remove crowded seedlings when they are quite small (about 12 mm tall) to a larger container. Fill the seedling tray with soil mix or potting mix then gently prise out a few seedlings with a pointed knife. Separate the seedlings on newspaper that covers a work bench or table. Take a seedling (gently but firmly) between thumb and forefinger in one hand and with the other use a dibble or a pencil to make a small hole in the mix. Lower the seedling roots into the hole and push a little soil mix around them with the dibble to firm the seedling. When the tray is full, gently water and keep in shade or under a fly screen or shade cloth frame for a few days until seedlings are well established. Grow seedlings on until they are 7–10 cm high and then transplant to garden beds.

TRANSPLANTING

Prepare the bed to receive seedlings two or three weeks before transplanting by adding a complete fertiliser (N.P.K. 5:5:4) at one-third of a cup per square metre. Level the bed and water well so the soil is dark and damp. The day before transplanting, water the seedlings as well.

Mark out the position for each seedling. Make a hole in the soil with a trowel or your hand, 7–10 cm deep and wide enough to accommodate the seedling. Gently ease out seedlings from seed bed or container, taking as much soil as possible with each one. Lower the seedling into the hole and press soil around it, making a small depression at the same time to direct water to the roots. For seedlings in individual pots, simply tap the pot to remove the seedling and plant it slightly deeper than it was in the pot. If you have garden compost or other organic mulch available, spread some around each plant in an area about 30 cm in diameter. Then water each plant well with a hose or watering-can to settle soil around the roots. It is best to transplant seedlings in the late afternoon or evening. If planting during the day, provide protection with pieces of brush or a handful of straw, especially in hot weather. Scatter snail and slug baits over the bed to protect the young plants and repeat application if heavy rain falls.

PROPAGATING PLANTS

SEEDS WITH SPECIAL NEEDS

Seeds that need light to germinate:
ageratum, alyssum, aquilegia, begonia, coleus, impatiens, lettuce, petunia, primula, snapdragon

Seeds that need darkness to germinate:
calendula, coriander, cyclamen, delphinium, gazania, larkspur, nasturtium, nemesia, pansy, schizanthus (poor man's orchid), verbena, vinca, viola

Seeds that are sensitive to low temperatures:
aster, calendula, beans, capsicums, carrots, celosia, coleus, cucumbers, eggplant, marigold, parsley, petunia, pumpkin/squash, salvia, tomato, verbena, zinnia

Seeds sensitive to high temperatures:
alyssum, candytuft, coriander, cress, dahlia, freesia, gazania, larkspur, lettuce, nasturtium, nemesia, peas, phlox, poppy, spinach

Marigold seeds are sensitive to low temperatures.

Nasturtium seeds need darkness for germination.

CHECKLIST TO GERMINATION TROUBLE

PROPAGATING PLANTS

Too wet	Seed needs to be damp, not wet, for germination. Excess water prevents oxygen getting to the seed. Poorly drained soils may also have a high incidence of soil fungus diseases. The condition of wet soils can be improved with the addition of peat and compost and by raising the beds above the surrounding levels. To improve the germination of seeds, sow them in a band of seed-raising mix.
Too dry	A certain amount of water is essential for germination, so maintaining constant moisture during the germination period is vital. Cover containers with glass or paper to prevent drying.
Too cold	Cold temperatures result in slow, uneven germination; disease becomes prevalent and seedlings may be injured. Each species has a different optimum temperature for germination. Do not sow summer plants too early, e.g. beans, tomatoes, sweet corn, pumpkins, melons, cucumbers, petunia, portulaca and zinnia.
Too hot	High temperatures result in excessive drying and injury to seedlings.
Planting too deep	This will result in delayed emergence. Seeds may not be able to grow suffciently to reach the surface on the limited food reserve within the seed. Soil temperature is also lower with depth. As a guide, sow seed to a depth equal to twice the thickness of the seed. Very fine flower seed, e.g. begonia and petunia, is best just pressed into the surface. In dry weather, seed can be planted a little deeper as the surface may dry out.
Planting seeds too shallow	Shallow planting can cause seeds to dry out.
Seed beds too loose	Soil which has not been firmed down results in too much air surrounding the seeds; they will not absorb moisture, and are likely to dry out.
Seed beds too firm	Firming soil down too hard prevents oxygen getting to the seed. Drainage is also impeded.
Presence of soil fungus diseases	Seeds may rot or seedlings topple. Overwatering, poor drainage and lack of ventilation will increase the incidence. Sow seeds in sterilised seed-raising mix and ensure containers are clean. Plan a rotation of crops to prevent the build up of soil disease (leaf crops followed by root crops). Spray with Champion Copper.
Slugs and snails	During late autumn, winter and spring, slugs and snails may destroy seedlings as soon as they appear. Bait areas with Mesurol or Blitzem Snail & Slug Pellets.
Birds, cats, dogs, insects	Animals are often responsible for destroying seeds and seedlings. Cover seed beds with a fine-meshed netting. Seeds can be damaged or eaten by insects. Spray with Carbaryl or Mavrik.
Fertiliser burn	Seed in direct contact with fertiliser can be burnt. Fertiliser should be worked into soil several weeks before sowing seed, or placed in a band below or beside the seed. Seedlings in the presence of high soluble salts are also more prone to 'damping off' diseases.
Seed viability and storage	Always use fresh seed. Some seeds such as parsnip and lettuce have a short life once the foil packet is opened. Seed deteriorates quickly if stored in a damp place, or exposed to high temperature. Always treat and handle seed with care to prolong its life. As a general guide, once the foil sachet has been opened the seed should be used within six months.

THRIFTY GARDENING

A beautiful garden need not cost the earth. Propagating plants from seeds or cuttings is both an economical and satisfying way to expand your stocks of garden material. Self-propagation also allows you to indulge in some of the more unusual plants not available through regular channels. Commercial seed packets, plant networks, mail order nurseries and friends are good sources of new plant material.

One of the best ways to import quick colour into a garden is with flowering annuals. Propagating annuals from seed is an extremely inexpensive way to supply plants for the garden. The number of seeds per packet varies with seed size, but for an outlay of only a few dollars you will often receive from between 250 to 1000 of the smaller flower seeds.

Expert advice on fleshing out a garden with perennials always calls for planting in drifts. Drifts require several plants of the one type to be used. Select and purchase one perennial plant; it will clump up quickly and can then easily be divided into several plants to fill out garden space.

If the budget doesn't stretch to buying a whole row of shrubs for a hedge or low edgers, buy one plant and take cuttings – you'll have a whole row in no time.

Stem cut lines

Internodal cut lines

SMART SEED SOWING

When using old pots and punnets for propagating, firstly clean them with soapy water, then sterilise them with bleach or antiseptic.

Use Black Magic Seed Raising Mix or make up your own mix using peat moss, coarse sand and pumice.

TYPES OF CUTTINGS

Softwood (spring)   *Semi-hardwood (summer/autumn)*   *Hardwood (winter)*

seeds remain viable after being kept for a long period of time: tomatoes, eucalypts and grevilleas may germinate after being stored for ten years or more. Others don't. Check the use-by date on the seed packet and sow prior to that date.

Avoid overcrowding seeds. The root system of each emerging seedling needs room to grow to its full capacity and take up the available nutrients in the soil.

Sow seeds at the depth recommended on the pack. If the seeds are sown too close to the surface of the soil they may dry out or become dislodged when watering. If seeds are sown too deeply, they are literally buried and will be deprived of light and oxygen.

FIVE NEVER-FAIL SEEDS

• nasturtium • alyssum • sunflower • cosmos • Mexican sunflower

TOOLS OF THE TRADE

• seed-raising mix • tamper (to press the mix down firmly) • punnets and pots • labels and indelible marker • seeds • plastic bag cloches or mini greenhouse • secateurs • rooting hormone powder

CUTTING TO MAKE MORE

Some plants are harder to strike than others. Knowing the age of wood to use will help. See the three types opposite. Make sure the section of stem being used has at least one bud. Cut just below a node and remove the bottom leaves. Wounding the stem is particularly useful for those species difficult to root and those which have older wood at the base. To wound, use a sharp knife or razor blade. Scrape off a little of the outer tissue on either side of the bottom of the stem. Dip into hormone rooting powder and pot up, several cuttings to a pot, using a mixture of sand and peat moss.

SOFTWOOD CUTTINGS

Soft, succulent new spring growth can be taken from plants in spring or summer. *Fuchsia*, lavender, pelargonium, penstemon and Marguerite daisy are readily propagated from softwood cuttings.

SEMI-HARDWOOD CUTTINGS

Take cuttings of new growth which has begun to harden up for hebes, *Choisya ternata*, *Camellia*, *Daphne*, *Gardenia* and *Buxus* (box).

HARDWOOD CUTTINGS

Hardwood cuttings of the previous season's growth can be taken in winter for *Hydrangea*, crepe myrtle, rose rootstocks and *Wisteria*.

FIVE NEVER-FAIL CUTTINGS

• *Impatiens* • Marguerite daisy • *Fuchsia* • *Pelargonium* • *Coleus*

CHAPTER 8

NEW PLANTS FROM OLD

Vegetative propagation means causing plants to multiply by means other than seeds. Two advantages of this process are that gardeners are certain that new plants will be identical to old ones, and that they will have a usable plant in less time than one grown from seed. In some cases, plants set seed poorly or not at all, so one must use vegetative methods. With others, you have a choice – you can sow seed or propagate.

Examples of vegetative propagation in the garden are easy to find. Strawberries have stolons or runners which form new shoots and roots at every node or joint. Common mint has underground stems called rhizomes. These make a dense mat and each small piece can become a new plant. Potatoes have swollen underground stems or tubers. Each bud or eye on a potato is a potential potato plant. Bulbs and corms provide other examples of the ability of plants to multiply and grow. Unfortunately, many of our most troublesome weeds also have this ability.

All forms of vegetative reproduction depend on small regions of tissue which produce new plant cells. Growing tissue, where cells are actively dividing, is located in the tips of stems and roots and in lateral buds. Stems and roots increase in diameter too, especially in larger plants. To achieve growth in diameter there is another area of growing tissue called the cambium layer. It is best described as a thin, unbroken cylinder of dividing cells which connects every part of the plant. The cambium layer splits off new cells from both its inside and outside layers.

The cambium layer is the vital part of any plant when taking cuttings, or in layering, budding or grafting. For this reason, cuttings are taken just below a node or joint in the stem, or below a leaf axil, where one finds the greatest concentration of dividing cells which heal the wound ('form a callus') from which new roots will grow. In budding and grafting, the cambium layers of the two plants are placed in contact. This allows the bud or graft (the scion) to draw on food from the growing plant (the stock), and the two plants join together.

PLANT DIVISION

With the exception of taprooted plants, all perennials which form clumps of roots, shoots and foliage can be lifted and divided into a number of pieces for replanting. This is a quick and simple way to get new plants. Some clumps divide easily, but in others you must be more ruthless and use a spade or a sharp knife. Often you can cut off pieces with sufficient root without lifting the parent plant. Division is a useful method for herbaceous perennials (perennial roots and annual flower stems) like perennial phlox, Michaelmas daisy, gerbera, chrysanthemum and dahlia, and also for true perennials such as agapanthus, iris, canna, strelitzia, violet, nandina, New Zealand flax and ornamental grasses. Many perennial plants become too large and overcrowded and benefit from division every two or three years.

LAYERING

Layering is another easy method of propagation. It has the advantage that the 'layer' is not completely cut from the parent plant and continues to draw nourishment from it. Layering is a good way to multiply many small trees and shrubs, including azalea, rhododendron, magnolia, gardenia and daphne. Carnations, sometimes rather difficult as cuttings, take to this treatment too.

When layering small trees or shrubs, select a thin, supple branch close to the ground. Bend the branch towards the soil and make a slanting cut 5–7 cm long with a sharp knife on the underside of the branch. Finish the cut at a node, but take care not to cut more than halfway through the branch.

PROPAGATING PLANTS

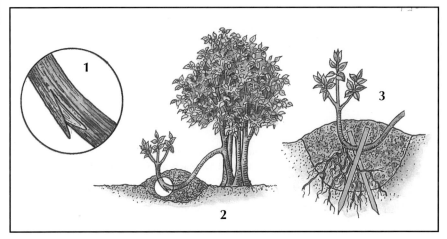

Layering is an easy method of propagation. (1) Make a slanting cut 5–7 cm long on the underside of a branch, finishing the cut at a node. (2) Bend the branch towards the ground and cover with soil. (3) Anchor the branch in the soil with wire in the shape of a U. When a good root system is formed, cut the layer from the parent plant.

The cut can be kept slightly open with a matchstick or a sliver of wood and the cut portion dusted with hormone cutting powder.

Hint

Hostas' most active period of root growth is late summer to autumn, so the best time to divide established plants is late January to early March. This lessens the chance of plants developing crown rot. The longer hostas are left untouched, the better they look.

BARRY SLIGH
TAUNTON GARDEN AND NURSERY

Now bury the cut portion of the branch in the soil and anchor it with a piece of stout wire bent to form a 'U'. If the soil is hard and lumpy, scrape it away and replace it with lighter soil or, preferably, a mixture of sand and compost or leaf mould. The end of the branch can be kept in an upright position by tying it to a small stake.

You can, of course, layer a number of branches at once. Keep the soil damp, but not wet, to encourage roots to form. If the branch is layered in late winter or early spring, roots are usually formed by the following autumn. You can gently scrape away the soil occasionally to check if roots are showing. When a good root system has formed, cut the branch from the parent plant. Leave the new plant for three or four weeks to adjust to its independent status, then lift it carefully and replant in its new position.

Much the same method can be used for carnations, but start layering in December or January. The rooted plants will be ready for planting in April or May. Remove the lower leaves (next to the parent plant), leaving a tuft of leaves at the end of the stem. These leaves can be shortened slightly.

Many climbing and trailing plants are layered easily. Bend down well-ripened stems and peg them in the ground so that one or two nodes are covered with soil. Cutting the stems from the parent plant is rarely necessary.

AIR-LAYERING

If branches or stems are too large and stiff to bend to the ground, air-layering is an alternative method. Again, make a slanting cut in the stem, finishing at a node. Keep the cut open with a sliver of wood. Then wrap the cut with damp sphagnum moss and cover with aluminium foil or plastic tied in place

PROPAGATING PLANTS

Hint

If you collect cuttings but can't plant them for a few days, keep them fresh by wrapping in slightly damp newspaper and keeping in a cool place such as the refrigerator or a chilly bin. When ready, prepare cuttings as usual.

JACK HOBBS
GARDEN WRITER AND BROADCASTER

with string or budding tape. This keeps the cut moist. Inspect periodically to ascertain whether the roots are well developed and the time has come to cut it from the parent plant. Air-layers need careful attention for the first few weeks after removal until the plants have become adjusted to relying on their new root system.

CUTTINGS

Many garden plants are grown from cuttings. A cutting is a piece of stem, leaf or root which, when planted under favourable conditions, produces another plant. You can collect, prepare and grow cuttings without too much effort, and little space or gardening skill is needed.

Cuttings fall into three main groups: stem cuttings, leaf cuttings and root cuttings. Stem cuttings are further divided into three subgroups depending on the type of wood used: softwood, semi-hardwood and hardwood cuttings. But before you start, there are a few other aspects to consider.

TOOLS AND EQUIPMENT

You need a good quality knife for a start. A razor blade with one edge covered with insulating or adhesive tape is useful for small cuttings. A good pair of secateurs should be kept in top condition by regular sharpening. A plastic collection bag for cuttings is useful to prevent them drying out and wilting, especially for softwood cuttings or if you are collecting cuttings away from home.

Low-growing branches of azaleas will sometimes layer and form roots where they contact the soil.

Top Five Plants to Grow from Cuttings

LAVENDER

Take lavender cuttings in early spring or autumn. Select a shoot 5 cm long (without a flower bud), pull it downward sharply so it comes away with a heel, dip it in rooting gel and plant in potting mix.

MARGUERITE DAISY

One of the easiest plants to strike from cuttings taken at almost any time, although spring is the best. Select a 5–10 cm shoot, remove all flower buds and the lower one-third of foliage, insert straight into good free-draining garden soil or potting mix.

FUCHSIA

Grows easily from tip cuttings taken either in early summer or mid-winter.

GERANIUM

All types of geranium (*Pelargonium*) are easily grown from cuttings. Softwood cuttings may be taken in early spring, or stem tip cuttings any time over the growing season provided all flower buds are removed.

BOX

One of the most popular hedging plants, often required in large numbers. Using your spring prunings, select healthy shoots, 7–10 cm long, remove the lower one-third of foliage and insert into potting mix. Semi-hardwood cuttings may also be taken in autumn, and will be ready to plant out into the garden in spring.

LAVENDER

FUCHSIA

CONTAINERS AND ROOTING MIXTURES

The best containers are plastic pots, punnets or trays. These are easy to clean, so wash thoroughly before using. All containers must have free drainage. The rooting mix must be as free as possible from disease, insects and weed seeds. Leading nurseries sterilise the rooting medium and the containers they use, but this sophisticated treatment is difficult for the average home gardener.

The materials recommended below are relatively sterile and relatively free of these problems. Coarse river sand is often used but dries out quickly. Try a mix containing two parts of coarse sand and one part of peat moss. A mix which holds more moisture is one part of coarse sand and one part of peat moss. Charcoal, when crushed and screened, may be added to keep the mixture clean and more open. A suggested mix is two parts coarse sand, one part peat moss and one part charcoal. Proprietary potting soils are not recommended for cuttings, but good-quality seed-raising mixtures are suitable.

ROOT-PROMOTING HORMONES

Hormone 'cutting' powders or gels can help cuttings form a callus and make roots quickly. There are a number of proprietary brands, Seradix and Clonex Rooting Hormone Gel being the most widely available. Dip the cleanly cut ends into the powder before planting. Full directions are given on the pack. Cutting powders are also useful for dusting the cut surfaces of stems for layering (see pages 115–116).

PROTECTION FOR CUTTINGS

Successfully striking cuttings depends a lot on providing a suitable microclimate. High humidity to prevent moisture loss is important. A mini greenhouse with a clear plastic lid can be useful if you grow a lot of cuttings. An inverted glass jar or a clear plastic bag supported on a wire frame placed over a pot of cuttings offers a simple solution. Large boxes (with the bottoms knocked out) or frames with glass or plastic covers are good for a number of pots. Stand them on a 2–3 cm layer of moisture-holding material – peat moss, charcoal, pine bark –

Geraniums grow easily from softwood cuttings.

so water will evaporate continuously. Boxes and frames should not be too deep; about 50 cm is sufficient. This allows about 15 cm between the top of the cuttings and the cover. Provide some shade because direct sunlight will build up too much heat. Most cuttings strike best at a temperature of 20–25°C, so keep your pots in a shady spot or place newspaper or shade cloth over the top of your box or frame for a week or so. Then harden them to direct sunlight. Ventilation is also needed, so prop the jar up slightly, open the plastic bag, or raise the frame cover a little.

Hint

Strips of white plastic ice-cream containers make cheap, effective plant labels.

JILL FISHER
HORTICULTURALIST

The three main groups of cuttings are as follows. Stem cuttings are divided into three further subgroups according to the type of wood used.

STEM CUTTINGS
Softwood cuttings

These are taken in spring from shrubby plants with soft green shoots. Because the plants are in active growth, take care to prevent cuttings wilting before you plant them. Take softwood cuttings early in the morning when the plant is full of sap. If they start to dry out, cover them with moist newspaper. There are exceptions to this rule – very sappy plants like geranium and cactus will tolerate wilting even for a day or two. This gives the cut section time to dry out and start to heal.

With tip cuttings, remove the leaves from the stem where the cut is to be made. Make a clean cut at a slight angle just below a node or leaf axil. For plants with large leaves, remove all but a few top ones. These can be reduced to about half their length. Tip cuttings are usually 5–10 cm in length and have four to six nodes. This method suits azaleas, gardenias and similar evergreens with large leaves. Heel cuttings are good for conifers and many other plants. Take off side shoots so that a small heel of the older branch is attached. Trim off any excess bark.

PROPAGATING PLANTS

Semi-hardwood cuttings

Take cuttings 10–15 cm long from evergreen trees and shrubs where the stems have started to mature into firmer brown or grey wood. These cuttings can be side shoots with a heel or a section of the lower, more mature part of the stem with the cut just below a node. Again, reduce the number or size of the leaves to avoid excessive moisture loss.

Hardwood cuttings

These are taken from deciduous trees or shrubs in winter when they are dormant. Select wood about 6–20 mm in diameter and about 20 cm long, with four to six nodes on each cutting. These cuttings usually root easily, in the same way that branches of willows, poplars and coral trees will grow when simply pushed into the ground. To avoid planting hardwood cuttings upside down, make a slanting cut at the bottom just below the node and a straight cut about 6–12 mm above the top node. This way you will be reminded to plant the cutting point down.

LEAF CUTTINGS

These are used for many indoor plants. The leaves of Rex begonia, for example, can be cut in sections and laid on a moist rooting medium, or a single leaf can be laid flat and the veins cut with a sharp knife or razor blade. For propagating African violets, remove a mature leaf with about 25 mm of petiole (leaf stem) and bury the petiole in the rooting mix. Shoots and roots develop from the base of the leaf. Sansevieria (mother-in-law's tongue) can be propagated from 5 cm sections of leaf. The bases of these sections are placed vertically in a rooting medium.

ROOT CUTTINGS

This is not a common method of propagation in the garden but some plants can produce buds from their thick fleshy roots. Root sections 8–10 cm long and 12 mm in diameter are covered with 1–2 cm of rooting mix. Perennial phlox, albizia, bouvardia, lagerstroemia and wisteria have been propagated by this method.

African violets can be propagated from leaf cuttings by burying the leaf stem in rooting mix.

PROPAGATING PLANTS

Coloured-leaf begonias grow readily from leaf cuttings.

PLANTING CUTTINGS

Pot up cuttings as soon as possible. Fill the pots with a rooting medium, which should be slightly damp. Dip the cut surface into water and then into hormone powder. Make holes with a dibble or pencil about 5 cm apart in the damp mix around the edge of the pot. Set the cuttings in the holes about one-third of their length deep. Firm the mix around them and water the pots gently. Protect cuttings as described above for the first week or two, and then allow more sun and ventilation. Always keep pots moist but not wet. Roots take time to develop. It may be many weeks before they will support the new plant, so do not try to move cuttings too early. It is best to transfer rooted cuttings to individual 7–10 cm pots and grow them on until the root system is well advanced.

Hint

Hemerocallis (day lilies) can be planted at any time of the year. Division can be done year round, but mid-summer, after flowering, is best. As the soil is warm a new root system will quickly form. Divide day lilies with a sharp spade or knife.

BARRY SLIGH
TAUNTON GARDEN AND NURSERY

BUDDING AND GRAFTING

These methods of propagation involve the union of a cut portion of one plant (the scion) with a stem or branch of a growing plant (the stock). In other words, the cambium layers of both scion and stock must be in contact. Both methods are used by nurseries, especially when a selected variety is budded or grafted onto a more vigorous or disease-resistant root stock.

Budding and grafting are really tasks for the specialist, and few home gardeners have the skill or experience to undertake such methods successfully. Only a brief summary with diagrams is given here. Those who wish for more detail should consult one of the books available on this subject.

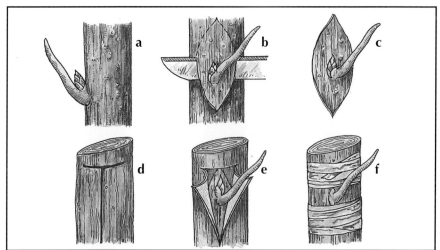

Shield budding is the method used for grafting fruit trees, citrus and roses. Diagrams a, b, and c show how the bud is sliced from the scion. d. A T-shaped cut is made in the stock. e. The bud is inserted in the stock, closing the bark flaps over the edges of the shield. f. Tie the shield firmly to the stock with plastic grafting tape, but take care not to cover the bud.

SHIELD BUDDING

Shield budding is mostly used for propagating citrus trees, deciduous fruit trees and roses. Spring or early autumn is a suitable time for budding.

1. To prepare the stock, make a T-shaped cut in the bark on one- or two-year-old wood. The flaps should lift easily from the wood.
2. Cut the bud from a pencil-thick shoot of the scion. Use a very sharp knife to slice an oval-shaped piece of bark and wood with the bud in the centre. Make the shield 2–4 cm long. Remove the piece of wood behind the shield if it will lift out easily.
3. Place the shield into the T-shaped cut, closing the bark flaps over its edges. Trim off surplus bark at the top of the shield.
4. Starting at the bottom, use budding tape to tie the shield firmly to the stock along its full length. Take care not to cover the bud.
5. After three weeks, cut the tape away. If the shield is still green and the bud plump, it has taken.
6. If budded in spring, cut off the stock above the bud when binding is cut. If budded in autumn, the bud remains dormant until early spring when the stock is cut back.

WHIP-TONGUE GRAFT

This method is used when the scion and the stock are of the same diameter – to about 2.5 cm thick.

1. Cut the top of the stock and the bottom of the scion with a slanting cut 4 cm long. The scion should be about 10 cm long.
2. Cut along the grain on both faces, one-third of the length from the tips to a depth of 6 mm.
3. Fit scion to stock so that the tongues interlock and the cambium layers match on at least one side.
4. Bind the graft carefully with budding tape to make it firm and airtight.

CROWN OR RIND GRAFT

This method is used for one or more scions on a trunk or branch of stock over 2.5 cm in diameter.

1. Saw off the stock at right angles. Smooth the cut surface with a sharp knife.
2. Make a vertical cut 5–7 cm long for each scion. The knife should penetrate the bark to the wood, but not further.
3. Prepare 15 cm scions with a long, slanting cut to the base to form a tapered wedge.
4. Slip the thin end of the wedge between the bark and the wood of the stock and push down until the cut surface of the

scion fits snugly against the exposed tissue of the stock.

5. When all scions are in position, bind them with budding tape and cover the whole cut surface with grafting wax to exclude air and rain.

TISSUE CULTURE

Plant tissue culture is essentially a laboratory technique and very few home gardeners would have the necessary skills or equipment to successfully undertake such a task.

Tissue culture is the vegetative propagation of plants on artificial nutrient under aseptic (sterile) conditions.

The main objectives of plant propagation under the tissue culture system are: the rapid regeneration of plant specimens ensuring genetic homogeneity; the multiplication of important plant species which are difficult to propagate by conventional means (for example, orchid hybrids); and the elimination of viruses from infected plants.

The plant parts which are suitable for plant tissue culture range from plant organs, plant tissue, diminutive shoot tips, seeds, anthers, pollen grains and plant cells.

The general method employed for cultivating larger plant tissue is to sterilise the surface of the tissue and place it on a sterile nutrient base under aseptic conditions for exclusion of microorganisms, such as fungi and bacteria. The cultured tissue and nutrient are usually maintained in a flask or bottle and are incubated under artificially controlled conditions of light and temperature.

Plants which are commonly regenerated by plant tissue culture for commercial or scientific purposes are strawberries, forest trees, azaleas, ferns, grapes, carnations, chrysanthemums, roses and several foliage plants.

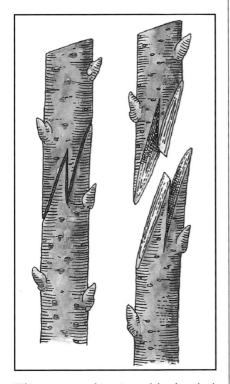

Whip-tongue grafting is useful when both scion and stock are the same thickness. The diagram shows how the cuts are made and fitted together before binding with insulating or grafting tape.

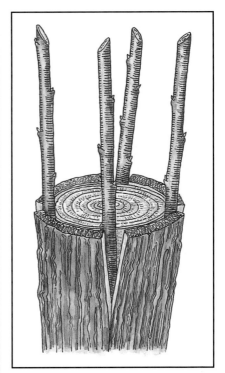

Crown or rind graft is used for grafting one or more scions into a thick trunk or branch of the stock. Slits are made in the bark of the stock, and scions cut to tapered wedges are inserted and held in place with budding tape.

PART IV:
GROWING YOUR GARDEN

CHAPTER 9

THE PERFECT LAWN

L awns have been a feature of home gardens for centuries. New Zealand gardeners have followed this tradition, but there are many other reasons why we grow lawns. A lawn is the best way to cover and maintain large sections of garden easily and quickly. The initial cost of establishment is relatively low and a lawn will last indefinitely. A lawn blends the house with the garden, softens harsh outlines, and complements trees, shrubs and colourful annuals. Even in the smallest garden an attractive lawn adds a touch of spaciousness. On hot summer days a lawn reduces temperature and glare to give a feeling of coolness. Last, but not least, a lawn is a place for relaxation, pleasant to look at, delightful to walk or lie on, and the ideal surface for children to romp and play.

LAWN PLANNING

In many respects, a lawn is an unnatural way to grow millions of grass plants which are all competing for light, water and nutrients. We cut them constantly, which makes their task of growing more difficult. We remove grass clippings everytime we mow. This is an added drain on soil nutrients. Fortunately, lawn grasses are well adapted to this harsh treatment and will thrive if we understand their needs and go about providing for them in the right way. Because a lawn is permanent, it pays to spend some time planning it. This will help with maintenance and often makes the difference between a good lawn and a poor lawn.

Always shape the lawn area with flowing curves. Curves are easier to water and mow than square or sharp corners. Small beds and specimen trees or shrubs can detract from the space of the lawn and make mowing more difficult. Very steep slopes are also hard to mow. Concrete mower strips adjacent to gravel paths, driveways, gardens, rockeries or other features will reduce edge clipping enormously. It is best to construct mower strips or paving after the lawn has been established and there is no longer any risk of lawn subsidence.

Avoid growing grass to the building line. Pathways or paving adjacent to walls are better, because they eliminate wetting and drying effects in the foundation area when watering the lawn. Grass that is grown under overhanging eaves misses out on rain and will need extra watering.

Avoid heavily shaded areas for lawns – especially the southern side of buildings, beside fences or underneath dense shrubs or trees. Trying to grow grass under trees has limited success – there is competition for moisture and nutrients as well as for light. These areas are best paved or separated from the lawn by a mower strip and covered with gravel, pebbles or pine bark. Shade-loving ground covers are an attractive alternative and are discussed later in this chapter.

Avoid growing grass in situations liable to excessive wear – at the corners of buildings, outside doorways and so on. Paths or paving are the best solution here, although a few stepping stones may be enough to solve the traffic problem.

PREPARING THE SITE
SOILS AND DRAINAGE

Whether you sow lawn seed, plant sprigs of running grasses or lay turf, soil must be well prepared. The success of the lawn largely depends on the effort you put into soil preparation. Most grasses prefer well-drained loam or sandy loam soils rather than heavier, wetter soils. Good drainage means better penetration of water, air and grass roots. On very heavy soils it is wise to import some sandy loam soil, spread it over the area to a depth of 8–10 cm and incorporate it

Keep lawn grasses away from the base of trees to avoid competition for light, water and nutrients.

into the topsoil. In extremely wet situations, artificial drainage may be needed. (See Chapter 1.) Very sandy soils may drain too

> ## Hint
>
> *When sowing grass, cover the lawn-to-be with shade cloth or frost cloth until the seed germinates. The cloth will lessen evaporation and will provide a protected environment for germination. Remember to water daily.*
>
> ATHOL McCULLY
> GARDEN EXPERT

easily, so improve them by adding animal manure, spent mushroom compost, or other organic matter to increase their water-holding capacity.

Start preparing the soil well before the time for sowing or planting. This allows you to form the correct levels and contours, to prepare a crumbly soil structure and to destroy any weed seedlings. You can dig small areas with a fork or spade, but it is worthwhile in the long run to hire a rotary hoe to save time and labour for large areas. There is no need to dig the soil deeply. On most sites, a depth of 15 cm is ample. Always dig the soil, especially heavy soil, when it is damp, but keep in mind that cultivating heavy soil when it is either too wet or too dry will spoil its structure. After the initial cultivation remove large stones, gravel and other rubbish.

Allow the soil to remain in a loose or fallow condition for several weeks. Exposure to weather will often help to break down large clods and form a crumbly structure, but further cultivation may be necessary. Watering (or rain) will germinate many weed seeds. Destroy them by hoeing, raking or spraying with glyphosate herbicides. Dig out the underground parts of persistent, perennial weeds, or use an appropriate herbicide. (See Chapter 6.)

SOIL pH AND USE OF LIME

Grasses grow happily in medium acid or slightly acid soils (pH 5.5–6.5). In high rainfall districts, soils may be strongly acid (less than pH 5.5). To these, apply lime at the rate of 25 kg per 100 square metres. This is equivalent to one cup per square metre. Lime also helps to improve the structure of heavy soils, so a good time to apply it is soon after initial cultivation. After spreading the lime, rake it into the topsoil.

LEVELLING AND GRADING

Levelling with pegs and lines is rarely necessary unless the lawn is to be used for tennis or bowls. Lawns need not be flat. Those which follow the natural slope of the ground are usually more attractive. For drainage reasons the lawn should slope away from the house. Grading the soil is necessary to fill in noticeable hollows and to scrape off high spots. You can make an improvised grader from an old window frame or wooden gate, or you can nail together some pieces of 75 mm x 50 mm hardwood to make a frame for the same purpose. These do a good, if somewhat rough, grading job when dragged across the surface. The amount of bite taken into the soil by the leading edge depends on where you attach the rope. If it is too far forward the grader skims over the high spots rather than levelling them. A rake is useful for final grading and for spreading soil evenly. Grading must be done when the soil is loose and fairly dry. When you are satisfied with the lawn's levels and contours, water the area well and leave it for approximately a week. Then rake and cross-rake again and adjust any spots by further grading.

CONSOLIDATING

During the fallow period, natural settling or consolidation of soil below the crumbly surface will occur. Walking over the area for grading, raking or destroying weeds (plus occasional watering or rain) does this for you. If soil is still soft and spongy all over, rolling may be necessary. If soft in spots, tread these firmly one by one. To avoid compaction, only roll or tread when soil is damp, but not wet. Rake the area again after rolling or treading.

Hint

When sowing lawn seed split the volume in half, sowing the first half north to south and the second half east to west. This ensures even coverage.
PETER GREEN
AGRONOMIST

FERTILISER

If you now have a 12–20 mm layer of loose, crumbly surface soil and firmer soil below, it is now in good condition for sowing seed, planting sprigs or laying turf. Apply a base fertiliser or pre-planting fertiliser. All soils for lawns need fertiliser. Having a dark, rich-looking loam is no guarantee of its fertility. Soils in high rainfall districts are deficient in phosphorus, which is the nutrient most needed by developing seedlings. Phosphorus is important for new root growth of sprigs and turf too. Use a mixed fertiliser with 5 per cent phosphorus or more, such as Gro-Plus Complete Plant Food which has an approximate N.P.K. analysis of 5:5:4. Avoid using lawn fertilisers at pre-sowing or pre-planting. These are low in phosphorus and high in nitrogen, and are intended for regular feeding of established lawns only. A recommended rate for a pre-sowing or pre-planting fertiliser is 10 kg per 100 square metres. This is equivalent to one-third of a cup per square metre.

Technological innovation in lawn fertilisers has developed very concentrated, controlled-release fertiliser granules which have the advantage of covering a large area and, because they are coated, of releasing the nutrients slowly without burning the grass.

SPREADING FERTILISER

It is essential to spread fertiliser evenly. Mechanical spreaders are available but fertiliser can be broadcast very effectively by hand. Probably the best method is to divide the total quantity of fertiliser into halves. Then spread the first half in one direction (say, north/south) and the other half at right angles to it (east/west). This way you cover the area twice. You can be even more accurate if you divide the area into strips with garden twine stretched between pegs at two metre intervals. This is a convenient width for scattering fertiliser by hand. Calculate the quantity of fertiliser for each strip. After spreading the first half of the fertiliser, move the twine and pegs to make strips at right angles for spreading the second lot. After spreading, water well. Any weed seedlings can be killed easily by raking and cross-raking.

Hint

A newly seeded lawn needs special protection for its first cut. No more than one third of the grass should be removed, and the blade height should be set at a minimum of 2.5 cm above the soil level. Mow the lawn regularly at this height to ensure best growth.

MIKE WEAVER
GROUNDS SUPERINTENDENT
UNIVERSITY OF AUCKLAND

SOWING SEED

Lawn grass seed is small and light, so choose a calm day for sowing. A good time of the day is early morning when there is generally little or no wind. Only sow an area which you can effectively water. It is better to sow small sections over a few weeks than to have patchy germination of the whole lawn because of inadequate watering. For even sowing, use the same method as suggested for spreading fertiliser. That is, sow the seed in two directions. Best sowing rates and sowing times are given in the section 'Selecting your grass' (see page opposite).

After sowing, lightly rake the crumbly surface. A light roller may be used to press the small seeds into contact with the soil particles, but this is not essential. On sandy soils, a very light covering of dry, sieved mushroom compost retains moisture and helps to prevent soil washing away during rain or watering. On sloping sites, hessian can be stretched over the surface and anchored with pieces of light timber to prevent soil wash, but remove it as soon as seeds start to germinate. Keep the surface soil moist with light watering until seeds germinate and seedlings are well established. As they grow stronger, water the lawn more heavily but less frequently. This will encourage roots to go deeper.

PLANTING SPRIGS OR RUNNERS

This method is often used to establish creeping grasses such as buffalo grass and kikuyu. A sprig or runner is a small piece 7–15 cm long, with one or more nodes (joints) from which leaves and roots grow. Planting runners does not require as much attention as sowing seed. It is a fairly inexpensive method, but time-consuming.

Prepare the soil in the same way as for sowing seed. Plant runners into damp soil about 30 cm apart, by hand or with a trowel. Alternatively, make a furrow 5–7 cm deep, lay runners in the furrow and firm the soil around the roots. Make sure some of the leaves are above ground. On very large areas, runners can be 'chaffed' (chopped into small pieces), broadcast and covered with a light sandy soil. Some landscape contractors will quote for the complete operation.

Only plant sections you can handle and water. Cover unplanted runners with a wet bag or hessian to prevent drying out. Keep soil moist for the first few weeks, especially in hot, dry weather. The best time to plant runners is spring and early summer, but autumn is satisfactory in warmer areas.

LAYING TURF

Laying turf is a more expensive method of laying a lawn but provides an instant lawn with little chance of erosion or loss of planting material. It is a good method for sloping sites. Soil preparation need not be as thorough as for sowing seeds or planting runners, but the surface should be crumbly and well graded. Early maintenance, especially watering, is less critical. Turfing is usually confined to amenity rye, brown top and fescue, an ideal mix for all areas of New Zealand. Turf supplies are available from turf farms and contractors. Turf comprised of Kentucky bluegrass and tall fescue is being trialled by some turf nurseries for its performance in hot weather. Obtain

your turf from a reliable supplier of 'cultivated' turf. The turf must be free of weeds such as onion weed and oxalis and also of the 'grassy' weeds (paspalum and couch).

Cultivated turf is machine-harvested and cut to an even thickness. It comes sometimes in 30 cm squares, more often in rolls 30 cm (or more) wide, which are laid in place like a carpet. Place individual squares or edges of rolls to fit snugly against each other, and fill cracks between them with dry, sandy soil. Tramp or roll the turf after laying, and water well. Turfing can be done at almost any time of the year, but late winter or early spring is probably best. It is important to lay turf as soon as possible after delivery. The turf tends to deteriorate, especially in warm weather, if stored for more than a few days.

SELECTING YOUR GRASS

Lawn seed mixes are a blend of different grass species. The choice of mix will depend on the climate and intended use of the lawn. When planning a lawn, selecting the correct lawn mix can mean the diffference between success and failure.

Lawn grasses are abused more than any other group of plants. They are repeatedly trodden and crushed. As soon as they hold their leaves up, a mower cuts them down, but they must still look green and keep growing. This requires special qualities!

The following species are commonly used in lawn seed mixes.

Brown top

Brown top (also known as New Zealand Bent or Highland Bent) was at one time the most widely grown cool-season grass, either by itself or in grass seed mixtures. While it makes a beautiful, evergreen, fine-textured lawn, and is preferred for top-class bowling and golf greens, it is less favoured by home gardeners these days as it requires a continual high level of maintenance.

Brown top is best suited to cool–temperate or cold climates, but will grow in warmer areas provided plenty of water is applied throughout summer. It prefers full sunlight but will tolerate partial shade and is resistant to wear when very well established.

Sow seed in early spring or autumn. For oversowing couch lawns to provide winter green, sow in autumn. Seedlings emerge in seven to ten days, sometimes sooner in favourable weather.

Kentucky bluegrass

Kentucky bluegrass is hardier than brown top and makes an attractive lawn. It withstands extreme cold and frosts in climates like Otago's, but also does well in warmer districts. Kentucky bluegrass lawns are more resistant to wear than most cool-season grasses, but thin out when poorly grown or too closely cut. Apply fertiliser in both spring and autumn (but not in summer when it is dormant). Lenient mowing at a cutting height of 2.5–4 cm is strongly recommended. Sow seed in spring or autumn at 2 kg per 100 square metres. Seedlings emerge in two to three weeks.

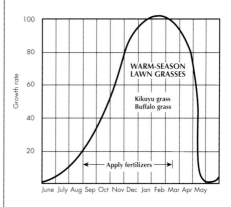

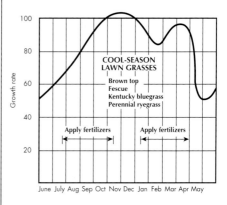

Growth pattern of warm- and cool-season grasses

GROWING YOUR GARDEN

Chewings fescue

This grass is seldom grown alone as a lawn species but is widely used in lawn grass mixtures with Kentucky bluegrass and brown top. Seeds germinate in seven to ten days and seedlings grow quickly. This gives good protection to slower seedlings in the mixture. Chewings fescue prefers full sunlight but will tolerate partial shade. It needs lenient mowing and, for this reason, is a good companion grass to Kentucky bluegrass.

Perennial ryegrass

Perennial ryegrass forms a rather open turf when sown alone. For this reason it is usually combined with brown top and fescue. Ryegrass mixtures are sown at heavier rates to give an attractive, hard-wearing lawn. Ryegrass mixtures are less expensive than those containing 'fine' turf grasses only. They are popular for play areas, swimming pool surrounds and nature strips. They are widely used to give quick cover for large-scale planting on playing fields and parks. Perennial ryegrass has deep roots and withstands heat and dry weather better than brown top and Chewings fescue, but requires lenient mowing – a 4 cm cut – for best results.

Tall fescue

A great deal of recent research and development has gone into modern, turf-type fescue grasses.

They no longer deserve the title 'tall' as the newer varieties are much more compact in growth, have greater tolerance to low mowing heights. They have a delightful deep-green leaf colour. Tall-fescues are non-running grasses. They are best planted in autumn, as their drought tolerance depends on the establishment of a deep root system, and they perform best if they have time to establish their root system before the onset of very hot and dry weather.

Tall fescue is hard-wearing, prefers full sun but tolerates partial shade. Being a drought- and frost-resistant grass, it is suitable for a wide range of climates and retains good colour throughout the year. Tall fescues should never be cut lower than 4 cm.

Sow seed in spring and autumn at the rate of 3.7 kg per 100 square metres. Seedlings emerge in ten to fifteen days.

Turf grass

A new superfine ryegrass. The leaves are so fine they can be compared in appearance to a fescue rather than the traditional ryegrass. It is fast germinating and produces a quick, dense ground cover. It also has a slow growth habit and requires less mowing.

Turf grass is suited to all soil types and climatic zones in New Zealand. It is extremely hard-wearing and popular in sportsgrounds.

Clover

Clover is sometimes added to lawn mixes. It has the advantage of staying green over the summer in dry areas where fine grasses may brown off. Can be slippery when wet and may be unsuitable for children's play areas as it attracts bees when in flower.

LAWN GRASS MIXTURES

A wide range of lawn seed mixtures are available in home-garden packs or in bulk for larger areas.

Coated lawn seed, which has a thin covering layer of fertiliser and bird repellent, is often a popular choice. While it would appear to offer advantages, there can be problems associated with its use. Coated seed is slower to germinate which means it is vulnerable to drying out and the lawn is more susceptible to weed invasion during the early establishment stage. Uncoated seed is quicker germinating and more economical.

One kg of uncoated seed contains twice the number of seeds as 1 kg of coated seed because half the weight is in the 'coat'. Different mixes are formulated for particular uses.

ALTERNATIVE LAWNS

Dichondra

Dichondra repens or Mercury Bay weed is a native of New Zealand. It is a popular alternative to grass lawns, particularly in the warmer northern areas where it establishes quickly and fine grass lawns are more difficult to keep. The main advantage of dichondra lawns is that they require little, if any, mowing. In full sun, dichondra gives a soft, almost shagpile effect. In shady areas where the growth tends to be lanky, some mowing may be necessary. Dichondra is ideally suited to contoured or undulating lawn areas where mowing is difficult.

Thorough preparation is essential before planting dichondra, preferably in light, free-draining soils. Incorporating peat into more difficult heavy soil types will be beneficial. Difficult weeds such as kikuyu, paspalum and couch should be removed with Roundup or Grass Killer.

Spring, when the soil temperatures begin to rise, is the best time to sow dichondra seed. Germination takes from 5 to 30 days, the warmer the soil temperature the quicker the germination. In northern districts where moderate winter temperatures are experienced, late summer and autumn are also suitable for sowing, as the dichondra will continue to grow through the winter.

Ten grams of seed per square metre gives a good cover in five weeks. Rates as low as 3 g per square metre can be used but total ground cover may take three months. Bulk the seed up with sand, sow in alternate directions and rake seed into the top 1 cm of soil. Firm the seed bed down.

As the seed bed is germinating keep it well watered. Drying will cause uneven and slow germination. A light mulching with peat will minimise the water loss and encourage germination as well as suppress some weeds.

Cotula

There are many different species but for the home garden a low-growing species which will need little mowing is most suitable. (The species used in bowling greens tend to be more vigorous and robust.) The small fern-like leaves are pale green in colour. If grown in full sun the lawn will be low and compact.

Establish by taking runners or strips from an established lawn.

Other plants which can be used for making an alternative lawn include thyme, chamomile, hydrocotyle, yarrow and moss.

Buffalo grass

Buffalo grass has broad, light-green leaves and forms a dense, coarse-textured lawn which resists wear and weeds. Buffalo was previously one of the most popular lawn grasses but now appears to be losing favour. It does not set fertile seed and must be established from runners. Buffalo prefers full sunlight but tolerates shade better than most warm-season grasses. It tends to become dense and spongy after a few years and requires frequent cutting and renovation to preserve its well-kept appearance. Generally suited to warm coastal climates, it tolerates heat and dry weather well. Plant runners or lay turf in spring or early summer.

Kikuyu grass

Kikuyu, a native of the highlands of East Africa, is now naturalised in many coastal

Once established, buffalo tolerates heat, dryness and a little bit of shade.

GROWING YOUR GARDEN

LAWN SEED MIXES

NAME	COATED MIX		COMMENTS
'Superfine Showlawn'	Yes	Fescue, brown top	Decorative, luxury lawn with very fine grasses. Requires constant care.
Coated 'Mow-it-Less'	Yes	Turf grass, fescue, brown top	A fine grass lawn which is also durable. Will withstand moderate neglect.
'Mow-it-Less'	No	Turf grass, fescue, brown top	Faster germinating and easier to establish than Coated Mow-it-Less.
Coated 'Country Touch'	Yes	Ryegrass, fescue, brown top	A vigorous, hardwearing lawn which is suited to a wide range of conditions.
'Country Touch'	No	Ryegrass, fescue, brown top	Faster germinating and easier to establish than Coated Country Touch.
'Colonial'	No	Perennial ryegrass, clover	Fast germinating, easily established and hardy. Inexpensive.

regions of New Zealand. It is the most vigorous of all lawn grasses, with stout stolons and rhizomes. For this reason it has often been regarded as undesirable in home gardens. But when kept within bounds, by mower strips and the use of weedkillers, kikuyu makes an attractive, hard-wearing lawn. It stays greener in winter than other warm-season grasses and tolerates partial shade, growing well to the base of trees. It revels in warm weather, tolerates dry spells but needs watering in very hot conditions. Kikuyu responds dramatically to nitrogen fertilisers and the dense turf resists weeds, insects and disease. Runners can be planted in spring or summer.

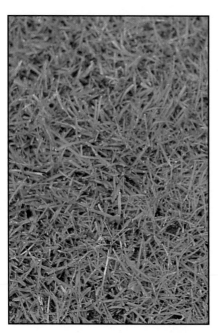

Kikuyu is a very rapid-growing lawn grass.

Country Touch is a hard-wearing lawn grass.

Mow-it-Less is a shade-tolerant grass mix.

above the soil. This will encourage new shoots at the base of each plant. The next three or four cuts should be repeated at the same height – a light 'topping' only. Once grass is established, reduce the cutting height to 2.5–4 cm.

FERTILISER

A pre-sowing or pre-planting fertiliser will keep the new lawn green and vigorous for eight to ten weeks after sowing or planting. At this stage, the need for nitrogen will be increasing. Lack of this nutrient will cause yellowing of leaves and a generally unpromising appearance. Nitrogen fertilisers, such as sulphate of ammonia, can be used occasionally, but a lawn food such as Gro-Plus Lawn Food is recommended for regular application. Lawn foods contain about 12 per cent nitrogen. Should young grass seedlings be stunted and show a reddish-brown or purple pigment in the leaves, this points to a phosphorus deficiency. It may occur only in patches due to uneven spreading of the base fertiliser. Correct it by watering each discoloured patch with a water-soluble fertiliser like Thrive.

CARE OF NEW LAWNS
WATERING

Lawns sown from seed need frequent watering until the grass is growing strongly. When the grass is about 2 cm high, allow the soil to dry out for a few days to encourage roots to go deeper. Then give a good watering and repeat the process. Unless the weather is very hot, you will find that watering may now be reduced to one good soaking each week. Always aim to wet the soil thoroughly to a depth of 15–20 cm with each watering. Lawns from planted runners need care in watering, too, because there can be a lot of bare soil between individual plants. Again, encourage deep rooting by a few days' spell between waterings. Unless the weather is very hot, lawns from turf will get by with a good soaking each week after laying.

MOWING

Don't allow grass to grow too high before you cut it. When warm-season grasses are 3.5–4 cm tall, mow with the blades set at 2.5 cm

Hint

Make your own lawn fertiliser by mixing together 3 parts sulphate of ammonia, 1 part potash and 1 part superphosphate. Apply at 25 g per square metre.

TERRY WALKER
ENVIROSCAPES

LAWN MAINTENANCE

For good lawn maintenance you must consider the kind of grass and its growing season.

WATERING

There are no set rules on when to water or how much water to use. This will depend on the kind of grass, the soil type and the weather conditions. Brown top and other

Hint

Once autumn days set in, apply a high-nitrogen fertiliser to your lawn. This will help prevent frost damage to the grass during the coldest seasons. Make sure you water the fertiliser in thoroughly to avoid burning the grass.

KATHERINE BALL
AGRICULTURAL CONSULTANT

cool-season grasses need more water than tougher summer growers like kikuyu, especially in hot weather. Heavy soils hold moisture well and may only need a good soaking once a week in summer, but sandy soils may need watering every day or two under the same conditions.

Encourage deep rooting by thorough watering. Frequent surface watering makes for soft, sappy growth which is more prone to disease. Generally, it is best to have a fairly dry surface soil and damp soil below. Check this by removing a square or plug of lawn to see how far water has penetrated. The plug can be replaced without damage to the lawn.

Early morning is the best time to water lawns because the sun will dry out the surface during the day. Watering in the evening or at night creates a high humidity layer in the lawn. This also favours the spread of disease. A very common mistake is to apply too much water, especially on kikuyu and other summer growers which are dormant in winter. Watering at this time of the year does nothing for the lawn and very often encourages annual weeds like daisies to germinate and grow.

FERTILISERS AND LIME

Only fertilise lawns when they are growing or starting to grow actively. This is when they make best use of it. Use lawn foods which are high in nitrogen, because this is the nutrient removed in greatest amounts in grass clippings. Apply them little and often at about 3 kg per 100 square metres every five

or six weeks during the growing season: for summer grasses, from spring through to autumn; for cool-season grasses, from late winter to early summer and again from late summer to autumn. Except in subtropical climates with very mild winters, fertilising lawns in the colder months is unnecessary and wasteful.

When applying fertilisers, make sure to spread them evenly. Water into the lawn as soon as possible to avoid fertiliser burn. Some lawn foods are soluble and may be applied with a watering-can or through hose-end sprayers. Continuous use of sulphate of ammonia, or of lawn foods containing it, increases soil acidity. The degree of acidity can only be determined accurately by a soil test. In high rainfall districts a general recommendation is to apply lime at 25 kg per 100 square metres every second or third year. Avoid using too much lime, as this encourages weeds.

MOWING

Always mow lawns regularly at a constant cutting height. This develops a balance between the shoot and root system. Mowing too closely results in shallow roots and weakens the turf, which in turn encourages weeds. Close mowing of couch in autumn causes premature browning and interferes with food storage in the stolons, on which spring growth depends.

For home lawns made up of warm-season grasses or bent grass, a cutting height of at least 2 cm is suitable. A slightly higher cut of 2.5 cm helps to lower soil temperatures in summer. Kentucky bluegrass, ryegrass and fescues need a higher cut at all times (at least 4 cm).

In the growing season, mow once each week, but during winter mowing every four or five weeks will probably be sufficient. Remove the clippings to improve the appearance of the lawn and provide material for compost, or use a mulching mower. Removing clippings also helps to prevent a spongy surface developing, especially in running grasses.

RENOVATION

Renovation is any mechanical measure to improve the surface of lawns and to allow free entry of air, water and nutrients. Always renovate lawns when they will recover quickly – in spring for summer growers, in late winter or early autumn for the cool-season grasses.

'Mat' or 'thatch' is an undecomposed layer of old roots and runners which builds up between the grass leaves and the soil. Thatch prevents the entry of air, water and fertilisers into the soil. To get rid of it, cut the lawn closely and rake severely. Then cut again and repeat the raking until there is a bare cover of grass over the soil. Follow with a ration of fertiliser and water well. The use of organic lawn fertilisers can help reduce thatch.

Bare patches may occur in compacted heavy soil, or perhaps as a result of severe traffic. Compacted soil, like thatch, prevents the entry of air, water and nutrients to the roots of the grass. Give the soil a thorough soaking and use a garden fork to penetrate the soil 10–15 cm deep and the same distance apart. Work the fork back and forth to enlarge the holes. Special hollow-tined forks can be bought for this coring treatment, and mechanical corers can be hired for very large areas.

TOPDRESSING

Fortunately for most gardeners, topdressing is no longer the annual ritual advocated in the past. The main purpose of topdressing is to correct any unevenness in the lawn surface, so it is still very important in turf used for cricket, tennis, bowls and golf putting greens. It has little place in home lawns once the correct levels and grades are made. Topdressing is useful as a light soil covering after de-thatching or coring, and also for oversowing cool-season grasses on couch lawns in autumn.

Soils for topdressing are usually light, sandy loams and provide little in the way of nutrients; that is, they are no substitute for fertilisers. If topdressing is used for any reason, spread it thinly with the back of a rake or a dummy rake. Do not bury the grass completely, as deep covering will retard it. After rubbing in the topdressing, the tips of the grass should show through the soil. Usually, a bucket of topdressing soil per square metre is sufficient. Apply a mixed fertiliser at 3 kg per 100 square metres. This is equivalent to one and a half tablespoons per square metre.

WEED CONTROL

A healthy, vigorous turf which is difficult for weeds to invade is the first line of defence in the battle for weed control. Adequate and regular fertilising is essential to achieving this. Low nutrient supply means poor, open turf which invites weed invasion. Nitrogen and potassium are the key nutrient elements necessary in achieving excellent turf growth. Phosphorus needs to be supplied during establishment, but once the turf is growing well, special lawn fertilisers that have a low phosphorus content will give best grass growth and will discourage the growth of clovers and some grass weeds.

Deep but infrequent watering and regular mowing are important factors in having a weed-free lawn. A wide range of herbicides can be applied to lawns as selective sprays. These chemicals, together with those to control insects and diseases in lawns, are discussed in Chapter 6.

GROUND COVERS

A grass lawn is the most popular ground cover but there are some situations where grass will not grow, is difficult to maintain or ought not to be grown. Such situations include shady areas under trees, steep banks or batters which are difficult to mow, rocky outcrops, and damp, soggy spots with poor drainage.

The answer to these problem areas is ground cover. Gravel, pebbles, quartz chips and pine bark can be considered as ground covers. The materials can be used alone or can be combined with plants. Very often the

Hint
Onehunga weed (prickle weed) can be a painful problem with lawns. Treat it with Prickle Weedkiller in Novemebr before plants set seed.
DENISE CLEVERLEY
HORTICULTURAL CONSULTANT

GROWING YOUR GARDEN

LAWN PESTS

PEST	SYMPTOMS	MOST OBVIOUS	CONTROL
Earthworms	'Wormcasts' or small mounds of soil are left on surface causing unevenness and reducing stability of the lawn.	During autumn rains. During winter until spring.	Carbaryl. Keep lawns acidic (pH5–5.5). Do not lime. Remove grass clippings.
Porina	Feed on grasses, chewing them off at ground level. They do not eat roots. Leave tunnels (about diameter of 1–2 mm) and soil casts with silken threads. Grub is a grey colour with dark head; grows up to 6 cm.	February–April	Granular insecticide (Soil Insect Killer) applied in autumn or spring. (Do not apply in frosty weather as grubs will be inactive.)
Grass grub	Grubs feed on roots causing yellow patches and stunted lawn growth. Adult beetles feed on foliage taking notch-shaped bites and can cause considerable damage on ornamentals in November.	Autumn, early winter.	Soil Insect Killer applied in autumn or, more effectively, in spring as the adults are emerging.

best solution to a damp, shaded area is a mulch of one or other of these materials softened by shade-loving plants such as mondo grass (*Ophiopogon*), plantain lily (*Hosta*), leather leaf (*Bergenia*), bugle flower (*Ajuga*) or Tasmanian violet (*Viola hederacea*).

Most ground cover plants are prostrate perennials which spread rapidly by above-ground stolons or underground rhizomes. When established, ground covers need little attention and maintenance. An annual dressing of fertiliser – slow-release fertilisers are the most suitable – and occasional pruning to keep the plants from getting out of hand is about all that is necessary.

It does pay dividends to prepare the site thoroughly before you establish your ground cover. If possible, start preparation in winter and keep the soil cultivated through the spring months to destroy weeds, especially perennial weeds with persistent underground parts. The herbicide glyphosate, known as Zero or Roundup, is very useful because it does not have a residual effect on the soil. Early summer is a good time for planting. Close planting will give a quick cover (assisted by scattering a mixed fertiliser, such as Gro-Plus Complete Plant Food, before planting). You may need to continue with some weeding until the ground cover is well established and forms a dense mat.

On a bank or sloping site, prostrate shrubs can be used to bind the soil and form a weed-resistant cover. One of the best native shrubs is *Coprosma prostrata* with rich-green, highly polished foliage. It is tolerant of most climatic extremes including drought and heat, and is an excellent coastal plant. Another attractive, shrubby ground cover is shore juniper

(*Juniperus conferta*), which has tiny, grey-green leaves and grows to 60 cm in height. Creeping juniper (*J. horizontalis*) is not quite so tall (30 cm), but spreads over the ground covering 2–3 metres. Bulbous plants like agapanthus, clivia and hemerocallis are also good, low-maintenance soil binders for steep banks.

Climbing plants are very suitable for ground covers on sloping or flat sites. Ivy is one of the most popular. There are many varieties of this adaptable plant. Creeping boobialla (*Myoporum parvifolium*) is another attractive ground cover plant. It forms a dense green mat with white, tubular flowers followed by purple berries. Other climbing plants which are useful for soil binding or covering rock faces are ivy (*Hedera*), star jasmine (*Trachelospermum*), Australian sarsparilla (*Hardenbergia*), ivy geranium (*Pelargonium*), creeping fig (*Ficus pumila*) and Virginian creeper (*Parthenocissus*).

Many perennials make suitable ground covers, among them bugle flower (*Ajuga*), chamomile (*Anthemis*), ground morning glory (*Convolvulus*), pig face (*Mesembryanthemum*), lamb's ear (*Stachys lanata*), snow-in-summer (*Cerastium*) and violets (*Viola odorata*).

Other widely grown ground covers are Japanese spurge (*Pachysandra*), with glossy foliage and greenish-white flowers; London pride (*Crassula*), a shrubby succulent with oval leaves and small, pink flowers; Spanish shawl (*Schizocentron*), with a dense mat of short foliage and small carmine flowers; Dalmatian bellflower (*Campanula portenschlagiana*), with small violet-like leaves and a profusion of small, star-shaped, violet flowers; and thyme (*Thymus*), of which there are many forms, all with aromatic leaves. Lemon-scented thyme (*T. citriodorus*) and wild thyme (*T. serpyllum*) are both prostrate, creeping species.

Creeping mint (*Mentha requienii*) is also a good carpeting plant with aromatic leaves. Lippia (*Lippia nodiflora*), which forms a loose mat of small leaves with clusters of tiny white flowers, is also a very popular ground cover.

Most of these ground covers will tolerate shade but will not stand heavy traffic. You will need to lay stepping stones or discs of sawn hardwood in areas where people are likely to walk.

TOP FIVE EXOTIC GROUND COVERS

SPANISH SHAWL

When this mat-growing plant produces its mass of rosy purple flowers, you can see why it's called 'Spanish Shawl'. Protect from frost.

IVY GERANIUM

Smooth, shiny, slightly ivy-shaped leaves make a perfect foil for clusters of brightly coloured flowers on these easily grown plants. Plenty of sun is essential.

SHORE JUNIPER

This low-growing conifer is remarkably hardy and is especially useful in exposed coastal locations.

CREEPING THYME

Good for carpeting small areas, creeping thyme will release its attractive perfume when walked on or brushed against. It won't, however, take heavy traffic.

CONVOLVULUS MAURITANICUS

This sweet little plant develops a dense carpet of grey-green leaves that are studded with lavender-blue blooms throughout the warm season.

JUNIPER

THYME

CHAPTER 10

THE FLOWER GARDEN

There are many hundreds of flowering plants available around the world, but in this chapter we have restricted ourselves to those of most interest to New Zealand home gardeners. Full growing details for a particular variety – soil preparation and cultivation – are only given where there is a special requirement. New gardeners would probably find it helpful to read the general information on soil and fertilisers in Chapters 3 and 4, and the methods for sowing seed and raising seedlings in Chapter 7.

ANNUALS

These plants complete their life span in one year, and most of them flower in three to four months from the time of sowing. Flowering finishes as the seeds ripen and the plants die. Annuals are divided into two groups: summer-flowering and winter-/spring-flowering. The former are sown in spring; the latter in summer and autumn. Some flowers have both annual and perennial types – alyssum, lupins and statice are good examples. Many so-called annuals are really short-lived perennials. In cool climates they may last for three or four years, but in warmer districts their effective life is much shorter.

Annual flowers are always favourites for the home garden; no other plants give such a colourful display in such a short time and for so little trouble. They can be changed seasonally to create varied effects and colour combinations. The brilliant colours look wonderful in large masses, clumps or drifts, but they can be used effectively in narrow borders too. Annuals complement other garden plantings and can be arranged so that flowers are in bloom (except in very cold districts) at almost any time of the year.

BIENNIALS

These plants usually live for two years. They spend their first year building up a good strong leaf and root base. Growth then slows down, and in colder climates they may die back to total dormancy. The following season the plant breaks into fresh growth and flowers. After flowering in its second season the plant sets seed and dies in the same way as an annual.

Cool and temperate climates suit most biennials, but there are a few exceptions, such as Canterbury bells. Many others are grown successfully in warm climates if treated as annuals. It is the cooler conditions between flowerings which encourage the dormant period. Without a cold period the plant is less likely to make a good flush of growth in the second year. In cold climates, biennials are usually sown in spring. They flower in late spring and summer and then remain dormant through autumn and winter to restart growth for flowering again in warmer weather.

PERENNIALS

This term applies to plants which have an effective life of three years or more. Some, under favourable conditions – especially in cool climates – may remain in the garden permanently. But in this chapter we will concentrate on those perennials which flower the first season from seed. Most perennials bloom at the same time each year, but a few, such as carnations, have been bred and selected to bloom over a longer time. As a rule, perennials which flower quickly from sowing seed (say, within six months) are those which should be freshly sown each year, especially in warm climates. This does not mean that some, for example snapdragons, will not stand cutting back at least once to give a good display at their second flowering.

Flowering bulbs, like anemones and ranunculus, are perennials because under good conditions they continue to flower each season without special attention. Dahlias and chrysanthemums, which are grown from tubers, are in the same category because the tubers carry over from year to year. These are not usually classified as perennials in the same way as carnations and hollyhocks, where it is the plant itself which persists.

Carnations, chrysanthemums, dahlias and some other perennials may be propagated from seed or by vegetative methods: plant division, cuttings or layers. (See Chapter 8.) They are not always grown from seed because many named varieties do not breed true to type.

Plants grown from seed will vary in type and colour, so if you grow a good strain from seed, you may discover a plant of particular quality which is worthwhile propagating vegetatively.

DWARF, MEDIUM AND TALL FLOWERS

DWARF FLOWERS – 30 CM OR LESS

Ageratum, alyssum, aster (dwarf), begonia (bedding), bellis (English daisy), calendula, candytuft, carnation, celosia (dwarf), chrysanthemum (dwarf), cineraria (dwarf), cockscomb, dianthus, Californian poppy, forget-me-not, fairy pinks, gazania, globe amaranth, godetia (dwarf), impatiens, linaria, livingstone daisy, lobelia, lupin (dwarf), marigold (dwarf), mignonette, nasturtium (dwarf), nemesia (dwarf), nemophila, nigella, ornamental basil, ornamental chilli, pansy, phlox (dwarf), polyanthus, portulaca, primula, salvia (dwarf), stock (dwarf), sweet pea (dwarf), verbena, viola, Virginian stock, zinnia (dwarf).

MEDIUM-HEIGHT FLOWERS – 30–60 CM

Acroclinium (everlasting daisy), antirrhinum (snapdragon), aquilegia (columbine), arctotis, aster, balsam, boronia, brachycome (Swan River daisy), calendula, candytuft, Canterbury bells, carnation, celosia, centaurea (cornflower), chrysanthemum,

cineraria, coleus, dahlia (dwarf), dianthus, gaillardia, geranium, gerbera, godetia, gomphrena (globe amaranth), gypsophila, helichrysum (strawflower), honesty, linaria, lupin, marigold (French), molucella (bells of Ireland), nasturtium, ornamental chilli, petunia, phlox, poppy (Iceland), rudbeckia (gloriosa daisy), salpiglossis, salvia, schizanthus, statice, stock, sweet William, viscaria, wallflower, zinnia.

TALL FLOWERS – 60 CM OR OVER

Amaranthus, aster, cleome, cosmos, chrysanthemum, dahlia, delphinium, hollyhock, larkspur, lupin (tall), marigold (tall), salvia (tall), scabiosa, sunflower, sweet pea, zinnia (tall).

FLOWERS FOR SHADE OR SEMI-SHADE

Ageratum, alyssum, aquilegia, begonia (bedding), calendula, cineraria, coleus, cyclamen, Canterbury bells, forget-me-not, foxglove, impatiens, linaria, lobelia, mimulus, nasturtium, nigella, pansy, polyanthus, primula, schizanthus, viola, Virginia stock, wallflower. (Viola and pansy require at least half sunlight.)

SPRING FLOWERS

Acroclinium, ageratum, alyssum, antirrhinum, aquilegia, candytuft, Canterbury bells, centaurea, chrysanthemum (annual), cineraria, delphinium, dianthus, forget-me-not, gaillardia, godetia, gypsophila, helichrysum, larkspur, linaria, lobelia, lupin, marigold (French), mignonette, nasturtium, nemesia, pansy, polyanthus, poppy, primula, scabiosa, schizanthus, statice, stock, sweet pea, sweet William, viola, wallflower.

SUMMER AND AUTUMN FLOWERS

Amaranthus, antirrhinum, aster, balsam, begonia (bedding), carnation, celosia, chrysanthemum (perennial), cleome, cockscomb, cosmos, dahlia, dianthus, Californian poppy, gaillardia, gerbera, gomphrena, gypsophila, hollyhock, marigold (African), petunia, phlox, portulaca, salpiglossis, salvia, sunflower, verbena, viscaria, zinnia.

Garden flowers of varying heights can add interest to a landscape.

GROWING YOUR GARDEN

SOWING GUIDE FOR FLOWERS

FLOWER	TEMPERATE												COLD											
	J	F	M	A	M	J	J	A	S	O	N	D	J	F	M	A	M	J	J	A	S	O	N	D
Acroclinium (see Everlasting daisy)																								
Ageratum	●	●	●	●	●	●		●	●	●	●	●	●	●							●	●	●	●
Alyssum	●	●	●	●	●	●		●	●	●	●	●	●	●	●	●					●	●	●	●
Amaranthus							●	●	●	●	●										●	●	●	●
Antirrhinum (see Snapdragon)																								
Aquilegia (Columbine)	●	●	●	●	●										●	●	●				●			
Arctotis (Aurora daisy)	●	●	●	●										●	●	●					●	●		
Aster						●	●	●	●	●	●									●	●	●	●	●
Aurora daisy (see Arctotis)																								
Baby blue eyes (see Nemophila)																								
Balsam						●	●	●	●										●	●	●	●	●	●
Begonia, bedding						●	●	●	●											●	●	●		
Begonia, tuberous						●	●	●	●											●	●	●		
Bellis (English daisy)				●	●	●	●						●	●	●						●	●		
Bells of Ireland (Molucella)	●	●	●	●			●	●	●					●	●	●					●	●		
Brachycome (see Swan River daisy)																								
Calceolaria	●	●	●	●									●								●	●	●	●
Calendula (English marigold)	●	●	●	●	●	●									●	●	●					●	●	
Californian poppy (Eschscholtzia)						●	●	●	●	●											●	●	●	●
Candytuft	●	●	●	●	●										●	●	●					●	●	
Canterbury bells	●	●	●	●	●										●	●	●							
Carnation		●	●	●			●	●	●					●	●	●	●			●	●	●		
Celosia						●	●	●	●	●											●	●	●	●

HOW TO SOW: SEED TRAYS (S) DIRECT (D)	SOWING DEPTH (MM)	SEEDLINGS EMERGE (DAYS)	TRANSPLANT OR SOW DIRECT AND THIN TO . . . CM APART	APPROX. TIME TO FLOWERING (WEEKS)
S or D	6	14–21	15–20	14
S or D	3	10–14	7-10	8
D	6	14–21	40	14
S	3	21–28	30–40	28
S or D	6	18–21	30–40	16
S	6	10–14	20–30	16
S or D	6	10–14	30	12
S	1	14–21	20	16
S	1	14–21	pots	28
S	3	10–14	10–15	12
D	6	14–21	20–30	12
S	12	14–21	pots	20
S or D	12	10–14	30	10
S or D	3	10–14	30	8
S or D	6	14–21	20–30	12
S	3	14–21	30	14
S or D	6	10–14	30–40	28
S or D	6	10–14	20–30	12

GROWING YOUR GARDEN

FLOWER	J	F	M	A	M	J	J	A	S	O	N	D	J	F	M	A	M	J	J	A	S	O	N	D
	TEMPERATE												**COLD**											
Centaurea (see Cornflower)																								
Chrysanthemum (Star Daisy)								●	●	●	●									●	●	●	●	
Cineraria		●	●	●	●									●	●	●	●							
Cleome (see Spider flower)																								
Cockscomb							●	●	●	●	●	●									●	●	●	●
Coleus							●	●	●	●	●	●									●	●	●	●
Columbine (see Aquilegia)																								
Coreopsis			●	●	●		●	●	●					●	●						●	●	●	●
Cornflower (Centaurea)	●	●	●	●									●	●	●							●	●	
Cosmos							●	●	●	●	●										●	●	●	●
Cyclamen	●	●	●	●	●	●						●	●	●	●	●	●							●
Dahlia (seed)							●	●	●	●	●										●	●	●	●
Delphinium	●	●	●	●	●	●	●						●	●	●				●	●				
Dianthus (Fairy pinks)	●	●	●	●	●	●	●	●	●				●	●	●				●	●				
English daisy (see Bellis)																								
English marigold (see Calendula)																								
Eschscholtzia (see Californian poppy)																								
Everlasting daisy (Acroclinium)	●	●	●	●			●	●	●				●	●	●					●	●			
Fairy pinks (see Dianthus)																								
Forget-me-not	●	●	●	●	●								●	●	●	●								●
Gaillardia	●	●	●	●			●	●	●				●	●	●					●	●			
Gazania							●	●	●	●	●	●								●	●	●	●	●
Geranium (seed)							●	●	●	●	●	●								●	●	●	●	
Gerbera							●	●	●	●	●	●								●	●	●	●	

HOW TO SOW: SEED TRAYS (S) DIRECT (D)	SOWING DEPTH (MM)	SEEDLINGS EMERGE (DAYS)	TRANSPLANT OR SOW DIRECT AND THIN TO . . . CM APART	APPROX. TIME TO FLOWERING (WEEKS)
S	6	10–14	75–100	24
S	3	10–14	30–40	20
S or D	6	10–14	30	12
S	6	14–21	30 or pots	10
S	1	7–21	30	12
S	3	14–21	40–50	14
S or D	6	14–21	40–50	12
S	3	28–42	Pots	64
S	12	14–28	50–100	16
S	3	21–28	50	20
D	3	10–14	15–30	20
D	12	21–28	20–30	14
S	3	21–28	20–30	12
S or D	6	14–21	30	16
S	6	14–21	20	12
S	3	14–28	40–50	16
S	6	14–21	40–50	30–50

GROWING YOUR GARDEN

FLOWER	TEMPERATE												COLD											
	J	F	M	A	M	J	J	A	S	O	N	D	J	F	M	A	M	J	J	A	S	O	N	D
Globe amaranth (Gomphrena)							•	•	•	•	•										•	•	•	•
Gloxinia						•	•	•	•												•	•	•	
Godetia	•	•	•	•	•	•								•	•	•						•	•	
Gypsophila	•	•	•	•	•	•	•	•	•	•	•		•	•	•	•	•	•			•	•	•	•
Helianthus (see Sunflower)																								
Helichrysum (see Strawflower)																								
Hollyhock		•	•	•	•								•	•	•	•								
Honesty (Lunaria)		•	•	•	•		•	•	•				•	•	•						•	•		
Impatiens		•	•	•	•		•	•	•				•	•	•						•	•		
Larkspur		•	•	•	•	•							•	•	•						•	•		
Linaria	•	•	•	•	•	•							•	•	•						•	•		
Livingstone daisy (Mesembryanthemum)		•	•	•	•								•	•	•						•	•		
Lobelia		•	•	•	•								•	•	•						•	•		
Lunaria (see Honesty)																								
Lupin	•	•	•	•	•	•	•						•	•	•	•					•	•		
Malope					•	•	•	•	•	•											•	•	•	•
Marigold, African						•	•	•	•	•											•	•	•	•
Marigold, French	•	•	•	•	•	•							•	•	•	•	•	•			•	•		
Marmalade daisy (see Rudbeckia)																								
Mexican sunflower (Tithonia)							•	•	•	•											•	•	•	•

HOW TO SOW: SEED TRAYS (S) DIRECT (D)	SOWING DEPTH (MM)	SEEDLINGS EMERGE (DAYS)	TRANSPLANT OR SOW DIRECT AND THIN TO . . . CM APART	APPROX. TIME TO FLOWERING (WEEKS)
S or D	6	14–21	30	12
S	3	21–28	pots	30
S or D	6	10–14	30	12
D	6	10–14	20–30	10
S	6	14–21	30–40	28
S	3	14–21	40–50	12
S	3	14–21	30–40	12
D	3	14–21	20–30	20
D	6	10–14	10–15	10
S or D	3	14–21	10–15	20
S	3	10–14	10	14
D	12	10–14	20–50	16–32
S or D	5	14–21	25–30	12–14
S or D	6	10–14	20–40	12
S or D	6	10–14	20–40	12
D	5	7–21	60	12

FLOWER	TEMPERATE												COLD											
	J	F	M	A	M	J	J	A	S	O	N	D	J	F	M	A	M	J	J	A	S	O	N	D
Mignonette	•	•	•	•	•	•	•	•						•	•	•							•	•
Molucella (see Bells of Ireland)																								
Nasturtium	•	•					•	•	•	•	•										•	•	•	•
Nemesia		•	•	•	•																		•	•
Nemophila (Baby blue eyes)		•	•	•	•									•	•	•							•	•
Nigella		•	•	•	•									•	•	•								
Ornamental basil						•	•	•	•	•											•	•	•	•
Ornamental chilli						•	•	•	•	•											•	•	•	•
Painted daisy		•	•	•	•	•								•	•	•							•	•
Pansy	•	•	•	•	•	•							•	•	•	•							•	•
Petunia							•	•	•	•	•										•	•	•	•
Phlox							•	•	•	•	•										•	•	•	•
Pinks (see Dianthus)																								
Pin-cushion flower (see Scabiosa)																								
Polyanthus		•	•	•										•	•	•								
Poor man's orchid (Schizanthus)	•	•	•	•									•	•	•	•								
Poppy, Iceland	•	•	•	•									•	•	•	•								
Portulaca						•	•	•	•	•											•	•	•	•
Primula	•	•	•	•	•								•	•	•	•								
Rudbeckia (Marmalade daisy)						•	•	•	•	•											•	•	•	
Salpiglossis						•	•	•	•	•											•	•	•	
Salvia						•	•	•	•	•											•	•	•	•

HOW TO SOW: SEED TRAYS (S) DIRECT (D)	SOWING DEPTH (MM)	TRANSPLANT OR SEEDLINGS EMERGE (DAYS)	APPROX. SOW DIRECT AND THIN TO . . . CM APART	TIME TO FLOWERING (WEEKS)
D	6	10–14	15–20	12
D	12	14–21	20–30	10–12
S or D	6	10–14	15–20	14
D	3	10–14	15	12
S or D	3	21–28	20	14
S or D	6	10–14	20–30	–
S or D	6	10–14	60	20
S	6	14–21	40–50	12–14
S	6	21–28	20–30	16
S	3	10–14	25–40	12
S or D	3	14–21	10–15	10
S	3	21–28	15–20	24
S	3	14–21	30	14
S	3	10–14	20-30	24
S or D	6	10–14	10	6
S	3	21–28	15–20	24
S or D	6	10–14	30	14
D	6	14–21	15	5–12
S or D	3	14–21	20–40	12

GROWING YOUR GARDEN

FLOWER	TEMPERATE												COLD											
	J	F	M	A	M	J	J	A	S	O	N	D	J	F	M	A	M	J	J	A	S	O	N	D
Scabiosa (Pin-cushion flower)		•	•	•	•								•	•	•							•	•	
Schizanthus (see Poor man's orchid)																								
Snapdragon (Antirrhinum)	•	•	•	•	•	•		•	•	•	•	•									•	•	•	•
Spider flower (Cleome)	•	•					•	•	•	•	•	•	•	•							•	•	•	•
Star daisy (see Chrysanthemum)																								
Statice			•	•	•	•	•	•	•	•				•	•	•						•	•	
Stock	•	•	•	•	•								•	•	•	•								
Strawflower (Helichrysum)		•	•	•	•			•	•	•				•	•	•						•	•	•
Sturt's desert pea (Clianthus)						•	•	•	•	•	•										•	•	•	•
Sunflower (Helianthus)							•	•	•	•	•	•									•	•	•	•
Swan River daisy (Brachycome)						•	•	•	•	•	•										•	•	•	•
Sweet pea	•	•	•	•	•								•	•	•	•						•	•	
Sweet William (see Dianthus)																								
Verbena	•	•					•	•	•	•	•	•	•								•	•	•	•
Vinca	•	•	•					•	•	•	•	•	•	•	•	•						•	•	
Viola	•	•	•	•	•	•							•	•	•						•	•	•	
Virginia stock		•	•	•	•	•								•	•	•						•	•	
Viscaria							•	•	•	•	•	•									•	•	•	•
Wallflower	•	•	•	•	•								•	•	•	•								
Zinnia							•	•	•	•	•	•									•	•	•	•

HOW TO SOW: SEED TRAYS (S) DIRECT (D)	SOWING DEPTH (MM)	SEEDLINGS EMERGE (DAYS)	TRANSPLANT OR SOW DIRECT AND THIN TO . . . CM APART	APPROX. TIME TO FLOWERING (WEEKS)
S or D	6	14–21	40	14
S	3	10–14	25–40	16
D	3	14–21	50–60	12
D	12	28	30–40	20
S or D	3	10–14	20–40	20
S	3	10–14	30	16
S or D	6	14–28	40	24
S or D	6	10–14	50–60	12
S or D	3	14–21	20	16
D	25	10–14	5–7	14
S or D	6	21–28	25–30	10
S or D	2	7–10	20–30	11–12
S	6	21–28	20	16
S or D	6	10–14	15	14
D	6	14–21	15	12
S	6	10–14	20–30	24
S or D	6	7–10	20–40	12

GROWING YOUR GARDEN

HOW TO GROW INDIVIDUAL FLOWERS

ACROCLINIUM

See Everlasting daisy.

AGERATUM

Sometimes known as floss flower, ageratum, an attractive blue annual, is usually grown for spring, summer and autumn display.

All varieties make splendid border plants, and their soft blue flowers are excellent for garden display and indoor decoration. They will succeed in a variety of soils but respond to good conditions and added fertiliser. They are fairly drought-resistant but need regular watering in dry weather. They are at their best when grown in full sunlight, but will give reasonable results in semi-shade.

Hint

To get the best out of plants grown in containers, situate the pots in positions that are appropriate to their contents. So, place pots containing shade-loving plants in cool areas, put sun-lovers in a bright location, and protect frost-tender plants in winter. Lightweight plastic pots are easier on your back.

THE TWO ANNS
A & A CONSULTANTS

Spring and summer sowings are best. Seed can either be sown in seed beds, and the seedlings transplanted, or sown direct in the garden bed. The seeds need light for germination so press them into the top of the seed-raising mix or soil and keep moist until seedlings emerge. Seedlings are transplanted or thinned to a distance of 15–20 cm apart. Plants need very little care apart from normal cultivation and watering. Liquid feeds of Thrive at regular intervals will promote flowering. Cut back all spent blooms. 'Blue Mink' is a popular dwarf variety.

ALYSSUM

Sweet Alice, as this plant is often called, is popular for edging and borders. It is ideal for rockeries and wall gardens, as it flowers all the year in most climates. It does quite well in semi-shade but flowering is more prolific in open sunlight. It grows well in all types of soils, but thrives in good, friable soil with added fertiliser. Good drainage is essential as it resents damp conditions.

In temperate climates you can sow seed at almost any time of the year but in cold districts it is best to sow during spring and autumn months. Seedlings can be raised in boxes or punnets for transplanting, or seed can be sown direct in the garden in clumps 7–10 cm apart and thinned as necessary. Cover seeds lightly with seed-raising mix and keep damp until seedlings emerge. Water plants regularly in dry weather, giving a good soaking once or twice a week rather than frequent sprinkling. Control weeds while they are small, otherwise the fine roots of the plants will be damaged when large weeds are pulled out. Give regular liquid feeds of soluble fertiliser as plants grow. This will promote flowering over a longer period. Cut back all spent flowers.

Varieties

'Carpet of Snow' has masses of pure white flowers on dwarf bushes 10 cm tall. It is excellent for borders and edging, in rockeries and between bricks or stones in paths or paving. 'Royal Carpet' has deep violet flowers on bushes the same height as 'Carpet of Snow', with which it combines for a beautiful colour combination. 'Cameo Mixture' is a delightful blend of 'Carpet of Snow', 'Royal Carpet' and other subtle colours and is ideal for mass planting. *Alyssum saxatile* (also known as aurinia) grows to about 15 cm with clusters of deep-yellow flowers. It is spring blooming but plants last two to three years. Alyssum is ideal for borders, mass planting and for adding colour to rockeries.

AMARANTHUS

This is a popular summer annual in sub-tropical areas, widely grown for its brilliant foliage and its ability to stand very hot weather.

Plants grow to 1–2 metres. Amaranthus

revels in hot sunny situations, but requires ample water during dry times. Prepare soil well a week or two before planting. Use animal manure or compost, plus a mixed fertiliser such as Gro-Plus Complete Plant Food at the rate of one-third of a cup per square metre.

Sowing can be made in spring when the danger of frost is over and can be continued until early summer. It is best to sow a few seeds direct in the garden in clumps 40 cm apart and thin out to one or two seedlings. You can also raise seedlings and transplant to the same distance apart. Cover seed with seed-raising mix and keep damp until seedlings emerge. If transplanting seedlings, discard any plants which are not well coloured. Water regularly while plants are growing and keep down weed growth by shallow cultivation. As hot weather approaches, a mulch of compost will protect shallow roots and conserve moisture. When the plants are about 30 cm tall, give liquid feeds of soluble fertilisers and repeat this treatment every ten to fourteen days.

ANCHUSA

Sometimes known as summer forget-me-not because it is similar to, but later flowering than, the common forget-me-not, anchusa has vibrantly blue flowers with small, creamy-white centres. It can be sown either direct in the garden or in seed punnets filled with seed-raising mix. The compact bushy plants grow to 25 cm. After the first flush of blooms is finished, the plants can be cut back and fed with Thrive Flower and Fruit to promote further flowering. These plants need good drainage and dislike humid conditions.

ANTIRRHINUM

See Snapdragon.

AQUILEGIA (COLUMBINE)

This unusual and attractive flower has been improved by selection in recent years and the present-day strains are well worth a place in the garden. Aquilegia is a perennial best suited to cool climates. Plants prefer a sunny position, but they can be grown in semi-shade. Sow seed in autumn, but in cool climates you can sow in early spring too.

Sow seed in seed beds or punnets and transplant seedlings when 5–7 cm tall,

spacing 30–40 cm apart. Water regularly, especially in dry weather, and scatter a mulch of compost around each plant. Apply liquid feeds of Thrive or other soluble fertilisers as buds start to form. In cold districts, flowering in the first year is not as prolific as it is in subsequent years. In cool climates, plants will last for many years but in warmer climates it is best to start new seedlings at least every second year.

ARCTOTIS (AURORA DAISY)

This is a beautiful annual, flowering during winter, spring and summer. The large daisy-like flowers are produced freely on long, strong stems about 40 cm tall and come in a wide range of brilliant colours, including tangerine, rose, pink, red, claret, lemon, orange and white. Some flowers show attractive two-tone effects while others are one colour.

Plants will grow on a wide range of soils and do very well on light sandy soils. Sow seed in autumn (for winter flowering) and also in spring. Seed may be sown direct in the garden bed or seedlings may be raised in boxes or punnets and transplanted when 5–7 cm tall. Space plants 30–40 cm apart. Water well during hot, dry weather and give liquid feeds of soluble fertilisers as flowering commences. A sunny position is best.

ASTER

Rich, bright flower colours have made asters a firm favourite with gardeners. Although subject to aster wilt, good strains such as 'Giant Crego' will give good results if not planted in soil which has grown asters the previous year. Good drainage and a well-structured soil also help plants to resist the wilt problem.

Asters prefer a light sandy soil which is not heavily manured. Improve heavy clay soils by the addition of compost for better crumb structure. In preparing the bed, apply a mixed fertiliser such as Gro-Plus Complete Plant Food at the rate of one-third of a cup per square metre. Careful soil preparation, well before the seedlings are transplanted, will pay dividends. Asters prefer an open sunny position.

There is little advantage to be gained from sowing seed too early in spring. Later sowings will bloom at the same time – about mid-summer. You can sow seed from spring (but wait until frosts are over) through until mid-summer. Raise seedlings in seed beds, boxes or punnets as described in Chapter 7. After sowing, cover the seeds lightly with a light sandy soil or seed-raising mixture.

When the seedlings are large enough, transplant them into the prepared bed, spacing them 20–30 cm apart each way.

On heavy soils seedlings may have difficulty in establishing their root systems. You can assist root development by mixing some seed-raising mix or a handful of sand into the hole where the seedlings are planted.

In hot weather, spread a mulch of compost over the surface of the bed to conserve moisture and keep the roots cool. With normal attention plants should be flowering in three months from sowing the seed.

Later sowings will bloom a little more quickly. It is important to remember that asters are very susceptible to frost, so do not sow too late in summer because this will not give sufficient time for the plants to flower.

Varieties

'Dwarf Colour Carpet' is a colourful dwarf aster growing to 20 cm high. It is ideal for borders and rock gardens. There are many other strains and cultivars. Some of the better known are 'Giant Crego', which has large double flowers in an excellent colour range and made up of long, curled and twisted petals, and 'King Aster', a free-flowering variety with large, fully double blooms made up of attractive quilled petals.

Hint

Green flowers are hard to find but they are beautiful. Euphorbias, Daphne laureola, Helleborus argutifolius, and Helleborus lividus are all shade-loving and refreshingly green. Different shades of green can complement each other in any garden design.

DENNIS GREVILLE
GARDEN WRITER

Impatiens is a versatile plant; grow it in full sun or on the shady side of the house.

AURORA DAISY

See Arctotis.

BABY BLUE EYES

See Nemophila.

BALSAM

This colourful flower is an excellent plant for borders or massed display. It can also be grown in window boxes, pots and troughs. Balsam likes the sun but will do well in semi-shade too. Prepare soil well and add organic matter and a pre-planting fertiliser. Balsam is sometimes also called impatiens.

Raise seedlings in boxes or punnets in early spring, but direct sowing is best delayed until all danger of frosts is past. Transplant or sow in clumps 30 cm apart each way. Plants eventually grow to a height of 50 cm and flower in about three months from sowing. 'Superb Double Mixed' is the most widely grown variety.

BEGONIA
Bedding

Few other flowers grow so well in heavily shaded places as the bedding or fibrous-rooted begonia. Begonias are well suited to southerly and westerly aspects which receive little direct sunlight. While these plants thrive in shade, they do quite well in a sunny position also, but need regular watering in dry weather. Prepare soil well with added compost plus a mixed fertiliser such as Gro-Plus Complete Plant Food at one-third of a cup per square metre. Spring is the best time to sow seed in most climates.

The seed is almost as fine as flour, so seedlings need to be raised in seed boxes or punnets. Mark out rows 3–5 cm apart with the point of a nail, or lay the edge of a ruler on the surface and press down gently. Sprinkle seed thinly along the rows and press it in. Do not cover, as the seeds need light for germination.

Water gently with a very fine spray so as not to disturb the surface. Alternatively, stand containers in shallow water until moisture seeps to the surface. Keep damp until seedlings emerge in two to three weeks. Prick out seedlings when they are small to a seed tray and grow them on until 5–7 cm high before transplanting to the garden bed. Space seedlings 20 cm apart for the dwarf bedding types. Water regularly until well established. Liquid feeds of soluble fertiliser at intervals of ten to fourteen days will promote more rapid growth, especially towards flowering time.

Varieties

'Strawberry Sundae' is a delightful dwarf bedding begonia with dense compact growth. It is covered in flowers in all but the frosty months of the year. Flower colours include dark and light reds, pinks of various shades and white.

Tuberous

Tuberous begonias are usually grown in pots or in shadehouses. They make beautiful pot plants and can be raised from seed or grown from bulbs. Showy tuberous begonias often have double flowers in a very wide range of colours. Tubers are planted during winter and spring.

BELLIS (ENGLISH DAISY)

Although perennial, these hardy daisies are best treated as annuals and should be sown from fresh seed each autumn. They are very attractive and make a splendid edging plant with their fully double blooms carried on stems up to 15 cm high.

They prefer open sunlight, but grow quite well in semi-shade. The plants are adapted to a wide range of soils but respond to good soil structure, so it is worthwhile adding organic

matter and a pre-planting fertiliser when preparing the bed. In northern areas the seeds should be sown in autumn, but in cold districts you can sow seed in spring too.

Raise seedlings in seed beds, trays or boxes as described in Chapter 7, covering the seed with seed-raising mixture. Transplant seedlings 10–15 cm apart each way. Give them ample water during dry weather and keep down weeds by shallow cultivation. This is important, as the plants are small and could easily be choked by weeds. When the first flower buds appear, give the plants liquid feeds of a soluble fertiliser. This will promote flowering over a long period. Cut off all faded flowers regularly.

BELLS OF IRELAND (MOLUCELLA)

Bells of Ireland is also known as molucella or molucca balm. It is an attractive bedding or accent plant with closely packed, pale-green, bell-shaped flowers (bracts) borne on stems 60 cm long. The stems are much in demand for modern flower arrangements. Sow seed in autumn or spring, direct in the garden, because seedlings do not transplant easily. Sow a few seeds in clumps spaced 20–30 cm apart and cover with seed-raising mix. Thin each clump to the strongest one or two seedlings. The plants are very adaptable to different soil types and need little attention apart from regular watering.

Fibrous-rooted begonias come in a range of leaf and flower colours.

BRACHYCOME

See Swan River daisy.

CALCEOLARIA

Calceolarias make very attractive pot plants for spring flowering or short-term indoor use. The plants are excellent for greenhouses (in cold climates), but are not really suitable for outdoor planting. They are rather particular in their soil and temperature requirements and care must be taken to grow them successfully. In mild climates they can be grown in a greenhouse with moderate warmth during the flowering period.

In temperate climates, sow the seed from mid-summer to early autumn, but in cold districts seed can be sown in both spring and summer and the plants grown successfully. Raise seedlings in seed boxes, trays or punnets of seed-raising mix. Sow the seed on the surface, barely covering it with a sprinkling of sand or sifted compost, but firm the soil down. Water gently with a very fine spray or by standing the box or punnet in a dish of water until moisture seeps to the surface.

Transfer young seedlings from the box or punnet into 7–10 cm pots and as they grow larger move them into larger pots, with a final planting into pots about 20 cm in diameter. When the plants are finally growing strongly, give them weak liquid feeds of soluble fertiliser. Calceolarias resent excessive heat and need only moderate warmth at the flowering period.

CALENDULA
(ENGLISH MARIGOLD)

Calendula is another flower which has become very popular with the development of superior modern strains. This improvement has been possible due to the efforts of plant breeders who have developed and selected plants for vigour, flower size, colour and quality. Calendulas are hardy and easy to grow. In temperate climates, plants come into bloom during the winter months, provided sowings are made early enough. Calendulas grow best in fertile, well-drained soil but succeed on a variety of soil types. They prefer an open, sunny position but must be watered regularly during dry weather. Sow seed any time from January to April, or to June in warmer areas.

Seed can be sown directly in rows, or in clumps in the garden bed, or the seedlings can be raised in seed beds or boxes for transplanting. Whichever method you use, cover the seed to a depth of 12 mm with seed-raising mixture. Transplant when seedlings are large enough to handle easily. It is better to have them on the large side rather than too small. Whether sowing directly or transplanting, always apply a pre-planting fertiliser to the bed when preparing the soil. This will improve the vigour of the plants and increase the size of the flowers. Remove spent blooms to prolong flowering, and keep down weeds by shallow cultivation.

Rust is the most serious disease of calendulas and can be prevented by regular spraying with fungicide. (See Chapter 6.) Badly affected plants should be removed and burnt.

Varieties

'Pacific Beauty' is a delightful tall strain. It reaches 60 cm and the colour range includes some lovely pastel shades. 'Honey Babe' is a dwarf variety suitable for mass plantings and rockeries. The colours include yellow, gold, orange and shades between. 'Bronze Babe' grows to about 40 cm and is a free-flowering compact plant with a strong main colour of yellow or orange with a bronze highlight on the underside of the petal.

Calceolaria thrive best in warm conditions.

CALIFORNIAN POPPY (ESCHSCHOLTZIA)

This is another addition to the list of sun-loving plants with brightly coloured flowers which thrive in warm summer months. Seed can be sown in spring and summer in both temperate and cool climates. You can sow seed direct in the garden or raise seedlings for transplanting. With either method, cover seed lightly with seed-raising mix and keep damp until seedlings emerge. The seedlings are thinned or transplanted to 30 cm apart. Keep down weeds by shallow cultivation and give liquid feeds of soluble fertilisers as plants commence to flower.

CANDYTUFT

There are two distinct types of candytuft. The most popular is called *Iberis umbellata*, and carries its flowers at the top of the stem. The second is called *I. coronaria* or hyacinth-flowered candytuft. It produces a mass of pure white florets, which resemble the hyacinth flower. Candytuft grows well in most soils, but it must be well drained. The plants prefer a sunny situation, sheltered from strong winds. Plants must not be crowded because they become too spindly and flowers are poor. In temperate climates, sow seeds from autumn to early winter. In cold districts, seed can be sown in spring too.

Prepare the bed well with organic matter plus a pre-planting fertiliser at one-third of a cup per square metre. Seed can be sown direct in the garden in clumps 20–30 cm apart, or seedlings can be raised in seed boxes or punnets for transplanting at the same distance. The hyacinth-flowered varieties can be spaced more closely at 20 cm apart.

Candytuft is an easy plant to grow. Keep down weeds by shallow cultivation and give liquid feeds of soluble fertiliser when plants are establishing.

Varieties

'Fairy Mixed' has massed heads in a wide range of pastel colours covering the compact plants. 'White Flash' has a profusion of white flowers.

CANTERBURY BELLS

Canterbury bells form a spire of large 'cup and saucer' flowers with the texture of fine porcelain. They are excellent for garden display in clumps or drifts and for cut flowers in spring. Colours range from dark blue to mauve, rose, soft pink and white. Sow seed in autumn in seed boxes or punnets, just covering with seed-raising mix; firm down gently. Keep soil moist until seedlings emerge – usually in two to three weeks. Transplant seedlings when 5–7 cm tall into the garden bed, spaced 30 cm apart. Give liquid feeds of soluble fertiliser when flower buds appear.

CARNATION

Like most garden flowers, this fragrant favourite had humble beginnings. It was introduced to England in a wild form about the sixteenth century, but it was not until about 1900 that the Perpetual Flowering types were developed.

In New Zealand we are mainly interested in two types (either of which can be grown from seed): the Chabaud (bedding carnation) and the Perpetual Flowering. Chabaud is the most widely known and is easily recognised by its deeply serrated or fringed petals and a strong, clove-like scent. Perpetual Flowering types are the source from which most named varieties are obtained. It should be understood, however, that named varieties of carnation will not breed true to type from seed. If you require these named varieties, they must be started from cuttings or purchased as plants from nurseries.

When starting carnations from seed it is best to raise seedlings in beds, boxes or punnets using seed-raising mix. Germination may be slow and rather erratic. For this reason the seed bed or containers need close attention for ten to fourteen days – perhaps longer – until seedlings emerge. Carnation seed can be sown direct but it is difficult to give the germinating seeds the same attention. Seed can be sown at almost any time of the year but spring or autumn are regarded as the best periods.

Whether carnations are started from seed, cuttings or nursery plants, the requirements for soil, cultivation and general care are the same. Carnations prefer an open position exposed to full sunlight and resent being crowded by other plants or shrubs. It is best if they are protected from westerly and southerly winds too. They will grow in a wide range of soils from heavy (but well structured) to light sandy soils. On heavy soils add organic matter and sand to improve both structure and texture. On sandy soils add organic matter in the form of animal manure, garden compost or peat moss to improve structure and increase water-holding capacity. Manure, compost, peat moss or any other materials for soil improvement should be dug into the soil some weeks beforehand. At the same time lime and a pre-planting fertiliser such as Gro-Plus Complete Plant Food should be added.

In areas with acid soil, mix in some horticultural lime before planting. As a general guide, use one handful of lime per square metre on sandy soils but double this amount on heavier soils.

Hint

Sweet peas come in different flowering types. Winter flowering seed should be sown in February and grown under cover; spring seed should be sown in the open garden in April or May. Summer flowering seed should be sown between July and September. Check seed packets to determine variety.

KEITH HAMMETT
PLANT BREEDER

The rate for mixed fertiliser is the same for both soil types: one-third of a cup per square metre. Dig the bed to a depth of 10 cm to thoroughly mix the soil, moisture-holding materials, lime and fertiliser. Leave for a few weeks and then gently break the surface soil a few days before planting, to destroy any weeds. The bed should contain sufficient nutrients to feed the plants through the main growing period.

Just before flowering, scatter another ration of mixed fertiliser around the plants at the rate of three tablespoons per square metre. Alternatively, give liquid feeds of soluble fertiliser. Bad drainage is probably the greatest enemy of carnations and the plants

are likely to be attacked by root rot and collar rot diseases. Beds should be raised above the surface – about 10 cm for light soil and 15 cm for heavy soil.

Short stocky plants are the best. Space plants 30–40 cm apart. When planting out, keep the lower leaves well out of the ground so that no more than 12 mm of soil covers the top of the roots. To avoid weeds, keep the soil surface well stirred, but not too deeply.

The greatest number of good blooms come from compact, sturdy plants. You can encourage sturdiness by nipping back the early flowering stems regularly. When the plants are about 15 cm tall, pinch them back to induce side shoots, which in turn are pinched back when they reach the same height. When plants have developed eight to twelve shoots (depending on the growth habit of the variety), allow these to send up flower stems. When picking flowers, always break them off near the base of the plant. Each main stem should bear only one bloom if first-class flowers are desired. This means the removal of all side buds growing from the leaf axils to leave the main bud only at the top of the stem. In some varieties, buds will have a tendency to burst at the calyx (the green collar beneath the flower). You can prevent this by fitting small rubber bands around them.

After about twelve months of flowering, plants may begin to look straggly. But if they still appear healthy and vigorous, cut them back hard to within 5 cm of the centre stem. With normal attention, these plants should produce a further flush of blooms as good as the previous flowering. In some soils, especially light ones, plants which have flowered abundantly may not be worth this treatment so it is best to renew them – either from seedlings or cuttings taken in autumn.

Pests and diseases are not a serious problem in growing carnations. Aphids and thrips are the most common pests but can be controlled by spraying with insecticides. Rust and collar rot are the most serious fungus diseases. For control of both pests and diseases see Chapter 6.

Varieties

'Fragrance' is a dwarf strain which has similar flowers to the Chabaud type. This variety

Red is the classic celosia colour, but other shades are available.

does not need stakes for support and cut flowers have good lasting quality. 'Chabaud Gems' is a beautiful mixture of fringed and plain-edge types in a good colour range.

CELOSIA

This annual bedding plant revels in a hot sunny situation. Plants are susceptible to frost and seed must be sown into warm soil in spring and early summer. Plants grow well in almost any garden soil but prefer a soil to which organic matter plus a ration of mixed fertiliser has been added. Seed can be sown direct in the garden in rows or clumps, or seedlings can be raised in seed beds, boxes or punnets for transplanting. Thin seedlings or transplant to 20–30 cm apart.

Celosia is an easy plant to grow. Water plants regularly, especially in hot weather, and give liquid feeds of soluble fertilisers as flowering commences. Destroy any weeds by shallow cultivation only to avoid damaging surface roots. A mulch of compost around the plants discourages weeds and conserves moisture.

Varieties

'Painted Ostrich' grows to about 75 cm with brilliantly coloured plumes. 'Forest Fire' is a semi-dwarf variety to 90 cm tall with spectacular scarlet plumes and contrasting dark foliage. It is an excellent variety for background borders or for mass bedding. 'Flamenco Feather' is an unusual variety of celosia, with spikes of soft-pink flowers that fade as they age.

CENTAUREA

See Cornflower.

CHRYSANTHEMUM

The most widely grown species of chrysanthemum is *Chrysanthemum indicum.* This is a perennial which can be grown from seed, although named varieties must be propagated by root divisions or cuttings taken in July or August. Shasta daisy (*C. maximum*) is another popular perennial type. There are also annual chrysanthemums, of which the small, white-flowered, yellow-centred star daisy (*C. paludosum*) is one of the most popular. The colourful painted daisy (*C. tricolor*) is another widely grown annual.

The perennial variety of chrysanthemum (*C. indicum*) includes a very wide range of flower types: decorative single, semi-double and fully double. It is the source of all modern named and exhibition varieties. Named varieties must be propagated vegetatively from root divisions or cuttings. Plants are usually available from nurseries in October or November. Seed of perennial chrysanthemums will produce plants with a variety of flower forms and colours – an interesting (and economical) way of growing them.

Chrysanthemums grow well in a variety of soils, but both heavy and light soils are improved with garden compost plus the addition of a mixed fertiliser at the rate of one-third of a cup per square metre. It is a good idea to dig the soil over two or three times before planting, to bring it to an open, friable condition.

Chrysanthemums dislike poorly drained soil. Raising the beds above the surrounding level is probably the easiest method of ensuring good drainage. Plant them in a warm, sunny position, avoiding shady sites and those exposed to wind.

Spring is the best time for sowing seed. Raise the seedlings in seed beds, boxes or punnets as described in Chapter 7. Make up a good seed bed soil, sow the seed and cover with a sprinkling of seed-raising mix about 6 mm deep. Keep damp until seedlings emerge in ten to fourteen days. Seedlings are ready to transplant when 7–10 cm high.

For exhibition, space plants 100 cm apart, but for general garden display or cut flowers this distance can be reduced to 75 cm. Firm the soil well around the roots of each plant and water well. Continue regular watering until plants are established. Keep the plants growing strongly by giving liquid feeds of soluble fertiliser and cultivate the soil surface regularly to control weeds. Liquid feeds can be discontinued when the flower buds show colour.

Hint

Coleus plants make wonderful fillers and add a subtropical look to any summer garden. Remember they are frost-tender.
DIANA SELBY
LANDSCAPE ARCHITECT

When setting out to grow chrysanthemums, management practices will largely determine the habit of growth, the number of flower stems and the size and quality of the flowers. 'Stopping' consists of breaking out the growing tip of the plant to promote three or four lateral stems to develop. This is done when the plants are about 20 cm tall. Lateral stems can also be stopped when 5–10 cm tall to induce further laterals and a bushy plant. 'Disbudding' (the removal of surplus buds) influences the size and quality of the flowers. If you wish to have very large blooms, disbud to leave the centre or top bud only. Small-flowered types of chrysanthemum are usually not disbudded.

The eight main varieties of perennial chrysanthemums are: Large Flowered Exhibition, which has giant, waratah-shaped blooms to 15 cm diameter with broad, in-curving petals; Decorative, which has similar flowers to the Exhibition type but rather smaller; Spider or Quilled, on which the petals are loose and finely rolled or quilled; Anemone-centred, which has a tightly packed centre and is surrounded by a row of outer petals often in contrasting colours; Singles,

having daisy-like flowers with a distinct centre and three to five rows of petals; Pompon or Button, which displays clusters of small, double, anemone-like flowers 3–5 cm in diameter; Cascade, which has small, single blooms on trailing stems giving a cascade effect (suitable for pots, troughs and window boxes); and Charm, consisting of compact plants to 60 cm tall with masses of small daisy-like flowers for massed display.

Exhibition, Decorative and all but the low-growing types of chrysanthemums (Anemone-centred, Pompon, Cascade and Charm) need staking by the time buds form. It is best to surround the plants with two or three light stakes and tie garden twine around them at intervals of about 30 cm.

Varieties

The following varieties can be grown from seed. 'Autumn Brilliance' is a perennial strain with a bright colour range of single and double flowers in late autumn. Star daisy (*C. paludosum*) is another dwarf annual chrysanthemum with small, daisy-like white flowers with yellow centres. Plants grow to 30 cm and are covered in blooms which are excellent for cut flowers. 'Snowlands' is an improved form of star daisy. Sow spring or autumn. Painted daisy (*C. tricolor*) also grows readily from seed.

CINERARIA

Cinerarias are among the few garden flowers which prefer semi-shade. The plants can be grown in shady aspects in the open garden or in pots in a shadehouse. The pots can be moved indoors for decoration when flowering commences.

Modern varieties have a much wider colour range than older varieties, and both large-flowered, tall types and compact, dwarf types are available.

Sow seed during the late summer and autumn for flowering in late winter and early spring. The seeds are quite small and should be sown in seed boxes or punnets. Lightly cover with seed-raising mixture and water gently.

To grow strong seedlings it is a good idea to prick them out as soon as they are large enough to handle into 5–7 cm pots, or into larger boxes or trays, spacing them about

10 cm apart. If you wish to grow the plants on in pots, transfer them to 15 cm pots and finally to 20 cm pots for flowering. The soil for potting should be an open, friable mixture which drains easily. Add a ration of mixed fertiliser to each batch of soil. As the plants grow, give regular liquid feeds of a soluble fertiliser, especially towards flowering time. The main insect pests of cinerarias are aphids and leafminer. Spray regularly with insecticide to control them. (See Chapter 6.) Cinerarias are frost sensitive and in cool climates should be protected from cold.

Varieties

The best dwarf cineraria strain is 'Starship', which has medium-sized flowers on compact plants. It is excellent for growing in pots. 'Exhibition Strain' is a taller variety with a mass of larger flowers held above a compact, robust bush.

CLEOME

See Spider Flower.

COCKSCOMB

Cockscomb is an annual bedding plant, very similar to celosia but with flowers that have velvet-coated, twisted crests (which look somewhat like a rooster's comb) instead of feathery plumes. See Celosia for cultivation notes.

COLEUS

Coleus has brilliant, coloured foliage and is an ideal plant for growing in pots in a shadehouse or in shaded parts of the garden. Although they prefer semi-shade, the plants need a warm, sheltered position and are very susceptible to frost.

Sow seed in boxes or punnets in spring or early summer using the soil mixture described in Chapter 7. The seeds are quite

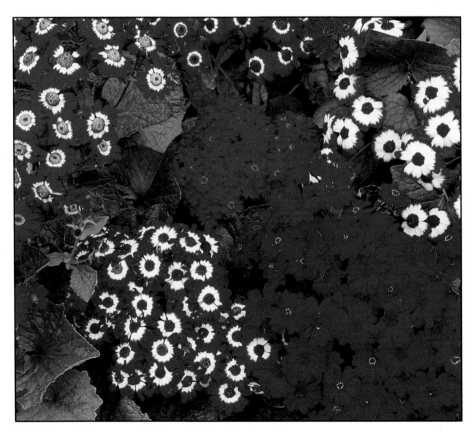

Cinerarias will tolerate semi-shade conditions.

small, so cover lightly with seed-raising mixture. Transplant seedlings when 5 cm high and space them 30 cm apart in the garden. If growing the plants in pots, select seedlings with the best colouring – this can be determined when the plants are quite small. The stems of seedlings are soft and tender so handle them carefully to prevent damage. When the plants are established, water regularly so that the soil is always damp but not wet. Pinch back main shoots to encourage lateral branching. Give liquid feeds of soluble fertiliser every seven to ten days to promote large leaves and to intensify the colours. Pinch out any flower buds to prolong leaf growth.

COLUMBINE
See Aquilegia.

COREOPSIS
This is a very hardy daisy that flowers during the warm weather. It comes in both annual and perennial forms and will provide hot colour from mid-spring to autumn. 'Summer Glow' is a perennial coreopsis that has yellow daisy flowers with dark-red centres. Plants need full sun, good drainage and should be watered sparingly. Flowers are excellent for picking. Remove faded blooms to promote further flowering.

CORNFLOWER (CENTAUREA)
Centaurea cyanus is the well-known blue cornflower. Seed mixtures also contain other colours: rose, maroon, lavender and white. Cornflowers grow well in temperate climates, needing good drainage and a well-structured and fertilised soil. Plant them in a position which receives morning sun. Sow seed from early autumn until early winter in prepared seed boxes or punnets. Cover the seed with seed-raising mixture and water gently. Transplant seedlings to the garden and space them 40–50 cm apart. Cultivate regularly to control weeds and give soluble fertilisers every ten to fourteen days after plants show flower buds.

'Mystic Blue' is a good example of the traditional blue cornflower. 'Double Mixed' is the best mixed colour. Plants grow to 60 cm and display a wide range of flower colours.

COSMOS
These tall, colourful plants make an excellent background for low-growing annuals and supply plenty of cut flowers for indoor decoration. Cosmos are easy plants to grow and need little attention. Newer varieties are much improved in both flower form and colour range. The flowers, with their fine colours and lasting quality, make cosmos well worth growing in any garden. Cosmos will grow on a wide range of soils but respond best to well-drained, friable soils with a mixed fertiliser such as Gro-Plus Complete Plant Food added. The plants need a sunny position and because of their height should be sheltered from strong winds.

You can start sowing seed in spring and continue through to summer. Seed sown as late as January in northern areas will produce plants which will flower before cold weather or frost arrives.

It is best to raise seedlings in seed beds, boxes or punnets for transplanting into the garden, but as the seeds are quite large you can sow a few seeds direct in clumps spaced 40–50 cm apart in the garden and thin to the strongest one or two seedlings. When transplanting seedlings space them at the same distance apart. Keep the soil between the plants well cultivated and in hot weather spread a mulch of compost over it to keep the roots cool and moist. Staking plants is rarely needed because when they are grown close together they support each other.

Varieties

'Sonata Mixed' and 'Sensation' are similar, with large rose and crimson flowers with a sprinkling of white. Plants grow to a height of about 90 cm and are highly recommended. The flowers of 'Seashells' have unusual recurved edges on the petals, creating a fluted effect.

CYCLAMEN
Delicate flowers in white, pinks, mauves and reds make cyclamen one of the most popular plants for winter and early spring flowering. They can be grown in an open, friable soil in a semi-shaded position in the garden but are more often grown in pots. They do well indoors but need a well-lit, well-ventilated but draught-free spot – preferably with an hour or two of sunlight each morning.

The plants form a corm or bulb and can be carried on from year to year. Corms more than two or three years old, however, are best replaced by new plants grown from seed. Sow seed from late summer to early autumn in a seed box or punnets using a soil mixture made up of garden loam or peat moss and coarse sand. (See Chapter 7.) Stand containers in water until moisture seeps to the surface, allow to drain for at least a day and press the seeds into the damp soil mixture to a depth of 6 mm, spacing them 2–3 cm apart.

Seedlings emerge over a period of four to six weeks. Prick them out when small into individual 5–7 cm pots using a similar soil mix, and transfer them to larger pots as they grow. Give liquid feeds of Thrive (at half-strength) every three or four weeks. Water regularly by standing the pots in water until soil is wetted and then allow to drain. Do not overwater – plants will benefit from short spells of dryness.

Buds form in autumn and respond to regular liquid feeds until flowering ceases in late spring. Then, as leaves turn yellow, reduce the water supply and tip pots on their sides for final drying. The corm or bulb which has formed during the flowering period can remain in the pot or can be taken out and stored in damp sand or peat moss before repotting in late summer. Water sparingly until new growth starts.

DAHLIA

Named in honour of Dr Andreas Dahl, a Swedish botanist, this popular flower is a native of Mexico and found its way to the Botanic Gardens, Madrid, in 1789. At that time, only three kinds of flowers were known: a double purple, a single rose colour and a single red. Tubers from each of these were sent to Kew Gardens, London, but they did not survive. Some years later, another lot brought from France was grown successfully. Today there is a tremendous array of dahlias, both in colour range and flower form. They are easy to grow and, given reasonable attention, will produce a mass of blooms for many weeks in late summer and autumn.

You can grow dahlias from seed or from tubers of named varieties which are usually available in late spring.

> ### Hint
> It is important not to plant dahlia tubers too early. Wait until the soil has warmed up, as this reduces the chances of the tubers rotting or suffering frost damage. Plant them from September onwards in the north, and October onwards in the south. Dahlias will flower right through summer — great reward for little effort.
> KEITH HAMMETT
> PLANT BREEDER

There is a lot of interest in growing them from seed because there is always the possibility of obtaining an unusual variation in colour or flower from the plants you grow. Plants will flower within three or four months after seedlings are planted out and will continue flowering for many weeks. During this time, the plants are forming small tubers. Save tubers of the best plants for replanting next season. Named varieties of dahlias will not grow true to type from seed.

Dahlias prefer a sunny position which is sheltered on the southern and western sides. They need a well-drained soil with an open, friable structure. In sandy soils add organic matter in the form of compost, leaf mould or peat moss. Animal manure is also suitable but too much of it will produce excessive leaf growth at the expense of flowers. If the bed for dahlias has been in constant cultivation, you will need to dig this over before planting and add well-rotted organic matter at the same time. Do not use lawn clippings which have not been decomposed. When soil has been idle for a season or two, dig it roughly in winter and again just before planting in spring. Very deep digging is not necessary. Spade depth is ample in most soils. A ration of lime is recommended if the soil is acid. Apply no more than two-thirds of a cup per square metre on heavy soils. A light scattering of a mixed fertiliser will be beneficial.

Hint

Blue and white delphiniums planted in a perennial bed provide stunning structure, form and colour. They also make a perfect companion for red roses.

TERRY DOWDESWELL
HORTICULTURALIST

Sow seeds in spring or early summer – plants from early sowings will flower in January and those from late sowings in autumn; autumn blooms will appear fresher and not be bleached by hot sun. Use seed boxes, trays or punnets, covering the seeds with about 12 mm compost or seed-raising mixture. Seedlings may take two to four weeks to emerge so keep the containers damp for this length of time. Transplant seedlings when 5–7 cm tall.

Growing plants should be supported by a stake to protect them against wind damage. After planting out, water regularly to make sure that the soil does not dry out. Slugs and snails should be controlled as soon as young shoots appear. When the plants are about 30 cm tall, apply a ration of mixed fertiliser, giving about 50 g to each plant. Spread the fertiliser in a circle around the plant, rake it in and water thoroughly. When the buds appear, give liquid feeds of soluble fertilisers every ten to fourteen days to promote large blooms and to prolong the flowering period. It is important to remove all spent flowers regularly to encourage further bud formation.

Flowers for indoor decoration should be picked in the cool of the evening and the stem ends dipped in boiling water for about 30 seconds. Take care that the rising steam does not scald the blooms. Do this by tilting the container slightly or covering them with a double thickness of newspaper wrapped around the stems.

If you wish to propagate dahlias from tubers, these should not be lifted until the plants have completely died down – usually early in winter. Dig them with a garden fork, taking care not to damage the crown and tubers attached to it. The lifted crowns can be stored in the shade under trees or in a corner of the garden shed during winter. As warm weather starts in spring, tubers will form 'eyes' or shoots. Cut between the shoots to leave some stem tissue surrounding the shoot and with one or two tubers attached. Set the tubers so that the root end is covered by about 10 cm of soil but the shoot is at soil level.

Varieties

Like chrysanthemums, there is a wide range of dahlias, summarised as:

Decorative: Large, heavy, double flowers 15–25 cm in diameter produced on long stems; mature plants are 2 m or more tall.

Hybrid Cactus: Flowers with narrow, curled petals but smaller than Decorative types; plants grow to 1.5 m tall.

Charm: Rather smaller flowers than Cactus dahlias, usually in pastel colours, free-flowering; plants grow to 1.2 m tall.

Collerette: Flowers have a distinct centre with space between petals; 60–75 cm tall.

Nymphaea or Water Lily: Daisy-like flowers with space between petals, pastel shades with one colour fading into another; plants 60–75 cm tall.

Paeony-flowered: Small semi-double flowers in soft colours.

Pompon Small: Tightly packed flowers in a wide colour range.

All tall-growing dahlias need some support. Place three stakes about 15 cm apart around the base of the plant. Spread these outward so that they are about 30 cm apart at the top. Encircle with twine at 40 cm height and again at 80 cm. Then join the centre of each tie to form a second triangle and encourage the branches to grow naturally through the crossing sections. As with the chrysanthemums, stopping (that is, pinching out the growing point) and disbudding are often practised in the tall-growing dahlias, but this is rarely necessary with dwarf bedding types.

The large-flowered, tall-growing types are the Decorative, Hybrid Cactus and Charm Dahlias. These are grown from tubers available from nurseries as named varieties. Both types may reach a height of 150 cm or more so need to be planted about 1 m apart. The smaller dahlias usually grow to 60–75 cm tall and can be spaced about 50 cm apart.

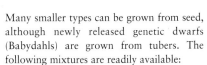

Many smaller types can be grown from seed, although newly released genetic dwarfs (Babydahls) are grown from tubers. The following mixtures are readily available:

"Pompom Mixed': A wide colour range of golf ball-size flowers, some of which are two-tone. Ideal for cut flowers.

'Cinderella': This relatively short variety grows on a compact bush to about 40 cm in height. It has a delightful colour range including pastels, reds and bicolours. Ideal for a massed border or containers.

'Silk Symphony': Brightly coloured single flowers that sit on top of 1.2 m tall stems. They give a long lasting garden display.

DELPHINIUM

Delphiniums have few equals for tall, stately spikes of flowers in rich shades of colour. Delphiniums are best treated as annuals in warm–temperate climates but in cold districts the plants will last for several years, providing the summer months are mild. Delphiniums prefer a well-drained, fertile soil with plenty of organic matter and a ration of mixed fertiliser added.

Prepare the bed well to have the soil in friable condition for transplanting the seedlings. In temperate climates you can sow seed in autumn, winter and early spring, but in cold districts restrict sowing to autumn and spring only. Once established, delphiniums are very hardy and tolerate frost well, but in very cold districts seedlings from autumn sowings should be protected during the first winter.

Sow seed in a good soil mixture in seed boxes, trays or punnets. Cover them well because seeds must be dark for successful germination. Germination is often slow and seedlings may take three to four weeks to emerge. Transplant seedlings, spacing them about 50 cm apart each way. As the plants grow, keep the soil well cultivated to control weeds. During summer months a mulch of compost will prevent evaporation and keep the roots cool. Delphiniums are gross feeders and will respond dramatically to dressings of liquid fertiliser at regular two to three weekly intervals.

Varieties
'Pacific Giants' is a magnificent, tall hybrid

variety. The giant flower spikes are closely packed, with satin-textured blooms in glorious colours which range from white through shades of pink and lavender to pale-blue, mid-blue, royal blue and purple. 'Belladonna' has mixed single flowers with a slightly looser arrangement on the stems than 'Pacific Giants'.

Dwarf delphiniums, like 'Blue Pygmy', are small growers (to about 25 cm) that produce intensely blue flowers.

DIANTHUS

Dianthus is a close relative of carnation and its sowing times and cultivation requirements are the same (see Carnation in this chapter). The plants are possibly more adaptable to a wider variety of soils and they tolerate very

The stately spires of delphiniums

dry conditions. They make excellent rockery and edging plants and produce large quantities of fragrant flowers in reds, mauves, pinks and white. Dianthus is usually treated as an annual, but if the plants are cut back after the first flowering and given liquid feeds of soluble fertiliser they will flower again in the second year.

Varieties

Dianthus 'Peppermint Pinks' is a delightful dwarf variety growing to 10 cm high, excellent for rockeries and low borders. Fairy pinks or pinks (*Dianthus plumarius*) are grown in the same way. The plants persist from year to year and are useful as perennial borders or rockery plants. Flowers are single or semi-double. Double pinks grow to 20 cm and produce quantites of fragrant double flowers in mixed colours. Sweet William (*Dianthus barbatus*) is another close relative.

ENGLISH DAISY

See Bellis.

ENGLISH MARIGOLD

See Calendula.

ESCHSCHOLTZIA

See Californian Poppy.

EVERLASTING DAISY (ACROCLINIUM)

Everlastings are always handy for indoor decoration because they can be dried and kept without water for many weeks. Everlasting daisies will grow on a wide range of soils but need good drainage and an open sunny position. A ration of mixed fertiliser such as Gro-Plus Complete Plant Food will promote vigorous growth and increase the size of flowers. Everlasting daisies can be sown in both autumn and spring.

It is best to sow seeds direct into the garden where the plants are to flower. Mark out shallow rows 12 mm deep, sprinkle seed sparsely along them and cover with seed-raising mix. Thin seedlings to 20–30 cm apart.

Alternatively, sow a few seeds in clumps at this distance and cover as before. Keep the soil moist until the seedlings are well established. The plants usually need very little attention apart from regular watering and shallow cultivation to destroy weeds. Take care not to cultivate too closely to the plants. When buds start to form, apply a side dressing of mixed fertiliser and water in. Alternatively, give liquid feeds of soluble fertiliser every ten to fourteen days. If flowers are required for indoor decoration, cut them in full bloom, tie in bunches and hang head downwards for a few weeks until the stems are dry. See also Strawflower.

FAIRY PINKS

See Dianthus.

FORGET-ME-NOT

Forget-me-not is a very popular flower for edging, borders and rockeries. Although the flowers are traditionally blue with yellow centres, there are also pink and white varieties. The plants thrive in moist, semi-shaded situations with morning sun for a few hours each day. An open, friable soil is needed to grow them to perfection. Sow seed in late summer or early autumn in seed boxes, trays or punnets. Cover the seed very lightly with seed-raising mix as described in Chapter 7. Seed may be slow to germinate and seedlings may take three to four weeks to emerge. Keep the containers damp but not wet for this period. Transplant seedlings when large enough to handle and space them 20–30 cm apart. Although best treated as annuals, forget-me-nots will very often seed naturally and new seedlings will appear each year.

FOXGLOVE

Although foxgloves are really biennials, some of the newer varieties will flower the first year and can be treated as annuals. They have exquisite, bell-shaped blooms in cream, salmon, purple and rose colours. The flattened tubular flowers open gradually from the bottom to the top of the spike (which usually reaches about 1 m). After the main spike has finished flowering, it can be cut off and smaller spikes will develop from the base. Foxgloves prefer moist soil and a semi-shaded garden situation. Sow the fine seed direct into the garden position, in soil that has been well prepared with some complete fertiliser and old compost. Cover very lightly with

Foxgloves look particularly good in cottage gardens.

seed-raising mix. 'Foxy' is the most widely grown foxglove variety.

GAILLARDIA

There are both annual and perennial species of this plant and each has its own special merits. The annual types flower quickly from seed but the perennials have a longer flowering period and can be cut back several times. You can sow seed of the annual types either in autumn or spring in most districts; the perennial is best sown in autumn. Seed can be sown in seed boxes or punnets and the seedlings transplanted, spacing them 30 cm apart each way. Alternatively, sow a few seeds direct in clumps at the same distance apart and thin to the strongest two or three seedlings.

There is an annual species with flowers in shades of yellow, gold and crimson. Plants grow quickly from seed to a height of 40 cm and flower throughout the summer. The perennial gaillardia (*G. grandiflora*) has larger single flowers in shades of gold, orange and scarlet, many with contrasting colours in the centre.

GAZANIA

This dwarf perennial plant with slender, leathery leaves and daisy-like flowers in shades of cream, yellow, pink and mahogany is a native of South Africa. It revels in full sunlight and does well in dry situations. Excellent for banks, rockeries and low borders. Established plants can be divided after flowering in spring and summer. Sow seeds in boxes or punnets in spring or summer and transplant seedlings when 5 cm tall, spacing them 20 cm apart. Give liquid feeds of soluble fertiliser when buds appear in spring.

GERANIUM

Geraniums are ideal perennial plants for pots, window boxes, or massed flower displays in beds and borders, especially in sunny situations. Plants of named varieties can be purchased from nurseries or started from cuttings, but geraniums can also be grown from seed. Sow seeds in boxes or punnets in spring or early summer – remember, the seeds need a temperature of 25°C to germinate.

Fill the containers with seed-raising mix. Scatter seeds on the surface, cover lightly and press down firmly. Water gently or stand the container in water until moisture seeps to the surface. Ensure the soil is kept moist until seedlings emerge.

Transplant seedlings when large enough to handle into pots filled with a similar soil mixture and grow on until well established for transplanting into tubs or the open garden. When planting for massed colour in the garden, space plants 40–50 cm apart. Geraniums, or more correctly pelargoniums, are very adaptable perennials. Provided the plants are in full sunlight they will thrive in both warm and cool climates. They withstand light frosts. The soil in which they grow must be well-drained but not overly rich. Too much nitrogen or animal manure tends to promote excessive leaf growth at the expense of flowers.

Geraniums may become straggly as they grow, so regular pruning is needed to keep the plants compact and to encourage more flowers. Light pruning can be done after each flush of flowers during the warmer months, followed by a general pruning and 'clean up' in autumn when flowering is over. Vigorous stems should be cut back by one- or two-thirds, making the cut just above a node or

GROWING YOUR GARDEN

joint with a bud facing outwards. At the same time, remove dead or diseased wood and any inward-growing or crossing stems. When new growth starts, 'tip pruning' or 'pinching out' may be necessary to encourage further branching.

Hint

Prolong the flowering season of poppies and sweet peas by removing blooms before they fade. Never let these flowers set seed. The more you pick them, the more you get.

MARY LOVELL-SMITH
CHRISTCHURCH *PRESS*

Geraniums are very easily propagated by cuttings, which are best taken in autumn. Both tip cuttings and stem cuttings develop roots easily. Take the cuttings with two to four nodes or joints and make the cut just below the lowest one. With tip cuttings, remove all but the top leaves. With stem cuttings, remove lower leaves and retain the top leaf only, which may be cut in half to reduce loss of moisture by transpiration. Cuttings may be planted directly in the garden if the soil is crumbly, but it is more reliable to place them 4–5 cm deep in pots filled with coarse sand or a mixture of coarse sand (three parts) and peat moss (one part). Most of these cuttings will develop roots within three or four weeks of planting.

GERBERA

Gerberas, which are naturally adapted to hot, sunny conditions, do well in temperate climates too, providing they are grown in a sunny position sheltered from strong winds. The dainty flowers come in a wide range of colours and are excellent for indoor decoration. Gerberas are adapted to light soils but will grow well on heavier ones provided the soils have been improved by the addition of organic matter and sand. The soil must be open and well-drained and, because they are susceptible to a condition known as 'crown rot', it is best to grow them on beds raised at least 20 cm above the surrounding level. On acid soils, gerberas respond to an application of lime. Mixed fertiliser can be added when the bed is being prepared.

Sow seed in spring or early summer when

A mixture of cottage garden favourites (including foxgloves, irises and columbines) planted under established trees.

the weather is warm. Prepare an open, friable soil mixture to use in seed boxes, trays or punnets as described in Chapter 8. A mixture with rather more sand than usual (say, one part sand and one part other materials) is recommended. Press the pointed end of the seed into the surface of the seed-raising mix, and press firmly so the seeds make contact with the dark, damp soil.

Seed containers must be kept in a warm spot until seedlings emerge – usually about two or three weeks. The soil in the containers can be kept warm if they are kept indoors and covered with glass or a clear plastic bag. The cover should be removed when seedlings appear and the container transferred to a warm, sheltered, but shady spot in the garden.

It is best to prick out the seedlings when they are quite small. Transfer them into a larger container spaced 5 cm apart or into individual 5–7 cm pots. They can then be grown to a good size before planting in the open garden, spaced 40–50 cm apart. When planting it is important to keep the crowns well above the surface, especially on heavy soils. Soil washing into the centre of the crowns often promotes rotting.

Gerberas can be grown in the same position for two or three years. Old plants can be lifted, divided and replanted. This is best done in late summer or early autumn before cold weather sets in.

GLOBE AMARANTH

This attractive summer-flowering annual grows to a height of 30 cm and has round, clover-like, 'everlasting' flowers in rich purple. It is an adaptable plant in regard to soil but responds to good soil preparation plus added fertiliser. It is excellent for bedding, low borders or edging in a sunny position.

Sow seeds in spring or early summer in seed boxes or punnets and transplant seedlings to the garden, spaced 30 cm apart. Alternatively, sow a few seeds direct in clumps at the same distance and thin to two or three seedlings at each position. Keep the plants well watered in dry times and mulch with compost to conserve moisture and deter weeds. Give liquid feeds of soluble fertiliser when buds appear.

'Little Buddy', with masses of purple, globe-shaped blooms, grows to 20–30 cm tall and is popular. Flowers may be used fresh for indoor decoration or may be bunched and hung, head downwards, in a cool place to dry for 'everlastings'. *Gomphrena* 'Global Harmony' grows to about 60 cm with 5 cm heads of ball-shaped flowers in a mixture of purple, lilac and white.

GLOXINIA

These exquisite pot plants are ideal for growing in a glasshouse, shadehouse or fernery and flower well indoors in a well-lit position. The velvety, bell-shaped flowers have rich colours overlaid with mottling or spotted effects. Deep red, rose, violet or purple are the predominant colours overlaid with white, pink, mauve or lavender-blue markings.

Sow seed in winter or early spring; under glasshouse conditions, autumn sowing is possible. Seed is extremely small and rather

Gerberas provide great colour for a hot, sunny spot.

GROWING YOUR GARDEN

slow to germinate, so extra care is needed. Sow seed in seed trays, punnets or pots using an open, friable, rather sandy soil mixture as outlined in Chapter 7. Enclose containers in a plastic bag until seedlings emerge.

When seedlings are large enough to handle, prick them out into small individual pots and transfer to larger pots as they grow. They reach a height of 30 cm and flower in mid to late summer. Give liquid feeds of soluble fertiliser when buds appear. Small bulbs are formed during the flowering period. These can be replanted the next spring.

GODETIA

Godetias are attractive annuals which have been aptly called 'farewell to spring' because they flower late in spring, helping to bridge the gap between spring and summer flowers. The dwarf type, to 60 cm tall, has masses of single blooms on top of the plant and is more widely grown than the tall azalea-flowered type with double flowers.

The plants prefer a sunny aspect sheltered from strong winds. They will grow on a wide range of soils but tend to make too much foliage in fertile soils. Prepare the bed with a mixed fertiliser such as Gro-Plus Complete Plant Food at one-third of a cup per square metre, but avoid fertilisers high in nitrogen, along with side-dressings of water-soluble fertilisers. In most climates, sow seeds in autumn to early winter; spring sowings can be made in cold districts. You can raise seedlings in boxes or punnets for transplanting when 5–7 cm high.

Space seedlings 30 cm apart. Alternatively, sow a few seeds direct in clumps spaced at the same distance and thin to two to three seedlings at each position.

The plants tolerate dry conditions well but respond to occasional watering as they grow. Cultivate or hand-weed around the plants but take care not to disturb the rather shallow root system. 'Dwarf Mixed' is the leading variety of godetia.

GOURDS

Ornamental – see Chapter 13.

GYPSOPHILA

Gypsophila is an extremely useful plant for flower arrangements. It is also attractive grown in odd clumps in the garden. The plants need a well-prepared soil with organic matter and mixed fertiliser added. If soil is acid an application of lime is recommended, as these plants like a relatively high pH. Select a sunny but sheltered position. Seeds can be sown at almost any time of the year except in the very coldest or hottest months. By making small successive sowings you can have a continuous supply of flowers for indoor decoration. Sow seeds direct in the open garden, either in rows 20–30 cm apart or in clumps at the same distance. Cover with seed-raising mix and keep damp until seedlings emerge. Thinning the seedlings is rarely needed as plants flower well when closely spaced. This way plants support each other too.

Varieties

'Baby's Breath', with tiny, double white flowers, is the most popular for picking. 'Pink Gins' has a range of single, starry flowers in a mixture of pink, white, carmine, rose and crimson.

HELIANTHUS

See Sunflower.

HELICHRYSUM

See Strawflower.

HOLLYHOCK

Among the tallest flowers in the garden, hollyhocks are an old English favourite. The plants grow to 2–3 m or more with magnificent spikes of large, closely packed flowers. They prefer full sunlight and a well-sheltered position. In exposed situations, plants need staking or a support such as a trellis to which to tie them. Hollyhocks are adapted to both light and heavy soils but will respond best to fertile soil with organic matter and a mixed fertiliser, such as Gro-Plus Complete Plant Food, added.

The best time to sow is late summer and autumn. In most temperate climates, when frosts are not severe, annual types will flower in spring. Perennial types often do not flower well until the second year. Sow the seed in boxes or punnets and cover with seed-raising mix or compost to a depth of 6 mm.

Seedlings emerge in two to three weeks and are ready for transplanting in six to eight weeks. Space the seedlings 30–40 cm apart. Do not crowd hollyhocks with other plants and leave space around them for cultivation. Small bedding plants which grow no more than 30–40 cm are suitable companions. When hollyhocks are 30 cm tall, give them a side dressing of mixed fertiliser and another application when buds appear.

Hollyhocks are very attractive to snails and slugs, so protect the plants with a regular scattering of Mesurol or Blitzem Snail and Slug Pellets. Plants are also susceptible to rust fungus, especially in humid weather, so spray regularly with fungicide to control. (See Chapter 6.)

Varieties

'Double Elegance' is an early-flowering annual hollyhock growing to 2 m in height with magnificent spikes of double flowers in a wonderful colour range. 'Double Mixed' is a perennial type but similar in size and flower colours.

HONESTY (LUNARIA)

Honesty is a biennial plant but is usually grown as an annual. Plants grow to 60 cm with attractive but rather insignificant lavender or purple flowers in spring. The decorative seed pods, which are prized for dried flower arrangements, mature in mid-summer. Plants do best in a cool, partly shaded position in the garden.

Sow seed in autumn in most districts; spring sowings can be made in cold climates. Raise seedlings in boxes or punnets using an open, friable soil mixture as described in Chapter 7. Transplant seedlings when large enough to handle, spacing them 40–50 cm apart. Give liquid feeds of soluble fertilisers towards flowering time. To preserve the pods for indoor decoration, cut the stems when pods are ripe and allow them to dry. When completely dry, peel the outside of the pod by flicking between forefinger and thumb to reveal the silvery, transparent lining.

IMPATIENS

Sometimes known as Sultan's balsam or busy Lizzie, it is a close relative of balsam, but the plants bear flowers in shades of white, pink, purple, salmon and deep rose. Impatiens is an excellent plant for moist, shady areas but also does well in full sun if temperatures are not too high and water supplies are adequate. It grows well in pots, troughs, window boxes and hanging baskets. Seeds can be sown in autumn (in warm areas only) or spring and are best raised in seed boxes, trays or punnets. Press the seeds into the top of the mix and avoid covering, as the seeds need light for germination. When seedlings have grown their second leaf, prick them out into small individual pots. At a height of 5–7 cm, transfer the seedlings to larger pots or plant in the open garden, spacing them 30–40 cm apart. Water regularly in dry weather and give liquid feeds of soluble fertiliser as flowering commences.

There is quite a range of impatiens varieties available and much breeding work is currently under way, especially in the development of dwarf varieties. One of the best of the new varieties is 'Rouge', a carpet variety carrying masses of delightful pink blooms atop attractive foliage. With well-grown plants, the foliage is almost hidden by the blooms. Ideal for growing in pots and hanging containers.

LARKSPUR

Larkspurs are tall, spring-flowering annuals which are ideal for accent planting or as background plants to low-growing bedding or border plants. They are closely related to delphiniums. Larkspur grows to 60–75 cm and the flower spikes, in pink, rosy-red, light blue and dark blue, make excellent cut flowers.

Larkspurs are adaptable to a wide range of soils but perform best in well-drained fertile

Hint

Larkspur seeds need to be in the dark to germinate. Put newspaper or cloth over the seed tray for successful germination.

ALAN MCDONALD
YATES NEW ZEALAND

soils with added organic matter plus a mixed fertiliser. If soil is acid, an application of lime is recommended. Soil should be prepared well beforehand and in 'dark damp' condition for sowing the seeds direct in position. Plants prefer full sunlight and protection from strong winds. In exposed situations they may need staking.

In temperate climates sow seed in autumn, but in cold districts spring sowing will be more successful. Seeds germinate best at a temperature of about 15°C, so early sowing in late summer or early autumn may not be as successful as later sowing when soil is cooler. Sow a few seeds direct in clumps or stations spaced 20–30 cm apart. Cover seeds with seed-raising mix about 3 mm deep and keep moist until seedlings emerge in two or three weeks. Thin seedlings to two to three in each position. This close spacing gives a good mass of colour and helps the tall plants to support each other. Control weeds by regular, shallow cultivation and give liquid feeds of soluble fertiliser when buds appear. 'Rainbow Mixed', the most widely grown variety, has an excellent range of colour from pale pink to deep blue.

LINARIA

Linaria is an adaptable and colourful little annual for flowering in winter and spring. Plants grow 30–40 cm tall with spikes of flowers like tiny snapdragons in delicate pastel shades. Like larkspurs, linarias are adaptable to a wide range of soils but respond to good soil structure, added fertiliser and an application of lime if soil is acid.

Prepare the bed well beforehand to have it in friable, 'dark damp' condition for direct sowing. Seed can be sown from early autumn to early winter in temperate climates but spring sowings are successful in cold districts too. Like larkspur, seeds germinate well in cool soil. Sow seeds direct in shallow rows quite thickly. Thinning is only needed if the seedlings are overcrowded. Alternatively, sow a few seeds in clumps about 10–15 cm apart – usually all seedlings can be retained to give a dense mass of colour. Plants can be smothered by weeds in the early stages of growth. Shallow cultivation or hand-weeding is needed from the seedling stage onwards to avoid weeds becoming too large. Water

plants regularly, especially in dry weather, and give liquid feeds of soluble fertilisers every ten to fourteen days when the plants are well established. After the first flowering, cut back plants to promote a further flush of blooms. 'Fairy Bouquet' is the leading dwarf variety with flowers in shades of cream, yellow, gold, apricot, pink and mauve. It is excellent as a low border or for growing in clumps in rockeries, and flowers very quickly from sowing.

LINUM (SCARLET FLAX)

This flower is an ornamental version of the economic flax plant from which linen is derived. It has glowing red flowers with a satin sheen that sit on top of low mounds of mid-green foliage. Each individual flower lasts for a short time, but the overall display goes on for weeks through spring and early summer. Sow linum seeds direct where they are to grow, as these plants resent disturbance. The plants must have full sunlight to produce their best flower display.

LIVINGSTONE DAISY

Livingstone daisies are among the brightest of flowers for late winter and spring. The dwarf plants are 15 cm tall and covered with tightly packed flowers in yellow, pink, cerise and purple. They are ideal plants for carpeting, edging and rockeries. The plants are very adaptable to light or heavy soil, withstand dry conditions well but need good drainage. They must be grown in full sunlight, as in shade or even on cloudy days the flowers remain closed. In temperate climates, seed can be sown from early autumn to early winter, but in cold districts early spring as well.

Sow seed in boxes or punnets for transplanting 10–15 cm apart or sow a few seeds direct in clumps at this distance and cover with seed-raising mixture. Seeds may take two or three weeks to germinate so keep moist until seedlings emerge. Thin each clump to 2–3 seedlings. Water regularly until the plants are established and then only if the weather is dry.

Providing a pre-planting fertiliser has been added to the garden bed before sowing or transplanting, additional fertiliser is rarely necessary.

LOBELIA

Lobelia, another dwarf, spring-flowering plant, is excellent for massed colour effects, for edging, rockeries and window boxes. A few plants have flowers in the richest and deepest blue of lobelia, which blends dramatically with white alyssum, yellow violas or dwarf marigolds. Plants respond to a friable, fertile soil with mixed fertiliser added. A sunny aspect, especially morning sun with protection from strong winds, is preferred. Sow seed in autumn in boxes or punnets. Seed is small and needs light for germination so use a good quality seed-raising mix which holds moisture well. Sow seed on surface and press lightly and firmly into the mix.

Water gently or stand the container in water until moisture seeps to the surface. Transplant seedlings when small (2–3 cm), spacing them 10 cm apart. Water regularly and give liquid feeds of soluble fertiliser when buds appear.

Varieties

'Crystal Palace' grows to 15 cm tall with bronze-green foliage and dark-blue flowers. 'String of Pearls' grows to a similar height but has flowers in shades of pink, mauve and rose-purple as well as crisp white and clear sky blue. 'Sapphire Streamers' is an interesting variety with trailing stems up to 30 cm in length. The leaves are bright green and the flowers, rich blue with a white eye, are borne in great profusion. Ideal for hanging pots. Use four seedlings per 30 cm container. 'Cascade Mixture' provides a wide colour range and flowers over a long period. 'Lightning Blue' has rich blue flowers with a white eye.

LUPIN

Lupins belong to the legume group of plants and are able to add nitrogen to the soil because of the nitrogen-fixing bacteria contained in their root nodules. (See Chapter 4.) New Zealand blue lupins are frequently used as a green manure crop to improve the soil. Most garden varieties of lupins are winter-growing annuals which flower in spring and early summer. They are very adaptable to climate and soil and grow well in warm and temperate districts.

The Russell lupin is a perennial type which is best suited to cooler areas.

Lupins do not need very fertile soil. Too much fertiliser – especially those high in nitrogen – tends to favour an abundance of foliage at the expense of flowers. Prepare the soil well beforehand so it will be in a friable, 'dark damp' condition for direct sowing in autumn. On most soils, an application of lime (about two-thirds of a cup per square metre for light soil, one and a half cups per square metre for heavy soil) is recommended. Also add a ration of mixed fertiliser high in phosphorus, such as Gro-Plus Complete Plant Food, at one third of a cup per square metre.

Select a well-drained, sunny position to grow lupins. The seeds are quite large (although size varies with different species and varieties) so are easy to handle for direct sowing into the garden. If the soil is in 'dark damp' condition at sowing, seeds will germinate quickly and easily with little need for extra watering until seedlings emerge. Too much moisture in the early stages of germination may do more harm than good. (See Chapter 7.) Dust seed with fungicide before sowing. It is best to sow a few seeds in clumps, the spacing depending on the size to which the plants will grow. For dwarf varieties allow 20 cm between plants, for tall, large-seeded types (and Hartwegii) allow 30–40 cm, and for Russell Lupins allow 50 cm. For dwarf types, thinning is rarely needed, but for larger varieties thin each clump to one or two seedlings.

Once established, lupins need very little attention apart from regular watering in dry weather. When buds appear, weak liquid feeds of a flower-promoting soluble fertiliser, such as Thrive Flower and Fruit, will promote larger blooms and prolong flowering. For cut flowers, stand stems in boiling water for 15–20 seconds; take care steam does not damage lower blossoms.

MALOPE

Malope is a member of the mallow family and is related to hibiscus. The soft plants reach about 1 m in height and should be grown in a sunny, sheltered position. *Malope trifida* has large, rosy-pink single flowers with darker veining. Plants are grown from seed sown in early spring.

GROWING YOUR GARDEN

MARIGOLD

Marigolds are summer-flowering annuals and are best sown in spring or early summer because they prefer the warm weather and are susceptible to frost. African marigolds are tall with large flowers while French marigolds are shorter, more compact – some are dwarf types – and have smaller flowers. Marigolds prefer friable, fertile soils with added organic matter and fertiliser but they tolerate poor soils too. They need a warm sunny aspect, well sheltered from wind.

Commence sowing seed in spring after all danger of frost is over; sowing can be continued until mid-summer for late summer and autumn flowering. Generally speaking, a frost-free period of five months is needed from sowing. You can sow seed in boxes or punnets for pricking out into larger containers when the seedlings are about 1 cm tall and are ready for transplanting when 7–10 cm high. As the seeds germinate quickly and seedlings are quite vigorous, you can sow seeds direct in rows or in clumps. The distance apart for

....

Hint

Try using subtle mixes of colour in the flower bed: related colours look better than a canned fruit salad mix. Kick your composition into life with small touches of an opposite colour.

DENNIS GREVILLE
GARDEN WRITER

....

transplanting or sowing direct depends on the height and spread of the plants. Generally, allow a distance of 40 cm apart for tall varieties, 30 cm apart for shorter varieties and 20 cm apart for dwarf types.

Marigolds are shallow-rooted plants, so they need regular watering in dry weather. A mulch of compost will prevent moisture loss, keep the roots cool and discourage weeds. Give liquid feeds of soluble fertiliser as buds appear and remove spent blooms regularly to prolong flowering.

Varieties
African Marigolds:
'African Queen' is a robust-growing variety with very large, double golden blooms on bushes reaching about 50 cm in height. The blooms have very good wet weather tolerance and are highly recommended for home gardens.

'Jubilee' has vigorous, sturdy bushes to 75 cm tall with huge, tightly ruffled flowers in lemon, gold and orange. 'Crackerjack' is even taller and has a wide colour range of double blooms. These varieties are extremely showy and produce masses of flowers suitable for cutting. 'Cupid Mixed' is low growing – to 40 cm – with softly curled flowers in orange, yellow and gold.

French marigolds:
'Honeycomb' grows to about 30 cm and is covered in flowers in shades of rich brown and yellow. An excellent bedding variety. 'Petite Yellow' is a very dwarf type, growing to 15–20 cm high. It is very free-flowering with double, clear yellow blooms prominently displayed for many months. It is excellent for mass bedding, low borders or as a rockery plant.

'Safari Mixture' is a mixture of semi-dwarf marigolds to 40 cm high. Plants have attractive, fern-like foliage and double flowers in shades of yellow, gold, orange and red.

MARMALADE DAISY

See Rudbeckia.

MEXICAN SUNFLOWER

Also known as tithonia, this daisy bears orange or scarlet flowers which bloom continuously from midsummer to midwinter. One of the largest plants grown as an annual, with stems which may reach over 2 metres (although 1 metre is normal). The rich, intense colours of the flowers create strong effects. Plants will require staking in strong winds. Use as a background screen, at the rear of a border or for cut flowers. Sow seed outside in spring or indoors six to eight weeks prior to transplanting. Cover seeds sparsely, as light may assist germination. Tithonia prefers average, well-drained soil and tolerates heat and drought. Do not overwater. It is excellent for warm climates.

MIGNONETTE

This dwarf, spring-flowering annual is an 'old world' favourite, loved more for its spicy aroma than for its small, orange-yellow flower spikes. It is a good subject for low borders, edging and rockeries and for growing in containers. The plants respond to friable, fertile soils to which organic matter and mixed fertiliser has been added. On acid soils, an application of lime is recommended.

Seedlings of mignonette do not transplant well so it is best to sow seed direct in the garden bed. You can sow seed in autumn and spring in warm–temperate climates but in cold districts spring only. It is best to scatter seed thinly in shallow rows or a few seeds in clumps where the plants are to flower. Cover the seeds with seed-raising mixture. Seed germination is often erratic so keep the soil moist but not wet for about two weeks.

When seedlings emerge, thin them if overcrowded. Established plants need little attention apart from occasional watering. Give liquid feeds of soluble fertiliser every ten to fourteen days, especially when buds appear. Remove spent flower spikes to prolong flowering.

MIMULUS

These low-growing plants are spring bloomers that do well in light shade but must have moist soil at all times. The unusually marked blooms come in shades of red, orange, yellow, cream and white. They have a tubular shape that flares out into a 'grinning' face, hence are often given the name 'monkey flower'. The seeds germinate in moderate temperatures and, in most climates, are sown in autumn for spring blooming. Sow seeds in trays of seed-raising mixture and water from below so as not to disturb the small seeds. The seedlings are tiny and very delicate when they first emerge and need gentle handling.

The attractive plants are good in shaded borders or can be used in pots and hanging baskets, as long as the potting mix is kept moist. They associate well with ferns and azaleas, and other shade-lovers, and are well-suited to stream-side planting

MOLUCELLA

See Bells of Ireland.

NASTURTIUM

Nasturtiums are very adaptable, colourful annuals. Old varieties were rather straggly plants, but plant breeders have made great improvements and the modern varieties are more compact than the old types and their flowers are produced well above the foliage to give a brighter display. Both the leaves and flowers are edible; seed heads can be pickled and used as mock capers. Nasturtiums will grow on a wide range of soils, but they do best on moderately fertile soils on which the plants produce less foliage and flower more prolifically. Nasturtiums prefer open sunlight and rather dry conditions but will make quite a good floral showing in partial shade.

Nasturtiums make excellent bedding plants and are also good for growing in rockeries, troughs, tubs or large hanging baskets. Plants flower in ten to twelve weeks from sowing. In warm–temperate climates, sow seed from spring to early autumn; in cold districts make sowings in spring only. Seed germinates best if soil temperatures are not too high. Prepare the bed for direct sowing to have the soil in 'dark damp' condition, but avoid using compost or animal manure, both of which provide conditions favouring excessive leaf growth. A mixed fertiliser such as Gro-Plus Complete Plant Food which is high in phosphorus can be scattered over the soil at one third of a cup per square metre and raked in before sowing.

Seeds are large, easy to handle and germinate in two to three weeks. Sow a few seeds in clumps spaced 20–30 cm apart. Thinning is rarely needed. Water moderately until plants are well established, but then keep them on the dry side to encourage flowering. Do not give liquid feeds of soluble fertilisers as these will encourage leaf growth.

Varieties

'Jewel Mixed' has compact plants and contains a mixture of the choicest colours available – primrose, gold, orange, red and mahogany. 'Cherry Rose' is one of the brightest varieties with semi-double cherry rose flowers which contrast dramatically with the foliage.

TOP FIVE
SUMMER ANNUALS

PETUNIAS

Favourites because of their long flowering habit and their profusion of blooms, petunias are often regarded as symbols of summer.

SUNFLOWERS

Sunflowers are easily grown from seed and are beloved by children. Almost every part of the plant can be eaten, so they're useful as well as good looking!

MARIGOLD

An old-time favourite with scores of varieties to choose from which provide brilliant hot colour for a very long season from early spring to late autumn.

PHLOX

Phlox will grow rapidly to blooming stage. If sown direct where it is to grow, it will produce a mass of (inexpensive) summer colour (see picture on page 180).

NICOTIANA

Unavailable in New Zealand for many years because of quarantine restrictions, seed-grown nicotianas are now readily available in seedling form. The starry flowers are very showy and last for months.

NICOTIANA

NEMESIA

Nemesia is one of the brightest and most colourful bedding and border plants for late winter and spring flowering. The trend has been to develop dwarf *compacta* types in preference to the tall *strumosa* types. Nemesias are adapted to light or heavy soil but prefer friable, fertile soil to which organic matter and mixed fertiliser have been added. Prepare the soil well beforehand. Direct sowing is the best method, although seedlings can be raised and transplanted if preferred. The plants need a warm, sunny aspect with good drainage. In warm climates, sow seed in autumn or early winter but in cold districts sowings are best made in spring. For the dwarf varieties, sow seed direct in rows or, better still, a few seeds in clumps spaced 15–20 cm apart. Cover the rows or positions with a light sprinkling of seed-raising mixture. Seedlings usually emerge within ten to fourteen days and thinning is rarely needed. Alternatively, seedlings can be raised in boxes or punnets, pricked out into larger containers if crowded and transplanted when 5–7 cm high. If transplanting seedlings, harden them off by withholding water for a few days and then give a good watering the night before you transplant. Space seedlings 15 cm apart each way. When the plants are established they need little attention. For bushier plants you can pinch out the leading stems. Water regularly and give liquid feeds of soluble fertilisers every two or three weeks, especially towards flowering time. Plants will flower in fourteen to sixteen weeks from seed sowing.

Varieties

'Carnival Mixture' is the leading dwarf variety. It has large flowers in cream, yellow, gold, orange, scarlet and red on strong, bushy plants 20–30 cm tall.

NEMOPHILA (BABY BLUE-EYES)

Nemophila is another charming dwarf annual for late winter and spring flowering. Plants grow to 20–30 cm with fern-like foliage and small, sky-blue, saucer-shaped flowers. It is an excellent fill-in plant for clump plantings in garden beds or in rockeries. Like nemesia, the plants prefer a friable, fertile, well-drained soil in a warm, sunny position. Seedlings do not transplant well and it is best to sow seeds direct in the garden. In most districts, autumn sowings are best, but in cold districts spring sowings can be made too. Sow seeds thinly in rows, or a few seeds in clumps spaced 15 cm apart, and cover lightly with seed-raising mix. Thin out seedlings if overcrowded. Water regularly and give liquid feeds of soluble fertiliser when buds appear.

NICOTIANA

Quarantine restrictions have recently been eased on the import of these lovely plants and dwarf annual types are readily available. They cover themslves with star-shaped flowers right throughout the warm weather. Nicotianas are heat tolerant and bloom in shades of red, white, pink and an unusual lime-green. Although they are extremely hardy, they are heavy feeders and will appreciate regular applications of soluble plant food such as Thrive.

NIGELLA

Nigella is also called love-in-a-mist because its attractive flowers are quaintly hidden in a fern-like foliage. Seed is sown during autumn or spring in boxes or seed beds and seedlings are afterwards transplanted about 20 cm apart. Best results are obtained in a moderately rich loam and a position sheltered from winds and the hot sun. Plants grow to about 40 cm in height and are excellent for indoor decoration. The dried seed heads are popular for long-lasting arrangements.

NOLANA

A low-growing plant that can be used as a ground cover, nolana has bluebell flowers on a mat of creeping foliage. Its prostrate habit looks especially effective in a hanging basket. Sow seed (when soil has lost its winter chill) directly where the plant is to grow. Although nolana must have plenty of sun the flowers can look a little tired in very hot sunlight. 'Bluebird' is the most popular variety.

ORNAMENTAL BASIL

This attractive annual is also known as 'Dark Opal' basil because of its purple-bronze foliage. Plants grow to 30–40 cm tall and leaves have the same spicy aroma as the herb, sweet basil. The spikes of small, lavender-white flowers are not spectacular but the plants are recommended for their foliage and aroma. They are ideal for troughs, pots or rockeries or spotted here and there among summer bedding plants. Sow seeds in spring or early summer in boxes or punnets for transplanting seedlings 20–30 cm apart, or sow direct in the garden in clumps at the same distance. Plants grow well in sun or semi-shade and need little attention apart from regular watering and weeding. To keep a neat and tidy appearance remove flower spikes as they appear.

ORNAMENTAL CHILLI

Ornamental chilli is a non-edible variety of capsicum or pepper. The fruits are much smaller but very attractive and change colour with maturity from green or purple to yellow, orange and scarlet. In mild climates, plants will overwinter to grow again the following spring but they are usually grown as annuals. They are warm-season plants and frost susceptible, so the best sowing time is spring to early summer. They need a warm, sunny position with shelter from strong winds. They prefer a fertile soil to which organic matter and a mixed fertiliser has been added during preparation. Ornamental chillies are excellent for individual specimens here and there in the garden or for container growing in tubs or large pots. Regular watering, together with mulching, is needed in dry weather. Do not give extra fertiliser until the small, white flowers appear. Then give liquid feeds of soluble fertiliser every two or three weeks to encourage and prolong flowering and fruiting. The fruits, or berries as they are often called, are extremely hot, so take care to keep young children away from them.

PAINTED DAISY
(SEE ALSO CHRYSANTHEMUM)

This annual chrysanthemum is a good subject for clump planting here and there in the garden or as a background plant. The plants grow to 60–75 cm with large, white flowers zoned with yellow, red and purple. They flower in spring and early summer from seed sown in autumn. In cold districts, seed can be sown in spring too. They do best on well-drained, fertile soils with organic matter and fertiliser added. They need a warm, sunny position sheltered from strong winds. Sow seeds in boxes or punnets, covering the seed

GROWING YOUR GARDEN

with seed-raising mix to a depth of 6 mm. Transplant seedlings when 7–10 cm high, spacing them 40–50 cm apart. Water regularly and give liquid feeds of a soluble fertiliser, such as Thrive, when buds appear. Plants flower within twelve to fourteen weeks from transplanting. Remove any spent blooms to prolong flowering.

PANSY

The pansy was originally known as hearts-ease or wild pansy and is closely related to violas and violets, all of which belong to the genus *Viola*. Pansies come in a wide colour range but are distinguished by velvety black or dark-coloured blotches or markings. These spring-flowering, biennial plants are treated as annuals and are excellent for carpet bedding or low borders. They need a well-drained, friable, fertile soil but the tender roots should not be in contact with concentrated fertiliser. It is best to prepare the bed well beforehand by adding old compost or animal manure together with a ration of mixed fertiliser (one-third of a cup per square metre) thoroughly incorporated into the top 10–15 cm of soil. Pansies prefer sunlight for most of the day, but shade from hot afternoon sun is an advantage.

Seed can be sown from midsummer to early winter in most districts, in cold areas autumn and early spring are recommended sowing times. Sow seed in boxes or punnets using an open, friable soil mixture as described in Chapter 7. Sow the seed thinly in shallow rows covering lightly with seed-raising mix. Germination may be slow (three to four weeks) so containers must be kept moist, but not wet, for this length of time. Prick out the seedlings when quite small, spacing them 5 cm apart in seedling trays filled with a similar soil mixture. Grow them on for a few weeks in partial shade until the seedlings are sturdy enough for planting out.

Transplant the seedlings into the well-prepared 'dark damp' soil of the garden bed, spacing them 20 cm apart for bedding and 30 cm apart for large exhibition blooms. Water plants regularly but do not overwater. Keep weeds under control by careful shallow cultivation, or with a mulch of compost tucked around the plants. This will help to conserve moisture, keep the soil crumbly and encourage a thick mat of surface roots.

Once the plants are well established, give weak liquid feeds of soluble fertiliser every two to three weeks. If the first flowers are

Pansies are excellent for carpet bedding and provide a colourful display.

small, remove some of the buds to increase the size of those which remain. Always pick spent blooms regularly to encourage new buds and prolong flowering. The main pests are aphids, which cluster under the foliage. (See Chapter 6 for control.)

Varieties

'Antiquity' is a variety noted for very vigorous growth. A profusion of flowers in bronze and pink pastel colours with complementary veining, and the lack of typical blotches of colour make this variety unique. It also flowers over a long period. 'Giant Supreme' is a popular strain with glorious flowers in various shapes and colours. 'Joker Mix' is a cheerful mixture of strongly coloured blooms with bicolour or tricolour contrasts that make distinct 'faces'. It stands up well to cold and hot weather conditions, flowering for a long period into the warm weather. Colour-themed pansies like 'Raspberry and Rose' (red shades), 'Denim and Lace' (blue with white edging), 'Oranges and Lemons' (orange and yellow tones) 'Blue Wash', 'Lemon Wash' and 'Rose Wash' are useful for outdoor decorating. One very unusual pansy is 'Black Knight', which produces striking black flowers.

PAPER DAISIES

The Australian paper daisies, or everlastings, are grown for their general hardiness and their long life as dried flowers. Yellow paper daisy (*Schoenia filifolia*) is an Australian native with yellow flowers borne on top of stems that are 30–40 cm tall. Pink paper daisy (*Rhodanthe chlorocephala*), which used to be known as acrolinium, flowers at its best in spring but may also produce a good show from spring plantings.

Both of these should be sown where they are to grow. They are suitable for planting here and there in the garden or ideal for open meadow plantings. For cultural directions see Strawflower, to which they are related.

PETUNIA

Petunias are one of the most colourful annuals for the summer garden. Like many other flowering plants, petunias have been improved tremendously by plant breeders in recent years. The multiflora (bedding) type of petunias are sturdier and more compact with flowers in strong, clear colours. The grandiflora types have magnificent single, double or frilled blooms and the plants are stronger and sturdier than old varieties.

All petunias are sun-loving plants and will tolerate dry conditions once they are established. Plants should be sheltered from strong winds, especially the taller, large-flowered types. They grow well on a wide range of soil textures, from light to heavy, but respond to fertiliser applied when the bed is prepared. Too much fertiliser and water produces sappy plants which flower poorly.

Petunias are excellent for mass bedding and borders but can also be grown (especially the grandiflora types) in tubs, troughs and large pots on a sunny terrace or patio. There are semi-trailing types too for a cascade effect in window boxes and hanging baskets.

Seed can be sown in spring, after all danger of frost is over, and continued through to midsummer in most districts. In cold areas with a shorter growing season, sow seed in early summer. Petunia seed is very small and extra care should be taken in raising the seedlings in boxes or punnets. Like many small seeds, petunias need light for germination. Prepare an open, friable soil mixture as described in Chapter 7. Scatter the seed on the surface and cover very lightly with seed-raising mixture. Press firmly and water very gently. Alternatively, stand the container in water until moisture seeps to the surface. Petunia seed needs fairly warm (25°C) conditions to germinate so it is best to keep the containers indoors until the seedlings emerge – then move them outside immediately, but to a sheltered position. Small containers can be covered with glass or plastic bags. This helps to maintain an even temperature and prevents drying out. Prick out the small seedlings into seedling trays, spacing them 3–5 cm apart, and grow them on until 5 cm high for transplanting into the garden.

Transplant the small-flowered bedding types at a spacing of 25–30 cm, but allow 30–40 cm for the large-flowered varieties. Always scatter snail baits around the newly planted seedlings to protect them from slugs and snails. When established, petunias need little attention apart from occasional watering if the soil becomes dry. Plants in tubs, pots or hanging baskets dry out very quickly and need more regular watering. Give weak liquid feeds of soluble fertiliser as the plants are developing.

After the first flush of flowers, plants can be cut back and given a liquid feed for a second flush of flowers in late summer or early autumn. If left until the end of their flowering season, petunias will often seed themselves around the garden. Because most of the modern petunias are hybrids, these second-generation plants will rarely be the same as the parents and are often of inferior quality. Start with fresh seed or plants each year.

There have been some interesting develop-ments with perennial petunias in recent years. They only come in a limited range of colours at this stage, and are best in areas with a warm winter but are of good value for hanging baskets or containers.

Varieties

Small-flowered multiflora bedding petunia (30–40 cm tall):
'Dazzler' is a hybrid, small-flowered type with compact vigorous plants which are very resistant to wet weather. A superb petunia for garden display.

'White Innocence' has clear white flowers that provide a good contrast. 'Waterfall' is a new variety in mauve and pink shades that stands up particularly well to summer rains.
Large-flowered grandiflora petunia (40–60 cm tall):
'Colour Parade' was one of the first Japanese F1 hybrids and is still the most popular strain. Single flowers are a cheerful mixture of colours including carmine, salmon, bright red, dark blue, clear white and several different shades of pink.

PHACELIA

Phacelia is also known as Californian bluebell. Apart from its pretty, bell-shaped flowers, it is grown for its wonderful ability to attract hoverflies, bees and other useful insects. Phacelia produces copious quantities of pollen, which is an important food source for the larvae of hoverflies. Successive sowings throughout the warm part of the year will maintain a good population of friendly insects in the garden. As the plants finish blooming, dig them into the soil. These plants make useful green manure.

Phlox seeds can be sown direct where they are to grow.

PHLOX

Phlox is one of the brightest summer flowers for mass bedding or borders. Dwarf varieties, the most widely grown, are 20 cm in height, but tall varieties reach 40 cm or more. The range of flower colour is magnificent, many with contrasting white centres and others star-shaped with pointed petals. The plants prefer full sunlight but perform well in any situation which has sun for part of the day. They respond to friable, well-drained soil with added organic matter plus a mixed fertiliser. Prepare the soil well for direct sowing in spring or early summer. In warm northern areas, sow in late summer and autumn too, providing there are no frosts.

Seeds can be sown in boxes or punnets if preferred but direct sowing is best because seeds germinate easily. Phlox seeds are ideal for sowing in clumps spaced 10–15 cm apart. Scatter a few seeds in each clump or station and cover with seed-raising mixture to a depth of 3 mm. Alternatively, seeds can be sown thinly in rows at the same distance apart. With both methods, thinning is rarely needed and this close spacing of plants gives a denser mass of colour.

When seedlings have emerged (two to three weeks) keep them well watered until plants are established. Then water regularly but do not overwater; phlox will tolerate fairly dry conditions. Give the plants liquid feeds of soluble fertilisers when buds appear. When flowering commences, avoid overhead watering as flowers last better when dry. Watering around the base of the plants and adding a mulch of compost helps to keep soil moist and protects the shallow roots. Remove spent flowers to promote new buds.

Varieties

'Drummondii Dwarf' is the most widely grown variety and is ideal for carpeting, low borders and in rockeries. The plants are compact and grow to 20 cm with a very wide colour range which includes pink, lavender, salmon, scarlet, crimson, blue and white, with some flowers having light-coloured centres. 'Sparkling Dwarf' is a free-flowering, compact strain with bushy plants covered with heads of flowers in beautiful colours. 'African Sunset' has unusual deep-red flowers.

PINKS

See Dianthus.

PIN-CUSHION FLOWER

See Scabiosa.

POLYANTHUS

These spring-flowering, primrose-like plants are herbaceous perennials but are often grown as annuals. The modern strain, 'Pacific Giants', has clusters of large florets on tall, strong stems in a range of colours which include apricot, gold, pink, scarlet, red, blue and white. Polyanthus grows well in a cool, sheltered, partially shaded position or in a shadehouse. When grown in shaded situations, the plants may last for two or three years and can be divided when they are dormant. The plants can also be grown in open beds in full sun and make ideal pot plants. If grown in the open, move the plants to shade after flowering and take plenty of soil with the roots. Polyanthus prefer a friable soil and respond to liquid feeds of a soluble fertiliser such as Thrive.

Sow seeds in late summer and early autumn in boxes, punnets or pots. Seeds are small and germination may be slow and erratic. Use a good seed-raising mix as outlined in Chapter 7. Scatter the seed along shallow rows in the boxes or on the surface of the soil mix in punnets or pots. Cover to a depth of 3 mm with a moisture-holding material such as compost or seed-raising mixture. Press down gently but firmly with a board and keep the surface moist until seedlings emerge in three or four weeks. As germination is erratic, the seedlings may not all be ready for transplanting at the one time. Transplant seedlings when large enough to handle. If growing the plants in pots, use the same mixture as for raising seed. Do not let the pots dry out, and give liquid feeds, especially near flowering time. 'Pacific Giants', with a superb colour range, is the leading variety.

POOR MAN'S ORCHID (SCHIZANTHUS)

These spring-flowering annuals with orchid-like flowers in shades of pink to violet are very adaptable and should be more widely grown. They thrive in semi-shaded positions but can be grown in the open garden provided they are shaded during the hottest part of the day. They are ideal for growing in pots or hanging baskets under trees or in ferneries and shadehouses. When grown in pots or baskets, the soil mixture should be open and friable with equal parts of garden soil, sand and moisture-holding material such as compost or peat moss. Add a mixed fertiliser such as Gro-Plus Complete Plant Food at the rate of one heaped tablespoon for each bucket of mixture.

In temperate climates, sow seed from late summer to early winter, but in cold districts, late summer and autumn only. Seed is quite small and is best sown in boxes or punnets. Germination may take two to three weeks. Cover the seed very lightly, firm down with a piece of flat board or the bottom of a punnet and keep the surface damp until seedlings emerge. Transplant seedlings to the open garden when 5 cm tall, spacing them 30 cm apart, or transfer to small pots for growing on to larger pots or hanging baskets.

To promote bushy growth of the fern-like foliage, pinch back the leading stems regularly. Keep the plants well watered and, when established, give liquid feeds of soluble fertiliser every ten or fourteen days to promote flowering.

POPPY, ICELAND

Iceland poppies are among the most popular flowers for late winter and spring. They are magnificent bedding plants, growing to 60 cm, and the cut flowers are unsurpassed for indoor decoration. Modern strains of Iceland poppies are a vast improvement on old varieties, both in flower size and colour range. Colours include lemon, yellow, gold, orange, pink, salmon, red shades and white. If spent blooms are picked regularly, the plants will flower for many months.

Iceland poppies need plenty of sunshine, good drainage and a friable, fertile soil. They revel in 'good going', so it pays to prepare the bed well beforehand with plenty of compost or animal manure, together with a pre-planting ration of mixed fertiliser. Sunlight, especially morning sun, is needed to 'pop' the buds, so select a warm, sunny (but wind-sheltered) bed to grow them.

In most temperate climates, you can start sowing in late summer and continue through to autumn. Early sowings will produce plants to flower in winter. In cold districts summer to early autumn sowings are recommended. Iceland poppy seed is small and the seedlings are delicate.

It is best to sow seed thinly in boxes or punnets as described in Chapter 7 and cover with a very light scattering of seed-raising mix. Keep the surface moist until seedlings emerge in ten to fourteen days. Prick out the seedlings when quite small, spacing them 3–5 cm apart in other boxes or seedling trays. Grow them on to a good size, hardening them off to more sunlight as they grow.

Transplant seedlings 20–30 cm apart each way into the garden bed. Plant out on a cool day and keep the crown of the plant slightly above the surface. Planting seedlings too deep may cause the crown to rot. Keep the seedlings well watered with a gentle spray until established. With a spacing of 20–30 cm between plants the foliage will eventually cover the soil, but mulching with compost will conserve moisture, keep down weeds and avoid possible damage to surface roots when cultivating. Root damage weakens the plants and may result in twisting of flower stems.

Give liquid feeds when buds appear and then at two-week intervals. Pinch out early buds until the plants have formed good clumps. Remove spent blooms to prolong flowering. For indoor decoration, pick flowers early in the morning in full bud or bud-opening stage. Dip the stems into boiling water for 30 seconds before arranging the blooms.

Other types of poppies are best sown directly where they are to grow.

Varieties

'Artist's Glory' is the most popular Iceland poppy for general garden display. It is a specially formulated mixture containing strong-stemmed flowers in shades of lemon, yellow, gold, apricot, rose pink, salmon and white, and many with distinctive picotee edges. This strain flowers over a long period. 'Matilda' is an Australian-bred variety with short, sturdy, wind-resistant stems, large flowers in a range of colours (many with two colours on the one bloom). 'Flanders Poppy' is a form of the wild European field poppy. It is traditionally associated with the battlefields of World War I. It has a strong, red, single flower with a black centre. 'Shirley' poppies were bred from the wild European poppy by the Reverend Wilks who lived in the English town of Shirley in the late nineteenth century. They have large, single and semi-double blooms in a mixture of salmon, rose-pink and red.

PORTULACA

Also known as pig face or sun plant, this summer-flowering annual is excellent for low borders, edging, banks and rockeries. The plants are 15–20 cm tall and covered in bright daisy-like flowers in lemon, mauve, pink, salmon, crimson and white. Portulaca will grow on a variety of soils but responds to added fertiliser, which should be incorporated into the soil when the bed is prepared. The plants do best in full sunlight, need good drainage and will tolerate dry conditions.

Sow seed in spring (after soil has become warm) or early summer. Seeds can be raised in boxes or punnets if preferred. Seedlings transplant easily, but it is best to sow seeds direct in the garden, either in rows, patterns or in clumps spaced 10 cm apart. Cover the seed with a very light covering of seed-raising mix and keep damp until seedlings emerge in ten to fourteen days. With direct sowing there is usually no need to thin the seedlings unless they are very crowded. If thinning is necessary, seedlings – if lifted carefully – can be replanted. The plants are prostrate and creep over the ground, protecting their roots and smothering weeds, but a light mulch of compost will assist them to become established. Water the plants in dry weather but do not overwater as they prefer rather dry conditions.

Give liquid feeds of soluble fertilisers when buds appear about six weeks after sowing. A popular strain, 'Sundancer', has a wide range of colours and the large blooms will open more freely under lower light conditions than older types.

PRIMULA

Primula malacoides is really a perennial but is always grown as a spring-flowering annual. It has come a long way from the old-type primula with small, mauve flowers on long stems. The modern primula is more compact

TOP FIVE
SPRING ANNUALS

PANSIES

Newer varieties of pansies flower over a long period and are much more heat tolerant than the old varieties, which means that they are able to continue blooming from spring into early summer (see picture on page 180).

POPPIES

Poppies create new magic each year when their hairy buds open to release the brightly coloured 'crepe paper' petals.

PRIMULAS

Each stem of *Primula malacoides* supports its own self-contained bunch of dainty flowers. As long as they have got plenty of water, primulas will do well in full sun or light shade.

LOBELIAS

The bluest of blues makes low-growing lobelia an unforgettable sight in the garden. It can also be planted as a ground cover in large tubs, or made to trail from hanging baskets.

CINERARIAS

A mix of brilliant, jewel-like colours makes cinerarias a popular choice. They grow happily in the shade but won't handle frost.

PANSIES AND POPPIES

GROWING YOUR GARDEN

and the flowers are much larger, with a range of colours which include mauve, carmine, pink, purple, ruby red and white. Most of this improvement in flower size and colour range has been carried out in Australia and breeding work is still going on. Primulas have traditionally been regarded as shade-loving plants, but most varieties available in this country grow equally well in full sunlight. They are ideal plants for bedding or borders but are also attractive when grown in troughs, pots and window boxes. They prefer friable, fertile soil with added organic matter and mixed fertiliser as a pre-planting dressing. On acid soils they benefit from an application of lime (one to two cups per square metre, according to soil type – see Chapter 4) during preparation of the garden bed.

Seed should be sown from mid-summer to early autumn. Like Iceland poppy, the seed of primula is small and the seedlings delicate. Use specific seed-raising mix for filling seed boxes or punnets. Sow seed in very shallow rows or scatter on the soil surface and press firmly with a board. Seeds should be barely covered with seed-raising mix. Seedlings may take three to four weeks to emerge, so keep surface moist for that period. When small, prick out seedlings into other boxes or seedling trays, spacing them 3–5 cm apart. Grow them on until large enough to transplant. Space seedlings in the garden 15–20 cm apart. Choose a cool, cloudy day for transplanting and keep the new plants well watered until they are established. Give regular liquid feeds of soluble fertiliser when buds appear. Primulas do well in pots but should always be given plenty of water.

Varieties

Primula malacoides:
'Carmine Glow' is a vigorous variety with compact, sturdy plants 20–25 cm in height. It has been selected over many years for its large, carmine-rose flowers which hold well in open sunlight. 'Gilham's White' is very similar in growth form but the flowers are pure white. It does well in open sunlight or shade. 'Royalty' has flowers in an attractive shade of pink and prefers semi-shade. 'Lollipops' is a specially formulated mixture of the dwarf annual primulas. Colours include carmine-rose, lavender-pink, ruby red

and white. An excellent mixture for bedding or borders in open sun or shade.
Primula obconica:
This is an evergreen perennial best suited to shady situations or for growing in pots or baskets in ferneries or shadehouses. The plants grow to 15–20 cm with large flowers in shades of rose, mauve, lavender-blue, crimson and white. The plants are excellent indoor pot plants when in flower. This type of primula is usually available as potted plants in flower. It is best to replant or repot obconicas in early winter. Plants sometimes cause skin allergy problems for some people, but newer varieties are allergy-free.

QUEEN ANNE'S LACE
This tall-growing plant (to 1 metre) is popular as a 'filler' in flower arrangements. The delicate-looking white flower heads are made up of dozens of minute white flowers. These lace-like flower clusters look wonderful in cottage gardens, especially when placed behind lower, more colourful plantings. *Daucus carota*, a flowering form of carrot, is also known as Queen Anne's lace. It has similar white flowers and finely dissected foliage.

RUDBECKIA (MARMALADE DAISY)
Rudbeckia is an attractive bedding or border plant growing to 40 cm high with masses of flowers in summer. The blooms are gold-yellow with a purple-black centre cone. The plants are best treated as annuals but in cold districts they can be grown as herbaceous perennials. They are adapted to a wide range of soils and climates but prefer a fertile, friable soil and full sunlight. Sow seed in spring or early summer in seed boxes or punnets for transplanting, or direct in the garden in clumps spaced about 30 cm apart. Give liquid feeds when flower buds appear. Pink rudbeckia (*Echinacea purpurea*) has pink flowers with a raised 'cone' centre. Its leaves, or an extract from the plant, are used for herbal remedies.

SALPIGLOSSIS
Salpiglossis is a tall bedding or background annual for summer flowering. The trumpet-shaped flowers are 5 cm long in shades of gold, bronze, red and violet. The plants require a friable, fertile soil with organic matter and mixed fertiliser added. Prepare the soil well

Rudbeckias are also known as black-eyed Susan because of their dark centres.

beforehand for direct sowing in spring or early summer. Plants need a warm, sunny aspect.

As seedlings do not transplant well, it is best to sow seeds direct in rows spaced 15 cm apart and thin seedlings to the same distance. Alternatively, sow a few seeds in clumps or stations and thin each position to one or two seedlings. Cover seeds to a depth of 6 mm with seed-raising mix and keep damp until seedlings emerge in two to three weeks. Once plants are established, water regularly, especially in dry weather, and give liquid feeds of soluble fertiliser every two or three weeks. Plants will flower twelve to fourteen weeks after sowing. The most widely grown variety is 'Emperor Mixed', which has a good range of flower colour.

SALVIA

Salvias are summer-flowering perennials but are best grown as annuals. While there are many hundreds of species of salvia available from specialist nurseries, here we will confine ourselves to the bedding plants that are usually treated as annuals.

In far northern areas, some types will continue flowering in autumn or winter and may be worth growing on into the second year. Plants grow 30–60 cm in height and are excellent for mass bedding or borders. Modern varieties, in traditional scarlet and a number of other colours, are more compact and bushier than older strains.

Salvias prefer a well-drained, friable soil to which organic matter and mixed fertiliser has been added during soil preparation. Plants do best in full sunlight and need protection from strong winds.

Sow seeds in spring or early summer when the weather is warm, because the seed is difficult to germinate in cold soil. You can raise seedlings in boxes or punnets for transplanting or sow seeds direct in the garden. Space seedlings or sow a few seeds in clumps 30–40 cm apart for tall varieties, but 20–30 cm apart for dwarf, compact plants. When plants are established, they can be pinched back when 10 cm tall to encourage lateral shoots for bushy plants.

Plants prefer moist but not soggy

conditions so do not overwater. Occasional liquid feeds of soluble fertiliser will keep them growing strongly.

Varieties

Salvia splendens 'Bonfire' is the traditional salvia with fiery scarlet blooms on long spikes. The modern strain of this variety is not as tall as older strains and rarely grows higher than 60 cm. 'Dwarf Scarlet' has compact, semi-dwarf plants to 30 cm tall. Flowers are equal in size and colour to 'Bonfire'.

'Touch of Blue' (*Salvia farinacea*) grows to a height of 45 cm and is excellent for colour effect when grown in clumps here and there in the garden. The deep Wedgwood-blue flowers are borne on long, slender spikes. This variety can be cut back in warm weather for further flowering, and in warm districts the clumps can overwinter for another flowering in late spring. There is a similar strain with white flowers.

SCABIOSA (PIN-CUSHION FLOWER)

Scabiosa or pin-cushion flower is a spring-flowering annual which has recently been improved in flower size and colour range. Suitable for bedding or background planting, plants grow to about 60 cm. They require a sunny aspect sheltered from strong winds. Prepare the bed well beforehand, adding a mixed fertiliser at one-third of a cup per square metre, and a ration of lime at one to two cups per square metre, depending on soil texture. The soil must be well drained but plants need ample water in dry weather.

Sow seed in autumn to early winter in temperate districts, but in autumn and spring where colder. Seed is best sown in boxes or punnets. Covered with 6 mm of seed-raising mix and keep soil moist until seedlings emerge in two or three weeks. Transplant seedlings when 5–7 cm high, spacing them about 40 cm apart. Give liquid feeds of soluble fertiliser when flower buds appear about twelve weeks from transplanting. Flower colours include shades of pink, mauve, purple and white.

SCHIZANTHUS

See Poor man's orchid.

SNAPDRAGON (ANTIRRHINUM)

A severe rust fungus led to a decline in the popularity of snapdragons for the home garden in recent years. However, many of the new varieties are more resistant to this disease and more effective fungicide sprays should encourage gardeners to grow these magnificent flowers. Snapdragons are perennial plants but are best treated as annuals and sown from seed each year, although they can be cut back after the first flowering to give a second flush of blooms.

The plants need well-drained friable soils to which organic matter has been added in liberal quantities. Also apply a pre-planting fertiliser and a ration of lime when the bed is being prepared. Keep the soil in good condition by cultivating when it is 'dark damp' until ready for transplanting. Snapdragons prefer full sunlight but do quite well if they are in sun for only part of the day.

Seed can be sown at almost any time of the year in temperate climates, but autumn is the best period for a spring display. In cold districts you can sow seeds in spring or early summer. As seeds are small, they should be sown in seed boxes or punnets using a friable, moisture-holding soil mixture as described in Chapter 7. Scatter the seed in shallow rows or broadcast on the surface and press firmly with a piece of board. Cover the seed very lightly with seed-raising mixture and keep damp until seedlings emerge – usually in ten to fourteen days. Seedlings are ready for transplanting in about six weeks from sowing when they are 3–5 cm high. Seedlings of tall varieties should be spaced about 40 cm apart, but dwarf varieties can be planted at 30 cm or even closer. If plants tend to produce buds too soon, nip them back to encourage lateral growth and leave eight to ten flower spikes. Give liquid feeds of soluble fertiliser at this stage. When cutting flowers for indoor decoration, or removing spent blooms, cut the stalks back to 5–7 cm from the crown to encourage a second crop of flowers on long stems. Continue to give liquid feeds while flowering continues.

Varieties

'Tetra Mixed' is a tetraploid strain which grows to 60 cm with large, ruffled flowers in shades of yellow, gold, rose, lilac, tango, deep red and white. It has shown some resistance to rust fungus and is an excellent variety for cut flowers. 'Excalibur' grows to 40–50 cm and is best suited for bedding and borders. The large flowers on strong, straight stems are excellent for cutting and come in lovely mixed shades. 'Tom Thumb' is a compact-growing mound-shaped bush with attractive blooms in a beautiful range of clear colours. The bush grows to about 20 cm and has a beautiful flower display.

SPIDER FLOWER (CLEOME)

Spider flower is an unusual, shrubby annual growing to a height of 1–2 metres. It is an excellent background plant or for planting here and there in the garden. The flowers are pink, lilac, mauve or white, with long, spidery stamens followed by decorative seed pods. The plants are very adaptable and flower well providing they are exposed to sunlight for part of the day. They do well on light or heavy soils which are well drained and have had a mixed fertiliser added during preparation. Sow seeds in spring or early summer or again in early autumn. It is best to sow a few seeds direct in the garden in clumps or stations spaced 50–60 cm apart, and thin to the strongest seedlings.

Water regularly and cultivate between plants. Give liquid feeds when buds appear.

STAR DAISY

See Chrysanthemum.

STATICE

Statice or sea lavender has attractive 'everlasting' flowers for garden display or for cutting and drying. The plants reach 60 cm and are suitable for accent in the garden bed. They need a moderately fertile soil and a well-drained, warm, sunny aspect. Statice is a perennial plant but it is usually grown as a spring-flowering annual. Cut back for a second flowering.

In temperate climates, sow seed from autumn to early spring, but in cold districts avoid sowing during the colder months. It is

The unusual spidery flowers of cleome look good in mass plantings.

best to sow seed direct into a well-prepared bed to which a mixed fertiliser has been added. Sow a few seeds in clumps or stations spaced 30–40 cm apart and thin to the strongest seedling. The seeds are large and may have some pieces of the dried petals attached. It does not matter if these show above the soil.

Cover the seeds with about 12 mm of seed-raising mix. Seedlings often germinate slowly and erratically and may take 28 days or more to emerge, so keep the soil damp for this length of time. When the plants are established they need little attention. Providing a pre-planting fertiliser has been added before sowing, the plants usually flower well, but give them a side-dressing of mixed fertiliser towards flowering time if they appear backward. The flowers are borne on long stems in clusters and range in colour from white through yellow to rose and blue. For everlastings, cut the flowers when mature, tie them in bunches and hang them head downwards in a cool, dry place. If well dried, the flowers will last for a long time without losing colour. The most widely grown variety is sinuata hybrid, with an excellent colour range.

STOCK

Stocks are one of the most popular spring-flowering annuals. They are magnificent for garden display in beds and borders, excellent for indoor decoration and worth growing for their fragrance alone.

Stocks have come a long way from the sixteenth century when Peter Mathioli, an Italian botanist, first classified them in a group of plants which included his own name (*Mathiola incana*). At that time, flower colour was limited to purple only, but today, as a result of plant breeding and selection, there is a tremendous colour range: white, cream, yellow, pink, lilac, mauve, red, port wine and purple. Dwarf and tall stock varieties are now available, but possibly the greatest advance has been the development of strains with a very high percentage of double flowers.

Oddly enough, stocks belong to the same botanical family (*Brassicaceae*) as many of our important cool-season vegetables – broccoli, cabbage, cauliflower, and turnips – so many of their requirements for climate, soil and fertiliser are very similar. Stocks, like the cabbage group, are really biennials but are

grown as annuals. The plants prefer friable, fertile soils with plenty of organic matter (in the form of compost, animal manure or leaf mould) added. Also apply a mixed fertiliser such as Gro-Plus Complete Plant Food at one-third of a cup per square metre and a liberal ration of lime, except on alkaline soils. All these should be added to the soil beforehand and dug in to a depth of 15–20 cm so that the soil is in first-class condition for either transplanting seedlings or direct sowing. Drainage is also important because stocks will not tolerate wet feet. Raising the beds 15–20 cm above the surrounding surface will usually give adequate drainage. Generally, the plants prefer rather dry conditions but should be given sufficient water to keep them growing steadily during the season. Stocks prefer a sunny position; tall varieties should be sheltered from strong winds.

In temperate and cold climates, seeds can be sown from midsummer to autumn, but in warm northern districts autumn sowings are best. Seeds can be sown in seed boxes or punnets for transplanting and this method may be preferable for early sowings. Good results are possible by sowing direct, especially when a moisture-holding material, such as seed-raising mix, is used to cover the seeds. Stock seeds germinate quickly (ten to fourteen days) and seedlings grow rapidly, so direct sowing avoids transplanting shock. When sowing direct, scatter a few seeds in clumps or stations and keep moist until seedlings merge. Thinning the seedlings in each clump is only necessary if they are too crowded. It does not matter if a few seedlings are close together, providing there is sufficient space between each clump.

Whether you transplant seedlings or sow direct, the planting distance will depend on the variety (dwarf or tall). As a guide, dwarf and column varieties are spaced 20–30 cm apart, but you should allow 30–40 cm for taller branching types.

When the plants are well established, cultivate regularly between individual plants or clumps to control weeds and water them when necessary, but do not overdo it. Give liquid feeds of soluble fertiliser as the plants grow, especially towards flowering time. An exception is the column type, which may develop lateral branches and new buds from the centre of the florets when it is fed too generously. Another point of interest is that plants which produce single flowers can often be discarded at the seedling stage. Seedlings which are tall, thin-leafed, dark green and vigorous usually produce single flowers, so many gardeners discard them when transplanting or thinning out. The method is not infallible, but has been used with some success. Most double strains available today will produce from 60 to 85 per cent double-flowered plants, giving good results. When plants are flowering well, remove all spent blooms to promote new buds to form and prolong the display.

Varieties

'Austral' is a beautiful strain bred and selected by Yates in Australia. Plants are vigorous, growing to 50 cm with a brilliant colour range including white, cream, apricot, various shades of pink and lavender, red and purple with other attractive bicolours. A short, closely packed central spike is soon followed by many lateral spikes. This is an excellent garden variety. 'Giant Perfection' ('Giant Imperial') is the popular, semi-bush stock. The central flower spike is followed by lateral spikes. Individual flowers are large, with a high percentage of double flowers. Colours include white, cream, buff, many shades of pink, lavender, lilac, purple and

brilliant red. Because they are non-branching, space between plants can be reduced to 20–30 cm. Dwarf stocks are available that grow to 25 cm tall with tightly packed flower spikes of double florets. They have the perfume and full colour range of the taller, branching types. They are excellent for borders and combine well with low bedding plants like alyssum, nemesia, pansy and viola. They are also suitable in exposed situations where taller strains may be damaged by wind.

STRAWFLOWER (HELICHRYSUM)

Strawflower is a popular 'everlasting' with paper-textured flowers in white, gold, mauve, pink and red. The plants grow to 75 cm or more and are ideal for background planting or for planting here and there in the garden. They will do well on most garden soils with base fertilisers added, but need a warm, sunny position. They also tolerate hard conditions better than most garden annuals but respond to regular watering in dry weather. Sow seeds either in autumn or spring in boxes or punnets, covering the seed lightly with seed-raising mix.

Transplant seedlings when 5–7 cm high, spacing them 30 cm apart. Cut flowers when half open, tie in bunches and hang head downwards in a cool place to dry. Dried flowers will last for months.

Strawflowers are great for colour in the garden or in the home.

GROWING YOUR GARDEN

SUNFLOWER (HELIANTHUS)

Although sunflowers are the 'giants' of the summer flowering annuals, some modern varieties are much shorter than older varieties, which grew to 3 metres or more. Flower form and colour range have been improved in recent years. Plants must be grown in full sunlight in a sheltered position to avoid wind damage. They are adapted to both light and heavy soils but do best when the soil has been improved by adding organic matter and a mixed fertiliser at one-third of a cup per square metre. The soil must be well drained. Sow seed in spring or early summer when weather and soil are warm. Although seed can be sown in boxes or punnets and transplanted when small, it is best to sow seeds direct in the garden by scattering a few seeds in clumps 50–60 cm apart and thinning to one or two seedlings. The plants need little attention when established, apart from watering in dry weather and cultivation to control weeds. Flowers for indoor decoration should not be too old before cutting. Remove spent blooms to prolong flowering.

Varieties

'Yellow Empress' is a tall strain with extra-large blooms. 'Bronze Shades' is a medium grower (150 cm) with single flowers which are excellent for picking. Flowers are in shades of bronze and terracotta, and many are tipped with yellow and pink.

SWAN RIVER DAISY (BRACHYCOME)

This delightful little annual grows to 20–30 cm tall with dainty single flowers in blue, mauve or white. It is useful for low borders or as an accent plant. Its rather spreading growth makes it ideal for rockeries or container growing. Brachycome will grow on quite poor soil and prefers light, well-drained soil in a sunny position.

Sow seed in spring or early summer, either in seed boxes or punnets for transplanting seedlings 20 cm apart, or sow a few seeds direct in clumps at the same distance. The seed is quite small so cover very lightly with seed-raising mix. When the plants are established they need little attention, as they withstand hot, dry conditions. Do not over-water.

SWEET PEA

Sweet peas are one of the most popular spring-flowering annuals for garden display and for cut flowers. Most varieties grow 2–3 metres tall, so need support in the form of a trellis, tripod or wire mesh cylinders. There are also dwarf strains. The dwarf plants grow 25–60 cm tall and are ideal for borders, rockeries, window boxes and pots. Sweet peas have been improved tremendously in flower form, size and colour range since they were first introduced to England from Sicily in the seventeenth century. Most sweet peas grown in New Zealand are early bloomers that flower during winter. In today's modern sweet pea strains, colours range from pure white and cream through numerous shades of pink, lavender and mauve to light and dark reds, blue and purple. Bicolours and 'flakes' with veined markings on the petals are also becoming more popular.

Sweet peas need ample sunlight and usually do poorly when shaded. If growing on a trellis the rows should run north–south so that the vines receive as much sun as possible. Good drainage is essential and it is best to raise the bed 15–20 cm above the surrounding surface so that water is shed quickly after heavy rain. Soil preparation is most important, too. Except on naturally alkaline soils, lime should be added to the soil at about one cup per square metre on light soils and two cups per square metre on heavier soils. Spread a generous layer of compost, animal manure or well-rotted grass clippings on top of the soil and add a mixed fertiliser such as Gro-Plus Complete Plant Food at one-third of a cup per square metre or at a heaped tablespoon per metre along the row where seed is to be sown. The organic matter will improve the structure of both light and heavy soils, but as these materials are very often low in phosphorus and potassium the addition of fertiliser will make good any deficiency. On the other hand, avoid using fertilisers which are high in nitrogen. Dig the lime, organic matter and fertiliser into the surface soil to a depth of 10–15 cm so that the materials are mixed well. Then dig the bed over to spade depth, loosening rather than turning the soil so the topsoil stays on the surface. Always remember to dig or cultivate the soil when 'dark damp' – especially on heavy soil – to preserve a good crumb structure. Give the bed a gentle but thorough watering and leave it to settle for a week or two. Then rake the surface to destroy any weed seedlings and to bring the soil to a crumbly condition for sowing the seeds direct.

In most temperate climates, seed can be sown from midsummer to late autumn, but March or April are usually the best months. In cold districts, spring sowings can be made as well. As the germinating seeds are susceptible to damping off (especially in cold soil) it is advisable to dust the seed with fungicide before sowing. (See Chapter 7.) It is often a good idea to erect the support before sowing. This will avoid disturbing or treading on the bed after the seeds are sown. Mark out shallow drills 2–3 cm deep and press the seeds into the soil, spacing them 5–7 cm apart. If the soil is loose and crumbly, cover the seed and lightly tamp down with the back of a rake. On very heavy soils, cover the rows with seed-raising mix. If the soil is 'dark damp' at sowing, additional watering is usually unnecessary until the seedlings emerge in ten to fourteen days. In very dry weather, or on very sandy soil, give extra water.

Overwatering is one of the main reasons for poor germination. For the same reason, soaking seeds in water before sowing may do more harm than good (see Chapter 7). If you wish to pre-germinate seeds, spread them out on wet blotting paper or towelling, or mix them with moist seed-raising mixture in a saucer or dish. This way they absorb water quickly but also get plenty of air, which is essential to germination. You can plant out the swollen seeds in a few days but handle them very carefully if they have started to germinate. Another point to remember is that some seeds may be smaller than others and may look pinched or shrivelled. These seeds are often the darker colours – red, mauves and blues – and if you discard them you may not have a full colour range.

Always sow all seeds in the packet or, if you have too many seeds, sow an average sample.

When the plants are 15–20 cm tall, place some twigs along the length of the row to help the tendrils to reach the netting. If the plants are spindly it may be necessary to cut them back slightly to promote sturdier growth. Laterals will appear when the plants are

Smaller-growing sweet pea varieties make excellent pot subjects.

20–30 cm tall. For general garden display allow these to grow on, but for exhibition blooms cut some out. Water the plants regularly, especially in dry weather, and every ten to fourteen days when buds appear. Remove spent blooms to prolong flowering. Sweet peas are usually not unduly troubled by pests and diseases. For control measures see Chapter 7.

Varieties

'Early Sunshine Mixture' has a splendid colour range of early-flowering, large-flowered sweet peas. 'Old Fashioned' is a rather later-flowering strain. The plants are extremely vigorous and bear large, ruffled blooms on long, sturdy stems. The flowers are heavily perfumed and very suitable for exhibition purposes.

Hint

If soil is too moist, sweet pea seeds rot away before they germinate. If in doubt, build a raised-up 'mini planting bed' using see-through plastic cups. Remove the bottom from each cup and sit upright on top of the soil. Fill with good-quality seed-raising mix and sow the sweet pea seeds inside. After the seeds germinate in the well-drained mix, the roots can move down into the soil and the plants will start to grow happily.

JUDY HORTON
GARDEN ADVISER, YATES

'Colorcade' is the most widely grown and popular of all the strains of sweet peas. This mixture of early-flowering blooms contains a complete range of all sweet pea colours and shades.

'Tiffany' is an early-flowering, tall, vigorous sweet pea featuring very large flowers on strong stems. Many blooms are true doubles, deeply frilled and bicoloured. A highly recommended variety.

'Bijou' is an outstanding dwarf sweet pea. Plants grow to 60 cm tall and flowers are beautifully perfumed in a full colour range. The flowers are as large as those of tall varieties and are borne on stems 20 cm long. An excellent variety for borders, rockeries, window boxes and pots, but remember that plants need full sunlight.

'Pixie Princess' is excellent for borders, rockeries, window boxes and pots. It grows to about half the height of 'Bijou', flowers a little later than 'Bijou' and is available in a wide range of colours.

One of the most interesting developments in recent years is the release of a range of Bicolour sweet peas. Following years of development work by a New Zealand plant breeder, Dr Keith Hammett, the Bicolour

sweet peas are notable additions. They have a wide range of colours and all, except one, have darker colours on the main petal with paler colours on the wing petals. This represents a major breakthrough in sweet pea colouring and, coupled with vigorous 2-metre high plants and blooms carried on strong stems, makes Bicolours a major new force in the sweet pea world.

SWEET WILLIAM

Sweet William (*Dianthus barbatus*) is a biennial or short-lived perennial growing to 40 cm tall. It is usually treated as an annual; seeds can be sown from mid-summer to autumn in most climates, but in both autumn and spring where colder. The cultivation of this free-flowering, attractive plant for beds, borders or rockeries is very similar to dianthus and carnation, to which it is closely related.

VERBENA

Verbena is a trailing perennial which may persist for two or three years, but is usually grown as an annual. The plants grow to 30 cm tall and continue to flower for many months. Flower colours include pink, mauve, red and purple, many with a white eye. Verbena is very adaptable and grows well in most garden soils, but it does need good drainage. It prefers full sunlight but will tolerate some shade. Seed can be sown in all the warm months, from spring to autumn.

You can raise seedlings in boxes or punnets for transplanting or sow a few seeds direct in clumps spaced 25–30 cm apart, thin each clump to two or three seedlings. Seed is slow to germinate, seedlings taking 21–28 days to emerge, so take care that the soil is kept damp but not wet for this length of time. Once established, the plants need very little attention. They tolerate quite dry conditions and grow well without extra fertiliser. Cultivate between plants to destroy weeds in the early stages but the bushy plants will soon cover the ground to form a dense mat. Cut back plants after flowering to promote a second flush of blooms.

'Vitality' is a new, compact variety, free-flowering with a brilliant range of colours, excellent for planting in odd corners of the garden and in rockeries. It is hardy and makes an ideal border plant.

excellent for borders, rockeries and containers and it flowers prolifically from early spring to summer.

VIRGINIAN STOCK

Virginian stock is a dainty little spring-flowering annual with tiny flowers in white, cream, lavender and pink. The plants grow to 20 cm tall and are excellent for low borders, edging and odd corners. Virginian stock is often sown over bulbs to disguise the bulb leaves as they die down after flowering. Virginian stock plants prefer a warm, sunny aspect but tolerate part-shade. They are very adaptable little plants and grow well on most soils, but add a mixed fertiliser when preparing the bed. In temperate climates, sow seed in autumn; in cold districts, sow in both autumn and spring.

Seedlings can be raised in boxes or punnets for transplanting, but it is best to sow direct – thinly in rows or a few seeds in clumps spaced 15 cm apart. Thinning is rarely necessary. Plants flower very quickly from seed. Give liquid feeds when buds start to show.

VISCARIA

Viscaria gives masses of dainty summer flowers in shades of pink, mauve, lavender and blue. The plants have thin, branching stems and grow to 30–40 cm. They need a warm, sunny position but are adaptable to both light and heavy soil to which a mixed fertiliser has been added during preparation. Sow seed in spring or early summer direct in the garden, scattering a few seeds in clumps spaced 15 cm apart. Cover with seed-raising mix.

Seedlings rarely need thinning, providing there is sufficient space around each clump. Water regularly in dry weather and mulch around plants to conserve moisture and discourage weeds.

WALLFLOWER

Wallflower is another old-world spring-flowering annual which has been improved in flower form and colour range but is still as fragrant as ever. The plants grow to 60 cm and are excellent for bedding or borders or for planting here and there in clumps or drifts in the garden. They prefer a warm, sunny aspect sheltered from strong winds. Like stocks (wallflowers belong to the same family) the

Violas are old-time favourites. Grown widely in Victorian times, they are now undergoing a resurgence in popularity.

VIOLA

Violas are close relatives of pansies and are grown in exactly the same way, although violas can be planted rather more closely together than pansies. The plants will continue flowering for a very long period, especially if the spent blooms are picked regularly. For general notes on soil, sowing and cultivation, refer to Pansy in this chapter.

Varieties

'Toyland' and 'Space Crystals' have large, velvety flowers and are excellent for beds or borders. They are self-coloured and without markings. As with pansies, colour-themed viola mixes like 'Surf Blues' and 'Beach Yellows' are becoming increasingly popular. 'Johnny Jump Up' is the original *Viola tricolour*, a delightful, small-flowered purple viola with streaked yellow centres. It is plants respond to friable, fertile, well-drained soil. Prepare the bed well beforehand, adding liberal quantities of compost or animal manure. On most soils, except those which are alkaline, add a ration of lime at one to two cups per square metre, depending on soil type. Then apply a mixed fertiliser such as Gro-Plus Complete Plant Food at one-third of a cup per square metre. Fork or spade these additives into the soil to a depth of 15–20 cm and leave in the rough state for four to six weeks. Cultivate again about a week before transplanting so that the soil is in a crumbly condition.

In most districts, seed can be sown from midsummer to autumn. Seed sown before April will produce plants which flower in late winter and early spring. Prepare an open, friable seed-raising mixture for boxes or punnets as described in Chapter 7. Sow the seeds in shallow rows and cover lightly with seed-raising mix. Water gently and keep damp until seedlings emerge in ten to fourteen days. Prick out seedlings when small into other containers (filled with the same soil mix) spacing them 3–5 cm apart. Grow them on until 5–7 cm high and then transplant them to the garden bed, spacing them 20–30 cm apart. Keep the plants growing strongly by regular watering and destroy weeds by surface cultivation, taking care not to damage the shallow roots. When buds appear, give liquid feeds of soluble fertilisers at intervals of ten to fourteen days. The double-flowered 'Winter Delight' is very fragrant and has double blooms in many colours. It blooms early and is ideal for cutting.

ZINNIA

Zinnias are one of the most popular summer-flowering annuals. Modern varieties, both tall and dwarf, have a wide range of flower forms and a tremendous range of colours. Zinnias are excellent for mass bedding, but many of the dwarf varieties make suitable border plants.

Zinnias, with their bright, paintbox-coloured blooms, do well in warm conditions.

Zinnias must be grown in full sunlight for best results and need shelter from strong winds. Soil should be well drained and improved with compost or animal manure, and a ration of mixed fertiliser and lime if the soil is too acid.

Prepare the bed well in advance so that the soil is in a crumbly condition for transplanting or direct sowing.

In temperate districts seed can be sown in early spring to mid-summer; in cold districts late spring or early summer sowing is best. Seed germination is often disappointing if seeds are sown in cold soil too early in the season, especially when sown direct in the garden. Germination is much improved if sowing is delayed until the soil warms up to 20°C or more. The seeds are quite large and can be handled easily, but it is advisable to dust them with fungicide to protect against damping off.

Early sowings can be made in seed boxes or punnets using an open, friable seed-raising mixture. Extra warmth can be provided by covering the containers with glass or clear plastic until the seedlings emerge (usually in seven to ten days). Grow seedlings on until 5–7 cm high before transplanting. When sowing direct, scatter a few seeds in clumps or stations and cover lightly with seed-raising mix. Thinning each clump is rarely needed unless the seedlings are overcrowded.

Whether transplanting seedlings or sowing direct, the distance between plants or clumps will depend on the variety and the size to which it will grow. As a general guide, space tall types 40 cm apart and semi-dwarf types 20 cm apart. Always pinch back the centre shoot of zinnias to promote the growth of laterals and produce a bushy plant.

Once established, the plants need little attention apart from regular watering (especially in dry periods) and cultivation to destroy weeds. In very hot weather, a good mulch of compost will conserve moisture and keep the roots cool. Give liquid feeds of soluble fertiliser when the plants are half-grown.

For ways to control mildew, a fungus which attacks the plants in later summer and autumn, see Chapter 6.

Varieties

'Gold Medal' (dahlia-flowered) is a blend of the best colours in this strain and has large double blooms on strong stems. Plants grow up to 1.2 m in height.

'Pallette d'Artiste' grows to 60 cm and is the most suitable variety for cut flowers. It produces a profusion of double blooms.

Zinnia linearis has masses of small, star-shaped yellow flowers over a long period. Plants are dwarf (to 30 cm tall) and are excellent for borders or rockeries.

Hint

Regular maintenance will ensure your garden remains healthy and vigorous: for perennials, this means pruning, trimming and cutting back; for annuals, it means dead-heading to prolong flowering.

CARAL OTHMAN
HORTICULTURALIST

FLOWER SEED MIXTURES

A number of mixtures of flower seeds for spring or autumn sowing are available for mass display, borders or special situations. These mixtures provide a wide variety of flower form and colour range.

BOUQUET OF BLUE

This mixture contains annual and some perennial blue flowers of medium height. It includes ageratum, centaurea (cornflower), delphinium, forget-me-not, larkspur, lupin, nigella, stock and other interesting blue flowers.

BOUQUET OF SUNSHINE

This is a blend of yellow, gold and orange flowers such as snapdragons, celosia, and dahlias.

COTTAGE GARDEN MIXTURE

This mix contains twenty hand-picked varieties designed to recreate the charm of the old-fashioned cottage garden.

COLONIAL COLLECTION

Contains a range of old favourites packaged according to height: low, medium and tall growing types in individual packs.

FESTIVAL OF FLOWERS

This will grow flowers year round for continuing colour and fragrance. The varieties are selected for suitability for all areas and include such colourful favourites as cosmos, dianthus, petunia and saponaria. Sow in spring.

HANGING BASKET AND PATIO COLLECTION

This is really two collections, both separately packaged. One is a collection of trailing plants for sowing around the edge of the container; the other a selection of more upright growing types. It has an overall range of 25 different flowers.

ROCKERY MIXTURE

This is a blend of attractive and useful plants for rockery planting. The mixture contains about twelve different flowers, most of which are dwarf types that vary in colour and flowering season.

SPRING BOUQUET

A cheerful mixture of spring-flowering annuals, it contains carnation, cornflower, everlasting daisy, painted daisy, poppy, snapdragon, stock and wallflower. Sow seed in autumn.

SUMMER FIESTA

This is a colourful mixture of summer-flowering annuals for spring sowing. It includes hot weather lovers such as aster, balsam, celosia, cosmos, marigold, petunia, phlox and zinnia.

WILDFLOWERS OF THE WORLD

As the name implies, this is a mixture of wildflowers gathered from many parts of the world.

Contrasting flower colours make a successful mixed planting.

PEST AND DISEASE CONTROL CHART
FOR FLOWERS AND ORNAMENTALS

GROWING YOUR GARDEN

PLANT	PEST OR DISEASE	SYMPTOMS	CONTROL
Aster	Aphids	Small insects under foliage and on flower buds.	Malathion, Target, Fruit Tree Spray, Confidor, Pyrethrum, Trigger Insect Spray, Mavrik
	Caterpillars	Caterpillar in leaves which come together.	Carbaryl, Malathion, Derris Dust, Pyrethrum, Mavrik
	Two-spotted mite	Foliage turns bronze and is unthrifty.	Mavrik
Azaleas and rhododendrons	Lace bug	Foliage becomes silver bronze.	Confidor
	Leaf miner	See Cineraria	
	Two-spotted mite	See Aster	
	Petal blight	Flecking and collapse of flowers.	Greenguard
Begonia	Powdery mildew	Powdery growths on leaves.	Greenguard, Baycor
Bellis (English daisy)	Rust	Bronze blisters on foliage.	Bravo, Baycor
	Two-spotted mite	See Aster	
Calendula	Rust	See Bellis	
	Two-spotted mite	See Aster	
	Powdery mildew	See Begonia	
Camellias	Dieback	Large, dark, dead areas on branches.	Remove and destroy infected twigs, spray with Champion Copper
	Balling	Flower buds do not open and bud scales are damaged due to bud mite.	Spray with Mavrik
Carnation	Thrips	White flecks on petals.	Malathion, Confidor
	Rust	See Bellis	
Chrysanthemum	Black aphids	Small, black insects underneath leaves and on flower buds.	See Aster
	Leaf spot and rust	Various spots on leaves.	Bravo, Fungus Fighter

GROWING YOUR GARDEN

PLANT	PEST OR DISEASE	SYMPTOMS	CONTROL
Cineraria	Leaf miner Two-spotted mite	Irregular yellow tracks on leaves.	Mavrik
	Leaf spot	Brown target spots on leaves.	Fungus Fighter
Cornflower	Aphids	See Aster	
	Powdery mildew	See Begonia	
	Collar rot	Plant rots at ground level.	Remove and destroy
Dahlia	Two-spotted mite	See Aster	
	Powdery mildew	Powdery film over foliage.	Greenguard
Delphinium	Powdery mildew	See Begonia	
Ferns	Mealybug	White insects with filaments under fronds.	Confidor
	Scale insects	Swellings along stem.	Conqueror Oil
	Aphids	Soft insects attack young growth.	See Aster
	Two-spotted mite	See Aster	
	Staghorn beetle	Holes in fronds and tips die.	Mavrik
Foxglove	Aphids	Insects on flower spikes and leaves.	Mavrik, Confidor
Geranium	Rust	See Bellis	
Gerbera	Thrips	Flowers deformed and flecked.	See Carnation
	Powdery mildew	See Begonia	
Gladioli	Thrips	Flecks on leaves and flowers.	See Carnation
Hibiscus	Caterpillars	Leaves stick together, holes in leaves.	See Aster
	Aphids	Young foliage distorted.	See Aster
	Beetles, weevils	Holes in foliage.	Carbaryl, Malathion
	Thrips	Flowers damaged.	See Carnation
Hollyhock	Two-spotted mite	Flowers become bronzed and dry.	See Aster
	Rust	See Bellis	
Larkspur	Powdery mildew	See Begonia	
Marigold	Two-spotted mite	Foliage becomes red-brown and unthrifty	See Aster
Pansy	See Violas		
Penstemon	Two-spotted mite	See Aster	

PLANT	PEST OR DISEASE	SYMPTOMS	CONTROL
Polyanthus	Two-spotted mite	See Aster	
	Mealybug	White fluffy insects under leaves and on roots.	Malathion sprays and soil drenches, Confidor
	Caterpillars	Holes in leaves.	Carbaryl, Pyrethrum, Mavrik
Roses	Aphids	Young foliage distorted.	Shield, Super Shield, Confidor
	Thrips	Flowers damaged by flecking.	Shield, Super Shield, Confidor
	Caterpillars	Leaf roll and holes in leaves.	Shield, Super Shield, Mavrik
	Two-spotted mite	See Aster	
	Black spot	Large black spots on leaves.	Greenguard, Fungus Fighter, Champion Copper, Baycor
	Powdery mildew	Powdery growth on leaves.	Greenguard, Fungus Fighter, Champion Copper
	Downy mildew	See Stock	
	Rust	See Bellis	
	Flower and bud blight	Grey fluffy growths on flowers and buds.	Greenguard
	Rose wilt virus	Leaves droop and bush is unthrifty.	Control aphids and remove and destroy infected bushes.
Snapdragon	Rust	See Bellis	
	Caterpillars	Green caterpillars on young flower buds.	See Aster
Stock	Aphids	Young plants deformed.	See Aster
	Caterpillars	On leaves and buds.	See Aster
	Downy mildew	Seedlings very unthrifty and white downy growths under leaves.	Fungus Fighter
Sweet Pea	Broad bean wilt virus	Plants wither and die, foliage becomes puckered.	Control aphids and plant later in season to avoid attack
	Thrips	See Carnation	
Violas	Aphids	Distorted foliage and shoots.	See Aster
Zinnia	Caterpillars	Holes in leaves and flower buds.	See Aster
	Powdery mildew	White powdery growth on older leaves.	See Begonia
	Leaf spot	Brown target spots on leaves and stems.	Fungus Fighter

FLOWERS FROM THE GARDEN

Picking flowers from the garden for the vase can be an intensely satisfying pastime. Each season will provide rich pickings for those who have established a cutting garden or are gathering from a mixed garden. Following a few basic rules will ensure your personal harvest stays fresher for longer.

CUTTING CLUES

- Invest in good-quality equipment. Maintain secateurs and scissors by regular sharpening with a whetstone. Blunt tools will crush stems, damage the parent plant and inhibit the cut flower from absorbing water.
- Cut in the cool of the day when transpiration is at its lowest. When picked early in the morning or in the evening, cut flowers are less likely to droop.
- Carry a bucket one-third filled with water when picking; plunge flowers straight in, rather than laying them in baskets. Collect a range of bucket sizes and use accordingly. Use a deep bucket for long stems and a shallow one for short stems. Separating sizes safeguards the flowers of the shorter, delicate plants from being crushed by the taller, heavier ones.
- Generally, flowers are best cut before they are fully open. The bud should be loose and showing a little colour. Dahlia, zinnia and rose flowers will not develop fully when picked at a tight bud stage.
- Where possible, cut long stems – the longer the stems, the easier the flowers will be to arrange. Strip off the bottom leaves as you go.
- When cutting flowers of bulbs leave the plant with some of its foliage. Without some remnant foliage to draw up new energy stores for the next season they will not survive.

STRAIGHT STEMS

To straighten long-stemmed flowers such as tulips, bind with string, wrap in stiff paper and leave overnight in water.

CONDITIONING FLOWERS

Directly after harvesting, bring flowers indoors. Place in a cool place out of direct sunlight and close to a bench and sink. Remove any leaves which will be below the vase water line.

Recut stems under water. Cut at an angle – a slight angle for soft stems, to prevent them from standing flat on the bottom of the bucket; at a 45 degree angle for woody stems to expose more of the fibrous centre which imbibes water.

Sappy and soft stems should be seared in boiling water. *Acanthus*, *Delphinium*, *Euphorbia*, *Helleborus*, hollyhocks, poppies, sunflowers and sweet peas benefit from this treatment. Keeping the flower heads

After treatment, leave all material to soak in deep tepid water for several hours – overnight if possible.

IN THE VASE

Keep vases in pristine condition by cleaning them with bleach rather than detergent. To prolong flower life check the water level every day and top up as required. In extremely hot weather change the water every second day. Avoid positioning arrangements in direct sunlight, close to ripe fruit (which emits ethylene) or near a heater during winter.

FLOWER FOOD

Add Floralife (available as a liquid or in sachets) or another floral preserver to the water to prolong freshness in cut flowers. As an alternative, add a teaspoon of sugar and a drop each of bleach and vinegar to the vase water.

away from the steam, dip the stems into 2.5 cm of boiling water for 30 seconds. Bubbles will emerge as the stem seals off. Immediately place the flowers in tepid water. Droopy roses will also revive with this approach.

Strip the leaves off woody-stemmed flowers – *Hydrangea*, lilac, *Camellia*, *Viburnum*, *Philadelphus*, *Rhododendron* – and leave the flowers to soak overnight before arranging them.

The long thin stems of tulips, roses and gerberas may bend after picking and will remain that way if not treated. To straighten them out, bunch stems together and wind string or florist's tape around the complete stem length. Wrap in stiff paper and soak overnight (see diagram opposite).

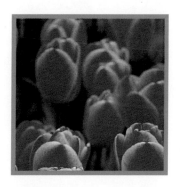

CHAPTER 11

FLOWERING BULBS

There are many kinds of flowering bulbs or bulbous plants which are easy to grow in the home garden. In this chapter we include the true bulbs and also those plants which are started from corms, rhizomes and tubers. To a botanist the differences are important, but for the average home gardener they are all sufficiently similar to be regarded as bulbs. However, it may be useful to describe briefly the characteristics of each kind of bulb.

TRUE BULBS

True bulbs have an onion-like structure consisting of layers of fleshy 'scale leaves' which are closely folded on each other. The fleshy scales enclosing the flower shoot are storage tissues filled with plant foods such as protein, starch and sugar, all of which are formed during the previous season's growth. For this reason, it is important to leave plants of true bulbs to die down naturally each year to provide as much nourishment as possible for the next season. It also explains why true bulbs can be grown successfully in bowls of fibre (or even water) which contain very little in the way of nutrients. When grown in soil, true bulbs will produce daughter-bulbs or bulbils which in time will become large enough to flower. Good examples of true bulbs are daffodil, jonquil, hyacinth, tulip and lilium.

CORMS

Corms do not have fleshy scales but consist of a shortened, swollen stem of solid storage tissue. The leaves arise in the axils of the scale-like remains of leaves of the previous season's growth. A new corm is formed on top of the old corm, which shrivels and dies. Small daughter-corms called 'cormels' may also develop. Examples of corms include anemone, crocus, freesia, ixia, gladiolus and ranunculus.

RHIZOMES

Rhizomes are underground stems, usually thick and swollen, containing storage tissue. They develop roots, leaves and flowering stems from the nodes or joints. Good examples are flag or bearded iris, lily-of-the-valley and Solomon's seal.

TUBERS

Tubers can be either swollen stems or swollen roots for storage. New shoots arise from axillary buds on stem tubers, or from buds on the short piece of stem on root tubers. Good examples of bulbs of this kind are cyclamen, arum lily and tuberous begonia.

BULBS IN THE GARDEN

Flowering bulbs are very adaptable and can be planted to give attractive garden effects. Some bulbs, especially anemone and ranunculus, are suitable for massed beds or borders. Lachenalias are good for low borders too. But most bulbs are best planted in bold clumps in the garden. Because of their different flowering times, many bulb varieties can be planted together to give a continuous and varied colour display. A garden that contains a good selection of many different bulbs is assured of some colour from late winter to summer or early autumn – jonquils and lachenalias in late winter or early spring, followed by daffodils, anemones and ranunculi. Spring brings hyacinths, freesias, tritonias and watsonias. Following on in summer are calla lilies and gladioli.

Terracotta pots filled with tulips create a stunning entrance. They can be easily moved when they are past their best.

Some spring-flowering bulbs can be planted under trees and on lawns or grassy slopes to become a permanent feature of the garden scene. In cold climates, bulbs such as bluebell, crocus, daffodil, grape hyacinth, jonquil, lily-of-the-valley, snowdrops, sternbergia and tulip become naturalised in these situations. In temperate districts, daffodils, jonquils, freesias, grape hyacinths and snowflakes are best for naturalising.

GENERAL BULB CULTURE

In the garden, a well-drained, sandy loam which is not overly rich is the best for bulbs and bulbous plants. But you can improve heavy soils by adding coarse sand and well-rotted organic matter to make them more friable. (See Chapter 3.) A light dressing of mixed fertiliser such as Gro-Plus Complete Plant Food or a specific bulb food should be incorporated into the soil during preparation and prior to planting. Avoid direct contact between fertiliser (or fresh manure) and the bulbs. Most bulbous plants will respond to feeds of liquid fertilisers when flower buds appear, and again after flowers have finished.

Some bulbs grow in full sunlight, others tolerate semi-shade. The best situation is given in the notes for each kind of bulb. Depth of planting varies with the size of the bulb, but a good general rule is to plant at a depth equal to twice the width of the bulb. Planting time,

together with approximate planting depth and plant spacing, is given in the notes and also summarised in the 'Planting guide for flowering bulbs' (on pages 219–221).

BULBS IN OUTDOOR CONTAINERS

Many bulbs grow to perfection in tubs, pots or troughs which can be moved about in the garden or on the terrace or balcony. Smaller containers can be brought indoors when the plants flower. Daffodils, jonquils, hyacinths (including grape hyacinths), bluebells, lachenalias, freesias and tulips can be grown this way. The containers, which must have drainage holes, should be at least 15 cm deep to allow for good root growth. Use a proprietary bulb potting mixture, or a friable, free-draining potting mix to which a little mixed fertiliser has been added, and fill the pots to the depth required. Set the bulbs in place – about half the distance apart for normal planting in the garden – and fill in the remainder of the mix to within 2–3 cm of the top to leave room for watering.

Keep the containers in a cool, shady place until leaves emerge and then move into a sunny but sheltered position. Keep the soil moist at all times but do not overwater. Give liquid feeds of soluble fertiliser if plants appear backward, and especially when buds appear.

BULBS FOR INDOORS

Hyacinths, crocuses, daffodils and tulips are favourites for bringing indoors. It is best to plant only one variety of daffodil or one colour of hyacinth in each bowl. This way all plants in the bowl will flower together. Make sure the bulbs you buy are firm and free from mould. If you are not quite ready for planting, store the bulbs in a cool, dry cupboard.

To promote earlier flowering on tall, strong stems, place bulbs of hyacinths and tulips in the crisper tray of the refrigerator (7–10°C) for three or four weeks before planting. Plant the bulbs in the moistened potting mix so that their tips are just below the surface. Space potted bulbs closely together, allowing 2–3 cm between bulbs.

....

Hint

Don't let soil type discourage you from growing certain plants. For instance, dahlias or bulbs planted in heavy soils often rot and die, especially when they are left dormant. To overcome this, incorporate a generous amount of coarse, gritty material such as pumice, sand or gravel into the soil before you plant. It will improve drainage and reduce waterlogging.

JACK HOBBS
GARDEN WRITER AND BROADCASTER

....

Water the pot well, drain, and keep in a cool, dark spot, or cover with another pot. Shoots emerge in six to eight weeks, although if bulbs have been chilled they may start a week or two earlier.

When shoots are clearly visible, move the bowls to a well-lit, airy room. When grown near a window, bowls need to be turned occasionally to keep the plants erect. Keep the mix damp, but not wet, while the plants are growing. If overwatered, tip the bowl on its side to drain.

Bulbs grown in pots are probably not suitable for reusing next season.

TOP FIVE BULBS FOR NATURALISING

FREESIAS

Because of their hardiness and their warm-climate origins (freesias come from South Africa), these plants will grow readily in most parts of New Zealand and can be left in place for many years (see picture on page 210).

SPANISH BLUEBELLS

Planted under trees, these heat-tolerant bulbs will let you create your very own bluebell wood.

IPHEION

Also known as star flower, this dainty little bulb has narrow, grass-like leaves. The flowers are blue or white and look good planted in drifts in well-drained garden beds.

SNOWFLAKES

Snowflakes can be aptly described by that well-worn phrase, 'harbingers of spring'. They are ideal for planting under trees and will multiply steadily over a number of years (see picture on page 213).

JONQUILS

The test of success in naturalising any bulb is to see it flourishing in old, abandoned gardens. Perfumed jonquils have proved themselves to be hardy survivors. Once established, they'll be with you forever.

IPHEION

SPRING-FLOWERING BULBS

ALLIUM (ORNAMENTAL ONION)

Allium, the ornamental onions, are easy to grow in all but the hottest subtropical gardens. *A. moly* (golden garlic) is a low-growing plant with star-like, bright yellow flowers, ideal for pots or naturalising under deciduous trees. *A. albopilosum* (star of Persia) provides late spring drama with huge metallic-violet flower heads on long stems. Plant in sun or part shade.

ANEMONE (WINDFLOWER)

Anemones produce excellent spring flowers in reds, pinks and blues for mass bedding and borders. They contrast well with ranunculus, which flower about the same time. Flowers of the St Brigid strain are semi-double or double, while the poppy-like flowers of the de Caen hybrids are single. Both are ideal for cutting. Anemones prefer full sunlight and a well-prepared, friable soil with a ration of mixed fertiliser added.

The best display is from new corms each year. Plant the corms in autumn, 3 cm deep and 15 cm apart, making sure the flat part of the corm is uppermost. In warmer climates delay planting until late autumn. Some gardeners prefer to start the corms in seedling trays and later transplant.

BABIANA

Babiana has violet-blue or mauve flowers, rather similar to those of freesias, which are produced on 20 cm spikes. The plants need full sunlight and, like other bulbs native to South Africa (freesia, ixia, sparaxis and tritonia), will tolerate rather dry conditions. Plant from late summer to autumn 5 cm deep and 7 cm apart. After the plants have died down the bulbs can be lifted and stored for replanting next season, but the plants can be left for several years if preferred.

BLUEBELLS

Also known as bells of the forest, these dainty, lavender-blue, bell-shaped flowers are ideal for clump planting in the garden or in a rockery. The plants are also useful for grassy banks and under trees where they become naturalised. They grow well in full sun or semi-shade. The larger Spanish bluebell is better suited to warm climates than the true English bluebell. Plants can be left undisturbed for a number of years. Plant bulbs in early to mid-autumn, 7 cm deep and 10 cm apart.

BRODIAEA (QUEEN FABIOLA)

Small, tubular blue flowers are borne on stems 30–40 cm tall. Plants prefer semi-shade and a well-drained soil and are suitable for borders, clump planting or in rockeries. Plant bulbs in autumn, 7 cm deep and 15 cm apart. They flower in late spring.

CHIONODOXA (GLORY OF THE SNOW)

This charming little plant from the mountains of Crete is only suitable for cold climates. Clumps grow 15 cm tall with blue and white star-shaped flowers in early spring. They need full sun and good drainage and should be left undisturbed once established. Plant bulbs in autumn, 7 cm deep and 10 cm apart.

CROCUS

One of the earliest spring-flowering bulbs, with small, cup-shaped flowers in purple, lavender and white on short stems, crocuses do best in a cool climate. Excellent for semi-shaded spots and rockery pockets with good drainage. Plants can be left undisturbed for many years. Plant in autumn, 5 cm deep and 10 cm apart.

CYCLAMEN

These attractive tuberous plants are usually started from seed sown in summer and early autumn and grown as pot plants. (See Chapter 16.) The tubers will carry over quite well but must be repotted 5 cm deep during late summer or early autumn.

DAFFODIL (NARCISSUS)

Daffodils are the best-known and most adaptable of all spring-flowering bulbs. They can be grown throughout New Zealand. They grow well in full sun or semi-shade and prefer a friable, well-drained soil to which a bulb fertiliser has been added. The plants respond to liquid feeds when buds appear. Daffodils can be grown in almost every garden situation. On grassy banks they can become a permanent feature, but are very popular for clump planting to combine with other spring annual flowers such as alyssum, nemesia, pansy, viola, linaria and Virginian

Beautiful striped flowers are features of some crocus varieties.

stock. They are excellent for growing in tubs, pots or troughs outdoors or for bowls indoors.

Daffodils come in a wide range of gold or cream shades and a variety of flower forms. Of the trumpet types, 'King Alfred' is still the best known, but 'Golden Lion' is another traditional yellow trumpet variety that does better in warmer climates than 'King Alfred'. 'Fortune', 'Ptolemy' and 'Salome' are also popular.

Smaller-growing or 'rockery' daffodils are useful for pots and small gardens. Plant bulbs in autumn (preferably before the middle of May in most districts), 12 cm deep and 10–15 cm apart. Bulbs in pots, troughs and bowls can be planted closer together than in a garden situation but will not be suitable to use again next season.

ERYTHRONIUM (TROUT LILY)

Trout lilies or 'dog's tooth violets' resemble small nodding lilies and are among the few bulbs that revel in a shady position. They thrive in a rich, moist, well-drained soil. During the winter–spring growing season plenty of moisture is required, but in summer they enjoy the relative dryness created by the

Hint

If you are picking daffodils or other sappy plants for display indoors, keep them separate from other flowers. The exudate from these plants will reduce the vase life of non-sappy flowers. Change the water daily to get the best out of your cut flowers.

MARILYN PAGE
HORTICULTURAL CONSULTANT

surrounding roots of trees and shrubs. The fleshy corms will not survive if allowed to dry out and must not be left out of the ground for too long. Plant corms as soon as they come available in late summer or early autumn. Lift and divide every few years to prevent overcrowding.

E. tuolumnense has dainty, bright yellow flowers. 'Pagoda' has large creamy-yellow flowers and large marbled leaves. 'White Beauty' has large white flowers and green-brown mottled leaves.

GROWING YOUR GARDEN

FREESIA

Freesias have been popular spring-flowering bulbs for a long time and are highly prized for their delightful perfume. The traditional New Zealand freesia is *Freesia* 'Burtonii', a small, creamy-white flower with an exquisite perfume. Many of the larger-flowered modern hybrids are also perfumed and come in shades of yellow, orange, rosy-red, ruby and blue. They are excellent for cut flowers too.

Freesias do best in a fairly sunny position but will grow well under shrubs and trees if not too shaded. They need a friable, well-drained soil which is not overly rich but with a scattering of mixed fertiliser worked into the soil during preparation. Usually this pre-planting fertiliser is all that is necessary. The plants are suitable for massing in beds or on grassy banks but are particularly attractive in clumps or in rockery pockets.

Freesias can be left in their permanent position for several years, or the corms can be lifted after the plants die for storing and replanting. Plant the corms in autumn at a depth of 7 cm at the same distance apart. Packs of red, blue, white, yellow and mixed colours are available.

FRITILLARIA

These attractive members of the lily family grow most successfully in cool climates. *Fritillaria imperialis* ('Crown Imperial') is the best known. The plants are 60 cm tall with drooping bell-shaped flowers in yellow, orange and bronze. They are best planted in clumps and should be left undisturbed unless they become overcrowded. Plant in autumn, 10 cm deep and 30 cm apart.

GRAPE HYACINTH (MUSCARI)

Grape hyacinths are one of the most attractive dwarf bulbs for spring, with spikes of bead-like, deep-blue flowers on stems 10–15 cm tall. The plants are very adaptable to soil and will grow in full sun or semi-shade. They are good for naturalising and ideal for clump planting in the garden or in rock pockets. Plant bulbs in autumn, 7 cm deep and 10 cm apart.

Freesias are some of the best bulbs for a warm climate.

HIPPEASTRUM (AMARYLLIS)

These plants produce magnificent trumpet-like flowers in salmon, red, rose and variegated white and red on strong stems 60 cm tall. The plants prefer friable, well-drained soil in a sunny position but will tolerate some shade during the day. They need plenty of water in spring when flower buds appear. Plant the bulbs in winter, keeping the neck of the bulb at the soil surface. Space bulbs 30–40 cm apart.

HYACINTH

New, improved varieties of hyacinth are very adaptable and will do well in all but very warm climates. They produce giant spikes crowded with large flowers in white, yellow, pink, red, light blue or dark blue. The plants prefer a sunny position and fertile, well-drained soil for best results. They are excellent for clump planting among spring annuals and are ideal for container growing, both outdoors and indoors. For container growing, select large, plump bulbs of good shape and free of blemishes.

Store bulbs in a cool spot in the house and pop them in the refrigerator crisper tray for three or four weeks before planting. Plant the bulbs in autumn (April or early May is a good time in most districts), 15 cm deep and 15 cm apart. Container-grown bulbs can be planted with the neck at soil level and the spacing reduced to 7 cm. Bulbs are available in separate colours or as assortments. Separate colours are best for pots as they will all flower at the same time.

IPHEION (SPRING STAR OR STAR VIOLET)

Dwarf plants with soft, green foliage and star-shaped, lavender-blue, mid-blue and white flowers on 15 cm stems. The plants become naturalised when grown under trees or shrubs and are attractive in borders, rockery pockets and containers. Plant in autumn, 5 cm deep and 7 cm apart.

IRIS

Bearded, Flag or German Iris

These plants grow from rhizomes into large clumps of attractive, grey-green leaves to 60 cm or more tall. The silky-textured, flag-like flowers come in a wide range of colours including yellow, gold, lavender, mauve, purple, brown and white. Many have combinations of more than one colour. Bearded iris does well in almost any garden situation but prefers a sunny aspect and well-drained soil. Add a ration of Gro-Plus Complete Plant Food when preparing the soil; an application of lime is recommended on acid soils. Plant in autumn through to winter, keeping the top of the rhizome at soil surface. Space rhizomes about 30 cm apart.

Dutch and Spanish Iris

Unlike Flag iris, the Dutch and Spanish types grow from bulbs and not from rhizomes. The plants form clumps and have flowers in a range of colours including blue, bronze, yellow and white on stems about 60 cm tall. The flowers of the Dutch iris are larger and rather earlier than the Spanish types. Plant bulbs in autumn, 10 cm deep and 15 cm apart.

IXIA (CORN LILY)

These attractive South African bulbs have clusters of bell-shaped flowers in shades of yellow, gold, pink, orange and port wine on stems 60 cm tall. Excellent for cut flowers. The plants need a sunny position and are best grown in clumps among annuals or between shrubs. Plant bulbs in autumn 7 cm deep and 10 cm apart.

JONQUIL (BUNCH-FLOWERED NARCISSUS)

A close relative of daffodils, jonquils are even more adaptable to climate and soil. They are one of the first bulbs to flower in late winter or spring, with small clusters of fragrant, daffodil-like blooms. They are useful for naturalising on lawns or grassy slopes and are attractive in clumps around shrubs. The plants can remain undisturbed for many years. The most popular variety is 'Soleil d'Or' with its orange-red cups surrounded by gold petals; many other varieties have cream or white blooms. Plant in autumn, 10 cm deep and 10 cm apart.

LACHENALIA (CAPE COWSLIP)

These are attractive dwarf plants from South Africa with 15 cm spikes of tubular, waxy flowers in shades of yellow, orange-red, red

GROWING YOUR GARDEN

or green, according to variety. The plants prefer full sunlight and a well-drained, friable soil. They are excellent for borders, clump planting, rockery pockets, outdoor pots and troughs, and indoor bowls as well. 'Pearsonnii' is a New Zealand-raised cultivar and one of the best, with many blooms per spike. The buds are reddish with the flowers opening golden-yellow and tipped red. 'Scarlet Bloom' has vibrant red, green-tipped flowers. Plants may remain in the ground for several years, or bulbs can be lifted when foliage dies for replanting the following season. Plant in autumn, 7 cm deep and 10 cm apart.

LILY-OF-THE-VALLEY (CONVALLARIA)

These dwarf plants grow from rhizomes and have tiny, fragrant, bell-shaped white or cream flowers in late spring. The plants need a shady, moist but well-drained position with plenty of organic matter in the soil. Plants can remain undisturbed for several years. Plant rhizomes in winter 3 cm deep and 10 cm apart. Plants can also be grown in pots for indoor decoration, especially in warmer climates where they do poorly in the garden.

Ranunculus grows from a claw-like corm. Always plant with the 'claws' down.

ORNITHOGALUM

There are three widely grown species of this spring-flowering bulb. All three need well-drained soil and prefer sunlight for at least half the day. They are best left for several years to form clumps but can be lifted after foliage dies and replanted next season if preferred. The plants prefer warm climates. *Ornithogalum thyrsoides* (Chincherinchee) grows to 30 cm with clusters of papery-white flowers which open from the base upwards. It is good for cut flowers, which are capable of changing colour when the stems are dipped in dye or coloured ink. *O. arabicum* (Arab's Eye) has papery-white petals surrounding a black centre and the blooms have an aromatic fragrance. *O. umbellatum* (Star of Bethlehem) has waxy, white flowers striped with green on the underside of the petals. Plant bulbs in autumn, 7 cm deep and 15 cm apart.

RANUNCULUS

Ranunculus, like anemone, is excellent for mass bedding, borders or for planting in clumps or drifts with other spring-flowering annuals. Plants grow to 60 cm and the semi-double and double flowers come in remarkable shades of red, crimson, scarlet, pink, orange, yellow, lemon, cream and white. Bulb packs of the Picasso strain are available as separate colours (red, pink, orange, gold, white) or as mixtures. Lower-growing strains are proving very popular, as they are less affected by winds. Ranunculus need full sunlight and a friable, fertile, well-drained soil to which organic matter and mixed fertiliser has been added during preparation. They respond to liquid feeds when buds form. You can dig and store the corms after the foliage dies down but results are usually better from fresh corms each year. Plant corms in autumn 3 cm deep and 15 cm apart. Make sure the corms are planted with the 'claws' downwards. The corms can be started in a shallow seedling tray for transplanting later.

SNOWDROPS (GALANTHUS); SNOWFLAKES (LEUCOJUM)

Both these small, spring-flowering bulbs have dainty, white bell-shaped flowers with a green spot on the outside of each petal. The

Hint

Zephyrantes are widely available in New Zealand. They are closely related to amaryllis, and are also known as flowers of the west wind. Their flat, papery seeds can be germinated by floating in water. Pot up as soon as the roots appear.

TONY PALMER
HORTICULTURAL SUPERINTENDENT
UNIVERSITY OF AUCKLAND

plants are excellent for clump planting and need a semi-shaded or shaded aspect for best results. They are excellent for planting under deciduous trees where winter sun can reach them, or on grassy banks. Plant bulbs in autumn. Snowdrops are usually only grown in cooler climates. Snowflakes are adaptable to a wide range of climates. Plant 7 cm deep and 10 cm apart.

Snowflakes are ideal for naturalising in lawns or under deciduous trees.

SPARAXIS (HARLEQUIN FLOWER OR WAND FLOWER)

These bulbs from South Africa need much the same conditions as freesias, including a sunny, well-drained position. They are excellent for naturalising on lawns or grassy slopes and suitable for rock gardens and outdoor container growing. The bell-shaped flowers are quite large and come in shades of red, orange and cream with black geometrical markings. Plant in autumn, 7 cm deep and 10 cm apart.

TRITONIA (MONTBRETIA)

This is another bulb from South Africa. The plants are very similar in height and flower form to sparaxis. Flower stems are rather longer, however, and flowers are in shades of orange, pink and red. Tritonias are grown in the same way as sparaxis or freesias. Plant bulbs in autumn, 7 cm deep and 10 cm apart.

TULIP

In the sixteenth century, single tulip bulbs fetched fantastic prices in Holland and other European countries. Tulips have large, beautifully formed, bell-shaped flowers in dazzling shades of cream, yellow, orange, pink, scarlet, red and deep maroon. The plants do best in cool climates but are very adaptable and should be grown more widely in temperate climates. The newer Monet series is adaptable to a wider climatic range and features large blooms on strong stems, some reaching 60 cm. These plants prefer full sunlight but will tolerate semi-shade. Bokassa tulips have short stems, are perfect for pots and flower very early, which also helps them to handle warm climates. Tulips need friable, well-drained soil which has been prepared before planting with compost and a mixed fertiliser. Tulips do not like acid soils so it is best to add a ration of lime if your soil has acidic tendencies. (See Chapter 4.) When flower buds appear, give liquid feeds of soluble fertiliser to promote long, strong stems and large blooms.

Tulips are best grown in clumps in the garden surrounded by dwarf annuals like alyssum, bellis or violas. They are ideal for container growing too. As for hyacinths, chill the bulbs in the refrigerator crisper before planting. Plant in autumn (late April or May are best in most districts), 12 cm deep and

12 cm apart. After flowers and foliage die, lift the bulbs for storing in a cool place and replanting next season. In warmer climates it may be best to buy new bulbs each year for a good display.

....

Hint

To hold gladioli flowers for up to three days, pick stems when the colour is just showing on the floret. Pick at dusk or dawn and place on a barely damp cloth in a cool, dark place. The day before using, snip off a few centimetres of stem and place in water.

MARILYN PAGE
HORTICULTURAL CONSULTANT

....

WATSONIA (BUGLE LILY)

Watsonias develop into large clumps of strap-like foliage 90–120 cm tall. The flower spikes are even taller, with dainty, tubular flowers in pink, salmon, red and white. Flowers are excellent for cutting in late spring when other flowers may be scarce. The plants are useful for background work and can be divided after the foliage dies in late summer or early autumn. Watsonias can become an environmental weed in some areas. Check local conditions before planting. Plant in autumn, 7 cm deep and 30 cm apart.

SUMMER-FLOWERING BULBS
AGAPANTHUS (AFRICAN LILY)

These vigorous, bulbous plants are evergreen and grow into large clumps 60–90 cm tall, although there are some lower-growing dwarf varieties. The large clusters of tubular flowers are blue or white. Agapanthus are good background plants but will grow almost anywhere – even on dry banks in full sun, or in shade under trees. Because of their vigorous roots and spreading habit, they crowd out weaker plants and can tend to take over the garden. Clumps can, of course, be thinned and replanted if necessary. Plant from late autumn to early winter. Just cover the fleshy rhizomes and space them 50 cm apart.

AMARYLLIS (BELLADONNA LILY BRUNSVIGIA)

These plants are also known as Naked Ladies. Large, fragrant, trumpet-shaped flowers are usually pink but also creamy white. Plants grow in full sun or under deciduous trees in semi-shade. They are best left undisturbed for a few years but can be lifted when dormant after flowering. Plant bulbs in late autumn or early winter, with the neck of the bulb protruding from the soil, and space them 30 cm apart. Brunsvigia is a close relative and is grown in the same way.

BEGONIA (TUBEROUS)

Usually grown in pots in a sheltered area, shadehouse or glasshouse, the magnificent semi-double or double blooms of tuberous begonia come in shades of red, pink, orange, yellow and white. The plants need a rich, friable, well-drained soil. Tubers can be carried over for repotting the following year. Plant or repot tubers in spring with the top or crown level with the soil surface.

CALLA

Callas prefer a sunny but damp position with fairly rich soil. Too much moisture when the bulbs are dormant in winter may cause them

Agapanthus will grow almost anywhere.

to rot, so lift them after foliage dies for replanting in late winter. *Zantedeschia elliotiana* grows to 60 cm with bright yellow lilies and white-spotted leaves. *Z. rehmannii* is smaller (30 cm) with dainty mauve-pink blooms. *Z. aethiopica* is the Lily of the Nile or arum lily. It is tolerant of poor drainage and, in warmer climates, the leaves are evergreen. Plant in late autumn or early winter, 10 cm deep and 20 cm apart.

CANNA

Canna is a vigorous plant 90–150 cm tall and forming dense clumps of brilliant green or bronze leaves from its tuberous roots. The large flower clusters, with lily like blooms, come in shades of cream, yellow, orange, pink and red. Some flowers are attractively spotted. Cannas prefer full sun but need damp or even wet conditions. After flowering, the stems can be cut down to ground level for regrowth in spring, or divided for replanting. Some varieties, however, tend to remain green all year round. Plant rhizomes in winter or early spring, 5 cm deep and 50 cm apart.

CRINUM (VELDT LILY)

The white or pinkish, fragrant flowers of crinum resemble lilies and are borne on stems 60–90 cm tall. Some species are evergreen while others die down after flowering. The plants prefer an open, sunny aspect and do best in warm coastal areas. The unusually large bulbs may be planted with a light soil covering at almost any time of the year, spacing them 30 cm apart.

DAHLIA

Dahlias flower right through summer into autumn and are very easy to grow, offering a huge array of different flower forms and colours. There are dwarf forms for pots or large, long-stemmed forms ideal for picking. Tubers are available in spring. Plant them into well-drained soil, well prepared with compost and Gro-Plus Complete Plant Food. Dahlia tubers are best lifted in autumn for replanting in spring, especially in cold climates. Divide the tubers, at least every three years, when the buds are clearly visible, in autumn or in spring. Always leave a part of the old stem on divided tubers. Alternatively, dahlias are easily

propagated from cuttings taken from new growth in spring. Dahlias need full sun, shelter from strong winds and summer moisture. Feed with liquid fertiliser every few weeks and remove spent flower heads to encourage continuous flowering. Stake tall varieties to prevent wind damage. Dahlias may be attacked by insects and fungi, mainly in summer. These are easily controlled by spraying with Shield or Super Shield.

DICENTRA (BLEEDING HEART)

Dicentra grows to 25 cm tall with sprays of red, heart-shaped flowers. The plants do best in cool–temperate or cold climates and prefer deep, well-drained soils, but need plenty of water in spring to mid-summer when flowers appear. The plants are dormant from late summer to spring. Plant the tuberous roots in autumn or early winter, 10 cm deep and 60 cm apart.

GALTONIA (SUMMER HYACINTH)

A tall (120 cm) bulbous plant from South Africa with clusters of white, drooping, bell-shaped flowers, galtonia is a good background plant but needs a sunny position. It is best in warmer districts, as the plants are sensitive to frost. Plant bulbs in spring, 10 cm deep and 20 cm apart.

'Black Magic' is a stunning new dahlia by leading plant breeder Keith Hammett.

GLADIOLUS (SWORD LILY)

Gladiolus is one of the most spectacular of summer-flowering plants, both for garden display and cut flowers. The orchid-like blooms come in a wide range of clear colours and pastel shades. Packs of separate or assorted colours are available from garden stores and nurseries. The plants prefer full sunlight and are best planted in clumps alongside dwarf summer-flowering annuals. The plants, when well grown, may reach 150 cm in height, so it is best if they are sheltered from strong winds. To prevent wind damage, tie three or four plants in a clump to a garden stake just before the flower buds appear.

Gladioli adapt easily to a variety of climates and can be grown in hot, mild and cold districts. Flowering takes about 90 to 100 days from planting and it is best to plant so that flowers appear before or after the extreme heat of summer. They need a well-drained, friable soil which should be prepared in advance by adding compost and some mixed fertiliser. In warm districts, planting can be made from May to September so that the plants flower before the hottest months. In cold districts it is best to delay planting until August or later. It is good insurance to dust the corms with a fungicide such as Captan before planting. Plant the corms 10 cm deep, spacing them 20 cm apart. Thrips are a serious insect pest of gladioli so it is necessary to spray with insecticide every two weeks after the plants reach the four-leaf stage. (See Chapter 6.) In warm weather, always cut flower spikes when the first flowers open. The remaining buds will open indoors if the stems are in water. Corms can be lifted after the leaves turn yellow and start to die – generally about four to six weeks after flowering. Allow the leaves to dry out, then cut them off close to the corm. Dust the corms with fungicide and store in a dry, cool place until the next planting season.

GLORIOSA (CLIMBING LILY)

Gloriosa is a climbing lily that uses its leaf tips to cling onto a support. It grows 2–3 metres tall with orange or red, flared trumpet-shaped flowers in summer. The plants prefer a sunny position but tolerate semi-shade. The offsets must be carefully removed from the corm as the roots are brittle and easily damaged. Plant corms horizontally in early spring, 3 cm deep and 30 cm apart.

GLOXINIA

These spectacular tuberous plants are best grown in pots in shadehouses or glasshouses where they are protected from wind and rain. They can also be grown indoors in a well-lit spot, but not in direct sunlight. They need ample moisture and a fairly even temperature (about 20°C). The bell-shaped flowers have a velvety texture and come in many shades of cream, pink, red, blue and purple, many of which are spotted or have contrasting edges and throats. Tubers can be dried off like cyclamen at the end of the flowering season for replanting. (See Chapter 10.) Plant tubers in winter or spring with the top of the tuber at soil level. Gloxinias can be raised from seed.

HEMEROCALLIS (DAY LILY)

These bulbous plants produce clumps of pale-green foliage 60–75 cm tall with flowers in cream, orange and red. Flowers last one day, but new flowers open over a long period. They prefer a sunny position. Plant bulbous roots in autumn to winter, 10 cm deep and 30 cm apart.

KNIPHOFIA (TORCH LILY OR RED HOT POKER)

These attractive plants form large, dense clumps with long, poker-like stems bearing masses of small, tubular flowers which open from the base. Colours range from yellow through to orange and red. Plants prefer a sunny position and are useful as background plants. They are best left undisturbed for several years. Plant bulbs in autumn or winter, 10 cm deep and 60 cm apart.

LILIUM

These are the true lilies. There are many species and varieties and hundreds of hybrids with an endless array of attractive flower forms and colours. The most widely grown are the November Lily or Christmas Lily (*L. longiflorum*) with white trumpet-shaped flowers; Tiger Lilies, *L. tigrinum* (orange), *L. speciosum* (pink), *L. speciosum album* (white); *L. regale* (large creamy-white, purple-backed flowers) and Golden Rayed Lily of Japan (*L. auratum*) with large, white flowers spotted purple and striped yellow. Most of the liliums form large clumps which should ideally be left undisturbed. They need half-sun and a friable, well-drained soil, but respond well to generous watering in summer and mulching to keep the soil cool and moist. Plant the scaly bulbs in late autumn to winter, 10–20 cm deep (according to bulb size) and 30–40 cm apart. They flower in late spring to late summer, according to variety.

Hint

To encourage the formation of more double flowers on tuberous begonias, carefully pinch out the smaller single flowers growing on either side of each existing double flower.

DIANA SELBY
LANDSCAPE ARCHITECT

LYCORIS

See Spider Lily.

NERINE

See Spider Lily.

SOLOMON'S SEAL (POLYGONATUM)

Solomon's seal is a good bulbous plant for cool, shady situations or dappled sunlight. The slender, oval leaves grow in clumps (60 cm tall) from shallow rhizomes and the curving stems bear white, bell-shaped flowers tipped with green. Plant rhizomes in late autumn to winter, 3 cm deep and 25 cm apart.

SPIDER LILY (LYCORIS, NERINE)

These two plants have similar flowers and are usually grown in clumps which are best left undisturbed. They prefer a well-drained soil and sunny position. Lycoris flowers are yellow (*L. aurea*) or red (*L. radiata*). Nerines flower before the foliage appears, in the same way as Belladonna lilies. Flowers are pink (*N. bowdenii*) or scarlet (*N. sarniensis*).

All the spider lilies are excellent for cut flowers. Plant bulbs in winter or early spring, keeping the neck of the bulb above the soil surface. Space the bulbs 15 cm apart.

GROWING YOUR GARDEN

Liliums, the true lilies, are garden aristocrats.

Lycoris, one of the spider lilies, blooms in late summer and autumn.

SPREKELIA (JACOBEAN LILY)

Sprekelia have large, crimson, orchid-like blooms 10 cm in diameter and borne on naked stems 15–30 cm tall. The plants prefer sandy, well-drained soil in a situation with half-sun. Plant bulbs in late winter and early spring with the necks of the bulbs just above the surface. Space them 12 cm apart.

STERNBERGIA (AUTUMN DAFFODIL)

A dwarf, bulbous plant to 20 cm high, sternbergia needs full sunlight and rather dry conditions. The golden, crocus-like flowers appear with the leaves in autumn. Plant in early summer, 10 cm deep and 15 cm apart.

TIGRIDIA (TIGER FLOWER OR JOCKEY'S CAP)

These unusual, colourful flowers with broad pink or red petals surrounding smaller, spotted petals are borne on 30–40 cm stems in early summer. Individual flowers last for only one day but there is a succession of blooms. The plants need a well-drained, sunny position and are best planted in clumps to remain undisturbed for a few years. Plant late autumn and early winter, 7 cm deep and 7 cm apart. Plants can also be raised from seed.

TUBEROSE (POLIANTHES)

The fragrant, white flowers of tuberose are favourites for bridal bouquets. In warm and mild climates the plants will flower at any time of the year, but summer is the best flowering period. The plants prefer a warm, sheltered position with plenty of moisture in summer. Once an individual bulb has bloomed, it will not flower again but will develop a number of bulblets. These can be separated from the clump in spring. Plant in winter or early spring, just covering with soil and spacing them 20 cm apart.

VALLOTA (SCARBOROUGH LILY)

These evergreen bulbous plants grow to 40 cm tall with clusters of large, orange-scarlet, trumpet-shaped flowers on strong stems. The plants prefer a sunny position but are very adaptable to soil. The clumps are best left undisturbed. Plant bulbs in winter or early spring with the neck of the bulb level with the soil surface. Space bulbs 20 cm apart.

ZEPHYRANTHES (AUTUMN CROCUS OR STORM LILY)

Zephyranthes is an excellent bulbous plant to grow for late summer and autumn flowering. The clumps grow to 20–30 cm tall with white (*Z. candida*), pink (*Z. rosea*) or yellow (*Z. citrina*) crocus-like flowers. The plants are evergreen in most climates. Plant bulbs in late autumn, winter or early spring, 7 cm deep and 30 cm apart. They are called storm lilies because of their habit of bursting into flower after summer rains or storms.

PLANTING GUIDE FOR FLOWERING BULBS

NAME AND COMMON NAME	PLANTING SEASON	PLANTING DEPTH (CM)	DISTANCE APART (CM)	FLOWERING SEASON
Agapanthus (African lily)	Spring	Note A	50	Summer
Allium (Ornamental onion)	Autumn	15	20	Spring–early summer
Amaryllis (Belladonna lily Brunsvigia)	Late autumn–winter	Note A	30	Summer
Anemone (Windflower)	Autumn	3	15	Spring
Babiana	Late summer–autumn	5	7	Spring
Begonia (tuberous)	Spring	Note B	In pots	Summer
Bluebells (Scilla)	Autumn	7	10	Spring
Brodiaea (Queen Fabiola)	Autumn	7	15	Late spring
Brunsvigia (see Amaryllis)				
Calla	Late autumn–winter	10	20	Summer
Canna	Winter–early spring	5	50	Summer
Chionodoxa (Glory of the Snow)	Autumn	7	10	Early spring
Clivia (Kaffir lily)	Autumn	Note A	30	Late spring
Crinum (Veldt lily)	Autumn–spring	Note A	30	Summer
Crocus	Autumn	5	10	Late winter–early spring
Cyclamen	Late summer–autumn	6	In pots	Late winter–early spring
Daffodil (Narcissus)	Autumn	12	10–15	Spring
Dahlia	Spring	7	30	Summer–Autumn
Dicentra (Bleeding Heart)	Autumn	10	60	Early summer

Note A. Just cover with soil.
Note B. Plant with top of bulb at soil surface.

GROWING YOUR GARDEN

NAME AND COMMON NAME	PLANTING SEASON	PLANTING DEPTH (CM)	DISTANCE APART (CM)	FLOWERING SEASON
Erythronium (Trout lily)	Autumn	8	10	Spring
Freesia	Autumn	7	7	Spring
Fritillaria	Autumn	10	30	Spring
Galtonia (Summer hyacinth)	Spring	10	20	Late summer
Gladiolus (Sword lily)	Late winter–spring	10	20	Summer
Gloriosa (Climbing lily)	Winter–spring	3	30	Summer
Gloxinia	Winter–spring	Note B	In pots	Summer
Grape hyacinth (Muscari)	Autumn	7	10	Spring
Hemerocallis (Day lily)	Autumn–winter	10	30	Summer
Hippeastrum (Amaryllis)	Winter	Note B	30–40	Late spring–summer
Hyacinth	Autumn	15	15	Spring
Ipheion (Star violet)	Autumn	5	7	Spring
Iris, bearded, flag or German	Autumn–winter	Note B	30	Late spring
Iris, Dutch and Spanish	Autumn	10	15	Spring
Ixia (Corn lily)	Autumn	7	10	Spring
Jonquil (Bunch-flowered narcissus)	Autumn	10	10	Later winter–early spring
Kniphofia (Torch lily, red hot poker)	Autumn–winter	10	60	Summer
Lachenalia (Cape cowslip)	Autumn	7	10	Spring
Lilium	Late autumn–winter	10–20	30–40	Summer
Lily-of-the-valley (Convallaria)	Winter	3	10	Late spring

Note A. Just cover with soil.
Note B. Plant with top of bulb at soil surface.

NAME AND COMMON NAME	PLANTING SEASON	PLANTING DEPTH (CM)	DISTANCE APART (CM)	FLOWERING SEASON
Lycoris (see Spider lily)				
Nerine (see Spider lily)				
Ornithogalum	Autumn	7	15	Spring
Peacock Iris (Moraea)	Autumn	5	5	Spring
Ranunculus	Autumn	3	15	Spring
Snowdrop (Galanthus)	Autumn	7	10	Spring
Snowflake (Leucojum)	Autumn	7	10	Spring
Solomon's seal (Polygonatum)	Late autumn–winter	3	25	Summer
Sparaxis (Harlequin flower, Wand flower)	Autumn	7	10	Spring
Spider lily (Lycoris, Nerine)	Winter–early spring	Note B	15	Late summer
Sprekelia (Jacobean lily)	Late winter– early spring	Note B	12	Summer
Sternbergia (Autumn daffodil)	Early summer	10	15	Autumn
Tigridia (Tiger flower, Jockey's cap)	Autumn–winter	7	7	Early summer
Tritonia (Montbretia)	Autumn	7	10	Spring
Tuberose (Polianthes)	Winter–early spring	Note A	20	Summer
Tulip	Autumn	12	12	Spring
Vallota (Scarborough Lily)	Winter–early spring	Note B	20	Late summer
Watsonia (Bugle Lily)	Autumn	7	30	Spring
Zephyranthes (sp) (Autumn Crocus)	Winter–early spring	7	30	Autumn

Note A. Just cover with soil.
Note B. Plant with top of bulb at soil surface.

CHAPTER 12

ROSES

Roses have always been a favourite flower in the garden. They were cultivated by the ancient Babylonians, Greeks and Romans, and no other flower has received more attention from gardeners through the ages. Modern varieties, with their superb colour range, flower form and fragrance, make them irresistible for garden display or for cut flowers.

Roses are extremely adaptable to both climate and soil. In cool, temperate and cold climates, roses have successive flushes of bloom during warm weather, but in warm subtropical climates they flower almost all year round. Many of the rose blooms sold by florists during winter are grown under glasshouse conditions.

There are so many different types of rose that there is one to suit any situation in the garden, always providing there is sufficient sunlight and good drainage. Hybrid tea or bush roses can be used in garden beds, generally with low-growing winter or spring-flowering annuals, perennials or bulbs to give colour to the garden during their dormant period. Floribunda roses make good borders or low hedges, while climbing roses can be trained on walls, fences and pergolas. Standard roses or weeping standards, which are grafted on to tall root stocks, are excellent for borders or accent plants. They provide lots of cut flowers and allow other annual flowers (and even vegetables) to grow beneath them. In recent times there has been a strong interest in growing and understanding 'old-fashioned' roses. There are quite a few varieties available but devotees are best advised to seek out and consult specialist growers. One spectacularly successful new-generation rose is 'Flower Carpet'. It has good mildew resistance, flowers for up to ten months, is evergreen in all but the harshest of climates, flowers prolifically and does not require any fancy pruning. A two-year-old plant can produce up to 2000 flowers during its flowering period. 'Flower Carpet' grows into a broad bush about 1.5 metres wide and up to 80 cm high. It is excellent for borders, lawn substitutes, patio pots or hanging baskets.

SITUATION AND SOIL

Roses need a sunny position to grow and flower well. They should not be grown too close to other shrubs or trees which will compete with them for light, moisture and nutrients. Good drainage is necessary too. Raising the bed 15–20 cm above the surrounding level will usually provide sufficient drainage on heavy soils.

Roses are very adaptable plants which can be grown on both sandy and clay soils. While they tolerate clay soil better than most plants, they do not prefer or need a clay soil to grow well. The ideal soil is a loamy topsoil with good structure, and a clay subsoil which will give an even supply of moisture – provided the clay is well drained and allows excess water to move away from the root zone. Sandy soils, which hold moisture badly, should be improved by adding plenty of organic matter as described in Chapter 3.

Because roses are long-lived plants, it is worthwhile spending some time and energy in preparing the soil well before planting. It is best to add organic matter (animal manure, compost or spent mushroom compost) and dig it into the topsoil about four to six weeks before planting. If the soil is naturally acid, lime can be added at the same time. Use about two-thirds of a cup per square metre on sandy soils and double this quantity on heavy soils. As roses cannot make use of fertilisers until growth commences there is no need to apply them during the soil preparation stage.

TOP FIVE
ROSES FOR POTS

'BONICA'

Arching canes smothered with pastel-pink, double blooms on a small-growing bush make this a good choice for a wide pot.

'FLOWER CARPET'

Flowers for up to ten months of the year and amazing disease resistance make these roses, in pink, pale pink, red, white and yellow, ideal for pots.

'ICEBERG'

This popular rose grows to more than 1 metre so needs a good-sized tub, but its generous blooming qualities make it worth any extra effort.

'KAPITI'

A spreading shrub with clusters of rose-pink semi-double blooms, which are produced from spring to autumn.

'WHITEOUT'

A compact patio rose with clusters of small, pinky buds opening to formal white blooms.

FLOWER CARPET

Ensure the soil is in a good crumbly condition for planting by digging it over again about two weeks before planting to break up any clods and mix the organic matter through the soil more evenly. Always cultivate heavy soils when damp so that they crumble easily.

PLANTING

These days many roses are sold in containers and may be transplanted at any time of the year. Bare-rooted roses are planted during their dormant season and are available at garden stores and nurseries from late May to August. In mild climates, June and July are good months for planting because the plants are then completely dormant. In colder areas planting can be delayed until August.

....

Hint

To ensure that you get the best result from roses growing in containers, remove them from their pots when doing the winter pruning. Prune the roots lightly and repot in the same container, but use fresh potting mix. There is no need to disinfect the container, just give it a good wash.

THE TWO ANNS
A & A CONSULTANTS

....

Bare-rooted roses dry out quickly; when the roots have dried the plants will very often die. When buying plants, check that the stems, which may be bright green or reddish-brown in colour, are smooth and free of any wrinkling, especially at the top of the stem. Such wrinkling indicates that the plants have been allowed to dry out at some stage. Don't buy rose plants until you are ready for planting. The bed should be finally prepared and well settled so you can start planting when you bring the plants home. If you are unable to plant that day, unwrap the plants and heel them into a shady spot in the garden, cover the roots well with soil and water thoroughly. This way you can 'hold' plants until they can

Candy Stripe produces nicely shaped blooms on a medium-sized bush.

be put into their permanent positions. When you have a number of roses to plant, cover them with a wet bag or stand them in a bucket of water. These days, most bare-rooted roses are sold 'packaged', that is, their roots are protected by some moisture-holding packaging material, and this and the whole root system is wrapped in plastic. The protective material should be gently hosed off before the rose is planted. Discard the packaging material: don't put it into the planting hole. The planting hole should be large enough to allow the roots to spread out naturally without bending them. Holes should be not less than 30 cm in diameter and about 20 cm deep. Make a mound of crumbly soil on the bottom of the hole on which to rest the plant and spread the roots. The height of the mound should be adjusted so that the bud union (where the scion is budded onto the root stock) is slightly above or at soil level. Now, cover the roots with 7–10 cm of damp crumbly soil and firm it down well to prevent pockets of air remaining around the roots. Then add half a bucket of water gently, so that soil is not washed away from the roots. Let the water drain away and then fill in the remainder of the soil without firming. The leftover soil is used to form a raised ring around the plants to help direct later watering to the plant roots.

Keep the surface soil free and moist by scattering compost or leaf mould around the plant. Later watering will depend on the weather: check the newly planted roses once a week and if the soil is dry give them about half a bucket of water. After planting, use only a slow-release type of fertiliser such as MagAmp or Multicote as the plants are dormant and will not utilise it until growth commences in early spring.

GENERAL MAINTENANCE
WATERING, MULCHING, WEEDING

When rose plants are established, heavy watering encourages the roots to go deeper so that plants can tolerate longer periods of dryness. This approach is preferable to frequent light sprinklings which promote shallow roots close to the surface. During the main growing period (spring to autumn) a mulch of compost or leaf mould around the base of the plants will help to conserve moisture and control weeds. When rose bushes lose their leaves in autumn, little or no watering is required except in warm, subtropical climates where roses can behave more or less as evergreen plants. Contact herbicides like Zero and Roundup are also useful in controlling weeds among rose bushes if they are grown alone without annual plants. They can be sprayed around the plants, providing they do not contact leaves or green, sappy stems. These herbicides have no residual action in soil and break down quickly into harmless compounds.

English roses bred by David Austin combine the best characteristics of old and modern roses.

FERTILISING

Fertilisers are necessary for vigorous growth and good-sized, quality flowers. Immediately after planting use only slow-release fertilisers as recommended above. An application of mixed fertiliser can be given in late December or January to encourage an autumn flush of blooms. Specially formulated fertilisers, such as Gro-Plus Rose Food, are ideal. With established plants, apply fertiliser in late winter or early spring and again in late summer. This can be scattered around the plants (not too close to the main stem) and lightly raked into the soil. If the soil is mulched, the fertiliser can remain on the surface as the nutrients will wash down to the soil below. Always apply fertilisers when the soil is evenly moist and water well afterwards to disperse the nutrients safely to the root zone. Alternatively, slow-release fertilisers such as MagAmp are also suitable.

CUTTING BLOOMS

With young rose bushes, do not cut flowers with long stems, as the plants need as many leaves as possible to develop into vigorous bushes. Cut blooms with short stems only. With older bushes, cutting flowers with short stems leads to tall, leggy growth, so make the cut more towards the base of the stem to encourage new growth to come from eyes or buds where the stem is thicker and sturdier. Always make cuts about 6 mm above an eye and slanting back slightly behind the bud. Roses keep best if cut late in the afternoon and placed in a bucket of water overnight for arranging in the morning.

Hint

Cottage and shrub roses can be pruned with hedge shears in winter. You can also use hedge shears to dead-head these plants in summer. Always clear away clippings as they can harbour disease.

CATH AND BOB MATTHEWS
MATTHEWS NURSERIES

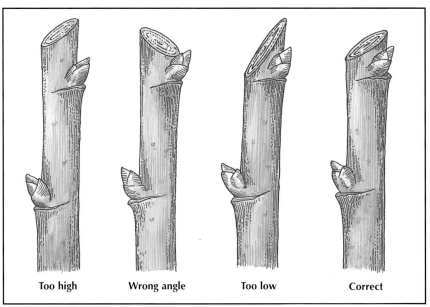

| Too high | Wrong angle | Too low | Correct |

When pruning roses, make sure the secateurs are clean and sharp to avoid bruising. The cut should be made just above a bud pointing in the direction you wish the new shoot to grow.

PRUNING

Summer pruning is often called 'summer trimming' and is usually done in late January or early February. It consists of a tidy-up, and entails removing any dead branches or those showing dieback by cutting back to the bud about 5 cm below the dead section. Any unproductive stems which have not produced good flowers or new shoots can also be removed.

It is important to distinguish between 'water shoots' and 'briar shoots'. The former are tall, vigorous, sappy shoots which suddenly develop from the crown of the plant (above the bud union) or from an old cane, while the latter arise from below the bud union. Always leave the water shoots because they are important in forming the future framework of the bush. They can be cut back when the wood is fully matured in winter.

Winter pruning is done in late July or early August in most districts but may be delayed until late August or early September in cold climates. The objectives of pruning are to remove dead, old or diseased wood, shorten healthy branches to promote new growth (flowers are borne on new wood) and to keep the bushes an appropriate size and shape.

STEP BY STEP – PRUNING ROSES

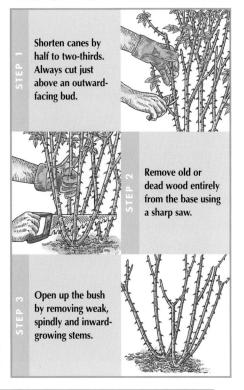

STEP 1
Shorten canes by half to two-thirds. Always cut just above an outward-facing bud.

STEP 2
Remove old or dead wood entirely from the base using a sharp saw.

STEP 3
Open up the bush by removing weak, spindly and inward-growing stems.

GROWING YOUR GARDEN

Hint

To maximise the flowering potential of your roses, dead-head them after each flush of flowers. Leave them to set hips for winter from the end of March onwards; this will help them through their natural cycle.

CATH AND BOB MATTHEWS
MATTHEWS NURSERIES

Make sure that the secateurs are clean and sharp and use a pruning saw for cutting thick, woody stems.

For dwarf or bush roses, cut out all dead, yellowing and diseased wood. Also discard thin or weak stems, those which rub against each other or are too crowded. Leave the strongest stems and shorten these by one-third of their length, cutting just above a bud pointing in the direction in which you wish the stem to grow. Floribunda or polyantha roses are usually cut back harder than bush roses, shortening stems by one-half. Standard roses are pruned in the same way as bush roses, but cut each stem to an outward growth and retain a neat shape. Climbing roses require slightly different treatment. Some gardeners give them a light pruning in winter and their main pruning after flowering in spring, removing old canes and dead wood and shortening the canes which remain. Rambling or wichuriana roses, most weeping standard roses, banksia roses and Dorothy Perkins types flower in spring on wood grown the previous year. Canes are cut out after flowering, but if this is too severe they can be cut back halfway to stimulate new growth.

Climbing roses are wonderful for landscaping. Here, on the right, 'Leander' tumbles over an arch.

Floribunda roses, like this 'Picasso', with its abundant flowering, make good garden subjects and mix well with other plants in garden beds.

PESTS AND DISEASES

Rose bushes can be attacked by a number of pests and diseases. Aphids (there are several kinds which attack roses) are the worst pests. Colonies of green, brown or pink insects cluster together on young, sappy shoots and flower buds. Thrips, also sap-sucking insects, are just visible to the naked eye and damage both buds and flowers. Two-spotted or red spider, a small mite, infests the lower surface of leaves, causing yellowing or browning and premature ageing. Some caterpillars chew holes in leaves and others roll leaves together. There are also several scale insects which attack roses.

The most serious diseases of rose plants are black spot and powdery mildew. Black spot causes small blackened areas, yellowing leaves and premature leaf fall. Humid weather, moderate temperatures and heavy night dews favour its spread. Powdery mildew produces a white powdery growth on leaves, stems and buds. It is most active in warm humid weather.

Pests and diseases can be effectively controlled by dusts or sprays of insecticides and fungicides. The recommended chemicals for control are given in Chapter 6. Many gardeners prefer to use an all-purpose rose dust or rose spray to control both pests and diseases rather than use individual chemicals. A number of such all-purpose sprays and dusts are available. The specially formulated Shield, Super Shield or ready-to-use Rose and Ornamental Aerosol are recommended.

After winter pruning, while bushes are still leafless, spray roses with lime sulphur. This can also be used to spray the soil underneath the rose bushes. It will help control fungal spores and rose scale.

Hint

For convenience in a can, try the new range of aerosol products from Yates to solve any problems you might be having with pests on your roses.

NICK HAYHOE
YATES NEW ZEALAND

TYPES OF ROSES

There are many different types of roses. To observe and learn about roses in your district, visit your local public rose gardens. There you can discover landscape ideas and new introductions and smell and touch rare and unusual varieties. Look for roses you like and observe their growing habits.

Hybrid tea rose 'Saratoga'. Hybrid teas are classic long-stemmed roses that are good for picking.

HYBRID TEA ROSES

Hybrid teas are the most popular type of rose and produce the largest, most perfectly formed flowers in a wide range of colours. They make a good garden display and are beautiful cut flowers.

FLORIBUNDA ROSES

Floribunda roses produce an abundance of flowers in a wide variety of colours. Borne in clusters or trusses, the flowers are inferior to those of the hybrid teas but they provide a greater display of colour, are reliable and longlasting.

CLIMBERS AND RAMBLERS

There is a vast range of climbing and rambling roses. Ramblers have long, pliable stems and bear large trusses of small flowers. They produce several strong stems from their base each year. Climbers make strong stems from any part of the plant and their height potential is far greater than that of ramblers.

Floribunda rose 'Sexy Rexy'. Floribundas flower abundantly from spring through to autumn.

Climbing rose 'Albertine'. Climbing roses may have long, arching canes or rambling, multibranched growth.

SHRUB ROSES

Most shrub roses are hybrids between wild species, hybrid tea roses and floribundas. They are extremely varied in habit, leaf shape and flower form.

Shrub rose 'Aotearoa'. 'Shrub rose' is a modern term for a bush rose that combines some characteristics of other rose types.

SPECIES ROSES

Species roses are those which are grown in their original wild form. They produce single, fine-petalled flowers, mainly in spring, followed by a display of decorative berry-like hips in autumn. They are particularly resistant to pests and diseases and require little pruning apart from the removal of soft tips and straggly growth.

Rosa rugosa. Rugosas are species roses which are renowned for their attractive rosehips (seed bearing fruit). They are the best for seaside plantings.

OLD ROSES

Old-fashioned roses encompass a broad group including Species, Old European, Tea and China roses. In recent years there has been a great upsurge in interest in them, due to their good garden qualities. They are particularly fragrant and hardy, and have a delightful, informal character. Heritage Roses attract enthusiasts and there are specialist growers throughout New Zealand.

Moss rose Rosa centifolia muscosa. Moss roses, like other old-style and heritage roses, have made a comeback in recent years.

MINIATURE ROSES

Miniature roses look like tiny floribundas, but have miniature leaves and flowers in perfect proportion. They normally grow betwen 20–50 cm high and are almost thornless. Miniature roses are rapidly increasing in popularity due to their novelty and versatility. They can be used for edging, growing in containers, rockeries, window boxes or indoors as temporary houseplants.

Patio rose 'Little Nugget'. Patio roses have gained in popularity recently. They have been bred so their leaves, stems and blooms stay in proportion.

CHAPTER 13

PERENNIALS, VINES AND CREEPERS

Perennial plants are those that grow for a number of years. This definition is very wide and could cover a vast array of plants including trees, shrubs, climbers, ferns, bulbs, cacti, succulents and many others – in fact, any plants which are not strictly annuals or biennials. In this chapter, however, we have concentrated on the most popular flowering perennials and climbing plants for the home garden.

PERENNIALS

Perennials – or, more precisely, flowering perennials – are defined as plants (mostly with non-woody stems and branches) which die back to the roots or an evergreen crown at the end of the flowering season. They burst into renewed growth the following spring. They repeat this cycle year after year, gradually spreading and increasing in size and number.

There are many perennials which can add interest and colour to the garden and they come in all shapes and sizes. Some grassy perennials such as New Zealand tussock grass (*Carex*) and New Zealand flax (*Phormium tenax*) have become popular as accent plants around buildings and pools.

Herbaceous perennials are those plants which, after flowering in summer, die down in autumn and become dormant in winter. They usually prefer cool conditions and have been used in the traditional herbaceous border or in English cottage gardens. Evergreen perennials are mostly natives of warmer climates and flower in spring. Whether herbaceous or evergreen, perennials can complement shrubs, annual flowers and bulbs. Many provide excellent flowers for indoor decoration, often at a time when annual flowers are scarce. Others have attractive, varied foliage in bronze, yellow-greens, grey and silver.

SOIL PREPARATION AND PLANTING

As most perennials will remain undisturbed for several years, it is important to prepare the soil well. Most perennials can be planted in late autumn and winter, so start preparation in early autumn. Dig the bed to spade depth and remove all tree roots and persistent weeds. Add organic matter in the form of animal manure or compost and a ration of mixed fertiliser such as Gro-Plus Complete Plant Food at one-third of a cup per square metre. Slow-acting blood and bone, or fertilisers based on blood and bone (such as Gro-Plus Camellia and Azalea Food) or other slow-release fertilisers (Multicote), are also suitable for providing nutrients over a long period. Raising the bed 10–15 cm above the surrounding level will ensure good drainage.

Select plants of the right height and size – dwarf plants in front and taller plants at the back of the bed. Make sure that each plant has sufficient space to develop without crowding or overlapping its neighbours. While a description of some popular perennials is given in this chapter, there are more comprehensive garden catalogues to help you plan your display. While many perennials can be started economically from seeds and cuttings, quicker results will be obtained by using established plants or divisions of good size. These can be purchased from garden suppliers and nurseries, or perhaps obtained from friends.

Most perennials are planted with the crowns slightly above soil level so that they do not collect water and rot during the dormant season. Plant the crowns so that the roots spread outwards and downwards. After planting, lightly fork the soil between clumps and water well.

MAINTAINING AND DIVIDING PERENNIALS

As the plants grow, cultivate between clumps to keep down weeds, or discourage the weeds by mulching with compost, pine bark or leaf litter. Taller plants may need hardwood stakes or circular wire supports (available from garden stores) to protect them against wind.

Remove spent flowers regularly during the summer months and cut out spent shoots of herbaceous perennials as they die down. Cut back shrubby, evergreen perennials

-----

Hint

To divide perennials, lift the entire clump and take the outside segments for replanting. Discard the old root-bound centre of the plant.

JACK HOBBS
GARDEN WRITER AND BROADCASTER

-----

to a tidy, compact shape after flowering. Removing the spent growth will also make it easier to fork over the surface between the plants.

Apply a ration of complete fertiliser in late winter or early spring each year. Slow-release fertilisers, such as Multicote, or organic plant foods like Bio-Gold, are ideal. They can be scattered liberally between and on plants without fear of fertiliser burn. Thinning or dividing perennials is usually necessary when the clumps become overcrowded after four or five years.

Often, the centre of the clump becomes old and straggly, so the best parts for replanting are on the outside. It is best to stagger the task of lifting and dividing, and do only a few plants each year. This way, you maintain the overall effect of the bed. After lifting clumps, dig the area well, adding more organic matter and fertiliser for the next few years. You will probably have more plants than you need for replacement, but your friends will be grateful for any leftovers.

FAVOURITE PERENNIALS

Abbreviations: H – herbaceous, E – evergreen, FS – full sun, HS – half sun, SS – semi-shade, S – shade. The height and spread of plants (given in cm) are shown in parentheses, for example (20–30).

ACANTHUS (BEAR'S BREECHES)

H, FS to S (200–120). Large, glossy-leafed plants with white and purple snapdragon-like flowers in summer.

ACHILLEA (YARROW OR MILFOIL)

A. filipendula H, FS (90–30). *A. tomentosa* E, FS (20–30). Both with lacy, finely divided leaves and rounded white, yellow, pink or red flower heads in summer.

ALSTROEMERIA (PERUVIAN LILY)

E, SS or FS (60–60). Large flowers in red, pink or yellow are ideal for picking. Dwarf varieties are ideal for pots.

ANTHEMIS (CHAMOMILE)

E, FS to SS (40–30). Semi-trailing plant with fern-like foliage and yellow or white daisy-like flowers in spring and summer. Good drainage.

ARENARIA (SANDWORT)

E, HS or SS (10–16). Moss-like trailing plant with tiny white flowers in spring.

ARMERIA (THRIFT)

E, FS to SS (40–20). Tufts of grassy foliage with globe-shaped heads of white or pink flowers in spring. Good drainage.

ARTEMESIA (WORMWOOD OR GHOST BUSH)

E, FS (120–60). Background plant with handsome, divided, greyish white leaves and yellow flowers in summer. Good drainage.

ASTER (MICHAELMAS DAISY)

E, FS or HS. Tall (120–50); medium (75–50); dwarf (20–25). White, pink, mauve, lavender or blue daisies in late summer and autumn.

ASTILBE (GOAT'S BEARD)

H, HS or SS (60–40). Clumps of attractive foliage with plumes of white, pink and red flowers in late spring. Moist position.

AURINIA (BASKET OF GOLD)

A. saxatile, E, FS or HS (30–30). Dwarf carpeting plant with soft mounds of foliage covered with brilliant yellow flowers in spring. Good drainage.

BERGENIA (SAXIFRAGA)

E, SS or S (30–40). Rosettes of large, rounded, glossy leaves with stems of waxy, pink or rose-coloured flowers in winter.

BRACHYCOME (SUSAN RIVER DAISY)

E, FS (30–50). Low-mounding plants have fine foliage and masses of daisy flowers in shades of purple, pink or blue. Good drainage.

CAMPANULA (BELLFLOWER)

H or E, SS (15–20). Neat dwarf mounds of green, covered with blue or white bell-shaped or star-shaped flowers in summer.

CERASTIUM (SNOW IN SUMMER)

E, FS (10–50). Dwarf carpeting plant with silvery-grey foliage and masses of white, cup-shaped flowers in late spring. Plants spread rapidly. Good drainage.

CHRYSANTHEMUM

(*C. maximum*, Shasta daisy) H, FS (100–75). Large daisy flowers with white petals and golden centres in summer. Protect from strong winds.

CINERARIA

(*C. maritima*, groundsel or dusty miller) E, FS or HS (60–30). Decorative, finely divided, silver foliage with brilliant yellow daisy-like flowers in late summer. Often listed as *Senecio cineraria*.

CONVOLVULUS

(*C. mauritanicus*, ground morning glory) E, FS (30–100). Ground cover and rockery plant with trailing stems and lavender-blue flowers in summer and early autumn. Good drainage.

CYPERUS

(*C. papyrus*, Nile grass) E, FS to SS (250–100). Broad clump of thick stems tipped with green, pendulous, thread-like flower spikes. *C. alternifolius* (umbrella plant) is similar but shorter (120 cm), with broader leaves. Very moist conditions for both.

DIMORPHOTHECA

(*D. aurantica*, African daisy) E, FS (60–100). Cheerful orange daisies in spring and summer. *D. ecklonis* has white flowers with a purple centre. *D. barberia* has mauve flowers. Good drainage for all three.

ECHINOPS (GLOBE THISTLE)

H, FS (150–100). Background plant with spiky, grey-green leaves and tall, steel-blue, globe-shaped flowers in summer. Good drainage.

ERYNGIUM (SEA HOLLY)

H, FS or HS (60–40). Thistle-like plant similar to echinops with cone-shaped blue flowers in summer. Good drainage.

EUPHORBIA

(*E. wulfenii*, yellow spurge) E, HS (100–100). Compact, rounded clumps of foliage covered with yellow-green or lime-green flower bracts in winter and spring. Good drainage required. Susceptible to frost.

Euphorbia wulfenii is valued for its unusual yellow/green flowers.

Euphorbia 'Jade Dragon' has striking blooms.

GROWING YOUR GARDEN

FELICIA

(*F. amelloides*, blue Marguerite) E, FS or HS (50–50). Mounds of foliage with dainty, sky-blue, daisy-like flowers in most seasons. *F. bergeriana* (kingfisher daisy) is a low-growing annual that is studded with bright blue flowers for months during the warmer part of the year. Good drainage for both.

FESTUCA

(*F. glauca*, blue fescue) E, FS or HS (25–25). Small attractive grass clumps with fine, blue-grey leaves. Good sun and drainage.

FILIPENDULA

H, HS or SS (100–40). Panicles of pink, mauve or white flowers with attractive, deeply cut, fern-like foliage. Prefers moist conditions.

HELIANTHUS (PERENNIAL SUNFLOWER)

H, FS (100–60). Bushy plants with many flowering stems with small sunflowers in autumn. Good drainage.

Variagated markings on hosta leaves can brighten shady spots in the garden.

Luscious hosta foliage is favourite snail food.

HELLEBORUS (WINTER ROSE)

H, HS to SS (50–40). Hand-shaped leaves with lime-green, mauve or purple flowers in winter and spring. Semi-shaded moist conditions.

HEUCHERA (CORAL BELLS)

E, FS or HS (50–25). Mounds of attractive, scalloped foliage with clusters of small, coral-pink bells in spring and summer. Requires moist conditions.

HOSTA

(*H. plantaginea*, plantain lily) H, FS to SS (25–40). Handsome, variegated or green foliage with small, bell-shaped, white or lilac flowers in summer. Moist conditions. Protect from snails.

HYPERICUM

(*H. reptans*, gold flower) E, FS or HS (10–30). Trailing plant with attractive foliage and yellow, five-petalled flowers in late spring. Good drainage.

LAVENDULA

(*L. spica*, lavender) E, FS or HS (50–30). Attractive clumps of silver-grey, aromatic foliage and lavender-blue flower spikes in early summer. Good drainage.

LIATRIS (GAY FEATHER)

H, FS or HS (60–30). Clumps of grass-like leaves with tall spikes of rose-purple flowers in summer. Good drainage.

LYCHNIS (MALTESE CROSS)

H, FS or HS (60–30). Compact clumps (evergreen in mild climates) with red flowers on wiry stems in late spring.

MECONOPSIS (BLUE TIBETAN POPPY)

H, FS to SS (100–40). Beautiful large, crepe-petalled poppies in late spring. Good drainage but regular watering. Notoriously difficult to grow.

MESEMBRYANTHEMUM (PIG FACE OR ICE PLANT)

E, FS (25–75). Drought-resistant carpeting plant with succulent leaves and silky-petalled flowers in late spring. Very wide colour range. Good drainage.

MONARDA
(BERGAMOT OR BEE BALM)

H, HS or SS (60–50). Large clumps with many stems bearing pink, mauve or red flowers in summer. Moist conditions.

NEPETA (CATMINT)

H, FS or HS (25–25). Soft mounds of sage-green foliage (attractive to cats) with dainty sprays of lavender-blue flowers in late spring and summer. Good drainage.

NIEREMBERGIA
(BLUE CUP FLOWER)

E, HS or SS (20–25). Dwarf border or rockery plant with lacy foliage and masses of blue, cup-shaped flowers in summer.

Bergamot can be a feature in the late-summer garden.

Hint

The foliage of *Helleborus orientalis* **should be cut back** in early May, before the flower buds appear. This will improve the flower display during winter, and keep the risk of botrytis to a minimum.

TERRY HATCH
JOY PLANTS

OPHIOPOGON
(MONDO GRASS)

E, SS or S (25–25). Clumps of green or black, strap-like leaves with white or cream flowers in muscari-like spikes in summer.

PAEONIA (PEONY ROSE)

H, SS (75–50). Cool-climate plant with large, fragrant, ruffled or single flowers in spring. Flower colours in shades of pink, mauve, red and white. Good drainage.

PENSTEMON (BEARD TONGUE)

H, FS (75–50). Bushy 'gloxinia-flowered' types have spikes of pink, mauve and red flowers in late spring and summer. Good drainage.

PHLOX

(*P. paniculata*, perennial phlox) H, FS to SS (60–50). Good herbaceous border plant with flowers in every shade of pink, mauve, salmon and white. Flowers in late spring to early autumn.

PHORMIUM
(NEW ZEALAND FLAX)

E, FS or HS (150–75). Background or accent plant. Green, bronze, red-purple or variegated (green–white) strap-like leaves. Red or yellow flowers on tall spikes in summer. Handles tough conditions and salt air.

PLATYCODON
(BALLOON FLOWER)

H, HS or SS (60–60). Herbaceous border plant with balloon-like buds which open to star-shaped, violet-blue flowers in summer. Good drainage but regular watering.

STACHYS (LAMB'S EAR)

E, FS to SS (20–30). Dwarf clumps of furry, silver-grey leaves for edging or ground cover. Spikes of small purple flowers in summer. Frost susceptible.

STOKESIA (STOKES' ASTER)

H or E, FS to SS (60–40). Dense clumps with large, lavender-blue daisy flowers in late spring and summer. Good drainage but adaptable to climate and soil.

GROWING YOUR GARDEN

Flower spikes of veronica (speedwell).

THALICTRUM (LAVENDER SHOWER)

H, HS or SS (150–50). Mass of fern-like foliage (similar to aquilegia) with tall, shivery stems bearing tiny lavender flowers on lateral branches in summer.

VERONICA (SPEEDWELL)

H, FS to HS (30–30). Rosettes of glossy, pointed leaves and pink, mauve or blue flower spikes in spring and summer. Good drainage.

VINCA

(*Catharanthus rosea*, Periwinkle) E, FS (35–25). This plant produces masses of five-petalled, single flowers in spring and summer, in shades of pink and white, often with a contrasting darker eye. It has been greatly improved in recent years with many compact and colourful forms being developed. The plant looks somewhat like a dwarf impatiens but will grow happily in full sun and stand up well to heat. Vincas are perennial in a frost-free climate. Cut back well in early spring to encourage bushy growth or replace plants annually.

VIOLET

(*V. odorata*) E, HS or SS (20–40). Attractive clumps of rounded leaves with fragrant purple (occasionally white) flowers in winter and spring. Good drainage but regular watering. Best replanted every few years.

Refer also to perennial plants described in Chapters 10 and 11.

VINES AND CREEPERS

'Climbers' is perhaps a better word than 'vines and creepers' to describe this group of plants because most, if not all of them, need support of some kind. Because climbing plants grow vertically, they are good space savers in the garden. They can be used to provide large masses of foliage as a background to shrubs and annuals. Many have attractive and fragrant flowers. Climbers are also useful to cover a bare wall, an ugly fence, an old stump or dead tree. They add more privacy to a corner of the garden. Deciduous vines and creepers growing over a trellis or pergola are ideal for shade in summer but let in winter sun. (See also Chapter 13.)

TYPES OF CLIMBERS

Vines and creepers cling to their support in different ways. Some, like honeysuckle and wisteria, grow by twining their long stems around the available support – and other plants, if they are growing too close. Others develop thin tendrils or claws which grasp wire or timber to keep the stems upright. Good examples are clematis, pyrostegia (flame vine) and vitis (ornamental grape). Another group of climbers – ficus, hedera (ivy) and Virginia creeper – have aerial roots or sucker pads which cling to brick or stone walls, bark of trees and timber. The last group are the woody scramblers like bougainvillea, which lean on their supports and bustle their way upwards.

SOIL PREPARATION AND PLANTING

Because most climbers will become a permanent garden feature, it is advisable to prepare the soil well by digging to spade depth and adding organic matter in the form of animal manure or compost. Sites against walls may contain builder's rubble, which should be removed and replaced with good soil. Add a ration of complete fertiliser at one-third of a cup per square metre. Slow-release fertilisers and fertilisers based on blood and bone are also useful for a pre-planting ration. Climbers, like most plants, need good drainage, so make provision for this, especially against brick or stone walls which are likely to trap water. It is a good

idea to plant vines or creepers at least 20 cm from a solid wall – 30–40 cm is even better if there is room.

Most climbers can be propagated from cuttings, layers or root divisions or you can buy started plants from garden stores or nurseries. Deciduous types are planted in winter but most evergreens are best planted in early autumn or spring. Some quick-growing evergreen vines which are most useful in a new garden are *Pandorea pandorana* (wonga-wonga vine), *Solanum jasminoides* (white potato vine) and *Clematis paniculata* (New Zealand clematis).

SELECTING VINES AND CREEPERS

It is important to choose suitable plants for your climate and for each situation in the garden. Some creepers spread quickly by self-layering and tend to take over the whole garden if not kept in check. Akebia, macfadyena, ficus, hedera, jasmine and wisteria all layer readily. Others, such as bougainvillea, clematis, hardenbergia and solandra, are very vigorous in warm, moist situations and may need cutting back regularly. A selection of climbing plants is given below with brief notes on the growth characteristics of each.

Abbreviations: D–deciduous, E–evergreen, SD–semi-deciduous, A–annual, FS–full sun, HS–half sun, SS–semi-shade, S–shade.

AKEBIA

(*A. quinata*) D, FS or HS. Vigorous twining creeper with divided foliage and fragrant, umbrella-shaped, lime-green to purple flowers in spring. If too vigorous, prune back after flowering and shorten the leaders. All climates.

BOUGAINVILLEA

E, FS. Large, woody scrambling creepers with hard, hooked thorns. Plants need full sun and tolerate dry conditions. The showy flower bracts make a dazzling display in spring and summer. Needs strong support and hard pruning if plants are too vigorous. Warm–temperate, subtropical. The best-known variety is 'Scarlet O'Hara', a bright red form. There are many others, including some double-flowered dwarf varieties.

CAMPSIS

(*C. grandiflora*, Chinese Trumpet Vine) D, FS. Fast-growing climber with attractive foliage and vibrant orange trumpet flowers. Ideal for summer pergolas and fast screening

Perfumed racemes of wisteria blossom produce a magnificent display.

GROWING YOUR GARDEN

White clematis in full bloom encloses a garden seat.

of sizeable areas. Tolerant of coastal conditions. Prune after flowering to control size and renew healthy growth.

CLEMATIS

D or E. FS or HS. There are two distinct forms of deciduous clematis commonly grown in New Zealand. The large-flowered hybrid clematis whose exotic flowers appear in spring and summer, and the various cultivars of *Clematis montana*, a very hardy and quick-growing climber which becomes a mass of pink or white flowers in early spring. *Clematis paniculata*, the New Zealand

Hint

Sweet peas are frequently grown on a trellis, frame, fence or garden shed. But they don't have to be. Sow them among other plants and just let them clamber about. You'll be surprised how good they look.

GORDON COLLIER
TITOKI POINT

clematis or puawhananga is one of the most admired of all New Zealand native plants, with masses of white flowers in early spring which adorn treetops and pergolas alike. Fast growing and evergreen.

FICUS

(*F. pumila*) E, FS to SS. Aerial root creeper with dense foliage if clipped regularly. Suitable for low walls, fences or natural covering for rocks. Temperate, subtropical.

GELSEMIUM

(*G. sempervirens*, Carolina jasmine) E, FS or HS. Small, attractive twining creeper with pointed leaves and fragrant bell-shaped, yellow flowers in late winter and spring. Suits all climates.

HARDENBERGIA

(*H. violacea*, Australian sarsparilla) E, HS to SS. Native, twining creeper with lavender-blue to violet, pea-shaped flowers in spring. All climates except coldest regions.

HEDERA (IVY)

E, FS to S. Foliage creepers with aerial roots. Very adaptable to climate, soil, sun and shade. Useful for covering fences, walls, banks or tree stumps or as ground cover. The most popular species are *H. canariensis* 'Variegata' with large, glossy, green and cream leaves, and *H. helix* (English ivy) with smaller leaves, but there are many varieties with deep greens, silver variegated, yellow variegated and yellow centred leaves. All climates.

HOYA

(*H. carnosa*, wax plant) E, HS or SS. Small twining plant useful for trellises or in containers with wall support for frame in a warm, sheltered position. Clusters of pink, star-shaped flowers in summer. New buds arise from old flower spurs. Temperate, subtropical.

JASMINUM (JASMINE)

E, HS or SS. Vigorous, twining or scrambling vine with sweetly scented flowers in spring or summer (depending on species). Temperate, subtropical but frost susceptible. *Jasminum polyanthemum*, or Chinese Jasmine, is the most widely grown but is best planted where it will not interfere with other plants, as it is inclined to take over. The sale of this plant is prohibited in the more northern areas of New Zealand, as it is a threat to native forests. *Jasminum azoricum* or Azores Jasmine, is easier to keep under control and better suited to small gardens. It will flower almost all year round with pure white fragrant flowers good for picking. Protect from frost when young.

MANDEVILLA

(*M. laxa*, Chilean jasmine) SD, FS or HS. Handsome vine with heart-shaped leaves and clusters of fragrant, white, trumpet-shaped flowers in summer and autumn. Prune back after flowering to prevent overcrowding. Warm–temperate, subtropical, but frost susceptible. (*M. sanderi* cultivars, Brazilian Jasmine) E, FS. Bright red, pink or white trumpet flowers have a yellow throat and appear almost throughout the year in a warm climate. Frost tender. Ideal for containers. (*M. splendens* 'Alice du Pont') E, FS. A spectacular climber for a subtropical climate. Vigorous intertwining stems bear large deeply veined leaves and magnificent warm pink trumpet flowers during summer and autumn.

MONSTERA

(*M. deliciosa*, fruit salad plant) E, FS to S. Vigorous climber with aerial roots which

TOP FIVE FLOWERING CLIMBERS

TRACHELOSPERMUM

This creeper produces deliciously fragrant white, lace-like flowers.

BOUGAINVILLEA

The papery bracts of bougainvillea are long-lasting and showy, with a range of 'almost-too-bright-to-be-real' colours.

WISTERIA

Pendulous clusters of white or lavender flowers bring a feeling of heady abundance to any spring garden.

PANDOREA JASMINOIDES

This Australian native produces clusters of showy pink bells right throughout the warm part of the year.

CLEMATIS

Entire books have been written about the many hundreds of types of clematis. Unlike most climbers, they perform especially well in colder climates (see picture opposite).

PANDOREA

BOUGAINVILLEA

TOP FIVE
CLIMBERS FOR SHADE

TECOMANTHE

Creamy yellow flowers will be more abundant with some sun, but the large glossy leaves are spectacular in shade.

MANDEVILLA

Mandevilla splendens is also known as dipladenia, and its attractive flowers are seen at their best in a morning sun–afternoon shade position.

IVY

Some of the variegated and coloured-leaf ivies are very pretty and all will cope with bright, shaded conditions.

TRACHELOSPERMUM

Commonly called star jasmine, this climber has thick waxy leaves and white, perfumed blooms. It looks wonderful in semi-shade.

FICUS PUMILA

Shade-tolerant climbing fig is grown for its flattened leaves, but must be clipped regularly to keep it under control.

Hint

For vibrant year-round colour in warmer districts of New Zealand, plant bougainvillea (choose from red, scarlet or white) and the bright orange Pyrostegia venusta *(flame vine) together, and train them along your fenceline or over a pergola.*

DIANA SELBY
LANDSCAPE ARCHITECT

cling to masonry, and with large, round but deeply divided leaves. Also useful as indoor plant in large pots or tubs. Arum-type yellow flowers develop into long, cylindrical fruit with a delicious flavour. Warm–temperate, subtropical climates.

PANDOREA

E, FS or HS. *P. jasminoides* is an attractive creeper with glossy leaves and pink, trumpet-like flowers flushed rosy-purple in spring. *P. pandorana* is commonly known as wonga-wonga vine. A similar creeper but the small, creamy-white, tubular flowers are in clusters. Warm–temperate, subtropical climates for both species.

PARTHENOCISSUS

(*P. tricuspidata* or *P. quinquefolia*, Virginia creeper or Boston ivy) D, FS or HS. Vigorous self-clinging creeper, grown for its soft, deciduous leaves which colour brilliantly in autumn. Ideal for brick walls and stonework. All climates.

PASSIFLORA (PASSIONFRUIT)

See Chapter 20.

PELARGONIUM (IVY GERANIUM)

E, FS or HS. Geraniums with long stems for training over walls and fences or for trailing over banks or batters. Also for hanging baskets. Ivy-shaped leaves and white, pink or red flowers in spring and summer. All climates.

MANDEVILLA

FICUS PUMILA

PETREA

(*P. volubilis*, Purple Wreath) E, FS. An elegant twining plant with a late spring flower show. Masses of tiny purple flowers are produced on gracefully drooping, 30 cm long racemes. Best in a frost-free climate with well-drained soil.

PHAEDRANTHUS

(*P. buccinatorius*, Mexican blood trumpet) E, FS or HS. Previously known as *Bignonia cherere*. Vigorous creeper with strong stems and clusters of orange-red trumpet flowers in spring and summer. Warm–temperate, subtropical.

PODRANEA

(*P. ricasoliana*, Port St John Creeper) E, FS. Bright pink flowers and lush glossy foliage characterise this rampant-growing creeper. Flowers from mid-summer to autumn. Suits most soils but needs a sunny position. Requires tying back or support to grow.

PYROSTEGIA

(*P. venusta*, flame vine) E, FS. Previously known as *Bignonia venusta*. Vigorous, adaptable creeper for covering fences, trellises or outbuildings with brilliant orange, tubular flowers in late winter and spring. Temperate, subtropical, but tolerates light frosts.

ROSA

(*R. wichuriana*, rambler rose) SD, FS. Spectacular spring-flowering roses for trellis, pergola or for weeping standards. All climates. For rose cultivation, see Chapter 12.

SOLANDRA (CUP OF GOLD OR HAWAIIAN LILY)

E, FS to SS. Sprawling, rampant vine which needs solid support and regular cutting back to keep it under control. Large, creamy-yellow trumpet flowers to 25 cm diameter in spring. Warm–temperate, subtropical. Frost susceptible.

SOLANUM

(*S. jasminoides*, White Potato Vine) E, FS or SS. Small starry white flowers can be seen all year round on this quick-growing twiner. Very hardy and easy to grow in most soils. Trim occasionally to encourage foliage cover at the base of the plant. Evergreen in warm climates.

Parthenocissus is a self-clinging vine and is best in autumn.

Pyrostegia smothers itself in hot-orange flowers in winter. Great for warm coastal climates.

Hint

Locate scented plants near doorways, so you can enjoy their fragrance without going out.

DENNIS GREVILLE
GARDEN WRITER

(*S. wendlandii*, Blue Potato Vine) D, FS. Fast-growing vine with stunning purple-blue flowers in spring and summer. Requires a frost-free climate.

STEPHANOTIS (MADAGASCAR JASMINE)

E, FS or HS. Handsome creeper which needs light support and training. Fragrant, white, trumpet-like flowers in late summer are favourites in bridal bouquets. Needs a warm, sheltered position. Temperate, subtropical.

TECOMANTHE

(*T. speciosa*) E, FS or SS. Attractive large glossy leaves and creamy-yellow trumpet flowers in winter. Grows best in sun or partly shaded areas and mild climates.

THUNBERGIA

E, FS. Several species are attractive climbers which flower intermittently throughout the year. The best known is *T. alata* (black-eyed Susan) with orange petals and black centres. *T. grandiflora* (sky flower) has pale-blue flowers. All species prefer a warm, sheltered position. Temperate and subtropical. Can become weeds.

TRACHELOSPERMUM (STAR JASMINE)

E, FS to SS. Sometimes known as *Rhynchospermum*, this useful creeper has rich, glossy foliage and fragrant, lace-like white flowers in spring and summer. All climates except coldest regions.

VITIS (ORNAMENTAL GRAPE)

D, FS. Vigorous tendril vine with cool, green summer foliage and brilliant autumn colours. Ideal for training on a trellis or pergola, especially to let through winter sun. All climates.

WISTERIA

D, FS to HS. One of the most popular spring-flowering creepers with pendulous clusters of pea-like flowers in white, lavender and lilac (depending on species or variety). Vines may be slow to establish but become very vigorous and long-lived and therefore need strong support. Ideal for covering a pergola for summer shade, winter sun and spring blossom. All climates.

Tecomanthe venusta *'Montana'; rare but special.*

Thunbergia grandiflora *is a popular choice for tropical plantings.*

The delicate appearance of wisteria blossom belies the vine's hardiness.

CHAPTER 14

TREES AND SHRUBS

Trees and shrubs can make an important contribution to the general outline and colour of your garden. They provide an easy-care background for annuals, bulbs and perennials which change with the seasons. They can ensure privacy and protection against winds, screen unsightly views and diminish traffic noise. They provide a leafy canopy on hot summer days, and deciduous species let warm winter sun penetrate to indoor and outdoor living areas. From the hundreds of kinds of trees and shrubs available, it is essential to choose those which suit your climate, situation and soil. Plant form, shape and height when mature is very important in deciding their position in the garden, either as a single specimens or in groups. Lists of popular trees and shrubs are given in this chapter as a guide, but the best plan – especially for new gardeners – is to visit a garden centre where the plants are displayed. Alongside each kind should be a label which gives the size of the plant when fully grown.

PLANTING

Some plant nurseries still sell open-ground plants, but these are mostly deciduous kinds such as roses, flowering fruit trees and others which lose their leaves in winter. Most shrubs and trees are sold in plastic pots or plastic bags. This has made year-round planting possible, although the cooler months of autumn or spring are the best. Containers of different sizes also offer the choice of small, semi-advanced, or advanced specimens.

Before planting, check the position to make sure it is suitable for the plant when fully grown. Avoid sites close to sewerage or drainage lines which could be invaded by strong-rooting species and cause future problems – especially with trees like willows, poplars and rubber trees. Also avoid planting trees under overhead wires where they may eventually be dangerous or cause expense and trouble in keeping them lopped. Do any drainage work necessary beforehand, as many shrubs and trees resent wet, soggy conditions. If the soil is a very heavy clay, organic matter in the form of animal manure, leaf mould or compost should be incorporated to improve the structure. The addition of coarse sand or gypsum (calcium sulphate) also makes heavy soils more crumbly.

The potting mix in the container and the soil in the garden should be damp (but not wet) at planting time. Dig a wide but shallow hole – about twice the width of the container but not much deeper. Roots will travel faster through soil which has been well broken up. The potting mixture in the container is often of a different texture from that of the garden soil, which may create an 'interface' problem, that is, the two soils fail to merge, causing a root barrier. Add compost or peat moss to the soil removed from the hole and mix it well. Now fill the base of the hole with the soil mixture to bring the root-ball of the plant level with the top of the hole so that the plant is not deeper in the soil than it was in the container. Take the plant from the container and set it at the correct level. If the plant is slightly root-bound (roots tangled round and round), tease the roots away gently, spread them out and cover with soil progressively. Alternatively, hose the root-ball gently to wash away the outside soil so that roots can be separated and covered. Add the rest of the soil gradually, firming it down to exclude air spaces, but avoiding heavy pressure by treading. The leftover soil should be used to form a raised ring around the plant.

Water well and then spread leaf mould or fibrous compost for a mulch. Keep the mulch away from the stem as it might encourage collar rot or other root rots. The mulch will prevent the surface soil from caking and will conserve moisture. Only stake if absolutely necessary; stakes should be driven in outside the root-ball to avoid damage. Tie trees or shrubs to the stake with

STEP 1 Container-grown plants can be planted year round, providing the soil is not too wet. Avoid planting in extreme heat or cold conditions so as not to stress the plant.

STEP 2 Dig the planting hole twice as wide and to the same depth as the root-ball, loosening the soil at the bottom. Add compost or peat to the soil removed from the hole.

STEP 3 Take shrub out of its container. Cut away any circled or tangled roots so they radiate out from the root-ball. Plant the shrub no deeper in the soil than it was in its container.

STEP 4 Fill the hole in with enriched soil, gradually firming it down to exclude air spaces. Avoid compacting the soil through through heavy treading.

STEP 5 Form a raised ring around the plant, creating a basin so that water will be concentrated in the area where it is needed most. Water thoroughly.

STEP 6 Stake if necessary, placing it on the side of prevailing winds. Drive in the stake outside of the area of the root-ball to avoid damage. Tie the plant to the stake.

plant ties or lengths of old rag or nylon stocking. Do not use wire, as this will cut into the stem or trunk.

Water thoroughly when needed, making sure that the root-ball is wetted because this will tend to dry out more quickly than the surrounding soil. Avoid using strong powdered or granular fertilisers, either at planting time or immediately afterwards. Slow-acting fertilisers such as Gro-Plus Camellia and Azalea Food are safe to scatter on the mulched surface. Slow-release fertilisers such as MagAmp can be placed in the planting hole. Slow-release fertilisers like Multicote may be scratched into the soil surface.

PRUNING

Many trees and shrubs are more or less self-shaping, so pruning is only rarely necessary. Others can be improved by regular or occasional pruning. Briefly, the objectives of the pruning are:

- To shape the plant – especially young shrubs and trees – and ensure a balanced framework for the future. For hedges the aim is to promote a dense growth down to ground level.
- To reduce competition by thinning out crowded growth, reduce competition with plants nearby or prevent obstruction of pathways and light to windows.
- To stimulate new growth and encourage flowers (and fruits). With flowering shrubs, the removal of spent blooms prevents fruits and seeds from forming and so directs plant energy into more flowering or vegetative growth.
- To remove diseased or dead wood and cut away unwanted branches such as those which have reverted from a variegated leaf to a plain leaf, or from a dwarf form to a tall form.
- To remove suckers from root stocks on which some shrubs on trees are grafted.

Only sharp tools (secateurs or pruning saws) should be used, because jagged cuts provide a resting place for disease spores and a greater area for the plant to form a callus (see Chapter 7). Always make cuts just above a bud or level with the joint to a larger branch to protect large areas from dieback.

The shaping of a tree, shrub or hedge should begin as soon as possible. If early

PINCHING

The first opportunity to control or direct plant growth is to remove or to pinch out the terminal bud. This is especially useful with young plants when you want to make them bushier, for example petunia. Conversely, if you want the plant to gain height, keep side growth pinched back so the terminal bud on the main stem continues to elongate. Nipping out the axillary laterals on tomatoes will produce a smaller crop of larger-sized fruit.

PRUNING CUTS

There is a correct way to make pruning cuts which helps direct new growth and facilitates the healing of the wound. A pruning cut should be made close to an outward-facing bud. The lowest point of the cut should be even with the top of the bud and slanting upwards at 45 degrees. Large branches should be removed in stages to avoid unnecessary damage. Trim back to a stub of 45–60 cm which can then be removed safely, leaving a clean surface.

THINNING

Thinning removes stems or branches, opening the plant up. It enables old and unproductive wood to be removed, removes branches that are growing in awkward directions and produces a taller and more open plant. The removal of superfluous branches also allows for better air circulation within the framework of the tree or shrub, thereby minimising the likelihood of entry of disease. This leads to improved plant health and vigour.

CLIPPING BACK

Clipping back results in a stronger, more prolific growth of branches because the removal of the terminal portion of a stem destroys apical dominance and stimulates growth hormone in the lateral buds. This is particularly desirable in plants grown as hedges, which look their best when bushy and compact. To clip back, cut around the entire shape of the plant using a pair of sharp, clean secateurs.

GROWING YOUR GARDEN

pruning is neglected it is more difficult to achieve a balanced shape later. Shears are suitable for clipping or trimming hedges. While it is not possible to control the exact position of the cut on each stem, most hedge plants develop laterals freely and do not suffer from dieback at the cut ends.

Most slow-growing trees and shrubs need little pruning. Good examples are azalea (*Rhododendron*), camellia, daphne and gardenia. As a general rule, most flowering shrubs and some flowering trees are pruned after they have flowered, although deciduous types fall into two groups. Those which flower (usually summer or early autumn) on current season's growth (new wood) are pruned in winter. Examples are cassia, hydrangea and lagerstroemia. Those which flower in spring on last season's growth (old wood) are pruned immediately after flowering. Pruning in winter would remove much of the spring blossom. Good examples are flowering peach and flowering almond. Other spring-flowering trees and shrubs are best pruned back (if they need it at all) after flowering. Multi-stemmed shrubs like Japanese bamboo (*Nandina*), may (*Spirea*) and barberry (*Berberis*) require little pruning except to remove older canes periodically at ground level to promote new growth.

REPAIRING DAMAGED TREES AND SHRUBS

Very often, a broken branch or stem, if not completely severed, can be repaired by fitting the broken section together using a splint (a piece of dowel stick for small branches or stouter hardwood for larger limbs) and then binding the break and splint tightly together with plastic budding tape. Heavy branches may be propped with stakes from below or, better still, secure the branch to the main trunk or stem with rope or garden stakes tied at each point. Pruning the foliage from the damaged branch will reduce its weight and prevent any further possible wind damage. Closely bound branches should mend in three or four months. If a break is beyond repair, saw the branch off cleanly. Make the first cut underneath to about halfway or until the saw binds. Make the second cut about 5 cm in front of the first and take it through until the branch falls. Now make a third cut right

> ## Hint
> Lagerstromeria (crepe myrtle) is the best small urban tree for the new millennium. Interesting bark, glossy foliage with autumn colour, and beautiful flowers provide something great to look at for every season. It is particularly suitable for sub-divided sections.
> **DALE HARVEY**
> GARDEN WRITER

through to remove the stub, which is easily handled. In some cases it may be best to remove the branch entirely, cutting just outside the 'wrinkle' where the branch joins the trunk.

Trees which have been blown over can often be salvaged because usually only half the roots are broken and exposed. Trim the broken roots cleanly and paint them with tree wound dressing. Lift the tree upright while the soil is still moist, using one or more forked poles for extra leverage. Move them in closer to support the tree as it is raised. A permanent support of a guy wire (fencing wire or clothes-line wire) fixed to one or more stakes on the windward side should be sufficient. Thread the wire through a short piece of old garden hose to prevent damage where it loops around the trunk of the tree.

Shrubs and small trees can be moved successfully if handled carefully when they are dormant. Winter is the safest time for most kinds, but warmth-loving shrubs like gardenia and hibiscus are often best moved in very early spring. Dig around the plants so that a wide, rather shallow root-ball is taken. Slide or juggle the plant onto a piece of canvas or heavy-duty plastic to carry or drag the plant to the new site. Take care that the root-ball remains intact.

TREE OR SHRUB?

Defining whether a plant is a tree or a shrub can be difficult. As a general rule, a tree grows taller (usually more than 4 metres) and has a single main trunk. A shrub is usually smaller and most often has multiple shoots from the base. The line between the two can be blurred, however, and many shrubs can be grown in a tree-like shape, while many small trees can be used as shrubs. For landscaping purposes, a tree can easily be grown as a freestanding specimen in a lawn but it is far better to have shrubs in mixed garden beds, or 'shrubberies'.

In the following lists, these plants have been divided into either the tree or shrub group, depending on their most common usage, but the line between the two is often blurred.

Hint

In frost-prone areas it pays to leave the pruning and trimming of frost-susceptible plants until spring, as leaving the top growth on during winter will protect the lower leaves. Minimise any frost damage by watering before sunrise.

ATHOL MCCULLY
GARDEN EXPERT

SELECTING TREES AND SHRUBS

The height to which a tree or shrub grows, whether it is evergreen or deciduous and whether it is grown for foliage, flowers or fruits are important factors to consider in making a selection. A summary of some of the most popular trees and shrubs is given in this chapter. It is far from being complete but may be a useful reference for the new gardener. Further information can be gathered from nursery catalogues or one of the many good reference books which deal specifically with this aspect of gardening. The most practical way of learning about trees and shrubs is to see them actually growing in your own district. Most leading nurseries employ trained horticulturists who can give valuable information to help you make your final selection. In the summary which follows, plants are listed in alphabetical order by their botanical name, followed by their common name.

TOP FIVE FLOWERING TREES

JACARANDA

This glorious South American native usually flowers when the tree is bare of leaves, which enhances the magnificent effect.

MAGNOLIA

Another tree that usually blooms on bare branches, every deciduous magnolia is a garden aristocrat.

GORDONIA

On the borderline between a tree and a shrub, but able to be pruned into a tree-like shape (which shows off its attractive bark), gordonia's 'fried egg' flowers can be close to 10 cm across.

PRUNUS (FLOWERING CHERRY)

Pink or white blossom smothers these shapely trees during spring. There are many beautiful varieties.

SOPHORA (KOWHAI)

Golden-yellow flowers appear in great profusion in early spring on one of New Zealand's favourite native trees.

MAGNOLIA

PRUNUS

JACARANDA

GROWING YOUR GARDEN

Abbreviations: E–evergreen, D–deciduous, SD–semi-deciduous, FS–full sun, HS–half sun, SS–semi-shade, S–shade, H–height, W–width. Measurements shown in metres (m) or centimetres (cm).

ABELIA (GLOSSY ABELIA)

E, FS or HS, H 2–3 m, W 1–2 m. Arching shrub with small leaves and white to pink bell-shaped flowers in summer and autumn. All climates except coldest districts. Makes good specimen or hedge plant.

ABUTILON (JAPANESE LANTERN)

E, FS to SS, H 1–2 m, W 1–2 m. Attractive, usually mottled foliage and pendulous, hibiscus-like flowers in white, yellow, orange or pink (depending on variety) in summer. All climates except coldest districts.

ACACIA (WATTLE)

E, FS or HS, H 1–9 m, W 1–9 m (quite variable). There are over 600 species of this genus, ranging from small shrubs to large trees. All are evergreen with yellow flowers in late winter or spring, but the foliage may be feathery, flat or needle-like. All prefer full sun or half sun and are usually fast growing but short-lived.

ACER (MAPLE)

D, FS to SS, H 2–18 m, W 1–15 m. Attractive trees with spectacular autumn foliage for cold and temperate climates. Japanese maples (*A. palmatum*) have many leaf forms and colours (some of them variegated) and are usually small to medium-size trees. Box elder (*A. negundo*) and Norway maple (*A. platanoides*) are larger trees for cool climates.

AGATHUS (KAURI)

See Chapter 15.

AGONIS (WILLOW MYRTLE)

E, FS or HS, H 5–6 m, W 3–5 m. Attractive tree with willow-like branches and small, white, tea-tree-like flowers in spring. Frost susceptible. Temperate and warm climates.

ALECTRYON (TITOKI)

See Chapter 15.

ARBUTUS (IRISH STRAWBERRY TREE)

E, FS or HS, H 5–6 m, W 3–4 m. Rounded, densely foliaged tree with masses of small white blossoms from summer to winter followed by large, rough, multi-coloured (green, yellow and orange) berries. Very adaptable to climate and soil.

AUCUBA (GOLD DUST TREE)

E, HS to S, H 1–2 m, W 1 m. Large, oval, glossy leaves flecked with gold; may produce red berries when both male and female plants are grown together. Prefers a damp, cool, shady position but may scorch in hot, dry climates. Can also be grown as indoor plant.

AZALEA

E or SD, HS to S, H 30 cm–3 m, W 30 cm–2 m. The best known and most useful of spring flowering shrubs. There are several species from dwarf (*A. kurume*) to large *magnifica* or *splendens* types (*A. indica*) with hundreds of hybrids and named varieties in single and double flowers in almost every colour. The evergreen types will grow in almost any climate except the tropics but deciduous kinds prefer cooler conditions. They must have an acid soil and will not grow in alkaline soil. They require good drainage but the shallow roots need to be cool, moist and shaded. Azaleas make excellent plants for pots or tubs.

Hint

When choosing perennials and shrubs for the garden, select a range of foliage shapes and colours, so that you can use them in vases in winter when flowers are in short supply. Vases of foliage can look stunning, and often last for weeks. Good varieties to use include barberry, griselinias and pittosporums.

BOB EDWARDS
EDITOR, *COMMERCIAL HORTICULTURE*

BACKHOUSIA (LEMON-SCENTED MYRTLE)

E, FS or HS, H 2–4 m, W 1–2 m. Attractive shrub with glossy lemon-scented leaves and clusters of small, greenish-white flowers in early summer. Frost susceptible. Temperate and warm climates.

BAECKEA

E, HS or SS, H 1–2 m, W up to 1 m. Small attractive shrub with white flowers, not unlike those of boronia, blooming in spring and summer. Temperate and warm climates.

BANKSIA

E, FS or HS, H 3–6 m, W 2–5 m (variable). Quaint but attractive shrubs or trees with thick, often serrated leaves and large erect cones of stiff, wiry flowers in shades of greenish-white, yellow, orange and red. Prefer well-drained sandy soils in warm coastal climates.

BERBERIS (BARBERRY)

E or D, FS or HS, H 1–2 m, W 1–2 m. Small, compact, usually spiny shrubs with yellow flowers in spring and red berries in autumn. Most deciduous species have brilliant autumn foliage. Very adaptable but prefer mild–temperate or cold climates. Those barberries with purple-bronze foliage (*B. thunbergii* 'Atropurpurea') make good accent plants. All can be used as hedge plants.

BETULA (BIRCH)

D, FS or HS, H 6–9 m, W 3–6 m. Slender trees with graceful foliage and pendulous catkins in spring. In autumn they have brilliant foliage. Silver birch (*B. pendula*), with silvery-white bark, is the best known of all birch trees. Adapted to cool–temperate and cold climates

BORONIA

E, HS or SS, H 60–90 cm, W 30–60 cm. Many species of small shrubs with spicy fragrance and attractive delicate flowers: mostly pink, but some brown and yellow. All prefer well-drained, slightly acid, shady soils similar to those of their natural habitat. Mulch with compost or leaf mould to avoid root disturbance and hold moisture.

BRUNFELSIA (BRAZIL RAIN TREE)

E, HS or SS, H 2–3 m, W 2–3 m. This handsome shrub is also called yesterday, today and tomorrow because the fragrant flowers in spring open deep-blue, fade to lavender and then to white on successive days. Adaptable to all climates except the coldest districts and prefers well-drained soil in a semi-shaded situation.

BUDDLEIA (SUMMER LILAC OR BUTTERFLY BUSH)

SD, FS or HS, H 2–3 m, W 2 m. Fast-growing shrub with long sprays of slightly fragrant lilac or purple flowers in spring and summer. Attractive to butterflies. Adaptable to all climates – evergreen in warm districts and deciduous where colder.

BUXUS (BOX)

E, FS or HS, H 2 m, W 1 m. Attractive, tidy, small tree or shrub with small shiny foliage. Often used as a low hedge or as accent plants in formal gardens. Box is very adaptable to all climates.

CALLISTEMON (BOTTLEBRUSH)

E, FS or HS, H 2–6 m, W 2–5 m. Attractive shrubs or small trees with brush-like flowers in shades of cream, yellow, pink and red in spring and early summer. Very adaptable plants to both wet and dry conditions with good tolerance to salty soils. Appropriate for all climates except the coldest districts. Many named varieties are readily available.

CAMELLIA

E, HS to S, H 3–5 m, W 1–3 m. Camellias compete with azaleas for the most popular shrub or tree. The most widely grown is *C. japonica*, which flowers in winter and early spring. There are hundreds of named varieties with single, semi-double or double flowers which range in colour from pure white through pinks and mauves to deep red. Another species is *C. sasanqua* with mostly single flowers in late autumn and winter; it is useful as a background plant or trimmed as a tall hedge. Like azaleas, camellias will not tolerate alkaline soils and need good drainage, plenty of organic matter and a cool root area. Camellias prefer semi-shade or shade, as strong sunlight can scorch the blooms. They make excellent tub specimens.

Hint

Betula dalecarlica (swedish silver birch) doesn't set seed, so it is a good choice if you are looking for a tree to plant near buildings or other areas where seed might be a nuisance.

GORDON COLLIER
TITOKI POINT

CASSIA

E, FS or HS, H 1–6 m, W 1–3 m. There are several species of these showy shrubs or small trees with yellow pea-like flowers in spring, summer or autumn. Buttercup tree (*C. corymbosa*) is the most widely grown, with masses of yellow blooms in spring. Most species are fast-growing and adaptable to all climates except cold districts. A dwarf Australian species, *C. artemisoides*, is very suitable for hot, dry regions.

CERATOPETALUM
(CHRISTMAS BUSH)

E, FS or HS, H 3–6 m, W 2–3 m. Small, shapely tree with showy pink or red bracts in summer. Prune back after flowering. Prefers well-drained soils but water regularly from spring onwards. Temperate to warm coastal climates.

CERATOSTIGMA

D, FS, H 3 m, W 3 m. Small shrubs with pale-green, bronze-tinted leaves and bright-blue flowers in summer. Foliage colours in autumn. Cut back hard in winter to promote new growth and flowers. Very adaptable to most climates.

CESTRUM

E, FS or HS, H 2–3 m, W 1–2 m. Fast-growing shrubs with showy, tubular flowers in light green, orange or red, according to species. The best known is night jessamine

(*C. nocturnum*), which has strongly perfumed flowers on warm nights in summer. Temperate and subtropical climates.

CINNAMOMUM
(CAMPHOR LAUREL)

E, FS or HS, H 15 m, W 9 m. Vigorous, self-seeding tree with dense foliage with camphor odour and green berries turning black in summer. Takes a lot of space and is not suitable for small gardens. All climates except coldest districts.

CLIANTHUS

See Chapter 15.

COLEONEMA
(PINK DIOSMA)

E, FS or HS, H 1–2 m, W up to 1 m. Compact, delicate foliage with white or pink star-shaped flowers in spring. Good dwarf shrub for accent and rock gardens. Prune back after flowering. All climates.

COPROSMA

See Chapter 15.

CORDYLINE
(CABBAGE TREE)

See Chapter 15.

CORNUS (DOGWOOD)

D, FS to SS, H 2–4 m, W 1–3 m. Beautiful small trees for cool climates. Delightful flowers, foliage and handsome stems. Prefer deep, rich, well-drained, acid soils.

COROKIA

See Chapter 15.

COTONEASTER

E or D, FS to SS, H 1–4 m, W 1–4 m. Many species and varieties, from prostrate spill-over shrubs to small trees, all of which have attractive clusters of orange or red berries. Mostly evergreen but some deciduous. Excellent garden shrubs; also useful for hedges and espalier training. Small types for rockeries. All climates.

CRATAEGUS (HAWTHORN)

D, FS to SS, H 4–6 m, W 2–3 m. Thorny shrubs or small trees with white or pink rose-like flowers in spring followed by brilliant yellow, orange or red berries according to species. All climates except very hot districts.

CUPHEA
(CIGAR PLANT)
E, FS to SS, H 30–60 cm, W 60 cm. Small spreading shrubs with red tubular flowers tipped with ash grey. Excellent for rockeries. Adapted to most climates.

DAPHNE
E, HS to SS, H 1 m, W 1 m. Charming dwarf shrub with glossy foliage and highly perfumed, waxy, white, pink or red flowers in winter and early spring. Needs good drainage. Mulch to keep roots cool and moist. Prefers morning sun or semi-shade. For temperate or cool climates.

DEUTZIA
(WEDDING BELLS)
D, HS or SS, H 2–3 m, W 1.5 m. Attractive shrubs with long canes and clusters of white or pink flowers in late spring and early summer. Cut back after flowering. All climates except very hot districts.

DREJERELLA (SYN. BELOPERONE, SHRIMP PLANT)
E, FS or HS, H 1 m, W 1 m. Small softwood shrub with overlapping, shell-like bracts in yellow or pink, suggesting a prawn or shrimp. Very adaptable to climate but prefers warm, sheltered position.

EPACRIS
E, FS to SS, H 1 m, W 30 cm. Heath-like shrub with sprays of slender, tubular red flowers with white tips. Needs well-drained, slightly acid, sandy soil and resents root disturbance. Temperate and cold climates.

ERICA (HEATH)
E, FS, H up to 2 m, W up to 1 m. Heath-like plants in many varieties and forms with needle-like leaves and masses of tubular or bell-shaped flowers in shades of yellow, orange, pink and mauve. They need well-drained, slightly acid soils, as for azaleas, to which they are related. Best in cool–temperate or cold climates.

Pure white flower bracts with a characteristic pointed tip are the most striking feature of Cornus kousa.

ERIOSTEMON
(WAXFLOWER)
E, HS or SS, H 120 cm, W 90 cm. Compact shrub with fragrant foliage and white or pink star-shaped flowers showing in winter and early spring. Prefers well-drained, slightly acid sandy soils. Suits temperate and warm climates.

ESCALLONIA
E, FS to S, H 2–3 m, W 1–2 m. Glossy foliage shrubs with rose-pink or white flowers in late spring and summer. Cut back after flowering. All climates except very cold areas.

EUCALYPTUS (GUM TREE)
E, FS to SS, H 6–90 m, W 3–12 m. Over 600 species of eucalypt trees are recorded and dominate the Australian landscape. They range in size from small trees to forest giants. Most are fast growing and very adaptable but it is best to consult your local nursery for advice on suitable varieties for your own district. Some have showy flowers while others are suitable for windbreaks, street planting or as specimen trees.

EXOCHORDA (PEARL BUSH)
D, FS to SS, H 2–3 m, W 2–3 m. Attractive shrub with pale green foliage and pearly

GROWING YOUR GARDEN

The pendulous habit of fuchsias makes them suitable for hanging baskets.

white flowers like apple blossom in spring. Prune lightly after flowering. Temperate and cool climates.

FAGUS (BEECH)

D, FS or HS, H 9–18 m, W 9–12 m. Large but slow-growing deciduous tree. For cool–temperate and cold climates only. Magnificent foliage trees with many varied forms and colours of leaves. Silver beech and copper beech are the most widely grown.

FICUS (FIG)

E, FS or HS, H 9–15 m, W 6–15 m. Many species of medium-sized to very large trees (Port Jackson fig and Moreton Bay fig). Small species are India rubber plant (*F. elastica*) and weeping fig (*F. hillii*) with dense, pendulous foliage. *F. pumila* is an evergreen creeper (see Chapter 13).

FRANGIPANI

See Plumeria.

FRAXINUS (ASH)

D, FS or HS, H 6–12 m, W 4–6 m. Fast-growing, attractive trees with brilliant

autumn foliage for cool–temperate and cold climates. Golden ash, desert ash and claret ash are the most popular species.

FUCHSIA

E, SS or S, H 1–2 m, W 30–60 cm. Decorative softwood shrubs which flower from late spring to early winter. Flowers are pendulous with a tubular corolla surrounded by sepals in contrasting colours. There are hundreds of named varieties. All prefer semi-shade and a friable, well-structured soil. Most are suitable for pots, tubs and hanging baskets. All climates except very cold districts.

GARDENIA

E, FS or HS, H 1–2 m, W up to 1 m. Attractive shrubs or small trees with dark, glossy foliage and highly fragrant, waxy, white flowers from late spring through to summer. If necessary, prune back plants in winter. They need a sheltered, sunny position and do well in most climates except extremely cold ones.

GARRYA (SILK TASSEL OR CURTAIN BUSH)

E, SS to S, H 3 m, W 2–3 m. Dense-foliaged shrub with pendulous clusters of greyish-yellow catkins in winter and early spring. Prefers semi-shade or shade and does best in cool–temperate and cold climates, with low humidity.

GINKGO (MAIDENHAIR TREE)

D, FS or HS, H 9–12 m, W 4–6 m. Pale-green, two-lobed leaves turning golden yellow in autumn. Suits cool–temperate and cold climates.

GORDONIA

E, FS or HS, H 3–4 m, W 2–3 m. Tall, fast-growing shrub with glossy foliage. Autumn to spring flowering with large single white flowers with prominent yellow centres. Flowers fall intact to form a floral carpet beneath. Best in temperate climates but has some cold tolerance.

GREVILLEA (SPIDER FLOWER)

E, FS or HS, H 1–3 m, W 1–3 m. There is a great range of these Australian native shrubs from all climates, about 250 species in all, so there is one to suit every garden. The spider-like flowers are usually pink or red but there are yellow and orange flowers too. Plants need good drainage, a slightly acid soil and resent root disturbance. Consult a nursery or catalogue for the best species and varieties for your district. Silky oak (*G. robusta*), the largest of the family by far, is a handsome, self-shaping tree which grows to a height of 12–15 m and a spread of 6 m, with fern-like foliage and showy orange flowers in late spring or early summer.

HAKEA

E, FS or HS, H 4–6 m, W 2–3 m. Fast-growing shrub with rather thick, leathery leaves for screening or windbreaks.
● Pin-cushion hakea (*H. laurina*) has red, globe-shaped flowers in spring.
● Willow leaf hakea (*H. salicifolia*) has bronze-tipped foliage and can be trained as a hedge. All climates except coldest districts.

HIBISCUS

E or D, FS or HS, H 2–4 m, W 1–2 m. One of the best summer-flowering shrubs for warm–temperate and subtropical climates. There are many species (most of them evergreen) and hundreds of named varieties. The magnificent large flowers (some to 20 cm across) are single or double and range in colour from pure white through to lemon, yellow, gold, orange, pink, red and maroon. All species are frost susceptible. In cool–temperate climates select a sunny, sheltered position, preferably facing north.

HYDRANGEA

D, SS or S, H 0.5–3 m, W 0.5–2 m. Popular deciduous shrubs for shade and moist situations. Have large, showy flower heads in summer. Most flowers are in shades of pink or blue but colour can change depending on soil reaction (pH) – alkaline soil produces pink flowers and acid soil produces blue. In some varieties the flowers are white or greenish and do not change colour with soil pH. Prune back plants when dormant in winter. All climates.

HYPERICUM

E, FS to SS, H 3–5 m, W 1–2 m. Handsome shrubs or small trees with glossy foliage and yellow flowers followed by brilliant red berries in winter. Plants may be trimmed to shape and make a dense hedge. Adapted to cool–temperate and cold climates only.

JACARANDA

SD, FS or HS, H 9–12 m, W 9–12 m. Graceful tree with fine, fern-like leaves which turn golden bronze in winter. Masses of lavender-blue flowers appear in late spring and early summer. Adapted to all climates except very cold regions. Young trees may need protection from frost until established.

Hint

If you are looking for hardy plants for coastal and other harsh environments, try specimens that have silver leaves, as they often perform well in adverse conditions. Try astelias, lambs ears and olearia

SIMON FARRELL
GARDEN WRITER

KNIGHTIA (REWAREWA)

See Chapter 15.

KOLKWITZIA (CHINESE BEAUTY BUSH)

D, HS or SS, H 2 m, W 1.5 m. Attractive shrubs with long, arching canes covered with pale-pink, trumpet-shaped flowers in spring. Adapted to cool–temperate and cold climates.

LAGERSTROEMIA (CREPE MYRTLE)

D, FS or HS, H 2–3 m, W 1–2 m. Large shrubs or small trees, often with gold autumn leaves. They have showy clusters of pink, mauve or carmine flowers in late summer. Prune hard in winter. Suits all climates except the coldest districts.

LEPTOSPERMUM

See Chapter 15.

LIQUIDAMBAR (SWEET GUM)

D, FS or HS, H 6–12 m, W 4–9 m. Tall conical trees with maple-like leaves in brilliant autumn colours of yellow, orange, red and purple. Adaptable but best suited to temperate and cold climates

LIRIODENDRON (TULIP TREE)

D, FS or HS, H 9–12 m, W 4–5 m. Attractive large tree with fiddle-shaped leaves turning bright yellow in autumn. Flowers are lime-green and tulip shaped. Cool–temperate and cold climates only.

LOROPETALUM (CHINESE FRINGE FLOWER)

E, HS or SS, H 1–2 m, W 1–2 m. Graceful shrub with rounded leaves and spidery, cream flowers in spring. Temperate and cold climates, but frost susceptible.

LUCULIA

E, HS or SS, H 2–3 m, W 2–3 m. Attractive shrub with rounded heads of fragrant pink flowers in early winter. Cut back after flowering. Suits temperate climates but is susceptible to frost.

Deciduous magnolias make good lawn specimens and grow to a manageable size for a smaller garden.

MAGNOLIA

E or D, FS or HS, H 5–9 m, W 3–6 m. Several species exist, but the deciduous tree (*M. soulangeana*) is the most popular species. Large, tulip-shaped flowers in white, pink, mauve or purple appear in early spring before the foliage. Temperate or cold climates. The evergreen tree (*M. grandiflora*) has large, fragrant, waxy, white flowers in summer. Suits all but the very coldest climates.

Hint

As a general rule of thumb, native plants with glossy foliage are a good choice for growing in windy situations. The selection is huge and includes coprosmas, pittosporums, flaxes, pohutukawa and griselinias. Secure with a stout stake when young.

TERRY HATCH
JOY PLANTS

MALUS (CRABAPPLE)

D, FS or HS, H 3–5 m, W 3–5 m. A most delightful spring-flowering tree with blossoms in white, pink or red followed by small, multi-coloured apples used for jam or for decoration. Prune trees to shape and size. All climates.

MELALEUCA (PAPER BARK)

E, FS or HS, H 2–9 m, W 2–6 m. Shrubs or small trees noted for their showy flowers (similar to those of bottlebrush) and their decorative, papery bark. Many tolerate swampy conditions, strong winds and salt spray. All but coldest climates.

MERYTA (PUKA)

See Chapter 15.

METROSIDEROS (NEW ZEALAND CHRISTMAS TREE; POHUTUKAWA)

See Chapter 15.

MURRAYA (SATIN WOOD)

E, HS or SS, H 2–3 m, W 2–2.5 m. Dense, rounded shrub with glossy foliage and fragrant clusters of white flowers like orange blossom in spring and summer. Susceptible to frost. Suits temperate and subtropical climates.

NANDINA (JAPANESE BAMBOO)

E, FS to SS, H 1–2 m, W 1 m. Multi-stemmed shrub with finely divided foliage, cream flowers and red berries. Attractive autumn foliage, especially in the dwarf variety (*N. domestica* 'Pygmaea'). All climates.

NERIUM (OLEANDER)

E, FS to SS, H 3–5 m, W 1–2 m. Adaptable shrub with lance-shaped, rather leathery leaves and masses of single or double flowers (white, cream, yellow, pink and crimson) from early summer to late autumn. Suits all but cold climates.

NYSSA

D, FS or HS, H 6–9 m, W 4–6 m. Handsome tree with attractive foliage in both spring and autumn. Reddish-brown flowers in late winter. Mild, temperate and cold climates.

OLEARIA

See Chapter 15.

PHILADELPHUS (MOCK ORANGE)

D, HS or SS, H 2–3 m, W 2 m. Cane-like shrubs with sweetly scented white flowers in late spring. Prune back after flowering. All climates.

PHORMIUM (FLAX)

See Chapter 15.

PHOTINIA

E, FS to SS, H 2–5 m, W 1–3 m. Foliage plants with brilliant red new growth, often used as hedge plants. All climates.

PIERIS (LILY-OF-THE-VALLEY SHRUB)

E, HS to SS, H 1–2 m, W 1–2 m. Small attractive shrubs with sprays of cream flowers in spring. Well-drained soil and cool, sheltered position, similar to azaleas. Cool–temperate and cold climates.

PIMELEA

E, FS, H 1–2 m, W 1 m. Attractive shrub with small glossy leaves and dense clusters of cream, yellow or pink flowers in spring to early summer. Temperate climates.

Hint

If you have to transplant a tree, always dig the new hole first. Then dig a circular trench around the tree, about a metre away from the trunk. Cut away any surface roots by digging vertically into the ground. Chip away the soil to reveal the root ball and lighten the load, then move to the new location.

NICK HAYHOE
YATES NEW ZEALAND

PITTOSPORUM

See Chapter 15.

PLUMERIA (FRANGIPANI)

D, FS or HS, H 3–4m, W 2–3 m. Small deciduous tree with fragrant, waxy, white (or pink) flowers in summer. Frost susceptible, warm–temperate and subtropical climates only.

POLYGALA (SWEET PEA SHRUB)

E, FS to SS, H 1–2 m, W 1–2 m. Small, fast-growing shrub with purple, pea-like flowers from winter to early summer. Prune after flowering to keep within bounds. Temperate and subtropical climates, but dislikes excessive moisture.

POPULUS (POPLAR)

D, FS to HS, H 9–24 m, W 3–12 m. Beautiful deciduous trees with brilliant autumn colours, but rather large and greedy for small gardens. The tall, slender Lombardy poplar, the silver poplar and cottonwood are

GROWING YOUR GARDEN

the best known. Very adaptable but prefer temperate and cold climates.

PROSTANTHERA (MINT BUSH)

E, FS or HS, H 2–4 m, W 2–3 m. Several species of attractive shrubs with small aromatic leaves and masses of mauve, purple or blue flowers in spring. They prefer good drainage and resent root disturbance. Prune back after flowering to prevent bushes becoming leggy. Cool–temperate to subtropical climates.

PRUNUS

D, FS or HS, H 3–6 m, W 1–6 m. This large genus includes not only the flowering plum but also most of the spring-flowering blossoms – peaches, almonds and cherries. There are many species and varieties which differ in size, leaf and flower colour, flower form (single or double) and the time of flowering. All are pruned after flowering. Generally, this group of beautiful trees prefers full sunlight, good drainage and a cool winter climate. Leading nurseries can advise you on the kinds and varieties suitable for your district.

PSEUDOPANAX

See Chapter 15.

PSORALEA (BLUE BUTTERFLY BUSH)

E, FS or HS, H 2–3 m, W 2–3 m. Fast-growing shrubs with masses of pale-blue, pea-like flowers in spring. Prune back by one-third after flowering. Frost susceptible. Prefers temperate to warm climates.

PYRACANTHA (FIRETHORN)

E, FS to SS, H 2–3 m, W 2–3 m. Often confused with the deciduous hawthorn, these spiny, evergreen shrubs have clusters of small white flowers followed by yellow, orange or red berries. Good hedge plant. Temperate and cold climates.

QUERCUS (OAK)

D, FS or HS, H 9–18 m, W 5–9 m. Large trees in varying shapes and sizes. English oak is round-headed and spreading. Pin oak is conical with red autumn leaves. Temperate and cold climates.

Hint

I often hear certain plants referred to as common or ordinary, and therefore not worthy of a place in the garden. Ordinary plants don't exist, ordinary plantings do. It is how plants are used that counts.

DENNIS GREVILLE
GARDEN WRITER

RAPHIOLEPIS

E, FS or HS, H 2 m, W 1–2 m. Compact shrubs with pink or white flowers in spring followed by black berries. Very adaptable to most climates.

RHODODENDRON

E, SS or S, H 3–6 m, W 2–4 m. Spectacular spring-flowering shrubs or trees for mild–temperate and cold climates. Need similar conditions (semi-shade, good drainage and acid soil) to azalea, to which they are closely related. Many varieties and flower colours.

RONDELETIA

E, HS or SS, H 2–3 m, W 1–2 m. Attractive shrub with dark-green foliage and rounded masses of pink blossoms in late winter and early spring. Frost susceptible. Temperate to warm climates.

ROSMARINUS (ROSEMARY)

E, FS to SS, H 1–2 m, W 1 m. Attractive small shrub with glossy, aromatic leaves (used as a herb in cooking). Pale-blue flowers in early spring and autumn. Good hedge plant. Very adaptable to most climates.

RUSSELIA

E, FS or HS, H 1–2 m, W up to 1 m. A stemmy, rush-like plant with scarlet tubular flowers in summer. Can be tied to a stake or used as spill-over plant for walls and rockeries. Temperate and warm climates.

SALIX (WILLOW)

D, FS to SS, H 6–9 m, W 6–9 m. Graceful trees suited to wet conditions. Weeping willow is the best known. Tend to invade drains in small gardens. There are smaller, less vigorous species: pussy willow with silvery catkins in spring, and tortured willow with twisted stems and leaves. All climates.

SOPHORA (KOWHAI)
See Chapter 15.

SPIRAEA (MAY)
D, FS to SS, H 1–3 m, W 1–3 m. Several species of cany shrubs with masses of white single or double flowers in spring. Prune back after flowering to preserve shrub's compact shape. Adaptable to all climates.

STREPTOSOLEN (SYN. *BROWALLIA JAMESONII*)
E, FS or HS, H 1–2 m, W 1 m. Cany shrubs with clusters of bright-orange flowers in spring and early summer. Needs occasional pruning and thinning. Frost susceptible. Temperate and subtropical climates.

SYRINGA (LILAC)
D, FS or HS, H 2–3 m, W 1–2 m. Attractive, suckering shrub with fragrant clumps of flowers in white, pink, red, mauve and purple. Cool–temperate and cold climates only.

TAMARIX (FLOWERING CYPRESS)
D and E, FS or HS, H 3–9 m, W 2–5 m. Small trees with cypress-like pendulous foliage and feathery masses of pink flowers in spring and summer. Very adaptable and tolerates dry heat, strong winds and salty soils. All climates.

ULMUS (ELM)
D or SD, FS or HS, H 9–18 m, W 9–18 m. Several species of medium to large trees with attractive foliage in spring and autumn. Golden elm and Chinese weeping elm are widely grown as lawn specimen trees. Cool–temperate to cold climates.

VIBURNUM
E, D, FS to SS, H 2.5 m, W 1–3 m. More than 100 species and many more named varieties of these attractive shrubs are grown for their fragrant, hydrangea-like flowers and attractive berries. Prune both evergreen and deciduous types after flowering. Suitable for most climates.

VIRGILIA
E, FS to SS, H 4–6 m, W 3–4 m. Fast-growing small trees with fern-like foliage and sprays of mauve flowers in spring. Very adaptable but sometimes short-lived. All climates except cold districts.

WEIGELA
D, HS or SS, H 2–3 m, W 1–2 m. Cany shrubs with white or pink–red trumpet-like flowers in spring. Cut back after flowering. Temperate and cold climates.

Blossom trees like this Prunus *'Pink Cloud' make a glorious display in spring.*

WHAT CAN GO WRONG WITH AZALEA, CAMELLIA AND RHODODENDRON?

PROBLEM	SYMPTOM	SOLUTION
Aphids	Cluster of insects on young growth.	Spray with Mavrik or Confidor when detected.
Mites	Leaves yellow (stippled or mottled) and dehydrated in hot, dry weather.	Spray with Super Shield, Mite Killer or Mavrik.
Thrips	Leaves silver and dry. Brown-black specks appear on underside of leaves.	Spray with Confidor, Super Shield, Mavrik, Baythroid Aerosol when first observed.
Leaf gall	Developing leaves and flowers are thickened, fleshy and pale-green. As the thickenings enlarge, they become white or pink, with a powdery appearance during wet weather.	Remove and destroy all infected parts.
Petal blight	Earliest symptom is light-brown or whitish coloured circular spots on petals. Spots enlarge to form irregular blotches until whole flower collapses. Petals feel slimy when rubbed between fingers. Diseased flowers dry up and cling to the plant (leaves and stems are not affected).	Avoid overhead watering. Pick off diseased flowers. Spray at two weekly intervals with Greenguard from expanded bud stage until end of flowering.
Sooty mould	Black sooty mould on leaves and twigs.	Sooty mould fungus lives on honeydew excreted from sapsucking insects. Spray with Mavrik or Confidor or use Conqueror Oil on scale infestation.
Lack of fertiliser	Leaves yellow and/or developing dark purple tone. Slow, stunted growth.	Fertilise with Gro-Plus Camellia and Azalea Food in late spring after flowering finishes and again just before new growth starts.
Soil too alkaline	Decline in vigour and new leaves turn yellow while the veins remain green.	Fertilise with Gro-Plus Camellia and Azalea Food in late spring after flowering finishes. Do *not* lime soil.

CONIFERS

This is the group of cone-bearing plants. Most are evergreen, grow to a definite (usually symmetrical) shape and almost never need pruning. They vary in size, shape and leaf colour from small, prostrate trees or shrubs suitable for tubs or rockeries to magnificent specimens growing to 30 metres or more in height.

As a group, conifers are slow growers but respond to attention in watering, mulching and fertilising. As with other trees and shrubs, slow-acting fertilisers based on blood and bone or slow-release fertilisers such as Multicote are the most suitable and effective.

Conifers are best suited to temperate and cold climates where, as evergreens, they are valuable for winter effect. There are dozens of species and hundreds of varieties and the reader is advised to consult a nursery catalogue or, better still, visit a specialist nursery where advanced specimens can be seen. The following is only a brief summary of the most important conifers.

ABIES (FIR TREES)

Tall, pyramid-shaped trees with beautiful foliage. Best suited to cool and cold climates with high rainfall. Silver fir (*A. alba*) H 15 m: green-silver foliage. Colorado white fir (*A. concolor*) H 15 m: bluish foliage. Caucasian fir (*A. nordmanniana*) H 18 m: green-silver foliage.

ARAUCARIA

Tall, symmetrical trees but rather too large for the average garden. Monkey puzzle (*A. araucana*) H 12–15 m: cool, moist climates. Bunya pine (*A. bidwillii*) H 8–13 m: all climates except coldest. Hoop pine (*A. cunninghamii*) H 24–45 m: moist coastal climates. Norfolk Island pine (*A. heterophylla*) H 18–30 m: moist coastal climates.

CALLITRIS (CYPRESS PINE)

These ornamental Australian native trees are very useful for light-textured soils, where many of them grow naturally. White cypress pine (*C. columellaris*) H 15 m: dark-green foliage. Port Jackson pine (*C. rhomboidea*) H 12 m: olive-green foliage.

CEDRUS (CEDAR)

Shapely, pyramidal trees with needle-like leaves and upright, barrel-shaped cones. Adaptable trees but best in cool–temperate and cold climates. Atlas cedar (*C. atlantica*) H 15–18 m: grey-green foliage; var. *glauca* with silver-blue foliage; var. *aurea* with yellow foliage. Deodar (*C. deodara*) H 15–18 m: green or grey-green foliage; var. *aurea* yellowish foliage. Cedar of Lebanon (*C. libani*) H 12–15 m: similar to *C. atlantica* but a more flattened shape.

CHAMAECYPARIS (SYN. RETINOSPORA, FALSE CYPRESS)

Shapely, ornamental, medium-sized or dwarf trees, useful for garden landscape effects. Need good drainage and do best in cool–temperate or cold climates with good rainfall. Lawson cypress (*C. lawsoniana*) H 12–15 m: pyramidal growth to ground level with many varieties and differing foliage colours. Dwarf varieties range in height from 60 cm to 3 m. Hinoki cypress (*C. obtusa*) H 9–12 m: flattened, fan-like foliage; var. *crippsii* has yellow foliage and is a smaller tree (6 m). Many dwarf varieties exist, ranging in height from 60 cm to 2 m. Sawara cypress (*C. pisifera*) H 9–12 m: similar to *C. lawsoniana* with many leaf forms and colours.

CRYPTOMERIA (JAPANESE CEDAR, C. JAPONICA)

H 12 m. Stately tree for cool–temperate and cold climates; var. *nana* is dwarf, 1–2 m tall.

CUPRESSUS (CYPRESS)

Fast-growing, attractive conifers for screen or windbreak planting or for specimen trees. Very adaptable but prefer temperate or cold climates. Arizona cypress (*C. macrocarpa*) H 15–18 m: fast-growing conifers for hedges and windbreaks. Smaller varieties are *C. brunniana* H 12 m, with gold foliage; Italian cypress (*C. sempervirens*) H 12–18 m, with an erect pyramidal shape; var. *stricta*, which is more slender (often called pencil pine); Bhutan cypress (*C. torulosa*) H 12–18 m, with a tall, pyramidal shape, useful for screens or windbreaks.

A mixed display of conifers in this garden demonstrates the diversity of this plant group.

JUNIPERUS (SYN. SABINA, JUNIPER)

A large group of conifers with interesting shapes and leaf colours, especially in the dwarf species and varieties. Very adaptable and suited to most climates. Bermuda cedar (*J. bermudiana*) H 12–15 m: frost sensitive. Chinese juniper (*J. chinensis*) H 9–12 m; var. *aurea* with yellow foliage; var. *variegata* with grey and cream foliage. Pencil cedar (*J. virginiana*) H 12–18 m: narrow column shape, very adaptable. Alligator juniper (*J. pachyphlaea*) H 3 m: erect habit, silver-blue foliage. Creeping juniper (*J. horizontalis*) H 60–90 cm: prostrate, creeping habit, blue-green foliage, good spill-over plant for rockeries and banks. Meyer juniper (*J. squamata* 'Meyeri') H 2–3 m: erect habit, blue-grey foliage. Savin Juniper (*J. sabina*) H 1–2 m: spreading habit, blue-green foliage.

PICEA (SPRUCE)

Handsome, symmetrical, cone-shaped trees. Best in cool–temperate and cold climates. Norway spruce (*P. abies*) H 9–15 m: fast-growing, green foliage. White spruce (*P. glauca*) H 9–15 m: upturned branches, grey-green foliage; var. *albertiana conica* is dwarf (1–2 m). Blue spruce (*P. pungens*) H 6–9 m: slow-growing with blue-green foliage; var. *glauca* has blue-grey foliage; var. *kosteriana* has silver-blue foliage.

PINUS (PINES)

Large, fast-growing conifers with needle-like leaves. Pyramidal in shape when young but may lose their symmetry when mature. Very adaptable to climate but generally prefer temperate regions. Canary Island pine (*P. canariensis*) H 9–15 m: pendulous, grey-green foliage; all but coldest districts. Cuban pine (*P. caribaea*) H 18–24 m: fast-growing pine for coastal and subtropical areas with summer rainfall. Aleppo pine (*P. halepensis*) H 18 m: drought resistant, suitable for poor soils in low rainfall regions. Mexican pine (*P. patula*) H 12–15 m: fast grower, with pendulous, blue-green foliage; temperate and warm climates. Monterey pine (*P. radiata* syn. *P. insignis*) H 18–24 m: dense, fast-growing pine, excellent for shade, shelter or windbreaks; very adaptable to all climates.

PODOCARPUS (*P. ELATUS*, ILLAWARRA PLUM PINE)

H 12 m. Attractive, round-headed, Australian tree with glossy foliage, plum-coloured when young. Adaptable to all but cold and dry climates. Yellowwood (*P. falcatus*) is a similar tree from South Africa with blue-green foliage.

RETINOSPORA

See Chamaecyparis.

SABINA

See Juniperus.

TAXODIUM (*T. DISTICHUM*, SWAMP CYPRESS)

H 15–18 m. Large deciduous tree with green, feathery foliage turning russet-brown in autumn. Useful in wet situations. All climates except very cold regions.

THUJA

Ornamental conifers with attractive shapes and flattened frond-like foliage of various colours. Best suited to cool–temperate and cold climates. American arbor-vitae (*T. occidentalis*) H 15 m: fast-growing tree with conical shape. There are many smaller and more colourful varieties including 'Fastigiata' (H 2–3 m), green foliage; 'Lutescens' (H 2–3 m), tipped foliage; 'Hoveyii' (H 1 m), green foliage; 'Rheingold' (H 1 m), golden foliage; 'Little Gem' (H 60 cm), green foliage. Bookleaf cypress (*T. orientalis*) H 9–12 m: fast-growing conifer with dense, compact shape. Smaller, coloured-leaf varieties are also available. Western red cedar (*T. plicata*) H 12 m: dark-green foliage which droops at the ends; var. 'Aurea' is smaller with gold-tipped foliage and var. 'Zebrina' has striped foliage.

THUJOPSIS (*T. DOLABRATA*, FALSE ARBOR-VITAE)

H 9–12 m. Slow-growing conifer with heavy, coarse foliage. A smaller variety (4 m) is *variegata* which has cream patches through its foliage.

GROWING YOUR GARDEN

PALMS

This large family of woody, evergreen plants contains over 1000 species. In their natural habitat, most species are found in tropical and subtropical climates, but can be grown successfully in temperate climates too. They are not really suited to cold climates, unless planted in a warm, sheltered position or grown as indoor plants in containers. Some palms have a single trunk (others have several) with a distinctive crown of leaves or fronds. The fronds may be fan-shaped (palmate) or deeply divided (pinnate). Generally, palms are ornamental and easy to grow.

ARCHONTOPHOENIX

(*A. alexandrae*, Alexander palm) H 10–13 m (2 m): attractive specimen for garden or pot, requires ample moisture and frost-free area. (*A. cunninghamiana*, Bangalow palm) H 9–12 m (2 m): graceful Australian native palm with smooth grey trunk, dense crown of feathery fronds and pendulous bunches of flower spikes and fruit; good container plant when young.

ARECASTRUM

(*A. romanzoffianum* syn. *Cocos plumosa*, plume or queen palm) H 12 m (2 m): slender, smooth trunk and a head of arching, blue-green fronds; prefers full sunlight or semi-shade conditions.

BUTIA

(*B. capitata*, jelly or wine palm) H 6 m (1 m): short trunk with head of blue-grey fronds and orange-red bunches of fruit; sunlight or shade; good container plant.

CARYOTA

(*C. mitis*, fish tail palm) H 6 m (1 m): multiple trunks with long, yellow-green fronds with toothed, wedge-shaped leaflets.

CHAMAEDOREA

(*C. elegans* syn. *Neanthe elegans*, parlour palm) H 2 m (1 m): delightful pot or tub plant for patio or terrace in semi-shade or indoors; bright green, papery fronds in a spiral around the thin, dainty stem.

CHAMAEROPS

(*C. humilis*, European fan palm) H 5 m (1 m): clumps of several stems, bearing shiny, deeply cut, fan-like leaves; good for small gardens and containers, both indoors and outdoors; tolerates cooler conditions more than most palms and does well in full sun or shade.

CYCAS (SAGO PALM)

(*C. revoluta*) H 3 m (1 m); not a true palm, but a cycad. Very slow growing. In a botanical class of their own, they are the most primitive plants in existence. Fern-like in youth and palm-like in maturity. Ideal for containers.

HOWEA (SYN. KENTIA)

There are two attractive species, native to Lord Howe Island: *H. belmoreana* (sentry or curly palm) H 6 m (1 m): stout ringed trunk with feathery fronds curving inward; good container plant for indoors or outdoors; sunlight or semi-shade. *H. forsteriana* (kentia or thatch leaf palm) H 7–9 m (1 m): a more slender palm. Ideal for indoors. Mature palms of both species have long spikes of green fruit turning yellow and red as they ripen.

LINOSPADIX

(*L. monostachya*, walking-stick palm) H 3 m (1·m): attractive, mid-green fronds are broad and fringed and blend in well with other plants in a half sun or semi-shade position; ideal container plant for a shady terrace.

PHOENIX (DATE PALMS)

Several species, including the date palm (*P. dactylifera*), which is grown for its fruit. *P. canariensis* (Canary Island palm) H 6 m (2 m): arching fronds from ground level for 8–10 years. The fronds then grow from a thick, robust trunk. Heavy bunches of edible, orange berries are produced periodically. Very adaptable but prefers full sun. *P. roebelinii* (dwarf date palm) H 4 m (2 m): very slow-growing but extremely attractive palm with glossy, finely feathered, arching fronds. A good garden palm, ideal for container growing (indoors or outdoors). Grows in sun or shade.

RHAPIS

(*R. excelsa*, lady palm or ground rattan cane) H 4 m (1 m): attractive palm with several slender trunks topped by small fan-shaped fronds; an excellent container plant for indoors or outdoors.

RHOPALOSTYLIS

(*R. sapida*, nikau palm) H 6 m (6 m): New Zealand's native nikau looks like a giant feather duster. Fronds are borne in erect clusters from the top of distinctively ringed trees. Red, berry-like fruits appear below the leaves, after the rather insignificant flowers have fallen. *R. bauri* 'Cheesemanii' (Kermadec native palm) H 6 m (7 m): is faster and larger growing.

TRACHYCARPUS

(*T. fortunei*, fan or Chusan palm) H 9 m (2 m): slender trunks with persistent fibres and bearing fan-shaped fronds with stout spines at base. Large clusters of fragrant yellow flowers followed by black fruit. Full sun or semi-shade. Like the European fan palm, this species tolerates cooler conditions.

Palms and hibiscus by the pool help create a distinctly tropical atmosphere.

PRUNING

Plants are pruned for a variety of reasons. They will grow vigorously and look more attractive when dead, diseased or broken branches are removed.

It may be necessary to trim parts off a young plant to encourage a particular mature habit. For instance, to generate a shade tree with a single trunk and elevated canopy, the regular elimination of lower branches is required. It is also legitimate to prune plants for hedging, topiary or espalier where their natural habit or shape is modified in order to fulfil a particular function.

Pruning is sometimes carried out to keep a plant within bounds. However, proper selection of plants should eliminate the practice of severe annual lopping. If a plant needs to be pruned more than every five years to control its size, it is the wrong plant for the situation.

Judicious pruning of trees and shrubs can also promote greater production or better-quality flowers and fruit.

DO ALL PLANTS NEED PRUNING?

It is not necessary to prune everything annually. Some plants, like camellias, daphne and gardenias, can be left to assume their own neat habit and only need the occasional wayward stem to be corrected.

GOLDEN RULES OF PRUNING

- Never cut without good reason.
- Prune at the right time for the species concerned.
- Prune lightly, rather than severely – more can always be cut off later.
- Never prune with blunt tools.

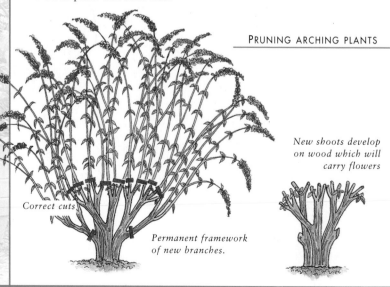

PRUNING ARCHING PLANTS

New shoots develop on wood which will carry flowers

Correct cuts

Permanent framework of new branches.

PRUNING MADE EASY

Pruning shrubs or trees to enhance their flowering requires some knowledge of plant behaviour. Observe when growth occurs, when flowers appear and the type and age of the shoots that produce flowers. Without this information there is a tendency to prune in the wrong season, causing a complete loss of the flowering period.

FLOWERS GROW ON THREE TYPES OF WOOD:

1. FLOWERS BORNE ON CURRENT SEASON'S GROWTH

Plants which flower in summer on new growth made in mid to late spring are pruned in late winter. Pruning out older wood encourages fresh new growth; the more abundant the new growth the more prolific the flowers. If plants are sensitive to frosts, delay pruning until early spring.

FIVE PLANTS PRUNED IN LATE WINTER

roses • hibiscus • crepe myrtle
Bouvardia • *Fuchsia*

2. FLOWERS BORNE ON WOOD FROM PREVIOUS YEAR'S GROWTH

In this category new growth commences in spring, ripens through summer, becomes dormant in late autumn, rests during winter and bears flowers in spring on wood that is then one year old. Prune in spring, immediately after flowering, to allow sufficient time for the subsequent new growth to mature.

FIVE PLANTS PRUNED IN SPRING IMMEDIATELY AFTER FLOWERING

Spiraea • *Weigela*
Forsythia • flowering peach
Wisteria

3. FLOWERS BORNE ON ONE-YEAR-OLD WOOD, OLDER WOOD AND SHORT SPURS

These need little pruning except to maintain their naturally tidy habit and remove any old or dying wood. Trim immediately after flowering.

FIVE PLANTS WHICH REQUIRE MINIMAL PRUNING

magnolia • crab apple
Taiwan cherry • flowering plum
Japanese flowering cherry

TRIMMING TIPS

● Retain the natural arching shape of plants like mock orange, *Weigela*, may bush, *Prunus glandulosa* and *Abelia* by removing old woody canes at the base of the plant.
● To prevent fruit from forming on ornamental flowering fruit trees, shorten the flowered shoots after blooming has finished.
● Natives benefit from a light annual trim to maintain compact growth.

CLEAN CUTS

Invest in good-quality tools and keep them sharpened using a whetstone. Cutting with blunt or burred blades causes bruised and torn tissue, providing an entry point for fungal diseases and insects.

Sterilise tools with household bleach after pruning to prevent transmission of diseases from one plant to another.

Cut immediately above a healthy growth bud and at an angle sloping away from the bud so that moisture is readily shed.

CHAPTER 15

NEW ZEALAND
NATIVE PLANTS

Until arrival of Europeans, apart from some burning-off by moa hunters in the south, the native forests and plants of New Zealand maintained balanced growth over most of the country. Then in the days of pioneer farming, a major aim was the destruction of native plants over vast areas to make room for grazing livestock. In addition, the gardens of the early pioneers were stocked with plants from Europe, North America, Japan and the Himalayas.

Even today New Zealand gardeners are often better informed about plants from other lands than they are about New Zealand plants.

The New Zealand flora consists of approximately 2000 flowering plants and 150 ferns. Many of these plants are unique, because New Zealand has been isolated from other land masses for many millions of years. Our native flora offers a varied collection of species of different size, form and texture and colourful flowering plants. Their value as garden plants has been recognised overseas and many are now exported to Europe and America. In addition the foliage of many native plants is used by exponents of floral art in New Zealand and overseas and there is a growing export industry of foliage for this purpose (phormium, coprosma, leptospermum, lophomyrtus, pittosporum and hebes are just a few of the plants used.)

The great majority of natives are easy to grow and will thrive in any good garden soil. For quick, successful establishment, choose young nursery-grown plants and plant in winter in well prepared soil. The drainage of heavier soils can be improved by adding extra topsoil and peat to provide raised planting sites. Staking is usually necessary for the first two years and early training of trees is essential to prolong life and good health. For the first few summers keep weeds away from the bases of newly planted trees, which will require regular watering. Mulching with organic materials will conserve moisture and help suppress weeds as well as improving soil structure. Most trees will respond well to an annual light dressing (50 g per square metre) of Gro-Plus General Garden Fertiliser in early spring.

In recent years new cultivars have become available. Manuka is just one example where a whole range of white, pink and red flowering varieties are available in single and double forms with prostrate and pendulous habits.

Coprosmas, pittosporums and the flaxes (*Phormium*) are particularly valuable as garden plants.

COPROSMAS AS GARDEN PLANTS

There are approximately 50 species of coprosma in New Zealand. They are mostly shrubs or small trees and vary in height from a few centimetres to several metres. They are common throughout the country, some in the alpine regions which are different from those found among seashore vegetation or others which occur as undershrubs in the forests. Some taller tree species have large, attractive, glossy, leaves whilst others, especially the divaricating shrubs, have minute leaves. Many produce small brightly coloured fleshy fruits but if grown in the garden for their berries they must be planted in groups, because male and female flowers are formed on different plants.

Coprosma repens and its many cultivars are extremely useful in coastal districts as shelter and hedge plants; their shiny leaves make them excellent background shrubs. Cultivars such as

'Picturata', 'Variegata' and the hybrids 'Beatson's Gold' and 'Coppershine' add colour to any shrub planting. The divaricating species make interesting specimen shrubs in a bark or pebble garden. The dense prostrate species such as *C. acerose*, *C. brunnea* and *C.X. kirkii* and their cultivars make excellent quick growing ground cover in most situations.

Most cultivars are quick growing; they are best in open situations but will tolerate semi-shade. To keep them in an attractive form they need constant pruning and grooming in spring and midsummer to promote the new well coloured foliage. They are practically free of disease and insect pests; occasionally *C. repens* and its cultivars can be frost tender.

Pittosporums thrive in soil with good drainage.

A SELECTION OF COPROSMAS

	NAME	FOLIAGE COVER	COMMENTS
Shrubs over 1 m	*C. crassifolia*	Small, pale green	Much branched, wiry habit
	C. (coastal hybrid)	Shiny green	Compact, spreading shrub
	C. repens	Shiny green	Handsome foliage shrub
	C. repens 'Picturata'	Yellow margined with green	
Shrubs under 1 m	*C.* 'Beatson's Gold'	Small, gold centre	Dense habit
	C. 'Coppershine'	Shiny, brown shading	
	C. 'Greensleeves'	Shiny green	
	C. 'Williamsii Variegata'	Margined creamy-white	Requires shade
Groundcovers	*C. acerose* hybrids	Small, golden brown	Interlacing branches, variable
	C. X. kirkii 'Kirkii'	Small green	
	C. X. kirkii 'Prostrata'	Small, shiny green	Requires clipping to keep prostrate
Hedges	*C. repens*	Shiny green	Coastal hardy, quick growing
	C. repens 'Picturata'	Yellow, margined with green	

PITTOSPORUMS AS GARDEN PLANTS

Pittosporums and their variegated cultivars have won a place in horticulture as foliage shrubs. Most species produce in spring small, delightfully fragrant flowers. They are quick growing and will give maturity to a new garden; they can be used as hedges, background shrubs or small species and cultivars will give variety to any planting. Although some species are frost tender a number are resistant to salt spray and make excellent hedges in a windswept situation. Young nursery grown plants should be planted out in autumn; this is especially important when establishing plantings in exposed situations. To keep plants compact they will need trimming with shears in the spring before new season's growth is formed.

If grown in sheltered areas some cultivars are susceptible to an Alternaria leaf blight and are best planted in open situations. Aphids can be a pest on cultivars of *P. tenuifolium* whilst blister scale (psillids) will cause distortion of young growth of both *P. crassifolium* and *P. tenuifolium*. A spray of Target or Orthene in October and again in February will control this pest.

A SELECTION OF NEW ZEALAND PITTOSPORUMS

	COMMENTS
TREES	
P. eugenioides 'Tarata'	To 5 or more metres in ten years. Sweetly scented yellow flowers.
P. eugenioides 'Variegatum'	3 m. Light green leaves, heavily margined with creamy white.
P. tenuifolium 'Kohuhu'	3–5 m. Erect growing, black stems and pale green leaves 3–7 cm long.
P. tenuifolium 'Variegatum'	3–5 m. Dark stems, oval leaves variegated pale green and creamy white.
P. umbellatum	3–5 m. Pink flowered; dark green leaves. Handsome tree.
SHRUBS	
P. tenuifolium 'James Stirling'	Trim in early spring with shears. Dainty form, sparse foliage.
'Marjorie Channon'	Silver leaves with narrow cream margins.
'Rotundifolium'	Black stems, rounded leaves pale silvery green and variegated creamy white.
'Silver Sheen'	Silver-leafed form of kohuhu.
'Stirling Gold'	Small leaves with gold centres; red new stems.
'Sunburst'	Leaves variegated gold and lime green.
HEDGES	
P. crassifolium 'Karo'	Particularly good for exposed positions.
P. eugenioides 'Tarata'	Excellent informal habit.
P. tenuifolium 'Kohuhu'	Regular clipping makes a neat, formal hedge.

GROWING YOUR GARDEN

FLAX AS GARDEN PLANTS

Flaxes are large herbaceous perennials belonging to the genus *Phormium*. Named cultivars are available in a wide range of foliage colours and growth forms. They are amongst the most useful of our native plants, being equally at home in the shrub border, in pebble or bark gardens and as tub plants. Flax is a hardy coastal plant which will grow in almost any soil or situation. Modern cultivars of mountain flax require well drained soils. The quantity of flowers produced varies between cultivars. Tuis visit the flowers for nectar.

Flaxes are propagated by division. Lift and divide the rhizome in late autumn; each piece must bear one terminal fan and have the leaves shortened by one half. Many coloured cultivars are not completely stable. Discard fans with inferior colouring and replant the best in well drained soil. Do not bury the rhizome, plant at the same depth as the parent. A stake will be necessary in exposed situations until new roots anchor the plant. Plants should be divided every three to four years and established plants will benefit from a light application (50 g per square metre) of Gro-Plus General Garden Fertiliser in spring. Remove faded, damaged and dead leaves regularly.

Two pests require regular control. Leaf cutting moth is controlled by Carbaryl applied in November and March. Scale insect is controlled by Orthene and oil combined, applied in November and February. Spray must penetrate leaf bases of the crowns.

LEPTOSPERMUM AS GARDEN PLANTS

The New Zealand tea tree belongs to the genus *Leptospermum*. The two most common are the kanuka (*L. ericoides*), where the flowers are borne in clusters and the foliage is soft and feathery, and manuka (*L. scoparium*), where the flowers are borne singly and the leaves are stiff and pointed. They are found throughout the country from sea level to sub-alpine regions and in the wild show great diversity in growth forms and sometimes in flower colour and size.

The common name originated because early settlers used the leaves as a substitute for tea.

GARDEN USE

Until recently kanuka was rarely grown in gardens but it will quickly form an attractive small tree in exposed situations on difficult soils. In manuka a number of distinct growth forms and flower colours have been brought

The bold appearance of flax provides a focal point in many types of gardens.

Leptospermum are hardy plants, untroubled by cold and wind.

A SELECTION OF PHORMIUM CULTIVARS

SIZE	CULTIVAR	FOLIAGE COLOUR	HABIT	COMMENTS
Large, over 150 cm	P. 'Black Prince'	Bronze	Weeping	Requires sheltered position, leaf ends split, florists' foliage.
	P. 'Burgundy'	Bronze	Upright	Bold landscaping, erect habit, florists' foliage.
	P. 'Guardsman'	Bronze/red variegated	Upright	Brightly coloured form, regular grooming essential.
	P. 'Platt's Black'	Dark	Weeping	Darkest form available.
	P. 'Williamsii Variegatum'	Green/yellow variegated	Weeping	Good for bold landscaping.
Medium 100–150 cm	P. 'Dark Delight'	Dark	Weeping	Excellent dark form.
	P. 'Duet'	Green/yellow variegatedgood	Upright	Attractive plant, good flowerer.
	P. 'Sunset'	Bronze/yellow variegated	Weeping	Best apricot-variegated form for shade, tidy.
	P. 'Yellow Wave'	Green/yellow variegated	Weeping	Bright bold effect, divide and replant every two or three years.
Small 50–100 cm	P. 'Green Dwarf'	Green	Upright	Attractive flowers and foliage, good drainage essential.
	P. 'Rubrum'	Bronze	Weeping	Good florists' foliage.

into cultivation and hybridised to produce cultivars which are now well established garden plants in New Zealand and overseas. Cultivars vary from erect shrubs to dwarf forms suitable for rock and bark gardens to prostrate forms suitable for ground covers and crib walls. Flower colour varies from scarlet, deep rose and all shades of pink to white. Amongst the shrubs many attractive double-flowered cultivars have been developed. Some cultivars flower for nearly six months of the year.

CULTIVATION

Propagation of cultivars is from semi-ripe tip cuttings taken in autumn; the species grows readily from seed. It prefers a well drained soil and sunny position. Prune immediately after flowering to maintain a bushy habit by shortening the flowering wood to approximately one third its length. To retain the natural character of the plant, use secateurs to shorten growths individually rather than clipping to a 'neat shape' with hedge clippers. Plants benefit from a light

GROWING YOUR GARDEN

LEPTOSPERMUM CULTIVARS

SIZE	CULTIVAR	FLOWER COLOUR	FLOWER TYPE AND SIZE MM	FLOWERING TIME (AUCKLAND)
Shrub 2 m	L. 'Blossom'	White, flushed pale pink	Double 15	April–November
	L. 'Crimson Glory'	Deep red	Double 15	April–November
	L. 'Kare Kare'	Clear white	Single 15	August–November
	L. 'Keatleyi'	White, flushed with pink	Single 25	April–November
	L. 'Martinii'	Bicolour effect; pink/pale pink	Single 20	March–November
	L. 'Red Ensign'	Deep red	Single 15	March–November
	L. 'Rose Queen'	Bicolour effect and light pink	Single 20	March–October
	L. 'Rosy Morn'	Rosy pink	Double 15	March–November
Shrub up to 1 m	L. 'Cherry Brandy'	Rosy pink	Single 15	March–October
	L. 'Elizabeth Jane'	Rosy pink	Single 10	May–November
	L. 'Kea'	White, tinged pink	Single 10	May–November
	L. 'Ruru'	Rosy pink, darker centre	Single 10	May–November
Groundcover	L. 'Pink Cascade'	White, flushed pink	Single 20	March–October
	L. 'Red Falls'	Red	Single 10	April–September

application (50 g per square metre) of Gro-Plus General Garden Fertiliser in spring.

Most forms of *L. scoparium* are susceptible to a conspicuous black mould which covers all parts of the plant. Scale insects on the plant secrete a sweet syrupy liquid which forms a medium for fungus growth. Spray with Orthene and Conqueror Oil combined in November and repeat in February to control the scale and the mould will disappear. The 'Nanum' group appears relatively resistant. Leaf roller caterpillar and bag moth can infest plants; they will be controlled with an Orthene and Conqueror Oil spray. Preventative action is required to keep this condition at bay.

Flowering xeronema makes a good contrast to fern foliage.

NATIVE FERNS

Ferns are a dominant feature in our native flora. They grow in a variety of habitats from dry hillsides to sheltered humid valleys. Over the years a number of species have proved to be good garden plants.

Tree ferns such as the black mamaku are too large for a modern city garden but smaller species will provide interest in sheltered, cool, shady corners. When incorporated in an evergreen foliage shrub border, they give a New Zealand identity to the planting and provide an interesting form and texture. They also make excellent ground cover under deciduous trees or among young plantings of camellias, magnolias and rhododendrons. In scree gardens, species such as *Blechnum pennamarina* and *Doodia media* add variety to the planting.

Most species grow best when planted in friable, well-drained soil; however they will not tolerate wind and a number are frost sensitive. Care is needed not to plant too deeply; the crown should never be buried. Most ferns require moist, shaded conditions but will not tolerate wet, poorly drained soil.

Propagation depends on the species; a number can be increased by division whilst in others only a single crown is produced; these species must be produced from spores.

A few species such as *Asplenium bulbiferum* — the hen and chickens fern or moku — bud off small bulbils on the leaves; if mature bulbils are taken with a small portion of the leaf and placed in moist potting mix, roots are quickly formed and a new plant is obtained.

Pohutukawa is susceptible to frosts and should be protected when young.

Macropiper is an ideal plant to grow in difficult, shady spots.

GROWING YOUR GARDEN

A SELECTION OF NATIVE TREES

5–10 METRES (the height it will reach in 10–15 years in average conditions)		
Agathis australis	Kauri	Slow growing New Zealand conifer forming a stately, pyramidal-shaped specimen. Older trees are compactly branched, leaves are olive green.
Alectryon excelsus	Titoki	A spreading tree with handsome foliage, it requires shelter. When ripe, fruit splits revealing black seed in scarlet cup.
Dacrydium cupressinum	Rimu	Outstanding specimen tree with drooping foliage. Requires a rich moist soil sheltered from winds. Hardy.
Metrosideros excelsa	Pohutukawa or New Zealand Christmas Tree	One of the finest flowering trees. Excellent for coastal planting. Tolerant to most soil types.
Knightia excelsa	Rewarewa	A tall, slender, erect tree with leathery leaves and maroon, bottlebrush flowers.
Libocedrus plumosa	Kawaka	Upright conifer with feathery foliage. A good lawn specimen.
Podocarpus totara 'Aurea'	Golden totara	Compact conifer form with golden yellow foliage. Slow growing, requires pruning to maintain compact and upright habit.
2.5–5 METRES		
Dodonaea vicosa 'Purpurea'	Purple akeake	Good foliage plant with purplish-red leaves and purplish-red seed capsules in summer.
Leptospermum ericoides	Kanuka	Provides striking display in full bloom; masses of small white flowers in December. Feathery foliage, graceful habit.
Meryta sinclairii	Puka	Has large bright green leaves and tropical appearance. Best grown in sheltered position in good soil. Excellent tub plant.
Metrosideros kermadecensis 'Variegata'		Good foliage plant, dark green leaves variegated with broad creamy white margin. Deep crimson flowers. Excellent tub plant.
Sophora tetraptera 'Chevalier'	Kowhai	Selected free-flowering form bearing masses of large, yellow flowers.

A SELECTION OF NATIVE SHRUBS

OVER 1 METRE

Clianthus puniceus	Kaka beak	Spreading habit, bunches of large pea-shaped flowers in summer. Frost tender.
Corokia 'Red Wonder'		Spreading habit, red berries in autumn.
Corokia 'Yellow Wonder'		Compact habit, yellow berries in autumn.
Griselinia littoralis	Kapuka *	Dense habit, large, mid-green leaves.
Griselinia lucida	Puka *	Large foliage plant with large shiny leaves.
Lophomyrtus 'Kathryn'		Upright, dense habit, dark crinkled foliage. Susceptible to thrips.
Macropiper excelsum var. psittacorum		Compact habit with heart-shaped mid-green leaves.
Melicope ternata	Wharangi	Open habit, glossy green leaves.
Olearia thompsonii		Much branched shrub, dark green leaves, panicles of white flowers.
Pennantia corymbosa	Kaikomako	Forms handsome, slender tree with abundant white flowers.
Pisonia brunonianam 'Variegatum'	*	Large leaves irregularly margined with creamy yellow. Shelter from strong winds and frost.
Pomaderris kumeraho	Kumarahou	Well branched shrub, mass of yellow flowers in spring.
Pomaderris polifolia		Densely branched shrub bearing cream flowers in spring.
Pseudopanax 'Gold Splash'	*	Many branched, bright, gold-splashed leaves.

UNDER 1 METRE

Brachyglottis greyi	syn Senecio	Soft-grey foliage, good drainage essential.
Hymenanthera crassifolia		Densely branched shrub, dark green leaves and light grey bark.
Metrosideros carminea	Akakura	Forms a dense bush bearing brilliant carmine flowers in spring. Frost tender, susceptible to thrips.
Metrosideros diffusa		Dense habit, mid-green leaves.
Metrosideros perforata		Light green new growth, maturing to dark green; white flowers.
Meuhlenbeckia astonii		Much branched interlacing shrub, hardy.

GROUND COVER

Fuchsia procumbens		Slender, spreading plant bearing large red fruit; deciduous.
Myporum debile		Dense, prostrate habit, purple fruit in winter.

* Suitable for tub plants

CHAPTER 16

GARDENING IN CONTAINERS

G rowing plants in containers is an interesting hobby, especially for people who live in flats or home units and do their gardening on a windowsill or balcony. Potted plants are very decorative, especially if they are grown in attractive containers. They can be used to soften and beautify large paved areas like patios and courtyards or can create a focal point in the garden. Perhaps the best thing about container-grown plants is that they can be moved about from one place to another, providing the containers are not too heavy. This way you can give plants a suitable microclimate or show them off when they're looking at their best.

There are, of course, many other reasons why the popularity of this form of gardening is growing. Garden centres now offer a much bigger range of attractive tubs, pots, troughs, hanging baskets and window boxes and an even greater variety of plants to grow in them. Moreover, there are new, efficient potting mixtures these days which greatly reduce the chances of failure, and plant breeders have developed plants more suitable for tub culture.

However, the two outstanding advantages of gardening in containers are that they are portable and that almost any plant can be grown in them – flowering annuals, bulbs, ferns, creepers, herbs, shrubs, or even trees. There are even specially bred compact forms of plants which produce perfect fruit in a confined space.

SITUATION AND SOIL

To be a successful container gardener you must choose the right plant for your situation. Home unit balconies are often windy, so anything you plant should be able to stand up to the breezes. The amount of sunlight is very important and will also influence your choice of plants. Sun-loving plants – which include vegetables – need at least four to five hours of sunlight each day to grow successfully, so check the amount of sunshine before spending money on plants that may not be suitable.

Containers must have free drainage, otherwise your plants will drown. Most pots and tubs have one or several drainage holes 1–2 cm in diameter.

Ordinary garden soil is usually unsuitable for pot culture because it does not drain well and tends to set hard. Proprietary potting mixtures, which are available from garden stores and nurseries, are open, porous mixes which are very satisfactory and have the added advantage of being free from weed seeds, soil pests and plant diseases. Special potting mixes like Orchid Mix, African Violet Mix and Bulb Mix are available too. For best results purchase a good-quality mix. Cheap potting mixtures are just that: cheap. They are rarely a bargain.

When potting up most plants, don't be tempted to put a small plant into a large pot with the idea of saving yourself some work. Plants do not thrive in overlarge containers – some prefer to be crowded. It is best to move a plant into a slightly larger pot when the previous one fills with roots.

WATERING AND FEEDING

Whatever you decide to grow in your pots, remember that container-grown plants have a restricted root system and cannot forage for moisture as they would do in the open garden. On hot summer days, daily watering may be needed – perhaps twice a day if the plants are in full sunlight. Always water thoroughly – not just a sprinkle. Use a water-breaker or a watering wand rather than a hose nozzle. A water-breaker delivers a large volume of water gently onto the potting mix and causes minimum disturbance.

STEP 1
Before you begin, water the pot thoroughly and allow to drain. The potting mix should be moist but not overwet.

When potting, leave a margin between the soil level and the rim of the container. When watering, fill this space slowly with water until it weeps out of the drainage holes. A mulch of compost, coarse gravel, pebbles or pine bark helps to reduce evaporation and cools the surface soil.

STEP 2
Spread your opened fingers over the top of the mix before inverting the pot. Tap gently on the base to loosen root-ball. Ease plant out of the pot.

Hint

Don't be tempted into buying cheap potting mixes, thinking that you will be saving money. They're not always a bargain. The more expensive mixes designed specifically for containers and outdoor use have drainage and moisture-retention characteristics that will ensure your plants thrive.

THE TWO ANNS
A & A CONSULTANTS

STEP 3
Carefully remove some of the old potting mix, either by hand or with a jet of water from a hose. Gently tease out the outermost roots.

STEP 4
With sharp secateurs, trim off any diseased, dead or overlong roots. When finished, make sure you clean the secateurs to remove any potting mix residue.

Good drainage and frequent watering also means loss of plant nutrients. Regular, small amounts of fertiliser are needed to keep plants growing strongly. Always apply fertilisers to moist soil to avoid burning young roots. The water-soluble fertilisers, such as Thrive are suitable for regular liquid feeds. Use at half-strength for tender plants. Slow-acting fertilisers, controlled-release fertilisers (such as Multicote) or organic pellets (such as Bio-Gold) are also suitable to provide nutrients over a long period. Whatever fertiliser you choose, always use it according to the manufacturer's directions. Too much fertiliser for potted plants can be disastrous, especially if the soil becomes dry.

STEP 5
Repot into a slightly larger container using fresh potting mix. The top of the root-ball should be at the same level as it was in the previous pot.

PESTS AND DISEASES

Container-grown plants are not immune to attack by pests and diseases. Grubs, bugs, blights and mildews must always be guarded against. A few plants on a balcony can often be kept clear of caterpillars, snails and other leaf-eating pests by picking them off by hand or spraying with low-toxic insect sprays

STEP 6
Firm the mix gently into place. Water well. Add some controlled-release fertiliser. When finished, wash your hands well with soap and water.

which are suitable for controlling pests of potted and indoor plants. Pyrethrum-based sprays such as Nature's Way are ideal. A few pellets of snail bait at the base of potted plants will control snails and slugs.

FAVOURITE SHRUBS FOR TUBS

Camellias and azaleas with all-year-round foliage and exquisite flowers in season make excellent tub specimens. They prefer partial shade or filtered sunlight. Most proprietary potting mixes are suitable for growing azaleas and camellias in tubs. Yates Patio and Tub Mix is ideal.

Hydrangeas make magnificent tub plants for shady situations, although they do look rather bare in winter. They give a tremendous flower display in summer and can be brought indoors when flowering. Flower colour depends on whether the soil is acid or alkaline – blue in acid soil, pink in alkaline. If you want your hydrangeas to be a particular colour, grow them in a tub and treat the soil accordingly. (See Chapter 4.)

Fuchsias – and there are dozens of varieties – are dependable flowering shrubs for tubs, pots or hanging baskets. Flowers in white, pink, red and purple are produced over a long period.

Gardenias, with handsome glossy leaves and waxy, white fragrant flowers, make good tub specimens. Plants prefer full sun or half sun in a warm, sheltered spot. In the right position (especially in warm climates) some varieties of gardenias will flower from spring to autumn.

Daphne is another neat, evergreen shrub with exquisitely perfumed pink, red or mauve flowers in late winter and spring. Plants need good drainage and are often more reliable in a large pot or tub than in the open garden. They prefer morning sun but shade for the rest of the day.

Geraniums will provide a bright patch of colour on a sunny terrace or patio. Grow them in tubs, large pots or window boxes; with plenty of sun they will flower from early spring to late autumn. The ivy-leaf trailing varieties are ideal for hanging baskets.

Bougainvillea is another sun-lover, especially for warm northern climates. Dwarf varieties are now readily available. These are best for

Hint

Remove the saucers from underneath outdoor containers for the duration of winter: this will encourage free drainage and help prevent waterlogging. Replace them in spring.

DAVID JACOBS
YATES NEW ZEALAND

containers and give a magnificent, long-lasting display of flower bracts.

Citrus trees are both ornamental and useful tub plants for outdoor living areas. The smaller citrus trees like cumquats and limes are easy to grow in tubs, but lemons, oranges and mandarins need pruning to keep them within bounds. (See Chapter 20 for more information on citrus trees.)

Japanese bamboo (*Nandina*), with its lacy foliage, makes a good container plant and can be kept in bounds by pruning. True bamboo, which belongs to the grass family, gives an oriental effect for tub culture but only dwarf varieties up to 2–3 m tall should be chosen.

ROSES

Roses do well in tubs and pots and they are easy to grow, though obviously the miniature varieties and small floribundas will perform best. They are not fussy about climate and can withstand hot summers as well as freezing winters – provided you don't let the container dry out.

Choose a pot at least 50 cm or more in diameter to allow sufficient room for the roots to develop properly. Fertilise with controlled-release fertiliser in early spring, as new growth begins, and again in early autumn. Your display will last longer if you keep removing dead flower heads to encourage the formation of new buds. Never allow rose hips (fruits) to develop because they drain energy from the plant and inhibit the growth of more flowers. Here is a list of some roses suitable for container growing – and remember that roses generally

A bowl-shaped container effectively displays flowering annuals and bulbs.

look better massed than as single specimens. Try to group several pots together.

- Floribunda types: 'Apricot Nectar', 'Iceberg', 'Lilli Marlene', 'Regensberg'.
- Miniatures: 'Green Ice', 'Kaikoura', 'Ko's Yellow', 'Lavender Lace', 'Little Red Devil', 'Magic Carousel', 'Otago', 'Over the Rainbow', 'Snow Carpet', 'Sunspray', 'Wanaka'.
- Shrub types: 'Cottage Maid', 'Eyeopener', 'Flower Carpet', 'Lavender Dream', 'Seafoam', 'The Fairy'.

Hint

If you want to experiment with new colour combinations in the garden, using annuals in containers offers the perfect opportunity to be flamboyant. Be brave: stretch your imagination and see what happens!

LOUISE RUNDLE
INTERIOR DESIGNER

FLOWERING BULBS FOR POTS

Bulbs are the easiest plants to grow in pots. Favourite spring-flowering bulbs for this treatment are daffodils, jonquils, hyacinths, bluebells, lachenalias, freesias, triteleias and tulips. Daffodils, hyacinths and tulips are ideal for growing in bulb fibre indoors. In cool districts, lily-of-the-valley can be planted several bulbs to the pot and will be a great source of enjoyment either indoors or outdoors. Permanent plantings of large evergreen bulbous plants like agapanthus are suitable for large tubs around swimming pools, barbecue areas or on sunny patios. The strap-like leaves are attractive all year round, with large clusters of blue or white flowers in summer when outdoor living areas are most used.

Clivia, with orange-red blooms in winter followed by attractive red berries, is a good substitute for shady areas. Hippeastrums are popular container-grown bulbs in Europe and favourites for their large pink, white or red, lily-like flowers in spring. They are ideal for pots on balconies, patios and in courtyards and can be brought inside as temporary house plants when they flower. Many other bulbs and bulbous plants can be grown in this way. Hymenocallis (one of the many spider lilies), eucharis, eucomis (pineapple flower) and liliums are good examples. Gloriosa (climbing lily) can be grown in a hanging basket. For further information on flowering bulbs refer to Chapter 11.

....

Hint

Day lilies are a wonderful choice for container planting in hot, sunny locations. They should be planted into a good-quality potting mix. Feed them in spring with a slow-release fertiliser. Most varieties will be in full flower at Christmas. Dead-head after flowering and divide plants every three years.

BARRY SLIGH
TAUNTON GARDEN AND NURSERY

....

COLOURFUL ANNUALS

Annual flowers make a colourful display in pots or hanging baskets and are invaluable for brightening a balcony, terrace or patio. Potted annuals are also useful for special occasions like parties or weddings, which are planned well ahead.

For spring flowers, plant cineraria, lobelia, nemesia, pansy, polyanthus, primrose, primula, schizanthus, sweet pea (dwarf 'Bijou') and violas. These can all be raised from seed or seedlings planted in late summer to autumn. Use good quality potting mixes, as suggested earlier. Annuals for summer pots include petunia (especially colourful for hanging baskets), phlox, nasturtium ('Jewel Mixed' is a good trailing basket plant) and verbena. All need a sunny position but one which is sheltered from wind. Marigolds flower over a long period in containers – use dwarf varieties for small pots and troughs and larger ones for tubs where they will make a dazzling display. Celosia makes a striking pot plant for hot summer weather. Dwarf varieties in scarlet or gold can be combined or planted separately. Bedding

TOP FIVE CONTAINER PLANTS FOR FULL SUN

CITRUS

Many of the smaller-growing citrus trees, such as mandarins, cumquats and 'Meyer' lemons, grow well in pots. Their glossy leaves are green year round, the flowers have a delightful fragrance, and the fruits are decorative. In Asia, potted citrus are given as 'good luck' tokens at New Year.

HEBE

These neat, small-growing New Zealand plants are not particularly fussy about conditions, but always maintain a better profile if they're given a light haircut after flowering.

POHUTUKAWA (NEW ZEALAND CHRISTMAS TREE)

Almost unkillable (but no heavy frosts, please) and, if you're lucky, you'll get a good show of red blooms at Christmas. The pretty, variegated form is notoriously reluctant to flower.

GREVILLEA

There are hundreds of grevillea species around but *G. juniperina*, *G. intricata* and *G. 'Robyn Gordon'* are particularly attractive.

BOX

Renowned for their hardiness and their small, neat leaves, box plants are very popular for topiary work. Begin clipping when the plant is young to maintain a dense foliage cover.

GROWING YOUR GARDEN

begonias are delightful in quite small pots and make a good show in semi-shade planted in a strawberry pot. Impatiens (busy Lizzie) is an excellent pot plant for shady areas and flowers almost all year round in colours of pink, salmon and mauve. It is easily raised from seed and grows quickly. The more glamorous hybrids with double, rose-like flowers or handsome variegated foliage are a delightful feature on balconies or patios.

As a change from annual flowers in pots, ornamental chilli has interesting, multi-coloured fruits, and coleus, which has colourful leaves, is another attractive foliage plant which is ideal for container growing,

Plants in hanging baskets (like these tuberous begonias) can look stunning but must be in a suitable situation. Exposed baskets can heat up and dry out quickly.

even in shade. Most herbs, except the very tall ones, can be grown successfully in pots, as can many of the smaller vegetables.

Refer to Chapter 18 for information on vegetables and Chapter 19 for information on suitable herbs.

Hint

Herbs are ideal for growing in pots, either as a mixed group or as single specimens. Always plant mint in its own pot. Sensitive plants like basil can be brought inside when the weather turns. To get the best results, give them a liquid feed every fortnight during their growing season, and put down bait if slugs or snails are a problem.

THE TWO ANNS
A & A CONSULTANTS

HERBS FOR POTS

Many herbs are both decorative and useful in pots or tubs. Most herbs need some sunshine each day and an ideal place is a window box as close to the kitchen as possible. Herbs also need fresh air to thrive – they do not grow well indoors. Although they are not as fussy as more ornamental plants, herbs should be planted in a good soil mixture to encourage lush, attractive growth. The best herb plants to grow in pots are the low or dwarf varieties, like chives, parsley, thyme, tarragon, basil, geraniums, savory, mint, marjoram, oregano, thrift, pennyroyal, prostrate rosemary and dwarf lavender. A sprinkling of controlled-release fertiliser (such as Multicote), or regular applications of soluble fertilisers like Thrive, will improve plant growth, particularly if you are picking the leaves for cooking or infusions. Apart from chives (which can be cut to the ground when ready for harvest), never remove more than one-fifth of the plant in one cut, and let the plant start growing again before

GROWING YOUR GARDEN

harvesting any more leaves. Herbs with strong roots like mint, tarragon and lemon balm should be contained in pots and not mixed in with other plants. Dill, fennel, borage and sage are larger growing plants which tend to grow smaller when restricted in a pot. Don't grow these in amongst the more prostrate herbs as they will soon overwhelm the smaller plants. Grow aromatic herbs where they can be touched, brushed against or walked on. The fragrance is always pleasing and often wards off insects. Scented leaf geraniums are among the easiest to grow and come in a variety of perfumes, some peppermint, others nutmeg, rose, lemon and a number of other spicy flavours.

GROWING VEGETABLES IN CONTAINERS

VEGETABLE	MOST SUITABLE VARIETIES	RECOMMENDED MIN. DEPTH OF CONTAINER
Cabbage	Earliball	25 cm
	Sugarloaf	25 cm
Capsicum	All	40 cm
Carrot	Baby	25 cm
	Chantenay	25 cm
Cress	Salad Curled	10 cm
Cucumber	Salad Bush	40 cm
Eggplant	All	40 cm
Herbs	Many types	20 cm
Lettuce	Cos	25 cm
	Salad Mix	25 cm
	Buttercrunch	25 cm
Mustard	Quick Salad	10 cm
Onion	Spring or Shallot Bunching	20 cm
Pumpkin	Little Dumpling	30 cm
Radish	All	20 cm
Silver Beet	Fordhook Giant	25 cm
Tomato	Sweetie	30 cm
	Tiny Tim	30 cm
	Small Fry	30 cm
Zucchini-marrow	Blackjack hybrid	40 cm
	Greyzini hybrid	40 cm
	Lebanese	40 cm

Epiphytic cacti will flower in a well-lit indoor position.

INDOOR PLANTS

Indoor plants are especially popular with people living in home units or flats who do not have a garden. And few offices, foyers, hotels or restaurants are without indoor plants to soften the atmosphere. Yet it is

Hint

When potted maidenhair fern fronds dry out (usually because of lack of humidity), cut them all off, water the pot thoroughly, then apply liquid plant food and put it out under a bush in the garden surrounded by slug pellets. In a few weeks it will be a mass of new fronds and ready to come back indoors.

BOB EDWARDS
EDITOR, *COMMERCIAL HORTICULTURE*

curious that the popularity of indoor plants did not become apparent until after World War II. Certainly, the early Victorians grew plants indoors, but their choice was limited and the introduction of gaslighting and

regular winter heating killed so many that only the aspidistra survived to become the most remembered feature of the nineteenth-century home.

Millions of plants are sold today to be grown indoors, but there is really no such thing as an indoor plant. The natural place for plants is outdoors; certain species have merely been adapted to growing indoors. So it is not surprising that the most successful indoor plants are those from tropical rainforests which grow in the shade of large trees and rambling vines in a warm, humid atmosphere.

When you grow these plants in your home you should try to duplicate these conditions. Indoor plants need good light, but should never be placed in direct sunlight. If there is enough light to cast a shadow (test by holding your hand against a piece of white paper), there is enough for most indoor plants. Temperature should be fairly even (about 20°C), without extremes, if possible. In warm, dry weather, the humidity they need can be created by standing the pots on pebbles above a tray of water, and mist-spraying the foliage regularly. Plants grouped together are better off than a single plant because the massed leaves will create a microclimate to produce higher humidity. This point is easily demonstrated in nurseries which specialise in selling indoor plants; they often create a mini jungle of plants in tubs, hanging baskets, climbers and epiphytes.

The easiest plants to grow indoors are those with thick, glossy leaves, such as philodendron, rubber tree (*Ficus elastica*), umbrella plant (*Schefflera*), cast iron plant (*Aspidistra*), dragon plant (*Dracaena*), prayer plant (*Maranta*), *Monstera deliciosa*, mother-in-law's tongue (*Sansevieria*), dumb cane (*Dieffenbachia*), bromeliad (*Aechmea*) and fatsia.

Other plants well adapted to growing indoors are spider plant (*Chlorophytum*), madonna lily (*Spathiphyllum*), aglaeonema, arrowhead (*Syngonium*), grape ivy and kangaroo vine (*Cissus sp.*), aluminium plant (*Pilea*), coleus, peperomias, pelargonium or geraniums, English ivy (*Hedera*), Kentia palm (*Howea*), brake ferns and fatshedera.

These are the toughest and most reliable indoor plants, so begin with these before graduating to the more exotic kinds available from specialist nurseries.

There are many flowering indoor plants, too: African violet (*Saintpaulia*), tuberous and elatior begonias, calceolaria, cyclamen, gloxinia, *Primula obconica* and polyanthus are popular and readily available in nurseries in season.

These require more light and care than the hardier foliage plants listed above. Most of them are described in Chapter 11. Flowering chrysanthemums and dwarf poinsettias will produce long-lasting indoor blooms.

Most indoor plants will grow better if they are rested outside in a shady, sheltered spot periodically (never in full sun) – three weeks indoors and three weeks outdoors is a good timetable. If you have no sheltered place outside, rotate the plants to the best growing spot beside a well-lit window. Plants dislike dark, closed rooms. They need fresh air and light to grow. If you are away all day and your home is closed, try to arrange ventilation for your plants. Don't pull down the blinds or draw the curtains, but let in the light.

Indoor plants also need regular watering. This may mean daily watering in dry weather, but perhaps only once a week when it is cooler. In cold weather it is best to use tepid water because cold water will chill the soil

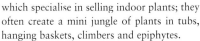

Hint

Check the water needs of your pot plants daily. Scratch the soil with your finger. If it is dry, fill the saucer to the brim, wait five minutes, then discard any water that has not been absorbed.

BOB EDWARDS
EDITOR, *COMMERCIAL HORTICULTURE*

and damage the roots. Don't water pots if the soil feels damp. More plants are lost through overwatering than underwatering – the soil becomes clogged and the roots drown or suffocate. Always check the soil mix at least 3 cm below the surface. Gadgets which can measure the degree of soil moisture are particularly useful to anyone with lots of potted plants.

Most indoor plants react to stress by dropping their leaves. This can mean they are too dry, too wet, too hot, too cold or too dark. You will have to assess the situation to decide which is the problem.

Fertilise indoor plants to keep them growing steadily. Small doses of liquid feed (such as Thrive) at half-strength every three to four weeks should be sufficient. Otherwise use controlled-release plant food such as Multicote according to directions.

Dust plants regularly and gently with a clean cloth or duster for glossy-leaved plants or a soft paintbrush or old shaving brush for those with furry leaves. Leaf Shine will give indoor plants a remarkable facelift. Milk is good for shiny leaves and should be wiped on with a thick wad of cotton wool.

It is a good idea to put your plants outside when it rains. Rain washes the leaves and helps leach the soil of any build-up of salts from tap water (but don't leave them outside to be burnt when the sun comes out).

Plants which grow too big for their containers can often be rejuvenated by cutting off the tops and letting them shoot again from the base. Rubber plants, dieffenbachia and umbrella plants can be treated this way.

GROWING YOUR GARDEN

HOUSEPLANT AILMENTS

PROBLEM	PLANT RESPONSE
Aphids	New leaves curl and become distorted. Presence of small, soft insects on buds, young stems and leaves. To control, spray with Mavrik.
Mealybug	White cottony or waxy insect on the underside of leaves and leaf axils. Infested plants become unthrifty. Control is difficult. If only a few present, wipe off with a damp cloth. Otherwise spray with Confidor or Baythroid Aerosol. Severely infested plants should be discarded.
Scale insects	Stems and leaves become covered with flattened reddish, grey or brown scaly bumps. To control, spray with Conqueror Oil. Repeat applications may be necessary.
Mites	Leaves yellow, become stippled and may fall. There may also be spider-webbing present. To control, spray with Mavrik at regular intervals.
Botrytis	Brown spots and blotches appear on leaves and sometimes stems. Under humid conditions infected portions may be covered with a fuzzy grey growth. Diseased and dead plant material should be removed promptly, particularly flowers. Avoid splashing water on foliage and growing plants in crowded conditions where the air is damp and still.
Powdery mildew	Faint white spots appear on leaves and gradually enlarge until the whole leaf surface is covered with white powder. Spray with Baycor.
Too little light	Leaves smaller and paler than normal. Flowers poor or absent. Lower leaves turn yellow, dry and fall. Spindly growth with long spaces between leaves. Variegated leaves turn green.
Too much water	Leaves limp. Soft areas may appear. Poor growth. Leaves curl. Leaves yellow and wilt, tips may brown.
Too cold	Leaves curl, brown and fall.
Too hot	Spindly growth when in good light conditions. Flowers short-lived. Lower leaves wilt, brown and fall.
Sudden change in temperature	Leaves fall after rapid yellowing.
Too little humidity	Leaf-tips brown and shrivelled. Leaf edges yellow. Buds and flowers shrivel and fall.
Draughts	Leaves turn yellow and fall. Leaves curl and fall. Brown tips or edges on leaves.

ORCHIDS

Orchids make lovely container plants. In mild–temperate climates, pots or tubs of cymbidium orchids can be placed under trees in filtered light. Orchids thrive in warm, subtropical areas but need glasshouse conditions in cold districts. When growing orchids in containers it is best to use proprietary orchid potting mixes. These special mixes do not contain any soil and the roots of the plants can move through them freely. Orchids are epiphytes (a plant attached to another plant but not a parasite) and under natural conditions they grow in the debris of bark and dead leaves of trees. It is a good idea to place a layer of crocks or pine bark at the bottom of the container before adding the orchid mix.

Some species of orchid are very easy to grow. The crucifix orchid (*Epidendrum*) can usually be grown in the open garden in mild climates but also makes an attractive pot plant for a sunny position. There are hundreds of species of tree orchids (*Dendrobium*), one of which is endemic to New Zealand, and which is the southernmost of the genus. Other tree orchids do best in warm, tropical areas and need glasshouse treatment for the cooler New Zealand climate.

Cymbidiums are the most popular orchids for mild climates where the temperature does not drop below 5°C. They make ideal plants for large pots and tubs which can be moved to a favoured position for flowering. They need light shade in summer but full sun in winter when the flower spikes are forming. Flower spikes last for many weeks. There are hundreds of varieties, coming in shades of white, yellow, pink, red, brown and green. Slipper orchid (*Paphiopedilum* syn. *Cypripedium*) is a reliable orchid for a small pot (they like to be crowded) and blooms in winter or early spring.

Dancing ladies (*Oncidium*) are also delightful orchids for pots or hanging baskets. Natives of Brazil, they need a warm, subtropical climate but can be grown in a shadehouse or glasshouse in cool areas. Angel orchid (*Coelogyne*) has pure white flowers with golden throats in autumn and winter. They are very adaptable to climate, providing there are no frosts. They like to be crowded in pots and prefer rather dry conditions when

flowering. Chinese ground orchid (*Bletilla*) is another adaptable orchid for pot culture. It is dormant in winter and flowers in spring. *Vanda* and *Cattleya* are probably the showiest of all the orchids, but they need a warm, humid, tropical climate so require glasshouse conditions in cooler areas. *Stanhopeas* are fascinating orchids for hanging baskets. Their vanilla-scented flowers bloom through the bottom of the basket. They are best potted using a bark liner so that the new spikes can easily force their way through.

Most orchids respond to supplementary feeding in addition to the compost in which they are growing. The soluble orchid foods, or liquid feeds of Thrive, can be used every two to three weeks during the growing period. Do not fertilise orchids when they are dormant.

Hint

If you are growing cacti and succulents in containers, use a potting mix developed specifically for these plants. Add extra broken terracotta or gravel to the bottom of your pots to encourage good drainage. Move the plants to a protected place when snow, frost or heavy rain is forecast.

THE TWO ANNS
A & A CONSULTANTS

CACTUS AND OTHER SUCCULENT PLANTS

Cactus plants and other succulents make ideal pot plants for a sunny windowsill, balcony or patio. They are easy to grow and require very little attention. They prefer a dry atmosphere so they need plenty of fresh air in humid climates. For pot culture, a suitable mixture consists of coarse sand or fine gravel, compost and leaf mould or peat moss. This mixture holds water but also drains well. Although these fleshy plants can go for long periods without water in their natural

GROWING YOUR GARDEN

habitat, the pots should be watered when the mixture is dry to the touch. Avoid heavy feeding because this promotes rapid, soft growth and plants may rot. A scattering of Multicote (used according to directions) is probably the most suitable fertiliser to use.

The spines of cactus plants are very sharp and may be difficult to remove from the skin, so care must be taken in handling the plants. People with sensitive skins are advised to consider those succulents without spines, such as *Kalanchoe*, hen and chickens (*Echeveria*), stonecrop (*Sedum*), jade plant (*Crassula*) and sempervivum. Most of these quaint, fleshy plants have attractive flowers. Crab cactus (*Zygocactus*) and orchid cactus (*Epiphyllum*) are also spineless with jointed, flattened stems and showy flowers in winter and spring. Both are ideal for pots or hanging baskets but prefer semi-shade.

FERNS FOR POTS AND BASKETS

Some of the smaller ferns of the dozens of different species available can be grown in containers indoors, or more often in a sheltered patio or courtyard. Most are grown in pots or hanging baskets but some, like staghorns and elkhorns, can be wired to wooden uprights or boards.

Ferns as a group require cool, moist conditions. When indoors, they are best in full light from a window facing south or where summer sunlight can be excluded by curtains. Free air movement is essential as ferns resent still, dry air and are prone to attack by insects (aphids, mealybug and scale) under poorly ventilated conditions. (See Chapter 6.) It is best to bring potted ferns indoors for decoration for short periods only (one or two weeks) and then

Container-grown cacti and succulents stand up well to hot, dry conditions.

return them to a shady, sheltered spot for the same length of time.

A suitable soil mixture for pots and baskets of ferns consists of equal parts of garden loam, sand and peat moss or leaf mould. Potting up is done in late winter or early spring when new fronds appear. Pots or baskets should not be too large as the plants prefer to be crowded. Wire baskets are usually lined with moisture-retaining bark or sphagnum moss. Ferns must be kept damp at all times, although they require less water in winter when growth is slower. Ferns need little feeding and do not like concentrated fertilisers. The safest method is to use water-soluble fertilisers. Apply them at half-strength every three or four weeks during warm weather. Maidenhair fern (*Adiantum*) is probably the most popular and widely grown fern for pots and baskets. The fronds are finely cut and come on long wiry stems – a favourite for flower arrangements and bouquets. There are over 200 species of maidenhair fern which differ in leaf shape and size. Hare's-foot fern (*Davallia*) has lacy fronds curving downwards and furry, creeping rhizomes. It is an ideal plant for baskets and tolerates warm conditions providing it is kept moist. Fish bone fern or sword fern (*Nephrolepis*), with bright-green upright fronds, is perhaps the easiest of all to grow. It tolerates tough conditions – even full sunlight – and spreads rapidly. It can easily become an invasive weed. Brake fern (*Pteris*) is easily propagated from new crowns which develop from the rhizomes. It is a handsome fern with curled or crimped, many-lobed fronds. Bird's nest fern (*Asplenium*) is a clump of shiny, undivided fronds which may grow to 1 m long. It is an epiphyte and may be grown on pieces of old tree or timber, but is equally at home in a pot filled with sand and leaf mould or peat moss. Propagate by quartering the plant and repotting each section, which will regain the rosette shape. Staghorn or elkhorn fern (*Platycerium*) is an epiphyte which can be attached to a number of surfaces, including stone or brickwork, cork or timber – and therefore popular in courtyards and ferneries where there is semi-shade. Tree ferns (*Cyathea*) are the giants of the fern family and are best grown in shady positions out of

doors. They can be grown in a large tubs or in a corner bed of a courtyard. Several species are popular, including black tree fern (*C. medullaris*), New Zealand or silver tree fern (*C. dealbata*), the coin spot tree fern (*C. cooperi*) and the Tasmanian tree fern (*Dicksonia australis*). All species are best in semi-shade and like plenty of moisture.

PALMS

Many palms are suitable indoor plants given the correct growing conditions. Palms do not mind root restriction so it is best to put them in a larger pot only when the previous one is filled to capacity with roots. Good drainage and an open, porous soil mixture are essential. Water regularly and feed with water-soluble fertilisers or controlled-release Multicote pellets. Palms hate low humidity, so rooms with heaters or air-conditioners are not suitable. If the air is too dry, leaf tips will brown off. Draughts, too, are damaging. Mist spraying the foliage several times a day when the weather is dry and hot helps prevent lasting damage.

Do not stand potted palms in a tray of water. Most varieties of palms loathe wet feet. Fill a shallow tray with pebbles and cover with water. Then stand the potted palm on top. Good indirect light is necessary for healthy growth, and if a window is not close by, then palms will absorb some light from an ordinary electric light placed 40–50 cm above the foliage. Wipe fronds regularly to remove dust. Use commercial leaf wipes, or a weak solution of soap in water.

Palms are often attacked by scale insects and red spider mites indoors. Spider mites usually only occur when the atmosphere is dry. Increase the humidity by mist spraying with water for effective control. Scale is easily removed by scrubbing with a toothbrush and soapy water. Avoid spraying with chemicals indoors unless absolutely necessary.

Palms most suited to growing indoors include kentia palms (*Howea* spp); parlour palms; *Arecastrum* – the plume or queen palm; *Caryota* – fish tail palm; *Chamaerops* – European fan palm; triangle palm (*Neodypsis*) and golden cane palm (*Chrysalidocarpus*); *Linospadix* – walking stick palm; *Phoenix* – date palm; *Rhapis* – lady palm or ground rattan cane. See detailed information on selected palms in Chapter 14.

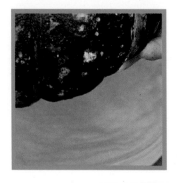

CHAPTER 17

GARDENING FOR KIDS

Gardening is a skill that used to be readily passed on from one generation to the next but, with changing social customs, many children grow up without learning any basic gardening skills. The saddest loss however, for children who don't garden, is that they fail to gain an appreciation of the importance of plants and of the natural world in our lives. Just as some children never learn that milk comes from a cow, others fail to appreciate that peas, broad beans and sweet corn are seeds, that they are not made in a factory and packed into plastic bags, but that they come from living plants.

GARDEN BASICS

The best way to teach children about gardening is for parents to show the way by gardening themselves. Try to make gardening a family activity. It is curious how many families will take a great deal of trouble to make sure that responsibility for domestic household chores is not gender related, but are content to have outdoor activities such as gardening seen as something that 'only dads do'.

GETTING STARTED

Children who are given responsibility for some potted plants are able to learn valuable lessons about nurturing other living things. Younger children are seldom successful in maintaining their own part of the garden – their enthusiasm rarely lasts for the required length of time – but a few potted plants are far less of an overall commitment. It is important that the basic equipment is at hand – hat, sunscreen, trowel (lightweight but sturdy), pots, potting mix and a small watering can – before the fun can begin.

Flowering annuals may be the best plants to grow in a pot. Because they don't last all that long, a child can have a break at the end of the season and come back to gardening further down the track. It is desirable, however, that children realise that these plants are only short-lived so they are prepared for the plant to come to the end of its life. Choose plants with lots of colour, like petunias; hardiness, like marigolds (although some children don't like their smell); good smells, such as sweet peas; and shade tolerance, like impatiens. Nasturtium seeds are relatively easy to handle and the plants are also relatively easy to cultivate. They make a good choice for container growing or garden beds.

If it is difficult to grow a pot outdoors, hardy indoor plants, like madonna lily (*Spathiphyllum* sp.), arrowhead (*Syngonium* sp.) or a kentia palm can be placed in a well-lit spot, out of direct sunlight, in a child's bedroom and even given a name. Teach the child to judge when the plant needs watering by feeling the top of the potting mix, or by using a self-watering pot. Make sure that the water can drain away and that the roots are not sitting in moisture all the time. If necessary, put a layer of fine pebbles in the saucer – this will raise the base of the pot above the residue of water in the saucer.

Feed the plant during the growing season with a long-lasting, controlled-release fertiliser such as Multicote.

GARDEN RULES AND SAFETY

Throughout their growing years children are learning the rules of life. This applies just as much to gardening as to any other activity.

GROWING YOUR GARDEN

Some commonsense rules are:
1. Don't touch someone else's garden unless you have their permission.
2. Never eat anything in the garden unless you know it is okay.
3. Ask before you pick flowers.
4. Wear sunscreen and a hat as a routine when you are outside in the garden.
5. Wear gloves when handling soil or potting mix, when moving anything rough or sharp or working where spiders may lurk.
6. Wear boots or solid footwear.
7. Always check inside boots before putting them on, especially if they have been stored outdoors.
8. Garden in suitable old clothes.
9. Wash hands well after handling potting mix, soil or compost.

Most children would love to 'adopt a pot' – especially if the fruit can be used to make lemonade!

POISONOUS PLANTS

Some common garden plants are poisonous and their planting should, if possible, be avoided in kids' gardens. This list is by no means exhaustive, but the inclusion of so many commonly grown plants serves to reinforce how important it is that children are taught never to eat anything in the garden unless they know it is safe. All parts of the following plants are poisonous:

✗ Caladium – coloured-leaf indoor plant
✗ Datura – angel's trumpet
✗ Delphiniums
✗ Foxgloves
✗ Helleborus species – also known as Christmas roses
✗ Lily of the valley
✗ Lobelia
✗ Rhododendrons and azaleas
✗ *Thevetia peruviana* – known as yellow oleander or be-still tree

The leaves of the following plants are poisonous:

✗ Box (*Buxus* spp)
✗ Calendula
✗ Elephant's ears
✗ Rhubarb
✗ Tomato

The flowers of the arum lily are poisonous.

The milky sap of the following is poisonous:

✗ Frangipani
✗ Oleander
✗ Poinsettia

The fruits and seeds of the following are poisonous:

✗ *Cestrum nocturnum* – night-scented jessamine
✗ Clivias
✗ Cycads
✗ Duranta – pigeon berry
✗ Laburnum
✗ *Melia azederach* – white cedar
✗ Moreton Bay chestnut – black bean
✗ Peppercorn tree
✗ Privet
✗ Sweet peas
✗ Wisteria
✗ Yew

These tubers and bulbs are poisonous:

✗ Daffodils
✗ Gloriosa lily
✗ Hyacinth bulbs

Kids can have a face-to-face meeting with a sunflower.

EASY-TO-GROW GARDEN PLANTS

A child can be given responsibility for a particular plant in the garden. Make sure that the plant chosen is not a particularly temperamental or fragile plant. Geraniums (pelargoniums) are almost indestructible. Clumping plants like agapanthus (there are some wonderful, smaller growing cultivars) and liriope, lavender, cuphea, abelia and citrus, as long as they are given the most basic of care, are hard to kill.

EASY-TO-GROW SEEDS

Growing plants from seed gives a child a chance to understand the very basics of nature. To achieve success, a child will need some guidance. Here are a few tips for successful seed raising:

1. Read the packet. If it says sow in seed trays, then do so.
2. Sow at the right time of year. Germination is very temperature dependent.
3. Sow into seed-raising mix.
4. Keep seed trays in bright light, but out of direct sunlight.
5. Keep seeds moist. Water gently with a watering-can or a very soft water-breaker.

Some seeds are easy for beginners as long as you follow basic instructions on the packet.

EASY FLOWERS FROM SEED

Nasturtiums, sweet peas, sunflowers, marigolds, cosmos, rudbeckia, pansies and violas are all relatively easy for children to grow. Avoid plants with tiny seeds, such as

Hint

To encourage children to take an interest in gardening, let them plant seeds that give quick or exciting results. This will keep their attention and sustain their interest. Try them out on plants such as beans, cherry tomatoes and sunflowers.

NICK HAYHOE
YATES NEW ZEALAND

petunias and lobelias. These can be difficult for the inexperienced seed grower.

Mixed packets of flower seeds (some of them especially labelled for children) can be scattered onto flower beds. Keep moist and something is bound to come up.

GROWING YOUR GARDEN

GARDENS KIDS CAN EAT

Most children like to have a productive garden but it is essential that the fruits and vegetables grown by children are things they are likely to eat. For example, radishes give satisfyingly fast results, but very few children enjoy eating them. Some vegies that are popular with kids are sweet corn, cherry tomatoes, beans straight off the plant (not cooked) and snow peas.

Easy-to-grow fruits include strawberries (which can even be grown in a hanging basket), citrus trees of most kinds, especially mandarins, passionfruit, and raspberries in colder climates.

Productive plants need a sunny position, compost-enriched soil, and plenty of water and fertiliser.

Hint

Most children will appreciate trees that bear fruit and trees that are good for climbing. However, if you are planning a new garden with children in mind, you will need to bear in mind the length of time it will take any trees you plant to reach maturity, and consider what age your children will be at that time.

DIANA SELBY
LANDSCAPE ARCHITECT

If given some encouragement, children will love learning the joys of cultivating their own garden plot.

A child's garden can be on his or her bedroom windowsill.

CONTAINER GARDENING

Gardening in pots or containers is a good way to kick-start a child's interest in gardening. The basics for success are:

1. Don't have too small a container – it will dry out too quickly and need to be watered too often.
2. Use a good quality potting mix, such as Yates Patio and Tub Mix.
3. Water with a water-breaker (not a nozzle) attached to the end of a hose.
4. Don't allow the base of the pot to sit in water.
5. Potting mixes need more fertiliser than soil. Feed regularly during the growing season with a soluble plant food, such as Thrive, or controlled release pellets.
6. Wash hands after handing potting mix or soil.

SECRET GARDENS

Children love parts of the garden that are a bit secretive and enclosed and where they can feel alone but secure. One of the most famous twentieth-century children's stories, *The Secret Garden* by Frances Hodgson Burnett, surely owes much of its enduring popularity to the fact that every child fantasises about having a secret outoor place to escape to.

If your garden can be designed with some slightly hidden or separate sections, it will have a special appeal for children.

GARDEN ACTIVITIES FOR KIDS

1. Use stalks from dead agapanthus flowers to build a 'cubby' around a simple frame.
2. Collect cicada shells, ask an adult to help you spray-paint them gold or silver, and use them as decorations on next year's Christmas tree.

TOP FIVE
TREES FOR CLIMBING

PLANE TREE (*PLANUS X HYBRIDA*)

Though rather large for the suburban garden, plane trees have excellent, well-spaced branches. The round seed balls are just right for squashing underfoot.

PLUM TREES
(*PRUNUS* VARIETIES)

Many old New Zealand gardens contain wonderful mature plum trees, ideal for climbing and not too large.

EVERGREEN MAGNOLIA
(*MAGNOLIA GRANDIFLORA*)

Strong, well-spaced branches and large shiny leaves with felted undersides make this an ideal evergreen tree for climbing and hiding in.

POHUTUKAWA
(*METROSIDEROS EXCELSA*)

New Zealand's native Christmas tree tends not to grow as gnarled and spreading in the garden as it does in its natural coastal environment, but makes a handsome tree which can be trained to any dimensions desired.

MULBERRY (*MORUS ALBA*)

Every child's dream and mum's nightmare! A tree you can sit in and feast from at the same time. Everyone can be happy if the child knows to wear old clothes – then the stains won't matter.

PLANE TREE

3. Write your name on a baby zucchini and watch it grow as the fruit expands into a giant marrow.
4. Have a competition to grow the biggest pumpkin.
5. Under supervision, make a Jack-o'-lantern out of a pumpkin.
6. Make poppy dolls out of poppy flowers by pulling down the petals and tying a ribbon or piece of grass around the 'waist'.
7. Make pictures on the ground or in the sandpit with seeds and flowers.
8. Gather winged maple seeds. They make fantastic helicopters if dropped from a height and allowed to corkscrew to the ground.
9. Pop any flower buds that are ready to open. Fuchsias and poppies are good.
10. Stick rose thorns onto a friend's forehead with a bit of moisture, and turn the child into an instant 'devil'.

Another activity for kids is to grow a hyacinth bulb in the top of a bottle. All you will need is a good-sized bulb, and a jar or bottle whose top is just about the right diameter for the bulb to sit on top. Fill the jar with water until it is just below the base of the bulb, and keep it topped up by carefully lifting the bulb and pouring water into the top. The roots of the bulb will grow down into the water and eventually the bulb will produce a flower.

Hyacinth bulbs can also be grown in a pot indoors. In order to develop a good flower stem, it is helpful to keep the pot in a dark cupboard, or covered with an upside-down pot until the shoot emerges. Then gradually introduce the hyacinth to more light as its shoot develops.

Never place your indoor bulb into direct sunlight or subject it to indoor heating. These stresses will spoil the flowering before it even starts to happen.

One word of warning: hyacinth bulbs have a special irritant in their scaly outer skin that can cause itchiness. Always wash hands well after touching hyacinth bulbs or, preferably, handle the bulbs with gloves.

FASCINATING PLANTS
FOR KIDS' GARDENS

Strelitzia (bird of paradise). This plant has colourful flowers that look like exotic birds on top of stiff stems. They are good for

Making a scarecrow is a fun garden activity.

adding mid-winter colour to a tropical-style garden and can also be grown successfully in containers.

Sensitive plant (*Mimosa pudica*) is a fun, potted plant. When touched, the leaves fold up and can take some time before they unfurl again.

Tortured willow (*Salix matsudana* 'Tortuosa') and twisted hazelnut (*Corylus avellana* 'Contorta') have curiously curled and twisted stems that children love. They can be cut during their dormant winter season, dried and used as floral decorations or for displaying light ornaments, especially for Christmas.

Pussy willows are also beloved for the fluffy catkins that decorate the stems in spring. All willows should be planted with care and never where there is any risk of these water-hungry plants invading drains.

Chain of hearts (*Ceropegia woodii*) is a delightful basket plant with leaves that do resemble tiny hearts.

Hint

Succulents are wonderful plants for children to grow as they require little maintenance and come in a wide variety of interesting shapes and colours. Take your children to your favourite nursery or garden centre and let them pick out a selection of their own succulents to look after.

JODY LUSK AND RICHARD DAVEY
WAIRERE NURSERY

Part V: Gardening for the Kitchen

CHAPTER 18

VEGETABLES

Of all gardening activities, being able to harvest fresh, vitamin-packed vegetables for salads or the kitchen pot is one of the most rewarding. Growing vegetables is an intensive form of cultivation, but it is very satisfying to plan a programme of small, successive sowings and plantings for a continuous harvest throughout the year. To do this, you should know when and how to grow different vegetables, how long each kind will take to mature and what yield to expect.

Vegetables are often divided into three groups depending on the part of the plants we usually eat:
1. Fruit and seed vegetables, such as beans, peas, capsicum, eggplant, tomato, sweet corn and vine crops (cucurbits).
2. Leaf and stem vegetables, such as cabbage, celery, lettuce, rhubarb, silver beet and spinach. Broccoli and cauliflower are usually included in this group, too, although the part we eat is the flower bud and not the leaves or stems.
3. Root and bulb vegetables, such as beetroot, carrots, onions, parsnips, potatoes, radishes and turnips.

All vegetables should be grown quickly, so there is not a great deal of difference in the way you grow different varieties. You do not need different soil for different vegetables. If you can grow good tomatoes there is no reason why you cannot grow good beans, cabbages or carrots, too. However, the grouping of vegetables into fruit, leaf and root plants does give good guidelines for fertiliser use.

Fruit and root vegetables need large quantities of potassium and phosphorus in fertiliser, because these elements stimulate flowers, fruits and seeds and root development. Fertilisers high in nitrogen may produce too much leaf growth and reduce yields of fruits and seeds. On the other hand, nitrogenous fertilisers are needed in greater quantities by leafy vegetables like broccoli, cabbage, cauliflower, lettuce, silver beet and spinach.

COOL- AND WARM-SEASON VEGETABLES

Most vegetables are disappointing if planted out of season.

Cool-season vegetables grow best at low temperatures of 10–20°C, but they tolerate even colder conditions and are usually frost-resistant. This group includes broad beans, broccoli, Brussels sprouts, cauliflower, onions, peas, spinach and turnips, which are sown to grow during the cooler months of the year. Warm-season vegetables grow best at a temperature of 20°C or above. They grow poorly in cool weather and are susceptible to frost. This group includes beans, capsicum, eggplant, potato, sweet corn, sweet potato, tomato and all the vine crops. They are sown in spring or early summer to grow during warmer months.

A third group has intermediate temperature requirements and grows best at 15–25°C. This group includes beetroot, cabbage, carrot, celery, leek, lettuce, parsnip, radish and silver beet. It is important to sow them at the correct time of the year for your climate because they tend to 'bolt', or run to seed, if they are sown too early or too late. Root crops like beetroot, carrot and parsnip may run to seed if sown too late in autumn or winter. Silver beet, a close relative of beetroot, may do this too. Some varieties of lettuce run to seed if sown in warm weather, so choose those varieties which have been selected for growing in summer. The best months for sowing each kind of vegetable in each climate zone – temperate and cold – are shown in the Sowing Guide on pages 348–351.

NEED FOR SUNLIGHT

An open, sunny site is a must for your vegetable garden. To grow quickly and well, vegetables need as much sunlight as possible, especially in winter when days are shorter. If possible, select a part of the garden facing north to north-east to catch the morning sun and at least four or five hours of direct sunlight each day. Make allowance for longer shadows in winter. Try to avoid shade from buildings, fences, or large trees and shrubs. Trees and shrubs with large root systems will compete for moisture and plant nutrients as well as light. A level site is best and easiest to manage, with both beds and rows running north–south. This way each plant in the row receives maximum sunlight. On sloping sites, garden beds should run across the slope with a retaining wall of timber, brick or concrete on the downhill side to prevent erosion and loss of soil. In this case it may be best for rows to run across the beds instead of along them.

SHELTER FROM WINDS

Vegetables need some protection from wind. Cold winds slow down growth, and hot, dry winds cause water to evaporate from soil and plants. Strong winds also damage leaves and stems and may loosen and weaken roots. Windbreaks of trees, shrubs or hedges growing on the south or west of the vegetable garden do not create shade problems and can be planted well back from the garden to give good wind protection. Artificial windbreaks of trellis, slatted timber or light brush fences make an excellent wind-barrier. They reduce wind velocity without creating turbulence. Brick or concrete walls (with about 50 per cent opening) have this effect too (see diagrams showing effects of windbreaks in Chapter 1). Wind-barriers on the south offer a bonus by providing support for climbing beans and cucumbers in summer, and climbing peas in winter.

SIZE AND LAYOUT

Available space and your own enthusiasm will dictate the size of your vegetable plot. Generally, it is best to have beds 150 cm wide and paths 30–40 cm between each bed. This allows you to work from both sides. This width is doubly convenient because it will accommodate three plants of broccoli, cabbage or tomato across the bed, or three

VEGETABLES TO GROW IN WINTER

VEGETABLE	SUGGESTED VARIETY	SOW COOL DISTRICT	SOW WARM DISTRICT
Broccoli	Winter Harvest	January/February	February/March
Cabbage	Eureka	January-March	March-May
Cauliflower	Mini Phenomenal Early	January-March	February/March
Carrots	All Seasons, Topweight	January-March	March-May
Lettuce	Winter Triumph	March/April	April/May
Leeks	Welsh Wonder	January/February	April-June
Parsnips	Yatesnip	January-March	April/May
Silver beet	Fordhook Giant	February/March	March-May
Spinach	English Improved	February-April	March-May
Broad Beans	Exhibition Long Pod	April/May	April-June

rows of beans, peas or sweet corn. With smaller, more upright growers – such as beetroot, carrots, lettuce and silver beet – you can fit in five or six rows across the bed. Beds may be of any length, but 9 m is a convenient length which can be divided into 3 m sections

....

Hint

If you are short of space, you don't need to be conventional: silverbeet and parsley look great growing amongst the roses! Companion plant with marigolds to minimise aphid attacks.
DENNIS GREVILLE
GARDEN WRITER

....

for successive plantings. To provide year-round vegetables for a family of four you need about six beds, each 9 m by 1.5 m, a total area of about 100 square metres. For new gardeners, a smaller area of three beds is suggested. It is better to look after a small garden well than to have a large garden which may be too hard to manage. You can always increase the area by adding extra beds or making them longer.

There is a modern trend to be less rigid about growing vegetables among flowers and in the ornamental garden bed, especially using attractive plants like red-stemmed silver beet, parsley, and coloured and frilly-leafed lettuce.

SOIL FOR VEGETABLES

Soil for vegetables should have a loose, crumbly structure which is capable of absorbing and holding water and nutrients, but it should be well aerated and drain easily.

As described in Chapter 3, you can improve sandy soils easily by adding moisture-holding materials such as animal manure, mushroom compost, garden compost or peat moss. The crumb structure of heavy soils also benefits from organic matter and their texture is improved by adding coarse sand. Always dig heavy soil when damp but not too wet. For most vegetables, including root crops, dig soil to

25–30 cm deep but do not bring subsoil to the surface. Extra drainage is usually necessary on heavy soils. Raise each bed 15–20 cm by shovelling soil from the pathway onto beds on either side. Slope the edge of the beds to between 45 and 60 degrees. This allows downward and lateral movement of water. Beds can also be contained by flat boards held in position with stout pegs, or surrounded by bricks or concrete, but remember to make provision for weep holes for drainage.

FERTILISERS AND LIME

It is best to apply a pre-sowing or pre-planting mixed fertiliser (such as Gro-Plus Complete Plant Food, with an approximate analysis N.P.K. 5:5:4) for each vegetable crop you grow. The high phosphorus content will ensure vigorous seedlings and good root development. Broadcast the fertiliser, apply in bands or scatter in furrows as described in Chapter 4. Root and bulb vegetables, once established, will often produce a good crop without side dressings of additional fertiliser. Leaf vegetables demand extra nitrogen in the form of liquid feeds of Thrive every ten to fourteen days during the growing period.

What about lime for vegetables? Most vegetables and herbs grow successfully in soil which is slightly or very slightly acid (pH 6.0–7.0). A few vegetables, such as potatoes, sweet potatoes and watermelons, will tolerate a strongly acid soil. In high rainfall districts near the coast it is a good idea to add agricultural lime to vegetable beds every year or two, but there is no need to apply lime before every crop. Too much lime can be harmful (see section on pH and lime in Chapter 5). A good time to apply lime is after summer crops have finished and before cool-season crops are established.

CROP ROTATION

The main reason for crop rotation in the vegetable garden is to prevent the spread of diseases (or insect pests) which may attack vegetables belonging to the same family or group. If disease in any crop is serious, it would be unwise to plant a closely related crop in the same bed. Complicated charts and diagrams for crop rotation are rather confusing and seldom work out as planned.

In New Zealand, there is a natural rotation between warm and cool-season crops. Providing you apply fertiliser and organic matter and are aware of the possibility of related plants contracting a disease from a previous crop, you need not be concerned about crop rotation.

WATERING AND MULCHING

The general principles of watering and mulching have been discussed in Chapter 3. To grow quickly, vegetables need adequate water at all times. Most of the water they absorb is passed through the plant and is evaporated or transpired by the leaves. In hot, dry weather, leaf vegetables may lose several times their weight in water each day. Once vegetables are established, a soaking will encourage deep roots. This helps them to withstand dry conditions for longer periods.

Hint
Avoid overhead watering to help prevent late blight of tomatoes. Water them at ground level only, rather than using a sprinkler system. For extra protection, spray your plants with Bravo according to directions.

RENE VAN TILBURG
YATES NEW ZEALAND

Sprinklers with a slow application rate and fine droplets are the best for vegetables. A vegetable garden can be watered by placing a pulsating sprinkler (set at 90 degrees) at each

Lavender and other flowering ornamentals will attract pollinating bees into your vegetable patch.

corner in succession. Soaker hoses or micro-irrigation systems are also useful for slow watering and can be laid between the rows. Furrow irrigation is suitable for flat beds, or for those with a gentle slope, especially for watering tomatoes, potatoes and other crops where it is desirable to keep the leaves dry to lessen the spread of leaf diseases. Make a deep furrow, with a gradual fall to one end, between the rows of plants. Water with a slow-running hose until the furrow is completely filled with water.

Mulching vegetable beds, especially in summer, will greatly reduce loss of soil moisture. It also provides a more even temperature and discourages weeds. The best mulching materials for vegetable beds are garden compost, well-rotted animal manure or lucerne hay. The mulch can be dug into the soil when preparing for the next crop.

CHOOSING YOUR CROPS

Naturally you will choose vegetables which you and your family enjoy eating, but some give better value than others. Yield for the area occupied is a good reason for growing a particular vegetable. Climbing beans, climbing peas and cucumbers grown on a trellis use vertical space but little soil space. Tomatoes and capsicum give high yields for space occupied. The cut-and-come-again vegetables – broccoli, celery (pick green outside leaves progressively), loose-hearted types of lettuce, rhubarb and silver beet – are good value for extended harvesting. Salad vegetables and leaf crops, which lose quality quickly after harvest, are excellent in the home garden because of their extra flavour and freshness.

New dwarf or bush varieties of some vegetables are now available, for example dwarf or mini tomatoes, bush pumpkin and baby beetroot. They take up little garden space and many can be grown in tubs or large pots on a sunny balcony.

Some of the best home garden vegetables (yield for space occupied) are: beans (dwarf and climbing), broccoli, Brussels sprouts, cabbage, capsicum, carrot, cauliflower, cucumber (on trellis), lettuce, marrow (bush), onion, parsnips, peas (climbing), pumpkin (bush), radish, rhubarb, silver beet, spinach, tomato, turnip.

GENERAL HINTS FOR VEGETABLE GROWING
SUCCESSIVE SOWINGS

For a continuous satisfactory supply of home-grown vegies, make small successive sowings. Always have an empty bed or section of bed in preparation for the next sowing or planting.

TALL VEGETABLES

Plant tall crops (tomatoes, sweet corn, broad beans) on the southern end of beds to prevent shading of low-growing vegetables. If making successive sowings of any crop in the one bed – say, dwarf beans or sweet corn – use the southern end first so that subsequent sowings get full sunlight.

GROUPING VEGETABLES

If possible, try to group vegetables which grow to the same height and mature about the same time (carrots, leeks and parsnips). This gives each a fair share of sunlight and, after harvest, the whole section can be dug and prepared for the next crops. Root and bulb crops are usually easier to handle in long rows of 2–3 m.

LONG-STANDING CROPS

Plant perennial crops such as asparagus and rhubarb in a separate section or at one end of a bed where they can grow undisturbed. Crops with an extended harvest period (capsicum, celery – picked green – and silver beet) will also occupy space for two or three months after your first picking.

MAKING WAY FOR NEW CROPS

Always pull out and compost crops which have passed their best as soon as possible. Why keep a whole row of beans or peas for just a few pods? Make the best use of this space by planting a fresh crop.

Hint

Grow red-leaf varieties of lettuce: birds don't seem to find them attractive, so you will have a better crop.

MARK ELLER
GARDEN CONSULTANT

PEST AND DISEASE
CONTROL CHART FOR VEGETABLES

PLANT	PEST OR DISEASE	SYMPTOMS	CONTROL
Broad beans	Black aphids	Small black insects on underside of leaves and shoots.	Target, Pyrethrum, Mavrik, Carbaryl
French and runner beans	Two-spotted mite	Bronzing and unthriftiness of foliage.	Mite Killer, Mavrik
	Bean fly	Larvae burrow into stalks and stems.	Rogor
	Green vegetable bug	Large green shield bugs.	Carbaryl, Maldison, Mavrik
	Rust	Red-brown blisters on leaves and pods.	Greenguard
Broccoli, Brussels sprouts, Cabbage, Cauliflower	Larvae of cabbage moth and white butterfly	Holes in leaves	Carbaryl, Baythroid, Derris Dust, Mavrik, Pyrethrum
	Aphids	Small green insects on underside of leaves.	Maldison, Mavrik, Pyrethrum
	Cutworms	Seedlings eaten at ground level.	Carbaryl drench
Capsicum	Aphids	Small green insects.	Maldison, Mavrik, Target
Carrot	Carrot rust fly	Small grubs underground.	Soil Insect Killer
Celery	Leaf spot	Brown spots over leaves.	Greenguard
Cucumber	Powdery mildew	Powdery white film on leaves.	Bravo, Baycor Aerosol
	Downy mildew	Leaf spots and downy tufts underneath.	Captan
Eggplant	Aphids	See Capsicum.	
Lettuce	Aphids	See Broccoli.	
	Downy mildew	Leaf spots and downy mildew tufts underneath.	Captan, Fungus Fighter
Marrows (zucchinis), Melon squash	See Cucumber		
Onion	Thrips	White flecks on foliage.	Mavrik, Maldison, Target
	Downy mildew	Leaves die from tips and downy tufts on leaves.	Captan

PLANT	PEST OR DISEASE	SYMPTOMS	CONTROL
Parsnip	Powdery mildew	See Cucumber	
Peas	Mites	See French beans	
Potato	Potato moth	Leaves or tubers infested.	Carbaryl, Derris Dust
	Late blight	Large black areas on leaves.	Champion Copper, Greenguard
Pumpkin	See Cucumber		
Seeds and seedlings	Damping off	Seeds fail to germinate or seedlings fall over at soil level.	Use Black Magic Seed Raising Mix
Silver beet, Spinach	Leaf miner	White tunnel streaks on leaves.	Carbaryl
	Leaf spot	Small brown spots on foliage.	Greenguard, Champion Copper
Sweet corn	Corn ear worm	Caterpillar in top of cob.	Dust or spray with Carbaryl
Tomato	Tomato fruit worm	Caterpillar attacks fruit at stalk end.	Carbaryl, Liquid Tomato Spray, Derris Dust, Pyrethrum, Mavrik
	Spotted wilt	Browning of young foliage.	Remove infected plants and control thrips – see Onion
	Root eelworm (nematodes)	Swellings on roots.	Basamid granules before planting
	Leaf spot	Brown target-like spots on foliage and fruit.	Fungus Fighter

Hint

When you use sprays on fruit or vegetables, always take notice of the withholding period marked on the label. Don't harvest any produce until the appropriate amount of time has passed.

CHARLIE GRAY
YATES NEW ZEALAND

HOW TO GROW INDIVIDUAL VEGETABLES

ARTICHOKES

The globe artichoke is a grey-green thistle-like plant which grows to a height of 1 m or more. It takes up a lot of space in the vegetable garden but you may find an odd corner where it can flourish undisturbed for three or four years. Often a few plants can be grown in a sunny spot in the flower garden. The best climate is one with a mild winter (no frosts) and a cool summer.

Seeds of globe artichoke may be sown in spring. Plants can also be started from shoots or suckers. Plant these in late winter in cool districts, or in autumn where it is warmer.

GARDENING FOR THE KITCHEN

Shoots should be about 30 cm in length with well-developed roots. Plant them 1 m apart and rake in a small handful of pre-planting fertiliser in a circle around each plant.

The globe-shaped buds appear in early spring and plants keep bearing until November. After flowering, keep plants watered and mulched through summer. In autumn, cut plants back to 30 cm high and apply a side-dressing of mixed fertiliser. Add a mulch of animal manure or compost to maintain good soil structure. Prune back to the four or five strongest shoots in winter for buds next spring. Plants will bear well for three or four years, after which they should be divided and replanted. Harvest buds when 5–10 cm in diameter and still tight and tender. For larger main buds, prune out lateral buds when about the size of a golf ball. Three to five plants should be sufficient for an average family.

The Jerusalem artichoke is really a large sunflower with tuberous roots like a potato. It is a perennial, but is grown as an annual from tubers planted in late winter or early spring. Plant tubers 10–15 cm deep and 50–60 cm apart with a pre-planting fertiliser scattered in a circle around each. The plants produce yellow flowers in summer, but pinch them out in the bud stage. Tubers are ready four to six weeks after buds appear, but can be left in the ground until winter if necessary. Nine to twelve plants should be sufficient for the average family.

ASPARAGUS

Once established, asparagus plants are very long-lived and can go on producing for twenty years or more. Asparagus is best suited to mild or cold climates. Frosts are no problem because the plant (often called asparagus fern) dies off each winter to produce new shoots or spears in spring. Light soils, through which the spears can easily push, are preferred.

Sow asparagus seed in spring in a seed bed in a corner of the vegetable garden. Seedlings should be two years old before planting out in their permanent position. Asparagus has male and female flowers on separate plants. Male plants produce bigger and better spears, so female plants (which develop red berries in the second autumn from sowing) should be

discarded. Some gardeners prefer to buy two-year-old crowns from nurseries in winter. 'Mary Washington' is the standard variety.

Hint

Some plants are very particular about their germination requirements. For instance, bean seed needs the soil temperature to be at 16°C. Most areas in New Zealand will have correct environmental conditions for sowing bean seed after Labour weekend. Have patience: if the weather is not right, wait until it is.

SIMON FARRELL
GARDEN WRITER

Before planting crowns, prepare the bed to spade depth and add a pre-planting fertiliser plus liberal quantities of organic matter for good soil structure. Acid soils should be dressed with a small amount of garden lime. Set crowns 15–20 cm deep and 30–50 cm apart at the bottom of a trench along the row. Cover with about 5 cm of soil, filling in the remainder as the fern grows. Do not cover new shoots. Water regularly and give liberal dressings of high-nitrogen fertiliser (N.P.K. 10:4:6) in summer to encourage vigorous top growth. Cut down the dry, yellow fern in winter to ground level and rake it up for composting. Fertilise again in late winter to encourage spears in spring. Do not cut any spears in the first spring after planting. Cutting can increase each year as plants grow older and reach full bearing in four or five years. Each year, start cutting when spears appear (August or September, depending on district). Harvest every day or two and continue cutting for eight to ten weeks.

'Green' asparagus is cut from level beds when spears are 15–20 cm long and before the tips open. For 'white' or 'blanched' asparagus (whose stems are deliberately deprived of sunlight), hill the soil over the row to a depth of 25–30 cm in late winter.

As the tip of the spear breaks the surface, push a sharp knife through the soil to cut the spear about 15 cm below. Hills may be levelled when the fern is removed in winter. Cultivate and fertilise, then rebuild the hills before spring. Whether you grow green or white asparagus, 20–25 plants are ample for the average family. Spears keep well for several days in the crisper tray of the refrigerator or, after washing and blanching (immersing vegetables in boiling water) for three minutes, can be packaged for the home freezer.

BEANS

Packed with vitamins and easy to grow, beans are among the most popular of all vegetables to grow in home gardens. They produce outstanding yields for the space occupied. Beans are warm-season vegetables and susceptible to frost. They can be grown all year round in warm northern regions. In temperate areas the growing season is five to six months, but in cold climates only three or four months. Beans do best on well-drained soils, but may suffer on very sandy soils, so add old organic matter to improve water-holding capacity. Mulching with compost is recommended in very hot weather but avoid direct contact with the bean plants. Beans are also susceptible to wind damage, so protect them with wind-breaks. Dwarf beans are ready to pick in eight to ten weeks. Climbing beans are great space-savers, and yield more pods over a longer period, but take ten to twelve weeks to picking. Cultivation methods for both dwarf and climbing beans are the same.

Dust seed with a fungicide before sowing. Sow dwarf beans in rows 50–60 cm apart, spacing seeds 7–10 cm along the row. A row 3–5 m long at each sowing is suitable for the average family. Make the next sowing when plants in the previous crop develop their first true leaves.

Sow climbing beans to grow on a fence or trellis, spacing seeds 10–15 cm apart. You can make a simple trellis by stretching two wires between steel droppers or timber posts, with the bottom wire at 15 cm and top wire at 2 m. Use garden twine between the bottom and top wires for the bean plants to climb. A row 2–3 m in length is suitable for the

TOP FIVE BEANS

'DWARF GOLDEN WAX II'

A most popular home garden butter bean. Holds its quality over a long picking period. Pods are bright yellow, slim and stringless. Adapted to a wide range of climatic conditions.

'CHEF'S CHOICE'

An all-new variety that produces copious quantities of medium-sized, straight, round, stringless beans. Dark green and tasty, ideal fresh or for freezing. Very disease resistant.

'TOP CROP'

An early-maturing, high-yielding variety. Pods carried high on the plant. Seeds are brown with buff mottling. Pods stringless, round and medium-green. Resistant to common bean mosaic. Suitable for freezing and canning.

'STRINGLESS SCARLET'

A new variety with pods that remain stringless right up until maturity, becoming 'stringy' only if left on the vine. High yielding, excellent flavour.

'SCARLET RUNNER'

These large beans taste wonderful but will really only bear reliably in areas with a cool summer.

'STRINGLESS SCARLET'

'TOP CROP'

'SCARLET RUNNER'

GARDENING FOR THE KITCHEN

average family. Another way to grow climbing beans is to form a tripod or A-frame of garden stakes and sow two or three seeds at the bottom of each stake.

When sowing dwarf or climbing beans, always apply a pre-planting fertiliser in a band, as suggested for sowing large seeds direct in Chapter 7. Be careful not to place bean seeds in direct contact with fertiliser because they are susceptible to fertiliser burn. If you press bean seeds into damp soil they absorb sufficient moisture to germinate. Avoid watering for a day or two after sowing and do not soak seeds in water overnight – this may hinder rather than help germination.

Bean plants usually give good yields without additional fertiliser as they grow, but a side-dressing of nitrogen fertiliser or liquid feeds of water-soluble fertilisers will increase yield and quality if applied when flowering

commences. Always pick beans when young and tender, before the seeds swell to make the pods lumpy. After the first picking the pods mature quickly, so pick them every three to five days. This will prolong flowering. Use the beans when as fresh as possible. They are best if picked and cooked the same day, although they keep well in the refrigerator for a few days. For quick freezing, wash and prepare pods as for cooking, blanch for three minutes, drain and package.

There are many varieties of beans: dwarf, climbing, string, stringless and wax-podded (butterbeans).

Dwarf beans

'Freezer Slims' are extra long and flat podded. Excellent quality which holds well into late maturity. White seeds. Pods medium green. Quite resistant to top yellow virus.

SOLVING PROBLEMS WITH BEANS

PROBLEM	CAUSE	SOLUTION
Excessive leaf growth.	Too much nitrogen fertiliser	Use a balanced N.P.K. fertiliser such as Gro-Plus Complete Plant Food.
Stem and stalks swollen and cracked. Young plants wilt, old plants break easily.	Bean fly	Where problem is prevalent apply Mavrik to young plants.
Fine yellow mottling of upper leaves. Masses of small insects fly from plant when disturbed.	Whitefly	Target, Baythroid Aerosol.
Pods twisted and distorted, may be lumpy and have rusty marks near stalk end.	Blossom thrip	Spray blossom with Super Shield or Mavrik. Note: both insecticides are toxic to bees.
Angular spots with wide halo around them on leaves. Leaves may be pale green with dark veins. Plants wilt.	Halo blight	Remove and destroy affected plants. Spray crop with Champion Copper.
Yellowish orange pustules on leaves which yellow and fall.	Rust	Bravo at first sign of problem.

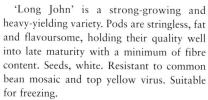

'Long John' is a strong-growing and heavy-yielding variety. Pods are stringless, fat and flavoursome, holding their quality well into late maturity with a minimum of fibre content. Seeds, white. Resistant to common bean mosaic and top yellow virus. Suitable for freezing.

'Scarlet Bush' is not only a beautiful sight with its glorious scarlet flowers but also a prolific producer of stringless juicy pods up to 25 cm.

'Tendergreen' is a popular snap pod, stringless bean. Seeds are a purple-brown mottled with fawn. Pods are round, dark green with some darker flecks. Resistant to common bean mosaic. Suitable for freezing.

Climbing beans

'Purple King' is an old garden favourite. The long, dark-purple, rather flat pods turn green when cooked. The plant bears over a long period but is rather susceptible to rust in warm, humid weather.

'Mangere Pole' is an excellent late season cultivar. Superb quality, prolific bean. Strong and reliable. Pods are long, shiny dark green, stringless, flat and very attractive. Seeds are large, flat and white. Recommended for all areas including subtropical and temperate zones. Quite resistant to rust. Suitable for outdoor and glasshouse production.

'Shiny Fardenlosa' is an early- and mid-season cultivar, prolific and vigorous. The attractive pods are long, flat, and a dark glossy green, straight and entirely stringless. The white seeds are large, flat and kidney-shaped. Long season producing over six to eight weeks. Suitable for outdoors and glasshouses.

Climbing runner beans

Runner beans are perennial plants which die back after cropping in summer but grow again from the crown the following spring. The pods are broader and shorter with a rough texture but are tender when cooked. They are popular in cool districts and are grown extensively in South Island home gardens. The flowers are large and ornamental. The most popular variety is 'Scarlet Runner', which has brilliant-red flowers. Although they flower profusely, runner beans will not set fruit in high temperatures.

A wigwam of garden stakes or sturdy bamboo poles can be used to support climbing beans.

Dried beans

Most varieties of beans can be used as dried beans. Allow pods to ripen on the bush or vine. When dry, shell the seeds. These can be used in soups, stews and bean salads.

Two varieties of French beans grown specifically for this purpose are 'Borlotti' (Italian or cooker bean) with speckled yellow and red seeds, and 'Canellini' (red kidney bean).

Other beans in this dried bean group include lima bean (harvested before the seeds ripen and shelled like peas) and soybeans, which are used (particularly in Asian countries) to make sauces and beverages, and as a milk or cheese substitute. Soybeans have a very high protein content.

VEGETABLES

WHAT TO LOOK FOR	NUTRITION	STORAGE	PREPARATION	METHOD OF COOKING
BEANS Firm. Long straight beans, crisp enough to snap. Good green colour.	Small mineral and vitamin content, particularly vitamin C. Some fibre. 126 kilojoules per 100 grams.	Wash, drain and store in vented plastic bag in refrigerator. Use soon after harvest.	Wash, top and tail and remove strings. Slice diagonally or leave whole.	Steam or boil. May be lightly tossed in butter to glaze. Do not overcook.
BROCCOLI Compact flower heads with no sign of yellow. Leaves and stems should show no sign of ageing.	Good source of folic acid. Excellent source of vitamin A and vitamin C. Fair source of calcium and fibre. 147 kilojoules per 100 grams.	Keep dry. Handle as little as possible as flowers bruise. Store in vented plastic bag in refrigerator. Use within 1–2 days.	Wash. Steam flowers whole in bunches. Stems may be sliced and served as a separate vegetable.	Steam, boil or oven bake. May be served raw if finely sliced. Remember, stems take longer to cook than flowers.
BRUSSELS SPROUTS Firm and compact with no limp leaves.	Excellent source of vitamin C. Good source of folic acid and fibre. 205 kilojoules per 100 grams.	Wrap in plastic. Store in refrigerator.	Wash. Trim stalk. Remove any poor quality leaves.	Steam or boil. May be deep-fried in batter after initial cooking.
CABBAGES Firm head. Outer leaves should be strongly coloured and not limp.	Good source of vitamin C. Some calcium and fibre. 109 kilojoules per 100 grams.	Trim lightly and remove outer leaves. Wrap in plastic and store in refrigerator. Use within a week of harvest.	Remove any poor quality leaves. Wash. Remove rib if desired. Slice finely or leave whole.	Drop a whole walnut into the water while cooking cabbage to minimise odour. May be boiled, steamed or stir-fried.
CAPSICUMS Well-shaped, thick-walled and firm, with a uniform glossy colour (deep red or bright green).	Very good source of vitamin C. Fair source of vitamin A. 109 kilojoules per 100 grams.	Store in plastic bag in refrigerator. Use within 5 days.	Simply wash and remove all seeds.	Delicious raw in salads. May be stuffed and baked or used in soups and casseroles.
CARROTS Firm, smooth and well formed. Deep orange to red in colour.	Outstanding source of vitamin A. Some fibre. 151 kilojoules per 100 grams.	Store in plastic bag in refrigerator.	Wash and scrape lightly. May be left whole, sliced or diced for cooking.	Steam, boil, braise or shred. Delicious raw or cooked.
CAULIFLOWERS Should not have a ricey appearance or obvious flowers. Look for firm white compact heads without spots or bruises.	Very good source of vitamin C, fair source of folic acid and fibre. 109 kilojoules per 100 grams.	Remove all leaves as they absorb moisture from head. Store in plastic bag in refrigerator. Use before heads turn brown.	Wash and break into flowerets or leave whole.	Steam or boil and top with cheese sauce. Use raw in salads and soup.

WHAT TO LOOK FOR	NUTRITION	STORAGE	PREPARATION	METHOD OF COOKING
CELERY Crisp, firm, well-coloured stalks with no blemishes or limp leaves.	Small mineral content, some fibre. 75 kilojoules per 100 grams.	Wash and store in plastic bag in refrigerator.	Remove leaves, wash stalks and cut to desired length. Remove any loose fibres.	Eat fresh, braise or stir-fry. May be added for flavour to stews or soups.
CUCUMBERS Should be green with no yellow colouring. Firm and fresh looking.	Low energy, high water content. 59 kilojoules per 100 grams.	Store in crisper in refrigerator. Use within a few weeks.	Wash and slice. Remove rind if desired.	Boil, steam or bake with filling. Most often eaten raw.
EGGPLANTS Dark purple to purple–black colour with glossy skin. Firm to touch.	High water content. Small amounts of most minerals and vitamins. Some fibre. 105 kilojoules per 100 grams.	Keep for about 7 days in refrigerator crisper.	Wipe over. Not necessary to remove skin. Discard stalk. Slice and leave sprinkled with salt 20 minutes to extract bitter juice. Rinse prior to cooking.	Bake, boil, fry or mash.
LETTUCES Choose firm, green heads with crisp, blemish-free leaves.	Some potassium, fibre and folic acid. 71 kilojoules per 100 grams.	Perishable. Store in plastic in refrigerator crisper and use as soon as possible.	Remove core, wash under running water, drain. Tear rather than cut leaves.	Usually eaten fresh. May be braised, stir-fried or added to soup.
MUSHROOMS Look for firmness, white or creamy colour and un-broken shape. Avoid withered mushrooms.	Good source of niacin and riboflavin. Excellent source of potassium. 92 kilojoules per 100 grams.	Perishable. Store in paper bag in refrigerator. Use within 2–3 days.	Do not peel. Wipe over cap. Only remove stem if desired. Do not wash under running water.	Can be eaten raw, baked with a filling or sautéed in butter. Cook only lightly.
ONIONS Firm, with clear outer skin, no dark patches or signs of sprouting.	Small amount of vitamins and miner-als. Rich in sugars. 147 kilojoules per 100 grams.	Store in cool, dry and dark area. May be stored in refrigerator.	Peel and cut in required style e.g. rings, quarters, etc.	Sauté, boil, bake, cream or fry.
PEAS Pods should be bright green in colour. Very firm and full pods indicate over-maturity.	Some protein and iron. Fair source of thiamin and folic acid. Good source of dietary fibre. 335 kilojoules per 100 grams.	Store in plastic bag in refrigerator. Use as soon as possible.	Remove shell and discard, unless using snowpeas.	Boil, steam, or braise with lettuce.
POTATOES Firm and unbroken skin with no green tinge. There should be no dark spots or green shoots.	Fairly good source of vitamin C. Good source of potassium and dietary fibre. Some protein. 335 kilojoules per 100 grams.	Store in cool, dry and dark area. Do not store in refrigerator.	Do not soak in water. Only peel if necessary.	Bake, boil, fry, steam or mash.

GARDENING FOR THE KITCHEN

WHAT TO LOOK FOR	NUTRITION	STORAGE	PREPARATION	METHOD OF COOKING
PUMPKINS Firm, bright and well-coloured flesh.	Good source of vitamin A. Some fibre.130 kilojoules per 100 grams.	Cool, dark storage until cut. Then remove seeds, wrap in plastic, and store in refrigerator.	Wipe over. Cut into suitably sized pieces, remove seeds, stringy pieces and skin if desired.	Bake, boil, steam or mash.
ROCK MELONS Smell is a good indication of flavour and ripeness. Avoid soft spots and look for a clean stem scar.	Excellent source vitamin C. Good source vitamin A. Fair source dietary fibre. Some iron. 105 kilojoules per 100 grams.	Ripen at room temperature for finer flavour. Wrap cut melon in plastic and store in refrigerator away from butter and milk.	Tends to flavour other foods when cut. Remove seeds and serve chilled. Slice as required.	Use in fruit salad, eat alone or with ice cream. Ideal as an entree, slice and serve with prosciutto, or fill with port.
SILVER BEET Glossy, bright-green leaves that show no sign of limpness.	Excellent source of vitamin A. Good source of folic acid and vitamin C. Fair source of calcium and iron. Some fibre. 96 kilojoules per 100 grams.	Buy on day required. Store in plastic bag in refrigerator. Highly perishable.	Wash carefully. Tear rather than cut leaves. Stems may be served as a separate vegetable.	Eat raw in salad, steam or boil. Used as a wrapper for fillings.
SWEET CORN Husks fresh and green in colour. Kernels well-filled, tender, milky, and pale yellow in colour.	Some protein and vitamin A. Good source of dietary fibre. 406 kilojoules per 100 grams.	Wrap in vented plastic bag and keep refrigerated.	Remove corn silk and outer leaves.	Boil, bake or steam.
TOMATOES Free of blemish, firmly fleshed. Should weigh heavy in the hand.	Good source of vitamin C, some vitamin A. 88 kilojoules per 100 grams.	Only refrigerate when over-ripe. Always remove from refrigerator 1 hour before eating to improve flavour.	Wash, dry and remove stalk. Remove skin only if necessary by plunging into boiling water.	Use fresh or stew, bake, sauté, stuff, or prepare as a sauce.
WATERMELONS Large, well-coloured bright fruit that is heavy in the hand. A yellowish underside is a good guide to ripeness.	Fair source of vitamin C. Some vitamin A. 113 kilojoules per 100 grams.	Store in cool place in refrigerator. When cut, use promptly.	Wipe skin, serve chilled in slices or wedges. Use a melon baller for a quick dessert.	Great for picnics and in fruit salad, jams and pickles. Rind can be steamed and served with butter and nutmeg. Lovely as a refreshing drink.
ZUCCHINI Well-shaped with firm, glossy skin and good colour.	Low energy, high water content. 66 kilojoules per 100 grams.	Place in plastic bag in refrigerator.	Wash or wipe over. Use unpeeled, sliced or halved or cut in strips.	Boil, steam, bake or eat raw.

BEETROOT

Beetroot is an attractive and tasty cooked vegetable for salads and for pickling. Beetroot is adaptable to all climate zones but plants may bolt (run to seed) if sown out of season. Sow seed from July to March in temperate climates but only from September to February where colder. In warm areas sow beetroot in most months of the year, although sowing during the wet season can be risky.

The 'seed' is a cluster of two to four true seeds in a corky cluster which absorbs water slowly, so it is a good idea to soak seed for a few hours before sowing. Apply a pre-planting fertiliser in a band where the seed is to be sown and rake into the soil. Dust seed with fungicide and sow thinly in drills 20–30 cm apart and 12 mm deep. Cover seeds with seed-raising mix. Keep damp with light watering until seedlings emerge in ten to fourteen days. Thin seedlings (two or three seedlings may emerge from each cluster) early to 5–8 cm apart. Roots are ready to pull about ten weeks after sowing. Start pulling alternate roots early. This spreads the harvest, and roots left in the soil have room to gain in size. Roots grow at, or slightly above, soil level so do not cover them with soil when cultivating between rows.

Beetroot is best when grown quickly and responds to liquid feeds of Thrive. Sow successive rows 2–3 m long every four to six weeks during the season. Beetroot keeps well in open storage for a few weeks but it will keep for two or three months when stored in the refrigerator.

....

Hint

Turn friends gourmet-green with envy by sowing Yates Salad Mix into pots at regular intervals to ensure a delicious, varied and continuous crop of lettuces. Red oak leaf, lollo rossa and cos make up this wonderful blend of designer lettuces.

SEAN DUGGAN
YATES NEW ZEALAND

....

Varieties

'Derwent Globe' is a deep, round beet with flesh of good texture and flavour. 'Baby' is a small variety with good colour and flavour. It matures quickly and pulling can commence six to seven weeks after sowing. Pull alternate plants unless harvesting the whole row. 'Cylindra', as its name suggests, has a cylindrical shape which makes it excellent for slicing.

BORECOLE

Borecole (also called Scotch kale or curly greens) is a loose-leafed member of the cabbage group of plants. It is widely used in the British Isles and Northern Europe. It is very hardy and withstands severe winter conditions, but is not widely grown in New Zealand. Borecole is grown in exactly the same way as cabbage. It can be used by harvesting the outside leaves progressively, like silver beet, or by cutting the whole plant at once.

BROAD BEANS

Unlike other beans, broad beans are a cool-season vegetable and provide useful meals in spring and early summer when other vegetables are often scarce. It is a useful legume for soil improvement too. Broad beans are best suited to mild–temperate and cool climates and are sown from early autumn to late winter in most districts.

Broad beans are a tall leafy crop and they need plenty of space to grow. Sow seeds in rows 60–75 cm apart after banding a pre-planting fertiliser alongside. Another way is to sow double rows 25–30 cm apart with 75–90 cm between each pair of rows. Dusting seed with fungicide before sowing is recommended. Press the large seeds into damp soil at the bottom of a furrow about 5 cm deep, spacing them 15–20 cm apart. Cover with soil, tamp down and rake surface. If sown in damp soil, extra water is not needed until seedlings emerge in ten to fourteen days.

Extra fertiliser is usually unnecessary while the crop is growing. Too much fertiliser, especially fertiliser high in nitrogen, promotes leaf growth at the expense of flowers and pods. Plants of broad beans may need some support. An easy way is to use garden twine stretched between stakes at each end of the row. Flower-drop is a common problem in early spring and is due to low temperatures. Pod setting improves with warmer weather and greater activity of bees. You can pick pods when young and slice them like French beans, or leave them to fill. Then shell the half-ripe seeds. A 5–6 m row is usually sufficient for one sowing for the average family.

Varieties

'Exhibition Long Pod' has thick fleshy pods approximately 30 cm long. 'Coles Dwarf' or 'Dwarf Prolific' grows to 1 m with smaller pods. A dwarf variety is often preferred by home gardeners as the plants are more compact and less liable to wind damage.

BROCCOLI

Broccoli is an excellent cool-season vegetable for use in late autumn, winter and early spring, although newer varieties are more tolerant to heat. It is a close relative of cauliflower but the tightly packed heads are green. The large centre head may reach 20 cm in diameter. When this is cut, new shoots with smaller heads form in the leaf axils, so a single plant will bear for many weeks. Broccoli does best in temperate and cold climates but is adaptable to all climates with a cool winter. In cold districts, sow seed in December or even November. Early sowing allows plants to grow a large frame before cold weather. In temperate and warmer climates, sow from late summer to autumn. Successive sowings may be made. Usually nine to twelve plants at each sowing, four to six weeks apart, are sufficient for the average family.

Broccoli is usually raised as seedlings, because only a few plants are required. Sow seed in punnets, prick out seedlings early into 10 cm pots and grow on until 7–10 cm high. Transfer plants to a well-prepared bed to which plenty of organic matter and a pre-planting fertiliser has been added. Seeds may also be sown direct in clumps or stations spaced 45–60 cm apart. Thin each station to one seedling. Broccoli, like all leafy crops, needs to be grown quickly and responds to side dressing with nitrogen fertilisers or liquid feeds of Thrive. Use dusts or sprays to control caterpillars and aphids. (See Chapter 6.)

Cut the centre head when still tightly packed and before the individual flower buds open. Take about 10 cm of main stem with a slanting cut. This prevents water lodging in the stem and causing rotting. Cut side shoots as they develop, again taking 10 cm of stem. Centre heads and side shoots store well in the crisper tray of the refrigerator for several days, or can be prepared as for cooking – blanched for 3–4 minutes, packaged and deep frozen.

Varieties

'Winter Harvest' broccoli is the best choice for growing into the colder months when other varieties do not thrive. It has firm, dome-shaped heads with an attractive green colour. 'Shogun' is a new release bred at Yates' research station. It is suited to summer production as it tolerates heat well. It carries a large, attractively coloured flower head. 'Summer King' is another heat-tolerant variety that can be sown even earlier in the season.

BRUSSELS SPROUTS

Brussels sprouts are another cool-season crop but they are less adaptable than broccoli. They do best in mild–temperate and in cold districts and are not really suited to warm northern climates. Make sowings from October to early February in cold districts and from December to late February in mild–temperate areas. Brussels sprouts are usually raised as seedlings in the same way as broccoli. Transplant seedlings at the same size into a prepared, well-manured and fertilised bed. The plants need more space to grow than broccoli, so allow 60–75 cm between plants. Apply side-dressings of nitrogen fertiliser or liquid feeds regularly from transplanting onwards. Hill soil around plants as they grow to lessen wind damage. Dust or spray to control caterpillars and aphids. For the average family, six to nine plants are usually sufficient for one sowing.

Brussels sprouts are ready to harvest four or five months after transplanting. The cabbage-shaped sprouts form in the leaf axils of the main stem and mature progressively from bottom to top. When bottom sprouts are quite small, start stripping lower leaves with a sideways pull. This allows sprouts to develop more easily. Pick the sprouts with a downward and sideways action. Discard any fluffy sprouts at the bottom of the stem. Continue stripping leaves and pick sprouts as they become usable. Modern varieties, especially hybrids, tend to form sprouts from bottom to top about the same time. If plants are well grown, cut the main stem at ground level and pick all sprouts at once. This makes harvesting easier but you may have to sacrifice a few small sprouts at the top of the stem. Sprouts store well in the refrigerator for seven to ten days or they can be washed, trimmed of loose outside leaves, blanched for four to five minutes, packaged and deep frozen.

Varieties

'Drumtight' is adaptable to a wide range of climatic conditions, is vigorous and very uniform. If well grown, the hard, tight sprouts can all be harvested at the one time.

CABBAGE

Cabbages are very adaptable to climatic conditions. In warm northern areas they are sown during most months of the year, although they may be difficult to grow well in the wet season. In temperate and cold districts they can be sown from early spring to autumn. Some old varieties tended to 'burst' or run to seed if sown out of season, but modern hybrid varieties are more reliable. Like other leaf crops, cabbages like good going, so the soil must have excellent structure (apply plenty of organic matter). Also, it is a good idea to use a pre-planting fertiliser when preparing the bed.

Cabbage plants can be raised as seedlings in the same way as broccoli, or sown direct in clumps in the garden bed and later thinned to one seedling. Plant spacing depends on variety. Space small varieties 40–50 cm apart

Flowers and vegetables can grow together as companions. The flowers attract pollinators and friendly insects for the vegetables while benefiting from the good soil and plentiful sunshine.

each way but give more room (60–75 cm) for large cabbage varieties.

Plenty of water (but good drainage) and regular side-dressings of nitrogen fertiliser or liquid feeds of water-soluble fertiliser every 2–3 weeks will promote quick growth and crisp heads. Dust or spray regularly to control caterpillars and aphids. (See Chapter 6.)

You can make successive sowings of cabbage over a long period. Usually nine to twelve plants are sufficient at each sowing for the average family. Make next sowing when seedlings of previous batch are 15–20 cm tall. Start cutting the first plants from each sowing when the heads are firm but quite small. Hybrid varieties have an advantage here because they 'hold' well in the garden and are slower to burst or run to seed. Cabbages store well in the refrigerator for a week or you can slice them, blanch for three or four minutes, package and deep freeze.

Varieties

Small early varieties mature in eight to ten weeks and weigh 1–2 kg. 'Earliball' is fast growing, with small, solid, round heads. 'Sugarloaf' has conical heads weighing up to 2–3 kg. Both are recommended home garden varieties. 'Green Gold' hybrid is an excellent winter cabbage. It is large with a firm solid head flattened into a semi-globe shape. It performs best when sown in summer and autumn, for maturity twelve to fourteen weeks from transplanting. 'Savoy Hybrid' is a very large cabbage with dark-green, blistered leaves. 'Racer' is a newer hybrid variety that matures quickly and has a very tight head.

CAPE GOOSEBERRY

Cape gooseberry, also known as ground cherry, husk tomato or Chinese lantern plant, is grown for its small, globe-shaped, yellow or red fruits which are enclosed in papery husks. The fruit may be eaten fresh but is more often used to make jams or jellies. Cape gooseberry is a warm-season plant. In frost-free, warm and subtropical climates, the bushes are perennial and reach a height of 1 m or more. In cool–temperate climates it is grown as an annual during summer. It needs a warm, sheltered position. In suitable areas it may be grown as an ornamental shrub.

Generally, the cultivation of cape goose-

berry is very similar to that of capsicum. Sow seeds in punnets in spring when the weather is warm. Transplant seedlings to the garden when 8–10 cm tall, spacing them 100 cm in the row. For the average family two to three plants should be ample. Plants take five or six months before fruit is ready for picking. In warm, frost-free districts cut plants back hard after fruiting to induce new growth for next year's crop. Plants may bear well for three or four years.

CAPSICUM

There are two kinds of capsicum or pepper. The sweet (mild) ones are eaten raw in salads or used in cooked dishes, soups and stews. The hot pepper or chilli is used fresh or dried as a flavouring and for sauces and pickles. Whether sweet or hot, capsicums are warm-season plants like tomatoes, and in warm subtropical climates you can grow them almost all year round. In temperate zones sow seed from August to December and, in cold climates, September to November only. In frost-free areas, capsicums will die back over winter and shoot again in spring, but they are most successfully grown as annuals.

You can sow seed direct but, because of the short growing season in most districts, it is best to raise seedlings for transplanting to the open garden as soon as it is warm enough. You only need a small number of plants – four to six well-grown plants are sufficient for the average family. There is hardly time, even in a mild climate, for successive sowings. Seedlings transplanted in mid-September will bear fruit about Christmas and keep bearing until autumn. It is easy to raise seedlings in plastic punnets. Keep the punnets indoors until seedlings emerge, then prick them out into 10 cm pots to grow on in a sunny, sheltered spot until about 15 cm tall. Transfer them to a bed well-prepared beforehand with organic matter and pre-planting fertiliser. Space plants 50–60 cm apart.

Capsicums have a fairly deep root system and are adaptable to both heavy and light soils, but they need regular watering. Do not force plants, especially with nitrogen fertilisers, in the early stages. This makes too much leaf growth. After flowering has started, a side-dressing of mixed fertiliser, such as Gro-Plus Complete Plant Food, scattered around each plant will promote good fruiting. Repeat every four or five weeks while the plants are bearing. Capsicums rarely need staking, but well-grown plants may need support if carrying a heavy crop and exposed to wind. Drive in a stake close to each plant and tie the main stems to it with garden twine. Capsicums can be useful and ornamental when grown in large pots or tubs on a sunny terrace or patio. A pot 40 cm in diameter and the same depth will grow a good-sized plant, but pay special care to watering because pots dry out quickly.

You can pick sweet capsicums at any stage; there is no need to wait till they are full size. Frequent picking encourages more flowers and fruits. Hot capsicums (chillies) can be picked when immature or left on the bush until full-coloured and shrivelled.

Varieties

'Giant Bell' ('Californian Wonder' type) is a popular variety of sweet capsicum with large, bell-shaped, dark-green fruits turning red as they mature. 'Sweet Banana' has green and yellow tapered fruit. Hot capsicums have rather smaller, green, tapered fruit turning red at full maturity. 'Hot Pepper', 'Jalapeno' and 'Inferno' are typical names of some of the most popular varieties.

CARROTS

Carrots are an adaptable crop in the home garden and give a good yield for the space occupied. In warm northern zones, you can sow seed almost any month of the year, although midsummer sowings are often avoided. Best months to sow in temperate zones are July through to March and in cold districts August to February. Sowings in late autumn or winter may run to seed without forming roots.

Deep sandy soil or heavy soils with good structure allow roots to grow and expand quickly. On clay soils, add coarse sand to improve texture, and organic matter to improve structure. If you add organic matter the roots can be forked and misshapen; avoid this by mixing it evenly through the soil. For carrots, you will need a well-prepared bed for direct sowing, firm soil below and a loose, crumbly surface. After scattering pre-planting fertiliser in a band where seed is to be sown, mark out shallow furrows

> ## Hint
>
> *When you sow carrot seed, mix it with radish seed. As you harvest the radishes, your rows of carrots will be naturally thinned and there will be less wastage of young plants.*
>
> RAYMOND REES
> GARDEN EXPERT

20–30 cm apart and sow seeds 6 mm deep by tapping the seeds from the packet as described in Chapter 7. Cover with seed-raising mixture and water gently. Seedlings may take two to three weeks to emerge so keep the bed damp until they do.

When seedlings are 5 cm high, thin them to 2–3 cm apart. Later, when 15 cm high, thin again to 5 cm apart. The seedlings removed will have tender roots large enough to eat. While thinning, remove weed seedlings too. If space between rows is then cultivated and mulched, further weeding is seldom needed. The base fertiliser applied before sowing may be sufficient to grow a good crop, but liquid feeds every few weeks will promote faster growth. Do not overfeed, especially with high-nitrogen fertilisers.

Most varieties take three to four months from sowing to harvest. For the average family a row 4–6 m long is sufficient for each sowing. Make further sowings at 4–6 week intervals during the season. Pests and diseases are usually not a serious problem. Start pulling early to spread the harvest and allow remaining roots to grow larger. Carrots keep well in open storage (remove tops) but even better in the refrigerator crisper tray. For freezing, slice or dice carrots as for cooking, blanch for five minutes, package and freeze.

Varieties

'Topweight' has been the leading carrot variety in New Zealand for many years. It has a strong top with long, tapering roots of good colour. 'Egmont Gold' is another popular long-rooted variety. It is a strong and vigorous carrot suited to sowing from early spring to mid-summer.

'Majestic Red', bred in Australia, also has tapering roots of a good colour and flavour.

Shorter, stump-root varieties are often preferred in the home garden and are better suited to shallow soils. 'Early Chantenay' has excellent colour and has been a favoured home garden variety for a number of years. 'Express Hybrid' is a reliable cylindrical carrot attaining good size while still retaining excellent colour and taste. 'Manchester Table' is a very popular old variety with a cylindrical shape and deep-orange flesh.

'Baby' is a sweet, tender, finger-size carrot which is ready for harvest in ten to twelve weeks from sowing. It can be sown more thickly in rows 10–15 cm apart and rarely needs thinning when grown in light, friable soil. Because of early maturity it can be sown later in the autumn than other varieties. Very suitable for growing in pots or troughs in a sunny, sheltered position.

CAULIFLOWER

Cauliflower, like broccoli, is a valuable winter vegetable but is not so adaptable to climate. Cauliflower takes longer to grow – 14–24 weeks, depending on variety – and there is only one head per plant. Cauliflowers are best grown in cool to cold climates but are also successful in mild–temperate areas. In warmer areas, select an appropriate variety. Cauliflowers need low temperatures for flower heads (called 'curds') to form, so they must be sown from mid-summer to autumn to develop a good-sized plant before cold weather sets in. The best months to sow them are shown in the sowing guide in this chapter. You can have an extended harvest by

SOLVING PROBLEMS WITH CARROTS

SYMPTOM	CAUSE	SOLUTION
Branched and misshapen roots.	Stones, clods or lumps of bulky organic manure in soil.	Prepare a deep, crumbly, well-drained soil which allows roots to expand and grow quickly.
Pale colour.	Pale variety, or strongly acid soil, or excess nitrogen, or high temperature during growth.	Plant deeply coloured carrot such as 'Chantenay', or add lime to soil and avoid nitrogen fertiliser. Potash increases intensity of colour.
Seedlings burn off.	Hot, sunny weather at tender stage of growth.	Sprinkle with water, keep soil moist.
Green tops on carrot roots.	Sunlight on exposed crowns.	
Roots cracked or split.	Interior of carrot grows faster than skin; caused by heavy rain following a dry spell, or overfertilising.	Pile earth up to cover crowns during growth.
Bolting – running to seed prematurely without forming roots.	Seedling subject to cool weather during early spring growth.	
Excessive leaf growth.	Excess nitrogen.	Avoid nitrogenous fertiliser, and use balanced ones.

sowing two varieties of different maturity at the one time or a packet of mixed varieties.

Cauliflower seeds, like those of broccoli, Brussels sprouts and cabbage, are usually sown in boxes or punnets and the seedlings transplanted when 7–10 cm high. Space the plants 50–75 cm apart. Late varieties need rather more space than early varieties. Like other leafy plants in this group, cauliflowers are hungry plants. Prepare the bed with plenty of organic matter and a ration of pre-planting fertiliser as described previously for broccoli. Give regular side-dressings of nitrogen fertiliser every two to three weeks, or liquid feeds every ten to fourteen days. Dust or spray regularly to control caterpillars and aphids.

Cut the curds when tight and solid for best quality; do not wait until they become soft and fuzzy. Protect the white curds from direct sunlight (and yellow discolouration) by breaking outside leaves inward or by tying the ends of longer leaves together with string to form a shady tent over the centre. Start cutting early to extend the harvest. Curds store well in the refrigerator crisper for up to a week, but you can break them into serving-size pieces, blanch for four or five minutes, package and freeze.

Varieties

All varieties produce top-quality curds when grown quickly and harvested at the correct time. The main difference in varieties is the time they take to mature. The most popular cauliflower varieties (maturity in weeks from transplanting to harvest is shown in brackets) are 'Mini' (ten to twelve weeks) and 'Phenomenal Early' (fourteen to eighteen weeks). 'Mini' is a unique early-maturing mini cauliflower with solid snow-white heads on small compact plants. It is very easy to grow and ideal for the small garden. 'Phenomenal Early' has a medium-sized head and is a consistently reliable performer in most conditions.

'All Year Round' is a newer hybrid cauliflower that can reach maturity as early as fifteen weeks. It can be sown all year round in warmer districts, although it would be wise to avoid heatwave periods.

Broccoflower is an unusual cauliflower with green curds. The heads resemble broccoli but have a true cauliflower taste. There are, of course, other varieties which may be available as seedlings from nurseries.

CELERY

Celery is a very good home garden vegetable, especially if the outside stems are picked like silver beet. These green stems give a continuous harvest over two or three months for use in salads, soups, stews or as a cooked vegetable. If you like white celery, blanch the stems by excluding sunlight. Celery prefers a mild to cool climate but grows well in warmer areas in late summer and autumn. Raise seedlings in boxes or punnets in much the same way as other vegetable seedlings. Seeds are small and it may take two to three weeks for the seedlings to emerge. Seedlings grow slowly, too, and it is best to prick them out into small pots or mini punnets to grow on until large enough (eight to ten weeks) to plant out in the garden.

Prepare the bed with liberal amounts of compost or animal manure, if available, and add a ration of pre-planting fertiliser as well. Space plants 30–40 cm apart and water well. For the average family, sixteen to twenty plants for each sowing are sufficient. Celery is shallow-rooted and regular watering is needed, every day or two in hot weather. Plants need generous feeding to grow quickly, otherwise stems become coarse and stringy. Give nitrogen side-dressings or liquid feeds of fertilisers like Thrive every two weeks or so. Leaf spot disease may be troublesome but can be controlled with a fungicide spray. (See Chapter 6.)

For green celery, simply pick outside stems with a sideways pull to break them off at ground level, but leave as many younger leaves as possible for regrowth. You can 'blanch' celery plants three to four weeks before harvesting time by wrapping black polythene or even a few thicknesses of newspaper around the stems from ground level to about 40 cm high, and tying loosely with string or raffia. Empty milk cartons work well in a home garden situation. A scattering of snail bait will deter snails and slugs from sheltering inside the cover. Blanching by setting seedlings in a trench and covering with soil as they grow is not recommended because of disease problems.

Celery keeps well in the refrigerator crisper for up to a week, or you can trim off leaves, chop stems into 5 cm lengths, blanch for three minutes and freeze for later use. Leaves can also be dried until brittle and chopped or crushed into small pieces to use for flavouring in the same way as dried herbs.

Varieties

'Green Crunch' is stringless, has good flavour and a crisp texture.

CELERIAC

Celeriac (turnip-rooted celery) is grown in the same way as celery. The tops may be used as green celery. The tuberous roots, which may reach a diameter of 5–8 cm and the same length, can be grated for salads or used in soups and stews.

CHICORY

Chicory, or witloof, is not widely grown in home gardens in New Zealand. Chicory roots can be dried, ground and used as a coffee substitute. Roots can be dug up in late summer and buried upright in damp sand or peat moss with an 8–10 cm covering of the material on top. New growth forms plump white shoots called 'chicons' which can be used for winter salads.

Radicchio is a form of chicory that has become a popular salad component. Sow radicchio in the same way as lettuce and thin seedlings to the same distance. Fertiliser and cultivation requirements are almost identical. Good watering and fertilising will encourage rapid growth that will prevent the piquant leaves from becoming bitter.

CHINESE CABBAGE

Chinese cabbage is a close relation of cabbage but is a different species. It is widely grown in Asian countries where is called pe-tsai, pak choy, bok choy, Hong Kong, michili, kim chee and other names. There are many different varieties available. Generally, plants of Chinese cabbages are smaller than ordinary cabbages. Plants are more upright, with loose heads, and the leaves have a texture like lettuce, but with a mustard-like flavour.

Chinese cabbage is grown in the same way as cabbage, but is best sown to grow when temperatures are mild. Chinese cabbages tend to run to seed when temperatures are cold. They can also perform poorly when temperatures are high. Seed is best sown direct in clumps 30–40 cm apart and seedlings thinned to the strongest. For the average family, six to nine plants are usually sufficient for each sowing. Protect plants by dusting or spraying against caterpillars and aphids. (See Chapter 6.) Chinese cabbages, like other leaf crops, need generous feeding, so follow the same programme as for cabbages. Plants grow quickly and are ready for harvest eight to ten weeks from sowing. Chinese cabbage can be used in salads or coleslaws or cooked in the same way as cabbage.

Varieties

Seeds of Chinese cabbage have been sold under many of the Chinese names given to it, 'Pe-tsai' or 'Wong Bok'. Another variety is 'Pak Choy', which does not form a head. It has mid-green leaves and white stalks, not unlike silver beet. The outside leaves can be picked separately or the whole plant cut at ground level.

CHOKO

Choko, also known as chayote or alligator pear, is a vigorous vine crop which is adapted to mild temperate and subtropical zones. It is frost susceptible and needs a warm growing season of five to six months. The pear-shaped fruits have a texture and flavour rather like marrow or summer squash. The choko vine is best grown on a fence or trellis in an out-of-the-way part of the garden where it can run wild. The vine is started from a single sprouted fruit but it is important to select a well-matured fruit with a smooth skin free of prickles. Keep the fruit indoors until it sprouts.

Prepare soil well by adding organic matter and a pre-planting fertiliser. Plant the choko into damp soil with the shoot and top of the fruit just above soil level. One well-grown vine is sufficient for the average family but plant two or three fruits about 100 cm apart in case of failure. While the vine grows, give side-dressings of high-nutrient fertiliser such as Gro-Plus Citrus Food every five or six weeks. Plants started in spring will flower in late summer to bear fruit in autumn. In

winter, cut the old vines down, leaving two to four young shoots for the next crop. Cultivate around the plants in early spring and work in organic matter and fertiliser in the same way as for starting a new vine.

Pick the fruit when lime-green and 5–7 cm long. If left on the vine too long, the fruit becomes coarse and loses flavour. Chokoes store well in the refrigerator crisper for a week or more. They are not suitable for freezing as the flesh becomes soggy on thawing out.

CUCUMBER

Cucumber is a warm-season vegetable but is adaptable to all climate zones. In temperate areas, best months for sowing are September to January. In cold districts, with a short growing season, October to December.

You can sow seed direct into a well-prepared bed with added compost or animal manure plus a pre-planting fertiliser. For direct sowing, soil must be warm, 20°C or above, for good germination. Dusting seed with fungicide is recommended as cucumber seeds (and those of all vine crops) are liable to damping off. Press four or five seeds into 'dark damp' soil at each clump or station, spaced about 100 cm between rows and 40–50 cm between clumps. Thin seedlings to the two strongest. Although clumps are often called 'hills', they should really be saucer-shaped depressions so that water is directed to plant roots. To save space, cucumbers can be grown on a fence or trellis. The vines need some help to climb when young, so tie the stems to the wire support. Later, tendrils cling to the wire quite well. 'High-rise' cucumbers not only save garden space, but fruits are not in contact with the ground so shape and quality is improved.

For early cucumbers, sow seeds in punnets. Prick out seedlings into 10 cm plastic pots to grow on before planting in the garden. (See Chapter 7.) Prick out seedlings at the cotyledon stage before they form the first true leaf. This way so they can be easily handled without root damage.

Cucumbers and other vine crops like 'good going'. Thorough soil preparation with organic matter and pre-planting fertiliser will see the plants through to flowering; after flowering commences, scatter a mixed fertiliser around the base of the plants. Repeat this side-dressing at four to five week intervals while plants are bearing. For the average family, four to six plants are sufficient. These will continue to fruit well into autumn. The worst enemies of cucumbers and other vine crops are mildews. Some varieties are resistant to mildew but refer to Chapter 6 for control of these diseases.

You can pick long, green varieties as gherkins when 5–10 cm long, to use fresh or for pickling. For high-quality salad use, pick green varieties when 15–20 cm long, or round (apple-shaped) cucumbers when no larger than a cricket ball. Early and regular picking promotes further flowering and fruit setting. Like all vine crops, female flowers are pollinated by bees after visiting the male (pollen) flowers. Failure to set fruit is often due to cold weather or the absence of bees. Fruit setting will improve in warm sunny weather.

Varieties

Green cucumbers are long and thin, sometimes rather oval-shaped. They start bearing eight to ten weeks from sowing. The best green variety is 'Burpless'. It is tolerant to downy and powdery mildew and has long, thin fruit which may grow to 40 cm but is still fleshy and tender. This is an excellent home garden variety especially suitable for trellis growing. 'Long Green' is another long slim variety with dark-green skin and a white spine. It has good disease resistance and matures in nine weeks from seed. 'Slicemaster' is a high-yielding, disease-resistant variety, of very uniform and high-quality, long, straight fruit, tapering at the blossom end. It matures from seed in only eight weeks. 'Pickling' or 'Gherkin' have tender crisp fruit which may be picked when less than 5 cm in length and produce a heavy crop or left to reach 15–18 cm if larger fruit is preferred.

Lebanese cucumber has dark-green fruit that should be picked and eaten when small, approximately 10 cm in length. The sweetly flavoured burpless fruit may be eaten whole or sliced for salads. Plants usually have male and female flowers on separate plants – so always sow a good range of seeds.

Round or apple-shaped cucumbers have a

lime-green, cream or white skin. They take ten to twelve weeks to fruiting but are extremely prolific.

'Crystal Apple', with a cream to white smooth skin, is the most popular of the round varieties.

There are many other cucumber varieties. 'Salad Bush' is a compact-growing variety that can be used in pots. It is ready for picking in eight weeks.

EGGPLANT

Eggplant or aubergine is closely related to potato but is grown for its purple, egg-shaped or pear-shaped fruits which vary in length from 10 to 25 cm. It is a native of Africa and southern Asia so needs a long, warm growing season. In mild–temperate climates, sow from September to December. In cold districts, sow eggplants only in the period from October to November because the plants take fourteen to sixteen weeks to bear.

You can grow eggplants in the same way as capsicums. In areas with a short growing season, it is best to raise plants in punnets. Prick out seedlings into pots and transfer them to the garden bed when weather is warm. Plants grow 60–90 cm tall, so space them 60–75 cm apart. The plants may need to be staked for support. For the average family, four to six plants are usually sufficient.

Harvest fruit when the skin is smooth and rich purple in colour. If the skin has started to wrinkle with maturity, the flesh will be coarse and tough. The fruit stalks are hard and woody so cut them with a pair of secateurs to avoid damaging the plants. When well grown, you can expect six to eight fruits on each plant.

Varieties

'Blacknite' has a traditional oval shape and dark-purple fruit.

'Black Gnome' produces smaller, narrower fruit that is ready in eleven weeks from sowing. Unusual, white varieties are now available.

ENDIVE

Endive is closely related to chicory but is grown for its serrated, frilled leaves which form a loose heart and add an interesting taste to salads. It is similar in appearance to lettuce and is grown in much the same way. Endive is usually sown in late summer and early autumn for winter harvest. In warm northern zones it can be sown from autumn to spring. For the average family six to nine plants are sufficient. The leaves may have a slightly bitter taste which can be removed by blanching. To do this, cover plants with large plastic pots or a thick layer of straw about three weeks before cutting. 'Green Curled' is the most popular variety.

KOHLRABI

Kohlrabi is easy to grow and delicious to eat. The plant forms a swollen stem above the ground, so it is in fact really a turnip-rooted cabbage. It can be sown in all climates from late summer to autumn. In temperate and cold districts, early spring sowings are also successful.

Prepare soil well for direct sowing, adding plenty of organic matter. Scatter a mixed fertiliser in a band where seeds will be sown and rake into topsoil. Sow seeds in clumps 10–15 cm apart with 30–40 cm between rows. Cover seeds with seed-raising mix and water gently. Thin seedlings at each position to the strongest. Kohlrabi is best when grown quickly with regular watering and side-dressings of nitrogen fertiliser or liquid feeds. Do not hill plants. Remove weeds by shallow cultivation between the rows. Control caterpillars and aphids as for cabbage. For the average family a 1–2 m row is sufficient for each sowing at four to five week intervals from mid-summer to autumn.

Kohlrabi is ready to pick in eight to ten weeks. Start pulling the 'bulbs' early to spread the harvest. For top quality, bulbs should not exceed 5–7 cm in diameter. They store well in the refrigerator for a week or two. For freezing, select young bulbs, peel and dice or slice, blanch for two minutes, package and freeze. 'Early Purple' is a good variety, with flattened globe-shaped bulbs and purple stems.

KUMARA

Kumara (or sweet potato), which is a close relative of convolvulus, is a warm-season, frost-susceptible vegetable which needs a growing season of five months. Sweet potato is suitable for subtropical or very warm temperature areas. The plant is a vigorous, rather untidy vine. It prefers light soils.

Start plants from cuttings, which may be available from nurseries in spring, or buy a few kumara and bury them in a box of moist sand placed in a warm spot. When tubers shoot, divide them up for planting. Prepare soil as for potatoes and apply a pre-planting fertiliser in a band 30 cm wide at three tablespoons per metre where plants are to grow. Planting on a raised ridge makes for better drainage and easier harvesting. Set cuttings 40–50 cm apart and 5–7 cm deep with 100 cm between rows. For an ample supply of tubers, 18–24 plants are sufficient.

Lift vines occasionally as they grow to prevent rooting at the nodes along the stems. Do not give additional fertiliser, especially not nitrogen, which promotes top growth at the expense of tubers. Diseases and pests are not a problem. It is best to wait until plants are completely yellow and tubers fully mature before digging. Mature tubers have firm skin and when cut, dry quickly to a creamy white colour. After digging, leave tubers in the sun for a few days to cure. Discard diseased or damaged ones and store remainder in sacks in a cool, dry, airy place.

LEEKS

Leeks are close relatives of onions but are grown for their long, white (blanched) stem and bulbous base. They are more adaptable to climate than onions and grow more quickly. In temperate and cold climates you can sow seeds from spring to autumn but in warm or subtropical areas the best sowing period is late summer and autumn for plants to grow during the cooler months.

Leeks are best raised as seedlings in boxes or punnets. Grow them on to 20 cm tall before transplanting into a bed well prepared with organic matter and with mixed fertiliser added. The easiest method of planting is to make holes with a dibble or rake handle, 2–3 cm wide and 15 cm deep. Drop seedlings into holes so that the roots rest on the bottom. When watered, enough soil will wash into the hole to cover roots. As plants grow, regular watering will fill the hole with soil.

Another method is to set seedlings at the bottom of a trench 20 cm deep. Fill in the trench with soil as plants grow. With either method, space plants 15–20 cm apart.

Leeks need regular watering and respond well to side-dressings of nitrogen fertiliser or liquid fertiliser feeds every two or three weeks. Generous feeding promotes quick growth and plump, tender stems. For the average family, 40–50 plants are sufficient for each sowing. Successive sowings every four to six weeks can be made.

Start harvesting when stems are 2 cm thick, usually twelve to fourteen weeks after transplanting. This way you can harvest three to four leeks each week for several weeks. On heavier soils, dig each plant with a long trowel so that stems are not damaged. Some plants may form small stems around the main one. Separate these carefully and replant to grow on. Leeks store well in the refrigerator crisper for several weeks. 'Welsh Wonder' is the most widely grown variety.

LETTUCE

Lettuce is not difficult to grow but, of all vegetables, needs to be grown quickly for crisp, tender hearts. The main requirements for lettuces are:

1. Friable, well-prepared soil which absorbs and holds moisture but drains readily.
2. The right lettuce varieties for the time of the year.
3. Regular and thorough watering.
4. Generous feeding.

Hint

Plant garlic on the shortest day and harvest it on the longest day plus two weeks: this will ensure you get nice, plump bulbs. Don't use garlic from the supermarkets as it won't grow very well. Only use certified garlic; this is available from all good garden centres.

RENE VAN TILBURG
YATES NEW ZEALAND

GARDENING FOR THE KITCHEN

Lettuce, by nature, is a cool-season crop, but plant breeders have evolved sure-hearting varieties which can be grown in summer. You can sow lettuce all year round in each climate zone. Lettuce is the mainstay of summer salads so make successive sowings from early spring to January or early February.

Prepare the bed with plenty of organic matter for good soil structure and add a pre-planting fertiliser. Broadcast fertiliser at one-third of a cup per square metre or scatter in a band where plants are to grow and rake it into the topsoil.

You can raise seedlings in a good seed-raising mixture for transplanting, but direct sowing in clumps or stations is more reliable, especially in warm weather. Make shallow, saucer-shaped depressions 20 cm apart for small varieties or 30 cm apart for large varieties. Tap out several seeds at each depression, then cover with seed-raising mix and water gently.

Keep the bed moist (a light mulch of compost helps tremendously) until seedlings emerge, usually in six to seven days but sometimes sooner. Scatter snail baits to protect the seedlings from snails and slugs. Thin each clump to the strongest seedling.

Poor germination of lettuce seeds may be a problem when sown direct in very hot weather. You can overcome this by moistening the seeds, spreading them on a piece of damp flannel or paper towel, and keeping them in the refrigerator for a day or two. Then sow them direct as before. For the average family, nine to twelve plants should be more than adequate for each sowing. Make successive sowings every three to four weeks.

Lettuce plants have shallow roots so they need plenty of water – every day in summer. Mulch plants with compost. Give light side-dressings of nitrogen fertiliser or liquid feeds of Thrive every ten to fourteen days while the plants are growing. Start picking lettuce early when hearts are just forming. The young plants are crisp and tender and this spreads your harvest. Each sowing should give a two-to three-week harvest if you start picking early.

Lettuce keeps well in the refrigerator crisper for about a week. Lettuce cannot be frozen because leaves become soggy when thawed out.

Varieties

'Great Lakes' is a large, sure-hearting variety for growing in summer. It has crisp, solid hearts and will not run to seed when well grown. 'Greenway', bred by Yates at their Narromine Research Station in Australia, is a medium-large lettuce with dark-green leaves and good hearts. Ideal for late-winter and spring sowings, or late-summer/early-autumn in some districts. Resistant to downy mildew. 'Winter Triumph' is a large, cool-weather variety for winter cutting, while 'Crisphead' is suitable to use between seasons (that is, to cut in spring, early summer and autumn). They are all excellent lettuces with solid hearts.

'Red Coral' variety is a loose-leaved, red-pigmented lettuce with unusual frilly leaves. Of great sweetness and flavour, it is much sought after by restaurateurs.

Small varieties are often preferred in the home garden. They can be planted closer but do not form hearts as solid as the large types. They may run to seed in hot weather, too. 'Red Oak Leaf' has similar colouring to 'Red Coral' but has leaves that are slightly less 'frilly'. 'Mignonette' is an old garden favourite and is sown all year round in many climates. 'Green Mignonette' has pale-green loose hearts. 'Buttercrunch' ('Butterhead' type) is a small variety with leathery, light-green outer leaves and yellowish green hearts, an excellent variety for tossed salads. 'Cos' or 'Romaine' lettuce has rather upright leaves forming a tall, loose heart. All small varieties are excellent for growing in large pots, tubs or troughs, but keep them well-watered.

MARROWS

Marrows belong to the warm-season group of vine crops, often referred to as 'cucurbits' after the family name. This family includes cucumbers, marrows, melons, pumpkins and squash. The climatic requirements, time of sowing, soil preparation and fertiliser, cultivation and pest control for each of these vegetables is much the same. This has been described for cucumbers and the reader is referred to this section. There are a few minor differences in detail, such as sowing depth, plant spacing, time to maturity and number of plants for the average family. These figures are given for marrow in the Sowing Guide.

MELONS

Melons are another vine crop group. For details of sowing and growing see the section on cucumbers. Refer also to melons in the Sowing Guide.

Rock melon or cantaloupe

'Hales Best' is the leading variety of rock melon. It is powdery mildew-resistant. Fruit weighs about 1 kg with a netted yellow skin and sweet, salmon-coloured flesh. 'Planters Jumbo' is a new, large-fruited variety of good-quality deep-coloured flesh and excellent flavour. 'Honey Melon' has oval fruit to 3 kg in weight. Fruits have smooth white skin and sweet green flesh. 'Greenflesh' is an interesting honeydew melon with cream-coloured skin and green flesh. It is a medium-sized globe shape, and matures late in the season. An unusual and interesting melon for desserts or salads. Rock melons are ready to harvest when the stem pulls easily from fruit. Ripen indoors for a day or two for full flavour.

Watermelon

'Candy Red' is the leading large-fruited variety. It has large, oblong fruit to 14 kg in weight with grey-green skin and deep red flesh. It is resistant to fusarium wilt and to a disease called anthracnose. 'Sugar Baby' matures at the same time but has small round fruit to 4 kg in weight. Close planting is recommended. 'Minilee' is a particularly small melon with a very high sugar content. 'Country Sweet' is a big, roundish melon with dark-green, striped skin. The fruit is dense and full-flavoured, and is ideal for fruit salads and with desserts.

Harvest watermelons when the underside (the part in contact with the soil)' turns yellow and the fruit gives a dull, hollow sound when tapped. All varieties of melons are running types so they need plenty of room in the garden.

MUSHROOMS

The mushroom is not a vegetable but a fungus which has a fleshy, fruiting body (the mushroom) arising from the underground web of hair-like filaments known as mycelium. The stalk of the mushroom is topped by the pileus or cap, underneath which are the gills containing the spores or reproductive cells. Mushrooms are prized for their delicate flavour and are used as a vegetable in cooking, either alone or combined with many ingredients.

In their natural habitat, mushrooms and their inedible, and sometimes poisonous, relatives called toadstools occur in open grassland in autumn or spring when favourable conditions of moisture, temperature and humidity are present. Care must be taken when gathering field mushrooms because edible and inedible species are similar in appearance. Identify field mushrooms by the shape and texture of the cap, the colour (pink turning brown) of the gills and the characteristic smell of mushrooms.

Mushrooms can be grown artificially on compost. Those bought in shops are nearly all produced this way. Commercial mushroom growing is a highly specialised process which involves careful preparation and pasteurisation of the compost, the addition of the mushroom inoculum (called spawn) and a covering of peat or soil (the casing layer). The commercial crop is grown in specially constructed growing houses in which the temperature, humidity and ventilation are controlled. Similar, but less sophisticated, methods were used by home gardeners in the past, but preparing the compost from fresh animal manure, straw, soil and lime is a laborious task and accurate control of moisture and temperature during the composting process is not easy.

However, an offshoot of commercial mushroom growing is the marketing for home growers of 'mushroom farm' compost in large plastic bags or boxes. The compost is already inoculated with spawn and a casing layer is also supplied, together with instructions. For best results, the 'farm' should be placed in a well-shaded location with still, fresh air, a high humidity level and a temperature between 15–18°C. A good spot for the mushroom farm is a corner of the garage or garden shed, in the cellar or underneath the house. Complete darkness is not necessary.

After spreading the casing layer of peat, sprinkle the surface with water to keep it damp but not wet. A light sprinkle two or three times each week is usually sufficient. The whitish-grey strands of the mycelium will cover the surface of the peat in ten to fifteen days and a few days later the filaments will clump together to form 'pin heads' which then develop into the first flush of mushrooms. After picking the first crop, sprinkle again regularly to keep the surface damp, and new pin heads will form for the next flush. A well-grown bag of mushrooms should produce a crop about every ten days over a period of two to three months.

If, after several crops, no mushrooms appear for two or three weeks, the compost is exhausted and a new bag should be started. Use the spent compost for mulching or digging into the vegetable or flower garden.

Mushrooms can be picked in the button, cup or flat stage, whichever you prefer. Hold the cap of the mushroom in your fingers and gently twist the stalk from the casing layer. It is a good idea to keep a small amount of peat in reserve for filling in small holes which may occur on the surface when removing the mushrooms.

Success with mushrooms grown in plastic bags depends largely on their location (which must be free of draughts) and on very careful attention to watering. Growth rate depends on temperature, so the flushes of mushrooms take longer in cold weather. Mushroom farms are sold ready-prepared and usually produce most mushrooms in autumn and spring, when temperatures are close to the optimum of 15–18°C.

Keep the area around the farm clean at all times, especially before starting a new box or bag. Pests such as slugs, slaters, cockroaches and mice may be a problem, so scatter appropriate baits on the floor around the mushroom farms.

MUSTARD

See Cress and Mustard in Chapter 19.

NEW ZEALAND SPINACH

New Zealand spinach is a leafy vegetable with characteristic bright green triangular leaves. It is the only vegetable species native to New Zealand. It flourishes in dry summers when it is too hot for true spinach and has become popular throughout the world. It is a succulent plant which spreads over an area of about 1 metre. Although it is frost tender it often re-establishes itself during the next spring. Growth is rapid and plants respond best to light, fertile soils in sunny positions with adequate moisture. The seeds are tough, so should be soaked for one to two hours prior to sowing, to help germination. Sow seed directly in soil 2 cm deep and thin to 50 cm apart after emergence.

Harvest by picking about 8 cm of the growing tip. This will encourage new shoots to develop. Can be picked over a long period. New Zealand spinach is a little coarse in texture for use in salads, but it cooks well and can be treated in the same manner as true spinach.

OKRA

Okra or gumbo is an annual plant related to hibiscus. It is most suited to subtropical climates or warm–temperate climates with a long growing season. Plants grow to 90 cm tall and have large, hibiscus-like, yellow flowers with red centres. These form the edible pods 7–10 cm long.

Raise seedlings in late spring or early summer in a similar way to those of capsicum. Transplant seedlings when 10 cm high to a well-prepared bed, spacing plants 50–60 cm apart. For an average family, four or five plants are sufficient. Plants are grown on in the same way as capsicum, with a side-dressing of mixed fertiliser when flowering commences. The tender pods are ready to pick four or five days after the flowers have opened. They become very tough if left on the bush, and plants stop flowering. The pods, fresh or dried, are used for flavouring soups and stews.

ONIONS

Onions are a very good winter crop in the home garden. For best results, it is important to choose the right variety for sowing at the right time of the year in different climate zones. Generally, onions are classified as early, mid-season and late-maturing types. In warm northern areas, early onions are sown from February until May. In temperate climates, sow early onions from March to May and mid-season onions June to July. In cold southern areas sow early, mid-season and late onions in succession from April to August or September. It is important to sow early onions first, mid-season onions next and late onions last. Premature bolting (running to seed) may occur if maturity groups are sown out of sequence or season.

You can raise onion seedlings in beds, boxes or punnets for transplanting when 10–15 cm tall, spacing plants 7–10 cm apart in rows 20–30 cm apart. Do not plant deeply; just cover roots and the base of the stem. Direct sowing saves double handling and is less trouble. Prepare the bed well, as for sowing carrots, scatter a pre-planting fertiliser in a band where seed is to be sown, and rake in. Make a shallow furrow 6 mm deep and tap out seeds thinly onto the 'dark damp' soil. Cover with seed-raising mix and water gently. Seedlings generally emerge in ten to fourteen days, but may take longer in colder weather. Thin seedlings early to 2–3 cm and later to 7–10 cm. For the average family a 4–6 m row is sufficient. Make successive sowings with varieties of different maturity.

If the bed is well prepared and fertilised, additional fertiliser is seldom necessary. A light side-dressing of mixed fertiliser or liquid feeds when bulbs start to form will boost plants along if they are not growing strongly. Control weeds by hand, weeding between plants and shallow cultivation between rows. Do not hill the plants; bulbs sit on the soil surface, not below it. For control of diseases and pests see Chapter 6.

Onions take six to eight months to picking. Bulbs are ready to pull when tops dry and fall over. After pulling, leave them in the sun for a few days to cure. When outside skin is quite dry, screw off tops and rub off remaining roots. Select sound bulbs without blemishes for storage in a cool, dry place. Wire baskets or plastic mesh bags give good ventilation.

Varieties

Onions not only vary in maturity but come in different shapes, colours and degree of onion flavour (strong or mild). Generally, early-maturing onions do not keep as well as mid-season and late onions. 'Early Barletta' is the earliest onion, with flat, white bulbs. It is a favourite for early sowing. 'Hunter River Brown' is another early onion producing small- to medium-sized, globe-shaped bulbs with fair keeping quality. They are the main varieties for early sowing in warm and mild–temperate climates.

'Odourless' is a mid-season, large, flat onion with light-brown skin and mild cream flesh. It is popular with home gardeners. 'Sweet Red' is also mid-season in maturity with purple-red, globe-shaped bulbs which keep fairly well.

'Pukekohe Long Keeper' is the best main crop variety maturing in late summer. Golden-brown skin covers medium-sized globe-shaped onions with firm, pungent flesh. It keeps for up to ten months.

Many varieties of onion can be used as green salad or spring onions, but it is best to sow seed that is labelled 'Spring Onion' or 'Shallot Bunching Onion'. You can sow both varieties direct at almost any time of the year, from spring through to autumn. Sow seed more thickly with rows 5–10 cm apart. Thinning is seldom necessary. Spring or bunching onions are ready to harvest in 8–12 weeks. Make successive sowings every 4–6 weeks as required. Both varieties are ideal for growing in pots or troughs.

Potato onion (multiplier onion) is grown from small sets of bulblets planted in autumn. Groups of bulbs are formed below the ground. Tree onion (Egyptian onion) is grown from sets in the same way. Bulbs are formed below ground and at the top of the flowering stem.

PARSNIPS

Parsnips, like carrots, yield well for the space they occupy. They can be grown in all climate zones. In warm areas, sow seed from February to September in order to avoid the hot season. In temperate districts, sow parsnips from July to March and in cold districts from August to February. Late sowings in autumn and winter may produce small roots and plants may run to seed prematurely.

Parsnips like a friable, open soil and good drainage for best root development. Compost or animal manure, if added well before sowing, will not result in forked or misshapen roots. Dig the bed to spade depth and prepare the bed for direct sowing in the same way as for carrots. Add mixed fertiliser in a band and rake into the soil. Sow seed thinly in a furrow 6 mm deep. Rows should be 30–45 cm apart. Cover seed with seed-raising mix and water gently. Parsnip seeds are slow to germinate (three to four weeks,) so keep the bed damp with light watering until seedlings emerge. A light compost mulch helps to control moisture loss in hot weather. For the average family, 3–5 m of row is sufficient. Late summer and early autumn sowings are the most useful for harvesting the roots for baking, stews and soups.

Thin seedlings to 5–7 cm apart and control weeds by hand-weeding and row cultivation. If parsnips are grown on a well-prepared and fertilised bed, extra fertiliser is rarely needed, but liquid feeds, when roots start to form, will promote faster growth. Do not overfeed, especially with nitrogen fertilisers.

Parsnips take eighteen to twenty weeks to grow. Start pulling roots early to spread the harvest. The remainder keep well in the soil, especially in winter when growth is slow. Roots store well for a week or two in an airy cupboard (remove the tops) but for several weeks in the refrigerator crisper. Roots can also be washed, sliced or diced, blanched for two or three minutes, packaged and frozen for later use.

PEANUTS

Peanuts are sometimes called ground nuts, earth nuts or monkey nuts. Americans call them 'goobers'. Commercially, peanuts are grown on a large scale for eating raw or roasted, or to be ground for peanut butter or crushed for peanut oil. They are very nutritious and contain 50–55 per cent oil and 40–45 per cent protein. Peanuts are not commonly found in the home vegetable garden but they are an interesting crop to grow. The plants are semi-erect, annual legumes which add nitrogen to the soil in the same way as beans and peas. They are natives of Brazil and need a long, warm growing season of about five months to mature. For this reason, they are best adapted to subtropical and warm–temperate climates. The plants are very susceptible to frost damage.

Peanuts are grown in much the same way as dwarf beans, but peanuts are strange plants. After the small, yellow flowers are pollinated, the flower stalks (called 'pegs' by peanut growers) lengthen and push downwards into the soil. The pods, containing one to four kernels, develop underground. The

crop is dug when the top growth begins to yellow and die down.

Peanuts prefer a well-drained, sandy soil through which the 'pegs' can penetrate easily. Heavy soils are less suitable but satisfactory if they contain plenty of organic matter to give them a friable structure. When preparing the soil, add a dressing of lime, if necessary, to raise the pH level to 6.5 or 7.0 (see Chapter 4). Seeds (raw peanuts – roasted ones will not germinate) are usually available from health stores and are sown direct in the garden when soil temperatures reach about 20°C. Like bean seeds, peanuts are susceptible to fertiliser burn, so put a band of pre-planting fertiliser such as Gro-Plus Complete Plant Food or superphosphate alongside the line where the seeds are to be sown. Also dust the seeds with fungicide before sowing (see Chapter 7). Press the seeds into 'dark damp' soil at the bottom of a furrow about 50 mm deep, spacing the seeds 10–15 cm apart. If sowing more than one row, allow 60–75 cm between each. Cover the seeds with soil and tamp down firmly with the back of the rake. Then level the surface and scatter mulch over the whole bed to retain moisture and prevent the soil caking. If seeds are sown in 'dark damp' soil, there is usually no need for extra watering until the seedlings emerge in 7–10 days.

Cultivate between the rows to destroy weeds and water the plants regularly, especially in hot weather. As the plants grow, hill the soil slightly against them for support. Alternatively, apply a mulch of compost between the rows. If a pre-planting fertiliser has been used, additional fertiliser is rarely needed. However, if the plants lack vigour at any stage, apply a complete fertiliser with about 10 per cent nitrogen as a side-dressing or give liquid feeds of Thrive. Well-grown peanut plants should reach a height of 30–40 cm at flowering time.

When the foliage turns yellow and starts to die down it is time to dig the plants, usually sixteen to twenty-two weeks after sowing the seed. If dug too early, yields will be reduced and the kernels may be shrivelled. If left too late, the pods may break off the 'pegs' and remain in the soil. Lift each plant with a large fork and turn it upside down to dry in the sun for a few days. After the plants have wilted, shake the roots and pods free of soil and dry them further under cover. When the pods are quite dry, strip them from the plants and store them in bags or boxes. After shelling, the kernels can be eaten raw, or roasted on a shallow tray in the oven.

PEAS

Peas are one of the best cool-season crops for the home garden. The yield for space occupied is not as high as some of the other vegetables, but peas are easy to grow and space is usually available in winter to sow them. You can grow peas in all climates. In warm northern zones, sow seed from March to July. In temperate climates sow from February to August, and in cold climates sow from June to September or early October. In any district where frosts are likely, make sowings so that the crop is not in flower during the frost period. Frost will damage both flowers and young pods.

Peas are adaptable to heavy and light soils but need good drainage and a friable, well-structured soil. If your soil is acid, apply lime as described in Chapter 4. Prepare the bed free of clods and in 'dark damp' condition for direct sowing. Apply pre-planting fertiliser such as Gro-Plus Complete Plant Food in furrows along-side where the seed is to be sown to avoid fertiliser burn. (See Chapter 7 for direct-sowing large seeds.) Dusting seeds with fungicide before sowing is strongly recommended.

Mark out a furrow 25 mm deep and press the seeds into the soil 3–5 cm apart. For dwarf peas allow 40–50 cm between rows. For climbing peas, space seeds at the same distance against a fence or trellis on which the plants can climb. If making large sowings of climbing peas, allow 100 cm between rows. For the average family a 3–5 m row is sufficient for each sowing of dwarf peas. A smaller row of 1–3 m is usually ample for a sowing of climbing peas because they yield more pods over a longer period.

After sowing pea seeds, cover in the furrow with soil, tamp down and rake the bed. If seeds are pressed into 'dark damp' soil, no further watering is required until seedlings emerge. Too much moisture, especially in the first 36 hours after sowing, may do more harm than good (see Chapter 6). Birds can be a problem to emerging seedlings too. If you have bird trouble, cover the rows or the whole bed with pieces of wire netting or with black cotton thread stretched between short stakes. Remove these bird deterrents when the seedlings are 10 cm high. The birds have usually lost interest at this stage. Peas nearly always crop well without extra fertiliser while they grow. Yellow, stunted plants are more often the result of wet soil and poor drainage than lack of nutrients. If drainage is adequate and the plants still lack colour and vigour, apply a mixed fertiliser or give liquid feeds.

Climbing peas need support but dwarf peas yield better if their tendrils can cling to brush, twigs or wire netting. This keeps the bushes upright and the pods are easier to pick. For all pea crops, cultivate regularly (a day or two after watering) to destroy weeds. Plants can be slightly hilled at the same time. This discourages weeds close to the row and gives the stems more support. Pests and diseases of peas are usually not a problem. (See Chapter 6.)

Pick well-filled pods before any etching of veins shows on the surface. Pick peas every few days for high quality and to prolong flowering. Peas in the pod keep well in the refrigerator crisper for a week or two, or you can shell the peas, blanch them for one minute, package and freeze them.

There's nothing like the taste of fresh garden peas for bringing back memories of childhood.

Varieties

'Earlicrop Massey' is an early dwarf variety. It is ready to pick twelve to fourteen weeks from sowing. 'Greenfeast' is the main crop variety. It is rather taller and bears masses of pods from fourteen to sixteen weeks after sowing. 'Telephone' is the standard climbing variety. Pods are ready about the same time as 'Greenfeast' but plants bear for much longer (three to five weeks). 'Snow Pea' (Chinese pea) is an edible, podded variety. You can pick very young pods for cooking without shelling or you can slice them like beans. 'Snow Pea' is a climbing variety with white or purple flowers but there are dwarf varieties too. 'Sugarsnap' is an edible podded pea that has enjoyed wide acceptance. It is available as a vigorously growing, heavy cropping climber and produces delicious pods over a long period. Highly recommended.

POTATOES

Potatoes are warm-season plants and are very susceptible to frost. Severe frosts will kill the tops completely. In subtropical zones, providing the district is frost-free, potatoes can be grown all year round, but the most suitable months are January to August. In warm to mild temperate districts, most gardeners prefer to grow a spring crop of potatoes (planted July to September) and an autumn crop (planted January to February). In cold districts the planting season is restricted to warmer months only, from August to December. The time of spring sowings depends on late frosts and soil temperatures.

Potatoes are adaptable to light and heavy soils but good drainage is essential. They do best on friable soils with good crumb structure. Potatoes are grown from tubers and not from true seeds. Tubers (or seed potatoes) are available from nurseries and garden stores at planting time in spring. When buying seed potatoes, look for government-certified tubers as these are free of virus diseases. If you want to grow an autumn crop too, you can save some seed potatoes from healthy, high-yielding plants in your spring crop.

For planting, tubers should be 30–60 g in weight. Cut large tubers into chunky pieces with at least one eye or sprout on each. Do not rub the cut surface in ashes or similar material,

Hint

When growing kumara, avoid using nitrogenous fertilisers such as blood and bone, but make sure you apply sufficient potassium. Plant your runners in a warm, frost-free location, with well drained soil, to ensure a bumper crop.

RENE VAN TILBURG
YATES NEW ZEALAND

just let it dry out naturally. Spread tubers out in a shady spot for a week or two before planting. This allows the young sprouts to 'green' or harden. As a guide, a 3 kg bag of certified seed potatoes should provide 50–60 plants, which is sufficient for an average family.

Prepare the bed to spade depth well beforehand to have the soil in friable, 'dark damp', condition at planting. Mark out furrows 15 cm deep and 75 cm apart. Scatter fertiliser along the bottom of the furrow at

Seed potatoes should be planted about 30 cm apart.

Hint

The simplest way to cultivate pumpkins is to throw the seeds in the compost heap in early spring, then sit back and watch them grow for autumn harvest. All pumpkin varieties can be grown in this way.

PETER LINDROSS
YATES NEW ZEALAND

one-quarter of a cup per metre and cover with about 5 cm of soil from the sides. Place tubers 30–40 cm apart, cover with soil and rake the surface level. Sprouts emerge in 3–4 weeks.

Cultivate between rows to keep down weeds and gradually hill the plants to form a furrow between the rows. Hilling supports the plants, protects new potatoes from exposure to light and prevents them being attacked by caterpillars of potato moth (see Chapter 6). On level or slightly sloping beds, the furrow between rows can be used for irrigating. On well-prepared and fertilised soil, no extra fertiliser is needed, but water regularly to promote smooth, well-developed potatoes. It is possible to start digging 'new' potatoes about 3–4 weeks after plants have flowered and the lower leaves have turned yellow. If potatoes are to be stored, allow the tops to die off completely before digging. Discard any damaged or blemished potatoes and store in a cool, dry place, which must be dark to prevent the skin from 'greening'. Wooden crates, wire baskets or hessian sacks are good containers for storage.

PUMPKINS

Pumpkins are grown in the same way as cucumbers. Refer also to the Sowing Guide.

Most pumpkins have large running vines and may take up a lot of space. If you can, grow them in an odd corner where they can scramble over a fence or garden shed; this is an ideal place. Some varieties have smaller vines and are described as 'bush' pumpkins. These are excellent for small gardens. Generally, all pumpkins are harvested when the vine dies and the fruit stalk is dry and

brittle. Fruit is then fully mature with best flavour.

Mature fruit stores well for many months, although some varieties keep better than others. Store fruits in a cool, airy cupboard or in cardboard cartons. Fruit for storage must be free of blemishes or broken skin through which storage rots can invade. Inspect stored pumpkins periodically for signs of damage by rot, rats and mice.

Varieties

Of the large pumpkins, 'Queensland Blue' is an old favourite with green, turning grey, creased fruit and deep-orange flesh. It is a good, long-keeping variety. 'Jarrahdale' is a smoother, grey-skinned variety with deep-orange flesh. Its fruit is somewhat larger than 'Queensland Blue' but has a similar shape. The fruit quality is first class (it is not susceptible to bone – hard sections in the flesh), it cuts well, its flavour is sweet and it has good storage qualities. 'Crown Prince' is New Zealand's first true hybrid pumpkin. It is of medium size with a sweet taste that is vastly superior to the older traditional crown-type pumpkins. Thin skin and a small seed cavity leaves copious solid orange flesh. It has excellent storage qualities, lasting for up to ten months. 'Whanga Crown' is still a popular variety for its keeping qualities. It is a flat, rounded shape with thick pale-grey, slightly corrugated skin. The solid deep-orange flesh is dry and moderately sweet.

Of the smaller pumpkins, 'Butternut' has yellow, pear-shaped fruit 1–2 kg in weight and with deep-orange flesh. It grows well on a fence or trellis to save space. It is a good keeper if fully mature when picked. 'Buttercup' is a fine-quality summer and autumn variety. It matures early, after a growth period of about fourteen weeks. The fruit is very uniform in both shape and size. The flesh is firm, deep-orange, sweet and dry, with good flavour. It has a trailing habit but is not recommended for long-term keeping, with a maximum storage of two months.

'Little Dumpling' is one of the popular new miniature varieties of pumpkin. The fruit is the size of a large apple and is a soft, lime-green with attractive contrasting markings. The flesh is pale and has a sweet flavour. It is ideal for the small family. 'Little Dumpling' is ready to harvest in nine or ten weeks but, for winter storage, should be left on the vine until the stalk withers.

RADICCHIO

See Chicory.

RADISH

Radish can be successfully sown almost the year round in all climate zones. Successive sowings from early spring to late summer will give crisp roots for the salad season. Radish is one of the quickest and easiest crops to grow. Seeds germinate in five to eight days and roots are ready to harvest in six to eight weeks.

Sow seeds direct in a well-prepared bed as for carrots. Broadcast fertiliser or scatter in a band where seed is to be sown. Space rows 10–15 cm apart and tap out seeds in a furrow 6 mm deep. Cover seeds with seed-raising mix and water gently. Thin seedlings to 3–5 cm apart when they have grown their second leaf. Water regularly and give liquid feeds every seven to ten days. Mulch between rows to keep soil moist in hot weather. Make sowings every two to three weeks as required. A short row 50–100 cm long is usually sufficient for the average family. Start picking roots early because they get old and tough quickly. Roots keep well in the refrigerator crisper for a week or so.

Varieties

Radishes come in different shapes and sizes. 'French Breakfast' (red with white top) is tankard-shaped. 'Salad Crunch' is the best of the globe-shaped (turnip-rooted) varieties. 'Long Scarlet' and 'Long White Icicle' have tapering roots to 15 cm. All varieties are ideal for growing in pots and troughs. 'Gentle Giant' is a hybrid that grows to a large size (up to 6 cm) without becoming too stringy.

RHUBARB

Rhubarb, one of the few perennial vegetables, is best grown in a separate bed where it can be left undisturbed for three or four years. It tolerates shade and stems are usually longer when plants are grown in semi-shade. Rhubarb is adapted to all climate zones and a variety of soils but needs good drainage, regular watering and generous feeding.

Grow rhubarb from crowns or sets by dividing established plants in late winter or early spring. This way you can select the best-yielding plants with certainty. Rhubarb crowns or sets are usually available from nurseries during winter months.

When plants are established, apply a nitrogen fertiliser or liquid feeds every four or five weeks during the main growing season, from early spring to autumn. For the average family, twelve or fifteen well-grown plants will provide a good harvest. In winter each year, loosen soil around the plants and fork in compost or animal manure plus another ration of mixed fertiliser to give them a good start for spring growth.

Pick stalks (outside ones first) as required with a downward and sideways action so that they pull away cleanly from the crown. Always leave the youngest stalks in the centre of each plant to promote new growth. If flowering stems appear, cut these off at the base and apply a nitrogen fertiliser or liquid feeds to encourage more stalks and leaves. After picking, cut the leaves from stems. Do not use the leaves, as cases of rhubarb poisoning have been reported. Stalks keep well in the refrigerator crisper for a week or two but it is better to cook them immediately. Cooked rhubarb will keep well in sealed containers in the refrigerator and can be served chilled as required.

Note that rhubarb does not always develop red stems. Green stems are quite safe to eat and the flavour is just as good.

ROCK MELON

See Melons.

SALSIFY

Salsify, often referred to as oyster plant or vegetable oyster, is grown for its cream-coloured roots which are used in the same way as parsnips. It is not widely grown in New Zealand but is adapted to all climates. Time of sowing, soil preparation, fertilisation and cultivation are the same as for carrots or parsnips. Salsify roots are long and thin and ready to dig in about twenty weeks from sowing. Wash, boil and scrape roots before baking or frying. For those who like the flavour of this vegetable, a row 1–2 m is sufficient for one sowing.

SHALLOTS

Shallots or eschalots are a different species from spring onions or bunching onions, which are often referred to as shallots. True shallots are grown from bulblets or cloves like garlic. The 'mother' bulbs are usually planted 5–7 cm deep in autumn or early winter. Space plants 15–25 cm apart. As plants and 'daughter' bulbs develop, push soil around them to blanch the stems. Grow them quickly with generous feeding as for leeks or spring onions.

You can harvest plants as chopped leaves (like chives), as green onions for salads, or as dry bulbs (like garlic) for flavouring. Small bulblets or cloves can, of course, be replanted. If you start with a few plants, you can grow shallots for ever.

The recent introduction of Mediterranean shallots, bulb-forming shallots that are grown from seed, has helped these plants to become widely available to the home gardener.

SILVER BEET

Silver beet or Swiss chard is a close relative of beetroot, in fact, a variety of the same species. Silver beet, with its large crinkly leaves and white stalks, is an excellent, cut-and-come-again vegetable and is easy to grow in the home garden. It is adapted to all climate zones. In warm northern areas it is sown almost any month of the year; in temperate and cold districts from early spring to early autumn. Late autumn and winter sowings may run to seed. (See Sowing Guide for best months to sow.) Silver beet, like other leaf vegetables, needs well-drained soils with plenty of organic matter for good structure and generous feeding.

Silver beet can be raised as seedlings in boxes or punnets but direct sowing avoids double handling and transplant shock. After scattering pre-planting fertiliser in a band where seed is to be sown, tap out a few seeds in clumps or stations 30–40 cm apart. Soak seeds for a few hours and then dust seed with fungicide before sowing. Cover seeds with seed-raising mix 12 mm deep and water gently. Seedlings emerge in ten to fourteen days and can be thinned to the strongest when 10 cm high. For the average family, nine to twelve plants are sufficient for one sowing. You can have a year-round supply with two to three sowings between spring and autumn.

A healthy crop of silver beet growing happily with herbs.

Grow silver beet quickly, like lettuce, with regular watering and side dressings of a nitrogen-rich fertiliser or liquid feeds every two to three weeks. Cultivate to control weeds and mulch around plants in hot weather. Diseases and pests are not serious but leaf spot may be troublesome. (See Chapter 6 for control.)

Start picking outside stalks and leaves when large enough. Break them off at the base with a downward and sideways action. Always leave four or five centre stalks for quick regrowth. Cut off any flower stems that appear, but once flowering commences plants become unproductive very quickly. Silver beet keeps well in the refrigerator crisper for up to a week but for the best flavour, cook leaves immediately after picking. Silver beet, like lettuce, does not freeze well.

Varieties

'Fordhook Giant' has been selected over many years for quality and high yield to become the leading variety for home gardens and commercial growing. It has dark-green, blistered leaves and creamy-white stalks. 'Compact Slobolt' is a compact variety that can be sown all year round and resists going to seed. Novelty varieties are 'Rainbow Chard' with leaf stalks in purple, red, pink and yellow, and 'Red-Stemmed' with bright crimson stalks. Silver beet 'Perpetual Green' has smooth, spinach-like leaves on slender stalks. It can be harvested over a long period.

SPINACH

Spinach is a cool-season, short-day crop which tends to run to seed in warm weather with long days. For this reason it is most widely grown from the Waikato, south. Home gardeners in warmer northern areas prefer to grow the more adaptable silver beet as 'spinach'. In warm northern areas, sow spinach in winter months only. For temperate climates, sow from late summer to early winter. In cold climates, sow from late summer right through to early spring.

Sow seeds direct into well-prepared beds with plenty of organic matter plus mixed fertiliser added. Plants prefer well-drained fertile soil with good structure similar to that for lettuce. Sow a few seeds in clumps 30–40 cm apart, cover with seed-raising mix and water. Thin seedlings in each clump to the strongest. For the average family, twelve to fifteen plants are sufficient. Plants grow quickly so make successive sowings every three to four weeks for a continuous supply.

Like lettuce, spinach needs regular watering and side dressings of nitrogen fertiliser or liquid feeds every ten to fourteen days. A straw mulch tucked around each plant will keep the leaves free of dirt. Major pests are leaf miners and mites. (See Chapter 6 for control.)

When plants are large enough, pick outside leaves individually like silver beet. Each plant will keep producing for about four weeks or so. Leaves keep well in the refrigerator crisper for up to a week but are best cooked immediately after picking. Like lettuce and silver beet, spinach leaves tend to collapse when frozen.

Varieties

Hybrid varieties have largely replaced open-pollinated varieties. 'English Hybrid' or 'Winter Hybrid', is the most widely grown variety. It has rather upright, plain, medium green leaves with excellent flavour. 'Winter Queen' and 'Summer Supreme' both have large leaves with a sweet flavour. 'Summer Supreme' is more heat tolerant. 'Native Spinach' (*Tetragonia expansa*) is a drought-resistant native vegetable that is long-lived and can be harvested for months. See New Zealand Spinach.

SQUASH

Squash is another warm-season vine crop grown in the same way as cucumber. Refer also to the Sowing Guide.

Varieties

There are two types of squash. Summer squash are picked when immature, like cucumbers or marrows. Winter squash are picked when fully mature, like pumpkins, and keep well in storage. Both types are, of course, grown during the spring, summer, autumn period.

'Early White Bush' is the most widely known variety of summer squash. The fruits are round, 15 cm in diameter with scalloped edges. Both skin and flesh are creamy-white.

Each fruit weighs 1–1.5 kg. 'Green Buttons Hybrid' is a recent introduction. It has lime-green fruits with scalloped edges. They are best picked when 5–10 cm in diameter. Pick regularly to encourage further flowers and fruit. 'Green Buttons Hybrid' can be grown in a large pot or tub about 40 cm in diameter and the same depth. An interesting mixture can be found in 'Sweet 'n' Kwik', which contains a selection of summer squash.

Of the winter squash, 'Green Warted Hubbard' is a running vine with round, dark green fruit with pointed edges. The fruit weighs about 5 kg and contains deep-orange flesh. 'Table Queen' (acorn squash) has a smaller grey-green, pear-shaped fruit to 1 kg in weight. Both varieties of winter squash are good keepers but are not as widely grown as they used to be.

SWEDES AND TURNIPS

Swedes and turnips are cool-season root crops which are grouped together because their climatic requirements and cultivation are almost identical. Both vegetables can be grown in all climate zones. In all climates, sowing takes place in late summer and autumn, but in cold districts both swedes and turnips can be sown in late winter or early spring as well (see Sowing Guide for best months to sow in each zone). Swedes take three to four months to grow and have large roots with yellow or buff-coloured flesh. The roots store well. Turnips take less time (ten to twelve weeks) to grow, have smaller globe-shaped roots with white flesh. Turnips do not store as well as swedes.

Prepare the soil well for direct sowing in the same way as for carrots. Both crops respond to liberal quantities of organic matter and a scattering of pre-planting fertiliser in a band where seed is to be sown. Mark out shallow drills 6 mm deep and 20–30 cm apart. Tap out seeds thinly along the drill, four to five seeds to each 5 cm, cover with seed-raising mix and water gently. Seedlings emerge in six to ten days, depending on temperature. Thin seedlings of both crops to 7–10 cm apart. For the average family, a 3–5 m row is sufficient at each sowing. Make successive sowings every three or four weeks.

Water regularly and if plants are backward, give side dressings of nitrogen fertiliser or liquid feeds. Cultivate between rows to keep down weeds but do not hill the plants. The roots are really swollen stems which sit on the soil surface, not below it. Control caterpillars and aphids as for other crops of the cabbage group. (See Chapter 6.)

Start harvesting early for best quality and to give the remaining roots more space to grow. Dig all roots before they become coarse and stringy. Swedes store better than turnips at normal temperatures but both keep well in the refrigerator crisper for eight to ten weeks.

Varieties

Best variety of swede is 'Champion Purple Top'. 'Purple Top White Globe' is the most popular turnip.

SWEET CORN

Sweet corn is a very popular vegetable, looks good in the garden and is easy to grow. Home-grown cobs are much tastier than the ones you buy, so if you like sweet corn it is worth the bit of extra space. A warm-season crop, sweet corn is adapted to all climates. In warm temperate and temperate climates, you can sow from August to January and in cold climates from October to December. Sweet corn grows well on both light and heavy soils, providing drainage and soil structure are good. Plenty of fertiliser and water are needed for a bumper crop.

Prepare soil well with organic matter added to have the bed in friable damp condition for direct sowing. It is best to grow sweet corn in a block of short rows rather than one long row. This way pollen from the male flowers or tassels at the top of the plants have the best chance of falling on the female flowers or silks halfway up the stems. You can grow three rows spaced 50–60 cm apart in a bed 150 cm wide.

Apply the pre-planting fertiliser in furrows where each row is to be sown so that seed is not in direct contact. It is best to dust seed with fungicide before sowing to protect against damping off. Mark out the seed furrow 25 mm deep and press seeds into 'dark damp' soil. Space seeds 15 cm apart. This allows for some misses when seedlings are thinned to 20–30 cm apart. Another method is to sow two seeds close together, with 30 cm between each pair, and thin to

GARDENING FOR THE KITCHEN

one seedling. Cover seeds with soil, tamp down, rake the bed and scatter a light compost mulch on the surface. If seed is sown in 'dark damp' soil seedlings will emerge without further watering. Scatter snail baits to protect seedlings from slugs and snails. For the average family, a sowing of three rows 2 m long will provide 20–24 plants after thinning out. Make the next sowing when the previous plants are 15–20 cm tall.

After thinning, scatter a side dressing of nitrogen fertiliser around each plant. Repeat this treatment when the tassel first appears between the top leaves. Regular watering is needed while the crops grow, especially in hot weather. A good soaking to field capacity once or twice a week is better than a light sprinkle every day. Cultivate between rows to control weeds and draw soil around the stems to hill the plants at the same time. Corn earworm and aphids are serious pests. (See Chapter 6 for control.) When tassels open out fully they are ready to shed pollen. Overhead watering in the early morning will create a humid atmosphere in the crop to promote good pollination of the silks. Pollen is shed, usually about mid-morning, for several days.

Cobs must be harvested at the right time. They are ready to pick when the silks have turned brown and cobs stand out from the stem at about a 30 degree angle. Make a further check by pulling open the husk from the top and pressing the grains with your thumb nail. If grain is soft and exudes juice with a creamy consistency, the cob is ready to pick. In over-ripe cobs, sugar quickly turns to starch and the grains are tough and doughy. Pick cobs with a downward and twisting action.

For top quality, remove husks and cook as soon as possible. Water must be boiling before cobs are put in saucepan. Cobs in-the-husk keep well in the refrigerator crisper for three or four days. To freeze corn on the cob, remove the husks, blanch the cobs for eight minutes, cool quickly and package each cob separately. For corn off the cob, blanch cobs for five minutes only, cool quickly, cut grains from cob, package and freeze.

Varieties

Most are now F1 hybrids, the older strains having been replaced by the superior high-yielding varieties such as 'Earlychief Hybrid' and 'Honeysweet'. 'Honeysweet' has attractive yellow kernels, extremely sweet, and a superb flavour. 'Earlychief' is a strong grower with good quality, even cobs. 'Sun'n'Snow' has white and yellow kernels on cobs of exquisite flavour and sweetness. 'Popcorn' is different from sweet corn but it is grown in the same way. The cobs are harvested when the grain is hard and fully mature. The very high starch content in the grains makes them explode or 'pop' when heated.

TOMATOES

In a popularity poll for home-grown vegetables, tomatoes would top the list. Tomatoes give a higher yield for space occupied than any other vegetable. A good average yield is 3–5 kg per plant but when well grown, each plant can yield 10 kg of fruit or more.

Hint

Basil is not only a great companion for tomatoes on your plate, they also work well together in the garden. Growing basil amongst your tomato plants will enhance the flavour of the fruit, and it seems to result in healthier crops of both plants. Pinch out growing tips when flowers appear to keep basil plants bushy and in full leaf.

JENNY WHITE
HORTICULTURALIST

Tomatoes are warm-season, frost-susceptible plants which need a growing season of about three months, so they are adapted to all areas of New Zealand. In frost-free, warm northern areas, tomatoes are grown throughout the year. In temperate climates the best months to start tomatoes are August to December and in cold districts September to November. In mild districts, an early crop (August sowing) and a late crop (November sowing) will supply tomatoes for about five months of the year (mid-December to mid-April).

Tomatoes grow well on light and heavy soils but the usual rules for vegetable soils apply: good drainage, organic matter for soil structure and adequate water and fertiliser. Phosphorus is a most important nutrient for tomatoes, and lack of it, especially in the seedling stage, will reduce yields of fruit. Nitrogen is needed too but not in excessive quantities as for leaf vegetables.

Seeds can be sown direct (especially for the late crop) but it is more usual to raise seedlings in boxes or punnets for transplanting. Seedlings for the early crop can be pricked out into 10 cm plastic pots and grown on for several weeks in a warm sunny spot. If the garden bed is not ready, transfer the seedlings to 15–20 cm pots. Spacing plants is an important consideration. For tall, staking tomatoes, set seedlings 50–60 cm apart each way. This relatively close spacing (much closer than commercial crops) gives quite enough light to each plant, but plenty of watering and fertiliser is needed. For an average family, twelve to fifteen plants are sufficient for one sowing. Cultivate around plants and between rows to destroy weeds. On flat or sloping beds you can make furrows between the rows for furrow irrigation. This is a useful method as many leaf spot and leaf blight diseases are spread by overhead watering.

With adequate base fertiliser (in seed bed soil or applied before direct sowing) extra fertiliser is not needed until plants have set their first truss of fruit. At this stage, scatter a tablespoon of mixed fertiliser around each plant and water in. Repeat treatment every four to five weeks as plants grow. Water regularly to field capacity, weekly when plants are small, but increase this to twice a week when plants are carrying a heavy crop.

Most tomatoes are grown on stakes about 2 m in length. Hammer stakes into the soil 5 cm from stem of plants after transplanting. Plants are pruned to two leaders (main stems), which are tied to the stakes. Break off laterals (which grow from leaf axils) with a sideways twist when small, or cut with a sharp knife when larger. The lateral to select

TOP FIVE TOMATOES

'GROSSE LISSE'

The name means 'large smooth' and these tomatoes are just that: perfect balls of bright red with a much-loved flavour.

'SWEET 100'

Miniature tomatoes hang like bunches of grapes from the stems of this easily grown variety. 'Sweet 100' seems to be pest and disease free.

'SUMMERTASTE'

Although it will grow anywhere, this Australian-bred tomato, because of its disease resistance, is a particularly good choice for warmer climates.

'ROMA'

The traditional egg tomato is a favourite for cooking and sauce making.

'TINY TIM'

Number one choice for pots, 'Tiny Tim' has compact growth that doesn't need staking. The fruit is yummy, but also ornamental.

'SWEET 100'

'ROMA'

'Grosse Lisse' is a favourite tomato.

for the second leader is the one immediately below the first flower truss. This lateral is more vigorous than others. Tie the leaders to the stake with garden twine just above a leaf stalk to stop it from slipping down the stem. Ties should be about 30 cm part. Make a figure–8 tie which allows the leader to increase in size. Take care that flower trusses are not squeezed between leader and stake. Carefully twist the leader so that each truss faces outwards.

Diseases and pests can be a problem with tomatoes. Tomato fruit worm is the worst pest and must be controlled. (See Chapter 6.)

For top quality fruit, pick when red ripe, although slightly coloured fruit ripens well indoors. Fruit keeps well in the refrigerator for one or two weeks (ripe) or four or five weeks (green). Fresh tomatoes cannot be snap frozen. Preserve them by bottling or cook them and then package for freezing.

There are more varieties of tomatoes than any other vegetable crop. This reflects their world-wide popularity and emphasises the many different types available for selection and breeding.

Varieties – large and medium
'Grosse Lisse', released over fifty years ago, is still the most popular garden variety. It is mid-season in maturity with medium to large globe-shaped fruits. 'Big Beef' is an improved strain of the very old and popular 'Beefsteak'. It has the wonderful 'Beefsteak' flavour with medium to large, thick-skinned fruit and increased disease resistance. One slice will cover a whole sandwich!

'Moneymaker' is another old favourite and still one of the most popular varieties today. It is a tall, vigorous grower with masses of medium-sized fruit. 'Summertaste' is an Australian-developed variety which is resistant to bacterial wilt and has good flavour. It is an excellent choice for warmer areas but will grow happily in a wide climate range.

'Roma' is an egg tomato with a slightly 'pear-like' shape. Although it can be used in salads, 'Roma' is most popular for cooking, saucing and soups.

Varieties – small
'Sweet 100' has prolific clusters of cherry-sized fruit. It is best grown on a sunny fence where the plant receives some support. 'Tiny Tim' is a true mini-tomato. Plants grow to 30–40 cm tall and bear masses of bite-sized fruit. This variety is ideal for growing in large pots or tubs, but don't forget to give it lots of water in hot weather.

SOLVING PROBLEMS WITH TOMATOES

PROBLEM	CAUSE	SOLUTION
Split fruit	Heavy watering or rain after soil has been dry	Water regularly through dry periods
Blossom drop	Low temperatures in spring or very high temperatures in summer	Grow a variety suited to the season e.g. 'Grosse Lisse' for early or late crops
Sun scald – papery brown patches on fruit	Exposure to bright sunlight	Do not remove too many old leaves at once
Blossom end rot – bottom of fruit sunken, leathery and blackened	Lack of calcium, together with irregular watering	Lime, water daily
Blotchy ripening – parts of fruit remain yellow or orange	Too much heat, too little potash	Add potash
Misshapen fruit	Poor pollination caused by cold weather at flowering or very high temperature. Also virus diseases	Apply Thrive plant food
Rolling of older leaves	Excess deleafing or a wide variation between day and night temperatures	Maintain leaf cover
Yellowing between veins beginning with lower leaves	Magnesium deficiency. Can also be nitrogen and potash deficiency	Apply Thrive
Insects clustered on young shoots	Aphids	Mavrik or Liquid Tomato Spray
Tiny white insects on underside of leaves which fly when disturbed	White fly	Mavrik, Target
Small caterpillar tunnel holes in fruit	Tomato fruit worm	Mavrik, Liquid Tomato Spray
Leaves become yellow (mottled) and deydrated in hot, dry weather especially in glasshouses. Minute insects under leaves	Mites	Mite Killer or Mavrik
Irregular green/brown or black patches on leaves spreading rapidly in wet weather.	Late blight	Champion Copper or Bravo

PROBLEM	CAUSE	SOLUTION
Small spots on older leaves increasing to 1 cm. Common in hot humid weather.	Early blight	Champion Copper or Bravo
Leaves yellow and wilt, followed by total collapse of the plant.	Verticillium wilt	Do not grow in same area more than one year in three.
Leaves pale and stunted, blackening of stems, followed by stunting and death.	Bacterial wilt	Destroy plants. If severe, grow future plants in a new area.
Plants suddenly stop growing and tops become yellow/purplish and bunched.	Spotted wilt virus	Destroy plants.

TURNIPS
See Swedes and Turnips.

VINE CROPS
See Choko, Cucumbers, Marrows, Melons, Pumpkin and Squash.

WATERMELON
See Melons.

ZUCCHINI
The best home garden varieties of marrows are zucchinis. Culture is the same as for marrows but the fruit is picked when immature. Zucchinis should be regularly harvested when small to encourage continuous cropping.

Varieties
'Blackjack' hybrid zucchini is a prolific bush variety with very dark-green fruit. Fruit can be picked at almost any size but most people prefer them about 15 cm long. 'Greyzini' is another excellent bush variety. It is similar to 'Blackjack' but fruits have grey-green, mottled skin. 'Golden' zucchini hybrid is a yellow-skinned variety. All can be grown in a tub on terrace or patio. Lebanese zucchini, which spreads slightly more than 'Blackjack', carries tear-shaped light-coloured fruit in great quantities. Easy and quick to grow.

ASIAN VEGETABLES
In addition to the popular Chinese cabbage and Chinese snow peas there is a wide variety of vegetables grown in Asia. Around them much of the specialised regional cooking has developed. Many of these vegetables are not commonly available in New Zealand so we have selected for description those few varieties whose seed supply is easily accessible.

Varieties
'Chinese Broccoli Kailaan' produces much smaller heads than common broccoli and is used, stem and all, when the flowers start opening. The plants are very heat tolerant.

Cabbage 'Michili' is upright growing to about 50 cm, with cylindrical firm heads weighing about 1.5 kg. The delicate flavour is much favoured in Asian cuisines.

Radish 'Daikon Long White' is widely used in Asian cooking and particularly in Japanese-style dishes. Grows easily from seed, and is ready for picking seven weeks from sowing. Its growing conditions are the same as for as other radishes.

Tatsoi is a versatile vegetable served cooked or in salads. Excellent flavour. The deep-green, spoon-shaped leaves of this vegetable are produced in profusion. For cultivation directions, treat as lettuce: ample water and regular applications of a nitrogenous soluble fertiliser such as Thrive. Pick young for best flavour.

Turnip 'Hakurei' is an economical vegetable, as both the root and leaves may be used. The root is white-skinned with crisp sweet flesh, excellent for salads, soups or stir-frying. Use the leaves in the same way as you would use Chinese cabbage.

All these vegetables are best grown from seed sown in summer and autumn in cool or temperate climates, or all year round in the subtropics.

Pot men guard the vegetable patch in the Hunterville garden 'Rathmoy'.

GARDENING FOR THE KITCHEN

SOWING GUIDE FOR VEGETABLES

VEGETABLES	TEMPERATE												COLD											
	J	F	M	A	M	J	J	A	S	O	N	D	J	F	M	A	M	J	J	A	S	O	N	D
Artichokes (suckers)			•	•	•	•	•	•												•	•	•	•	
Asparagus (2yr crowns)					•	•												•	•					
Beans (dwarf)	•	•				•	•	•	•	•												•	•	•
Beans (climbing)	•					•	•	•	•													•	•	•
Beetroots	•	•	•			•	•	•	•	•	•		•	•							•	•	•	•
Broad beans				•	•	•	•											•	•			•	•	
Broccoli	•	•	•	•	•				•	•	•												•	•
Brussels sprouts	•	•	•						•	•	•											•	•	•
Cabbages	•	•	•	•		•	•	•	•	•	•	•	•	•	•						•	•	•	•
Cape gooseberry						•	•	•	•	•												•	•	•
Capsicums (Peppers)						•	•	•	•	•												•	•	•
Carrots	•	•	•			•	•	•	•	•	•		•	•							•	•	•	•
Cauliflowers	•	•	•						•	•													•	•
Celery	•	•				•	•	•	•	•											•	•	•	•
Chicory	•	•	•			•	•	•	•	•	•		•	•							•	•	•	•
Chinese cabbages	•	•	•	•		•	•	•	•	•	•	•	•	•							•	•	•	•
Choko (see Note 1)						•	•	•							Not Suitable									
Cress	•	•	•	•	•	•	•	•	•	•	•	•	•	•	•	•	•	•	•	•	•	•	•	•
Cucumbers (see Note 3)	•					•	•	•	•													•	•	•
Eggplants						•	•	•	•														•	•
Endive	•	•	•			•	•	•	•	•	•	•									•	•	•	•
Herbs (see Note 4)	•	•	•	•		•	•	•	•	•	•	•	•	•	•						•	•	•	•
Kohlrabi	•	•	•			•	•	•					•	•	•						•	•	•	

Note 1 – Usually grown on fence or trellis.
Note 2 – Make successive sowings as required.

SOWING METHOD BED (S) DIRECT (D)	SOWING DEPTH (MM)	SEEDLING EMERGE (DAYS)	SOW AND THIN OR TRANSPLANT TO ... CM APART		TIME TO PICKING (WEEKS)	QUANTITY FOR FAMILY OF FOUR PLANTS (P) LENGTH (M)
			ROWS	PLANTS		
D	150	–	100	100	20–28	3–5p
D	150–200	–	100	30–50	16–24	20–25p
D	25	7–10	50–60	7–10	8–10	3–5m
D	25	7–10	100	10–15	10–12	2–3m
D	12	10–14	20–30	7–10	10–12	2–3m
D	50	10–14	60–75	15–20	18–20	5–6m
S or D	6	6–10	45–60	45–60	12–16	9–12p
S or D	6	6–10	60–75	60–75	16–20	6–9p
S or D	6	6–10	40–75	40–75	8–16	9–12p
S	6	14–28	100	100	20–24	2–3p
S or D	6	10–14	50–60	50–60	10–16	4–6p
D	6	10–21	20–30	3–5	12–16	4–6m
S or D	6	6–10	50–75	50–75	14–26	9–12p
S	6	14–21	30–40	30–40	20–22	16–20p
D	12	10–14	20–30	3–5	16–20	1–2m
D	6	6–10	30–40	30–40	8–10	6–9p
D	50–75	–	–	100	18–20	1–3p
D	6	6–10	Sow seeds in garden		4–6	(see Note 2)
D	12	6–10	100	40–50	8–12	4–6p
S or D	6	10–14	60–75	60–75	14–16	4–6p
S or D	6	10–14	20–30	20–30	8–12	6–9p
S or D	6	6-28	Sow seeds in pots or garden		12–20	(see Note 2)
D	6	6–10	30–40	10–15	8–10	1–2m

ote 3 – Early plants can be raised in punnets or pots.
ote 4 – Many herbs are perennials and will grow for several years.

GARDENING FOR THE KITCHEN

VEGETABLES	TEMPERATE												COLD											
	J	F	M	A	M	J	J	A	S	O	N	D	J	F	M	A	M	J	J	A	S	O	N	D
Kumara									•	•	•		Not suitable											
Leeks	•	•	•	•					•	•	•	•	•	•	•							•	•	•
Lettuces	•	•	•	•	•	•	•	•	•	•	•	•	•	•	•	•	•	•	•	•	•	•	•	•
Marrows (see Note 3)	•								•	•	•	•										•	•	•
Melons (see Note 3)									•	•	•	•										•	•	•
Mustard	•	•	•	•	•	•	•		•	•	•	•	•	•	•	•	•	•	•		•	•	•	•
New Zealand spinach	•	•						•	•	•	•	•	•									•	•	•
Okra									•	•	•	•										•	•	•
Onions			•	•	•	•	•	•												•	•	•	•	•
Onions (spring)	•	•	•	•	•	•			•	•	•	•	•	•	•	•					•	•	•
Parsnips	•	•	•					•	•	•	•	•	•	•							•	•	•	•
Peas (dwarf)			•	•	•	•	•	•	•												•	•	•	•
Peas (climbing)			•	•	•	•	•	•	•												•	•	•	•
Potatoes (tubers)	•	•					•	•	•													•	•	•
Pumpkins (see Note 3)								•	•	•	•											•	•	•
Radishes	•	•	•					•	•	•	•	•	•	•	•	•					•	•	•	•
Rhubarb (seed)								•	•	•	•											•	•	•
Rhubarb (crowns)	•	•			•	•	•	•	•	•	•	•	•	•							•	•	•	•
Salsify	•	•	•				•	•	•	•	•	•	•	•							•	•	•	•
Shallots (bulbs)			•	•	•	•	•						•	•	•	•	•							
Silver beet	•	•	•				•	•	•	•	•	•	•	•							•	•	•	•
Spinach			•	•	•	•	•								•	•	•	•	•	•	•			
Squashes (see Note 3)								•	•	•	•											•	•	•
Swedes	•	•	•										•	•							•	•		
Sweet Corn	•						•	•	•	•	•	•										•	•	•
Tomatoes							•	•	•	•	•	•										•	•	•
Turnips	•	•	•	•									•	•	•				•	•	•	•		
Zucchinis	•						•	•	•	•												•	•	•

Note 1 – Usually grown on fence or trellis.
Note 2 – Make successive sowings as required.

SOWING METHOD BED (S) DIRECT (D)	SOWING DEPTH (MM)	SEEDLING EMERGE (DAYS)	SOW AND THIN OR TRANSPLANT TO ... CM APART ROWS	PLANTS	TIME TO PICKING (WEEKS)	QUANTITY FOR FAMILY OF FOUR PLANTS (P) LENGTH (M)
D	50–70	–	100	40–50	18–20	18–24p
S	6	10–14	15–20	15–20	12–20	40–50p
S or D	6	6–7	20–30	20–30	8–12	9–12p
D	20	6–10	100	100	8–14	3–6p
D	20	6–10	150	100	14–16	2–3p
D	6	6–10	Sow seeds in pots or garden		4–6	(see Note 2)
D	2	7–21	80	50	8	4–6p
S or D	6	10–14	100	50–60	16–20	4–5p
S or D	6	10–14	20–30	7–10	24–32	4–6m
D	6	10–14	5–10	1–2	8–12	0.5–1m
D	6	21–28	30–40	5–7	18–20	3–5m
D	25	7–10	40–50	3–5	12–16	3–5m
D	25	7–10	100	3–5	14–16	1–3m
D	100–150	–	60–75	30–40	16–20	50–60p
D	20	6–10	100	100	14–16	3–6p
D	6	5–8	10–15	3–5	6–8	0.5–1m
S or D	12	10–21	40–50	40–50	16–20	12–15p
D	80–100	–	40–50	40–50	8–12	12–15p
D	6	10–14	30–40	5–7	20–22	1–2m
D	50–75	–	15–25	15–25	12–14	6–9p
S or D	12	10–14	30–40	30–40	8–12	9–12p
D	12	14-21	30–40	30–40	8–10	12–15p
D	20	6–10	100	100	12–14	4–6p
D	6	6–10	20–30	7–10	12–16	3–5m
D	25	6–10	50–60	20–30	12–16	20–24p
S or D	6	10–14	50-60	50–60	12–20	12–15p
D	6	6-10	20–30	7–10	10–12	3–5m
D	20	6–10	100	100	8–14	3–6p

Note 3 – Early plants can be raised in punnets or pots.
Note 4 – Many herbs are perennials and will grow for several years.

CHAPTER 19

HERBS

For gardeners, growing herbs is a rewarding experience. Herbs may be grown primarily for their fragrance or for their value in cooking, and even for their historical associations. Many herbs are regarded as practical medicinal remedies and a browse through old books will clearly show that a great deal of them were once used for these purposes.

Today there are hundreds of herbs that are being cultivated for medicinal or culinary uses in different parts of the world. This chapter will concentrate on the commonly available varieties, so if you want to learn about some of the more unusual herbs you will probably need to consult one of the excellent specialist books.

For thousands of years herbs have been used for medicine throughout the world and today the research into medicinal herbs is on the increase. Before the days of refrigeration and the wide availability of food in many forms, herbs played an essential part in the preservation and flavouring of foods. However, the major use for herbs in contemporary society is flavouring and garnishing food.

In recent years, there has been a resurgence of interest in the use of herbs for flavouring food. Today the most commonly used herbs are basil, chives, garlic, parsley, thyme, marjoram, sage and mint, but coriander, dill, horseradish, hyssop, oregano, rosemary and tarragon are also frequently used and are readily available.

CULTIVATION

Most herbs need a friable, well-drained soil and enjoy full sunlight, but a few grow well in partial shade.

Herbs may be grown in a separate, designated garden, but many of the smaller varieties can be grown as rockery plants or as borders to flower gardens. All but the very tall herbs can be grown in pots, tubs, or troughs. However, small containers are really not suitable for most herbs. Herbs grown in pots will benefit from an application of liquid fertiliser as they grow, but, once established, most herbs need only minimal care.

Harvest fresh herbs as required. For drying, cut off stems when the plants are well grown, tie them with string and hang them upside down to dry in a shady place. When completely dry, store the leaves and stems, uncrushed or crushed, in air-tight bottles or jars. Many herbs (such as parsley) can be preserved by lightly washing, shaking off the excess water, and then wrapping in plastic wrap before freezing.

Here are some brief notes on the most popular kinds of herbs.

ALOE (*ALOE VERA*)

This is a succulent perennial, with fleshy leaves that contain a bitter yellow juice used as a balm for insect bites and sunburn, and extensively in cosmetics. The sap is an ingredient in the manufacture of the drink additive known as bitters and in medications to discourage nail biting in children. The thick, leathery, strap-like green leaves grow to a length of between 20 and 60 cm and are usually edged with spines. When young the leaves are dotted with white spots. A semi-desert plant, it is quite low maintenance and can be grown outdoors in frost-free areas, or indoors, or in a pot on a terrace or patio. Propagate by detaching the small, rooted suckers that come up around the base of the plant, and planting them in pots of a light sandy, well-drained mixture.

Aloe vera can be easily propagated by detaching small suckers.

ANGELICA
(ANGELICA ARCHANGELICA)

This herb stands 1.5–2.4 m tall. It is a biennial with bright-green serrated leaves and branching hollow stems, and a celery-like texture. The hollow stems and stalks may be crystallised and used for decorating cakes and pastry, whilst the leaves may be added to salads. A tea can be made from either the leaves, stems, seeds, or the dried roots. It is raised from seeds.

BASIL OR SWEET BASIL
(OCIMUM BASILUM)

This is an attractive annual plant, up to 40 cm tall, with shiny oval leaves and white flowers. It prefers full sun but tolerates semi-shade. Basil is a useful border plant and grows well in pots or tubs. Leaves have a clove-like flavour and can be used fresh or dried. Sow seeds in spring and space plants 20 cm apart. There are several ornamental cultivars available. These are mainly grown for their colourful foliage.

BAY TREE (LAURUS NOBILIS)

This is a large evergreen, slow-growing tree to about 12 m. It is the laurel tree of ancient Greece and Rome. Bay trees have glossy, dark-green leaves which are narrow and about 4 cm long. The leaves are used extensively in many different types of cooking. Propagation is by seed or cuttings.

BORAGE (BORAGO OFFICINALIS)

An annual herb that grows up to 60–90 cm, with purple-blue flowers, its leaves and flowers are used for flavouring soups and stews. Sow seeds in spring and summer and space plants about 30 cm apart.

CARAWAY (CARUM CARVI)

A 60 cm biennial, requiring a sheltered, sunny position, it has finely cut frond-like foliage with white flowers in summer. Caraway is most often grown for its seeds which contribute a licorice-like flavour to many dishes. To harvest caraway seeds, cut the seed heads off in late summer as soon as the seeds turn brown. Do not leave them on the plant until they are thoroughly dry. Otherwise, they will scatter.

CATMINT (NEPETA CATARIA)

Noted for the way its leaves and blossoms attract cats, the leaves of this lemony, mint-scented herb are used for brewing tea and for flavouring meats and salads. This hardy perennial grows to 60–90 cm and features 5 cm long, heart-shaped, grey-green leaves with downy grey undersides. The flowers may be pale pink or white. Catmint flower spikes attract bees. Seed may be sown where the plants are to grow, or plants can be started from root divisions in the spring. The lower growing *Nepeta* X *faasenii*, with smaller grey leaves and mauve flowers is usually grown as an ornamental.

CHAMOMILE
(*ANTHEMIS NOBILIS*)

This is an ancient herb and a traditional ground cover for around the garden paths and walks. The flowers may be used to flavour dry sherry, and a tea may be brewed from the blossoms. The whole plant has a pleasantly pungent fragrance, and the dried flower heads are quite popular in hot tisanes for the relief of head colds. Chamomile oil is used for cosmetic purposes such as soaps and in body lotions. Grow from seeds or cuttings.

CHERVIL
(*ANTHRISCUS CEREFOLIUM*)

One of the classic fine herbs of French cooking, chervil will grow for eighteen months or more under good conditions. Plants grow to 30–60 cm tall and the divided parsley-like leaves have a mild aniseed flavour. Chervil grows well in partial shade and prefers a moist position. It loses its delicate flavour quickly when cooked and should only be added finely chopped to soups and sauces at the very last minute. It is ideal to add piquancy to salads, fresh vegetables and salad dressings. Chervil does not dry well. Sow seed in spring, summer or early autumn, spacing plants 30 cm apart.

CHIVES
(*ALLIUM SCHOENOPRASUM*)

Close relative of onions, shallots and garlic, chives are perennial plants which grow in grass-like clumps about 20–30 cm tall. They grow well in sun or semi-shade and are ideal plants for pot culture, probably in a relatively large pot (say about 30 cm diameter). Sow seeds in spring, summer or early autumn, spacing the clumps about 30 cm apart, or in rows with plants 10 cm apart. New plants can be started by dividing clumps if they become overcrowded. The chopped leaves are useful in salads, soups, and egg dishes.

TOP FIVE CULINARY HERBS

BAY

Use a whole, fresh bay leaf to flavour cooked dishes, but remember to remove it before serving. Bay trees are hardy ornamentals, especially for containers.

BASIL

Basil is a summer-growing annual. It's also reputed to function as an effective companion plant for tomatoes, repelling white fly and other insect pests.

CORIANDER

Use the leaves or seeds of coriander, according to your cooking styles. Coriander is one of the most cosmopolitan of herbs.

MINT

Mint loves a cool, moist spot and can become a pest if conditions are too much to its liking. Use mint in drinks and food for its fresh flavour.

PARSLEY

Legend says that you have to be wicked to be able to grow parsley successfully. The plants have a disconcerting habit of disappearing from the garden just when you think they're established for good. Replace on a regular basis.

BAY

BASIL

MINT

GARDENING FOR THE KITCHEN

Flat-leafed garlic chives (*Allium tuberosum*) have a mild garlic flavour. They are very hardy and will tolerate more neglect than common chives.

CORIANDER OR CHINESE PARSLEY (*CORIANDRUM SATIVUM*)

This is one of the ancient herbs and has been used for many hundreds of years in cooking and in medicine. An annual, it reaches about 40 cm tall and prefers a full sun situation but will tolerate partial shade. Sow the seed in spring, summer or early autumn and space the plants about 20 cm apart. The parsley-like leaves have a sharp taste and the mature seeds are used for flavouring salads, bread and confectionery. Heat and long days will cause coriander plants to go to seed, so if you are growing them for their leaves it is best to grow when conditions are milder.

CRESS AND MUSTARD (*LEPIDIUM SATIVUM* AND *BRASSICA ALBA*)

Garden cress and mustard greens make tasty additions to salads and are used for sandwiches and garnishes. They are grown in all climate zones and seed can be sown at any time of the year. Seeds are best sown in separate boxes, pots or punnets. Prepare a good seed-raising soil plus a mixed fertiliser as described in Chapter 7. Broadcast the seed freely on the surface to have plants spaced 1–2 cm apart. Cover seed lightly with compost or seed-raising mix and water gently. Keep damp until the seedlings emerge, usually in six to ten days, but often less in warm weather. Thinning is seldom necessary. Plants are ready to harvest in about four weeks' time but may take longer in the cooler months of the year. When plants are 10–15 cm tall, cut them with scissors just above ground level. Sow successively for a continuous supply.

An extract from Echinacea *(see Rudbeckia p. 186) is used for medicinal purposes.*

The crunchy, swollen base of Florence fennel with its aniseed flavour can be lightly cooked or used raw in salads.

Watercress, a close relative of nasturtium, grows in running streams. You can grow it in pots standing in water, placed in the shade. It is a perennial plant and is started from cuttings, root divisions or seed.

American or land cress is another cress. It prefers damp, shady conditions, but plants or seed may be difficult to obtain.

DILL (ANETHUM GRAVEOLENS)

A hardy, annual herb to 90 cm tall with light-green, feathery leaves and umbrella-shaped flower heads, it prefers full sun but will accept light shade. Sow seeds direct in spring or early summer in clumps spaced 30 cm apart. The leaves have a pungent, bitter-sweet taste. The seed can also be used for flavouring.

FENNEL (FOENICULUM VULGARE)

A perennial herb, and one of the oldest known culinary herbs, fennel is usually grown as an annual. Plants resemble those of dill but are taller and coarser. Sow seeds direct in spring or early summer, spacing plants 50–60 cm apart. Both leaves and seeds have an aniseed flavour.

Florence fennel is a variety that is not so tall and has a bulbous base which is eaten as a vegetable called finocchio.

GARLIC (ALLIUM SATIVUM)

Another close relative of the onion, garlic is a bulbous perennial with a clump of flat leaves growing to about 60–90 cm tall. Plants die back after flowering. Plants are grown from separate bulblets or cloves which make up the compound bulb. Dig the bulbs for use as flavouring or for replanting in autumn and winter.

Hint

For convenience and ease of picking grow herbs near the kitchen and you will remember to use them in your cooking.

DIANA SELBY
LANDSCAPE ARCHITECT

HELIOTROPE OR CHERRY PIE
(HELIOTROPIUM ARBORESCENS)

This is a tender perennial shrub which is used in preparations for perfumes and cosmetics. Usually treated as an annual, it grows to about 35 cm tall. In frost-free areas it is sometimes treated as a perennial. It grows from seed or from cuttings.

HORSERADISH
(COCHLEARICA ARMORACIA)

Horseradish is a plant with large spinach-like leaves and a long white taproot. Start plants in late winter or early spring from sections of root 15 cm long. Space them in well-prepared soil about 30 cm apart at an angle and cover the thick end with 2.5 cm of soil. When the shoots appear, reduce them in number to two or three. Although a perennial, horseradish is best grown as an annual. Take care to dig up all the pieces of root as the smallest piece will regrow. Well-grown roots are 5 cm in diameter and can be freshly grated or dried for use in spreads, dressings and horseradish sauce.

HYSSOP
(HYSSOPUS OFFICINALIS)

A strongly flavoured, perennial herb growing to a height of about 50 cm, it was once very popular as a household strewing herb as it is fragrant when walked upon. The leaves have a minty taste and are particularly useful for flavouring salads and soups. This herb is reputed to make rich food easily digestible.

LAVENDER (LAVANDULA SP)

This traditional herb is a hardy, perennial plant and is widely grown. The English lavender (*Lavandula spica*) is the most widely planted and the French lavender (*Lavandula dentata*) is also well known. Both species are compact bushes growing in excess of 50 cm. They need a warm, sunny location in the garden but must have free-draining soils.

LEMON BALM
(MELISSA OFFICINALIS)

A bushy, perennial herb, lemon balm grows to a height of 50 cm. The crushed leaves have a delightful lemon fragrance. Sow seed from

Herbs bordering a crossed path give a formal look to a garden.

spring to early autumn. A useful herb for adding to poultry, fish and pork. Also used for fruit jellies, tarts and custard.

LEMON VERBENA
(*LIPPIA CITRIODORA*)

This is an aromatic, semi-evergreen shrub. Scented leaves are used to flavour sweet dishes, beverages and fruit drinks, and to perfume colognes, soap and body lotions. Also used in pot-pourri. Lemon verbena grows to about 2 m and can be frost tender. Propagation is by stem cuttings of new growth taken in the spring.

LOVAGE
(*LEVISTICUM OFFICINALE*)

Lovage is the giant of the herb garden as, at maturity, it can reach more than 2 m. This size is reached over a period of several years as the plant dies back to the ground each winter. Somewhat resembling celery in appearance, taste and use, the dark-green leaves are used as a salad green or to flavour soups and stews. The seeds add a tasty celery and lemon-like flavour to many dishes, particularly cheese. The stems are sometimes used like angelica and candied, whilst the roots can be cooked as a vegetable. Usual method of propagation is by seed sown in late summer and autumn.

MARJORAM
OR SWEET MARJORAM
(*ORIGANUM MARJORANA*)

This is a perennial herb which grows to 30–40 cm tall, but is often grown as an annual. Sow seed in spring or autumn and space plants about 20 cm apart. Plants need full sun and rather moist conditions. The oval leaves and small white flowers are used fresh or dried for flavouring meat dishes.

MINT (*MENTHA SPP*)

A rambling perennial, spreading by means of rhizomes, it can often spread too well in the garden, so it is a good idea to grow it in a large pot or tub. Seed of some varieties is available or you can start plants from pieces of stem at any time of the year. It is one of the few herbs that prefers shade and very damp conditions. Leaves have a strong aroma and flavour and are used in mint sauce, mint jelly

Hint

Golden, silver and burgundy foliage (e.g. golden thyme, curry plant, purple sage) add interest to herb gardens. Add edible flowers such as heartsease violas and nasturtiums, which are great for garnishing.

DIANA SELBY
LANDSCAPE ARCHITECT

and for garnishing. Peppermint, spearmint and curled mint are the most common varieties but there are also others, including applemint, golden applemint (variegated leaves), eau de cologne mint (orange or bergamot) and pennyroyal.

NASTURTIUM
(*TROPAEOLUM MAJUS*)

This well-known climbing or trailing annual is cultivated mainly for its ornamental qualities, but sometimes used for its spicy, peppery-tasting leaves, seeds and flowers. The leaves are eaten in sandwiches and salads, the flowers are used as a garnish for salads and to flavour vinegar. For cultivation details, see Chapter 10.

OREGANO
(*ORIGANUM VULGARE*)

This herb is also known as wild marjoram or pot marjoram. A perennial herb very similar to sweet marjoram but with a distinct aroma and flavour. Sowing, spacing and cultivation are the same as for marjoram. Leaves have a sharper flavour than marjoram and are used fresh or dried in Italian, Spanish and Mexican dishes, especially those with spaghetti and tomato.

PARSLEY
(*PETROSELINUM CRISPUM*)

Undoubtedly the best known of all herbs, the most common variety is curled parsley. Another variety with stronger flavour is Italian plainleaf parsley. It is a biennial plant to 30 cm tall, but much taller when it runs to seed. It is

GARDENING FOR THE KITCHEN

best grown as an annual. Sow seeds direct in spring, summer and early autumn, either in clumps spaced 15–20 cm apart in the garden or broadcast in large pots or tubs. Seedlings may take three to four weeks to emerge, so keep the bed or container damp for this length of time after sowing. Parsley grows well in sun or semi-shade and prefers fertile soil and rather damp conditions. When established, plants respond to regular side dressings of nitrogen fertiliser or liquid feeds. Parsley leaves are used fresh as a garnish and fresh or dried for flavouring salads, vegetables, meats, stews, soups and egg dishes.

PYRETHRUM (CHRYSANTHEMUM PARTHENIUM)

Also called feverfew, pyrethrum is grown in gardens as a decorative plant for its attractive leaves and for its long blooming season. A related species is used in the manufacture of the insecticide, pyrethrum. A perennial, it is rather short-lived and is usually treated as an annual.

It reaches a height of about 60 cm and is topped with an abundance of button-shaped flowers with golden centres surrounded by white florets. It grows best in light, well-drained soil and prefers a sunny position. Seed is sown in spring or in autumn in mild districts.

ROCKET (ERUCA SATIVA)

This fast-growing salad herb mixes well with other salad greens. It has a peppery, bitter flavour and should be encouraged to grow quickly with good watering and liquid fertilising. Rocket is ready for picking in just a few weeks from sowing.

ROSEMARY (ROSMARINUS OFFICINALIS)

This is an attractive perennial herb that grows to 60–150 cm with dark-green, needle-like leaves and lavender-blue flowers. It grows well in sun or semi-shade but the soil must be well drained. Rosemary is very suitable for growing in large pots or tubs. Sow seeds in boxes or punnets in spring,

Dark-leafed basil, curled parsley and lettuce growing together in a tub near the door can be harvested as needed.

summer and early autumn, or start the plants from cuttings in late winter. The leaves have a pine-like appearance and flavour and are used, fresh or dried, with chicken or meat dishes and stews.

SAGE (*SALVIA OFFICINALIS*)

A perennial herb to 60 cm tall with long grey-green leaves and tall spikes of violet-blue flowers, sage is sown direct in spring, summer and early autumn in clumps 30 cm apart or seedlings are raised for transplanting at this distance. Plants need full sunlight and will tolerate quite dry conditions. Leaves, fresh or dried, are traditionally used for flavouring seasonings for poultry, pork, lamb and beef.

SALAD BURNET (*SANGUISORBA MINOR*)

Salad burnet is an old-fashioned herb whose cucumber-flavoured leaves were once popular in cooling drinks. The young leaves are also used in salads and as a flavouring for sauces. A hardy perennial, it grows to about 60 cm in height and produces thimble-shaped tufts of greenish flowers with purple-red stamens in early summer. It needs full sun and grows best in well-drained soils. It may be grown as a pot plant indoors but needs plenty of direct sunlight. Sow seeds in spring or early autumn.

SORREL (*RUMEX SCUTATUS*)

Sorrel is a perennial plant which grows to 60 cm tall, but flower stalks may reach as high as 120 cm. Sow seeds direct in clumps 20 cm apart in spring or early summer. Sorrel needs full sunlight and prefers rather damp conditions. Leaves have a sharp acid taste and are used as an addition to salads or cooked like silver beet or spinach. Also used for flavouring meat dishes, stews and soups.

SUMMER SAVOURY (*SATUREIA HORTENSIS*)

An annual herb to 30 cm tall. Sow seeds direct in clumps 15 cm apart in spring and/or early summer. Summer savoury needs full sunlight and well-drained soil and is suitable for container growing. Leaves have a peppery flavour and are used with meats, fish, eggs, beans, stews and soups.

Hint

To get a head start on the basil season, plant out in October, using a large bag of potting mix as your seed bed. Make small holes on one side for drainage, then flip it over and cut out a large square of the plastic to allow easy planting of the seeds. Soak with tepid water and cover with black plastic until the seeds germinate. Give your plants regular liquid feeds and you will reap a bountiful crop. You can never have too much basil: find a recipe for pesto and freeze batches for use during winter.

MARK ELLER
GARDEN CONSULTANT

TARRAGON (*ARTEMISIA DRACUNCULUS*)

A perennial herb 60–90 cm tall, with dark-green, pointed leaves that have a licorice flavour. Sow seeds direct into clumps 60 cm apart in spring or early summer. Tarragon needs full sunlight. Leaves are used in salads, egg and cheese dishes, with fish, and in sauces.

THYME (*THYMUS VULGARIS*)

Thyme is a small, prostrate, perennial herb 20–30 cm tall. Sow seeds in spring, summer and early autumn in clumps spaced 30 cm apart. It is a useful plant for ground cover and for rockeries and garden borders, and is also suitable for container growing. Plants prefer full sunlight and will tolerate rather dry conditions. There are many different varieties of thyme and all are suitable for flavouring. Use the fresh or dried leaves in soups and stews or in seasoning for poultry, meat and fish dishes.

CHAPTER 20

FRUIT TREES
AND FRUIT PLANTS

Wherever you live in New Zealand you can grow garden-fresh fruit. Fruit trees and fruit plants are not difficult to grow. Very often, a suitable microclimate exists or can be created in your garden. This means that the most unlikely fruits can be grown outside their natural climate. Once upon a time, fruit trees and fruit plants grew in nearly every New Zealand garden. Nowadays, gardens are smaller so it is difficult to find space for this very rewarding activity. But most home owners can grow two or three trees, especially citrus, which take up little room.

Many fruit plants – passionfruit, grapes and trailing berries – are great space-savers because you can train them on a fence or trellis. The aim of this chapter is to give background information on kinds and varieties of fruit together with recommendations for planting and management. Pests and diseases of fruit trees and fruit plants are dealt with in Chapter 6.

CITRUS TREES

Citrus (lemons, oranges, grapefruit, mandarins, limes and cumquats) have never lost their popularity. The vitamin-rich fruit can be picked progressively over a long time. This makes them ideal for home growing. But they are ornamental as well as useful, and make attractive trees with dark-green, glossy foliage and fragrant blossom in spring.

Citrus trees do well in all warm and mild climate zones. Providing frosts are not severe, trees will tolerate cool conditions. They also thrive in coastal areas with irrigation. Citrus require a sunny position, preferably facing north and protected from strong winds. They are most successful on sandy or loam soils and dislike clay soils or those with a heavy subsoil. Heavy soils become overwet and drain poorly, leading to rootrot problems. If drainage is poor, build the bed up 25–30 cm above the surrounding soil. Improve the texture of clay soils by adding generous amounts of sand and organic matter. (See Chapter 3.)

Advanced citrus plants are available from nurseries and garden stores. They usually come in large plastic pots or flexible plastic bags. Make sure the trees have not been in the container too long, as they may have become root-bound and trees so afflicted often fail to make satisfactory growth. The ideal tree is one year old from budding. It is best to plant trees in early autumn or early spring. This way, young trees avoid the effects of both winter cold and summer heat.

Make the planting hole shallow, but 30–50 cm wider than the container. Tip the tree from the pot or cut away the plastic bag. Gently tease out any roots which are pot-bound. For planting depth, keep the bud union (the knee-like joint where the tree has been grafted) above the soil level of the garden. Gently pack damp, crumbly soil, to which some sand and compost has been added, around the tree and water well. Mulch the soil with compost or leaf mould, but keep it 5–7 cm away from the stem.

An acceptable and simple method of applying fertiliser at planting is to use Multicote, which releases nutrients slowly and will continue to feed the tree for up to nine months. Do not use powdered fertilisers at planting as damage may occur. Wait for four or five weeks after planting, when organic fertiliser like Bio-Gold can be scattered around the tree in moderation. Do not overwater newly planted trees – a good drink every week is sufficient when the weather is dry.

Citrus trees tend to be self-shaping and so need little pruning. If growth is overcrowded, thin

TOP FIVE
CITRUS VARIETIES

'VALENCIA' ORANGE

Easily grown with sweet-tasting fruit (if you let it ripen on the tree), 'Valencia' is probably the best variety for making orange juice.

'SATSUMA' MANDARIN

A loose-skinned mandarin that's beloved by children because it's so easy to peel, 'Satsuma' has a typical sweet mandarin flavour.

'GOLDEN SPECIAL' GRAPEFRUIT

With very few seeds, this grapefruit has a juicy, tangy flavour and is cold tolerant.

'EUREKA' LEMON

An almost thornless variety that produces fruit just about year round, 'Eureka' is an ideal home garden lemon but must have good drainage.

'TAHITIAN' LIME

The small green fruit of the lime tree is used for drinks and, to a lesser extent, in cooked dishes. It needs warmer conditions than other citruses.

'TAHITIAN' LIME

'VALENCIA' ORANGE

GRAPEFRUIT

out the stems after fruiting because flowers and fruit are carried at the ends of the branches. Don't thin oranges and grapefruit severely, but mandarins can be cut back to the second or third shoot down the branch. Lemon trees are taller and less compact so prune them back well to keep them at a manageable height. Sappy water shoots of lemon and grapefruit should be cut away unless they can improve the tree shape. Any shoots below the bud union must be removed too. Old citrus trees can be 'skeletonised' in early spring by cutting back to the main branches. They will take a year or two to recover and bear again.

Hint
If you want to grow citrus trees in pots, grafted dwarf varieties are an excellent choice. Potted citrus tend to need extra fertiliser, and plenty of watering in spring and summer.

DIANA SELBY
LANDSCAPE ARCHITECT

Feeding roots of citrus are located at the 'drip-line' underneath the outer foliage, so do not cultivate deeply in this area. When applying fertiliser, scatter it around the 'drip-line' and not close to the trunk. Use a complete fertiliser containing about 10 per cent nitrogen. There are several brands of citrus fertiliser including Gro-Plus Citrus Food. A well-grown, mature citrus tree should be given 450–500 g of fertiliser each year. Apply two-thirds of this amount in late winter or early spring (July–August) and the balance in late summer (January–February). Water trees well both before and after fertilising.

Fruit drop is a common citrus problem, associated with irregular or uneven watering, especially when young fruits are forming. Lack of fertiliser (or too much of it) can aggravate this condition. Feed trees as suggested above and water them regularly through spring and summer.

CUMQUATS

These small attractive trees are suitable for the open garden or for tub specimens. The small, bitter fruit make excellent jams, jellies and liqueurs. 'Marumi' (round fruit) and 'Nagami' (oval fruit) are the best varieties.

GRAPEFRUIT

'Golden Special' is the most popular variety; a good cropper which is suitable for New Zealand's cooler summer and winter climates. The 'Wheeny' variety also bears well but fruits have an acid, lemon-like flavour and many seeds. 'Thompson' is a good variety for dry districts.

LEMON

'Meyer', a mild-flavoured lemon, is the most popular variety. It can be grown in most parts of New Zealand and will fruit for much of the year. 'Lisbon' and 'Eureka' are popular sharp-flavoured varieties ideal for cooking. 'Yen Ben' is a medium to large tree. It produces lots of seedless fruit with excellent sharp flavour. Though not without thorns, 'Yen Ben' is quick-growing and densely foliaged, bearing fruit in autumn and winter.

LIMES

The lime is a small, many-branched tree with green, thin-skinned fruit about 5 cm in diameter. 'Tahitian' is the most popular variety.

MANDARIN

Best early varieties are 'Clementine' and 'Satsuma Niyagawa'. Both are ready to pick in late autumn. A good late variety is 'Encore'. The tangelo (a mandarin-grapefruit hybrid) has large, juicy, mandarin-like fruits, the best variety of which is 'Seminole'.

ORANGE

The 'Valencia' orange is the most widely grown. It is a reliable cropper with fruit for picking from spring right through to the following autumn. 'Hardwood Late' is a New Zealand-raised form, and produces large, thick-skinned fruit in autumn and early winter. The 'Washington Navel' is an excellent quality orange and usually seedless. It bears from late autumn to spring. It is not as consistent a bearer as 'Valencia' and is more liable to fruit drop.

DECIDUOUS FRUIT TREES

These summer-fruiting trees lose their leaves in winter, so can be used where summer shade or winter sun is needed in any part of the garden. Most trees have a magnificent display of spring blossom and some, especially pear trees and persimmons, have attractive autumn foliage. Because they are dormant in winter, deciduous fruit trees can be grown in districts with cold winters and severe frosts, although late frosts in spring can damage flower and leaf buds. Apples and pears are attacked by codling moth, which can be controlled by spraying or setting a codling moth trap (available in most garden centres).

Deciduous fruit trees prefer an open, sunny position but will grow on a variety of soils. Like citrus trees, they need good drainage and will not tolerate heavy or waterlogged soil.

Plant all kinds and varieties of deciduous fruit trees in winter – June or July would be the best months in most districts. Unlike citrus, they are often sold as 'bare-root' trees, rather like rose bushes. Sometimes these bare-rooted trees are newly potted into fresh potting mix, which will fall away from the roots at planting time. Although the trees are dormant, roots must not dry out.

Dig shallow holes for planting but break up further soil at the bottom. Very wide holes are not necessary – for most trees a diameter of 60 cm is ample. Plant trees rather deeper than they were in the nursery but keep the bud union well above soil level. Spread roots carefully on a mound of soil, placing the longest and strongest in the direction from which prevailing winds will blow. Fill the hole with crumbly topsoil and firm it gently into place. Now add a bucket of water to settle soil around the roots and fill the hole with dry soil to ground level.

Trees cannot use fertiliser when they are dormant but they do require it when growth starts in the spring. A slow-release fertiliser, such as Multicote, can be applied to the perimeter of the planting hole at planting, or a mixed fertiliser such as Gro-Plus Complete Plant Food or Gro-Plus Citrus Food can be scattered around the tree at the rate of one-third of a cupful per square metre when growth begins. Chip or rake fertiliser into the topsoil and water to field capacity.

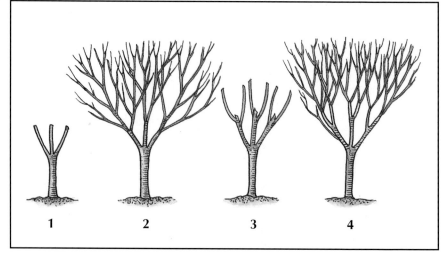

1   2   3   4

Deciduous fruit trees are pruned in winter to an open-centred vase shape. This shape forms a sturdy framework. Diagrams show: (1) tree pruned after first-year growth; (2) second-year growth; (3) tree pruned after second-year growth; (4) third-year growth.

Pruning aims to regulate growth of branches, allow light to enter the framework and encourage flowers and fruit. Most deciduous fruit trees are pruned to a 'vase' shape but many can be trained as an espalier, which requires a frame support. Generally, trees are pruned in winter, and usually hard for the first few years to make a sturdy framework and to shape the tree. Later, the main concern of pruning is to remove dead and diseased wood, ingrowing branches, thin overcrowded growth and to cut back leaders or main limbs.

Each kind of fruit tree has its own habit of growth. Fruit may set on current spring growth, on wood formed the previous year or on fruiting spurs which may bear for several years, so it is important to know the bearing wood for each kind before pruning. Brief notes are given in this chapter but detailed information on pruning each kind of tree is available from specialist books.

Fruit trees, like other plants, require feeding. On deep fertile soils it may be some years before fertilisers are needed, but in most gardens, yearly applications of fertiliser will improve growth and fruit yield. A mixed fertiliser that contains about 10 per cent nitrogen is recommended. For young fruit trees, apply fertiliser at the rate of 0.5 kg per tree for each year of age up to bearing. Scatter

the fertiliser in late winter or early spring when growth starts. On very poor soils, supplement this by a further application of 250 g per tree in mid-summer (December–January). Slow-release fertilisers used in late winter are also suitable. Animal manures, if available, are a useful way of supplying plant nutrients.

APPLES

Apples grow best in cool to cold climates with a mild summer and cold winter. Most varieties are self-sterile so two varieties are needed for pollination. Some nurseries can supply two or three varieties budded on to one root stock to solve this problem. Apple trees bear fruit on spurs and two-year-old or older laterals. Fruiting wood is encouraged by allowing laterals to develop on terminal branches to remain uncut until buds form. Then shorten them if necessary. Three popular early varieties are 'Gala', 'Oratia Beauty' and 'Gravenstein', any two of which will cross-pollinate. Late-maturing varieties, however, have better quality fruit. The best of the reds is 'Red Delicious', an excellent eating apple with a characteristic flavour, and 'Jonathan', good for eating and cooking. 'Granny Smith' is the most popular green apple, excellent for cooking and pleasant eating when fully ripe. Any two late varieties will cross-pollinate. The development of dwarf apple trees (and pears)

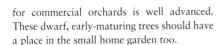

for commercial orchards is well advanced. These dwarf, early-maturing trees should have a place in the small home garden too.

APRICOTS

Apricots are very adaptable. They grow well in many parts of New Zealand. All varieties are self-fertile. Apricots bear fruit on laterals produced the previous year and on spurs which often bear for several years. Strong water shoots develop on some varieties. Cut these back in mid-summer to produce fruiting laterals and spurs.

'Newcastle' is a popular variety with a vigorous habit. It is a good cropper, maturing fruit in mid to late spring. 'Trevatt', the leading apricot variety for canning, is recommended for the warmer winter areas of New Zealand. 'Morocco' is a later variety but keeps rather better than 'Trevatt'.

CHERRIES

A climate with mild summers and cold winters is best for cherries. Soils must be deep and well drained. Trees grow to a large size, so are not well suited to small gardens. All varieties are self-sterile so two varieties are needed for pollination. Cherries bear fruit on spurs growing on two-year-old or older wood. After initial tree shaping, little pruning is needed. Pruning, when necessary, should be done in autumn as trees are subject to 'gumming'. Cuts heal quicker during this time than when trees are fully dormant.

Early varieties are 'Black Tartarian' and 'Early Burlat'. Both have dark fruit and will cross-pollinate. 'Dawson' is a dark red, mid-season variety with an upright, spreading habit. 'Bing' is also harvested mid-season, and has red-black fruit and vigorous, spreading growth. Ask your local supplier for the best regional pollinators.

FIGS

Figs, like apricots, are very adaptable to a wide climate range – cool, warm or hot. Trees flourish in humid climates but fruit may ferment on the tree in wet seasons. Figs are self-fertile and fruit ripens over a long period. Birds can be a problem – nylon netting over the tree is probably the best answer to this problem. Figs bear fruit on current season's growth. Trees usually form a well-balanced framework so little pruning is needed.

'Black Ischia' has dark skin and red flesh. 'White Genoa', with pale-green skin and creamy flesh, and 'Brown Turkey', a prolific cropper with dark-skinned fruit, are popular dessert varieties. 'White Adriatic', with green-brown skin and yellow flesh, is a smaller fig but excellent for making jam.

MULBERRY

Mulberry trees grow to about 6 m with large leaves and small fruit – about blackberry-size but rather longer. They grow well in subtropical, temperate and cool climates and are often grown as ornamentals for summer shade. Mulberries grow easily from cuttings and usually bear fruit in the second year. Apart from initial shaping, little pruning is needed. Top growth and long leaders on older trees can be cut back for easier picking. 'Black English' is the best variety for cool districts. 'Hicks', a variety of white or Chinese mulberry, is more suitable for warm climates. The fruits of both varieties make a pleasant, fresh dessert and are excellent for jam or jelly.

Leaves of Chinese mulberry are a favourite diet for silkworms if the younger members of your family keep them.

....

Hint

Before a sunny day makes you rush out to the garden centre, stop and consider what sort of plants you might like. Read up about them and see whether or not they are right for your garden. Alternatively, browse your garden centre first, then read about plants you have spotted and then go and buy them if they are suitable.

DENNIS GREVILLE
GARDEN WRITER

....

GARDENING FOR THE KITCHEN

PEACHES AND NECTARINES

Some varieties of peaches and nectarines (which are really a smooth-skinned peach) grow best in subtropical and temperate climates with a mild winter, while others have a high 'chilling requirement' and need a cold winter.

Selecting varieties suited to your area is important. All peaches and nectarines are self-fertile, with the exception of 'J.H. Hale', which requires a pollinator flowering at the same time. There are many peach varieties – white or yellow flesh, both clingstone and freestone with a range of in-betweens. Peaches and nectarines bear fruit on laterals produced the previous summer. Laterals fruit for one season only so there must be plenty of new ones coming on each year for continuity of cropping. Prune back trees each winter to encourage new growth but don't remove too much wood carrying buds for next spring.

For warm winter climates 'Royal Gold' (yellow, semi-freestone peach) is recommended. For cool, highland and cold inland regions, varieties must flower late enough to avoid frost damage. Popular cold-climate varieties are 'Compact Redhaven', 'Redhaven', 'Golden

....

Hint

Historically, man has been very harsh on the environment. As the caretakers of plants, we need to rectify the mistakes of the past in order to ensure a greener future for the new millennium. Nurture your garden, and leave your children something worth inheriting.

BILL WARD
GARDEN WRITER AND BROADCASTER

....

Queen' and 'Redskin'. 'J. H. Hale' is also very good but should be planted in the vicinity of another peach variety for pollination (most of those available in New Zealand will suit). An old favourite nectarine is 'Goldmine' (white freestone). It matures in mid-season and does well in all districts.

PEARS

Like apples, good quality pears require a mild summer and cool to cold winter. Nashi pears are a better choice for warm coastal districts. The trees are attractive with spring blossom and coloured autumn leaves. Pruning pear trees is the same as for apple trees. Trees take five years or more to bear but they are very long-lived. 'Williams' ('Bartlett') is the most popular variety for eating and cooking. Pick fruit when firm and ripen indoors. 'Williams' is self-fertile but usually crops better with another variety as a pollinator. 'Beurre Bosc' and 'Packham's Triumph' bear high-quality fruit which keep well. Fruit is left to ripen on the tree. 'Williams' is the best pollinator for both varieties.

PERSIMMON

Persimmons, like apricots and figs, are adaptable to a wide climate range. Unlike most deciduous fruit trees, they tolerate moist conditions and heavy clay soils. These attractive, spreading trees grow to about 5 m in height. They are ornamental, too, with brilliant autumn foliage. The salmon-pink fruit is picked when coloured but still firm.

Ripen fruit indoors until quite soft before eating. Persimmons have a unique texture and flavour. After the tree has been shaped, little pruning is needed. Fruit is produced on the current season's wood. Fruit on the topmost branches can be picked with a long-handled rake.

Most persimmon varieties are harvested in autumn or early winter. The most popular variety is 'Fuyu'. It has non-astringent fruit of excellent quality and a very sweet flavour. 'Fuyu' will produce better crops with a pollinator such as 'Gailey'. Persimmons sucker freely and you can establish new trees by digging these and replanting them when dormant in winter.

PLUMS

There are two types of plums: the European plum, which has a high chilling requirement suited to cool climates, and the Japanese plum, which has a low chilling requirement and grows best in warmer areas. The cherry plum is very similar to the Japanese type. While good drainage is recommended, plum trees usually tolerate heavy soil and moist conditions better than other stone fruits. Neither European nor Japanese plums (with the exception of 'Santa Rosa') are self-fertile and require a pollinator belonging to the same group. Cherry plums are usually self-pollinating.

After the plum tree is shaped it needs little pruning. Fruit is carried on two-year-old laterals (European type) or on one-year-old laterals (Japanese and cherry type) and on spurs which crop for a few years. 'Angelina', 'President' and 'Grand Duke' are the best European varieties. Any two will cross-pollinate. An early variety of Japanese plum is 'Santa Rosa' (red flesh). 'Santa Rosa' is self-fertile – if you only want one plum tree, this is it. A good mid-season Japanese variety is 'Mariposa' (dark red, blood plum). This is not self-fertile, but is able to be cross-pollinated by 'Santa Rosa'.

VINE FRUITS
GRAPES

Grapes are grown traditionally on a two-wire trellis but they can be trained over pergolas, arbours and screens. The vines are best suited to climates with a dry summer and cool to cold winter, such as Hawke's Bay. Gisborne, Nelson and Christchurch, but they can be grown with success in home gardens in most parts of the country. In humid climates, a disease-resistant variety is needed.

Grape vines are planted in winter about 3 m apart. The basic principle of pruning is that fruit buds are borne on one-year-old wood which arises from two-year-old wood. Water shoots grow from wood older than two years and are not fruit-bearing. Cut the strongest cane on the plant to two buds. Train growth from these in both directions along the bottom wire of the trellis or lateral support. Next winter, prune these main arms back to sturdy wood leaving three buds on each. The following winter, prune back at the base. Continue this process each year.

The American hybrid (labrusca) varieties are ideal for humid climates. The most widely successful in New Zealand home gardens is the juicy black grape, 'Albany Surprise'. Other recommended disease-resistant varieties are 'Niagara' (green) and 'Buffalo' (black). 'Lakemont' (green) is one of the best seedless varieties. 'Concord' (black) is both cold tolerant and disease resistant.

Grapes grow best in a relatively dry climate.

KIWIFRUIT

Kiwifruit, or Chinese gooseberries, as they were once known, are becoming more popular with home gardeners each year. The fruit is 5–7 cm long and covered with short, brown bristles. The flesh, which is light green with dark, soft seeds, can be used fresh or frozen or in jam, pickles or chutney.

The kiwifruit is a vigorous, deciduous vine suited to mild or temperate climates with warm summer months and freedom from late frost. The fibrous roots are shallow so regular watering is needed from spring to early winter when fruit ripens (usually May or June). Kiwifuit have male and female flowers on separate vines so you must buy one of each. Nurseries sell them in pairs although one male plant will provide enough pollen for several females. Female vines take four to five years to bear and keep on bearing for at least twenty years.

Vines, which are planted in winter, can be trained on trellises 2 m high with two or

Only the female kiwifruit vine will develop fruit.

three strands of wire. Space vines 3 m apart. Most home gardeners train the vines over a strong pergola about 2.5 m high and 3 m square. Wires spaced 60–75 cm apart on the sides and top provide support for the twining laterals. Fruit is formed on the first three to five buds or current season's growth. Each winter, prune laterals back to two or three buds beyond the previous season's crop. If overcrowded, cut some laterals out completely. In summer, shorten back growth if it is too vigorous. Many varieties, which vary in shape and size, have been selected. 'Hayward', with large fruit of good keeping quality, is the most popular.

PASSIONFRUIT

This evergreen, perennial vine is very prolific. The dark-green leaves and white and purple flowers are also attractive. Passionfruit do well in subtropical and temperate climates which are free of frost. They need a sunny aspect and prefer light soils with good drainage. Passionfruit are self-fertile and you can start by sowing seed from a good cropping vine. Started seedlings and grafted plants are also available from nurseries and garden stores. For trellis growing, wires at 1.2 m and 2 m should run north–south for maximum sun. Vines can be trained on fences, the railings of balconies or terraces and on pergolas. Provide wires or wire netting for the tendrils to cling to. One well-grown vine will give sufficient fruit for the average family but if more than one is required plant vines 2.5 m apart.

Passionfruit respond to generous feeding. Apply a complete fertiliser with at least 10 per cent nitrogen when growth starts in spring. Use 0.5 kg per vine and follow up with light side dressings of a high nitrogen fertiliser (for example, sulphate of ammonia) every three to four weeks through summer. Regular watering is needed because roots are quite shallow. Mulching is useful too, but keep mulch away from stems as this may favour collar rot.

Vines planted in spring often give a light crop in autumn but will bear well the following summer. After fruiting, cut the vines back if they are too dense. This allows better air movement and encourages new laterals on which fruit is formed. Vines may become weak and spindly after four or five years so it pays to have new ones coming on as replacements. Fruit colour changes from green to purple when ripe and fruit usually falls. Gather fallen fruit every day in summer. The banana passionfruit is a close relative grown in the same way. It has pink flowers and banana-like fruit with a soft yellow skin.

TROPICAL FRUITS
AVOCADO

This handsome, evergreen tree grows to a height of 9 m. The pear-shaped fruit – green or green turning black – contains cream-coloured, butter-textured flesh surrounding a large, oval seed. Although of tropical origin, avocado trees can be grown in sheltered positions in temperate climates. The trees prefer deep, well-drained soil and

Avocados are surprisingly easy to grow.

need regular watering in summer. Seedling trees are unreliable and may never bear fruit, so buy grafted plants from nurseries. The trees are self-shaping so no pruning is necessary. Scatter a complete fertiliser beneath the drip-line of the tree when flowering commences in spring. Repeat the treatment two or three times during summer and early autumn.

Avocados have a peculiar sex life. Flowers function as female for a few hours, close and then reopen as male flowers the following day, or vice versa. Fortunately, pollination of the variety 'Fuerte' is not so critical because these sex changes overlap in different flowers on the one tree. In New Zealand, 'Fuerte' fruit ripens thoughout summer. Fruit does not ripen well on the tree, so pick when the fruit is fully formed and the gloss on the skin fades, then ripen indoors.

'Hass' is a prolific cropper from mid-summer to autumn. It forms a large upright tree bearing medium-sized fruit with thick, wrinkled, leathery skin and a superb flavour.

BANANAS

Bananas are ornamental as well as useful. They will grow very well outside their tropical environment if they are planted in a sunny spot in a sheltered garden. Older plants will tolerate light frosts. Bananas are shallow-rooted and need fertile, well-drained soil with regular watering in summer. Start your banana tree from a vigorous sucker with a large, round base. Trim off roots (these will not grow again) and reduce the 'top' by one-quarter. Plant the sucker in spring with its base 20–25 cm deep. It will produce fruit in fifteen to eighteen months but may take longer under cooler conditions. Many new suckers will develop, so gouge these out but keep the strongest to replace the parent plant. Strip off any dead or wind-shredded leaves. A banana bunch is right for cutting when fruits have lost their angular shape. Still green, you can ripen them by hanging the bunch upside down in a warm place indoors. Protect bunches which form in cool weather with a blue plastic 'bunch cover'.

Most banana varieties grow to 6 m tall but 'Cavendish' is shorter at 3 m. Some popular varieties are 'Cavendish', 'Williams' (which are more tolerant to cool weather), 'Lady Finger', 'Orinoco', 'Gros Michel' and 'Pink

GARDENING FOR THE KITCHEN

Banana'. Friends and neighbours are a good source of planting material. Bananas are self-fertile and need no assistance to pollinate. In the home garden they are not overly troubled by pests or disease but plants can be sprayed if and when necessary.

CUSTARD APPLE

Custard apple or cherimoya is a small semi-deciduous tree growing to 6 m. It is suited to warm, humid districts. The fruit is heart-shaped, very knobby with a diameter of 5–8 cm. Flesh is custard-like with many seeds. It is best to buy grafted plants of the 'Cherimoya' or 'Peruvian' custard apple because plants from seeds are unreliable. Set plants in early spring or summer. Prune young trees to a vase shape over the first three to four years. Apply fertiliser each year in small doses as for mangoes. Flowering starts in October or November and may continue until January or February,

The strawberry guava makes a very handsome specimen tree and is found in many older gardens.

so the fruit ripens over a long period. Pick the fruit when skin turns a greenish-cream colour. They may take a few days to soften up for eating. 'African Pride' is the most widely grown variety. It is a compact tree, bearing fruit (March–June harvest) after three to four years. 'Pink's Mammoth' is a larger custard apple tree with better quality fruit (April–July harvest) but takes six to seven years to bear.

GUAVA

Guavas are not really tropical fruits and can be grown in warm temperate, frost-free climates. Yellow guava, an evergreen tree, is rather hardier than citrus and grows to 5 m tall. The yellow, oval or pear-shaped fruits are about 5 cm in diameter. Strawberry guava is a taller tree but fruits are smaller, purplish-red in colour with a tart flavour. Pineapple guava or feijoa is rather more adaptable to cool conditions and will tolerate light frosts. Fruit is oval, about 8 cm long with a greenish-yellow, waxy skin and pineapple-like aroma and flavour. Guavas can be eaten fresh but are more popular as jam or jelly. Fruits of the guava trees ripen in late summer.

PAWPAW

Pawpaw or papaya, like other tropical fruit, does best in warm, humid climates with good summer rainfall, but if you choose a sunny, sheltered site, this attractive tree will succeed in frost-free temperate climates. A well-drained loam or light soil is preferred.

Pawpaws have male and female flowers on separate trees but there are some bisexual trees. The fruit from bisexual trees is long rather than oval and the trees are not as tolerant of cool-climate-conditions. Hybrid bisexual trees are available from nurseries. Seeds from fruit of female trees germinate easily in punnets or pots. Transplant seedlings when 20 cm tall. You cannot tell whether seedlings are male or female, so it is wise to set four or five plants in a group spaced about 1.5 m apart. Odds are you will have at a least one male tree for pollination. Unwanted male trees are best removed, unless you want to keep them as ornamentals.

In favourable conditions, female or bisexual trees will bear fruit within fifteen months but take longer where it is cooler.

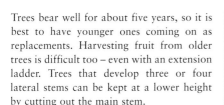

Trees bear well for about five years, so it is best to have younger ones coming on as replacements. Harvesting fruit from older trees is difficult too – even with an extension ladder. Trees that develop three or four lateral stems can be kept at a lower height by cutting out the main stem.

Pick the fruit when fully coloured, but if the weather is cool, pick when the fruit is showing a tinge of yellow and ripen indoors. Flowering takes place over several weeks so fruit at different stages of development will appear on the tree at the one time. Most pawpaws have bright-yellow or orange flesh, but there are some with red flesh.

TREE TOMATO (TAMARILLO)

This is a small umbrella-shaped tree growing to 3 m tall. The stem is quite brittle so it is best to support it with a stout stake or post. Tree tomato is not strictly a tropical fruit and grows well in temperate, frost-free districts. It prefers a sunny, sheltered aspect. You can raise tree tomatoes from seed but cuttings are easy too. Prune the main stem at a height of 1 m to encourage growth of three or four branches. The egg-shaped, purplish-red fruits are 5 cm long with many seeds. The fruits resemble tomatoes in appearance but have an acid-sweet flavour. They are used fresh or cooked.

BERRY FRUITS

GOOSEBERRIES AND CURRANTS

Both fruits grow on small bushes which are suited to cool to cold climates. The English or European gooseberry is started from cuttings in winter and planted 1.5 m apart each way. Gooseberry bushes bear fruit on one-year-old wood which is cut out after fruiting. The bush is trained as a vase-shaped, small tree which means that some pruning is needed. Prepare soil as for raspberries, adding manure or compost plus a mixed fertiliser.

Black currants and red currants need a similar climate and soil. Propagate them from cuttings and plant 1.5 m apart. Generally, black currants and red currants are grown as a many-stemmed bush, which may need thinning when crowded. They bear fruit on one-year-old wood and red currants have fruiting spurs as well. Widely grown varieties of black currant are 'Baldwin', 'Ben Sarek', 'Magnus' and 'Goliath'. Main red varieties are 'Red Lake' and 'White Versailles'.

STRAWBERRIES

Strawberries are very adaptable to climate and soil, so it is not surprising they are grown throughout New Zealand. The plants need a sunny position, a well-drained soil with good structure, regular feeding and watering.

Most home gardeners grow strawberries in a section of raised bed in the vegetable garden with plants spaced at 30 cm each way. Surface mulching between plants will prevent weeds, maintain an even soil temperature and prevent moisture loss in summer. A mulch helps to keep fruit clean, too. Compost, leaf mould, straw, sawdust, wood shavings or pine bark are all suitable for mulching. Black polythene sheeting makes an excellent mulch for raised beds, and fruiting is earlier because of the warmer soil. Spread the polythene and cut a small slit for each plant, making a depression in the soil below to direct water to roots. Strawberries do well in large pots, tubs or barrels with holes cut in the sides. There are a few non-running varieties suited to this kind of growing.

Prepare soil with organic manure, such as Bio-Gold or compost plus a ration of mixed fertiliser, such as Gro-Plus Citrus Food, at one-third of a cup per square metre. You can start plants any time between April and August, but early plantings will give fruit in October and November. Remove old dead leaves and trim any straggly roots before planting. After flowering commences, give plants liquid feeds of Thrive every few weeks. Many runners will develop, so pick these off progressively. Plants will bear well for about three seasons. Start a new bed in autumn of the third year. Strawberries are prone to a number of viruses which are spread by aphids. It is a good idea to replant every two or three years using only certified disease-free plants.

The 'Alpine' strawberry is a form of wild strawberry. It is fully perennial and quite different from the usual garden hybrids. The plants produce fruit in the first season after sowing and heavy crops of small-sized, flavourful fruit are borne on neat, bushy plants. Ideal for rockeries and pots on balconies. Sow autumn and spring.

Most soft berry fruits, like these raspberries, grow best in an area with cold winters.

RASPBERRIES

Raspberries grow best in cool temperate or cold climates. Districts where apples or cherries grow are ideal. The bushes need deep, well-drained soil with lots of organic matter. Prepare and fertilise the soil as for strawberries and set out the dormant canes 60 cm apart in rows 2 m apart. Raspberry bushes bear fruit on one-year-old wood, which is cut back to ground level each winter. Some 'ever-bearing' varieties have an autumn crop on the current season's wood. Thin the strongest of the new canes to 15 cm apart to prevent overcrowding and top them slightly for a manageable height. The canes can be tied together loosely with twine. Raspberries continue to bear for many years. Pick fruit when ripe and well-coloured. Fruit is delicious as a fresh dessert, freezes well and makes excellent jam or jelly.

Summer-fruiting varieties grown in New Zealand include 'Glen Moy', 'Glen Prosen', 'Leo', 'Malling Admiral', Malling Delight', 'Malling Jewel', 'Malling Joy' and 'Marcy'. Late summer and autumn varieties are 'Autumn Bliss', 'Fallgold', 'Heritage' and 'Southland'.

TRAILING BERRIES OR BRAMBLES

Loganberry, boysenberry and youngberry are the main trailing berries. They are hybrids derived from the dewberry or trailing blackberry. Loganberries prefer a cool to cold climate similar to that for raspberries, but boysenberries and youngberries are more adaptable to warm climates, providing that winter months are cool. They grow on a variety of soils, but drainage must be good. Propagate these berries by cuttings or rooted tip-layers. Plant these 2 m apart underneath a two-wire trellis. Like raspberries, they bear fruit on one-year-old wood. Canes produced the previous summer are tied to the top wire and then cut back to ground level after fruiting. New canes are tied to the bottom wire as they grow to keep them tidy, and transferred to the top wire when the old canes are cut away. Prepare the ground well by adding animal manure or compost plus a mixed fertiliser, as for strawberries. Each year, apply fertiliser such as Gro-Plus Citrus Food when growth starts in spring. Slow-release fertilisers are also suitable. Pick fruit when well-coloured (red for loganberries,

Dry weather can damage boysenberry leaves and cause fruit yields to be low.

and purplish-black for boysenberries and youngberries). Well-grown trailing berries will bear for up to fifteen years. A single vine may yield 5 kg of fruit each year.

NUT TREES

Nut trees are not widely grown in New Zealand gardens but some are quite ornamental as well as useful. A short summary is given as a guide to how and where the most popular kinds grow.

ALMOND

A deciduous tree, to 6 m tall, suited to winter-wet, summer-dry climates which are relatively free from early spring frosts. Both blossoms and young nuts are sensitive.

Almonds have similar soil and management requirements to peaches which are close relatives. Nuts are enclosed in a fleshy husk. The husk dries at maturity and splits open or is easily separated. Many varieties have been selected but two are needed for cross-pollination.

HAZELNUT

Hazelnuts or filberts grow on small, much-branched deciduous trees to 5 m tall. They are suited to cool climates. The shell is hard and woody but the smooth, brown kernel separates easily when cracked. Trees may take several years to bear.

MACADAMIA

This handsome tree, also known as Queensland nut, grows to 9 m tall. It is suited to warm, humid climate zones but grows quite well in temperate coastal districts such as Northland. The round white kernels are enclosed in a hard, woody shell. Nuts mature during late autumn and winter and fall when ripe. Seedling trees are extremely variable so it is best to buy grafted trees from nurseries.

OLIVE

The olive is included in this section because the fruit is useful for pickling and the trees are ornamental as well. Trees are evergreen and grow quickly to about 6 m tall. They are suited to temperate climates and withstand hot, dry summers and cool winters with some frosts. The leaves are dark-grey (silver underneath) and the white flowers in spring are followed by

Olives thrive wherever grapes grow.

green or black fruit in summer. Good varieties are 'Sevillano', 'Manzanillo', 'UC13A6' and 'Verdale'. Grafted plants from nurseries should be planted in well-drained, sunny situations in autumn or spring. Pruning is rarely needed unless the trees become too large.

PISTACHIO

The pistachio nut is a small deciduous tree to 6 m tall with compound leaves composed of three to five leaflets. It is suited to temperate climates with dry summers and cool to cold winters. The fruit is oval-shaped, about 2 cm long, containing the nut with a thin, woody shell which splits open when ripe. The kernel is smooth, light-green and richly flavoured.

WALNUT

The common walnut is a shapely, deciduous tree growing to over 15 m unless restricted by pruning. It thrives in cool to cold climates but is susceptible to late spring frosts. Nuts split open or are separated easily when mature. Many varieties are available. Two varieties are desirable for effective cross-pollination.

If you don't have the right climate for pistachio nuts, you may still be able to grow the ornamental Pistacia chinensis.

FRUIT

WHAT TO LOOK FOR	NUTRITION	STORAGE	PREPARATION	METHOD OF COOKING
APPLES Fruit should be the true variety colour, with skin free of bruises. Large apples do not keep as well as smaller fruit.	Fair source of vitamin C and dietary fibre. 222 kilojoules per 100 grams.	Keep in vented plastic bag in refrigerator.	Tart and sharp-tasting apples are best for cooking. Remove stalk, wash and dry well. Peel only if necessary.	As fresh juice or cider. Superb raw, pureed, in a tart or strudel, preserved as apple jelly. Use for fritters or bake.
APRICOT Firm, plump, fully developed fruit with a bright apricot colour. Avoid soft or shrivelled fruit.	Fair source of vitamin C, vitamin A and dietary fibre. Some iron. 188 kilojoules per 100 grams.	Keep in unsealed plastic bag in refrigerator for 2–3 days. Will deteriorate quickly at room temperature.	Wipe over, cut and remove stone.	As a snack. Use in fruit salad and jam. Cooking draws out the flavour. Serve with ham, lamb and duck.
AVOCADO Generally glossy and hard when unripe. When ripe, skin colour is dull, and a toothpick easily pierces flesh at stem. 'Hass' variety has rough dark skin.	Fair source of vitamin C, riboflavin and dietary fibre. Some iron, thiamin and niacin. Fair source of poly-unsaturated fat. 674 kilojoules per 100 grams.	Ripen at room temperature, then store in refrigerator.	Remove stone, discard skin. Slice flesh as required. Lemon juice will stop discolouration.	Use mashed on bread and sprinkle with lemon juice. Fill with seafood and dressing. Ideal accompaniment to smoked fish and as a soup. A great ice cream.
BANANAS Best eating quality will be bright, medium-sized fruit, yellow to gold in colour, well-rounded and free of bruises.	Fair source of vitamin A, vitamin C and dietary fibre. Some iron and thiamin. 364 kilojoules per 100 grams.	Store at room temperature to continue ripening process. Skin will blacken if refrigerated.	Simply peel, or if baking on the barbecue, slightly slit the skin. Lemon juice will prevent discolouration.	Sliced with cinnamon and cream. Ingredient in cakes, biscuits, desserts. Blend with milk for a nourishing drink. Bake on barbecue. Use for fritters.
CHERRIES Firm, fresh, bright uniformly coloured fruit, with green stems. Use the taste test.	Fair source of vitamin C and dietary fibre. Some vitamin A. 265 kilojoules per 100 grams	Keep in unsealed plastic bag in refrigerator to stop from drying out. Highly perishable. Eat soon after harvest.	Wash and remove stem. May be stoned before serving.	Use fresh, or as a tart filling. Blend stoned cherries for fruit sauce. Combine with walnuts and chicken in salad. As a soup.
GRAPEFRUIT Firm and heavy fruit. Skin should be smooth and bright yellow in colour.	Excellent source of vitamin C. 155 kilojoules per 100 grams.	Can be kept outside refrigerator in cool place. Keep in refrigerator crisper for longer storage.	Wipe over and peel. Use grapefruit knife to segment.	Popular as juice or served in halves for breakfast. Served spiced and grilled as entree. In salads, mix with prawns and mayonnaise.

GARDENING FOR THE KITCHEN

WHAT TO LOOK FOR	NUTRITION	STORAGE	PREPARATION	METHOD OF COOKING
KIWIFRUIT Firm, unblemished fruit. Look out for new hairless varieties.	Rich in vitamins A, C and D. 240 kilojoules per 100 grams.	Harvest fruit when still hard. Keep under cool conditions.	Eat raw. Scoop out flesh with a spoon or peel and slice for fruit salad or decoration.	Usually eaten raw, but may be made into jam. Use as a meat tenderiser.
GRAPES Select bunches of uniformly shaped berries, smooth and plump with natural bloom not rubbed off. Stems should be green with fruit firmly attached.	Some vitamin C, iron and thiamin. 276 kilojoules per 100 grams.	In vented plastic bag in refrigerator. Use as quickly as possible.	Wash, dry and remove stems. Pips may also be removed.	Great as a snack. Serve with cheese or pate, and in fruit salad. Combines well with duck, quail and sole.
LEMONS Firm and heavy fruit. Skin should be clean with fine texture. Choose lemons tinged with green for jam making.	Good source of vitamin C. Some calcium and iron. 134 kilojoules per 100 grams.	Keep in cool place, can be home-cured for longer storage. Juice can be frozen for use at later date.	Wipe over. Juice, slice for decoration. Cut into wedges and dip in parsley to serve with fish.	Use as a meat tenderiser (mix with mustard to coat meat before baking) and in sorbets. Helps stop apples and bananas from discolouring.
MANDARINS Firm and heavy fruit. Skin should be glossy with a strong orange colour. Heavy fruit gives high juice yield.	Excellent source of vitamin C. Some vitamin A, thiamin and calcium. 193 kilojoules per 100 grams.	Can be kept outside refrigerator in cool place for short time. Keep in crisper for longer storage.	Wipe over and peel. Best eaten raw.	Ideal for lunch box. Use in the same way as an orange, as a crystallised fruit, or in sorbets.
NECTARINES Smooth, plump and highly coloured fruit with no skin blemish. Avoid hard, dull and immature fruit.	Good source of vitamin C. Fair source of vitamin A and dietary fibre. Some iron and thiamin. 260 kilojoules per 100 grams.	Bruise easily. Handle with care. Refrigerate fruit that is riper. Use as quickly as possible.	Wash, cut and discard stone.	Delightful as a snack. Combine with roast beef, cheese and wholemeal bread as a sandwich. Enjoy with cereal or ice cream.
ORANGES Firm and heavy fruit. Skin should be glossy with a fine texture. Colour does not indicate maturity.	Excellent source vitamin C. Fair source dietary fibre. Some vitamin A, thiamin and calcium. 188 kilojoules per 100 grams.	Can be kept outside refrigerator in cool place for short time. Keep in crisper for longer storage.	Peel before eating, slice whole for salads, halve for juicing, quarter and freeze as a snack.	Serve with meat, rice. Use to flavour puddings, breads, biscuits, desserts and in fruit salad, marmalade. Ideal as juice.

WHAT TO LOOK FOR	NUTRITION	STORAGE	PREPARATION	METHOD OF COOKING
PAWPAWS Select well-coloured fruit. Skin should not be shrivelled or dull, and have no ripe rots or bruising. Aroma is good indicator of ripeness.	Excellent source of dietary fibre. Good source of vitamin C. Fair source of iron. Some riboflavin and niacin. 381 kilojoules per 100 grams.	Ripen at room temperature. Keep ripe fruit in refrigerator. Use as soon as possible.	Wipe over. Slice as required and remove seeds.	Use as meat tenderiser. Serve as accompaniment to smoked beef. Use in fruit salad, or with yoghurt and honey as dessert. Lovely water ice.
PASSIONFRUIT Select full heavy fruit with smooth dark purple skin. Avoid withered fruit.	Excellent source of vitamin C. Fair source of vitamin A. 172 kilojoules per 100 grams.	Keep in plastic bag in crisper of refrigerator. Pulp may be frozen for later use.	Wipe over. Cut in half. Remove pulp and use as required. Discard skin.	Use in fruit salad and fruit punch. Serve as topping over ice cream, pavlovas and flummery or as a fruit sauce. Include in icings.
PEACHES Firm fruit which is just beginning to soften, with a peachy smell. Avoid bruised or under-developed fruit.	Fair source of vitamin C and dietary fibre. Some vitamin A, iron, niacin. 172 kilojoules per 100 grams.	Keep in unsealed plastic bag in refrigerator. Will deteriorate quickly at room temperature.	Wash and discard stone. If peeled, use lemon juice to prevent discolouration.	Pies. Top with cinnamon and butter and lightly grill. Eat fresh with cereal, ice cream, cream or yoghurt. Use in compotes and mousses.
PEARS Pears ripen from the inside out after harvesting. Test for ripeness by applying gentle pressure at the stem area. Avoid immature fruit.	Fair source of vitamin C and dietary fibre. 234 kilojoules per 100 grams.	Store firm pears in vented plastic bag in refrigerator. Ripen at room temperature.	Wash and dry. Remove stalk for cooking. Peel only if recipe calls for it.	Eat raw with cheese and walnuts. Preserve. Serve with roast lamb, smoked fish or ham. Poach in vanilla syrup and coat with chocolate. Bake in wine.
PLUMS Firm, bright and fully developed fruit, with no sign of wrinkling.	Fair source of dietary fibre. Some vitamin A, vitamin C and thiamin. 247 kilojoules per 100 grams.	Ripen at room temperature. Then refrigerate and use as soon as possible.	Wash, cut and discard stone.	Jam, compotes. Serve chilled with camembert or blue cheese. With ice cream. Bake with roast lamb for added flavour. Use as a snack.
STRAWBERRIES Fruit should be clean and brightly coloured with no sign of soft spots or mould. Look for green stem cap and avoid fruit with white or green areas.	Excellent source vitamin C. Fair source dietary fibre. Some iron. 155 kilojoules per 100 grams.	Keep in refrigerator. Very perishable. Use as soon as possible.	Hull and wipe over.	Preserves, jams, tarts. Puree for fruit sauce. Combine with pineapple. Add to fruit salad. With cream or yoghurt. In fruit punch.

PART VI: YOUR GARDENING CALENDAR

AUGUST

With its temperamental weather changes, this month heralds new activity in the garden. It is time to establish the spring garden, with its array of vegetables, flowers and fruit.

Bulbs are flourishing in the flower beds and new buds are beginning to appear on the fruit trees. More seed can be sown in trays for transplanting later, while soil is prepared with fertiliser, peat and compost. Nature has a way of prompting the gardener to action in August, which will bring the reward of a satisfying harvest later on.

VEGETABLES

August is the time to begin planting the spring garden for vegetables, flowers and fruit. Seed can be sown in trays for transplanting in the warm weather to come.

Early carrots and radishes can be sown direct into the garden. Where the soil is cold and wet the bed should be raised with the addition of peat and compost to prepare for planting later. Work in a base dressing of Gro-Plus General Garden Fertiliser and lime.

Continue spraying winter crops of cabbage, cauliflower and broad beans with Champion Copper to combat ring spot, downy mildew and chocolate spot.

FRUIT

Make an application of fertiliser to the base of fruit trees. Spread 2–4 kg around the base of established trees and 0.5–1 kg around young trees. Spread fertiliser evenly over the roots, which should extend approximately 45 cm beyond the tips of the outermost leaves. Take care to keep fertiliser away from the trunk, and water in well.

Citrus fruits will be approaching maturity. High skin colour is caused by cold temperatures and is not always an indication of ripeness.

Green tip or early bud movement begins in peaches, nectarines, plums, apricots and cherries. This is the time to control leaf curl and bladder plum. These diseases attack the embryo leaves and fruit as they emerge from

Yates 'Fragrant Five' is a classic collection of spring-flowering bulbs that will bring both colour and perfume to your garden.

the bud scales and it is important to spray with Champion Copper at this stage.

Prune out overgrown passionfruit vines to stimulate fresh growth on which the new season's fruit will be produced.

FLOWERS

Daffodils, jonquils, hyacinths, narcissus and lachenalias are all in full bloom. Carefully cultivate to remove weeds and aerate surrounding soil.

LAWNS

Lawns can be top dressed with Gro-Plus Professional Lawn Food using 20–30 g per square metre. Take care to apply evenly. Damp mossy areas can be treated with Surrender.

CONTAINER PLANTS

Plant up new season spring vegetables in containers. Portable container gardens can be placed under shelter on patios or in porches for warmth and protection. Container-raised vegetables will mature earlier no matter how cold or difficult the climate may be. Repot overgrown pot plants. Trim back some of the old roots when repotting with fresh potting mix.

Hint

As newly planted and small-growing rhododendrons finish flowering, snap off the seed heads just above the point where new foliage is forming. This will channel the plant's energy away from seed production and into new growth.

DENISE CLEVERLEY
HORTICULTURAL CONSULTANT

SEEDS TO SOW

FLOWER	VEGETABLE
TEMPERATE CLIMATE	**TEMPERATE CLIMATE**
Ageratum, alyssum, amaranthus, aster, balsam, bedding begonia, tuberous begonia, boronia, Californian poppy, carnation, celosia, chrysanthemum, cockscomb, coleus, cosmos, dahlia (seed), delphinium, dianthus, everlasting daisy, gaillardia, gazania, geranium, gerbera, globe amaranth, gloxinia, gypsophila, honesty, impatiens, kochia, marigold (African), mignonette, nasturtium, ornamental basil, ornamental chilli, petunia, phlox, portulaca, rudbeckia, salpiglossis, salvia, snapdragon, spider flower, statice, strawflower, Sturt's desert pea, sunflower, Swan River daisy, verbena, viscaria, zinnia.	Beetroot, cabbage, cape gooseberry, capsicum, carrots, celery, chicory, Chinese cabbage, choko, cress, endive, kohlrabi, lettuce, mustard, spring onions, parsnip, peas, potatoes (tubers), radish, rhubarb (seed), rhubarb (crowns), salsify, silverbeet, tomatoes.
COLD CLIMATE	**COLD CLIMATE**
Balsam, tuberous begonia, gypsophila, marigold (African), polyanthus, portulaca, rudbeckia, salpiglossis, salvia, scabiosa, snapdragon, spider flower, stance.	Broad beans, cabbage, Chinese cabbage, cress, kohlrabi, lettuce, mustard, onions, spring onions, parsnip, peas, potatoes (tubers), rhubarb (crowns), salsify, silverbeet, spinach, swedes, turnips.

SEPTEMBER

A hectic time in the garden for seed sowing, spraying and fertilising. Buds, shoots, flowers and seeds are sprouting and growth becomes more rapid as days gain in length and become warmer, and soil temperatures rise.

Early spring gardening can be difficult in many districts with changeable cold snaps and late spring frosts likely. Remaining winter green crops can be dug into the soil.

VEGETABLES

Young seedlings are often attacked by downy mildew at this time of the year with yellowing of the leaves and poor growth being typical symptoms.

Spray with Champion Copper or Greenguard. Should aphids or mealybug be a problem, spray with Maldison or Confidor. Remember Blitzem or Mesurol slug and snail pellets to protect young seedlings when planting out.

Early sowings of broad beans will begin to flower. Growth will be quite rapid and plants may treble their size within six to eight weeks. It may be necessary to provide some sort of support. Spray with Bravo to prevent rust and chocolate spot.

Transplant cabbage and cauliflower seedlings.

Vegetables to harvest are broccoli, Brussels sprouts, cabbage, carrots, cauliflower, celery, leeks, lettuce, parsnips, radish, rhubarb, silverbeet, spinach and turnips.

FRUIT

Fruit trees require spraying: it is during this period that fungus infections can invade the growing shoots and continue to develop through the season. Diseases such as leaf curl of peaches can only be controlled by spraying with Champion Copper during the bud swelling and bud burst period. The other major devastating fungus disease is brown rot, which invades the fruit during the flowering and early fruit formation stages. It is necessary to follow a strict programme from bud swelling to petal fall to ensure a reliable crop. This is particularly important in warmer, northern districts where fungal diseases are prevalent.

Hint

Remove spent winter-flowering annuals now and replace them with summer-flowering annuals to ensure a well-established show for Christmas.

DENISE CLEVERLEY
HORTICULTURAL CONSULTANT

Fungus Fighter is an extremely effective fungicide against brown rot, and should be applied during the blossom period through to fruit formation at ten to fourteen day intervals.

Apples and pears are reaching various stages of bud development.

New season's growth on citrus is well advanced with new leaves and flower buds appearing. Black aphids are commonly found on young shoots. Control with Mavrik. Apply citrus fertiliser around the base of the tree using 1–4 kg per established tree.

Apply Champion Copper to grapes as buds burst open. An application of fertiliser will also be beneficial. Use 1–2 kg per established vine.

Plant young passionfruit vines. Drainage is important on heavy, wet sites, and a raised

The symmetrical lines of tulips bring elegance to a spring garden.

growing position can be built in which to place the young vine. Incorporate plenty of organic matter such as peat and compost.

Early season strawberry flowers will have set fruit. Apply regular sprays of Bravo to prevent leaf spot or botrytis.

CONTAINER PLANTS

Once flowering of cyclamen has finished, pot-grown plants can be transplanted outdoors in a sheltered place. In cooler southern areas stand the pot in a sheltered place outdoors.

FLOWERS

Roses are well advanced in growth. Regular sprays with Shield or Super Shield will prevent fungal diseases and insect pests. Apply a mulch to the base of all bushes, along with a dressing of rose fertiliser.

SEEDS TO SOW

FLOWER	VEGETABLE
TEMPERATE CLIMATE	**TEMPERATE CLIMATE**
Ageratum, alyssum, amaranthus, aster, balsam, bedding begonia, tuberous begonia, boronia, Californian poppy, carnation, celosia, chrysanthemum, cockscomb, coleus, cosmos, dahlias (seed), dianthus, everlasting daisy, gaillardia, gazania, geranium, gerbera, globe amaranth, gloxinia, gypsophila, honesty, impatiens, kochia, marigold (African), mignonette, nasturtium, ornamental basil, ornamental chilli, phlox, rudbeckia, salpiglossis, salvia, snapdragon, spider flower, statice, strawflower, Sturt's desert pea, sunflower, Swan River daisy, verbena, viscaria, wallflower.	Beetroot, cabbage, cape gooseberry, capsicum, carrots, celery, chicory, Chinese cabbage, choko, cress, eggplant, endive, kohlrabi, leeks, lettuce, marrows, melon, mustard, spring onions, parsnip, potatoes (tubers), radish, rhubarb (seed), rhubarb (crowns), salsify, silverbeet, squash, tomato.
COLD CLIMATE	**COLD CLIMATE**
Ageratum, alyssum, amaranthus, aquilegia, arctotis, aster, balsam, tuberous begonia, bellis, boronia, calceolaria, calendula, Californian poppy, candytuft, carnation, celosia, chrysanthemum, cockscomb, coleus, cornflower, cosmos, dahlia (seed), delphinium, dianthus, everlasting daisy, gaillardia, gazania, geranium (seed), gerbera, globe amaranth, gloxinia, godetia, gypsophila, honesty, impatiens, kochia, larkspur, linaria, Livingstone daisy, lobelia, lupin, marigolds, mignonette, nasturtium, nemesia, nemophila, nigella, ornamental basil, ornamental chilli, painted daisy, petunia, phlox, portulaca, rudbeckia, salpiglossis, salvia, scabiosa, snapdragon, spider flower, statice, strawflower, Sturt's desert pea, sunflower, Swan River daisy, sweet pea, verbena, viola, Virginian stock, viscaria, zinnia.	Beetroot, cabbage, cape gooseberry, capsicum, carrots, celery, chicory, Chinese cabbage, cress, eggplant, endive, kohlrabi, lettuce, mustard, spring onions, parsnip, peas, potatoes (tubers), radish, rhubarb (seed), rhubarb (crowns), salsify, silverbeet, swedes, turnip.

OCTOBER

Springtime in the garden brings the full flowering of fruit trees and shrubs.

Blossom provides delicate colour amongst new green growth, and in the flowerbeds the bulbs are giving way to a riot of other spring flowers.

This is one of the busiest months of a gardener's year, when soil must be carefully prepared and fertilised for the planting of early crops.

VEGETABLES

Most warm season vegetables can be sown towards the end of this month as the soils warm up. Concentrate on good preparation by using generous quantities of compost or peat. Raise the planting area 15–20 cm above the surrounding soil level. This not only improves drainage, but allows the soil to warm up more quickly.

Sowing summer vegetable seed outdoors too early, in cold soil, can result in poor germination and unthrifty plants. Beans, cucumbers, pumpkins and melons will require minimum germination temperatures of 15°C, the optimum temperature for even germination being 24°C. Do not be too impatient in getting these vegetables underway.

Germinate cucumbers and melons in pots or punnets indoors for an early start.

Young seedlings are often attacked by downy mildew at this time of the year. Typical symptoms include yellowing of leaves, pale brown patching with surface pitting and poor growth. Spray with Greenguard or Champion Copper.

Broad beans should be sprayed with Bravo if chocolate spot or rust appear.

Lay Blitzem or Mesurol slug and snail pellets when new seed emerges or when plants are transplanted.

Lightly scatter pellets every three to four days. During prolonged wet weather, Mesurol pellets are more effective than Blitzem.

FRUIT

Spring blossom is now complete on stonefruit trees, but apples and pears will be coming into full bloom. Warm sunny days encourage bees to work amongst the flowers and will result in a good fruit set. Continue with regular sprays of Greenguard to prevent fungus diseases.

New season's growth is well advanced on grapes, and flowering commences this month. Spray with Bravo at fourteen-day intervals to prevent downy mildew, powdery mildew and black spot.

Citrus fruits of most varieties will now have reached full maturity although tangelos will improve if left on the tree until next month. Apply Champion Copper spray as a pre-blossom treatment to prevent build-up of fungus diseases.

Early season strawberries start to ripen. Occasional applications of Lush liquid fertiliser over the leaves will assist plants to make sturdy growth and improve fruit size.

Plant vegetables now for prolific crops later in the year.

Continue to spray with Bravo and Greenguard to control botrytis, sclerotinia and leaf spot diseases.

LAWN

Rapid growth of lawn demands constant mowing and weekly trimming. Fertilise with Gro-Plus Professional Lawn Food.

FLOWERS

As late winter and spring flowering plants complete their season, beds will need cleaning up for planting of summer flowers.

Old plants should be removed and placed in a compost heap. Bulbs that have become overcrowded should be lifted and divided and then replanted or stored until the next growing season.

Once flowering is complete on spring flowering shrubs, prune back growth to retain shape and size.

Early flowering roses will appear this month. Bushes start to make their most rapid spring growth.

Keep a constant watch for any sign of pest and disease and spray with Shield.

SEEDS TO SOW

FLOWER	VEGETABLE
TEMPERATE CLIMATE	**TEMPERATE CLIMATE**
Ageratum, alyssum, amaranthus, aster, balsam, bedding begonia, boronia, Californian poppy, carnation, celosia, chrysanthemum, cockscomb, coleus, cosmos, dahlia, dianthus, everlasting daisy, gaillardia, gazania, geranium (seed), gerbera, globe amaranth, gloxinia, gypsophila, honesty, impatiens, kochia, marigold (African), nasturtium, ornamental basil, ornamental chilli, petunia, phlox, portulaca, rudbeckia, salpiglossis, salvia, snapdragon, spider flower, statice, strawflower, Sturt's desert pea, sunflower, Swan River daisy, verbena, viscaria, zinnia.	Beans, beetroot, cabbage, cape gooseberry, capsicum, carrots, celery, chicory, Chinese cabbage, choko, cress, cucumber, eggplant, endive, kumara (shoots), leeks, lettuce, marrow, melons, mustard, okra, spring onions, parsnip, pumpkin, radish, rhubarb, salsify, silverbeet, squash, sweet corn, tomato.
COLD CLIMATE	**COLD CLIMATE**
Ageratum, alyssum, amaranthus, arctotis, aster, balsam, bedding begonia, tuberous begonia, bellis, boronia, calceolaria, Californian poppy, celosia, chrysanthemum, cockscomb, coleus, cosmos, dahlia, delphinium, dianthus, everlasting daisy, gaillardia, gazania, geranium (seed), gerbera, globe amaranth, gloxinia, gypsophila, kochia, marigolds, mignonette, nasturtium, nemesia, nemophila, nigella, ornamental basil, ornamental chilli, painted daisy, pansy, petunia, phlox, portulaca, rudbeckia, salpiglossis, salvia, snapdragon, spider flower, strawflower, Sturt's desert pea, sunflower, Swan River daisy, sweet pea, verbena, viola, Virginian stock, viscaria, zinnia.	Beans, beetroot, Brussels sprouts, cabbage, cape gooseberry, capsicum, carrots, celery, chicory, Chinese cabbage, cress, cucumber, eggplant, endive, kohlrabi, leeks, lettuce, marrow, mustard, okra, spring onions, onions, peas, potatoes (tubers), radish, rhubarb, salsify, silverbeet, squash, sweet corn, tomato.

NOVEMBER

Early summer has arrived and this is another colourful and busy month. Growth is rapid and plants must be kept well watered to maintain growth. It is important to apply water before plants show visible signs of wilting.

Mulching will help preserve soil moisture and should be carried out now to be effective over the drier months. Mulching materials include peat, bark and compost, and should be spread around the base of plants to a depth of 3 cm.

VEGETABLES

Vegetables will benefit from a side dressing of Gro-Plus Complete Plant Food and regular watering. Spray with Target or Mavrik to control insects. Blight is best controlled with Bravo or Champion Copper.

Asparagus will continue to be harvested. Cultivate carefully to remove weeds from bed. Broad beans, cabbage, carrots, cauliflower, lettuce, onions, peas, potatoes, radishes, silverbeet and spinach can all be harvested.

Dwarf and climbing beans can be sown this month. For a continuous harvest make regular sowings at three-weekly intervals throughout the summer. 'Scarlet Runner' beans are best grown in warm sheltered positions to ensure a good fruit set.

Sow sweet corn. Sow quick- and long-maturing varieties at the same time to give a spread of harvest, or sow at two weekly intervals.

FLOWERS

Summer annuals can be transplanted. Gladiolus should also be planted now for late summer flowering. Amaryllis, another favourite, can be planted in a warm, sheltered position or grown as an indoor flowering plant.

Trim back shoots on roses which have had flowers, cutting to three or four buds below old flower heads. This will encourage further summer flowering. Roses will also benefit from a dressing of rose fertiliser and should be sprayed with Shield or Super Shield to prevent attacks from pests and diseases.

Shield can also be used to protect other ornamentals.

Canna lilies can be planted in warm, sheltered, sunny positions. Water lilies can be planted in ponds: they grow best in stagnant water and flower profusely when water temperatures increase in midsummer.

Chrysanthemums, carnations and impatiens are available from garden centres at this time and can be planted directly into the garden.

Roses will be at their best during November.

FRUIT

Apply fertiliser to citrus and other fruit trees. Berryfruit such as boysenberry and blackberries should be sprayed with Bravo for dry berry diseases. Spray citrus trees with Champion Copper for verrucosis and Orthene for insect pests.

Early varieties of plums and cherries mature in late November. Young trees should receive their first summer pruning. Trim out the strong vigorous growth and sappy growths in the centre of the tree. Old trees which are carrying a heavy crop of fruit will respond to a further dressing of fertiliser. Irrigate thoroughly if soil becomes dry.

New growth of grapes will be rapid and need tying in.

After fruit set in citrus, another application of fertiliser can be made. Nutrition is important at this time.

Newly planted trees and shrubs will need close attention. Irrigate if the soil is dry and apply a mulch of compost to conserve soil moisture around roots.

CONTAINER PLANTS

Daily watering of container plants is important, particularly in warmer weather, as plants can grow very quickly. Containers can be moved into partially shaded areas in the hottest months.

Turn compost heaps regularly. With warm summer temperatures, composting is rapid and may also need water.

Once a compost has turned a dark, chocolate-brown colour, it is sufficiently decomposed to incorporate into the garden soil or to use as a mulch.

SEEDS TO SOW

FLOWER	VEGETABLE
TEMPERATE CLIMATE	**TEMPERATE CLIMATE**
Ageratum, alyssum, amaranthus, aster, balsam, bedding begonia, Californian poppy, celosia, chrysanthemum, cockscomb, coleus, cosmos, dahlia (seed), dianthus, gazania, geranium (seed), gerbera, globe amaranth, gypsophila, kochia, marigold (African), nasturtium, ornamental basil, ornamental chilli, petunia, phlox, portulaca, rudbeckia, salpiglossis, salvia, spider flower, Sturt's desert pea, sunflower, Swan River daisy, verbena, viscaria, zinnia.	Beans, beetroot, cabbage, cape gooseberry, capsicum, carrots, celery, chicory, Chinese cabbage, cress, cucumber, eggplant, endive, leeks, lettuce, marrow, melons, mustard, okra, spring onions, parsnip, pumpkin, radish, rhubarb, salsify, silverbeet, squash, sweet corn, tomato, turnips.
COLD CLIMATE	**COLD CLIMATE**
Ageratum, alyssum, amaranthus, aster, balsam, bedding begonia, calceolaria, Californian poppy, celosia, chrysanthemum, cockscomb, coleus, cosmos, dahlia (seed), gazania, geranium, gerbera, globe amaranth, gypsophila, kochia, marigold (African), nasturtium, ornamental basil, ornamental chilli, petunia, phlox, portulaca, salvia, snapdragon, spider flower, strawflower, Sturt's desert pea, sunflower, Swan River daisy, verbena, viscaria, zinnia.	Beans, beetroot, broccoli, Brussels sprouts, cabbage, cape gooseberry, capsicum, carrots, cauliflower, celery, chicory, Chinese cabbage, cress, cucumber, eggplant, endive, kohlrabi, leeks, lettuce, marrow, melons, mustard, okra, spring onions, parsnip, pumpkins, radish, rhubarb, salsify, silverbeet, squash, sweet corn, tomato.

DECEMBER

Summer is in full swing, filling the garden with attractive colours and aromas. The vegetable garden is full of succulent green and root vegetables waiting to be picked and the 'Scarlet Runner' beans put out flowers to rival those in the flowerbeds.

Pay attention to watering, to keep all this burgeoning richness going. Remember pests will also be active amongst the foliage. The garden requires work in this season, but such activity is a pleasure amongst the wealth of greenery and flowers which crown the year's efforts.

VEGETABLES

With rapid growth of tomatoes, sweet corn and beans this month careful attention will have to be paid to cultivating, weeding, irrigation, feeding and spraying.

Caterpillars and white fly are likely to become a problem. Mavrik and Target provide best control; blights are best controlled with Bravo, while Greenguard is

Plant peppers in the sunniest spot you can find to ensure fruit reaches maturity.

better for powdery mildew on cucumbers and pumpkins.

Continue successive sowings of summer vegetables including beans, beetroot, carrot, celery, sweet corn, cucumber, lettuce, marrow, melons and tomatoes.

If earwigs appear, spray with Target or Mavrik.

Vegetables to harvest are asparagus, beetroot, broad beans, beans, cabbage, carrots, cauliflower, cucumber, lettuce, marrow, onion, peas, potatoes, silverbeet and tomatoes.

Sow dwarf beans at two to three week intervals. Sow climbing beans at six to eight week intervals.

'Scarlet Runner' beans produce masses of flowers. However, it is common for many of these flowers to drop off, due to climatic conditions such as strong winds or cold snaps at the time of flowering. Irrigate if soil becomes dry and apply a side dressing of fertiliser.

Aphids and white butterfly caterpillars are likely to cause damage on cabbages, broccoli, cauliflowers and Brussels sprouts at this time of the year. Spray with Target or apply Derris Dust.

Eggplant and pepper transplants will be ready to plant out. Choose the warmest and most sunny growing position where they will get maximum summer heat.

September and October plantings of peas will be ready for harvest. Potatoes will require mounding up with soil to prevent damage from potato tuber moth grubs.

FLOWERS

Anemones and ranunculus become available in December and can be planted for flowering during May, June and July.

Pinch and tie chrysanthemums if they have been grown as long-stem single blooms. Continue to water when weather is dry.

Maintain spraying of roses with Shield or Super Shield to prevent pests and diseases. Apply a side dressing of fertiliser to stimulate late summer growth. Keep bushes irrigated when dry.

Summer growth of lilium, dahlia, gladioli

and chrysanthemum is well advanced. Cultivate frequently around plants. Irrigate whenever soil is dry.

FRUIT

Further applications of fertiliser will help increase the size of fruit on fruit trees. Use 1–4 kg per tree depending on the size of the tree.

Continue spraying pip- and stonefruit with Greenguard for black spot and brown rot control.

Greenguard will also give excellent control on powdery mildew of tamarillos. Citrus should be sprayed with Champion Copper to prevent verrucosis and leaf curl.

Keep passionfruit well watered and apply Gro-Plus Complete Plant Food. Spray with Champion Copper to prevent fungus diseases.

Strawberries will be ready for harvest. Plants may need netting to prevent bird damage.

Main harvest of raspberries is starting. Leaf roller caterpillars can be troublesome. Spray fruits with Carbaryl, which has only a one day waiting period after application before harvest.

LAWNS

Summer weather causes drying out. Do not cut too closely, and water as often as possible.

CONTAINER PLANTS

Indoor plants should be moved away from hot windowsills to avoid burning at this time of the year. As the weather gets warmer the frequency of watering and feeding should be increased.

Repot winter- and spring- flowering indoor plants such as orchids.

Summer is a difficult time to care for container plants. Dry sunny conditions cause severe water stress. They will need daily watering, at times twice daily.

SEEDS TO SOW

FLOWER	VEGETABLE
TEMPERATE CLIMATE	**TEMPERATE CLIMATE**
Ageratum, alyssum, amaranthus, aster, Californian poppy, celosia, cockscomb, coleus, cosmos, cyclamen, dahlia (seed), gazania, geranium (seed), gerbera, globe amaranth, kochia, marigold (African), nasturtium, ornamental basil, ornamental chilli, petunia, phlox, portulaca, rudbeckia, salpiglossis, spider flower, Sturt's desert pea, sunflower, Swan River daisy, verbena, viscaria, zinnia.	Beans, beetroot, broccoli, Brussels sprouts, cabbage, cape gooseberry, capsicum, carrots, cauliflower, celery, chicory, Chinese cabbage, cress, cucumber, eggplant, endive, leeks, lettuce, marrow, melons, mustard, okra, spring onions, parsnip, pumpkin, radish, rhubarb, salsify, silverbeet, squash, sweet corn, tomato.
COLD CLIMATE	**COLD CLIMATE**
Ageratum, alyssum, aster, balsam, calceolaria, Californian poppy, celosia, chrysanthemum, cockscomb, coleus, cosmos, cyclamen, dahlia (seed), forget-me-not, gazania, geranium, gerbera, globe amaranth, gypsophila, kochia, nasturtium, ornamental basil, ornamental chilli, petunia, phlox, portulaca, salvia, snapdragon, spider flower, Sturt's desert pea, sunflower, Swan River daisy, verbena, viscaria, zinnia.	Beans, beetroot, broccoli, Brussels sprouts, cabbage, carrots, cauliflower, celery, chicory, Chinese cabbage, cress, cucumber, endive, leeks, lettuce, marrow, melons, mustard, okra, spring onions, parsnip, radish, rhubarb, salsify, spinach, squash, sweet corn.

JANUARY

January is a time for outdoor lunches under shady trees, for children to play under the hose on the lawn and for some of the hottest days of summer.

The garden looks beautiful and is also demanding: take care that soil moisture is constantly maintained. Fruits and flowers need attention, but there are often helpers on hand: holidaying children can be encouraged to take an interest, especially in easy tasks like pulling weeds. Planning and planting for the winter garden should also begin now.

VEGETABLES

This is the time to plant out cabbage, cauliflower, leeks, lettuce, silverbeet and spinach. Target or Derris Dust can be used to control white cabbage butterfly caterpillars, which are likely to be particularly troublesome.

Carrots and parsnips sown in November and December will be growing rapidly. Finger-size seedlings can be pulled out and eaten, to leave more growing space for the others. Carrot rust fly can be prevented with Soil Insect Killer.

Cucumbers and marrows will be ready for harvest. Marrows and zucchini will need daily picking to encourage continuous fruiting.

Garlic and onions may be ready for harvest. Garlic plants should be dug up and left to dry on the soil surface, even though they are still green and growing. Once the stems of onions have bent over, they need to be pulled and left to lie in the sun to dry and cure. Most will need ten to fourteen days to dry out sufficiently before storing.

New potatoes can be harvested as required once flowering is complete. Keep soil mounded up around potato plants, as cracked, dry, open soils will expose the tubers to the potato tuber moth.

Sweet corn in warm areas will be ready to harvest. Once the tassels have begun to shrivel and dry, the cobs are ready for picking. Tomatoes will be ready for harvest, and can be picked as fruit show colour. Trim off bottom leaves from plant as the fruit ripens, to help better air circulation around the base of the plant.

Continue to remove laterals and tie up the stems of tall-growing varieties.

Spray with Champion Copper or Bravo to control blight on tomatoes and potatoes.

FLOWERS

Marigold, zinnia, petunia and salvia will all be in full bloom. Pick off any old flower heads and keep the plants well watered.

Spray gladioli with Orthene or Confidor to prevent thrips damage.

In the midst of summer, the sumptuous scent of frangipani floats on the balmy night air.

Dahlias require plenty of water during the dry summer months.

Spray dahlias with Shield or Super Shield to prevent powdery mildew and caterpillars.

Rust disease and black aphids may be a problem on chrysanthemums; they should be treated with Shield.

Early season planting of spring flowering bulbs can be started. Prepare sites by cultivating soil, removing weeds and incorporating Gro-Plus Bulb Food.

FRUIT

Stonefruit should be sprayed with Greenguard at frequent intervals to prevent brown rot. Apples and pears should be sprayed with Carbaryl to control pear slug.

Summer pruning of peaches, nectarines and kiwifruit can be carried out.

New season's growth on grapes can be trimmed and tied down. Spray vines with Greenguard for downy mildew, powdery mildew and black spot control. Apply side dressing of fertiliser to citrus trees, check wood carefully for attacks of stem borer. If present, prune out infected branches and burn.

The main harvest of berryfruits is complete: prune out the old canes which have fruited and tie in the new season's canes, selecting only the strongest. Spray with Guardall and Garden Master for cane spot, blight and bud loss damage.

Tamarillos should be kept well watered and mulched in dry periods to avoid early fruit drop.

LAWNS

Keep lawns well watered to prevent grasses burning off; this will help prevent weed invasion.

CONTAINER GARDENS

Keep plants well watered, particularly those in smaller shallow containers (yellow leaves will indicate a nutrition problem). Include a liquid fertiliser at least once a week. Thrive is recommended.

Hint

When you are watering your garden over summer, remember to give your hedges a good soak too.

DENISE CLEVERLEY
HORTICULTURAL CONSULTANT

SEEDS TO SOW

FLOWER	VEGETABLE
TEMPERATE CLIMATE	**TEMPERATE CLIMATE**
Ageratum, alyssum, calceolaria, cineraria, cyclamen, forget-me-not, linaria, lupin, marigold (French), nasturtium, pansy, Iceland poppy, primula, stock, sweet pea, verbena, viola, wallflower.	Beans, beetroot, broccoli, Brussels sprouts, cabbage, carrots, cauliflower, chicory, celery, Chinese cabbage, cress, cucumber, endive, kohlrabi, leeks, lettuce, marrow, mustard, onions, parsnip, radish, rhubarb, salsify, silverbeet, swedes, sweet corn and turnips.
COLD CLIMATE	**COLD CLIMATE**
Ageratum, alyssum, calceolaria, cineraria, cyclamen, forget-me-not, gypsophila, hollyhock, lupin, marigold (French), Iceland poppy, primula, stock, sweet pea, verbena, viola, wallflower.	Dwarf beans, beetroot, broccoli, Brussels sprouts, cabbage, carrots, cauliflower, chicory, Chinese cabbage, cress, endive, kohlrabi, leeks, lettuce, marrow, mustard, spring onions, parsnip, radish, rhubarb, salsify, shallots, silverbeet, swedes, turnips.

FEBRUARY

If your garden has been well maintained, the green growth amongst trees and plants will still be lush and bright. Hibiscus are blooming and roses are still adding their brilliant splashes of colour to the flowerbeds.

As the hot, dry weather continues, many vegetables and fruits are coming to maturity, while the trees and shrubs are nearing the end of their main growing season.

The main concern is with moisture: plenty of water will be needed to maintain growth.

VEGETABLES

Cabbage, broccoli and leeks will be starting to make vigorous growth. These need to be encouraged so that they become well established for winter. Keep them well watered and apply a side dressing of Gro-Plus Complete Plant Food.

Earlier sowings of carrots will be ready to harvest.

Pick cucumbers as they mature to encourage more fruit production. Baby cucumbers can be used as pickling gherkins.

Eggplants, peppers, tomatoes and cape gooseberries will be ready to harvest, plus garlic and onions. After they have been well dried, the tops and roots of onions can be

Remove spent flowers from hanging baskets to keep them looking attractive.

trimmed and then stored in open-mesh wire trays or boxes. Alternatively, tops may be tied to a string and hung up, which is a very effective storing method.

Summer insects are likely to be a problem and should be sprayed with Target or Mavrik. Blights are best controlled with Bravo or Champion Copper while Greenguard is best for powdery mildew on cucumbers and pumpkins.

FLOWERS

Lightly prune roses and cut off dead heads to encourage more flowers. Spray roses with Shield or Super Shield to control insect pests as well as powdery mildew, rust and black spot.

Chrysanthemums should be disbudded, to encourage large blooms.

Thrips are a particular menace this month and are likely to attack gladioli, bottlebrush, ceanothus, fuchsia, azaleas and camellias, causing silvering of the leaves. Leaf roller caterpillar is also a problem on many shrubs, particularly manuka, camellia and chrysanthemum: they are easily recognised as they stick the young leaves together for protection. Psyllids attack pittosporum and pohutukawa, causing a blistering of the leaves. All of these insects can be quite devastating and are most effectively controlled by spraying at intervals of two to three weeks with Orthene or Confidor.

Early autumn rains often cause plants to become diseased. Once foliage starts to deteriorate, old plants should be removed. Dahlias will continue flowering in warm northern and central areas. Close attention should be given to controlling powdery mildew by spraying with Fungus Fighter.

February is the main month to plant bulbs.

FRUIT

The main autumn harvest of fruits begins. Late season peaches and plums mature rapidly. Apples develop a higher skin colour. Keep all trees well watered to swell fruit size.

As soon as harvest of stonefruit is complete, trees need to be summer pruned. Prune out overcrowded branches to open the trees' framework and allow light to penetrate the lower portions of the tree. Space out current season's growth along the main fruiting laterals and remove about two thirds of new growth on vigorous trees.

Pruning when trees are in full leaf is important for the prevention of silverleaf infection. Continue to spray apples and pears with Carbaryl to prevent codling moth and leaf roller.

Grapes may need a further trimming of vine growth before harvest. Continue to spray with Bravo to prevent mildew forming. Mealybug and leaf roller may also be troublesome. Spray with Target; citrus trees should be sprayed with Champion Copper for verrucosis plus Target or Orthene for insect problems.

CONTAINER PLANTS

Indoor plants tend to need more water in summer so keep a close watch on all pots, particularly those near windows and in the sun. As temperatures rise there are also more likely to be pest and disease problems.

LAWNS

The main lawn sowing season is rapidly approaching. New lawn areas require thorough preparation.

SEEDS TO SOW

FLOWER	VEGETABLE
TEMPERATE CLIMATE	**TEMPERATE CLIMATE**
Ageratum, alyssum, aquilegia, arctotis, bellis, calceolaria, calendula, candytuft, Canterbury bells, cineraria, cornflower, cyclamen, delphinium, dianthus, everlasting daisy, forget-me-not, gaillardia, godetia, gypsophila, hollyhock, honesty, impatiens, larkspur, linaria, Livingstone daisy, lobelia, lupin, French marigold, mignonette, nasturtium, nemesia, nemophila, nigella, painted daisy, pansy, polyanthus, poor man's orchid, Iceland poppy, primula, scabiosa, snapdragon, spider flower, statice, stock, strawflower, sweet pea, verbena, viola, Virginian stock, wallflower.	Dwarf beans, beetroot, broccoli, Brussels sprouts, cabbage, carrots, cauliflower, celery, chicory, Chinese cabbage, cress, endive, kohlrabi, leeks, lettuce, mustard, spring onions, parsnip, peas, radish, rhubarb, salsify, shallots, silverbeet, spinach, swedes, turnips.
COLD CLIMATE	**COLD CLIMATE**
Ageratum, alyssum, aquilegia, arctotis, bellis, calendula, candytuft, Canterbury bells, carnation, cineraria, cornflower, cyclamen, delphinium, dianthus, everlasting daisy, forget-me-not, gaillardia, godetia, gypsophila, hollyhock, honesty, impatiens, larkspur, linaria, Livingstone daisy, lobelia, lupin, marigold (French), mignonette, nemesia, nemophila, nigella, painted daisy, pansy, polyanthus, poor man's orchid, Iceland poppy, primula, scabiosa, snapdragon, spider flower, statice, stock, strawflower, viola, Virginian stock, wallflower.	Beetroot, broccoli, Brussels sprouts, cabbage, carrots, chicory, Chinese cabbage, cress, endive, kohlrabi, leeks, lettuce, marrow, melons, spring onions, parsnip, radish, rhubarb, salsify, silverbeet, spinach, shallots, swedes, turnips.

MARCH

Flowerbeds can be full of glorious colour this month, with petunias, salvia and marigolds providing rich contrasts. This is harvest month for most fruits, and orchardists will be busy picking plums, apples and peaches and tidying the orchard areas.

VEGETABLES

In vegetable gardens in cooler districts, the harvest of outdoor summer-grown vegetables such as tomatoes, beans, cucumbers, zucchini, pumpkins and sweet corn is complete. In warmer areas most of these vegetables continue ripening throughout the autumn, but careful attention to spraying is needed to prevent late attacks from pests and diseases.

March is the most important month for sowing and planting winter vegetables. Late plantings of broccoli, Brussels sprouts, cauliflower, kohlrabi, silverbeet and spinach may be made. In warmer districts lettuce can be sown, along with sugar snap peas.

If caterpillars or other summer pests are attacking vegetables such as beans, tomatoes or cabbages, spray with Target.

FLOWERS

Flower gardens become a blaze of autumn colour in March. Continue to disbud late-flowering chrysanthemums for large blooms.

Thrips, mealybug, leaf roller caterpillars and blister scale may be major problems. All of these insects are devastating, but can be effectively controlled by spraying with Orthene at two to three weekly intervals.

March is an ideal month for planting out anemones and ranunculus. It is a good idea to start them in seed-raising mix, as this will give a more reliable germination. Dust bulbs with Captan fungicide as an added precaution against damping off rots.

In cooler areas the flowering season for roses is coming to an end. Prior to autumn leaf fall, apply copper oxychloride to prevent overwintering of foliage and stem diseases.

FRUIT

March is predominantly a harvesting month for most fruit, particularly the main apple varieties and late stonefruits. Continue spraying the fruit with Carbaryl right up to harvest to prevent codling moth attacks. In all the areas, late varieties of stonefruits, particularly 'Golden Queen' peaches, are very susceptible to brown rot. This attacks towards the end of the season so it is important to continue spraying with Greenguard or Bravo up until harvest.

Tamarillos will need sprays of Fungus Fighter to protect from powdery mildew.

Citrus trees should receive an autumn dressing of fertiliser.

Gaillardia contribute to garden colour in March.

ORNAMENTAL TREES AND SHRUBS

Many shrubs and trees are easily propagated from semi-mature tip cuttings. Select young strong shoots from the upper portions of the branches. Those which receive full sunlight on outer parts of trees are the best propagating material.

Trim hedges to allow some growth before winter sets in. Young shoots give rich winter colour.

LAWNS

Final steps of soil preparation and levelling need to be completed for new lawn areas.

Choose a lawn seed mix which is best suited to your district and particular use. In the warmer northern areas successful establishment of fine-leaf turfs is often very difficult. Choosing a fine-leafed ryegrass is a far more suitable option under these circumstances.

To prepare an old lawn surface for over-sowing, give a vigorous raking. Fill in any dips and hollows with new topsoil before oversowing with seed.

CONTAINER GARDENS

Plant growth is slower, and watering and feeding are not so critical as they were during summer months.

SEEDS TO SOW

FLOWER	VEGETABLE
TEMPERATE CLIMATE	**TEMPERATE CLIMATE**
Ageratum, alyssum, aquilegia, arctotis, bellis, calceolaria, calendula, candytuft, Canterbury bells, carnation, cineraria, cornflower, cyclamen, delphinium, dianthus, everlasting daisy, forget-me-not, gaillardia, godetia, gypsophila, hollyhock, honesty, impatiens, larkspur, linaria, Livingstone daisy, lobelia, lupin, marigold (French), mignonette, nemesia, nemophila, nigella, painted daisy, pansy, polyanthus, poor man's orchid, Iceland poppy, primula, scabiosa, snapdragon, spider flower, statice, stock, strawflower, sweet pea, viola, Virginian stock, wallflower.	Beetroot, broccoli, Brussels sprouts, cabbage, carrots, cauliflower, chicory, Chinese cabbage, cress, endive, kohlrabi, leeks, lettuce, mustard, onions, spring onions, parsnip, peas, radish, salsify, shallots, silverbeet, spinach, swedes, turnips.
COLD CLIMATE	**COLD CLIMATE**
Alyssum, aquilegia, arctotis, bellis, calendula, candytuft, Canterbury bells, carnation, cineraria, cornflower, cyclamen, delphinium, dianthus, everlasting daisy, forget-me-not, gaillardia, godetia, gypsophila, hollyhock, honesty, impatiens, larkspur, linaria, Livingstone daisy, lobelia, lupin, marigold (French), mignonette, nemesia, nemophila, nigella, painted daisy, pansy, polyanthus, poor man's orchid, Iceland poppy, primula, scabiosa, snapdragon, statice, stock, strawflower, sweet pea, viola, Virginian stock, wallflower.	Broad beans, cabbage, Chinese cabbage, cress, leeks, lettuce, melons, spring onions, radish, shallots, spinach, turnips.

APRIL

April showers bring much-needed moisture to the garden. The cooler nights add freshness to lawns and young seedlings, and everywhere there will be a flush of new green growth.

This means weeds, too, which will need to be removed from flower beds, borders, shrubberies and under hedges.

Leaves on deciduous trees will be golden, red or brown and ready to fall. While tidying up the leaves, gardeners can pay attention to flower beds where the last of the summer blooms may be dying back. Bulbs can be planted in the freshly weeded earth.

VEGETABLES

In northern areas, late harvest of summer vegetables will continue. In colder southern areas the autumn harvest of broccoli, cabbage, cauliflower, swedes, turnips and spinach begins. Carrots and parsnips should be maturing along with celery. Further sowings of lettuces can be made. Choose hardy winter growing varieties, e.g. 'Winter Triumph'.

Sow sweet peas this month. They can be pre-germinated by placing on wet blotting paper.

Pumpkins stored for winter use should be inspected occasionally for signs of decay. Fruit with any symptoms should be removed to prevent infection spreading.

Old rhubarb crowns which have become overcrowded need to be dug up and divided.

Spinach is a valuable winter and early spring vegetable and successive sowings can be made now.

Yams can be harvested. Dig carefully once the tops have been frosted or are withered and store for winter use.

April is also an excellent month for sowing sugar snap peas.

Winter plantings are best made on raised beds or ridges to avoid waterlogging. This is particularly important on heavy clay soils.

If caterpillar and other summer insects are attacking vegetables now about to be harvested, spray with Carbaryl or Target. These can both be used close to harvest.

FLOWERS

Another busy month for tidying up. The last of the summer annuals can be removed and many of the summer flowering perennials cut back. Damage from summer insects, thrips, mealybug and leaf roller caterpillar is usually evident at this time. However, in many cases the insect has gone, leaving only the evidence behind.

Planting of anemones and ranunculus can still be made. For best results start them off in trays of seed-raising mix, using Black Magic Seed Raising Mix. April is also the last chance for daffodils, jonquils and other spring flowering bulbs. Cultivate winter and spring flowering annuals and bulbs and side dress with fertiliser.

FRUIT

Apart from the late varieties of apples, most pip and stonefruit have been harvested. In areas where silverleaf is known to be a problem, it is a good idea to carry out pruning while the weather is still dry. This helps prevent silverleaf infection.

When leaf fall commences, apply Champion Copper to protect leaf scars from fungus infections.

Tamarillos should be reaching maturity and a late spraying with Fungus Fighter to control powdery mildew will be required in warm areas.

The main planting season for strawberries is in April. In warm areas new beds will give best results, but in southern areas two-year-old beds are satisfactory.

Strawberries do best in rich, fertile free-draining soils. Before planting incorporate generous quantities of compost and Gro-Plus Complete Plant Food.

LAWNS

April is a good month for topdressing lawns to speed recovery from any damage suffered in dry weather. Apply Gro-Plus Professional Lawn Food at a rate of 30 g per square metre on established lawns.

A balanced fertiliser containing iron will help produce a deeper colour, and will promote fine grass species and discourage coarse grasses and weeds.

Late autumn is a good time for planting trees and shrubs as this allows for firm establishment before the onset of winter. Prepare the growing position carefully.

CONTAINER PLANTS

Place containers in warm, sunny situations. Growing mixes shrink with continued use. Add fresh potting mix to replenish.

SEEDS TO SOW

FLOWER	VEGETABLE
TEMPERATE CLIMATE	**TEMPERATE CLIMATE**
Ageratum, alyssum, aquilegia, arctotis, bellis, calceolaria, calendula, candytuft, Canterbury bells, carnation, cineraria, cornflower, cyclamen, delphinium, dianthus, everlasting daisy, forget-me-not, gaillardia, godetia, gypsophila, hollyhock, honesty, impatiens, larkspur, linaria, Livingstone daisy, lobelia, lupin, marigold (French), mignonette, nemesia, nemophila, nigella, painted daisy, pansy, polyanthus, poor man's orchid, Iceland poppy, primula, scabiosa, snapdragon, statice, stock, strawflower, sweet pea, viola, Virginian stock, wallflower.	Broad beans, broccoli, cabbage, Chinese cabbage, cress, leeks, lettuce, mustard, onions, peas potato (tubers), radish, shallots, spinach, turnips.
COLD CLIMATE	**COLD CLIMATE**
Alyssum, aquilegia, arctotis, bellis, calendula, candytuft, Canterbury bells, carnations, cineraria, cornflower, cyclamen, delphinium, dianthus, everlasting daisy, forget-me-not, gaillardia, godetia, gypsophila, hollyhock, honesty, impatiens, larkspur, linaria, Livingstone daisy, lobelia, lupin, marigold (French), mignonette, nemesia, nemophila, nigella, painted daisy, pansy, polyanthus, poor man's orchid, Iceland poppy, primula, scabiosa, snapdragon, statice, stock, strawflower, sweet pea, viola, Virginian stock, wallflower.	Broad beans, cress, lettuce, mustard, onions, radish, shallots, spinach.

MAY

In this month the hint of winter is apparent right through the garden, as the growth rate for most plants slows down. Weeding, cultivation, pest and disease control are less of a worry than they were earlier in the year.

This is the time to concentrate on soil preparation for spring and summer planting.

VEGETABLES

Continue spraying celery, cabbages and cauliflowers with Champion Copper or Bravo to check fungus diseases and leaf spots. Slugs and snails can also be a problem at this time of the year. Lay Blitzem or Mesurol pellets when transplanting young seedlings.

May is an important month to sow broad beans. Garlic can be planted now.

Main winter harvest of celery continues; select outer stalks and use as required.

January/February sowings of kohlrabi are ready for harvest. Use leaves as greens in salads and coleslaws, or eat cooked.

Any vacant garden areas can be sown in a cover crop of either lupins, barley or oats. These crops can then be dug into the soil during early spring. They are an excellent way to improve the soil structure for next season. Garden compost should also be incorporated into the soil now.

FLOWERS

Protea, camellia, leucodendron and banksia all provide winter colour.

Dahlia tubers and gladioli corms can be lifted. Dust with an insecticide and fungicide and store in a dry place. Cut back all old top growth of strong-growing perennials such as geraniums and Michaelmas daisies.

Overcrowding commonly occurs where different types of perennials are planted close to one another. The dominant ones will need trimming back to allow the less vigorous ones to be able to flourish.

Prepare new planting beds for roses, trees and shrubs before the soil becomes too wet.

There are scores of camellias from which to choose. Select a variety that is appropriate for your conditions.

Proteas are a unique group of plants; they require well drained acidic soils which are low in nutrient content.

Work in plenty of compost or peat. The addition of organic matter improves drainage and aeration which is particularly important in clay soils over the winter.

Prune back those shrubs that have finished flowering.

LAWN CARE

Gro-Plus Professional Lawn Food or sulphate of ammonia can be applied to the lawn at a rate of 30 g per metre (approximately one handful). This will boost the growth of grasses and suppress growth of broad-leafed weeds. If these are a major problem it may be necessary to use a selective weedkiller, e.g. Turfix. If moss is a problem in those shady or poorly drained areas spray with Surrender. Many bare or thin areas of lawn can be raked over and reseeded.

FRUIT

Harvest feijoas as they fall to the ground. Guavas will also be ripening and normally need to be picked.

Pick kiwifruit while flesh is firm; they ripen in storage. Once the skin colour of tamarillos begins to change from green to red

Leucodendrons make an excellent cut flower; they will last for several weeks in a vase.

(or to yellow on yellow varieties!) they can be harvested.

Set out young strawberry plants.

SEEDS TO SOW

FLOWER	VEGETABLE
TEMPERATE CLIMATE	**TEMPERATE CLIMATE**
Ageratum, alyssum, aquilegia, arctotis, bellis, calendula, candytuft, Canterbury bells, carnations, cineraria, cornflower, cyclamen, delphinium, dianthus, everlasting daisy, forget-me-not, gaillardia, godetia, gypsophila, hollyhock, honesty, impatiens, larkspur, linaria, Livingstone daisy, lobelia, lupin, marigold (French), mignonette, nemesia, nemophila, nigella, painted daisy, pansy, polyanthus, Iceland poppy, primula, scabiosa, snapdragon, statice, stock, strawflower, sweet pea, viola, Virginian stock, wallflower.	**Broad beans, broccoli, cress, lettuce, mustard, onions, spring onions, peas, potatoes, radish, shallots (bulbs), spinach.**
COLD CLIMATE	**COLD CLIMATE**
Gypsophila, marigold (French).	**Cress, lettuce, mustard, onions, shallots (bulbs), spinach.**

JUNE

This is the month when the skeleton and structure of the garden are most apparent. Established trees can be shaped and strengthened by judicious pruning and new sites can be prepared for fruit trees and ornamental plants which will enhance the general effect of the garden.

Roses and other flowering plants are also in line for pruning and cutting back. Other parts of the garden, especially the vegetable patch, should be full of healthy, green growth.

VEGETABLES

If planning has been thorough the garden will now be full of vegetables for winter use. Cabbage, cauliflower, broccoli and Brussels sprouts nearing maturity will benefit from an application of Thrive applied in soluble form so that the nutrients are instantly available. These vegetables are heavy feeders and a fertiliser at this stage will increase the size of the curd and sprouts and maintain good health.

Slugs and snails are likely to be active on young seedlings; lay Blitzem or Mesurol pellets if necessary. Lime can be added to build up soil structure along with peat and compost. If drainage is poor, raised beds offer a simple remedy.

Sow broad beans.

FLOWERS

Lift and divide overgrown, rootbound plants such as asters, phlox, cannas and dahlias. Prune hydrangeas. Thin out spindly growth and cut back strong growth to a pair of buds low down on the stem.

FRUIT

An ideal month for planting and pruning. Prune on a dry day to prevent infection of fungus spores which are transported in the rain. As an added precaution cover all pruning cuts with pruning paint. Begin pruning with stonefruit trees, as their spring growth commences earlier.

Winter need not be dull with the right selection of fruit trees for the home orchard.

Prune back hydrangeas to a pair of fat flower buds for a stunning display in summer.

Peaches and nectarines fruit on one-year-old wood. They are strong growers and need shortening back to maintain a manageable size.

Apples, pears and plums fruit on two-year-old spurs. Pruning aims at thinning out old, unnecessary growth and maintaining a desirable size and shape. All deciduous fruit trees should be sprayed with Champion Copper and Conqueror Oil for a general clean up.

ORNAMENTAL TREES AND SHRUBS

Prepare planting positions for new trees and shrubs. Incorporate topsoil in the bottom of the planting hole and leave exposed to aerate until ready for planting. Use MagAmp when planting new trees and shrubs.

Check deciduous trees for signs of disease and spray if necessary.

SEEDS TO SOW

FLOWER	VEGETABLE
TEMPERATE CLIMATE	**TEMPERATE CLIMATE**
Tuberous begonia, Canterbury bells, delphinium, dianthus, godetia, gypsophila, larkspur, linaria, lupin, mignonette, painted daisy, statice, sweet pea, viola, Virginian stock, wallflower.	Asparagus (crowns), broad beans, cabbage, cress, lettuce, mustard, onions, peas, potatoes, rhubarb (crowns), shallot (bulbs), spinach.
COLD CLIMATE	**COLD CLIMATE**
	Asparagus (crowns), cress, lettuce, mustard, onions, peas, spinach.

JULY

The cold days may make it seem unlikely, but the first days of early spring are only just around the corner.

A final tidying of the garden can take place, and meanwhile some seeds are being raised in containers for planting out later, as soon as ground temperatures are favourable.

New roses and other flowering shrubs and trees can be carefully planted in their chosen places and well cared for as they await the new spring growth.

VEGETABLE GARDEN

It is time to start preparing the vegetable garden. Cultivate any empty spaces by turning the soil and leaving rough clods exposed to the frosts. Weathering will help improve the soil structure. Apply garden compost which can be dug in later. Autumn green crops can also be dug in. The addition of sulphate of ammonia and lime will aid their breakdown. Avoid working waterlogged soils as you will damage the underlying structure.

Plants required for early spring planting can be sown in seed trays and kept in a warm place. Sprout potatoes for an early start. Place the tubers in flat boxes in a light, sunny position where the temperature is fairly steady at about 5–10°C. After six to eight weeks sprouts should appear from each tuber. Leave two or three short thick sprouts and remove the weaker ones.

Continue spraying winter crops such as cabbage, cauliflower and broad beans with Bravo or Champion Copper to combat fungus diseases (ring spot, downy mildew and chocolate spot).

Rhododendron 'Gilded Sunrise' flowers sporadically through the winter months.

The subtle beauty of Michelia *'Bubbles'.*

Buy only 'High Health' daphne to avoid problems with viral diseases.

FLOWERS

Roses and other flowering shrubs and trees can be planted. To keep established rose bushes vigorous and healthy, remove all diseased wood, spindly shoots and excessive growth. Spray with Champion Copper and Conqueror Oil to check scale, mites, aphids and fungus diseases.

Cut back untidy growth on perennials. Divide overgrown and root bound clumps.

FRUIT

Prune grapes. Cut out wood which has borne fruit and replace with young, new season's canes, selecting the strongest and removing those that are thin and weak.

CONTAINER PLANTS

Take care not to overwater indoor plants at this time of the year as they can be very susceptible to root rot. Move plants to a warm, well-lit location away from cold draughts.

Give maximum protection from cold weather to container plants outside. Stand pots in warm, sunny, sheltered positions.

SEEDS TO SOW

FLOWER	VEGETABLE
TEMPERATE CLIMATE	**TEMPERATE CLIMATE**
Begonia (tuberous), delphinium, dianthus, gloxinia, gypsophila, honesty, impatiens, kochia, mignonette, statice.	Asparagus (crowns), beetroot, broad beans, cabbage, carrots, Chinese cabbage, cress, kohlrabi, lettuce, mustard, onions, parsnip, peas, potatoes (tubers), rhubarb (crowns), salsify, silverbeet.
COLD CLIMATE	**COLD CLIMATE**
Carnation.	Asparagus (crowns), broad beans, cress, lettuce, mustard, onions, peas, spinach, turnips.

PICTURE CREDITS

t = top   b = bottom   c = centre   l = left   r = right

INDEX